THE
LOCKHEED
CONSTELLATION

by Peter J. Marson

AN AIR-BRITAIN PUBLICATION

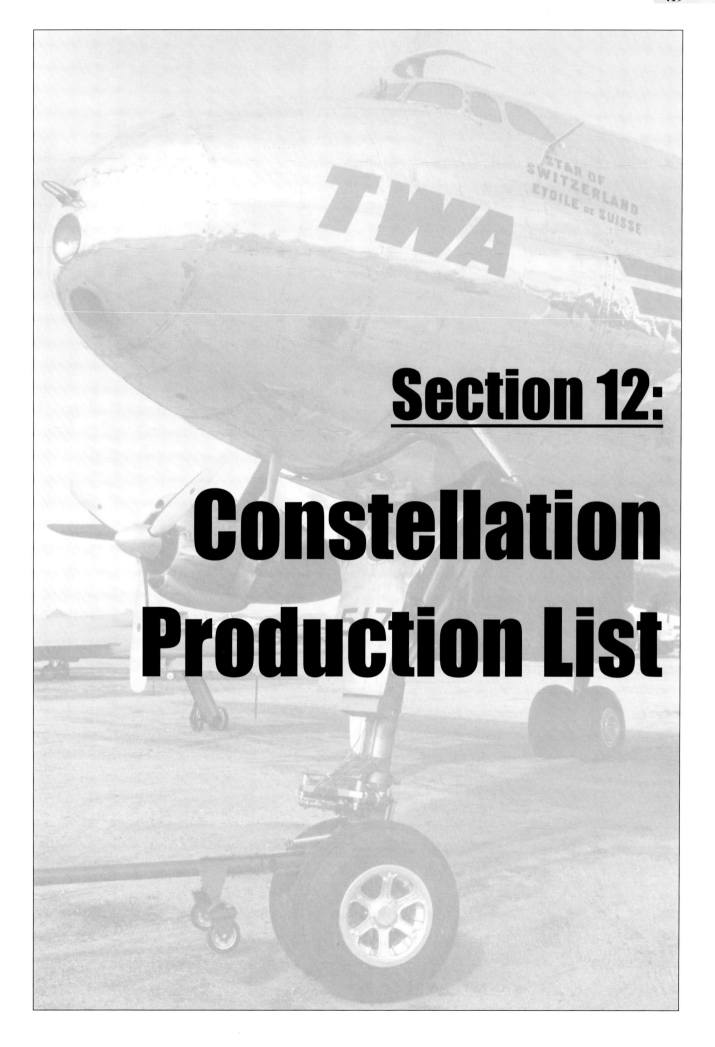

Section 12:
Constellation Production List

Introductory Remarks

In order to present as much information as possible, a number of abbreviations have been used. These will be found in the "Abbreviations" section (Section 11), or, in the case of commercial operators, full titles are given in the operators sections (Sections 7 to 10, as appropriate).

The Constellations are listed numerically according to the aircraft constructor's number (or manufacturer's serial), with the exception of the Model 1649 Starliner, which will be found at the end. Lockheed constructor's numbers should, strictly speaking, be prefixed by the aircraft model (e.g. 049-1963; 1049C-4501; 1649-1001). In preference to this, however, the full aircraft model number is given instead immediately after the constructor's number of each individual aircraft (with changes as appropriate in the aircraft's history).

The full Lockheed Constellation model numbers consist of three series of figures, e.g. 049-46-26. The first of these (e.g. 049) is the basic airframe model, the second (e.g. 46) is the engine type, and the third (e.g. 26) is the interior arrangement. All three series can, of course, change during the aircraft's career, and any confirmed changes are given in the individual histories. Full details of the meaning of each of these series of figures can be found in Sections 2 & 3, as can details of the military designations (e.g. C-121C or WV-2). Details of subsequent commercial conversions are given in Section 4.

The first date given is, in all cases where known, the Lockheed Acceptance Delivery Date (LADD), which is the most common date given in Lockheed-California Company's records. Other dates should be self-explanatory (e.g. 'Sold to..', 'CofA issued on..', 'wfu on..', 'registered to...on...'). If no explanation is given by a date, it is not known whether the date in question is a registration, sale, transfer of title, or lease date. Military unit transfer dates have been taken from official aircraft history cards (where available), or, failing that, from official unit sources, or in a few cases, from Lockheed records. Where no official (e.g. registration, or change of ownership) date is known for commercial aircraft operators, the first appearance in an official register is given (e.g. USCAR Jun 67).

United States civil registrations were prefixed NC, NR or NX officially until 31 Dec 48; from 1 Jan 49, merely N has been used. Where appropriate, both type registration prefixes are given. Individual aircraft names are given in inverted commas, e.g. 'Clipper Climax'. Trans World Airline's aircraft were normally named after a US location while in use on the international network and a non-US location while in use on the US domestic network. Renaming of the aircraft took place during the first repaint/touch-up after the change from the domestic network to the international network, or vice versa. By 1958, this custom ceased, and from this time onwards the aircraft carried no individual name at all.

Military Serials: With USAF aircraft, the official serial with Fiscal Year (FY) (e.g. 48-608) is listed. In early 1955, the Air Force introduced the digit "0" denoting that the aircraft was ten or more years old (i.e. obsolete). The use of the "0" has been interpreted in various ways (and often not used in a logical fashion). So far as the Constellation was concerned, an aircraft with a full serial consisting of five figures including FY (e.g. 48-608) was originally painted as "8608" on the aircraft. In 1956, an "0" was added, the serial on the aircraft becoming "80608". By about 1960, a further "0" was added, the serial painted on the aircraft becoming "0-80608". An aircraft with a full serial consisting of six figures including FY (e.g. 52-3411) was originally painted as "23411", and subsequently from the late 1950s/early 1960s as "0-23411". Exceptions to these two basic rules only are given in the production list (where known). One batch of aircraft - the EC-121Rs (FY 1967) - carried only the 'last five' of the serial, omitting any reference to the FY, throughout their career - i.e. 67-21471 to 67-21500 carried only "21471" to "21500" painted on the fins of the aircraft.

General: All full stops in abbreviations have been eliminated in the interests of saving space.

THE CONSTELLATIONS

1961 First prototype Constellation Model 49-46-10. Construction started Jun 41 and completed Nov 42. First taxy-runs 20 Nov 42. Painted in USAAF camouflage with military star and civil test registration NX25600. First flight Saturday, 9 Jan 43 from Burbank, CA, with Edmund T. Allen and Milo Burcham at the controls, and Rudy L Thoren (flight engineer) plus Dick Stanton (flight mechanic). Flight lasted 58 minutes, and ferried to Muroc Fld (part of Edwards AFB) on same day, with undercarriage lowered as a precautionary measure. Four take-offs and landings made at Muroc prior to return to Burbank. Eleven flights made up to 10 Feb 43 (TT: 11.77 hrs). Grounded 24 Feb 43 -17 June 43 after crash of Boeing B-29, which was also powered by Wright Duplex Cyclones, for engine modifications and rework. On 27 Jul 43, aircraft made 64th flight, ferried from Burbank to Las Vegas, NV, for official hand-over to USAAF on 28 Jul 43 (USAAF records give 29 Jul 43) as C-69 serial no. 43-10309. Loaned back 29 Jul 43 to Lockheed plants, though in fact ferried back to Burbank on previous day. Testing and modifications continued. Flown to Lindbergh Fld, San Diego, CA on 17 Jan 44 for fuel-tank work by Rohr Co. Returned to Burbank 15 Apr 44. Further tests and demonstration flights, including flight to Phoenix, AZ and return on 11 May 44 (110th and 111th flights respectively). Moved to Vega paint shop 3 Jun 44 for stripping of camouflage; reappeared in natural metal finish with USAAF star and bar and military serial on 12 Jun 44. Army test instruments installed 25 Jun 44, with first USAAF tests on 26 Jun 44. Tests completed 7 Jul 44 and Army test equipment removed, then original LAC test equipment re-installed. Further testing until 14 Oct 44, when the aircraft was taken out of commission for installation of the two-speed Model 3350-35A engines. Completed 24 Nov 44. Laid-up for conversion to Pratt & Whitney R-2800 engines and fitting of hot-air de-icing equipment for the 'hot wing tests'. On completion of conversion in Sep 45, aircraft re-designated Model 49-39-10. First flight with Pratt & Whitneys on 5 Oct 45. USAAF decided on re-designation to XC-69E on 21 Nov 45, officially changed to XC-69E on 22 Jan 46. Test flying with Pratt & Whitneys Oct 45 to Dec 45. Ferried to Minneapolis, MN, Ice Research Base for icing tests on 16 Jan 46 (USAAF records quote Minneapolis 24 Jan 46), which continued until Mar 46. Returned to Burbank and stored. Transferred to War Assets Administration and sold to Howard Hughes in mid-1946 for $20,000, being delivered to Hughes Fld, Culver City. (USAAF records quote Patterson, Culver City and TWA - i.e. Hughes, all on 14 Aug 46) . Regd NC67900 to Hughes Tool Co. Flew little during next four years, possibly only one flight. Bought back by LAC 1 May 50 for $100,000, at which time aircraft had TT 404.07 hrs (159.65 hrs of which were with Pratt & Whitneys). Reregd NC25600. Flew 2.92 hrs with LAC on return as c/n **1961A** for performance data as Model 049. Converted to prototype Super Constellation at Burbank during summer of 1950. Rolled out in deep blue colours with red and white trim Oct 50 as Model 049S c/n **1961S** and regd NX6700. First flight 13 Oct 50 with Jim White and Ray Meskimen at the controls, reregd N67900. Flew 22.40 hrs with four Pratt & Whitneys. Also flown by Roy Wimmer, Joe Ware and Jack Real. Paint scheme changed after first ten flights, with additional white on nose and cockpit roof, and engine nacelles painted deep blue. During early 1951, a Wright R3350-CA series engine was fitted in no.4 position and the outboard vertical stabilizers enlarged by 18 inches each for improved directional control. First flight with CA engine 4 Apr 51. Subsequently fitted with stepped cockpit roof (as on production Super Constellations). Late in 1951, the prototype R3350 Turbo-Compound engine (for the Lockheed Neptune) was fitted in no.1 position and made its first flight in the Super Constellation. Early in 1952, the aircraft was fitted with two 600-US gallon tip-tanks in connection with the planned turbo-prop development of the Super Constellation (first airliner to be thus equipped). In Jan 52, the R3350-CA engine in no.4 position was replaced by the updated R3350-CB engine. During 1952, the aircraft was converted to an aerodynamic test vehicle for Navy airborne early warning Super Constellations. The first flight in this configuration was made with the large fibreglass ventral radome (housing the APS-20 radar) and a small metal cap covering the mounting structure for the upper radome; on

SECTION 12: CONSTELLATION PRODUCTION LIST

43-10311 C-69 awaiting delivery at Burbank. (Lockheed)

subsequent flights the aircraft also had the large dorsal radome (housing the APS-45 radar). By 1953, weather warning radar had been fitted in the nose, and a DA-l series Turbo-Compound engine fitted in no.1 position (for the R7V-l/Model 1049C Super Constellation developments). During 1953-54, 'Old 1961', as the aircraft was called by Lockheed employees, was used to iron out several problems with the Turbo-Compound engines, including nacelle cooling and exhaust flames, and at one time had Turbo-Compounds in nos.1 and 4 positions (nos.2 and 3 still being Pratt & Whitneys). Was first transport aircraft to be fitted with the Turbo-Compound engine. Three different types of propellers were fitted at this time: one 43E60-313, one 43E60-605 and two 33E60-79s. Flew with two types of Curtiss Electric propellers and three types of Hamilton Standard propellers. As of Sep 53 had TT:767 hrs. By 1954, the tip-tanks and ventral/dorsal radomes had been removed, and during the first few months of 1954, an Allison YT-56 turbo-prop engine (for the Lockheed YC-130 Hercules) and a Curtiss three-bladed propeller were fitted in no.4 position. At the same time, the aircraft received its final paint-scheme of light grey with red cheat lines and two horizontal red bands on the fins and c/n changed to **1961ST**. The first flight with the YT-56 engine was made on 29 Apr 54. During 1954-55, the aircraft was used for development flying with this engine. At some time, a DA-3 Turbo-Compound engine was fitted in no.1 position, followed in Mar 56 by an EA-3 in no.1 position. From Aug 56, an EA-2 Turbo-Compound engine (for the Model 1649 Starliner) was fitted in no.1 position, and during the next three months several types of spinner and after-body were tried out with this engine, as were Hamilton Standard and Curtiss Electric propellers (of larger diameter than the usual Super Constellation propellers). At the same time, development of the Allison turbo-prop engine for the Model 188 Electra continued in no.4 position, first with a modified T-56 (to resemble the civil Allison 501, but with a three-bladed propeller). First flight with this engine was believed to be in Nov 56, followed by the first flight with the four-bladed propeller and civil Allison 501 D-13 in late Feb or early Mar 57. During Mar 57, tests on the Aeroproducts 606 propeller were flown to determine the torque characteristics. Late in 1957, 'old 1961' was withdrawn from use by LAC and stored at Burbank until at least Oct 59, after it was sold to California Airmotive for spares in Dec 58. The nose section up to the leading edge of the wing was used to repair c/n 2513 (qv) - the remainder of the fuselage, still fitted with wings, languished at Burbank for some time, before it was scrapped.

1962 49-46-10/C-69 First flight Aug 43 as 43-10310 for USAAF. Used for test and development flying at Burbank. TWA accepted aircraft on behalf of USAAF at Las Vegas 16 Apr 44 (USAAF records quote acceptance and delivery 17 Apr 44). Made record-breaking flight 17 Apr 44 from Lockheed Air Terminal, Burbank, CA to Washington, DC, piloted by Jack Frye and Howard Hughes, and in full TWA colours and markings with 'The Transcontinental Line' titling, but with USAAF serial number (although NC38936 was allocated to Trans-continental & Western Air Inc for this aircraft in 1944). USAAF history: Gravelly Point, DC, 22 Apr 44, Burbank 13 Jun 44 and to War Assets Administration 31 Mar 47, but already parked for disposal by 24 Feb 47 at Burbank (TT: 355hrs). Deleted by USAAF 28 May 47. Purchased by Paul J. Grosso, no regn allocated. Reportedly used for spares by A. Schwimmer for c/ns 1965, 1967 & 1968. By Jan 50 was a stripped shell awaiting scrapping at Burbank. Rebuilt by Intercontinental Airways (= A.Schwimmer) during 1952 and painted up in full Flying Tiger Line colours for lease to latter airline in Jan 53. Regd N38936. Destroyed by fire at Burbank, CA on 22 Jan 53 after wheels-up landing. Aircraft was being used for training, and circuit-breaker giving warning of 'undercarriage up' had been disconnected. Pilot had forgotten to reconnect, and perfect wheels-up landing made. Crew escaped unhurt (total 8 on board), but fuel valves left open and aircraft quickly enveloped by flames.

1963 49-46-10/C-69-1-LO USAAF 43-10311 27 Oct 44. USAAF records quote acceptance 25 Oct and delivery 27 Oct 44. Starboard main undercarriage collapsed during taxying 7 Dec 44. Repaired. USAAF history: Long Beach 10 Feb 45 (Pan American use), dep USA 14 Feb 45, ret USA 19 Feb 45. Flying 10 hrs daily from Miami, 18 hrs on one day. All four engines changed at Burbank early Apr 45. Brookley 22 Aug 45, Lowry 12 Oct 45, La Guardia 29 Oct 45 and grounded 29 Nov 45. Burbank 7 May 46, War Assets Administration 31 Mar 47, but parked for disposal by 24 Feb 47 (TT:1,427 hrs). Deleted by USAAF 28 May 47 on sale to Darius V. Phillips as NC67952, but ret to LAC by Oct 49. Cvtd to 049-46-59 for Capital Airlines as N67952 'Capitaliner Freedom' FN 751, deld 9 Aug 50, in svce 18 Aug 50. Flew in 56-pax configuration. Cvtd to 049D-46-59. TT: 29,307 hrs (a/o 1 Jul 57). Wfu and stored at Washington Natl by Aug 58. Nominally taken over by United Airlines 1 Jun 61. To Modern Air Transport 25 Sep 61. Stored at Mercer County, Trenton, NJ in ex-Capital markings by 1964. Sold to Curry Corp by early 64 and being used for spares

Constellations FOR SALE

The War Assets Administration invites you to bid on nine grounded Lockheed "Constellations" (Army Model C-69) aircraft which have been declared surplus.

These all-purpose low-wing Heavy Transports are of all-metal construction, with dual wheel tricycle landing gear and triple vertical tail surfaces. They are powered with four Wright 2200 HP engines and equipped with Hamilton Standard three-blade propellers. Their ability to carry heavy loads at high cruising speed for long distances makes them very desirable for either cargo or passenger operation.

These aircraft are available for inspection at Lockheed Air Terminal, Burbank, California, after February 24, 1947.

NOTE: *The hours of airplane and engine operation shown were taken from records (where furnished with the airplane) and such hourly figures are for information only.*

MODEL	IDENT. NO.	MFR.	MAKE OF ENGINE	H. P.	AIRPLANE HOURS	TOTAL ENGINE HOURS	ENGINE HOURS SINCE O. H.
C-69	42-94549	Lockheed	Wright	2200	280	L-280 L-280 R-280 R-280	L-New L-New R-New R-New
C-69	42-94550	Lockheed	Wright	2200	472	L-472 L-472 R-472 R-472	L-New L-New R-New R-New
C-69	43-10310	Lockheed	Wright	2200	355	L-121 L-308 R-328 R-305	L-New L-Unk. R-New R-Unk.
C-69	43-10311	Lockheed	Wright	2200	1427	L-422 L-152 R-422 R-372	L-New L-New R-New R-New
C-69	43-10312	Lockheed	Wright	2200	1303	L-854 L-854 R-854 R-259	L-Unk. L-Unk. R-Unk. R-Unk.
C-69	43-10313	Lockheed	Wright	2200	180	L-180 L-171 R-180 R-164	L-New L-New R-New R-New
C-69	43-10314	Lockheed	Wright	2200	552	L-533 L-468 R-151 R-42	L-New L-New R-New R-New
C-69	43-10315	Lockheed	Wright	2200	44	L-43 L-5 R-43 R-43	L-43 L-5 R-43 R-43
C-69	43-10316	Lockheed	Wright	2200	90	L-112 L-90 R-90 R-90	L-New L-New R-New R-New

Office of Aircraft Disposal: 425 Second St., N.W., Washington 25, D. C.

WAR ASSETS ADMINISTRATION

Offices located at: Atlanta • Birmingham • Boston • Charlotte • Chicago • Cincinnati • Cleveland • Dallas • Denver • Detroit • Fort Worth • Helena • Houston • Jacksonville • Kansas City, Mo. • Little Rock • Los Angeles • Louisville • Minnea-polis • Nashville • New Orleans • New York • Omaha • Philadelphia • Portland, Ore. • Richmond • Salt Lake City • St. Louis • San Antonio • San Francisco • Seattle • Spokane • Tulsa

To c/ns 1963 et seq. War Assets Administration advertisement for a batch of C-69s in "Aviation Week" dated 17th February 1947.

Section 12: Constellation Production List

ZP-CAS 049 stored at Viracopas, Brazil in 1964, with a Panair do Brasil DC-7C PP-PEG in the background and a BOAC van in the foreground. (P R Keating)

by Oct 64. To Trenton Aviation Inc by early 66. Broken up at Mercer County, Trenton, NJ mid 60s. Canx USCAR 16 Sep 66.

1964 49-46-10/C-69-1-LO USAAF 43-10312 14 Oct 44 and 18 Oct 44 (USAAF records give former as acceptance, latter as delivery date). Assigned to Sperry Instrument Co, Long Island, NY 1945 (presumably for auto-pilot tests). USAAF history: To Long Beach, dep USA approx 10 Feb 45, ret USA 19 Aug 45 at Gravelly Point, DC by TWA, but i/s with TWA a/o Apr 45 & 24 Jun 45. La Guardia approx Dec 45, Burbank 7 May 46, War Assets Administration 31 Mar 47, but parked for disposal by 24 Feb 47 (TT:1,303 hrs). Deleted by USAAF 28 May 47 on sale to Darius V Phillips.Tfd officially 16 Apr 48, and regd NC67953 on 28 Mar 49. Use unknown, but ret to LAC 21 Oct 49. Cvtd to 049-46-59 for Capital Airlines as N67953 'Capitaliner Spirit of World Peace' (christened by Eleanor Roosevelt 20 Sep 50), FN 753, to Capital 13 Sep 50 (FAA quote 14 Sep 50), in svce 23 Sep 50. Flew in 56-pax configuration. Cvtd to 049D-46-59. Ownership tfd to Trans American Aeronautical Corp 31 Dec 56 and lsd back same day by Capital. Wfu and stored at Washington Natl by Aug 58 (TT: 23,861 hrs). Sold to Regina Cargo Airlines Inc 27 Feb 60, later named Imperial Airlines Inc (officially changed 9 Nov 60). Sold to Miami Aircraft & Engine Sales Co 29 Nov 60 and lsd back to Imperial. Out of svce Nov 61 after crash of other Imperial 049 (c/n 1976). Lsd Coastal Airlines 1962, and ret Miami Aircraft 1963. Sold to International Export-Import Co Inc 29 Nov 63 & to Francisco Paes de Barros (a director of the Brazilian airline Paraense) 4 Dec 63 for lease to Lloyd Aereo Paraguayo. Regn ZP-CAS issued 24 Dec 63 to Lloyd Aereo Paraguayo (valid for one flight from Asuncion to Rio for overhaul). Aircraft deld Miami-Asuncion, and left Asuncion for Rio-Galeao 27 Jan 64. Suffered engine trouble and landed at Campinas-Viracopos (nr Sao Paulo). Planned to ferry to Rio on 3 engines, but other problems caused Lloyd Aereo Paraguayo to lose interest and the aircraft was dismantled at Viracopos in early 1965. Canx from USCAR 4 Jan 71. Reappeared on USCAR as "candidate" 1 May 80, but deleted Mar 99 as NTU.

1965 49-46-10/C-69-1-LO USAAF 43-10313 24 Jan 45. USAAF: acceptance 24 Jan 45, deld 25 Jan 45. Stored at Burbank prior dely and in full TWA colours and markings with 'The Transcontinental Line' titling, but with USAAF serial number. USAAF history: Deld to ATC 25 Jan 45. Held at Burbank for storage from 20 Oct 45, War Assets Administration 31 Mar 47, but parked for disposal by 24 Feb 47 (TT: 180 hrs). Deleted by USAAF 28 May 47. Sold to A W Schwimmer c 5 Dec 47 and regd NX90827. Cvtd at Burbank,CA to 049. Flew Burbank-Dallas, TX-Millvill, NJ 10-11 Mar 48. A W Schwimmer t/a Service Airways Inc requested cx of NX90827 11 Mar 48. Regd RX-123 for Lineas Aereas de Panama SA. Impounded at Newark, NJ, on 19 Mar 48 as "illegal export". Permission requested to fly Newark-Panama City 24 Mar 48 (CofA valid until 19 Jun 48), but apparently remained in storage Millville, NJ, and restored as N90827 to Service Airways Inc. RX-regn canx by Panamanian authorities 17 Sep 48. Sold by Schwimmer to The Jewish Agency Inc 3 Nov 49. Projected sale to Capital Airlines 1950 fell through. Tfd to El Al Israel Aviation Ltd 23 Jun 50. Cvtd to Model 149 and referred to by El Al as a 249. Deld Mar 51 (E-20450 21 Mar 51). N-regn canx 5 Apr 51, regd 4X-AKA. Sale in Switzerland as HB-IEA (regn issued 24 Feb 59) to Transazur Airlines ntu. Stored at Tel Aviv from at least autumn 1961 until sale to Universal Sky Tours in Feb 62. Canx from Israeli register 8 Jan 62 and regd G-ARXE 13 Feb 62 (TT:20,800 hrs), with dely to Luton, England Apr 62 in Euravia livery, as an 82-seater. Re-painted in Skyways livery Nov 62, and from Oct 62 to Apr 64 operated mainly on Skyways' scheduled services from Luton to Malta. Ownership tfd to Euravia (London) Ltd 23 May 63 and to Britannia Airways 2 Feb 65. Wfu Luton May 65 and broken up there between Jun 65 and end 1965. Canx from register 28 Jan 66. TT:24,231 hrs on wfu.

1966 49-46-10/C-69-1-LO USAAF 43-10314 6 Feb 45. Used for winterization tests at Edmonton,Alta, believed prior dely to USAAF. USAAF history: Acceptance & dely 7 Feb 45, deld to ATC, Ferrying Division. To Burbank 11 May 45, Gravelly Point, DC 27 Aug 45 for TWA (but already with TWA 1 Jul 45). Burbank 18 Nov 45, dep USA 19 Mar 46. Patterson 2 Apr 46, Burbank 15 Apr 46, War Assets Administration 31 Mar 47, and deleted 28 May 47. Also used for winterization tests at Ladd Fld, Fairbanks, AK late 1946/early 1947. TT: 552 hrs (a/o 24 Feb 47) when parked at Burbank. This was probably the USAAF C-69 that made a forced landing in the Mediterranean (date uk) - landed in the water just off a Mediterranean airport after the pilot had been confused by runway light reflections. Later salvaged and sold to the French Government. Aircraft was, however, handed over to Air France at New York 14 Dec 47 & deld to Toulouse Jan 48 as F-BECA. Used for spares. Parts used in rebuild of c/n 2512 after damage in cabin fire, Iceland on 27 Nov 48. Fuselage lying in hangar at Toulouse, France from 1949 until 1951. Purchased by Lockheed Air Service Intl & parts used in rebuild of c/n 1980 in 1951. Presumably remains scrapped after rebuild of c/n 1980.

1967 49-46-10/C-69-1-LO USAAF 43-10315 16 Feb 45. USAAF acceptance 17 Feb 45 dely 19 Feb 45. USAAF history: Dely to Wright Fld 19 Feb 45, Wichita 19 Nov 45, Burbank 26 Nov 45, War Assets Administration 11 Mar 47, but parked for disposal by 24 Feb 47 at Burbank (TT: 44 hrs). Deleted by USAAF 28 May 47. Sold to A.W. Schwimmer c 5 Dec 47 and regd NX90828. Panamanian records give this aircraft as RX- 123, but FAA records have no mention of a Panamanian registration and quote c/n 1965

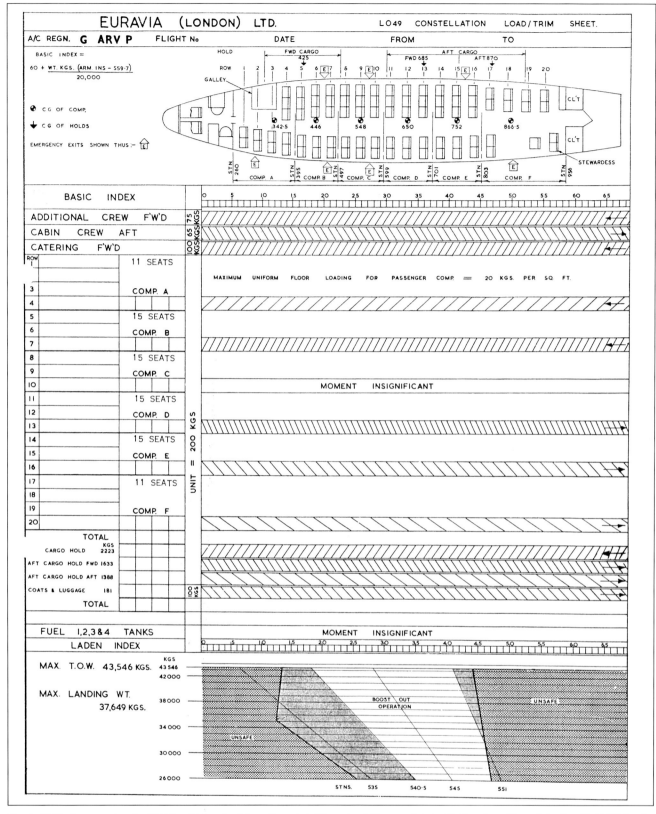

To c/n 1967. An example of a 1962 load/trim sheet from Euravia's 82-seater 049 pre-printed with the aircraft's registration G-ARVP (as the airline's original three 049/149 Constellations were each slightly different). This makes an interesting comparison with a similar item (see below c/n 2036) from 1945.

as RX-123. Assuming FAA records to be correct, this aircraft must be the third LAPSA aircraft, RX-124, and the aircraft's history as follows: Cvtd to 049 at Burbank, CA, for Lineas Aereas de Panama SA as RX-124. Aircraft never left the USA and remained in storage at Burbank, CA until flown to Millville, NJ, 7 Jun 48, joining c/n 1965. Impounded there as planned illegal export. RX-regn canx by Panamanian authorities 17 Sep 48. Reregd NC67930 to A W Schwimmer in 1949, later N67930. Sold to The Jewish Agency Inc, date uk. Projected sale to Capital Airlines 1950 fell through.

Tfd to El Al & regd 4X-AKB (E-20442 19 Dec 50). Arr in Israel 22 Dec 50, in svce Mar 51 'Mazal Tov' carried originally. N-regn canx 5 Apr 51. Minor damage to nose when hit by wingtip of BOAC 049 G-AHEJ while parked at London 13 Aug 51. Repaired. Cvtd to Model 049D and referred to by El Al as a 249. Tail damaged 26-27 Dec 55 during windstorm at Lydda Airport. Repaired. Sale in Switzerland as HB-IEB (regn issued 24 Feb 59) to Transazur Airlines ntu. Stored at Tel Aviv from at least autumn 1961 until sale to Universal Sky Tours in Feb 62 (TT: 23,001 hrs).

Canx from Israeli register 8 Jan 62 and regd G-ARVP 13 Feb 62, with dely to Luton, England 12 Apr 62 in Euravia livery, as an 82-seater. Ownership tfd to Euravia (London) Ltd 23 May 63 and to Britannia Airways 2 Feb 65. Wfu after CofA expiry 2 Apr 65 at Luton and broken up there during the summer. Canx from register 10 Sep 65. TT: 25,985 hrs on wfu.

1968 49-46-10/C-69-1-LO USAAF 43-10316 6 Mar 45 and 11 May 45 quoted by LAC, USAAF give acceptance 8 Mar 45 and dely 11 May 45. USAAF history: Retained at Burbank initially and apparently never left there. Aircraft was hangared at Burbank in Oct 45 and parked there for disposal by 24 Feb 47 (TT: 90 hrs). To War Assets Administration 31 Mar 47, and deleted by USAAF 28 May 47. Sold to A W Schwimmer c 5 Dec 47 and regd NX90829. Cvtd at Burbank,CA to 049 & del Burbank – Millvill, NJ 26 Jan 48. Request for canx of NX90829 by A W Schwimmer t/a Service Airways Inc 11 Mar 48. To RX-121 of Lineas Aereas de Panama SA. Flown via Newark, NJ, to Tocumen, Panama, arr Panama 13 Mar 48 (FAA files quote 14 Mar 48 as dep date from Newark). Flew via Paramaribo-Dakar-Casablanca to Zatec, Czechoslovakia 19-21 May 48. Used for arms airlift Czechoslovakia-Israel Jun 48 to 1949. En route Ekron AB, Israel to Zatec, suffered hydraulic failure, starboard undercarriage could not be lowered and damaged in subsequent landing at Zatec, Czechoslovakia, on 14 Jul 48. The aircraft swerved through 160 degrees to the right, causing damage to the lower fuselage, starboard wing, propellers and undercarriage. Withdrawn from svce. RX-regn canx by Panamanian authorities 17 Sep 48. Officially serialled 2401 with IDFAF Nov 48, but not painted on aircraft. Temporary repairs carried out at Zatec, reregd 4X-121 & flown to Schiphol, Amsterdam 17 Sep 49 with no.4 engine inoperative & prop feathered. Flew with Panama Air Lines titling. Further repairs carried out at Schiphol & dep for Burbank, CA, mid-Nov 49 for full repairs as NC90829 via Amsterdam-Keflavik-Gander-Chicago. Stored in Panamanian colours (a/o 18 Nov 49) at Burbank as N90829, with ex-regn 4X-121/RX-121 clearly visible. Projected sale to Capital Airlines 1950 fell through. Sold to El Al as 4X-AKC and deld Apr 51, regd 15 Jul 51. Cvtd to Model 149 and referred to by El Al as a 249. Struck jeep taxying Rome-Ciampino 21 Jan 52 on arrival from Lydda. Repaired. Shot down by Bulgarian anti-aircraft fire a few miles from the Greece-Bulgaria border at about 08.37 hrs (Israeli time) on 27 Jul 55 and crashed in flames in attempted forced-landing north of Petrich. Aircraft was on scheduled flight from London to Lydda-Lod via Vienna and Istanbul, and was approx 35 nmls off course.

1969 49-46-10/C-69-1-LO USAAF 43-10317 19 Apr 45. USAAF history: Acceptance 19 Apr 45, dely 21 Apr 45 to ATC Ferrying Division. Burbank 1 May 45, Gravelly Point, DC 14 May 45 (for TWA use). To La Guardia 24 Jan 46, Burbank 7 Jun 46 and to TWA for commercial use 15 Jul 46. LAC records give: purchased from War Assets Administration by Hughes Tool Co. To Transcontinental & Western Air 1 Jul 46, tfd to Hughes Tool Co 1 Jul 46 & regd NC67901 2 Oct 46. Modified by LAC for TWA as Model 049-46-25 (Feb 48 contract) a/o 9 Sep 48, mods completed 15 Nov 48. Regd NC90830 to Hughes Tool Co 24 Sep 48, to TWA 1 Feb 49. Deld to TWA at Burbank as 'Star of Zurich' FN 516 30 Nov 48 (TT: 274 hrs). In svce 3 Dec 48. Later N90830, regd to Trans World Airlines Inc 29 May 50. Damaged at Los Angeles, CA, 22 Jun 51 - inner wing panel ribs buckled, deflection of upper and lower wing skin and pulling away of fillet to no.4 nacelle from rivets, caused by partial collapse of no.4 tank. (TT: 8,410 hrs). Re-entered svce 13 Jul 51. Op last 1st-Class svce 19 Mar 53, and to LAS Burbank for Coach Class conversion 20 Mar 53. Re-entered svce 24 Apr 53. Sold to Falcon Airways 26 Jun 61 on behalf of Austrian Aero-Transport GmbH, and regd OE-IFA (E-50013 21 Jun 61). Deld Kansas City-Washington-Gander-Hurn, England 24-27 Jun 61 and to Vienna, Austria (arr 28 Jun 61). TT on sale to Austria 38,008 hrs. Op by M Kozubski t/a Falcon Airways on charter to Aero-Transport. Became first Austrian-regd transport aircraft to visit New York 18 Aug 61, Lisbon 30 Sep 61, Singapore 28 Oct 61 and Tokyo 12 Jan 62. Flight to Tokyo from Vienna via Rotterdam-Kuwait-Hong Kong was the longest flight at the time of an Austrian aircraft. Op on lease to Falcon Airways from 25 Aug 61 for a brief period. Seized by Austrian customs authorities at Vienna-Schwechat 16 Oct 63 for non-declaration of customs dues and taxes by owner M Kozubski. Forced sale 29 Apr 64 postponed due to objections by Kozubski until 27 Aug 64 (Price of 500,000 Austrian schillings in Apr 64 raised to 1,200,000 in Aug 64!). Aircraft had 2,796 hrs since general overhaul. No buyer found. Stored Vienna until sold to Martin Mitterhuber for scrap 24 Mar 66. Broken up Jun 66 and canx from register in Jun 66.

1970 49-46-10/C-69-5-LO USAAF 42-94549 28 Apr 45. USAAF history: Acceptance 30 Jun 45, dely Burbank 28 Jul 45 & kept at factory. Lsd TWA at Washington Natl 4 Aug 45, in use on Washington-San Francisco flights. To La Guardia 6 Jan 46, Burbank 30 Apr 46 (but in storage there by Mar 46, TT: 279 hrs), War Assets Administration 23 Jun 47, but parked for disposal by 24 Feb 47. Sold to Hughes Tool Co and modified by LAC for TWA as Model 049-46-25 (Feb 48 Contract). Deld to TWA at Burbank by Howard Hughes as NC90831 'Star of Switzerland' FN 517 1 Oct 48 (TT: 286 hrs), flown to Kansas City same day and in svce 7 Oct 48 as standard 1st Class 51-seater. Later N90831. Tfd to Transcontinental & Western Air 1 Feb 49, and to Trans World Airlines Inc 29 May 50. Last 1st-Class svce 24 Apr 53, and to LAS Burbank for Coach Class conversion 25 Apr 53. Re-entered svce 29 May 53. Damaged at Ontario, CA 12 Nov 53 en route Washington, DC-San Francisco, CA. Repaired. Damaged at St. Louis, MO, 19 Dec 57, when a ground loop occurred while the aircraft was making a left turn off a wet runway on to taxiway, causing right main undercarriage to collapse. En route Los Angeles-New York. Repaired. Damaged at Las Vegas, NV, 30 Mar 61, when left main undercarriage retracted while aircraft was parked on the ramp, settling onto one wing and stabilizer tip. Sold to Las Vegas Hacienda Inc in damaged condition 13 Apr 61 (TT: 37,905 hrs). Repaired, using port wing of N9409H (c/n 2074) and named 'Desert Queen'. Officially tfd to Hacienda 21 Jul 61. Lsd World Wide Airlines 13 Jul 62, Consolidated Airlines mid-63 and Standard Airways mid-63. Ret to Las Vegas Hacienda Inc 1964. Lsd to Dellair by Apr 64, and to Trans World Insurance Brokers 1 Dec 64. Stored at Long Beach, CA, by Jan 65, with Dellair markings removed. Ret to Las Vegas Hacienda Inc 23 Jul 65. Painted up in Air Belize Intl markings late 65, but never op by them. Sold to McCulloch Properties Inc 1 Dec 65 (FAA files give 18 Nov 65), t/a Lake Havasu City. Sold to Allied Aircraft Sales Inc 15 May 70. Sold to Harlow L Jones t/a Southwestern Skyways Inc 5 Jun 70. Flown from Lake Havasu City, AZ, to Tucson Intl, AZ 23 Jun 70 (TT: 41,908 hrs). Traded by Harlow L Jones to USAF Museum in exchange for HU-16B Albatross 51-7178 at Pima County Museum, AZ, in Sep 70. Flown from Tucson Intl to Davis Monthan AFB, AZ, 5 Feb 71 for Pima County Museum and ownership tfd to US Air Force Museum 6 Apr 71. Stored in open at Pima County. Canx from USCAR as "retired" 10 Jul 72. Restoration work began in 1977, by volunteer TWA personnel. Aircraft restored in full Trans World Airline markings as N90831 'Star of Switzerland' FN 517, with silver cabin roof. Handed over officially by TWA restorers, who had devoted over 7,000 man hours to the work, on 16 Feb 80. Oldest Constellation and only C-69 extant.

1971 49-46-19/C-69C-1-LO (prototype -19 interior, for planned wartime production C-69C/Model 549). USAAF 42-94550 4 Aug 45. USAAF history: Acceptance 31 Jul 45, deld Burbank 4 Aug 45. To TWA on lse a/o 16 Sep 45. To La Guardia 31 Jan 46, Burbank 30 Apr 46. Regd NC54212 to US Dept of War. TT: 285 hrs on lse to TWA for pilot training as NX54212 FN 548 (unnamed) on 10 Jun 46. Ret 30 Jul 46 (TT: 471 hrs). To War Assets Administration 28 May 47, but parked at Burbank by 24 Feb 47 for disposal. Kirk Kerkorian took out option on acft Jun 47, but lapsed. Cvtd to 049-46-26 by LAC for BOAC Jul-Oct 47. Regd 12 Aug 47 as G-AKCE 'Bedford'. To Montreal-Dorval for further mods 1 Nov 47-25 Apr 48, CofA 31 Mar 48 (no. V338), E-16112 dated 31 Mar 48. In svce 25 Apr 48 ex-Montreal. Arr London 29 Apr 48 on dely. Flew last Bermuda-Baltimore-Bermuda svce 17 Jan 49. Flew London-Azores-Havana inaugural 049 svce 2-3 Mar 50, ret 4-6 Mar 50 (diverted en route to Prestwick due fog at London). Cvtd to Model 049D & to 65-seater All-Tourist Class at Burbank 18 Nov 51-19

Apr 52. Cvtd to 049E Jun-Jul 53. Flew last BOAC 049 New York-Bermuda-New York svce 25 Mar 55 & last BOAC 049 New York-Nassau-Montego Bay-New York svce 26-27 Mar 55. Also flew last BOAC 049 svce London-Trinidad-London (via North Atlantic route) 16-20 Jun 55 & wfs 20 Jun 55. Sold to Capital Airlines as N2741A FN 761, dep London 23 Jun 55 as last BOAC 049, h/o to Capital 27 Jun 55, and in svce 5 (or 8) Aug 55. G-regn canx 27 Jun 55. Flew in 72-pax configuration (a/o May 59). Stored by Jan 61 (TT: 28,403 hrs), taken over nominally by United Airlines 1 Jun 61, and sold to Modern Air Transport 4 Aug 61. Used for spares prior to 1964 and broken up by Oct 64.

1972 49-46-10/C-69-5-LO USAAF 42-94551 23 Jul 45. USAAF history: Acceptance 30 Jun 45, dely 23 Jul 45 at Burbank. To Bolling 23 Jul 45. Reported as making first Atlantic crossing by a Constellation when it flew non-stop from New York to Paris-Orly on 4 Aug 45 in record time of 14 hrs 12 mins. USAAF history continues: To Lowry Fld 9 Sep 45, Higstey 8 Oct 45, Topeka 11 Oct 45, La Guardia 15 Jan 46, Tinker Fld 19 May 46, Reclamation 23 Jun 46, Complete 26 Jul 46. However, this Constellation crashed at Topeka, KS, on 18 Sep 45 while being op by Pan American for USAAF. En route San Francisco-La Guardia, had fire in No.1 engine. Engine fell off at 13,000ft during emergency descent, acft belly-landed at Topeka Airfield. (TT:449 hrs, 10C + 19P all ok). The USAAF subsequently grounded its Constellation fleet for a while, but ret them to service without any modifications. It was the following summer before some parts from the crashed Constellation were discovered which showed problems with the cabin-supercharger drive shaft. (See 18 Jun 46 accident to c/n 2058).

1973 49-46-10/C-69-5-LO USAAF 42-94552 2 May 45. USAAF history: Acceptance 30 Apr 45, dely 2 May 45 at Burbank. To Wright Fld 2 May 45. Classified OTL (?) 31 May 46 and to "School" 31 Jul 46. In fact tests at Wright Field were carried out 31 May 45-16 Oct 46, i/c pressure cabin tests, structural & strain tests, also load tests on all parts of the airframe. Aircraft was tested to destruction in these static tests at Wright Field by late in 1946.

42-94552 C-69 undergoing cabin pressurization tests to destruction at Wright Field in 1945/46. (US Army Air Corps via Smithsonian Museum)

1974 49-46-10/C-69-5-LO USAAF 42-94553 20 Sep 45. USAAF history: Acceptance 20 Sep 45, dely 10 May 46. To LAC for bailment to TWA. (TT: 20 hrs). Regd NC54214 to US Dept of War 1946. Used by TWA for pilot training from 15 May 46 until 27 Jul 46 as NX54214 FN 549 (unnamed). Ret to LAC 27 Jul 46 (TT: 82 hrs). USAAF history continues: Patterson 19 Jan 47, to War Assets Administration 25 Aug 47 at Bush Fld, GA. At one time, probably about Mar 46 (from evidence on photograph), this aircraft was painted up in full Eastern Air Lines colours at Burbank as NC70000 FN 325 with 'The Great Silver Fleet' cabin titling. In USAAF service, the Constellation carried the "buzz number" CM-553 (a/o 27 Jun 47 at Wright Fld). After War Assets Administration, used by the CAA for ground instruction at Oklahoma City, OK and presumably at one time for pilot duties, as the Constellation had TT: 180 hrs 55 mins, on sale by CAA to TWA on 23 Aug 51. Restored as N54214 to Trans World Airlines Inc 6 Sep 51. Ferried Oklahoma City - Fairfax 28 Sep 51, but

42-94553 C-69 with 'buzz-number' "CM-553" at Wright Field 27th June 1947. The remains of "The Great Silver Fleet" titling can just be made out on the cabin-roof after publicity photos for Eastern Air Lines at Burbank as "NC70000". (P M Bowers via John T Wible)

forced to land at Stillwater, OK, with mechanical trouble; all four engines changed and eventually arr Fairfax 18 Oct 51. Ferried to LAS Idlewild, NY, 7 Jan 52 for Coach Class conversion, completed 10 Sep 52. Restored as N54214 6 Sep 52, in svce with TWA 18 Oct 52 as 'Star of Piccadilly' FN 525. TT: 27,395 hrs (a/o 30 Jun 61). Sold to Nevada Airmotive 31 Mar 62, and to McCulloch Properties 15 Feb 64. Stored at Long Beach, CA, by Jun 65 and used for spares. Canx as scrapped 1 Aug 65, though a fin was still extant propped up against a hangar at Long Beach, CA as late as May 70. Regn canx 19 Apr 66.

1975 49-46-10/C-69-5-LO USAAF 42-94554, but ntu. Regd NC90602. Cvtd to 49-51-26 by LAS, New York, NY, for BOAC. LADD: 25 Apr 46. Deld to Dorval, Canada for BOAC 26 Apr 46 as G-AHEJ 'Bristol II', regd 6 Apr 46, CofA 21 May 46 (no. V237). In svce 1 Jul 46. Grounded 12 Jul-30 Aug 46. Cvtd to 049-46-26. Renamed 'Bristol' in Feb 48. Cvtd to 65-Seater, All-Tourist Class & Model 049D at Burbank 11 Mar-5 Jun 52. Cvtd 049E in May-Jun 53. Flew BOAC's first scheduled Constellation service to New York 1 Jul 46. Damaged when tyre caught fire landing, part of port undercarriage assembly failed taxying at Keflavik, Iceland 21 Dec 49, repaired. Flew 049 proving flight to South America (via Bermuda & Panama to Lima, Peru & Santiago, Chile) 22 Aug-3 Sep 50. Flew first BOAC mid-Atlantic svce London-Azores-Santiago, Chile dep 3 Oct 50. Wingtip damaged when hit El Al 049 4X-AKB taxying at London on 13 Aug 51. Repaired. Flew last BOAC 049 mid-Atlantic svce London-Azores-Kingston 7-8 Mar 52. Starboard wing root fairing severely damaged 22 Nov 54 after cabin-heater fuel-vapour explosion en route Prestwick-New York. Made emergency landing and temporary repairs carried out at Keflavik, Iceland, ret London for full repairs. Last svce 23 May 55, sold to Capital Airlines 28 May 55 as N2740A FN 760, deld from London 26 May 55, and G-regn canx 27 May 55. In svce with Capital 28 Jun 55, latterly in 72-pax configuration. Lsd Coastal Cargo 1958, later stored (TT: 29,975 hrs a/o May 59) until sold to Falcon Airways 19 Jan 61, E-42943 dated 17 Jan 61 (TT: 31,686 hrs on sale). Test flights at Washington as N2740A 17 Jan, reregd G-AHEJ for dely flight, dep Washington 20 Jan and arr Hurn (via Gander) 21 Jan 61, after CofA renewed 20 Jan 61. Used for crew training during Feb 61 but never entered svce with Falcon. Ferried to Biggin Hill 25 Feb 61 for use as spares. Sold to Trans European (for spares) Dec 61. Engines and components missing by Sep 62 and broken up at Biggin Hill Feb 63. Canx 12 Dec 62 as sold to Austria, so presumably Aero-Transport bought the remaining parts as spares for their Constellations.

1976 49-46-10/C-69-5-LO USAAF 42-94555, but ntu. Photographic evidence shows this aircraft did actually fly in USAAF markings. Regd NC90603. Cvtd to 49-51-26 by LAS New York, NY for BOAC. LADD: 30 Apr 46. Deld to Dorval, Canada for BOAC as G-AHEK 'Berwick II' 1 May 46, regd 6 Apr 46, CofA 21 May 46 (no. V238). Grounded 12 Jul-30 Aug 46. Cvtd to 049-46-26 & in svce 3 Sep 46. Renamed 'Berwick' Feb 48. Flew first New York-Bermuda-Baltimore svce 19-20 Jan 48. Flew inaugural 049 svce London-Azores-Bermuda-Kingston 7-8 Apr 50. Flew inaugural for the short-lived Panama-New York svce early Nov 50.

Carried titles "The Venezuelan Flying Cradle" painted along the fuselage 11-15 Dec 50 for a special charter from Munich to Caracas 11-12 Dec, carrying orphan German children to a new life in Venezuela. Cvtd to 65-seater, All-Tourist Class and Model 049D at Burbank 4 Jan-5 May 52. Cvtd 049E Jul-Aug 53. Last svce 21 Feb 55, sold to Capital Airlines 27 Feb 55 as N2737A FN 757, deld from London 26 Feb 55, G-regn canx 28 Feb 55 and entered svce 28 Mar 55 (TT: c32,000 hrs). Lsd Coastal Cargo summer 1958, later lsd Coastal Airlines (1959). Sold to Miami Aircraft & Engine Sales 14 Apr 61, and lsd Imperial Airlines 2 May 61. Made emergency landing at Prestwick, Scotland, en route Gander-Copenhagen 11 Jul 61. Bt by Imperial 14 Jul 61. Crashed at 2124 hrs (EST) 8 Nov 61 at Byrd Airport, Richmond, VA, with heavy loss of life. Aircraft was flying a charter for the US Army from Newark, NJ, and Baltimore, MD, to Columbia, SC. Ten miles west of Richmond, the plane developed engine trouble; as a result of fuel mismanagement, the crew allowed nos. 3 & 4 engines to run no.4 tank dry. On approach for a landing, the landing gear did not extend due to mismanagement of the hydraulic system. A go-around was initiated, and no. 1 engine failed as a result of over-boosting. The aircraft crashed and burned half a mile to the left of the extended runway 33 centreline and one mile short of the threshold. After the crash, the FAA suspended Imperial's operating certificate for unsatisfactory maintenance, pilot training and record-keeping. (TT: 32,589 hrs on crash).

1977 49-46-10/C-69-5-LO USAAF 42-94556, but ntu. Regd NC90604. Cvtd to 49-51-26 by LAS, New York, NY, for BOAC. LADD: 10 May 46. Deld to Dorval, Canada for BOAC as G-AHEL 'Bangor II', regd 6 Apr 46, CofA 24 Jun 46 (no. V239). In svce 4 Jul 46. Grounded 12 Jul-30 Aug 46. Cvtd to 049-46-26, renamed 'Bangor' Feb 48. Carried out the final Constellation charter flight on the Abadan airlift Abadan-London 23-24 Jun 51 with Anglo-Iranian Oil Company personnel. Cvtd to 65-Seater, All-Tourist Class and Model 049D at Burbank 4 Jan-29 Apr 52. Cvtd 049E Jun-Jul 53. Flew first direct svce London to Trinidad & Barbados (via Bermuda) 8-9 Oct, ret 10-11 Oct 53. Damaged port wing-tip in collision with Pan American DC-6B (N6518C) taxying at Trinidad 14 Nov 54. Repaired. Last svce 20 Jan 55, sold to Capital Airlines 28 Jan 55 as N2736A FN756, deld from London 26 Jan 55, G-regn canx 27 Jan 55. In svce with Capital 28 Feb 55, latterly in 72-pax configuration. Stored by Dec 60 (TT: 32,025 hrs). Sold to Falcon Airways Ltd Mar 61 (E-48503 23 Mar 61) and deld ex-Montreal via Gander to Hurn 24 Mar 61 as G-AHEL, and to Biggin Hill 25 Mar 61. Overhauled at London-Heathrow Jun 61 and sold shortly after to Trans European Aviation Ltd. Del Trans European 13 Jul 61, in svce 17 Jul 61. Operated for Falcon Airways by Trans European from end Jul 61 to 25 Aug 61 (as 82-Seater). Trans European ceased ops Aug 62. Flown to Luton, England 5 Oct 62 and stored there until sold to Euravia (London) Ltd 18 Apr 63, deld 23 May 63. Sold to Britair East Africa Ltd in Nov 64 as 5Y-ABF, in svce 22 Nov 64, but official dely 19 Dec 64 (and regd Mar 65). G-regn canx 30 Dec 64. Used for series of London-Gatwick to Rotterdam flts May 65. Last svce probably Jul 65. Ret to Luton late in 1965 and stored there, flown to Shannon, Ireland May 66 and stored there until broken up in 1968.

1978 49-46-10/C-69-5-LO USAAF 42-94557, but ntu. Regd NC90605. Cvtd to 49-51-26 by LAS, New York, NY, for BOAC. LADD: 22 May 46. Deld to Dorval, Canada, 23 May for BOAC as G-AHEM 'Balmoral', regd 6 Apr 46, to Hurn 12 Jun 46, CofA 24 Jun 46 (no. V240). Made first BOAC Atlantic proving flight New York-London 16 Jun 46. In svce 3 Jul 46. Grounded 12 Jul-30 Aug 46. Cvtd to 049-46-26. Inaugurated New York-London svces via Prestwick 11-12 Sep 46. Flew last First-class London-Montreal-London svce 30 May-1 Jun 50. Cvtd to 65-Seater, All-Tourist Class and Model 049D at Burbank 11 Mar-25 May 52, re-deld London 27 May 52. Cvtd to 049E Apr-May 53. Last svce 4 Oct 54, sold to Capital Airlines 11 Oct 54 as N2735A FN 755. Deld from London 8 Oct 54, flew a Paris-Boston charter, arr New York 10 Oct, G-regn canx 11 Oct 54. Deld Washington, DC 12 Oct, in svce 5 Dec 54. Lost nose-wheel door over Elyria, OH 19 May 55 en route Cleveland-Chicago. Ret to Cleveland and repaired. Crashed on landing in light rain at Kanawha Airport, Charleston, WV, at 1529 hrs (EST) on 12 May 59. On landing on wet runway, braking was ineffective, Captain chose to ground-loop the aircraft, which turned off the runway, slid over a steep embankment tail first, slid to a stop and burned. Aircraft was en route Pittsburgh, PA, to Atlanta, GA. TT: 29,589 hrs. 2 casualties.

1979 49-46-10/C-69-5-LO USAAF 42-94558. USAAF history: Acceptance 21 Jul 45, dely 31 Aug 45 (1946 quoted on another USAAF card, but '45 is believed to be correct). Retained at Burbank by Lockheed and used for development flying on the "Speedpak" cargo pannier & also for fuel-dump system tests. Took part in airshow at Long Beach, CA as 294558 1 Aug 46. To War Assets Administration 19 Jan 47, but already to Transcontinental & Western Air Inc 10 Dec 46 (LADD 18 Dec 46). Cvtd at Fairfax to Model 049-46-26 NC86536 'Star of Rome' FN 561 & deld for Intl ops Mar 47. To domestic ops 17 Aug 48. Regd to Trans World Airlines Inc 29 May 50. To Fairfax for Coach Class conversion 13 Feb 54. Re-entered svce 19 Mar 54. Re-regd N86536. Lsd to Eastern Air Lines 4 Dec 57. Ret TWA 20 Apr 58, re-entered svce with no paint 24 Apr 58 and with new paint 5 May 58. Sold Nevada Airmotive 31 Mar 62 (TT: 44,781 hrs). Believed stored at Las Vegas, NV until 1964, then scrapped. Canx from USCAR 5 Jan 65.

1980 49-46-10/C-69-5-LO USAAF 42-94559, but ntu. Cvtd to 49-51-26 by LAS, New York, regd NC90606 to LAC 21 May 46. Temporary CofA issued for production & demonstration flts & for dely to BOAC at Las Vegas, NV 27 May 46 (flown in British markings with "G-" masked off prior to handover). LADD: 29

N74192 049 in the colourful red and blue markings of California Hawaiian Airlines. A close look at the photo reveals the airline name appears in whole or part a total of six times! The photo was taken at San Francisco in 1952. (via Louis Barr)

May 46. Deld via Washington, DC to Dorval, Canada 31 May, for BOAC as G-AHEN 'Baltimore', regd 6 Apr 46, CofA 1 Jul 46 (no. V241), but N-regn not canx until 8 Apr 49. Flew special Montreal-Baltimore-Montreal flt 5 Jul 46. Grounded 12 Jul-30 Aug 46. Cvtd to 049-46-26. In svce 31 Aug 46. Made first BOAC Constellation flight to Canada (London-Prestwick-Gander-Dorval) on 15 Apr 47. Flew two special pre-inaugural return flts Baltimore-Bermuda 15-17 Jan 48, then inaugurated Baltimore-Bermuda-New York 049 svces 17-18 Jan 48. Flew last First-class New York-London svce 1 Apr 50. Severely damaged after overshooting at Filton-Bristol, England, on 8 Jan 51 on a training flight. Hit fuel-storage building, suffering damage to front portion of airframe, main spar and undercarriage. (TT: 11,350 hrs). British Aviation Insurance Co Ltd and other insurance companies paid BOAC a total loss on airframe of US $244,000. Remains sold at a good recovery price by insurers to Mel Adams & Associates, New York. Aircraft shipped as deck cargo, Avonmouth-New York Feb 51 for rebuild. Sold British Aviation Insurance Co Ltd 20 Feb 51, canx from UK register same day. Regd to Indamer Corp 22 Feb 51 & rebuilt in the open at LAS, New York, NY, with parts from c/n 1966, i/c port inner wing panel (qv). Regd to Kirk Kerkorian & Rose Pechuls (t/a Los Angeles Air Service Inc) 4 Apr 51, regn N74192 issued to them 19 Jun 51. Rebuild completed spring 1952 after 29 weeks & 40,000+ man hrs. Lsd to California Hawaiian Airlines in 60-Seater configuration Apr 52, sub-lsd at one stage to U S Airlines Inc (in CHA colours). CHA shown as operator/lessee a/o 3 Jul 52, but no official agreement. Tfd to Kirk Kerkorian t/a Los Angeles Air Service 20 Apr 53. For sale at $865,000 (a/o 28 Sep 53), with 1,655 hrs since major overhaul. Sold to El Al Oct 53, officially tfd 18 Dec 53, N-regn cx 22 Dec 53. Regd 4X-AKD. Flew Lod-Istanbul-Teheran 30 Jan 54 to operate a return immigrant charter from Teheran to Lod. Withdrawn for conversion to all-Tourist configuration, in svce 25 Jun 54. Port wingtip damaged while taxying into a hangar at Paris-Orly 21 Feb 55. Repaired. Damaged by fire at Lod, Israel 2 Apr 58. Repaired. Sale in Switzerland to Transazur A/L as HB-IED (regn issued 24 Feb 59) ntu. Stored at Tel Aviv by 1961 and canx from Israeli register 12 Mar 61. Regd to Katid Ltd 1961-62. Sold to Universal Sky Tours in Feb 62. Cvtd to 049D and regd G-AHEN 13 Feb 62. Painted in Euravia colours and deld Apr 62 (CofA 23 Apr 62). (TT: 26,718 hrs). Ownership tfd to Euravia (London) Ltd 23 May 63 and to Britannia Airways 2 Feb 65. Sustained damage to port tailplane at London-Heathrow during night of 6-7 Oct 63. Repaired. Op as 82-Seater. Wfu Luton, England, after CofA expiry on 21 Apr 65 and broken up from May 65. Canx 10 Sep 65 as "destroyed". (TT: 29,303 hrs).

Cancelled USAAF Constellation allocations and c/ns

2021 to 2070 (50 aircraft) 49-46-19/C-69C-l-LO Serials 42-94560 to 42-94609

2071 to 2110 (40 aircraft) 49-46-19/C-69C Serials 42-94610 to 42-94649

3001 to 3076 (76 aircraft) 549 Serials 42-94650 to 42-94725

3077 to 3147 (71 aircraft) 549 Serials 43-10238 to 43-10308

3148 to 3150 (3 aircraft) 549 Serials 42-94726 to 42-94728

These 240 aircraft (plus 1961-1980) represented the original order of 260 aircraft.

The second batch of Model 49s (2071 to 2110) was the first to be cancelled, the Model 549s (3001 onwards) then took over the serials 42-94610 to 42-94649 - the exact allocation of serials to c/ns is unconfirmed.

By 1 Mar 45, the USAAF order was cut back to 70 Model 49s and three Model 549-79-19s. At this stage, the allocation was:-

2021 to 2070 (50 aircraft) 49-46-19 Serials 42-94560 to 42-94609

3001 to 3003 (3 aircraft) 549-79-19 Serials 42-94610 to 42-94612

2071 onwards had been allocated to the commercial Model 49-46-21 by 29 May 45.

The final picture is shown in the production list, which continues with the 21st aircraft built (c/n 2021):-

2021 49-46-19/C-69C-1-LO USAAF 42-94560, ntu, but aircraft actually painted up in USAAF markings with serial. Cvtd to Model 49-51-25 for Transcontinental & Western Air Inc, LADD: 14 Nov 45. Regd NX86500 to LAC. First TWA 049 to be deld. Del to Kansas City on 15 Nov 45 as NC86500 'Star of the Mediterranean' FN 500 (TT: 14 hrs 59 mins). Cvtd to Model 049-46-25, later regd N86500. Damaged on landing at Pittsburgh, PA 22 May 50, when hit car & work stands - left main gear and wing fuel cell no.2 damaged (TT: 11,039 hrs). Regd to Trans World Airlines Inc 29 May 50. Ferried to Fairfax, KS 1 Jun 50 for repair. To Fairfax again for Coach Class conversion 13 Nov 50, re-entered svce 17 Dec 50 with new FN 524. In store by mid-61, awaiting sale. Sold to Nevada Airmotive 31 Mar 62 (TT: 45,709 hrs). Stored at Mid-Continent Airport, Kansas City, MO during 1963-64, and broken up there between Jun 64 and Dec 64. Canx from USCAR 19 Oct 64.

2022 49-46-19/C-69C-5-LO USAAF 42-94561, but ntu. Cvtd to Model 49-51-25 for Transcontinental & Western Air Inc, LADD: 9 Dec 45. Regd NX86501 to LAC. Deld to TWA on 7 Dec 45 as NC86501 'Star of the Persian Gulf' FN 501, in svce 17 Dec 45. Used for training at Kansas City Municipal from 19 Dec 45. Inaugurated svce to Albuquerque, NM 27 May 46, rn 'Zuni SkyChief'. Later reverted to 'Star of the Persian Gulf'. To 049-46-25 & re-entered svce 18 Oct 46, later regd N86501. Extensively damaged on landing at Chicago-Midway at 0817(CST) 18 Dec 49- ran off runway 13R, through fence and across road (excessive speed on landing on second ILS approach - pilot unsuccessfully attempted to ground-loop the aircraft). Aircraft finished up in parking lot - no injuries. TT: 9512 hrs. On flt TW154 San Francisco-Chicago-New York. Re-entered svce 16 Apr 50. Regd to Trans World Airlines Inc 29 May 50. To Mid-Continent Airport, Kansas City, MO 6 Nov 51 after last 1st-Class flight, in work same day for Coach Class conversion. Re-entered svce on 2 Jan 52. Slightly damaged near South Bend, IN en route Chicago-New York 4 Jul 57. Repaired. Sold to Nevada Airmotive 31 Mar 62 (TT: 44,479 hrs). Believed stored at Las Vegas, NV until 1964, then scrapped. Lapsed in USCAR 1967, canx 1970.

2023 49-51-25 Regd NX86502 to LAC. LADD 20 Dec 45 to Transcontinental & Western Air Inc as NC86502 'Star of the Pyramids' FN 502. To Engineering Dept 20 Dec 45. To 049-46-25 and re-entered svce 14 Oct 46. Later regd N86502. Regd to Trans World Airlines Inc 29 May 50. To Mid-Continent Airport, Kansas City, MO 28 Nov 53 for Coach Class conversion. Re-entered svce 15 Jan 54. Lsd Eastern Air Lines 17 Nov 57, ret to TWA 26 Apr 58. Sold to Nevada Airmotive 31 Mar 62 (TT: 45,985 hrs). Believed stored at Las Vegas, NV until 1964, then scrapped. Canx from USCAR 6 Sep 71 (failure to file 1973).

2024 49-51-25 Regd NX86503 to LAC. LADD 31 Dec 45 to Transcontinental & Western Air Inc as NC86503 'Navajo Sky Chief' FN 503. Deld 1 Jan 46, cvtd for domestic service, first flight 1 Feb 46. Renamed 'Star of California Sky Chief' (by 3 Feb 46) and inaugurated scheduled TWA domestic Constellation service Los Angeles-La Guardia, New York (also coast-to-coast schedule). Rn 'Star of the Nile' & used for proving flts for CAA with fuel-injection engines from 5 Sep 46. To 049-46-25, later regd N86503. Regd to Trans World Airlines Inc 29 May 50. To Mid-Continent Airport, Kansas City, MO 7 Jan 54 for Coach Class conversion. Re-entered svce 14 Feb 54. Sold to Nevada Airmotive 31 Mar 62

(TT: 46,953 hrs) and lsd shortly afterwards to ASA Intl. Stored at Burbank, CA by Jun 64, in ASA colours, parts missing by Dec 64. Condition deteriorated until finally broken up late in 1969 or first few months of 1970. Canx from USCAR 6 Sep 71 (failure to file 1973).

2025 49-51-25 Regd NX86504 to LAC. Prior to dely; LAC used the aircraft for the first demonstration flights outside the USA of the commercial Constellation series. Late in 1945, piloted by H Wegner and R Meskimen, with C R Mercer as Flight Engineer, the Constellation was flown to Canada for demonstrations to Trans-Canada Air Lines. En route, the aircraft landed at Jamestown, ND by mistake for Fargo, ND one day prior to the official opening of Jamestown. Later set up a record time on the Winnipeg-Montreal route. LADD 16 Jan 46 to Trans- continental & Western Air Inc as NC86504 (TT: 58 hrs). Named 'Star of France' FN504. In svce with TWA 5 Feb 46 after conversion for domestic use. To 049-46-25. Damaged by fire after hydraulic leak at San Francisco 31 Jan 48 while being serviced (TT: 3,849 hrs). Ferried to Van Nuys 14 Apr 48, ret to TWA 29 May 48 and re-entered svce 3 Jun 48. Later regd N86504. Regd to Trans World Airlines Inc 29 May 50. To Mid-Continent Airport, Kansas City, MO 16 Mar 54 for conversion to Coach Class. Re-entered svce 20 Apr 54. Sold to Nevada Airmotive 31 Mar 62 (TT: 44,777 hrs). Lsd Futura Air Lines May 62 FN 712. Lsd Paradise Airlines 7 Jun 63 (TT: 45,078 hrs), named 'City of Los Angeles'. Crashed 9 nm northeast of the Tahoe Valley Airport, CA at 11.29 hrs (PST) on 1 Mar 64, at 8,675 ft on a mountain ridge on the California-Nevada border. Aircraft was on Flight 901A from Oakland, CA to Tahoe Valley, via Salinas and San Jose. Pilot deviated from prescribed VFR flight procedures in attempting a landing approach in adverse weather conditions (snowstorm, ceiling 300 to 700 ft, winds of 30kts). In addition there was probably a heading error and altimeter error (11 reports of malfunction of the fluxgate compass system in eight months, discrepancies in both altimeters reported, both installed and repaired by mechanics without previous experience). TT: 45,629 hrs. All killed on board, FAA grounded Paradise Airlines afterwards for failing to conduct a safe operation. Canx from USCAR 6 Sep 71 (failure to file 1973).

2026 49-51-26 Regd NX86505 to LAC. LADD 21 Nov 45 to Transcontinental & Western Air Inc as NC86505, FN 550. Dely date also given as 28 Nov 45. Christened 'Paris Sky Chief' 3 Dec 45 and made preview flight New York-Paris 3-9 Dec 45. Also carried name 'Navajo Skychief' Dec 45 and 'Star of Cairo Skychief' in Feb 46. Was the first "Overwater" type to be deld to TWA. Left Chicago on 10 Feb 46 on a special flight to Rome with two cardinals. To 049-46-26. Crashed on small island one mile from the airport boundary at Rineanna-Shannon, Ireland while making an instrument approach at about 02.00 hrs (GMT) on 28 Dec 46. En route Paris-Shannon-New York. Cause: error in altimeter indication caused by the reversal of the primary and alternate static source lines, resulting in the pilot conducting an approach at a dangerously low altitude, with contributing factor of restriction of vision due to fogging of unheated windshield panels. Canx from USCAR 28 Mar 49.

2027 49-51-26 Regd NX86506 to LAC. LADD 6 Dec 45 to Transcontinental & Western Air Inc as NC86506 'Star of Dublin Sky Chief' FN 551, also named 'Star of Paris Sky Chief' (in Jan 46) Rn 'Star of Dublin'. Flew on Intl schedules until 2 Aug 48. To 049-46-26 and later regd N86506. Regd to Trans World Airlines Inc 29 May 50. Domestic 1st Class schedules until 23 Apr 55. To Fairfax, KS for conversion to Coach Class 24 Apr 55, completed 21 May 55, with new FN 506, although not applied to fins as late as 1959. Sold to Nevada Airmotive 31 Mar 62 (TT: 45,671 hrs). Lsd in 1962 to ASA Intl, FN 506 until early in 1963, then lsd to Paradise Airlines (airline grounded Mar 64). Stored Burbank (a/o Dec 64). Sold to Herman R (Fish) Salmon in May 66 and painted up in Aerospace Traveler markings at Burbank, CA and named 'Rosa'. Unconf whether actually flew for this travel club. Remained stored at Burbank. Still intact until 1970.

Condition deteriorated and eventually broken up at end of 1972 or in first few months of 1973. Canx from USCAR 15 Dec 71 (failure to file 1973).

2028 49-51-26 Regd NX86507 to LAC. LADD 13 Dec 45 to Transcontinental & Western Air Inc as NC86507 'Star of Madrid Sky Chief' FN 552. Flew on Intl schedules. Visited Brooklyn (now Ysterplaat-Cape Town), South Africa as 'Star of Madrid' from Washington, DC as part of world-wide sales tour Feb 46. Damaged starboard main undercarriage on landing when it hit a mound of earth on finals. Repaired. Inaugurated New York-Geneva, Switzerland service 31 Mar 46. To 049-46-26. Undershot runway on landing approach to New Castle County A/P, DE, after a training flight approx 1300 (EST) on 18 Nov 47. Landing gear struck ditch 130ft from runway end & 22ft in front of a 5ft embankment, forcing aircraft up into the air again. The Constellation skidded for 1,270 feet on its belly, lost starboard wing, overturned and caught fire, killing the 4 crew (3 Captains & a Flight Engineer) plus a CAA inspector. (TT: 3,256 hrs). Canx from USCAR 28 Mar 49.

2029 49-51-26 Regd NX86508 to LAC. LADD 30 Dec 45 to Transcontinental & Western Air Inc as NC86508 'Star of Athens' FN 553. Used on Intl schedules, also named 'Star of India'. To 049-46-26. Crashed during a transition training flight into Delaware Bay Ship Canal, approx 10 mls west of Cape May, NJ, on 11 May 47, killing the crew. While flying at 2,500 ft a left turn was started, which tightened as the turn progressed, with the aircraft entering a tight diving spiral. The spiral was stopped, but the aircraft continued a steep descent. A loud roar of engines was heard just before the aircraft struck the water at an angle of 45 degrees. Cause of accident unknown: no emergency call made, investigations hampered by deep water at place of accident, possibly due to loss of control. (TT: 2,214 hrs). Canx from USCAR 28 Mar 49.

2030 49-51-25 Regd NX86509 to LAC. LADD 29 Jan 46 to Transcontinental & Western Air Inc as NC86509 'Star of Africa' FN 509. Deld 30 Jan 46 (TT: 10hrs). To 049-46-25. Later N86509 and FN 505. Regd to Trans World Airlines Inc 29 May 50. Damaged at New York-La Guardia 23 Feb 55 while landing (after arrival from Los Angeles). Runway was wet & weather foggy, aircraft brakes partially ineffective during landing roll, so a ground-loop was attempted. The aircraft skidded sideways, slid off the end of the runway and across a drainage ditch, with the wing striking a ridge. Undercarriage was torn off, left wing buckled, fuselage and left stabilizer damaged. The Constellation ended up at the northeast end of Runway 04 against a dyke. (TT: 25,429 hrs). Interim repairs at La Guardia, wing panel from Model 749 (with outboard tank sealed) fitted, then after several months flown to Fairfax, KS for completion of repairs and converted to Coach Class at same time. Re-entered svce 27 Jun 55. Hit car with propeller at Denver, CO, 11 Mar 56, en route to Los Angeles. Repaired. TT: 39,459 hrs (a/o 31 Aug 59). Used for all-cargo flights 1959 onwards. Stored by mid-61, and sold to Nevada Airmotive 31 Mar 62 (TT: 42,955 hrs). Stored at Las Vegas-McCarran Fld, NV, until 1966, then scrapped. Lapsed in USCAR 1967, canx 6 Sep 71 (failure to file).

2031 49-51-26 5 Feb 46 to Pan American as NC88831. First transatlantic svce New York-Hurn, UK 20 Feb 46, ret Hurn-New York 20-21 Feb 46. Named 'UNO Clipper'. Later re-named 'Clipper London' and 'Clipper Carib' (a/o Sep 46). To 049-46-26. Damaged while landing at Shannon Airport, Ireland 24 Sep 46. After a normal landing, the captain called for "flaps up", but the co-pilot inadvertently moved the landing gear lever, the gear collapsed, and major damage was received to the airframe resulting in the aircraft subsequently being declared a write-off. After the accident, it was discovered that the landing-gear control handle locking installation was faulty, permitting the gear to retract while the weight of the aircraft was on the gear.

2032 49-51-26 Regd NX88832 to LAC. LADD 19 Feb 46 to Pan American as NC88832. Pan Am dely date 20 Feb 46. Originally

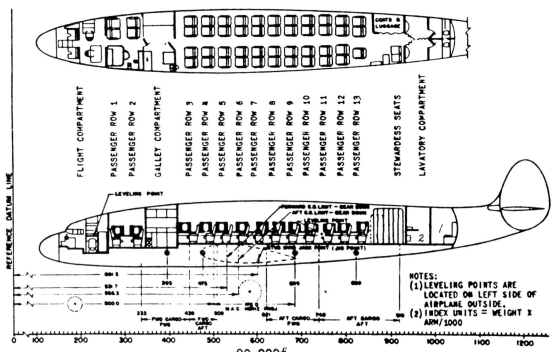

To c/n 2036. A loading chart for a Pan American transatlantic 049 from 1945 copied as an individual item from the Lockheed manual. Note the date is prior to the aircraft's entry into revenue service. The passenger seating makes an interesting comparison with the 1962 version (see above c/n 1967).

used in Pacific region & flew UNRRA charter 19-24 Apr 46, San Francisco-Shanghai-San Francisco. Return flight in record time of 21 hrs 26 mins flying. Named 'Clipper Flora Temple'. To 049-46-26 and later cvtd to Model 149 & regd N88832. Lsd Cubana as CU-T545 20 Aug 53-Feb 55. Restored as N88832 & tfd to Panair do Brasil as PP-PDJ, name unknown, deld 18 Mar 55 (E-17563, dated 24 Feb 55). Struck trees on a hillside at Villa Elisa, 6 miles from Asuncion Airport on an instrument approach in poor visibility to Asuncion Airport, Paraguay, on 16 Jun 55 and crashed. Had departed London 14 Jun 55, en route Rio de Janeiro and Buenos Aires. 14 of the passengers & crew killed. Cause: Descent below minimum prescribed altitude for an instrument approach to the runway in use, and unexpected low cloud.

2033   49-51-26 24 Feb 46 to Pan American as NC88833. Pan Am dely date 25 Feb 46. Originally used in Pacific region. Inaugurated UNRRA charter flights 24-30 Mar 46 (San Francisco-Tokyo & Shanghai-San Francisco), making first flights by commercial aircraft from Japan & China to the USA. To 049-46-26. Named 'Clipper Bald Eagle' (a/o Aug 47, Mar 48), 'Clipper Polynesia' and also 'Clipper Robin Hood' with Pan Am. Nosewheel would not extend, belly-landed off runway at Accra, Gold Coast 24 Mar 48. Repaired. Later N88833. Tfd to Panair do Brasil as PP-PDD, arr Rio de Janeiro 8 Dec 50 (TT: 12,078 hrs). Official transfer 31 Jan 51 and dely quoted as 18 Mar 51. Possibly originally on lse to Panair, as purchase date of 28 Sep 51 quoted. Damaged when the aircraft caught fire at Galeao Airport, Rio, on 1 Jun 55. Repaired. Later named 'Domingos Jorge Velho'. Damaged in heavy landing at Sao Paulo 12 Mar 58. Repaired. TT: 40,987 hrs a/o 23 Apr 63. Stored at Rio from Jul 63, although Brazilian CofA (No. 3261) did not expire until 23 Oct 63. Did not re-enter svce with Panair before the company's bankruptcy on 10 Feb 65. Continued in storage at Rio, and sold to ENGENAV 28 Apr 69. Dismantled for scrap shortly afterwards at Rio-Galeao Airport.

2034   49-51-26 Regd NX86510 to LAC. LADD 30 Nov 45 to Transcontinental & Western Air Inc as NC86510 FN 554 (TT: 11hrs). Christened 'Star of Rome' at La Guardia by Mrs Jimmy Doolittle (Feb 46). Inaugurated New York (La Guardia)-Rome service 11 Feb 46, and first US airline svce to Italy. Damaged beyond repair landing on wet runway at Washington, DC, 29 Mar 46. Aircraft landed far down the runway with flaps not completely extended. Braking was insufficient, the aircraft was turned 30°, went over the runway end and hit a concrete transformer building, turned 90 degrees to the right and ended up in a drainage ditch. (TT: 489 hrs). Cause: Pilot chose to use a near runway at the last minute, which did not allow enough time to make a satisfactory approach. No casualties.

2035   49-51-26 Regd NX86511 to LAC. LADD 18 Dec 45 to Transcontinental & Western Air Inc as NC86511 'Star of Paris' FN 555 (TT: 11hrs). TWA dely date 19 Dec 45. Used on Intl ops. Inaugurated New York (La Guardia)-Paris svce 5 Feb 46, USA-France airline svce and TWA Constellation service on same day. To 049-46-26. Later 'Star of Dublin'. Used for training Air France crew (a/o May 46). Damaged landing at Shannon Airport, Ireland 26 Jul 47. Braking partially ineffective on wet runway, landing in fog, and right main gear collapsed when full brakes were applied, with aircraft going slowly over runway end. En route Boston-Cairo. Slightly damaged. Repaired. Tfd to domestic network 24 Jul 48. (TT: 4,634 hrs). Re-entered svce 2 Aug 48. To N86511. Regd to Trans World Airlines Inc 29 May 50. Damaged landing at Long Beach, CA, 18 Nov 50 after trouble with nos. 2 & 3 engines. Emergency instrument approach made to the airport, with touchdown half way down runway. Brakes ineffective on wet runway, aircraft ran through a fence and over a spur track, collapsing right main gear. Aircraft came to rest 1,400 feet from runway. (TT: 12,082 hrs). Repaired, and ferried to Los Angeles 25 Feb 51. Re-entered svce 2 Mar 51. To Fairfax, KS 27 Feb 55 for Coach Class conversion, after op last 1st Class svce same day. Re-entered svce 1 Apr 55. TT: 38,206 hrs (a/o 31 Aug 59). Crashed shortly after take-off from Chicago-Midway Airport at 02.07 hrs on 1 Sep 61 into a cornfield near Clarendon Hills (a Chicago suburb). Aircraft lost longitudinal control on climb-out and was destroyed in the ensuing impact, killing all on board. Aircraft was flying a Boston, MA to San Francisco, CA, stopping flight TW 529. Cause: Loss of 5/16 inch nickel steel bolt from the parallelogram linkage of the elevator boost system, possibly due to omission of the cotter key. TT: 43,112 hrs. Canx from USCAR 24 Feb 64.

2036   49-51-26 Regd NX88836 to LAC. LADD 5 Jan 46 to Pan American as NC88836. Made first overseas flight of a Pan Am Constellation - New York (La Guardia) to Bermuda - on 14 Jan 46, this was also first commercial flight of Constellation. First transatlantic svce New York-Hurn, UK 24-25 Feb 46, ret Hurn-New York 25-26 Feb 46. Named 'Clipper Yankee Ranger' (a/o Mar 46), later 'Clipper Mayflower' (a/o Aug 47). To 049-46-26. Later N88836. Made emergency landing at Losey Fld, Ponce, PR, on 23 May 51 after no.4 engine malfunctioned and caught fire 45 minutes after take-off from San Juan, PR. Propeller could not be feathered or fire extinguished. Engine fell free of the aircraft, but nacelle continued to burn. Normal landing made, with no injuries. Repaired. Del to Cubana 15 Sep 53, probably as CU-P547, lsd 5 Oct 53 as CU-T547. Collided with CU-T532 (Cubana 049) on ground at Rancho Boyeros, Cuba, 6 Aug 54. Repaired. Sold to Bandes Bank (for Cubana) 30 Jun 55, ownership officially tfd 1 Jul 55. Sale to El Al as 4X-AKF in Oct 55 ntu. Used by Cubana in 1956 on Havana-Miami flights as the "Tropicana Express" with live entertainment on board - a baby grand piano and drums were fitted in the forward part of the cabin, and live entertainment provided by top artists from the, at the time, world-famous Tropicana night club in Havana. Lsd CINTA in 1957, later ALA-CINTA until at least May 59. Sold to Trans European Aviation Ltd as G-ARHK in Dec 60 and regd 9 Feb 61. However, while being ferried to the UK via Canada, the aircraft was seized at Charlotte, NC on 27 Jan 61, following legal action by Mr. J. Shapiro, who was attempting to collect US $750,000 compensation from the Cuban government for the seizure of his hosiery mill and department store in Cuba. The aircraft was released in late Feb 61 and continued to Dorval, Canada, carrying both Cuban and British registrations and Cubana livery. Trans European's interest in the aircraft lapsed, and the aircraft remained stored at Dorval until Jul 63, being canx from the British register 30 Apr 62 as "Sold in Israel". Carried "B" class markings BK-54 24 Feb 62 to 16 May 62 for Israeli Aircraft Industries. Regd to Mr. Leon Perez, Geneva, Switzerland as 4X-AOK on 16 May 62, and deld Dorval -Tel Aviv Jul 62 for the Israeli Aircraft Industries. Canx from 4X- register 16 Nov 62. Stored at Lod until 1967, when it was towed 8 kms from Lod Airport and the wings broken off. Broken up between Aug 68 and early 1969.

2037   49-51-26 12 Jan 46 to Pan American as NC88837, Pan Am dely date 11 Jan 46. Flew transatlantic proving flt New York-Hurn, UK 3-4 Feb 46, ret Hurn-New York 5 Feb 46 & op first scheduled 049 svce New York-Hurn-New York 11-12 Feb 46. Named 'Clipper Shannon' (a/o Mar 46) & 'Clipper Challenge' (a/o Aug 47). To 49-46-26, later cvtd to Model 149. To N88837. Sold to Panair do Brasil 11 Jan 54 as PP-PDG, deld 12 Jan 54 (TT: 20,698 hrs). Later named 'Joao Amaro Maciel Parente'. Panair bankrupt on 10 Feb 65. Stored at Rio-Galeao. CofA (No.3481) expired 21 Mar 65. Sold to ASL Arruda Industria e Comercia, subject to granting of a new CofA 28 Apr 69, and formally tfd to Arruda on 14 Jun 71. Tfd to Amazonense Importacao e Exportacao Ltda 20 Nov 71. TT: 44,569 hrs (a/o 7 Jan 72). Crashed near Cruzeiro do Sul Acre, Northern Brazil on 29 May 72 after all four engines failed. Was en route Rio Branco to Cruzeiro do Sul. All 14 on board killed, including the owner of Arruda and Amazonense, Senor ASL Arruda.

2038   49-51-26 21 Jan 46 to Pan American as NC88838 (Dely also quoted as 1 Feb 46). First transatlantic svce New York-Hurn, UK 25 Feb 46, ret Hurn-New York 27 Feb 46. Named 'Clipper Donald McKay'. To 49- 46-26, later became the first conversion to a Model 149. To N88838. Tfd to Panair do Brasil as PP-PDF 7 Dec 53 & deld 1 Dec 53, regd Jan 54. Later named 'Garcia Rodrigues Paes Leme'. Stored at Rio-Galeao after bankruptcy of Panair 10 Feb 65. CofA (No.3501) expired 14 Jun 65. Auctioned on 28 Apr

69, but not sold as did not reach reserve price. Sold Dec 69(?) to ASAS Importadora e Exportadero. Civil aviation authorities would not re-certify the aircraft. Repossessed by Panair creditors. Canx from PP-register 17 Dec 71 and scrapped at Galeao during Mar-Apr 74.

2039 49-51-26 Regd NX86512 to LAC. LADD 10 Jan 46 to Transcontinental & Western Air Inc as NC86512 'Star of India' FN 512. TWA dely date 11 Jan 46 (TT: 15hrs), new FN 556 shortly after. Used for training of Air France crews (a/o May 46). To 49-46-26. Crashed landing at Newcastle, DE on 12 Oct 46. The aircraft, while on approach to the airfield, was advised to divert, as a rain squall was passing over, but the captain refused. The squall was followed by a windshift, and the captain was advised to go around and land on another runway, which he also refused to do. On landing, braking was ineffective, a short burst of power was given, but then the landing was continued. The aircraft continued off the end of the runway, through trees, across a road, striking two cars, continued, for a further 650 ft, turning counter-clockwise, and stopped in an upright position and burst into flames. The crew escaped. TT: 1,195 hrs. Canx from USCAR 28 Mar 49.

2040 49-51-26 5 Feb 46 to Transcontinental & Western Air Inc as NC86513 'Star of Lisbon' FN 513. TWA dely date 8 Feb 46 (TT: 15hrs), new FN 557 shortly after. Crash-landed two miles northeast of Reading Airport, PA, on 11 Jul 46. An engine had caught fire while the crew had been practising stopping and re-starting engines during a training flight. In addition, smoke from a fire inside the aircraft blinded the pilots as they attempted to land. The aircraft ploughed through electric wires and scattered rocks, then slithered in rotary motion 1,000 feet across a hayfield and road before coming to a stop in a field. Five of the six crew were killed. Cause: The fire in the fuselage had been caused by a through-stud (a small bolt bringing electrical power from the generators in the wings into the fuselage without breaking the pressurization seal of the cabin). A bolt had worked loose, rubbed against the fuselage and thus created sufficient arcing to set fire to a nearby hydraulic line, which had a tendency to leak hydraulic fluid. After this accident, all Constellations (a total of 51 aircraft) were grounded by the CAA for 30 days while modifications were made to the design and installation of the through-studs, the hydraulic lines and fire-detection system, and also to the engines and cabin supercharger drive shaft. Canx from USCAR 28 Mar 49.

2041 49-51-25 Regd to LAC 22 Jan 46, to Transcontinental & Western Air Inc 9 Feb 46 as NC86514 'Star of India' FN 514, (TT: 10hrs). Shortly after FN 506. To 049-46-25. Made first visit of Constellation to Sky Harbor Airport, Tucson, AZ 26 Dec 46 (diverted in from Los Angeles on Flight TW95). Later N86514. Regd to Trans World Airlines Inc 29 May 50. To LAS, Burbank, for conversion to Coach Class 25 Feb 54. Re-entered svce 4 Apr 54. Lsd Eastern Air Lines 25 Nov 57. Ret TWA 23 Apr 58. TT: 40,091hrs (a/o 31 Aug 59). Sold to Nevada Airmotive 31 Mar 62 (TT: 45,459 hrs), official transfer date 13 Mar 62. Believed stored at Las Vegas, NV, until 1964, then scrapped. Lapsed USCAR 1967, canx 6 Sep 71 (failure to file 1973).

2042 49-51-25 15 Feb 46 to Transcontinental & Western Air Inc as NC86515 'Star of Arabia' FN 515 (TT: 9hrs), shortly after FN 507. To 049-46-25; later N86515. Regd to Trans World Airlines Inc 29 May 50. To Fairfax, KS for Coach Class conversion 23 Jan 55 after last 1st Class svce 22 Jan 55. Re-entered svce 1 Mar 55. TT: 40,103hrs (a/o 31 Aug 59). Sold to Nevada Airmotive 31 Mar 62 (TT: 45,591 hrs). Believed stored at Las Vegas, NV, until 1964, then scrapped. Lapsed USCAR 1967, canx 6 Sep 71 (failure to file 1973).

2043 49-51-25 19 Feb 46 to Transcontinental & Western Air Inc as NC86516 'Star of Ireland' FN 516 (TT: 11hrs), shortly after FN 508. To 049-46-25, later N86516. Regd to Trans World Airlines Inc 29 May 50. Last 1st Class svce 19 Dec 54, then to Fairfax, KS for Coach Class conversion 20 Dec 54. Re-entered svce 22 Jan 55. Lsd Eastern Air Lines 15 Dec 56. Ret TWA 17 May 57. TT: 40,312hrs (a/o 31 Aug 59). Sold to Nevada Airmotive 31 Mar 62 (TT: 44,692 hrs). Believed stored at Las Vegas, NV, until 1964, then scrapped. Lapsed USCAR 1967, canx 6 Sep 71 (failure to file 1973).

2044 49-51 25 Regd 14 Feb 46 to LAC as NC86517. LADD: 19 Feb 46 to Transcontinental & Western Air Inc as 'Star of Tripoli Sky Chief' FN 517, (TT: 9hrs), shortly after FN 509, named 'Star of Tripoli'. In svce 19 Feb 46. To 049-46-25, later N86517. Regd to Trans World Airlines Inc 29 May 50. Last 1st Class svce 7 Feb 53, then to LAS Burbank for Coach Class conversion, 8 Feb 53. Re-entered svce 20 Mar 53. TT: 41,203 hrs (a/o 31 May 59). Sold to Las Vegas Hacienda Inc 15 May 61 (FAA records), TWA quote 24 May 61. Lsd World Wide Airlines 13 Jul 62, lsd Standard Airways 8 Mar 63 until 30 Jan 64 (lost certificate), lsd Dellair by Apr 64. Sold to Trans World Insurance Brokers 1 Dec 64. Ret to Las Vegas Hacienda Inc 23 Jul 65. Lsd to Air Holiday and also to World Samplers. Sold to John W Ellis 2 Feb 67. Stored at San Francisco, CA, from Jan 69. Ownership tfd to the San Francisco Unified School District (Junior College, Adult & Adult Occupation Division) 29 Dec 69 after aircraft had been donated to the school for a nominal fee of one US dollar. The owner owed Butler Aviation Inc several thousand dollars for work carried out on the aircraft and could not pay it. The aircraft was subsequently moved off the airfield to a carpark on the perimeter and used as an instructional airframe by students at the technical school. To San Francisco Community College District (Adult & Adult Occupation Division) Apr 70. Canx from USCAR 1 Aug 72 as permanently retired from svce, used in aeronautical training. Continued in use until 1973, when a lorry hit it and ripped off the nose-wheel gear. Scrapping started in Jul 73 and the aircraft had been broken up by the end of 1973.

2045 49-51-26 24 Feb 46 to Pan American as NC88845. Pan Am dely date 25 Feb 46. First transatlantic svce New York-Hurn, UK 11 Mar 46, ret same day to New York. To 049-46-26. Named 'Clipper Dublin' (a/o Mar 46) & 'Clipper Eclipse'. Destroyed in forced-landing at Mayadine, Syria, on 19 Jun 47. While cruising at 18,500 ft, trouble developed in no.1 engine, which was feathered. Power on the other three engines was reduced after overheating occurred. When 75 miles northwest of Habbaniya, by which time the aircraft had descended to 10,000 ft, fire broke out in no.2 engine nacelle, and a rapid descent started. Six or seven minutes later, the no.2 engine fell from the aircraft, but the wing continued to burn. Less than a minute later, a wheels-up landing was made on hard-packed desert sand, striking the left wingtip, groundlooping, and skidding backwards for 210 ft, coming to rest in flames. 15 of passengers and crew killed. Cause: No.1 engine failed due to broken exhaust rocker arm, no.2 failed due to failure of the thrust-bearing, blocking oil from prop-feathering motor to the propeller dome, which subsequently ruptured due to the high pressure build-up in feathering the propeller. TT: 2,645 hrs (also quoted as 2,686hrs). Aircraft was en route Karachi-Istanbul-London. Canx from USCAR 9 Jun 64 (!)

2046 49-51-26 28 Feb 46 to Pan American as NC88846. Pan Am dely 1 Mar 46. First transatlantic svce New York-Hurn, UK 20 Apr 46, ret Hurn-New York same day. Re-inaugurated Pan Am Constellation svces New York-London after grounding, arr London 25 Aug 46, dep 26 Aug 46. Named 'Clipper Bermuda', later 'Clipper Great Republic' (a/o Aug 47, Aug 50). To 049-46-26. Later N88846. Crashed and burned out on a 1,500 ft hill in jungle near Sanoyea, fifty miles from Monrovia, Liberia shortly after 03.30 hrs (GMT) on 22 Jun 51. En route Johannesburg-New York. All killed. Cause: probably the action of the Captain in descending below en-route minimum altitude without positive identification of the aircraft's position; weather very bad with heavy rain. TT: 13,373 hrs.

2047 49-51-26 8 Mar 46 to Pan American as NC88847. Pan Am dely date 12 Mar 46. Originally used in Pacific region. Flew second UNRRA charter 4-13 Apr 46 San Francisco-Shanghai-San Francisco. Named 'Clipper Hotspur' (a/o Aug 47). To 049-46-26. Later N88847. Tfd to Panair do Brasil 30 Jul 53 (deld 20 Jul 53) as PP-PDE. Later named 'Estevao Ribeiro Baiao Parente'. Crashed in swampy jungle area near Parana de Eva, near a tributary of the

Amazon in Northern Brazil on 14 Dec 62, while on approach to Manaus late at night. All killed. En route Maceio-Recife-Belem-Manaus. The aircraft had departed Belem at 02.31 (GMT) & reported at 05.04hrs that it was "six minutes from Manaus". At 05.19 Manaus was asked whether the engines could be heard, to which they replied in the negative. It was assumed that the aircraft crashed immediately after the final message, approx. 45kms from Manaus. Cause: assumed to be navigation error as the NDB at Manaus was operating normally.

2048 49-51-26 This aircraft, the 48th production aircraft, was withdrawn from the military production line 7 Jun 45 to be completed as the prototype commercial model. LADD: 15 Mar 46 to Pan American as NC88848, but 18 Apr 46 also quoted (actual dely date?). Named 'Clipper Golden Gate'. Tfd to Panair do Brasil 27 Jul 46 (deld 21 Jul 46) as PP-PCB. To 049-46-26. Flew inaugural svce Rio-Rome 28 Sep 46. Later named 'Domingos Alfonso Sertao'. Withdrawn from use and stored, partly cannibalized at Rio de Janeiro from 1962. CofA (No.1507) expired 17 May 62. Panair bankrupt on 10 Feb 65. Sold to ENGENAV-Engenharia e Construcoes 28 Apr 69 and dismantled for scrap at Rio-Galeao.

2049 49-51-26 Regd NX88849 to LAC. Completed as NC88849 for Pan American, but deld direct to Panair do Brasil as PP-PCF, LADD: 22 Mar 46. Deld La Guardia-Rio de Janeiro 29-30 Mar 46. Brazilian CofA (No.1505). First foreign airliner to land at London-Heathrow 16 Apr 46 on European proving flt & first Panair 049 to visit Paris same day. Flew first scheduled flight Brazil-London 23 Apr 46. To 049-46-26. Later named 'Manoel de Borba Gato' and subsequently 'Antonio Rodriques Velho'. Damaged in a belly-landing at Rio-Galeao on 14 Jul 62 (TT: 41,338 hrs), and stored unrepaired. Panair bankrupt on 10 Feb 65. Sold to ENGENAV-Engenharia e Construcoes 28 Apr 69 and dismantled for scrap.

An aerial view of the apron outside the factory at Burbank in early 1946 shows seven 049s for Pan American awaiting engines or propellers, or both. NC88849 in the right foreground was actually delivered direct to Panair do Brasil and never flew in Pan American colours. (Lockheed)

2050 49-51-26 20 Mar 46 to Pan American as NC88850. First transatlantic svce New York-Hurn, UK 27 Mar 46, ret same day. Named 'Clipper Congo' (a/o May 46), also 'Clipper Intrepid' (a/o Aug 50). To 049-46-26, and later to Model 149. Later N88850. Sold to Panair do Brasil (TT: 21,323 hrs) as PP-PDH (E-17559, 30 Nov 54) and deld 4 Jan 55, Brazilian CofA (No.3657). Later named 'Manuel Preto'. Damaged landing at Galeao, Rio, 13 Dec 57. Repaired. Made last scheduled visit of PAB Constellation to London 20 Jun 57. TT: 40,732 hrs (a/o 27 Nov 64). Stored at Rio-Galeao after Panair bankruptcy 10 Feb 65, CofA expired 27 Feb 65. Auctioned at Rio 28 Apr 69, but not sold as the aircraft did not reach the reserve price. Sold 27 Dec 69 to ASAS-Importadora e Exportadaro. Painted up in ASAS colours, but not flown. Payments not completed, so aircraft repossessed by Panair creditors. Canx from register 17 Dec 71 (lack of inspection). Stored at Rio-Galeao until sold off for scrap in about Apr74. Scrapped between 11 May and 31 May 74.

2051 49-51-27 Regd NX90921 to LAC. LADD 9 Apr 46 to American Overseas as NC90921. First transatlantic svce New York-London 1 Jul 46. Carried names 'Flagship Sweden' (a/o Nov 49), 'Flagship Stockholm', and possibly 'Flagship Mercury' and 'Flagship London', but order unknown. To 049-46-27. Later N90921. Sold to Pan American 'Clipper Jupiter Rex' 25 Sep 50. Sold to BOAC 1 Dec 52 at Miami, ferried Burbank for conversion to 049D 9 Jan 53. Cvtd to 65-Seater, All-Tourist Class at Burbank 9 Jan-11 Mar 53. Regd G-AMUP 6 Feb 53 and deld Burbank-New York-London 11-13 Mar 53, named 'Boston' (E-22234, 9 Mar 53), CofA (A3880) issued 9 Mar 53. In svce 9 Apr 53 London-Montreal. Cvtd to 049E Aug-Sep 53. Last svce 27 Mar 55. Sold to Capital Airlines 28 Mar 55 as N2738A FN 758, deld ex-London 26 Mar 55, G-regn canx 29 Mar 55. In svce with Capital 27 Apr 55. Damaged at Washington, DC, 11 Sep 55 on local flt, when aircraft ran forward and hit APU on engine start-up. Repaired, used in 72-pax configuration. TT: 28,160 hrs (a/o May 59). Stored by 1960 and sold to Falcon Airways Dec 60 (TT: 30,611 hrs). Regn G-ARHJ reserved, but ntu, regd G-AMUP 4 Jan 61, deld Washington-Gander-London (Heathrow) 7-8 Jan 61 as N2738A (E-42941, undated), painted as G-AMUP after arrival LIIR. Capital's red colour scheme overpainted with Falcon's black scheme and cvtd to 82-Seater at London during Feb 61 and deld to London (Gatwick) 1 Mar 61 for entry into svce. Falcon ceased ops 21 Sep 61. Sold to Trans European Aviation 15 Jan 62 (CofRegn 13 Feb 62). Slightly damaged at Tel Aviv, Israel, 12 Jul 62. Repaired, impounded Tel Aviv for non-payment of maintenance work. Trans European ceased ops Aug 62. Aircraft stored at Gatwick, flown to Luton, England for storage Oct 62. Sold to Euravia (London) Ltd 18 Apr 63, CofRegn 23 May 63. Tfd Britannia Airways 2 Feb 65. Withdrawn from use at Luton after CofA expiry 5 Aug 65 and broken up there approx Oct 65, canx from register 28 Jan 66 (TT: 32,924 hrs).

2052 49-51-27 25 Mar 46 to American Overseas as NC90922. Carried names 'Flagship Copenhagen', 'Flagship Denmark' and 'Flagship Oslo'. To 049-46-27. Later N90922. Damaged when right undercarriage collapsed landing on a closed runway at Boston, MA, 3 May 47. Repaired. Sold to Pan American as 'Clipper Mount Vernon' 25 Sep 50. Starboard undercarriage caught fire at Miami, FL on 29 Jan 57, en route for Nassau. Received damage. Repaired. Lsd to Aeronaves de Mexico (E-17593, 13 Feb 57) as XA-MAG. Sold to Panair do Brasil 31 Dec 57 as PP-PDP (regd 2 Feb 59), Brazilian CofA (No.3982). Named 'Bras Cubas', later 'Francisco Nimes de Siqueira'. TT: 24,434 hrs (a/o 9 Jun 58). Stored at Rio-Galeao from Nov 63 (TT: 34,562 hrs). CofA expired 21 Jan 65. Panair bankrupt 10 Feb 65. Auctioned 28 Apr 69 at Rio, but not sold as the aircraft did not reach the reserve price. Sold for scrap 30 Jan 70 to unknown purchaser and scrapped at Rio-Galeao shortly afterwards.

2053 49-51-27 27 Mar 46 to American Overseas as NC90923. AOA dely date 29 Mar 46. Named 'Flagship Great Britain', 'Flagship Scotland', 'Flagship Oslo', and also possibly 'Flagship London' and 'Flagship Stockholm', order unknown. First AOA Constellation to visit London-Heathrow 31 May 46. To 049-46-27. Carried name 'Flagship XIV Olympiad' (for London Olympics Jul-Aug 48). Later N90923. Sold to Pan American 'Clipper Golden Rule' 25 Sep 50. Sold to Delta C & S 1 Feb 56 and cvtd to 72-Seater Coach Class, FN 503, in svce 29 Jun 56. Stored at LAS, Idlewild, NY, for sale by Jun 58. Sold to American Flyers Airline Corp 1 Apr 60, FN 503, later 923. Sold to California Airmotive 1967 and broken up at Burbank or Lancaster, CA, shortly afterwards. - Canx from USCAR 21 Jan 69.

2054 49-51-27 Regd NX90924 to LAC. LADD 4 Apr 46 to American Overseas as NC90924. First transatlantic svce New York-London 5 Jul 46. Named 'Flagship Holland', 'Flagship Amsterdam' and 'Flagship Shannon' (a/o Mar 50). To 049-46-27.

Later N90924. Sold to Pan American 'Clipper Lafayette' 25 Sep 50. Sold to Trans World Airlines Inc via Master Equipment Co and deld 12 May 52 at Miami, FL. Ferried next day to Fairfax, KS for modifications including cockpit standardization (TT: 11,185 hrs). Mods completed 2 Jun 52. Used for pilot training 3 Jun to 21 Sep 52. Retd Fairfax, KS for Coach Class conversion 21 Sep 52 (TT: 11,488 hrs). Deld to Kansas City Municipal 6 Dec 52 as 'Star of Algeria' FN 527 and first svce 7 Dec 52. Stored by mid-61 (TT: 38,586 hrs). Sold to Nevada Airmotive 31 Mar 62 and believed stored at Las Vegas, NV, until 1964, then scrapped. Lapsed USCAR 1967, canx 10 Sep 71.

2055 49-51-26 22 Apr 46 to Pan American as NC88855. Pan Am dely date 23 Apr 46. First transatlantic svce New York-Hurn, UK 1 May 46, ret Hurn-New York same day. Named 'Clipper Invincible' (a/o Aug 47) & 'Clipper Undaunted' (a/o Aug 50). To 049-46-26, later to Model 149. Later N88855. Sold to Delta C & S 1 Feb 56 and cvtd to 72-Seater Coach Class, FN 501, in svce 3 Sep 56. On 7 Feb 57, during an ILS approach to Shreveport, LA, the Captain took over from the co-pilot and started a missed approach procedure, but not in time to prevent the aircraft colliding with the ground. A pull-up was made, but the left gear could not be retracted. The aircraft returned to Jackson, MS, and landed, but the gear collapsed during the landing roll. En route Newark, NJ, to Dallas, TX. Received substantial damage, but repaired. Stored at LAS, Idlewild, NY, for sale by Jun 58. Sold to American Flyers Airline Corp 1 Apr 60, FN 501, later 855. Sold to California Airmotive 1967. Parked at Van Nuys, CA, by Jul 67 and stored subsequently at Lancaster, CA, until at least May 71, but scrapped shortly afterwards. Canx from USCAR 26 Jun 70.

2056 49-51-26 12 Apr 46 to Pan American as NC88856. Pan Am dely date 15 Apr 46. First transatlantic svce New York-Hurn, UK 23 Apr 46, ret Hurn-New York 24 Apr 46. Named 'Clipper Paul Jones' (a/o Aug 47), possibly also 'Clipper Portugal'. To 049-46-26. Fitted with an experimental periscopic sextant for the navigator's use, instead of the drag-producing astrodome, while in Pan American svce. Later N88856. Sold to Panair do Brasil in approx Oct 50 and deld as PP-PDC 31 Dec 50. Port undercarriage retracted while the aircraft was in a hangar at Rio on 19 Jan 56. Damaged. Repaired. Later named 'Domingos Dios Prado'. Belly-landed at Recife, Brazil, 14 Feb 59 following nose-wheel undercarriage failure. Repaired. Skidded off wet runway landing at Belo Horizonte, Brazil, on 26 Jan 61. Subsequently retired from service and used for spares.

2057 49-51-26 19 Apr 46 to Pan American as NC88857. First transatlantic svce New York-Hurn, UK 29 Apr 46, ret Hurn-New York same day. Named 'Clipper Unity', 'Clipper Africa' (a/o Apr 46) and also by Aug 47 'Clipper Flying Mist'. To 049-46-26, and later to Model 149. Later N88857. Sold to Panair do Brasil and deld 19 Jan 55 (E-17561, undated) as PP-PDI, Brazilian CofA (No.3656). Named 'Amador Bueno da Veiga'. Stored from Jan 62 at Rio-Galeao, and eventually used for spares, CofA expired 20 Jun 62. Panair bankrupt 10 Feb 65. Sold 28 Apr 69 to ENGENAV-Engenharia e Construcoes as scrap. Scrapped at Rio-Galeao and canx from register 17 Dec 71.

2058 49-51-26 24 Apr 46 (25 Apr also quoted) to Pan American as NC88858. Pan Am dely date 26 Apr 46. First transatlantic svce New York-Hurn, UK 5 May 46, ret Hurn-New York same day. Named 'Clipper America'. Damaged in belly-landing on grass at Windham Fld, Willimantic, CT, at 18.10 hrs (local) on 18 Jun 46. Shortly after leaving La Guardia, NY, for London, England, fire broke out in no.4 engine. Fire could not be extinguished, but engine eventually dropped out, with a small fire persisting in the wing. No injuries on forced-landing made 59 mins after take-off. Cause: Cabin supercharger drive-shaft broke, the engine-end of the rod flaying at the engine supports. Repairs carried out at Willimantic, with a strip of sheet metal riveted over the leading edge of the wing in place of the no.4 engine. Regd NX88858 - (as all Constellations had been grounded after the 11 Jul 46 crash of c/n 2040) - the aircraft was ferried to MacArthur Fld, Long Island, NY, on 25 Jul 46. After further checks, the only true Constellation

NX88858 049 was the only genuine Constellation trimotor. After a forced landing at Willimantic (Connecticut) on 18th June 1946, the aircraft was repaired by Lockheed Aircraft Service (Long Island) and ferried across the USA back to Burbank with a metal covering over the missing engine mounting and water in the outboard tank. The 049 is seen on approach to Burbank on 30th July 1946 after a successful ferry-flight. (Lockheed)

Trimotor left MacArthur Fld at 05.55 hrs (local) on 30 Jul 46 for its historic transcontinental flight via Wichita, KS, to Burbank, CA, flown by Joseph Towle (Captain), George McIntyre (First Officer) and C R (Chuck) Mercer (Flight Engineer), all of the LAC Flight Test Staff. Repaired at Burbank and re-entered svce as an 049-46-26 NC88858 'Clipper Empress of the Skies'. Crashed on second attempt at an ILS approach to Shannon Airport, Ireland on 15 Apr 48 at approx 02.34 hrs (GMT). Visibility was 2 to 3 miles with fog patches reducing visibility to 250 ft in places. The aircraft struck the ground 2,380 ft short of the runway-end, subsequently striking a stone wall which wrecked the undercarriage and tore out the port outer engine. After skidding along the ground for a further 750 ft the aircraft stopped and the fuel tanks exploded. There was one survivor. The aircraft was en route from Karachi to Shannon and New York. Cause: Probably the continuation of the ILS approach to an altitude insufficient to clear the terrain, with the failure of the pilot's fluorescent instrument light possibly a contributing factor.

The crew on the transcontinental "Connie trimotor" flight consisted of (from right to left): Charles R "Chuck" Mercer (Chief Flight Engineer) as flight engineer, Joe Towle (Director of Flying) as pilot, George McIntyre (Production & Training Pilot) as co-pilot, and Jake Jackson (Production & Training Flight Engineer) as assistant flight engineer. (Lockheed, with thanks for the precise information to Chuck Mercer & Jack Real)

SECTION 12: CONSTELLATION PRODUCTION LIST

2059 49-51-26 27 Apr 46, to Pan American as NC88859. Pan Am dely date 30 Apr 46. Named 'Clipper Flying Eagle' (a/o Aug 47), later 'Clipper Talisman' (a/o Aug 50). To 049-46-26, and later to Model 149. Later N88859. Lsd to Panair do Brasil 1 Jul 55 (E-17566) as PP-PDK. Ret to Pan American as N88859 in Dec 56. Lsd to Aero-naves de Mexico as XA-MAH 11 Feb 57 (E-17568). Sold to Panair do Brasil 31 Dec 57 and deld Mexico City to Rio de Janeiro 11 May 58 as PP-PDQ, Brazilian CofA (No.3978). Named 'Jeronimo Fragoso de Albuquerque'. Stored from 1962 at Rio-Galeao. Cof A expired 16 Feb 63. Panair bankrupt 10 Feb 65. Sold to ENGENAV-Engenharia e Construcoes 28 Apr 69 and dismantled for scrap shortly afterwards at Rio-Galeao.

2060 49-51-26 27 Apr 46 to Pan American as NC88860. Pan Am dely date 1 May 46. First transatlantic svce New York-Hurn, UK 22 May 46, ret Hurn-New York 23 May 46. Named 'Clipper New York', renamed 'Clipper London' and was first Pan American Constellation to visit London-Heathrow on 31 May 46. Also at one time named 'Clipper Courier'. To 049-46-26. Tfd to Panair do Brasil 24 May 47 as PP-PCR, deld 22 May 47 (TT: 2,005 hrs on arrival), Brazilian CofA (No.1786). Flew inaugural Rio-Frankfurt, Germany svce 2 Mar 48. Later named 'Domingos Barbosa Calheiros'. TT: 40,782 hrs a/o 22 Aug 61. Nosewheel undercarriage could not be retracted or fully extended again after take-off from Belo Horizonte Airport on 3 Mar 62. Belly-landed at Belo Horizonte or possibly at Rio-Galeao, as aircraft was subsequently stored at Rio in damaged condition (Brazilian CAR gives accident date as 28 Feb 62). Panair bankrupt 10 Feb 65. Sold to ENGENAV-Engenharia e Construcoes 28 Apr 69 for scrap and dismantled at Rio-Galeao shortly afterwards.

2061 49-51-26 10 May 46 to Pan American as NC88861. Pan Am dely date 14 May 46. First transatlantic svce New York-London (Heathrow) 5 Jun 46, ret London-New York same day. Named 'Clipper Atlantic' and 'Clipper Winged Arrow' (a/o Aug 47 & Aug 50). To 049-46-26. Later N88861. Flew first scheduled Calcutta-Bangkok-Hong Kong section of Pan American's Round-the-World schedule on 3 Nov 49. Lsd Cubana as CU-P532 9 Jun 53. Reregd as CU-T532 on arrival & flew inaugural Constellation svce Havana-Madrid 15 Jun 53. Collided with Constellation CU-T547 (c/n 2036) on ground at Rancho Boyeros, Cuba 6 Aug 54. Repaired. Bt by Bandes Bank (for Cubana) 30 Jun 55 & officially tfd 1 Jul 55. Sold to El Al Oct 55 and deld Dec 55 as 4X-AKE, in svce by Feb 56. Damaged taxying New York-Idlewild 19 Nov 57. Repaired. Sale in Switzerland to Transazur A/L as HB-IEC (regn issued 24 Feb 59) ntu. Canx from 4X-register 6 Feb 62, and tfd to Israeli Aircraft Industries. Stored at Lod for possible Israeli Air Force use, but ntu. Presumably scrapped at Lod in the mid-1960s (last report 1965).

2062 49-51-26 Completed as NC88862 for Pan American, but deld direct to Panair do Brasil as PP-PCG 14 May 46. To 049-46-26. Crashed 28 Jul 50 when it hit power lines on approach to Porto Alegre, Brazil, killing all on board.

2063 49-51-27 15 May 46 to American Overseas Airlines as NC90925. Named 'Flagship America', also 'Flagship Philadelphia' and 'Flagship Copenhagen', order unknown. To 049-46-27. Later N90925. Sold to Pan American as 'Clipper Courier' on 25 Sep 50. Struck Piper PA-20 after landing at San Salvador, El Salvador 26 Jul 53, badly damaged & three in light aircraft killed. Repaired. Sold to Delta C & S 1 Feb 56 and cvtd to 72-Seater Coach Class, FN 504, in svce 2 Aug 56. Stored at LAS, Idlewild, NY, for sale by Jun 58. Sold to American Flyers Airline Corp 1 Apr 60, FN 504, later 925. Broken up, believed at Ardmore, OK, by Sep 67. Lapsed from USCAR Jul 66, canx by 1970.

2064 49-51-27 15 May 46 to American Overseas Airlines as NC90926. Named 'Flagship Eire', 'Flagship Chicago' and 'Flagship Amsterdam' (a/o Sep 50). Leased to Linea Aeropostal Venezolana spring 47. To 049-46-27. Later N90926. Sold to Pan American as 'Clipper Ocean Herald' 25 Sep 50. Sold to Trans World Airlines Inc via Master Equipment Co 15 Apr 52 at Miami, FL (TT: 11,661 hrs) and deld same day to Fairfax, KS for modifications. Cvtd to Coach Class 28 Apr-3 Oct 52 as 'Star of Tunis' FN 526. In svce 3 Oct 52. Ferried Fairfax to Kansas City Municipal same day for use on special CAA and Engineering test with Hamilton Standard Integral Reversing Propellers on nos. 2 & 3 engines - first 049 series to be fitted with reversing props. Service test 10 May 53. Re-entered svce, date unknown. Lsd Eastern Air Lines 8 Jan 57. Ret TWA 17 May 57. Sold to Nevada Airmotive 31 Mar 62 (TT: 38,783 hrs). Lsd ASA International 1962 to 1963(?). Stored at Oakland, CA, from at least Oct 65 in ASA colours. Withdrawn from use in Apr 67 and stripped for useable spares Jul 67. Fuselage used for fire-practice at Oakland until about Oct 76 (last report), then scrapped.

2065 49-51-27 20 May 46 to American Overseas Airlines as NC90927. Named 'Flagship Norway', 'Flagship Detroit' and 'Flagship Glasgow', order unknown. To 049-46-27. Later N90927. Sold to Pan American 25 Sep 50 'Clipper Wings of the Morning'. Sold to BOAC 1 Dec 52 at Miami, ferried to Burbank for conversion to 049D 9 Jan 53. Cvtd to 65-Seater, All-Tourist Class at Burbank 9 Jan-27 Mar 53, also cvtd to 049E Mar 53. Regd G-AMUR 6 Feb 53. Flew Burbank-New York 27-28 Mar 53, then in svce 29 Mar 53 New York-London, deld to London 30 Mar 53, named 'Barnstaple' (E-22235, 27 Mar 53), CofA (A3881) issued 26 Mar 53. Damaged starboard wing-tip in collision with TWA 749A N6019C taxying Gander, Nfld 3 Jul 54. Repaired. Flew last BOAC 049 svce New York-London, dep 23 Mar 55, but had to return with problems, dep New York 26 Mar, arr London 27 Mar 55. Out of svce 11 Apr 55, sold to Capital Airlines 28 Apr 55, deld ex-London 26 Apr 55, G-regn canx & deld to Capital 28 Apr 55. Regd N2739A, FN 759, in svce 27 May 55. Later used in 72-pax configuration. Wfu and stored 18 Sep 60 (TT: 31,686 hrs). Transferred nominally to United Air Lines 1 Jun 61. Sold to Modern Air Transport via Miami Aircraft & Engine Sales 4 Aug 61, but never op by Modern. Flown to Mercer County Airport, Trenton, NJ, and used for spares. Major components missing by Oct 64. Sold to Curry Corp early 64, and to Trenton Aviation Inc early 66, and hulk broken up at Trenton.

2066 49-51-25 Completed as NC90616 for Pan American Grace Airways - PANAGRA, but deld direct to Pan American 23 May 46 as 49-51-26 NC88865. Pan Am dely date 24 May 46. Named 'Clipper Racer' (a/o Oct 46) and 'Clipper White Falcon' (a/o Aug 47). To 049-46-26. Sold to Panair do Brasil as PP-PDA and deld 15 Oct 47 (USA), 16 Oct 47 (Brazil). Damaged on 7 Dec 48, repaired. Crashed 4 miles short of the runway end at Sao Paulo, Brazil, on 17 Jun 53, while attempting emergency landing in bad weather. Engine failed and wing of aircraft hit hill on approach southwest of airport, aircraft caught fire, killing all on board. En route Paris to Buenos Aires, Argentina.

2067 49-51-25 Completed as NC90617 for Pan American Grace Airways - PANAGRA, but deld direct to Pan American 25 May 46 as 49-51-26 NC88868. Pan Am dely date 27 May 46. First transatlantic svce New York-London 22 Jun 46, ret 23 Jun 46. Flew last Pan Am Constellation svce to London prior grounding, dep London 11 Jul 46 for New York & mods. Named 'Clipper Golden Fleece' (a/o Aug 47 & Aug 50), and 'Clipper Peerless'. To 049-46-26, and later Model 149. Later N88868. Sold to Delta C & S 1 Feb 56 and cvtd to 72-Seater Coach Class, FN 502, in svce 5 Jul 56. Stored at LAS, Idlewild, NY, for sale by Jun 58. Sold to American Flyers Airline Corp 1 Apr 60, FN 502, later 868. Stored at Ardmore, OK, by Aug 66 and sold to California Airmotive late 67. In svce with unknown operator (American Flyers colours, no titles) from autumn 67. Sold to Fun Leasing Inc 1968 and to Tex Hou Inc 1970. Stored at Houston-Hobby, TX, by Apr 70, and later at Galveston, TX, by 1971. Canx by California Airmotive 12 Jul 70. Canx from USCAR 1972, and broken up at Galveston, TX, Jun 74.

2068 49-51-26 28 May 46 to KLM as PH-TAU 'Utrecht', but remained at Burbank and cvtd to 49-46-26. Officially regd 10 Sep 46 and deld early Oct 46 (E-9678, 3 Oct 46). KLM quote dely date as 10 Sep 46. Planned lse to Swissair Apr 49 & provisionally regd HB-IBI 27 Aug 49, but lse fell through. PH-regn canx 8 Jun 50. To LAC (trade-in on 749As) 8 Jun 50, FAA quote 22 May 50. Regd 5

Jun 50 to LAC as N86531. Cvtd to 049-46-59 for Capital Airlines as 'Capitaliner United States', FN 750, and deld 14 Jul 50. Ownership transferred officially 18 Jul 50, in svce 28 Jul 50. Cvtd to Model 049D. Later used in 72-pax configuration. Stored by Dec 60 (TT: 32,180 hrs), tfd nominally to United Air Lines Inc 1 Jun 61. Sold to Modern Air Transport 27 Jul 61 (United quote 8 Aug 61). Out of use by mid-65. Sold to Pasco Aviation Inc 15 Jul 66, and to Pinellas Central Bank & Trust Co 1 Sep 66. Sold to Harold W Harbican t/a Belizean Airlines Ltd 20 Mar 67, named 'The Belizean Belle'. Re-regd N864H 12 Feb 68. Repossessed by Diane H Summers on 10 Jun 69, renamed 'The Tiger', with the initials 'UH' on the rear fuselage and a white tiger emblem on the nose. Believed op as Gulf & Western Airlines Inc from Jun 69. Ownership transferred to First National Bank & Trust Co of Dunedin 14 Jan 71. Sold to Jack N Mangham 18 Jan 72 (also of Gulf & Western Airlines Inc). Stored at New Orleans, LA, by Jan 73. Owner reported as Antonio Fernandez in Jan 73 (no entry in FAA and files). Sold to Crash Landing 21 Jan 73, flown to Moisant Airport and dismantled for transportation to the "Crash Landing" bar/ nightclub at Metairic, New Orleans, LA. Canx from USCAR 14 Feb 73 as 'dismantled; salvaged and cvtd to a cocktail lounge'. In use as such by Nov 73. Closed down about a year later, and used as an attraction at the "Millionaires' Club", New Orleans, LA, by Nov 75. At the "Crash Landing" discotheque in New Orleans (a/o 1981), resold to the "Village Place" disco in 1982 (same location). Cut up for scrap New Orleans Feb-Mar 83.

2069 49-51-26 29 May 46 to KLM as PH-TAV 'Venlo', but remained at Burbank and cvtd to 49-46-26. Regd and deld 6 Sep 46 (E-9679, 29 Aug 46). Undercarriage failed landing at Santa Maria A/P, Azores 5 Nov 46 while en route Amsterdam-New York. Repaired. Planned lse to Swissair Apr 49, provisionally regd HB-IBJ 27 Aug 49, but lse fell through. PH-regn canx 19 Jul 50. To LAC (trade-in on 749As) 19 Jul 50. Cvtd to 049-46-59 for Capital Airlines as N86532 'Capitaliner Liberty', FN 754 and to Capital 1 Oct 50, in svce 7 Oct 50. Later Model 049D. Damaged when it hit another aircraft on the ground at La Guardia, NY, 20 Apr 56. Repaired. Sold to Trans American Aeronautical Corp on 31 Dec 56 and lsd back immediately to Capital Airlines Inc. Stored by May 59 in 56-pax configuration (TT: 29,807 hrs). Sold to Regina Cargo Airlines Inc 27 Feb 60, later named Imperial Airlines. Flew a BOAC charter from Frankfurt to Prestwick, Scotland, 16 Jul 61, then a round trip to London-Heathrow on charter to BOAC. Imperial grounded after crash of c/n 1976 on 8 Nov 61. Lsd to Coastal Airlines 1962 and sold to Magic City Airways 10 Jan 62. Sale to Compania Ciatra as LV-PWK (regn issued 20 Feb 63) ntu, aircraft remained at Miami, FL, painted up as LV-PKW. Canx from USCAR 31 May 63 as "Sold in Argentina". Restored to Magic City Airways 23 Jan 64. Sold to Alvaro Juan Adorisio 20 Mar 65, but remained in store at Miami during 1964 until at least Jun 65.

Impounded at Lima, Peru by Apr 66 and delivered to Oscar R Squella t/a Transportes Aereos Squella Aug 66 as CC-CAA. Stored at Los Cerillos, Santiago, parts missing, from Jan 76 until at least Apr 72, but believed little use (if any) with Squella. Transported to Apoquindo Avenida, Santiago de Chile, for use as a night club/restaurant called "Restaurant Aeropuerto" and painted in the then-current KLM (!) colours by 1974. Continued in use as such until 1976 at least. Then stood abandoned on same site until broken up during Feb-Mar 79. Canx from USCAR 28 Aug 70 (failure to file 1973).

2070 49-51-26 10 Jun 46 (16 Jun 46 also quoted) to KLM as PH-TAW 'Walcheren', but remained at Burbank and cvtd to 49-46-26. Officially regd 11 Sep 46 and deld 11 Sep 46 (but E-9680, dated 3 Oct 46). Planned lse to Swissair Apr 49, provisionally regd HB-IBY 27 Aug 49, but lse fell through. PH-regn canx 15 Oct 49. To LAC (trade-in on 749As) 15 Oct 49. Regd 1 Nov 49 to LAC as N6000C. Lsd to Hughes Tool Co 11 Nov 49, deld 12 Nov 49. Sold to Hughes 24 Feb 50. Hughes Tool Co resold to Transcontinental & Western Air Inc same day and deld at Burbank (TT: 6,782 hrs). Used by Howard Hughes 26 Feb to 6 Mar 50, when the aircraft was ferried to Fairfax, KS and modified to TWA requirements, completed 12 Apr 50. In svce 14 Apr 50 as 'Star of Newfoundland', FN 519; on intl ops from 1 May 50. Regd to Trans World Airlines Inc 29 May 50. Tfd to domestic ops 14 Aug 50. Last 1st Class svce 18 Feb 53, then to LAS, Burbank, for conversion to Coach Class same day. Re-entered svce 27 Mar 53. Used for all-cargo flights with TWA 1959-61. Sold to Las Vegas Hacienda on 15 May 61 (TT: 39,638 hrs). Lsd to World Wide Airlines from 13 Jul 62 (until Oct 62?), then lsd to Standard Airways in 1963 and to Dellair in early 64. Stored at Long Beach, CA, during early summer of 1964, and again, in ex-Dellair colours by Jan 65. Sold to Trans World Insurance Brokers 1 Dec 64 and to McCulloch Properties Inc 11 Mar 65. Sold to Allied Aircraft Sales Inc 15 May 70, and to Harlow L Jones 5 Jun 70. Sold to Full Gospel Native Missionary Inc 19 Mar 71, reportedly for use in Haiti. Aircraft stored at Long Beach, however, during most of 1971, and subsequently at Love Fld, Dallas, TX, by May 72 (still in Native Missionary colours). Sold 26 May 72 to Trans-Florida Airlines Inc and used by the Holiday Hunters Travel Club from 1973 until 1975. Sold to Quisqueyana in Dec 75 (TT: 45,180 hrs a/o 10 Jun 75), and deld to Dominica the same month as HI-260, with N- regn canx 11 Dec 75. Used on scheduled passenger services with Quisqueyana until Oct 77 (TT: 45,833 hrs a/o 12 Sep 76). Withdrawn from use and used for spares at Santo Domingo until Quisqueyana ceased ops in May 78. Damaged beyond repair while stored at the Las Americas Airport, Santo Domingo, during Hurricane David on 31 Aug 79. Aircraft was caught by high winds and thrown off the edge of the parking area on to its tail, buckling the main gear -had only one propeller and three engines with parts

The former N86533 049 which was preserved for many years at Asuncion, Paraguay and has now been restored by a Brazilian museum. (C J Mak)

SECTION 12: CONSTELLATION PRODUCTION LIST

missing at the time. During 1979, the derelict aircraft was sold to Amin Canaan dba TRADO for spares, and was stood up on its undercarriage again. Finally broken up during the last week of Jun 80 at Santo Domingo.

2071 49-51-26 7 Jun 46 to KLM as PH-TAX, but remained at Burbank and cvtd to 49-46-26. Re-regd 10 Sep 46 as PH-TDA 'Arnhem' (christened 18 Sep 46) and deld 10 Sep 46 (but E-9681, dated 3 Oct 46). Regn canx 21 Jun 50. To LAC (trade-in on 749As) 21 Jun 50. Cvtd to 049-46-59 for Capital Airlines as N86533 'Capitaliner Atlantan', FN 752 and deld 31 Aug 50, in svce 4 Sep 50, later Model 049D. In use as 56-pax configuration, TT: 31,572 hrs (a/o May 59). Stored by Dec 60 (TT: 33,628hrs). Tfd nominally to United Air Lines 1 Jun 61. Sold to Modern Air Transport 7 Sep 61. Damaged 30 Jun 64 at J F Kennedy, NY, when wing struck by National DC-8 N7181C. Repaired and remained in svce until Jun 65, when the aircraft was sold to Rymar of Montevideo - still as N86533. To International Caribbean Corp on lease 9 Aug 65 until 29 Sep 65, but impounded for smuggling at P.G. Stroessner Airport, Asuncion, Paraguay on 8 Sep 65. Canx from USCAR 21 Jun 71 (failure to file 1973). Stored at Asuncion until the spring of 1975, when it was prepared for preservation and painted in an overall yellow/orange colour scheme during Apr 75. Subsequently painted in a pop-art scheme, with nearly twenty different colours, cartoon figures on the outer fins and shark's teeth on the nose. Preserved at Asuncion airport, renamed Campo Grande, moved to Paraguayan Air Force recreation centre there in late 80s. Attempts by Brazilian museum to obtain the aircraft 1991 onwards blocked by legal problems. Paraguayan government eventually agreed to release the Constellation, and acquired by TAM Museum (set up by the airline's Chief Executive Officer Rolim Adolfo Amaro and his brother Joao Francisco Amaro) in late 1998. Dismantled at Asuncion late 2000 and transported on four trucks to Sao Carlos, Brazil, where the Constellation arrived after a 30-day journey on 11 Dec 2000. Fully restored during 2001-2006 at museum in final Panair do Brasil colour-scheme with registration "PP-PDD" and name "Domingos Jorge Velho".

2072 49-51-26 13 Jun 46 to Air France as F-BAZA (E-9682 18 Sep 46), but cvtd to 49-46-26 (amended E- 9682A not issued until 5 Mar 47!). In fact delivered to Air France, arr Paris-Orly 11 Jul 46 (TT: 24hrs), but with grounding of 049s & modifications necessary CofA not issued until 7 Jan 47, although the aircraft entered service on the Air France Paris-New York inaugural 3 Jan 47! Regd to SGAC until 30 Jan 50, when the aircraft was officially tfd to Air France. Wfs 11 Jan 50 (TT: 4343 hrs), sold to Hughes Tool Co same day & deld at New York-Newark 20 Feb 50 (TT: 4,390 hrs), as N9412H. Ferried Newark, NJ to Fairfax, KS 21 Feb 50. Deld to Howard Hughes at Las Vegas 3 Mar 50. Ret to Fairfax, KS 14 May 50 & tfd to TWA same day. Officially regd to Trans World Airlines Inc 5 Jun 50, but in svce 3 Jun 50 as 'Star of the Azores' FN 520. Cvtd to Coach Class at Fairfax, KS after last First Class svce 5 Feb 52. Re-entered svce 23 Mar 52. Sold to California Airmotive 26 Aug 59 (TT: 34,970 hrs) and deld Burbank, CA, same day. (FAA quote sale date 24 Aug). Resold to Las Vegas Hacienda 22 Sep 59. Lsd World Wide Airlines 13 Jul 62, then lsd Royal Air Burundi Dec 62 and named 'Umuganwa Ludovika Rwagasore'. Ret from lse 4 Jun 63 and stored at Oakland, later at Long Beach, CA. Lsd shortly afterwards to Edde Airlines. Ownership tfd 1 Dec 64 to Trans World Insurance Brokers, and back to Las Vegas Hacienda 23 Apr 65, with Edde lse continuing. Sold to McCulloch Properties Inc 10 May 66. Sold to Mineral County Airlines t/a Hawthorne Nevada Airlines 3 Jun 68, later t/a Air Nevada from 16 Mar 69. Named "Champagne Lady" at some stage. Stored at Long Beach, CA from Sep 69. Sold to Executive Party Club 15 May 70 and deld to Burbank same month. Stored at Burbank, CA, still in Air Nevada markings until mid-72. Sold to Produce Custom Air Freight Inc 20 Jul 72 and flown to Phoenix, AZ, in Mar 73. Stored at Buckeye, AZ, still in Air Nevada markings. Sold to Frank Lembo Jr, t/a Frank Lembo Enterprises Inc 23 May 76 for US$45,000 and flown on unknown date to Greenwood Lake, West Milford, NJ, landing on the 2,700 ft runway. (First report there Jul 77). The aircraft formed part of an exotic restaurant complex, with different sections of the fuselage and adjoining building representing different cultures (e.g. Far Eastern, Middle Eastern), with a wild game park next to the airport. Most of the interior art work on the Constellation had been completed when the owner, Frank Lembo, died early in 1979. Work on aircraft continued during 1980 under a new owner. Aircraft fuselage fitted out as a luxury restaurant. Advertized as "Kiwi Airlines - The only bird that doesn't fly". Opened Feb 81, closed Dec 81 with aircraft in good condition, President of restaurant was Frank McCormick. Remained stored at Greenwood Lake, repainted 1993. Renamed "Connie's Cafe" by Aug 98, manager Nick d'Ambrosio. Despite plans to restore the Constellation to fly again, it is still earthbound at Greenwood Lake. The airport, including the Constellation, was sold to the State of New Jersey in 2000. Interior refurbished and opened as flight school office in 2005.

2073 49-51-26 19 Jun 46 to Air France as F-BAZB, but remained at Burbank and cvtd to 49-46-26. Deld to Air France (E-9683, 4 Dec 46), but arrived Orly already 24 Oct 46 (TT: 52hrs), CofA issued 26 Oct 46. Used for trans-atlantic training flights 29 Oct 46-26 Dec 46. Aircraft regd to SGAC until 30 Jan 50, when the aircraft was tfd officially to Air France. Wfs 11 Jan 50 (TT: 4,953 hrs) & sold to Transcontinental & Western Air Inc 2 Feb 50, deld same day at Newark, NJ, as N9410H. Ferried to Burbank, CA for modifications 3 Feb 50 (TT: 4,986 hrs). Presumably cvtd to Coach Class and entered svce 18 May 50 as 'Star of London' FN 522. Regd to Trans World Airlines Inc 29 May 50. Lsd to Eastern Air Lines 28 Nov 57 and ret to TWA 18 Apr 58. (TT: 36,704 hrs a/o 31 Aug 59). Stored at Mid-Continent Airport, Kansas City, MO, believed by Jun 61. Sold to Nevada Airmotive Corp 31 Mar 62 (TT: 37,744 hrs), but remained stored at Mid-Continent until broken up there between Jun 64 and Dec 64. (USCARs Jun 63 to Jan 66 still give TWA as owner).

2074 49-51-26 24 Jun 46 to Air France as F-BAZC, but remained at Burbank and cvtd to 49-46-26. Deld to Air France (E-9684, 10 Dec 46), but arrived Orly already 24 Nov 46. CofA issued 26 Nov 46, in svce for transatlantic training flights 26 Nov 46–29 Dec 46. No.4 engine caught fire & would not feather en route Azores-Paris 19 Feb 47, prop detached & hit No.3 engine, continued to fly on Nos.1 & 2 engines for two & three-quarter hours & made safe emergency landing Casablanca, Morocco although ran off runway with nose-wheel u/c problems. Repaired. Aircraft regd to SGAC until 24 Jan 50, when tfd officially to Air France. Wfs 11 Jan 50 (TT: 4,302 hrs). Sold to Transcontinental & Western Air Inc 26 Jan 50 and deld same day at Newark, NJ, as N9409H. Ferried to Fairfax, KS 27 Jan 50 (for cockpit standardization mods), and on to Burbank, CA for Coach Class conversion 26 Feb 50. Accepted by TWA 27 May 50 (TT: 4,316 hrs) as 'Star of Egypt' FN 521. Regd to Trans World Airlines Inc 29 May 50. First flight for TWA 31 May 50 - in flight photos over the Grand Canyon, in non-revenue svce until ferried Los Angeles to Burbank 13 Apr 51 (TT: 6,976 hrs) and lsd to the Lockheed Aircraft Corp for Jet Stack tests (see Section 1.12). Flew 24 hrs 40 mins on these tests, and ret to TWA 17 May 51 as the first Jet Stack 049 (TT: 7,001 hrs). First revenue flight 20 May 51. Damaged when engine & hydraulic system failed, veered off runway & struck barracks landing at Kirtland AFB, Albuquerque, NM 21 Apr 54, en route New York-Los Angeles. Repaired. Sold to Las Vegas Hacienda 15 May 61 (TT: 38,887 hrs), and deld to Las Vegas, NV. At Long Beach, CA, in Oct 61 and believed never left there until broken up between Mar 66 and May 66. Port outer wing used in repair of c/n 1970.

2075 49-51-26 24 Jun 46 to Air France as F-BAZD, but remained at Burbank and cvtd to 49-46-26. Deld to Air France (E-9685, 13 Dec 46, but arrived Orly already 1 Dec 46 (TT: 55hrs), in svce same day, CofA issued 3 Dec 46. Aircraft regd to SGAC until 30 Jan 50, when transferred to Air France officially. Wfs 11 Jan 50 (TT: 4,655 hrs) & sold to Transcontinental & Western Air Inc 25 Jan 50. Deld 11 Feb 50 at Newark, NJ, as N9414H, being ferried same day to Burbank, CA for cockpit standardization & Coach Class conversion. Accepted by TWA 24 May 50 as 'Star of Lebanon' FN 523, in svce 26 May 50 (TT: 4,687 hrs). Regd to

Trans World Airlines Inc 29 May 50. Lsd Eastern Air Lines 25 Dec 56, ret TWA 18 May 57. (TT: 36,125 hrs a/o 31 Aug 59). Sold to Nevada Airmotive Corp 31 Mar 62 (TT: 41,630 hrs). Painted up in Nevada Airmotive colours as demonstration aircraft. Carried "McCulloch Site Six Marathon" titles in 1962. Lsd to Futura Air Lines FN 711 in May 62. Lsd to Paradise Airlines in late 63, until Paradise grounded Mar 64. Sold 64 to Pasco Aviation Inc, and later lsd (or sold) to Zephyr Hill Inc. Stored at Miami, FL, by Sep 65. Sold to Pinellas Central Bank & Trust Co 1 Sep 66. Lsd to Quisqueyana Jan 67, named 'Santiago'. Ret to Miami later same year and stored there. Continued in storage at Miami in Quisqueyana titling until broken up there Jul 70 to Aug 70. Canx 14 Oct 70.

2076 49-51-26 Cvtd to 49-46-26 prior dely to Transcontinental & Western Air Inc 7 Oct 46 as NC90814 'Star of Cairo' FN 558. Used on intl ops until tfd to domestic network 14 Jul 48 (TT: 4,600 hrs). To Fairfax, KS for domestic conversion 15 Jul 48, completed 27 Jul 48. Later N90814. Regd to Trans World Airlines Inc 29 May 50. To LAS, Burbank, CA, for Coach Class conversion 30 Nov 53. Re-entered svce 20 Jan 54. Badly damaged at Kansas City, MO when caught fire on landing 15 Oct 54, en route Los Angeles-New York. Repaired. (TT: 41,341 hrs a/o 31 Aug 59). Sold to Nevada Airmotive Corp 31 Mar 62 (TT: 46, 922 hrs). Lsd to Routh Aircraft Inc, but not flown. Ret Nevada Airmotive 21 Mar 63. Stored at Long Beach, CA, until broken up there late Dec 64.

2077 49-51-26 Cvtd to 49-46-26 prior dely to Transcontinental & Western Air Inc 21 Sep 46 as NC90815 FN 559. TWA dely date 22 Sep 46. Named 'Star of Lisbon' and 'Star of Detroit'. Used on Intl ops. Ret to Kansas City Municipal 8 Jun 48 (TT: 4,339 hrs), and used for pilot training there 10 Jun-20 Jun 48. Cvtd for domestic use & engineering tests 20 Jun-2 Jul 48. Damaged at Los Angeles 10 Oct 48 when the left undercarriage collapsed in a work dock, causing wing & engine nacelle damage. Repaired and re-entered svce 4 Nov 48. To N90815. Regd to Trans World Airlines Inc 29 May 50. To Fairfax, KS for Coach Class conversion 11 Nov 54 after last First Class svce 10 Nov 54. Re-entered svce 20 Dec 54. Lsd Eastern Air Lines 15 Dec 56, ret TWA 16 May 57. (TT: 40,095 hrs a/o 31 Aug 59). Sold to Nevada Airmotive Corp 31 Mar 62 (TT: 43,861 hrs). Sold to Fowler Aero Service late 64, and subsequently to Belmont Aviation. Stored at Long Beach, CA, by Apr 64 and broken up there early in 1965 (last report, semi-derelict in Feb 65), and canx from USCAR by Jan 66.

2078 49-51-26 Cvtd to 49-46-26 prior dely to Transcontinental & Western Air Inc 25 Sep 46 as NC90816 'Star of Geneva' FN 560. Used on Intl ops. Cvtd for domestic use at Fairfax, KS, arrived 27 Jul 48. To N90816. Regd to Trans World Airlines Inc 29 May 50. To LAS, Burbank, for Coach Class conversion 20 Jan 54. Re-entered svce 27 Feb 54. (TT: 41,184hrs a/o 31 Aug 59). Sold to Nevada Airmotive Corp 31 Mar 62 (officially 13 Mar 62), (TT: 46,958 hrs). Believed lsd Edde Airlines 1 Sep 62, then sold to Edde 10 Jul 64. Sold to AVEMCO Aircraft Investment Corp 15 Oct 66 and lsd out to Pacific Air Transport. Stored at Phoenix-Litchfield, AZ, by Mar 71, still in Pacific Air Transport markings, but believed no longer used by that company. Sold to Sergio A. Tomassoni dba S.S. & T.Aerial Contracting 21 Dec 72, and flown to Buckeye, AZ, but not used. Continued in storage at Buckeye until flown with gear down to Van Nuys, CA, in Apr 78 or May 78 by Herman 'Fish' Salmon. Sold to Asher Ward 21 May 78 and sale to Universal Pictures for $35,000 negotiated, for use in a film "Airplane" in which the Constellation was to be crash-landed in the desert and destroyed. Plans lapsed, and aircraft sold with TT of approx 48,000 hrs and fitted out as an 86-Seater to Cecil E. Wroton t/a Aero Sacasa Inc on 31 Mar 79 for US$ 34,000. Ferried Van Nuys, CA to Fort Lauderdale, FL, 7 May 79, but had to make approx nine intermediate landings as fuel tanks leaked so badly. At Mesa, AZ en route, the aircraft ran off the runway when the brakes failed. Occasional work carried out on aircraft until May 80. Stored at Fort Lauderdale & was the last Model 049 to fly. Aircraft stripped of pax interior. Advertized for sale Apr 81 by aircraft broker Landy Taylor for US $190,000 (!), airworthy ex-Fort Lauderdale. Reportedly sold to Air Wing (Florida) Oct 81, but sale fell through, as did reported sales to John Travolta (see c/n 2601) and Associated Air. Propellers removed Feb 83 for overhaul & use on C-46s. Condition deteriorated, derelict by Jun 88 & eventually scrapped in airport clean-up late 1988.

2079 49-51-25 Cvtd to 49-46-25 prior dely to Transcontinental & Western Air Inc 28 Sep 46 as NC90817 'Star of the Adriatic' FN 510 (reports of FN 561 unconf). TWA dely date 29 Sep 46 (TT: 10hrs), in svce 2 Oct 46. To N90817. Regd to Trans World Airlines Inc 29 May 50. To Fairfax, KS for Coach Class conversion 23 Mar 52 after last First Class svce 22 Mar 52. Re-entered svce 8 Jun 52. (TT: 42,253hrs a/o 31 Aug 59). Sold to Nevada Airmotive Corp 31 Mar 62 (TT: 47,100 hrs). Believed stored at Las Vegas, NV, until 1964, then scrapped. Canx from USCAR 1970.

2080 49-51-25 Cvtd to 49-46-25 prior dely to Transcontinental & Western Air Inc 5 Oct 46 as NC90818 'Star of the Red Sea' FN 511 (reports of FN 562 unconf). (TT: 7hrs). In svce 8 Oct 46. To N90818. Regd to Trans World Airlines Inc 29 May 50. To Fairfax, KS for conversion to Coach Class 30 Dec 51 after last First Class svce 29 Dec 51. Re-entered svce 15 Feb 52. Lsd Eastern Air Lines 30 Nov 57, ret TWA 24 Apr 58. (TT: 42,167hrs a/o 31 Aug 59). Sold to Nevada Airmotive Corp 31 Mar 62 (TT: 47,542 hrs). Believed stored at Las Vegas, NV, until 1964, then scrapped. Not current in USCAR Jun 63, but restored to USCAR Jan 64 until lapsed Jul 66, canx 1970.

2081 Completed as 49-51-25 for Transcontinental & Western Air Inc as NC90819 (FN 512 allocated). Cvtd to 49-46-25 and reworked by LAS to incorporate a navigator's station. Deld to Linea Aeropostal Venezolana as YV-C-AME FN302 'Simon Bolivar' 31 Oct 46 (E-14601, dated 4 Nov 46). Cvtd to 149. Sold to Braniff International Aug 55 as N2520B. Stored at Washington Natl by Aug 58. Lockheed quote sold to Trans American and used for spares 1 Nov 59. Sold to Empire Supply Co (H.M. Covert) 7 Nov 60, and tfd to Lloyd Airlines Inc 22 Nov 60. Tfd back to Hubert M Covert 10 Mar 61. Forced to land at Santa Cruz de la Sierra, Bolivia, on 30 Jul 61, on smuggling flight from Miami, FL, to Uruguay, with a planeload of whisky and cigarettes. A Bolivian Air Force P-51 Mustang that tried to force the Constellation to land, stalled and spun in the ground from 300 ft when the Constellation came down with flaps and undercarriage extended to this level - the Constellation's crew were accused on 2 Aug 61 by the Bolivian authorities of having shot down their Mustang! Constellation impounded at Santa Cruz de la Sierra and nominally became the property of the Bolivian Air Force (Fuerza Aerea Boliviana). Remained in storage at Santa Cruz, with owner officially Hubert M. Covert, until it lapsed in Jul 66 and was canx from USCAR after certificate revoked 4 Dec 70. By the early 1970s, the Constellation had been transported to the Parque Boris Banzer, a children's playground four miles from Santa Cruz airport, completely gutted and with much corrosion. By 1979, the interior of the Constellation had been converted into a library at Avenida Uruguay, Santa Cruz, complete with air-conditioning units, and still in use as such a/o Nov 87. Aircraft basically complete, but badly corroded; repainted in garish red, white & blue"Pepsi" colour-scheme late 1997. Repainted in turquoise & purple colours by Mar 03 with Aerosur titles plus small inscription 'Agencia de Viajes' (travel agency) & in use as office. Current.

2082 Completed as 49-51-25 for Transcontinental & Western Air Inc as NC90820 (FN 513 allocated). Cvtd to 49-46-25 and reworked by LAS to incorporate a navigator's station. Deld to Linea Aeropostal Venezolana as YV-C-AMI (FN30l) 'Francisco de Miranda', later 'Simon Bolivar' 31 Oct 46 (E-14603, dated 5 Nov 46). Suffered considerable damage to port wing, nose, undercarriage, port nacelles and engines when it struck trees on approach to an airport on the US East Coast, date unknown. Repaired by LAS, probably at MacArthur Fld, Long Island, NY. Cvtd to 149. Sold to Braniff International 10 Aug 55 (FAA files give 11 Aug 55). Canx from YV-register 23 Aug 55 and regd N2521B same day. Stored at Washington Natl by Aug 58. Lockheed quote sold to Trans American and used for spares 1 Nov 59 (no record in FAA files). Stored at Dallas, TX, in Oct 60. Sold to Hubert M Covert t/a Empire Supply Co 26 Mar 61 (FAA files give 24 Mar 61). Tfd to Lloyd Airlines Inc by mid-61. Ret to Hubert M Covert by Dec 62. To Hazel I Brown 14 Oct 63, and in use with Magic City Airways in 1965. Stored at Miami, FL, for long periods during mid-1960s. Sold to Omni Investment Corp 5 Jan 67 and to Miami Aviation Corp same day. Sold to Robert W Hollister 7 Jun 67, but remained in store at Miami. To Cov-Air Inc 1 Sep 67. Dismantling began at Miami, FL, Oct 67. Canx from USCAR 31 Oct 67. Broken up at Miami in Feb 68.

2083 Completed as 49-51-25 for Transcontinental & Western Air Inc as NC90821 (FN 514 allocated). Cvtd to 49-46-25 for KLM. A dely date of 21 Feb 47 is quoted in some sources. The cancelled order was taken over by KLM 14 Mar 47. Aircraft was flown to MacArthur Fld, Long Island, NY and a navigator's station plus long-range wings (i.e. Model 149 standard) installed by LAS. Regd PH-TEN 'Nijmegen' 8 May 47, KLM dely date 8 May 47, 23 May 47 (LADD); (E-15817, also dated 23 May 47). Made first Amsterdam-Batavia proving flight (fitted with Speedpak), dep Amsterdam 4 Jun 47. Flew into high-tension cables on approach to Prestwick, Scotland on 21 Oct 48, caught fire and crashed at 00.31 hrs (local) at Tarbolton, five miles east-north-east of the airport, killing all on board, including KLM's Chief Pilot, Captain K.D. Parmentier. Aircraft made a GCA and overshoot on Runway 31, but did not land owing to high cross-wind. On making visual circuit for Runway 26 at approx 700 ft, aircraft ran into low cloud, and failed to clear the high tension cables at 450 ft. Cause: Deteriorating weather, disorientation on visual circuit, and mistake in spot height on navigation chart (read 45 ft instead of 450 ft). Was en route Amsterdam-Prestwick-New York. Regn canx 21 Oct 48.

2084 Completed as 49-51-25 for Transcontinental & Western Air Inc as NC90822. Cvtd to 49-46-25 for KLM. A dely date of 21 Feb 47 is quoted in some sources. The cancelled order was taken over by KLM 14 Mar 47. Aircraft was flown to MacArthur Fld, Long Island, NY, and a navigator's station plus long-range wings (i.e. Model 149 standard) installed by LAS. Regd PH-TEO 'Overloon' 8 May 47, dely date 8 May 47 (KLM), 16 May 47 (LADD); (E-15809 dated 22 May 47). First Model 049/149 series to be deld with a Speedpak. Named 'Holland Michigan' for special flight 11 Aug 47 from Amsterdam to Holland in Michigan, USA on the occasion of the 100th Anniversary of Holland, MI. To LAC (trade-in on 749As), who resold to Hughes Tool Co in Nov or Dec 49. PH-regn canx 6 Feb 50. Re-sold to Transcontinental & Western Air Inc 3 Feb 50 (KLM quote 'sold to TWA' same date). Deld 4 Feb 50 (TT: 5,940 hrs), and cvtd to TWA standards as N86526 'Star of Greece' FN 518, in svce 22 Mar 50 on Intl routes. To domestic network 25 May 50. Regd to Trans World Airlines Inc 29 May 50. Tfd to pilot training 16 Jun 50. Damaged at St. Joseph, MO, 21 Jun 50, when fire broke out in no.2 nacelle prior to take-off. Wing and undercarriage damaged as a result of the fire in brake and wing. (TT: 6,372 hrs). Ret to svce 15 Jul 50. Damaged again, at Cincinnati, OH, on 2 Jan 51, when the aircraft contacted trees on final approach. Proceeded to Columbus, OH, for landing. Minor damage only (TT: 7,801 hrs). Repaired. To LAS, Burbank, 5 Jan 53 for conversion to Coach Class after last First Class svce 4 Jan 53. Re-entered svce 18 Feb 53. Badly damaged at Tucumcari, NM, on 23 May 54 after severe en-route turbulence (on New York-Los Angeles flight). Repaired. Lsd Eastern Air Lines 15 Dec 56, ret TWA 16 May 57. Again lsd Eastern Air Lines 2 Dec 57, ret TWA 16 Apr 58. (TT: 36,189hrs a/o 31 Aug 59). Stored at Mid-Continent Airport, Kansas City, MO, by Jun 61 (TT: 37,135 hrs) and sold to Nevada Airmotive Corp 31 Mar 62, but remained stored at Mid-Continent until broken up there between Jun 64 and Dec 64. (USCARs Jun 63 to Jan 66 still give TWA as owner).

2085 Completed as 49-51-25 for Transcontinental & Western Air Inc, but remained at Burbank and cvtd to 49-46-25. Regd NC90823 to LAC 18 Nov 46. Dely delayed to TWA, and officially sold to TWA 28 Mar 47 (TT: 44 hrs) as 'Star of the Yellow Sea', FN 512. To N90823. Regd to Trans World Airlines Inc 29 May 50. To LAS, Burbank for Coach Class conversion 14 Dec 52 after last First Class svce same day. Ret to svce 12 Feb 53. Damaged left rear wing spar approx 13 Jun 55 at unknown location. Repaired. (TT: 40,355hrs a/o 31 Aug 59). Several passengers on board sustained injuries on 25 Aug 60 due to severe in-flight turbulence near Chanute, KS, but no damage to aircraft. Sold to Nevada Airmotive Corp 31 Mar 62 (TT: 45,523 hrs), FAA quote 13 Mar 62 as change of ownership date. Sold to McCulloch Properties Inc 12 Feb 64 (FAA records: 5 Jul 64). Sold to Allied Aircraft Sales Inc 15 May 70, and to Harlow L Jones 5 Jun 70. To Southwestern Skyways Inc 30 Jun 70, and to Westernair of Albuquerque Inc 20 Aug 70. Stored at Long Beach, CA, during 1970. Reported to be used in Haiti (with c/n 2070) in Mar 71, but aircraft remained at Long Beach. Sold to Full Gospel Native Missionary Inc (owner C T Buchanan) 4 Oct 71, but still stored at Long Beach until sale to Trans-Florida Airlines Inc 26 May 72 and deld to Daytona Beach, FL. (TT: 49,129 hrs). Remained in storage at Daytona Beach and never entered service with Trans-Florida. Sold to Quisqueyana in Jul 76, deld 4 Jul 76 to Santo Domingo and N- regn canx 21 Jul 76. In svce Nov 76 as HI-270 on pax schedules until 19 Jan 78, when the aircraft operated the world's last 049 scheduled passenger svce from Santo Domingo to San Juan, PR, and return. Made one trip as a back-up cargo aircraft for Quisqueyana, before being wfu at Santo Domingo, Dominican Republic, by 3 Apr 78. Stored there in good condition and sold to Amin Canaan t/a TRADO in 1979 for spares or resale. Negotiations for restoration and dely to the Science Museum in London, England started in Apr 80, but deal fell through due to problems with financing arrangements. Continued in storage at Santo Domingo until broken up there during first week of Jul 80.

2086 Completed as 49-51-25 for Transcontinental & Western Air Inc, but remained at Burbank and cvtd to 49-46-25, with dely delayed until 6 May 47 (12 May 47 also quoted) as NC90824, FN 513, name unknown. Crashed on landing at Los Angeles at 05:52 (PST) 25 Nov 48 and burned out, no injuries to occupants. On final approach to runway 25L, the aircraft flew into a patch of ground fog at the moment of flaring out. The Captain pulled back on the control wheel and the aircraft hit the ground very hard, with both nose-wheel tyres blowing out and other serious structural damage occurring. The aircraft touched down 2,300 feet from the approach end of the runway, went off the runway, was turned sharply to the right to avoid a ditch and came to a stop, with part of the undercarriage knocked off, and subsequently bursting into flames. The right hand side of the aircraft was almost completely destroyed. Was on Flight TW 211 from Washington, DC via Kansas City, Albuquerque & Phoenix to Los Angeles. (TT: 4,343hrs).

2087 Completed as 49-51-25 for Transcontinental & Western Air Inc, but remained at Burbank and cvtd to 49-46-25, with dely delayed until 15 May 47 as NC90825 'Star of China', FN 514 (TT: 11hrs). In svce 17 May 47. To N90825. Regd to Trans World Airlines Inc 29 May 50. To LAS, Burbank, for Coach Class conversion 3 May 53, after flying last First Class svce 2 May 53. Re-entered svce 5 Jun 53. Lsd Eastern Air Lines 25 Dec 56, ret TWA 18 May 57. (TT: 40,384 hrs a/o 31 Aug 59). In store by mid-61 (TT: 44,754 hrs). Sold to Nevada Airmotive Corp 31 Mar 62, and reportedly at Burbank, CA, in Sep 62 being stripped for spares by California Airmotive. By 1964, however, the aircraft was stored at Long Beach, CA, where it was broken up during 1964. (USCAR gives final owner as Nevada Airmotive, canx by Jan 66).

2088 Completed as 49-51-25 for Transcontinental & Western Air Inc, but remained at Burbank and cvtd to 49-46-25, with dely delayed until 19 May 47 as NC90826 'Star of the China Sea', FN 515. In svce 20 May 47. (TT: 37 hrs). To N90826. Regd to Trans World Airlines Inc 29 May 50. Damaged when main undercarriage collapsed during landing roll at Phoenix, AZ, 5 Jan 51. Landing gear operating handle inadvertently raised instead of wing flaps, aircraft landed on its belly, and skidded a considerable distance before stopping. (TT: 11,402 hrs). Ferried to Fairfax for repairs 14 Jan 51 and re-entered svce 19 Feb 51. To LAS, Burbank, for Coach Class conversion 26 Mar 53 after last First Class svce 25 Mar 53. Re-entered svce 2 May 53. Damaged at Friendship Airport, Baltimore, MD, 6 May 56 when an oxygen bottle exploded and caught fire, damaging the cockpit and forward cabin. Repaired. Port wing damaged at La Guardia, NY, on 13 Sep 57. Repaired. Damaged again, on 13 Aug 58 approx, when jack collapsed at San Francisco, CA during maintenance (TT: 36,412 hrs). Repaired again. (TT: 38,937hrs a/o 31 Aug59). Sold to Nevada Airmotive Corp 31 Mar 62 (TT: 44,575 hrs) Believed stored at Las Vegas, NV, until 1964, then scrapped. Lapsed USCAR Jul 67, then canx 1970.

For details of cancelled serial numbers **2089** onwards, see note after c/n 1980.

2501 Laid down as Model 649-79-21 for Transcontinental & Western Air Inc as NC86518. Order canx. Changed to 749-79-22 and completed as Model 749 c/n 2584 for TWA (qv).

2502 Laid down as Model 649-79-21 for Transcontinental & Western Air Inc as NC86519. Order canx. Changed to 749-79-22 and completed as Model 749 c/n 2588 for TWA (qv).

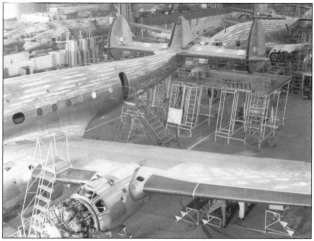

The order for this 649 c/n 2502 was cancelled, and the aircraft later appeared as a 749 c/n 2584. (Lockheed)

2503 Laid down as Model 649-79-21 for Transcontinental & Western Air Inc as NC86520. Order canx. Changed to 749-79-22 and completed as Model 749 and deld to Pan American on lse 6 Jun 47 as NC86520 'Clipper America'. Used to inaugurate 749 services, and flew the airline's first "Round-the-World" service La Guardia to La Guardia 17 Jun-30 Jun 47. Ret to LAC Aug 47. Re-deld to Aerovias Guest SA as XA-GOQ 'Veracruz' 6 Jan 48 (E-14768, dated 16 Dec 47). Flew inaugural 749 svce Mexico City-Madrid 17 Jan 48. Carried out Olympic Games charter to London, England, 9 Jul 48. Ret to LAC Dec 48, and regd NC86520 again. Sold to Air France as F-BAZR and deld 15 Jan 49 at Orly (TT: 1,325 hrs). CofA issued 30 Mar 49 and in svce same day. Damaged when the aircraft swerved off the runway at Maison Blanche, Algiers, on 2 or 3 Dec 54. Repaired. Last svce with Air France Casablanca-Paris (Orly) 19 Oct 60 (TT: 31,102 hrs), then stored at Orly 24 Oct 60. Withdrawn from storage 22 Feb 62, and overhauled at Orly, with CofA issued 1 Mar 62. Flown to Toulouse and cvtd to flying test-bed by Air France and CGTM-Compagnie Générale des Turbo-machines. Tfd to French Air Force 16 May 62, sold to L'Etat 2 Jan 63. Rolled out in new configuration 1 Apr 63, regd F-ZVMV. Transferred to Istres for fitting-out 12 Apr 63. Canx from F-civil register 5 Feb 63 on transfer to military marks. First flight with CGTM 26 Dec 63, last flight with CGTM 15 Feb 66, then transferred to CEV-Centre d'Essais en Vol, still at Istres. Made its last test flight (its 634th) 19 Dec 74 (TT: 32,471 hrs). During the period Dec 63-Dec 74, the aircraft flew a total of 1,363 hrs 40 mins on test-flying, including 1,106 hrs 30 mins at the CEV. Among the engines test-flown with the Constellation were: CF-700 (for Mystere) and the Turmo IIID (in Oct 64) at the CGTM; Turmo III (for Bréguet 941 in 1967-68), Astazou, Turbomeca Bastan (Sep 69), Bastan VI, Bastan VII (for Nord 262 series), Marbore, Turbomeca M49, various Larzac (for the Alpha Jet), including Larzac 01 (first flight 2 Mar 71), 02 and 04 (first flight

Mar 73), with further Bastan engines (for Nord 262) in Aug 72, for example. In addition to engine tests, including icing tests, wing sections were also test-flown. The aircraft's last flight on 19 Dec 74 was with the Turbomeca Bastan VII. After stripping the aircraft of some of its test equipment, it was flown to the Musée de l'Air at Le Bourget-Paris on 16 Jul 75, arriving at 11.40 hrs (local). Stored in open awaiting restoration. In 1982 the rear fuselage & fins were painted up in Air France colours for a television advert. In 1988, the aircraft was removed from the public display area and tfd to the museum storage area. Repainted grey overall with no dayglo orange cheat-line a/o Sep 02. Fifth engine removed. Painted in pseudo Air France colours during Apr 06 for filming of "La Mome". During filming carried registrations "F-BCN" and "F-UAZ", afterwards no registration or serial carried. Current.

2504 Laid down as Model 649-79-21 for Transcontinental & Western Air Inc as NC86521. Order canx. Changed to 749-79-22, and cvtd to 749-79-35 on line for Air India as VT-CQS 'Mogul Princess'. LADD: 30 Jan 48, but 9 Mar 48 also quoted. E- 14769 issued 30 Jan 48, actually dep Burbank 23 Feb 48 & deld 16 Mar 48 (arr in India), in svce Aug 48. Sold to Qantas as VH-EAF 'Horace Brimsmead' 24 Apr 51 for £333,000 (TT: 480hrs), CofRegn (No.1782) 27 Apr 51, arr Sydney same day. In svce 4 May 51, wfs 7 Jun 51 for standardization & tank-sealing, test flown 24 Aug 51. Cvtd to 749A Feb 52. Inaugurated London-Bangkok-Sydney service 18 Nov 53. While in Qantas svce, the aircraft was modified for use by Queen Elizabeth II & Duke of Edinburgh on the Royal Tour of Australia, and used for six of the Royal flights between 8 Mar 54 & 27 Mar 54 on sectors Melbourne-Brisbane, Brisbane-Townsville, Brisbane-Broken Hill & Brisbane-Adelaide-Kalgoorlie-Perth. Last QEA svce 13-22 Jul 54, Sydney-London-Sydney (TT: 8,188 hrs). Sold to BOAC and deld 23 Jul 54 (ex-Sydney), arr London 26 Jul 54, VH-Regn canx 28 Jul 54. Regd G-ANTF 16 Aug 54, 'Berkeley', CofA 15 Sep 54, in svce 27 Sep 54. Last svce 3 Mar 57 and stored London-Heathrow from 21 Mar 57, CofA expiry 28 Sep 57. CofA renewed 2 Dec 57, sold to The Babb Co 6 Dec 57, deld from London 8 Dec 57 as N9816F. Lsd to Transocean Airlines 3 Jan 58. Repossessed by The Babb Co Dec 58, ret 29 Jun 59 for resale. Nominal tf date to Babb Co 31 Jul 59. Lsd Capitol Airways by mid-Jul 59. Later stored at Oakland, CA. Tfd to International Aircraft Services Inc and cvtd to Freighter (rear cargo door), probably at Bradley Fld, CT, in 1960. BOAC negotiated lease of aircraft to Alaska Airlines approx Jun 61, but deal fell through. Stored at Bradley Fld, Windsor Locks, CT from Sep 62 until Jan 64. Sold in Britain and regd 23 Jan 64 to BOAC, as G-ANTF. Sold to Shackleton (Aviation) Ltd 17 Feb 64 for £39,285 for lse-purchase by ACE Freighters 21 Feb 64. Deld Newark-London (Gatwick) 23 Feb 64. In svce 6 May 64, London-Gatwick-Stockholm. Sold to ACE 1 Mar 66. Made perfect wheels-up landing at Aden 8 Mar 66, while on Ministry of Defence contract flight from Britain to Middle & Far East. Captain feathered all four propellers and positioned them to avoid damage on touch-down. Fire broke out in nose-wheel area shortly after touchdown, but was quickly extinguished. Aircraft returned to Britain after minor repairs and re-entered service shortly after. CofA expired 28 Mar 66. Stored at Baginton-Coventry, UK, after bankruptcy of ACE Sep 66. Sold by tender Dec 66 to unknown parties, but remained in storage at Baginton. Canx from G-register 4 Dec 67 as sold in the USA, but never deld. Condition gradually deteriorated, then set on fire 1 Feb 70, destroying most of the fuselage. Remains scrapped during late 1971.

2505 Laid down as Model 649-79-21 for Transcontinental & Western Air Inc as NC86522. Order canx. Changed to 749-79-22, and cvtd to 749-79-35 on line for Air India as VT-CQR 'Rajput Princess'. LADD: 13 Feb 48, also E-14770, same date. Arr in India 26 Mar 48, in svce 22 Jun 48. Sold to Qantas as VH-EAE 'Bert Hinkler' 30 Dec 49, del Sydney 11 Jan 50, in svce with Qantas (still as VT-CQR) Darwin-Sydney 17 Jan 50. CofRegn (No.1689) as VH-EAE 18 Jan 50, in svce as VH-EAE 8 Apr 50. Cvtd to 749A 1 Sep 51-22 Oct 51. Back-up aircraft for Royal Tour of Australia 8-27 Mar 54. Last svce 7-16 Aug 54 Sydney-London & return (TT: 11,718 hrs). Handed over to BOAC 18 Aug 54 at Sydney, sold

BOAC 20 Aug 54 on arrival at London. VH-regn canx 23 Aug 54, regd G-ANTG 10 Sep 54, 'Bournemouth', CofA 15 Oct 54, in svce 22 Nov 54. Made last BOAC Constellation flight on passenger service 6-7 Oct 58 (Abadan-London). Withdrawn from svce 12 Oct 58 & stored London-Heathrow. CofA extended to 16 Dec 58. Sold to Pacific Northern Airlines 30 Nov 58 & deld ex-London same day to Newark,NJ. Tfd to The Babb Co 1 Dec 58 for PNA, regd N1552V, FN52V & canx from G-register 2 Dec 58. Tfd to Western Airlines 1 Jul 67, FN 52V, later 552. Made last scheduled Constellation flight in North America, Juneau-Anchorage 26 Nov 68. Out of svce 27 Nov 68 and donated to City of Kenai, AK. (TT: 40,568 hrs). Kenai sold to an unknown person approx 1973 for use as a restaurant. Aircraft was towed to nearby parking lot, but nothing came of the idea and the aircraft was broken up, date unknown.

2506 Laid down as Model 649-79-21 for Transcontinental & Western Air Inc as NC86523, FN 525 & painted up (used in Eastern Air Lines film 1947). Order canx. Changed to 749-79-22, and cvtd to 749-79-35 on line for Air India as VT-CQP 'Malabar Princess'. LADD: 27 Feb 48, also E-14771, same date. Arr in India 26 Apr 48, in svce 8 Jun 48. Operated first Air India svce to Britain (Bombay-London), arr London 9 Jun 48. Crashed into snow-covered mountains 700 ft below the summit of Mont Blanc (15,781 ft), Swiss/French border, on 3 Nov 50 at 09.43 hrs (local). All on board killed. Aircraft was flying in a heavy snowstorm, with winds of 60 mph, and last radio contact with Geneva Airport, Switzerland, made at 09.30 hrs at which time the aircraft reported position north of Grenoble, France at 15,000 ft with strong headwinds. Was on seaman's charter flight Cairo-Geneva-London. Fuselage later found intact, and reportedly still there in late 1970s. Canx fromVT-register 11 Jan 51.

2507 Laid down as Model 649-79-21 for Transcontinental & Western Air Inc as NC86524. Order canx. Completed as Model 749 c/n 2577 for TWA.

2508 Laid down as Model 649-79-21 for Transcontinental & Western Air Inc as NC86525. Order canx. Completed as Model 749 c/n 2578 for TWA.

2509 Laid down as Model 649-79-21 for Transcontinental & Western Air Inc as NC86526. Order canx. Completed as Model 749 c/n 2579 for TWA.

2510 Laid down as Model 649-79-21 for Transcontinental & Western Air Inc, regn unknown. Order canx. Completed as Model 749 c/n 2580 for TWA.

2511 Laid down as Model 649-79-21 for Transcontinental & Western Air Inc, regn unknown. Order canx. Completed as Model 749 c/n 2581 for TWA.

2512 Laid down as Model 649-79-21 for Transcontinental & Western Air Inc, regn unknown. Order canx. Completed as Model 749-79-22 for Air France, cvtd to 749-79-46. LADD: 22 May 47 as F-BAZQ, TOC 26 May 47 at New York. E-13427 dated 19 Jun 47, dely Paris-Orly 10 Jul 47 (TT: 39hrs), CofA issued 25 Jul 47, in svce 26 Jul 47. Officially owned by SGAC until tfd to Air France 29 Mar 51. Badly damaged when cabin caught fire landing at Keflavik, Iceland 29 Nov 48 (also reptd as 27 Nov). Repaired with parts from c/n 1966. Ret to svce 7 Apr 49 (TT: 2,308 hrs). To 749A and cvtd to 65-Seater All-Tourist Class. Tfd to Air Maroc 8 Oct 57, regd CN-CCR 11 Oct 57 on issue of CofA, last Air France svce 15 Oct 57 (TT: 24,754 hrs). Rn Royal Air Maroc. Withdrawn from use 3 Jun 63 on expiry of CofA (TT: 36,605 hrs), tfd to the Centre de Formation Professionelle training centre 4 Jun 63 at Casablanca-Anfa. Used for student training until scrapped during Jun 75 at Casablanca-Anfa Airport.

2513 Laid down as Model 649-79-21. Completed as Model 749-79-22 for Air France, cvtd to 749-79-46. LADD: 18 Apr 47 as F-BAZI, E-13426 dated 26 May 47, dely Paris-Orly 1 Jun 47 (TT: 30hrs), CofA issued 13 Jun 47, in svce 14 Jun 47. Flew Paris-New

This aircraft (Air France 749 F-BAZI) was damaged beyond repair at Gander, Newfoundland in August 1954. A rebuild was started by Transocean Airlines at Oakland, California using the nose from the prototype Constellation (c/n 1961). The joining of the two aircraft can be seen in the photo. Unfortunately Transocean ceased operations and the restoration was abandoned. The registration N2717A had been allocated to the rebuild, which was photographed at Oakland in July 1960. (via Jennifer M Gradidge)

York-Antilles inaugural 9 Aug 48. Officially owned by SGAC until tfd to Air France 13 Nov 50. To 749A. Damaged when collided with 1049C F-BGNI at Orly 25 Feb 54. Repaired. Severely damaged when the aircraft ran off the runway at high speed while landing at Gander, Newfoundland, 25 Aug 54 & ran into a ditch (TT: 17,036 hrs). Declared a write-off by Air France 17 Sep 54, & canx from register 17 May 55. Remains bought by Transocean Associates, Inc in late 1954 & regn N2717A allotted. Repairs started, using nose section from c/n 1961, at Oakland in Dec 58, Russell Lawson of Oakland, CA, reportedly also involved, but rebuilding never completed. At end of Jul 60, the fuselage (complete with new nose section grafted on) was standing on trestles in a parking lot across the street from Transocean Airlines (who had, in the meantime, gone bankrupt). The fuselage was painted in green anti-corrosion paint, but was not being worked on. Subsequent fate unknown, but presumably scrapped.

2514 Laid down as Model 649-79-21. Completed as Model 749-79-22 for Air France, cvtd to 749-79-46. LADD: 9 May 47, as F-BAZJ, E-13428 dated 3 Jun 47, dely Orly 26 Jun 47, (TT: 28hrs), CofA 22 Jul 47, in svce 24 Jul 47. Officially owned by SGAC until transferred to Air France 18 Jan 51. Named 'Vincent Auriol' when used by President Auriol for flight Canada-Paris 9 Apr 51. To 749A, and by 1956 cvtd to 65-Seater All-Tourist Class. (TT: 22,101hrs a/o 1 Feb 56). Lsd to Air Algérie late May 60 to end Aug 60 (as Caravelle replacement). Withdrawn from svce 9 Nov 60 (TT: 32,819hrs), for tf to SGAC. Cvtd to special SAR configuration at Toulouse 14 Nov 60 to 6 Apr 61, officially tfd to SGAC 13 Apr 61, (CofA issued 24 May 61). Used by EARS 99 Squadron, Armée de l'Air, with call-sign F-SSFJ on SAR duties. Withdrawn from use after CofA expiry 31 Dec 69, but CofA renewed for ferry flight to St Yan for storage 6 Jan 70. Aircraft in fact deld to Toulouse-Blagnac 7 Jan 70 for use by the fire service (TT: 37,015 hrs). Scrapped by mid-1975, with fuselage in three pieces, and canx from F- register 30 Sep 76 as wfu.

2515 Laid down as Model 649-79-21. Completed as Model 749-79-22 for Air France, cvtd to 749-79-46. LADD: 6 Jun 47 as F-BAZK, but TOC at New York 9 May 47. Had landing gear accident Burbank, CA 6 Jun 47. Repaired, but was not deld to Orly until 27 Mar 48 (TT: 30hrs), E-13614, dated 22 Mar 48, & CofA issued 9 Apr 48, in svce 23 May 48. Officially owned by SGAC until tfd to Air France 13 Nov 50. To 749A, and by 1956 cvtd to 65-Seater All-Tourist Class. Port wing struck brace of radio mast taxiing at Hong Kong 20 Mar 56. Repaired. Withdrawn from svce 13 Nov 60 (TT: 31,982 hrs). Lsd to Air Inter 12 Mar-c.14 Dec 61. Sold to Royal Air Maroc 23 Jan 62, canx 27 Feb 62, and regd CN-CCM on CofA issue 17 Mar 62. Lsd to Air Afrique briefly at one time. CofA suspended at Casablanca 4 Jan 64 and wfu (TT: 35,879 hrs). Canx 13 Jan 64, used for spares and remains sold for scrap.

2516 Laid down as Model 649-79-21 for Transcontinental & Western Air Inc, regn unknown. Order canx. Completed as Model 749 c/n 2582 for TWA.

2517 Laid down as Model 649-79-21 for Transcontinental & Western Air Inc, regn unknown. Order canx. Completed as Model 749 c/n 2583 for TWA.

2518 649-84-24, cvtd on line to 649-79-12 for Eastern Air Lines. Regd NX101A for test-flying, including with Speedpak. Deld to Eastern at Miami, FL, 19 Mar 47, (probably for training). Ret to LAC May 47. Re-deld to Eastern as NC101A 10 Oct 47 FN 101. Believed cvtd to 649A, then to 749A in 1950. To N101A. Stored Louisville, KY Oct 60, later Miami. Reptd sold to Transit Equipment Corp 31 Jan 61, but not in FAA file. Sold to California Airmotive Inc 10 Jan 61. Lsd Associated Air Transport 'City of Puerto Rico' 10 Feb 62 until at least Aug 62. Lsd Standard Airways, then sold to them 7 Feb 63. Sold to LANSA and allotted OB-WAB-733 16 Dec 63, provisionally regd Feb 64, then re-regd OB-R-733 'Ciudad de Iquitos'. Withdrawn from use by late 1965, and cannibalized for spares at Lima, Peru by Jan 66. Officially regd 29 Mar 66(!). Derelict at Lima by Mar 68, and scrapped some time after, date unknown.

2519 649-84-24, cvtd on line to 649-79-12 for Eastern Air Lines. LADD: 13 May 47 as NC102A FN 102. Believed cvtd to 649A, then to 749A in 1950. To N102A. Still in use with Eastern for pilot training at Miami Oct 60. Reptd sold to Transit Equipment Corp 31 Jan 61, but not in FAA file. Sold to California Airmotive Corp 10 Jan 61, regd 16 Feb 61. Lsd Paramount Airlines 19 May-7 Sep 61. Sold to Great Lakes Airlines 1962, who cvtd aircraft to 98-Seater High-density Coach Class. Lsd California Hawaiian briefly in 1962, then lsd to Trans California mid- 1962 to Sep 64. Repossessed by California Airmotive as regd owner (CAR Jun 63). Ownership tfd to Cadelair Properties Corp 27 Jul 64. Sold to LANSA and allotted OB-R-785 28 Aug 65, regd 16 Sep 65 'Ciudad de Piura'. Withdrawn from use at Lima, Peru, probably about 1969. Stored there until scrapped some time after Jan 74.

2520 649-84-24, cvtd on line to 649-79-12 for Eastern Air Lines. LADD: 21 May 47 as NC103A FN 103, Eastern dely date 22 May 47. Believed cvtd to 649A, then to 749A in 1950. To N103A. Damaged at Washington, DC, 2 Jun 55, en route New Orleans, LA-Washington, DC. Repaired. Stored Louisville, KY Oct 60, later Miami,FL.Reptd sold to Transit Equipment Corp 31 Jan 61, but not in FAA file. Sold to California Airmotive Corp 10 Jan 61, regd 16 Feb 61. Lsd to Associated Air Transport 23 Jun 61 for unknown period. Lsd to Modern Air Transport 1964, in svce by Jun 64, sold to them 4 Aug 64. Out of use by mid-1965 and stored at Mercer County, Trenton, NJ, during 1965, later Miami, FL, 1966-67. Sold to Cov-Air Inc 25 Aug 67 and Bordas & Co, San Juan, PR same day. Sold to Quisqueyana and deld approx 30 Aug 67 as N103A. Regn canx 27 Oct 67, to HI-140, named 'Cibao' a/o Dec 67. Withdrawn from use at Santo Domingo, Dominican Republic approx Apr 72 after electrical problems and possible undercarriage collapse. Scrapped by 1976.

2521 649-84-24, cvtd on line to 649-79-12 for Eastern Air Lines. LADD: 27 May 47 as NC104A FN 104, Eastern dely date 28 May 47. Believed cvtd to 649A, then to 749A in 1950. To N104A. Damaged on landing at Jacksonville, FL, 10 Oct 50, when left gear retracted, aircraft swerved, causing right gear also to fail. Cause: Emergency hydraulic system not actuated properly due to lack of training in its use, left undercarriage leg not locked properly for landing. (TT: 10,435 hrs). Repaired. Stored Louisville, KY Oct 60, later Miami, FL. Reptd sold to Transit Equipment Corp 31 Jan 61, but not in FAA file. Sold to California Airmotive 10 Jan 61, sold Great Lakes Airlines 1961 or 1962 (lse-purchase), and cvtd to 98-Seater High-density Coach Class. Lsd Admiral Airways 20 Apr 62 in full colours until at least Sep 62. Lsd California Hawaiian briefly in 1962. Repossessed by California Airmotive as regd owner (USCAR Jun 63) & lsd Trans California by Jul 63. Out of svce Sep 64, after tf to Cadelair Properties Corp Jul 64. Sold to LANSA and allotted OB-R-771 7 Apr 65 'Ciudad de Iquitos'. Officially regd 6 Apr 66, but crashed approx 08:05hrs (local) on 27 Apr 66 between Huampara and Omas, in Andes mountains, 60 miles southeast of Lima, Peru, killing all on board. Was en route Lima to Cuzco on Flt 501 when it struck southeast side of Mt.Talaula at altitude of 12,600ft in a steep nose-up attitude & near stalling speed with engines set at METO power. Location was 5nm NE of San Pedro de Pilas & 29nm north of normal route. Cause: Possibly pilot error: Pilot is assumed to have decided to fly direct route from Las Palmas (7nm south of Lima-Callao Airport) to Cuzco as weather conditions were perfect, but found himself trapped in mountains with insufficient climb performance to clear the summits ahead, and insufficient manoeuvring space to turn back on a reciprocal course. The climb performance of the aircraft at its take-off weight of 90,572lbs was insufficient to clear the 14,000ft peaks safely. TT: 48,799 hrs.

2522 649-84-24, cvtd to 649-79-12 on line for Eastern Air Lines. LADD: 30 May 47 as NC105A FN 105. Believed cvtd to 649A, then to 749A in 1950. To N105A. Stored Louisville, KY Oct 60, later Miami, FL. Reptd sold to Transit Equipment Corp 31 Jan 61, but not in FAA file. Sold to California Airmotive Corp 10 Jan 61. Lsd Paramount Airlines 8 Jul 61 until at least Feb 62. Lsd Admiral Airways by Sep 62. Sold Great Lakes Airlines 1962 (lse-purchase), who cvtd to 98-Seater High-density Coach Class. Lsd Trans California Airlines spring 1963. Repossessed by California Airmotive as regd owner (USCAR Jun 63). Sold to Cadelair Properties Corp 27 Jul 64 (lse to Trans California continued). Stored Burbank, CA, by Sep 64. Sale to RIPSA as OB-R-849 Aug 66 ntu. Sold to Great Lakes Airlines 2 Oct 66, and to Huff Airsupply t/a California Pacific Air Supply, 4 Oct 67. Sold back to Great Lakes Airlines 22 May 68, then to MDL Nevada Corp 21 Jun 68 and to Mineral Mountain Mining Co 1 Jul 68. Sold to Pacific Air Transport 15 Aug 68. Out of svce and stored at Fort Lauderdale, FL, in Pacific Air Transport markings by Jun 70. Sold to Quisqueyana 19 Apr 71 (E-92333, dated 16 Jun 71). Canx from US register 7 Jul 71 and regd HI-207 'Duarte', but later unnamed. Made last scheduled Constellation passenger service in the world (with c/n 2085) on 19 Jan 78 Santo Domingo-San Juan, PR, and return. Used as a cargo aircraft by Quisqueyana from Feb 78 to May 78 (TT: a/o 5 Mar 78 was 55,068 hrs!) Then stored at Santo Domingo, Dominican Republic, after Quisqueyana ceased ops. Sold to Amin Canaan t/a TRADO and in svce by Aug 79, re-regd HI-332. Visited Miami, FL 28 Dec 79 with TRADO titles removed. Sold to persons unknown last week Feb 80 for a reported US $180,000 and impounded early Mar 80 for dope smuggling at Agua Jira, Northern Colombia. Reportedly struck off HI-register prior to last sale. Believed still stored at Agua Jira in 1981, riddled with bullets and abandoned. Remains used as shelter by local inhabitants. Final fate unknown.

2523 649-84-24, cvtd to 649-79-12 on line for Eastern Air Lines. LADD: 5 Jun 47 as NC106A, FN 106. Believed cvtd to 649A, then to 749A in 1950. To N106A. Stored Louisville, KY Oct 60, later Miami, FL. Reptd sold to Transit Equipment Corp 31 Jan 61, but not in FAA file. Sold to California Airmotive Corp 10 Jan 61. Lsd Admiral Airways 26 Jun 61 until at least Apr 62. Sold to Great Lakes Airlines and cvtd to 98-Seater High-density Coach Class. Stored by 1963. Lsd to Trans California Airlines by Apr 64, but out of svce by end of year. Sold to Cadelair Properties Corp Jul 64. Sale to COPISA as OB-R-819 1966 ntu (regn allocated 23 Mar 66). Sold to Nelson C Puente t/a American Aeronautical Exporting, who sold to Cosmos Corp 6 Dec 66. At Miami, FL as N106A 21 Dec 66 in full Quisqueyana colours. Sold to Quisqueyana same month and regd HI-129 by 10 Jan 67 (approx dely date from Miami), although N1060 was reserved or renewed 24 Jan 67. Named 'Santo Domingo', but later unnamed. Aircraft hijacked 26 Jan 71 en route Santo Domingo to San Juan, PR, when an attempt was made to force the pilot to fly to Cuba. Hi-jacking unsuccessful and aircraft reportedly crashed landing at Santo Domingo, but repaired and continued in svce with Quisqueyana until at least Jun 73. Withdrawn from use at Santo Domingo, Dominican Republic, the following year and used for spares until broken up during second half of Mar 77.

2524 649-84-24, cvtd to 649-79-12 on line for Eastern Air Lines. LADD: 8 Jun 47 as NC107A, FN 107. Believed cvtd to 649A, then to 749A in 1950. To N107A. Stored Louisville, KY Oct 60, later Miami, FL. Reptd sold to . Transit Equipment Corp 31 Jan 61, but not in FAA file. Sold to California Airmotive Corp 10 Jan 61. Lsd Admiral Airways from 16 Jun 61, for unknown period, and again from 20 Apr 62. Sold to Great Lakes Airlines and cvtd to 98-Seater High-density Coach Class. Stored at Burbank, CA, by Jul 63 in Admiral colours. To Trans California Airlines for spares use only spring 1964. Sold to Cadelair Properties Corp Jul 64, but remained in storage at Burbank, with parts missing by mid-1966. Broken up at Burbank between Feb 69 and Jun 69.

2525 Laid down as Model 649-79-22 for Transcontinental & Western Air Inc as NC86527. Order canx. Changed to 749-79-22 for Pan American. LADD: 20 Jun 47 as NC86527 'Clipper Glory of the Skies', Pan Am dely date 24 Aug 47. To N86527. Sold to Air France (TT: 5,573 hrs) with dely 3 Jan 50, arrived Orly 6 Jan 50. Cvtd to 749A-79-46. Regd F-BAZU, CofA issued 26 Jun 50, in svce 28 Jun 50. Flew inaugural Paris-Karachi-Saigon-Tokyo svce 24 Nov 52. Modified to 65-Seater All-Tourist Class by 1956 (TT: 23,377 hrs a/o 1 Feb 56). Withdrawn from svce 8 Oct 60, CofA expiry 10 Oct 60 (TT: 33,679hrs) and stored at Paris-Orly. Canx from F-register as wfu on 31 Aug 62. Tfd to Air France apprentice training school, the Centre d'Instruction de Vilgenis, near Paris, by Feb 66 and remained in use there until replaced by Caravelle F-BHRA by 5 Apr 76. Last report Jul 76, when the aircraft was outside at Vilgenis and awaiting scrapping, which followed shortly afterwards.

2526 Laid down as Model 649-79-22 for Transcontinental & Western Air Inc as NC86528. Order canx. Changed to 749-79-22 for Pan American. LADD: 21 Jun 47 as NC86528 ' Clipper Sovereign of the Skies ', Pan Am dely date 24 Aug 47. It is believed that this was the aircraft involved in a training accident 28 Jun 47 at New York-La Guardia, NY. Following contact with the ground on landing, the main undercarriage retracted, leaving the nosewheel extended and allowing the tail assembly to drag along the ground, causing also damage to propellers and other parts. Cause: Crew possibly failed to lock the gear down on landing, warning horn inoperative. Repaired. Ran off runway at La Guardia, NY into the bay 8 May 48. Repaired again.To N86528. Sold to Air France (TT: 4,217 hrs) with dely 23 Dec 49, arrived Orly 31 Dec 49. Cvtd to 749A-79-46, regd F-BAZV, CofA issued 3 Jun 50, in svce 5 Jun 50. Collided with tractor on icy patch of parking area at Orly 13 Feb 56. Repaired. Modified to 65-Seater, All-Tourist Class by 1956 (TT: 21,822 hrs on 1 Feb 56). Withdrawn from svce 8 Oct 60, CofA expiry 10 0ct 60 and stored at Paris-Orly (TT: 32,405 hrs). Canx from F-register 6 Nov 64 as wfu. Still stored a/o Jan 65, was reptd also to be tfd to the Air France training school at Vilgenis, but broken up approx 1968 instead.

2527 Laid down as Model 649-79-22 for Transcontinental & Western Air Inc as NC86529. Order canx. Changed to 749-79-22 for Pan American. LADD: 27 Jun 47 as NC86529 'Clipper Romance of the Skies', Pan Am dely date 24 Aug 47. To N86529. Sold to Air France (TT: 5,428 hrs) with dely 14 Jan 50, arrived Orly 17 Jan 50. Cvtd to 749A-79-46, regd F-BAZX, CofA issued 11 Aug 50, in svce 12 Aug 50. Modified to 61-Seater trans-atlantic Tourist configuration, and subsequently to 65-Seater European All-Tourist lay-out in 1956. (TT: 22,734 hrs a/o 1 Feb 56). Crashed and broke up on approach to Vienna-Schwechat Airport, Austria, at 22.59 hrs (Central European Time) on 24 Dec 58, at end of flight from Paris-Orly to Munich & Vienna, no casualties, but Captain & Flight Engineer severely injured. Aircraft hit ground hard 2,200 metres from threshold of runway 30, after entering sudden downdraft coupled with total loss of visibility of the ground on entering a cloud during the base leg turn to land. Canx from register 25 Mar 59.

2528 Laid down as Model 649-79-22 for Transcontinental & Western Air Inc as NC86530. Order canx. Changed to 749-79-22 for Pan American. LADD: 28 Jun 47 as NC86530 'Clipper

NC86530 049 "Clipper Monarch of the Skies". The passengers on this aircraft had a lucky escape en route from New York to London on 30th January 1949 when the 049 was hit at 4,000 feet by a Cessna 140. The Constellation landed safely with no injuries to passengers or crew, but the Cessna was less fortunate. (Associated Press via Lockheed)

Monarch of the Skies', changed to 'Clipper America' by Aug 47. Pan Am dely date 24 Aug 47. To N86530. Badly damaged in mid-air collision over Port Washington, NY, with Cessna 140 (NC76891) on 30 Jan 49. While climbing VFR following take-off from La Guardia en route for London, England, at approx 16.30 hrs (local) the Cessna hit the Constellation just aft of the flight deck at about 4,000 ft. A 15-foot hole was torn in the fuselage roof above the galley. The Constellation made an emergency landing at Mitchel Fld, NY, with no injuries to pax or crew. Repaired, and sold to Air France, dely as N86530 7 Jan 50, arrived Orly 12 Jan 50. (TT: 4,967hrs). N-regn canx 16 Jan 50. Cvtd to 749A-79-46, regd F-BAZY, CofA issued 21 Oct 50, in svce 22 Oct 50. (TT: 19,250hrs a/o 31 Dec 55). Named 'Ville Lumière' at one time. Modified to 65-Seater, All-Tourist Class by 1956. Operated BOAC flt BA631 London-Prestwick-Goose Bay-Montreal 24-25 Jun 57. Withdrawn from svce 18 Oct 60 for tf to SGAC (TT: 30,313hrs). Cvtd to special SAR configuration at Toulouse 20 Oct 60-1 Mar 61, with official tf to SGAC 21 Feb 61, CofA 24 Feb 61, sold 10 Mar 61. Used by EARS 99 Squadron, Armée de l'Air, with call-sign F-SSFYon SAR duties. Withdrawn from use 31 Dec 69, prior to CofA expiry on 24 Jun 70 (TT: 34,731 hrs), and ferried to St Yan for storage. Canx from register 2 Feb 70 as wfu. Auctioned by the Domaines at Macon 26 Oct 71 and sold for scrap. (NB: c/n 2528 was quoted for the 749A that was re-sold by the Domaines in Oct 73, but is believed to have been a mistake for c/n 2625-qv).

2529 649-84-24, cvtd on line to 649-79-12 for Eastern Air Lines, LADD: 17 Jul 47 as NC108A, FN 108. Believed cvtd to 649A, then to 749A in 1950. To N108A. Stored Louisville, KY Oct 60, later Miami, FL. Reptd sold to Transit Equipment Corp 31 Jan 61, but not in FAA file. Sold to California Airmotive Corp 10 Jan 61. Stripped to bare hulk for spares at Burbank, CA, during 1962, and practically taken apart by Sep 62, However, flown to Fox Field, Lancaster, CA, by late 1964 for storage. Derelict, with major components missing by May 71, and believed scrapped by early 1972. Canx from USCAR 12 Jul 70 at request of California Airmotive.

2530 649-84-24, cvtd on line to 649-79-12 for Eastern Air Lines. LADD: 20 Jul 47 as NC109A, FN 109. Believed cvtd to 649A, then to 749A in 1950. To N109A. Damaged when undercarriage collapsed Atlanta,GA 18 Dec 58 on training flight. Repaired. Stored Louisville, KY Oct 60, later Miami, FL. Reptd sold to Transit Equipment Corp 31 Jan 61, but not in FAA file. Sold to California Airmotive Corp 10 Jan 61. Sold to Great Lakes Airlines in 1962, used briefly then stored for spares use. Stripped to bare hulk for spares at Burbank, CA in 1962, and components missing by Sep 62. Broken up by about 1964.

2531 649-84-24, cvtd on line to 649-79-12 for Eastern Air Lines. LADD: 27 Jul 47 as NC110A, FN 110, Eastern dely date 23 Jul 47 (and also quoted by another LAC source). Believed cvtd to 649A, then to 749A in 1950. To N110A. Badly damaged in ground collision with Convair 240 Washington, DC 23 May 54. Repaired. Received substantial damage at Philadelphia, PA, at 01.43 hrs (EST) on 3 Jan 60. While taxying in after landing, the right main landing gear collapsed, causing damage to the starboard wing and engines. Cause: Fatigue failure of landing gear strut cylinder. Was en route Boston, MA to Washington, DC. Unrepaired. Reptd sold in an unairworthy state to Transit Equipment Corp on 31 Jan 61, but not in FAA file. Sold to California Airmotive Corp 10 Jan 61. Sold to Airmotive Suppliers Corp for reclamation for spares and broken up during 1961 at Idlewild, NY. Nose section used as a store for garden tools near Idlewild Airport from 1961 until removed between Jul 63 and Sep 63.

2532 649-84-24, cvtd on line to 649-79-12 for Eastern Air Lines. LADD: 19 Jul 47 as NC111A, FN 111. Possibly cvtd to 649A. Destroyed in landing accident at Boston, MA, 21 Jan 48. While on a scheduled flight from Miami to Newark, NJ, the aircraft was diverted to La Guardia. However, at La Guardia the approach was missed and the aircraft diverted to Boston. Here, an ILS approach was made, the aircraft landing 2,000 ft from the approach end of the runway and on half an inch of newly fallen snow. Shortly after touchdown, the left gear struck snow drifts, causing the aircraft to change direction sharply and crash into a large snowbank, with the undercarriage collapsing and fire breaking out in the vicinity of nos. 3 & 4 engines, subsequently spreading to the rest of the aircraft which was practically destroyed by fire. No casualties. Probable cause: Loss of directional control due to excessive accumulation of snow. (TT: 1,499 hrs).

2533 649-84-24, cvtd on line to 649-79-12 for Eastern Air Lines. LADD: 30 Jul 47 as NC112A, FN 112. Received substantial damage on 7 Feb 48. While flying from La Guardia, NY, to West Palm Beach, FL at 22,000 ft, there was a sudden loud noise and severe vibration. A descent was started, the cabin depressurized and engine instruments ceased to function and no.3 engine was vibrating. Soon after this, no.3 engine and propeller dropped from the aircraft, upon which the vibration ceased. It was discovered that parts of no.3 propeller had pierced the fuselage at the galley area and killed a steward. An emergency landing an hour and thirty minutes after the incident was made at Bunnell, nr Daytona Beach, FL, with no flaps (as these were also inoperative), the left outboard tyre blowing out on landing, and a small fire developing in the right main gear. Cause: Failure of the no.3 propeller while 155 miles out over the Atlantic, off Brunswick, GA. TT: 1,522hrs. Repaired. Believed cvtd to 649A, and then to 749A 7 Sep 50. To N112A. Damaged at Charlotte, NC, 24 Jan 55, when it struck a Cessna 120 on take-off, en route Birmingham, AL to New York, NY. Repaired. Crashed on ILS approach to Jacksonville, FL, at 03.43 hrs (EST) on 21 Dec 55, killing all on board. During final approach, aircraft deviated to left of glide path and below it, colliding with trees half a mile from the runway end, southwest of Imeson Co Airport. Acft was on flight EA642 Miami, FL to Boston, MA. Cause: Sudden decrease in visibility, with local fog patches, and pilot too late in executing a missed approach procedure, and descending below minimum altitude. (TT: 29,941 hrs).

2534 649-84-24, cvtd on line to 649-79-12 for Eastern Air Lines. LADD: 28 Jul 47 as NC113A, FN 113. Believed cvtd to 649A, then to 749A in 1950. To N113A. Lsd to unknown operator in 1954, restored to Eastern 6 Apr 54. Lsd to Aeronaves de Mexico approx 1958, believed as XA-MOA 'Ciudad de Guadalajara', for a short period. Ret Eastern Air Lines Nl13A. Stored Louisville, KY Oct 60, later Miami, FL. Reptd sold to Transit Equipment Corp 31 Jan 61, but not in FAA file. Sold to California Airmotive Corp 10 Jan 61. Lsd to Standard Airways 1962, and sold to them 7 Feb 63. Sold to LANSA and deld Mar 64 as OB-WAC-740 (allotted 19 Feb 64), re-regd OB-R-740 'Ciudad de Tacna', later unnamed. N-regn canx 10 Apr 64. Officially regd 29 Mar 66(!). Withdrawn from use at Lima, Peru, probably about 1971, and stored there (whole) until 1978, condition deteriorating. Still at Lima, in bad condition in late 1980, but had disappeared by Oct 81. Presumably scrapped.

2535 649-84-24, cvtd on line to 649-79-12 for Eastern Air Lines. LADD: 2 Aug 47 as NC114A, FN 114. Believed cvtd to 649A, then to 749A in 1950. To N114A. Stored Louisville, KY Oct 60, later Miami, FL. Reptd sold to Transit Equipment Corp 31 Jan 61, but not in FAA file. Sold to California Airmotive Corp 10 Jan 61. Lsd Pacific Northern for one year from 8 May 61. Ret California Airmotive 8 May 62. Lsd Standard Airways, then sold to them 7 Feb 63. Sold to LANSA and allotted OB-R-743 25 Mar 64. Dely due Apr 64, but remained in store at Long Beach, CA, in full LANSA markings until deld early 1965. Named 'Ciudad de Iquitos', later 'Ciudad de Cuzco' (unconf). Remained in svce with LANSA until about 1971, then stored at Lima, Peru. Derelict by Jan 74 and probably scrapped shortly after.

2536 Serial deleted - no details of any allocation known.

2537 Serial deleted - no details of any allocation known.

2538 Laid down as 649-79-22, cvtd on line to Model 749-79-22 for Air France, later 749-79-46. LADD: 19 Aug 47 as F-BAZL, E-13432, dated 6 Aug 47. TOC at New York 19 Aug 47, deld Orly 22 Sep 47 (TT: 35hrs), CofA 26 Sep 47, in svce 27 Sep 47. Officially regd to SGAC until tfd to Air France 20 Feb 51. To 749A, and modified to 65-Seater All-Tourist Class by 1956. Operated BOAC flt BA631 London-Prestwick-Goose Bay-Montreal 26-27 Jun 57. Withdrawn from svce 1 Nov 60. Stored at Paris-Orly 10 Nov 60 to 8 Mar 61. Restored to svce and lsd to Tunis Air, then to Air Inter,

LV-IGS 749 Freighter in the colours of Aerotransportes Entre Rios. The aircraft was photographed at Miami International on 12th November 1964 shortly after the fitting of a forward cargo door. (Harold G Martin)

8 Mar 61 to 28 Oct 61. Withdrawn from svce and stored again at Paris-Orly from 21 Oct 61 (TT: 32,558 hrs). Remained in storage until sold to the Government of Senegal (Gouvernement du Sénégal) 25 Mar 66 after cvtd to a 7-crew special configuration. CofA 18 Mar 66 as 6V-AAR 'Flèche des Almadies' and canx from F-register 25 Mar 66. Withdrawn from svce 7 Aug 69 (TT: 33,367 hrs). CofA expiry reptd also 27 Dec 71 at Paris-Orly. Stored there until ferried to Toussus-le-Noble early Oct 73. Stored at Toussus, unregistered, and reportedly owned by Monsieur Labadi, President of the Air France Aero Club, for a planned museum of aircraft used by Air France. Gradually deteriorated in condition, as plans were abandoned and eventually broken up during Jun 79 at Toussus, completely gone by Jul 79.

2539 Serial deleted - no details of any allocation known.

2540 Laid down as 649-79-22 for KNILM & regd PK-ALA, but ntu. Subsequently changed to 749-79-22. Taken over by KLM, and regd 12 Aug 47 as PH-TEP 'Pontianak', LADD: 13 Aug 47, E-13433, dated 1 Aug 47. Modified to 749-79-33. Cvtd from 46- to 61-Seater in 1950. Re-regd PH-LDR 16 Mar 54. Fitted with cargo door in forward fuselage by SALA at San Jose, Costa Rica, Sep 60 onwards. Reported cocooned at Amsterdam-Schiphol from Feb 61 until at least Jun 63, but also reported in svce Feb 62. On 14 Feb 64, the aircraft was at San Jose, Costa Rica, all silver, with no markings except the c/n on the nosewheel door. PH-regn canx 18 Feb 64. Regd to KLM as TI-1044P 20 Feb 64, canx 4 Mar 64 on sale to Aerotransportes Entre Rios 5 Mar 64, regd LV-PZX same day. Re-regd LV-IGS in Apr 64. Stored at Buenos Aires-Ezeiza after CofA expiry 1 Mar 67, but re-entered svce Jul 70 after crash of AER's Britannia Freighter. Again stored from approx Feb 72 at Miami, FL, but flying again later in the year and continued in svce in Uruguay until late 1973. Sold to ALAS - Atlantida Linea Aerea Sudamericana SA in Uruguay in 1973, AER markings painted over. Sale apparently not completed as acft listed again by AER in Apr 77. Stored at Montevideo-Carrasco in ex-AER colours from 1973, still complete in 1980, but looking rather weatherworn. Aircraft acquired the starboard nosewheel door from 1049G N6239G in approx 1970, with FN 239 visible. Legal problems over ownership resulted in acft eventually being abandoned. Auctioned at Montevideo-Carrasco 23 Jan 82, with reserve price of approx £2,650, parts missing but all four engines in place. Sold for scrap & broken up during fourth week of Jan 82.

2541 Laid down as 649-79-22 for KNILM, and subsequently changed to 749-79-22. Taken over by KLM and regd 12 Aug 47 as PH- TER 'Roermond', LADD: 14 Aug 47, E-13434, dated 5 Aug 47, by which time the aircraft had been modified to a 749-79-33. Flew to Prague 19 Sep 47 for demonstration flts to CSA - Ceskoslovenske Aerolinie. (see Section 10.2). Crashed into the sea a short distance off the coast near Bari, south-east Italy, at approx 10.30 hrs (local) on 23 Jun 49, killing all on board. The aircraft was flying from Batavia (Indonesia) to Amsterdam, via Cairo and Rome, and was flying at about 16,000 ft when it went into a steep dive, levelling off slightly at about 1,500 ft and then falling into the sea tail-first. Cause: Possibly malfunction of the auto-pilot. Regn canx 23 Jun 49.

2542 Serial deleted - no details of any allocation known.

2543 Serial deleted - no details of any allocation known.

2544 Laid down as 649-79-22 for Air France, but subsequently changed to a 749-79-22 for KLM. Regd PH-TDB 15 Oct 47, aircraft deld 14 Oct 47 (LADD), E-14756, also dated 14 Oct 47. Named 'Batavia'. Used for Amsterdam-Montreal inaugural 29 May 49. Renamed 'Walcheren' 10 Nov 49 in Indonesia on occasion of the 1000th Amsterdam-Batavia flight, retd Amsterdam 24 Nov 49. To 749A. Regn canx 7 Oct 53. To LAC as trade-in on Super Constellations, deld ex-Amsterdam 8 Oct 53, to Capital Airlines 9 Oct 53 as N90622, FN 863. Sold to BOAC on 26 Apr 55, and regd 28 Apr 55 as G-ANVD, E-21066 same day and deld to London-Heathrow 5 May 55 (CofA 30 Apr 55). Named 'Beverley', in svce 18 Jul 55 & used in 60-Seater Tourist Class configuration. Last svce 5-6 Mar 57. Stored London-Heathrow from 7 Mar 57, cocooned, awaiting disposal from 21 Mar 57. CofA expiry 16 Jun 57. Sold to The Babb Co 26 May 59 and deld ex-London 26 May 59 to Newark, NJ. Reregd N6689N & tfd to Avianca 27 May 59, carried dual regn G-ANVD/N6689N to Windsor Locks, CT, for conversion to 74-80 Seater domestic Tourist layout for Avianca. Deld to Avianca (E-41603, dated 16 Jul 59) as N6689N and re-regd HK-650. Sold to Trans-Peruana 31 Oct 67 and regd OB-R-914. Withdrawn from use at Lima, Peru by Sep 69 (bankruptcy of Trans-Peruana), and for sale by auction 8 Sep 70. Remained in storage at Lima and scrapped by Apr 75.

2545 Laid down as 649-79-22 for TWA as NC86531. Order canx. To 749-79-22, later modified to 749-79-46, for Air France as F-BAZM, LADD: 25 Aug 47, TOC 26 Aug 47 in New York. E-13442 dated 31 Aug 47, arrived Orly 12 Nov 47 (TT: 34hrs), CofA issued 18 Nov 47. Inaugurated sleeper-service New York-Paris 29 Nov 47. Officially regd to SGAC until tfd to Air France 18 Jan 51. To 749A. Damaged when carbon gas bottle exploded on ground at Douala, Cameroons, 25 Mar 55. Repaired. Modified to 61-Seater transatlantic Tourist Class, and subsequently in 1956 to 65-Seater European Tourist class. Operated BOAC flts BA637 London-Shannon-Gander-Montreal 5-6 Jun & London-Gander-Montreal 12-13 Jun 57. Withdrawn from svce 19 Jul 60 (TT: 30,700hrs) for tf to SGAC. Modified to special SAR configuration (12 pax + 8 crew) between 30 Jul 60 and 2 Feb 61. Officially tfd to SGAC 20 Jan 61, sold 2 Feb 61 & CofA 7 Feb 61. Used by EARS 99 Squadron, Armée de l'Air, with call-sign F- SSFM on SAR duties. Crashed into Mont Lapalme near Perillos, about 12 miles north of Perpignan, in south-west France, while flying from its base at Toulouse-Francazal 11 Jan 63, killing the crew. Aircraft appeared to have crashed head-on into a mountain peak at a height of 2,300 metres on the French-Spanish border, in fog. (TT: 31,766 hrs).

2546 Laid down as 649-79-22 for TWA as NC86532. Order canx. To 749-79-22, later modified to 749-79-46 for Air France as F-BAZN. LADD: 25 Aug 47, TOC 26 Aug 47 in New York. E-13443 dated 23 Jan 48, arrived Orly 28 Jan 48 (TT: 47hrs), CofA issued 26 Feb 48 & in svce 28 Feb 48. Officially regd to SGAC until tfd to Air France 11 Jan 50, and cvtd to 749A. Crashed into 3,500 ft Algarvia mountain on Sao Miguel Island at 20.50 hrs (CST) on 28 Oct 49, killing all on board. The aircraft was en route Paris-New York and was due to land at Santa Maria, Azores (60 miles away) five minutes after the accident occurred. Weather bad, with poor visibility. (TT: 3,399hrs). Regn canx 21 Nov 49.

2547 Laid down as 649-79-22 for TWA as NC86533. Order canx. To 749-79-22, later modified to 749-79-46 for Air France as F-BAZO. LADD: 17 Sep 47, but actually TOC 10 Sep 47 in New York. E-13444 dated 6 Feb 48, arrived Orly 16 Feb 48 (TT: 32hrs), CofA issued 27 Feb 48, in svce 21 Mar 48. Officially regd to SGAC until tfd to Air France 29 Mar 51. To 749A. Inaugurated Paris-Saigon svce via Karachi & Calcutta 1 Mar 50 & Strasbourg-Mulhouse-Geneva-Marseilles-Casablanca svce with couchettes 22 Jan 55. Modified to 65-Seater European Tourist Class by 1956. Lsd to Tunis Air Mar-May 61. Sold to SGAC 8 Jun 61 and modified to special SAR configuration (12 pax + 8 crew) at Toulouse 23 Jun-8 Aug 61. Officially tfd to SGAC 5 Jul 61, CofA issued 4 Jul 61. Used by EARS 99 Squadron, Armée de l'Air, with call-sign F-SSFO on SAR duties. Named 'Ciel de Guararapes' from 1968. Withdrawn from use 1 Sep 69, after CofA expiry on 31 Aug 69 (TT: 36,903 hrs). CofA renewed for ferry to St. Yan for storage 5 Sep 69. Stored at St Yan, and broken up there after being sold for scrap in auction by the Domaines at Macon on 26 Oct 71.

2548 Laid down as 649-79-22 for TWA as NC86534. Order canx. Then allocated to Air Ceylon. Modified to 749-79-32 for Aerlinte as EI-ACR 'Saint Brendan'. LADD 26 Aug 47, E-13435, dated 27 Aug 47, and deld ex-Burbank 16 Sep 47, arrived Shannon 20 Sep 47. In svce Nov 47. Stored from Feb 48 until sale to BOAC on 15 Jun 48. Regd G-ALAK 22 Jun 48, named 'Brentford', CofA (V349) 30 Jun 48. In svce 8 Dec 48. CofA no. changed to A2749 on renewal 8 Jul 50. Starboard rudder damaged when Air France DC-4 F-BFGS hit it while 'LAK was running up by Runway 23L

3 Jul 54. Repaired. Damaged in belly-landing at Karachi 21 Oct 54, en route London-Sydney, when nosewheel jammed in 'up' position. Sustained further damage 24 Oct 54 when lifting jacks moved as 'LAK weathercocked in strong cross-wind. Ferried to Burbank for repairs 31 Dec 54, under repair 1 Jan-9 Apr 55, retd to London 12 Apr 55. Modified to 60-Seater Tourist Class. Cvtd to 749A Jan-Feb 56. Flew London-Dar es Salaam inaugural 19-20 Aug 56. Last svce 17-18 Jan 58. Flew a London-Boston-London charter 10-14 Jun 58. Cof A renewed 27 Jun 58, but stored at London-Heathrow from 2 Aug 58. Lsd to Skyways 10 Jun 59, in svce 13 Jun 59, and fitted with rear cargo door by BOAC at London-Heathrow Apr-6 Jul 60, deld 5 Jul 60, test flown 11 Jul 60 & in svce 20 Jul 60. Sold to Skyways 5 Jun 62, CofRegn 22 Jun 62, and taken over by Euravia (London) Ltd on 1 Sep 62. Repainted in Euravia colours May 63 and used as an 82-Seater for IT flights (also for cargo). Rn Britannia Airways 16 Aug 64, but contd to carry Euravia titling. Sold to ACE Freighters and deld to Coventry-Baginton 6 Aug 65, with official tf 14 Sep 65. In svce Toulouse-London (Gatwick) 24 Jun 66, last svce Jeddah-Coventry 9 Sep 66. ACE bankrupt in Sep 66, and aircraft stored at Coventry. Sold by tender Dec 66 by liquidators of ACE, CofA expiry 24 Jun 67, and officially canx from G-register on 8 Aug 67 as sold in the USA. Regd N1489 to unknown buyer same day, but regn never carried and aircraft remained at Coventry. Painted up as CX-BHD for Aerolineas Uruguayas on 7 Jan 68, but regn deleted again on 13 Jan 68 (sale ntu). Painted as CP-797 for Trans-Bolivian (TABSA?) on 13 Jan 68 and deld ex-Coventry 15 Jan 68 via Shannon to Miami, FL. Stored at Miami after arrival and sold to COPISA in Jul 68 as OB-R-899 (in lieu of c/n 2549) and painted up in Sep 68. Manufacturer's construction number plate from this aircraft officially tfd to c/n 2549, in return for the plate from c/n 2549. This aircraft therefore officially "c/n 2549" from this point. Used by COPISA until company ceased ops around the end of 1971. Fate unknown, but probably scrapped at Lima, Peru, early 1970s.

2549 Laid down as 649-79-22 for TWA as NC86535. Order canx. Then allocated to Air Ceylon. Modified to 749-79-32 for Aerlinte as EI-ACS 'Saint Patrick'. LADD 28 Aug 47, E-13436, dated 15 Aug 47, and deld ex-Burbank 16 Sep 47, arrived Shannon 20 Sep 47. In svce Nov 47. Stored from Feb 48 until sale to BOAC on 15 Jun 48. Regd G-ALAL 22 Jun 48, named 'Banbury', CofA (V350) 30 Jun 48. In svce 1 Dec 48 on London-Sydney 749A inaugural. CofA no. changed to A1578 on renewal 1 Jun 51. Cvtd to 749A Oct-Dec 55. Modified to 60-Seater Tourist Class. Flew last svce 22-23 Nov 57. Last charter flight London-Lisbon-London 7 May 58. CofA renewed 23 May 58, carried out a training flight 1 Jul 58, but stored London from 2 Jul 58. Lsd to Skyways 21 Jul 59, del same day & in svce 25 Aug 59. Fitted with rear cargo door by BOAC at London-Heathrow Jan-5 Apr 60, in svce 20 Apr 60. Sold to Skyways 5 Jun 62, CofRegn 13 Jun 62, and taken over by Euravia (London) Ltd on 1 Sep 62. Repainted in Euravia colours May 63 and used as 82-Seater for IT flights (also for cargo). Rn Britannia Airways 16 Aug 64, but contd to carry Euravia titling. Sold to ACE Freighters 21 Jan 65, CofRegn 4 Feb 65. In svce May 65. Flew Lyneham-Far East inaugural charter dep 30 May 65. Sustained damage to no.2 engine and propeller at Karachi, Pakistan night of 5-6 Aug 65. Repaired. Last svce Gatwick-Coventry 28 Jul 66, CofA expired 27 Aug 66. ACE bankrupt in Sep 66, and aircraft stored at Coventry-Baginton. Sold by tender Dec 66 by liquidators of ACE, and officially canx from G-register 28 Mar 67 as sold in the USA. Deld Coventry-Miami, FL 22 Apr 67 as G-ALAL. No US-regn known, but transferred to W W Tilton on 15 Apr 67. Made test flight for COPISA on 27 Jun 67, last flight on 5 Jul 67. Was to have become OB-R-899 with COPISA, and was painted up as such at Miami. However, the aircraft was not accepted and was cancelled in favour of c/n 2548 (qv), the regn marks were painted out at the end of Jul 68 and the manufacturer's construction number plate from this aircraft was officially tfd to c/n 2548 in Jul 68. This aircraft therefore officially "c/n 2548" from this point. From Jul 68, the aircraft was stored with no identification marks at Miami. A lien was attached to the aircraft by Dade County Port Authority for parking fees owing in Jul 70 ($2,460 was owed for 1 Jul 69 to 31 Oct 69, at which time the regn was quoted as G-ALAL). Sold to Nelson C Puentes-t/a American Aeronautical Exports Sep 71. To Peter C. Shortell t/a Wade Trading Oct 72. Possessed by Air Agency (Miami Airport ramp operator) for non-payment of parking fee of $3,120. Sold to Lance W. Dreyer 20 Oct 72 for $300. Aircraft derelict by mid-1970; and was being used for spares in early 1971. Sold to John H Dreyer 1 Dec 72 (father of Lance W Dreyer), tfd Air Cargo Intl May 73, and the hulk was finally broken up by the autumn of 1974.

2550 Laid down as 649-79-22, and subsequently changed to 749-79-22 for Air France, later modified to 749-79-46, as F-BAZP. LADD 21 Sep 47, E-13447 dated 20 Feb 48, deld Orly 27 Feb 48 (TT: 23hrs). CofA 7 Apr 48, in svce 9 Apr 48. Officially regd to SGAC until transferred to Air France 14 Oct 50. To 749A. Flew inaugural extension of New York-Paris svce to Frankfurt-Rhein Main 2 May 51, inaugural Paris-Munich svce (en route to Damascus & Teheran) 18 Jun 51 & inaugural night-Sleeper svce Paris-Douala-Brazzaville 11-12 Nov 53. Modified to 65-Seater European Tourist Class by 1956. Operated BOAC flt BA637 London-Goose Bay-Montreal 27-28 Jun 57. Damaged when starboard wing struck building taxying at Lisbon 30 Oct 58. Repaired. Withdrawn from svce for tf to SGAC 5 Nov 60 (TT: 32,882 hrs). Modified to special SAR configuration (12 pax + 8 crew) at Toulouse Nov 60 to 9 May 61. Tfd officially to SGAC 4 May 61, with CofA issued same day, sold 17 May 61. Used by EARS 99 Squadron, Armée de l'Air, with call-sign F-SSFP on SAR duties. Named 'Château de Francazal' from 1967. Withdrawn from use 31 Dec 69 (TT: 37,544 hrs) and ferried to St. Yan for storage. Canx from F-register 2 Feb 70 as wfu prior to CofA expiry on 7 Jul 70. Sold in auction by Domaines at Macon 26 Oct 71 to Monsieur Jugnot. Dismantled for transport from St. Yan to Couchey, nr Dijon, and erected as attraction outside the "Bomotel" restaurant/motel on the N74 road at Couchey Nov-Dec 71. Remained preserved there until complaints by local residents forced M. Jugnot to scrap the aircraft on site during May-Jun 73.

2551 749-79-33 on 22 Oct 47 to KLM as PH-TDC, 'Curacao'. Regd 27 Oct 47, KLM dely date 23 Oct 47, E-14760 dated 22 Oct 47. To 749A. To LAC as trade-in on Super Constellations, deld ex-Amsterdam 17 Apr 52, to Capital Airlines 18 Apr 52 as N90607, FN 860, PH-regn canx same day. Sold to BOAC on 26 Jun 55, and regd 28 Jun 55 as G-ANUV, E-21073 same day and deld to London-Heathrow 4 Jul 55, CofA 1 Jul 55, and named 'Blan- tyre'. In svce 13 Sep 55. Used in 60-Seater Tourist Class configuration. Last svce 24-27 Feb 57 and stored London-Heathrow 27 Feb 57. Awaiting disposal from 21 Mar 57. CofA expired 20 Aug 57, renewed 8 Jan 58. Sold to The Babb Co 8 Jan 58, del ex-London 8 Jan 58. Regd 9 Jan 58 as N9830F & G-regn canx same day, tfd Transocean Airlines. Repossessed by The Babb Co Dec 58, ret 29 Jun 59 for resale. Stored at Oakland, CA, during 1959. Nominal tf date to The Babb Co 31 Jul 59. Sold to Korean National Airlines as HL102, in svce with Korean by Nov 59, and still in svce Aug 61. Withdrawn from use at Seoul. Sold to Marian Kozubski for £6,000 for lse to Aero-Transport in Oct 62. Air-tested 20 Oct 62, deld Seoul to Woensdrecht (Holland) via Hong Kong 24 Oct-1 Nov 62. Re-regd OE-IFE. This was probably the aircraft that was grounded at Djibouti, French Somalia, for alleged gun-running in Nov 63. Aero-Transport ceased ops 1964, and aircraft impounded at Schiphol-Amsterdam (for non-payment of landing-fees and parking charges) from Feb 64 until broken up on 26 Aug 66. Parts to scrap dealer in Nieuw Vennep, then in 1970 to Arnhem.

2552 Laid down as 649-84-12 for Eastern Air Lines, then allocated to KNILM as 649-79-22, later updated to 749-79-22. Taken over by KLM, as a 749-79-33 and regd PH-TES 'Soerabaja' 12 Sep 47, LADD 9 Sep 47, E-14749 same day. Made emergency landing at Miami, FL en route Montreal-Havana 17 Aug 51. Re-regd PH-LDS 29 Mar 54. Op an Air Ceylon flight 25 Aug 57 at London-Heathrow. Withdrawn from use at Schiphol-Amsterdam 5 Nov 59 and cocooned for storage. Used for spares Jun 62 at Schiphol, but also in use for ground training of aircrew at Schiphol till mid-1963, and scrapped shortly after. Regn canx 24 Jun 63.

2553 Laid down as 649-84-12 for Eastern Air Lines, then allocated to KNILM as 649-79-22, later updated to 749-79-22.

Taken over by KLM, as a 749-79-33 and regd PH-TET 'Tilburg' 1 Oct 47, LADD 25 Sep 47, KLM dely date 24 Sep 47, E-14748, undated. Original cost $750,000. Cvtd from 46- to 61-Seater in 1950. Suffered nosewheel collapse Amsterdam 24 Jan 51. Repaired. To 749A. Re-regd PH-LDT 7 Apr 54. Flew inaugural Amsterdam-Colombo-Tokyo svce 8 Apr 54, retd 16 Apr 54. Op an Air Ceylon flight 11 Jun 57, and again on 9 Mar 58 (both dates at London-Heathrow). Withdrawn from svce with KLM Sep 60, and cocooned at Schiphol, awaiting sale, from Feb 61 at least. Flown to San Jose, Costa Rica and fitted with large forward cargo door by SALA, second half 1962. KLM quote owned by them until 18 Mar 64, and sold to Don Gilbertson 1 Apr 64 for $107,356. However, the aircraft was regd TI-1045P on 15 Apr 64 (to KLM), after canx of PH-regn on 16 Mar 64, and officially sold 19 Apr 64. Ferried by Donald G. Gilbertson from San Jose to Burbank, CA, for modifications, prior to being placed on the US register as N7777G. Fitted with radar nose from Super Constellation c/n 4540 (CF-TGA) in May 64, US CofA 5 May 64 & STC completed 6 May 64 (TT: 31,285 hrs). Regd to Donald G. Gilbertson on 27 Jul 64, and lsd to Wien Alaska, named 'Arctic Liner Arlis'. Sold to Wien Alaska Airlines 30 Sep 64, t/a Wien Air Alaska from Jan 66. Believed withdrawn from svce at end of summer 1966, and stored

N7777G 749A Freighter. Close-up of the Rolling Stones insignia on the occasion of their Far East Tour 1973 (abbreviated to FET 73 on the aircraft). The photo was taken at Sydney, Australia in March 1973. (Peter Keating)

```
                    DEPARTMENT OF TRANSPORTATION
                    FEDERAL AVIATION ADMINISTRATION
                           SOUTHWEST REGION



                            NOTICE OF LIEN


     TO WHOM IT MAY CONCERN:

     PLEASE TAKE NOTICE THAT ON SEPTEMBER 19 AND NOVEMBER 21,
     1972, AND DURING THE PERIOD FEBRUARY 5, 1973  THROUGH
     APRIL 4, 1973, CIVIL AIRCRAFT N7777G, A LOCKHEED
     CONSTELLATION, WAS INVOLVED IN VARIOUS ALLEGED VIOLATIONS
     OF THE FEDERAL AVIATION REGULATIONS, AND IS THEREFORE
     SUBJECT TO THE PRIORITY LIEN ESTABLISHED BY SECTION 901(b)
     OF THE FEDERAL AVIATION ACT OF 1958, AS AMENDED, [49 U.S.C.
     1471(b)] TO SECURE CIVIL PENALTIES FOR WHICH THE OWNER/
     OPERATOR IS SUBJECT BY REASON OF THE VIOLATIONS, AND
     IS SUBJECT TO SEIZURE BY THE UNITED STATES OF AMERICA
     UNDER THE AUTHORITY OF SECTION 903(b)(2) OF THE FEDERAL
     AVIATION ACT OF 1958, AS AMENDED [49 U.S.C. 1473(b)(2)].
     LITIGATION IS NOW PENDING IN THE UNITED STATES DISTRICT
     COURT FOR THE SOUTHERN DISTRICT OF TEXAS, HOUSTON DIVISION,
     SEEKING FULL RECOVERY OF CIVIL PENALTIES FOR WHICH THE
     OWNER/OPERATOR IS SUBJECT BY REASON OF THE OPERATION OF
     THE AIRCRAFT, AND SUCH AIRCRAFT N7777G MAY BE SEIZED AT
     ANYTIME BY THE UNITED STATES OF AMERICA.


          Joseph A Kovarik
     JOSEPH A. KOVARIK
     REGIONAL COUNSEL
     SOUTHWEST REGION
     FEDERAL AVIATION ADMINISTRATION




          Dated this 22nd day of September, 1975, in Fort Worth, Texas
```

C/n 2553. Copy of lien issued by FAA Southwest USA region on 22nd September 1975 for alleged violations in late 1972 and early 1973. The aircraft had flown to Europe in late November 1973 and never returned to the USA.

at Fairbanks, AK. (TT: 33,403 hrs a/o 13 Jun 66). Tfd to Northern Consolidated Airlines 28 Mar 68, rn Wien Consolidated same day, but remained in storage until sold to Tex-Hou Corp Inc 24 Sep 68. Sold to Sky Leasing Inc 27 Sep 68, & ferried Seattle to Houston,TX 6 Oct 68. In Pennyrich (a lingerie firm) markings, on lse, during Mar-May 69. Sold back to Tex-Hou Inc 23 Jun 69, and to CHS Leasing Corp Inc 5 Dec 69, regd 16 Dec 69. Lsd to CJS Air Cargo Inc by 25 Jun 70, sold 29 Dec 70, and to Unum Inc 7 Mar 72. Lsd to Fun Leasing Inc Aug 72 (TT: 34,326 hrs). Regn N173X applied for on 12 Dec 72, reserved 21 Dec 72, but ntu. (The aircraft was, in fact, at Miami in May 72 with N7777G painted out). Sold to Air Cargo Intl Inc 2 Jan 73, regd 23 Feb 73 and lsd to the Rolling Stones pop group for their Far East Tour in Feb 73 (lessee quoted as Sunday Promotions of Houston), dep Long Beach, CA 6 Feb 73, retd 31 Mar 73. FAA placed lien on the aircraft on 22 Sep 75 for alleged violation of FARs on 19 Sep 72, 21 Nov 72, and 5 Feb 73 to 4 Apr 73 (the latter probably in connection with drug-carrying). (TT: a/o 4 Apr 73 33,383hrs!) Lse-purchase to Lanzair (Channel Islands) Ltd 3 Nov 73. Lien by Sherwood L McKendry for $1,059 against Air Cargo Intl for maintenance work 8 Nov 73, recorded 18 Nov 73 (not released until 8 Jan 80!). Dep Miami 24 Nov 73 for European charter work. Grounded at Amsterdam Dec 73-Jan 74, with engine problems, then flew to Coventry (Baginton), England, 17 Jan 74, where it stayed until 7 Mar 74. Flew to Dublin, Ireland, and made last flight from Dublin to Tripoli, Libya, and return on a cattle charter, on lse to Livestock Intl 7-10 Mar 74. Held by FAA at Dublin pending inspection and rectification of some problems, and replacement of no.3 engine. Due to be used in May 74 for oil-related charter work out of Southend, England, but never flew again, owing to legal problems about rightful ownership. Ownership tfd to Unum Inc 6 May 74, and in late 77 to Air International Inc, but aircraft remained at Dublin. Condition deteriorated, but as late as May 80, an inspection was made with a view to restoring the aircraft to flying condition (three engines found to be unserviceable). Parked next to the Irish Aviation Museum building at Dublin Airport. Sold to Aces High Ltd (Mike Woodley) 12 Mar 82, US regn canx 7 May 82 and regd G-CONI 12 May 82. Plans to restore to flying condition during summer 82 fell through with canx of film contract. Sold to Science Museum, London, England for £45,000 Jun 83. Dismantled & transported by sea & road from Dublin to Wroughton, UK, arrived 14 Jul 83. Reblt & restored in 1960s Trans World Airlines colours at Wroughton & completed for Science Museum Open Day 9 Sep 84. Current.

2554 Laid down as 649-84-12 for Eastern Air Lines, then to 749-79-22, and completed as 749-79-32 for Aerlinte as EI-ADA 'Saint Brigid'. LADD 16 Sep 47, E-13437, same day, and deld ex-Burbank on same day, formation flight over the Atlantic with c/ns 2548 & 2549, arr Shannon 20 Sep 47. Made first Aerlinte proving-flight Dublin-New York on 5 Oct 47, in svce Nov 47. Stored from Feb 48 until sale to BOAC 15 June 48. Regd G-ALAM 22 Jun 48, named 'Belfast', CofA (V351) 30 Jun 48. In svce 15 Dec 48. CofA no. changed to A918 on renewal 29 Jul 50. Slightly damaged when undershot landing Zurich on icy runway 2 Jan 54. Undershot runway and crashed while landing at Kallang Airport, Singapore at 07.34 (GMT) on 13 Mar 54. The aircraft's undercarriage cleared the seawall at the end of Runway 06-24 by a few inches, touched down on the grass with the starboard & nosewheels first, then hit the ridge 3.5ft from the threshold (a tarred stone bank). The aircraft became airborne briefly for a further 80 yds, then made a second touch-down, the starboard undercarriage leg collapsed, the starboard wing & tail unit were torn off & the plane turned over on to its back. Fire immediately broke out in the starboard wing stub & port wing, the fire quickly spreading to the rest of the aircraft, killing most on board. En route Sydney-London. Probable cause: Crew fatigue (the captain had been on duty continuously for at least 21.5 hours), the co-pilot was relatively inexperienced. Firefighting services at the airport were criticized as inadequate.

2555 Laid down as 649-84-12 for Eastern Air Lines, then to 749-79-22, and completed as 749-79-32 for Aerlinte as EI-ADD 'Saint Kevin'. LADD 29 Sep 47, E-13438, dated 29 Sep 47, deld Burbank-La Guardia-Shannon 5-9 Oct 47. Regd 8 Oct 47, in svce Nov 47. Stored from Feb 48 until sale to BOAC on 15 Jun 48. Regd G-ALAN 22 Jun 48, named 'Beaufort', CofA (V352) 30 Jun 48. Lsd Qantas 28 Jul 48-24 Apr 50. In svce with BOAC 29 May 50. CofA no. changed to A2487 on renewal 3 Jun 51. Took part in Air Display, Bristol (Whitchurch) 14 Jul 51. To 60-Seater Tourist Class. Cvtd to 749A 26 Dec 55-Feb 56. Flew last Constellation Hong Kong-Singapore-London svce 13-15 Sep 57. Tfd to disposal pool Mar 58 & stored London-Heathrow. CofA renewed 11 Jun 58, one of last three BOAC 749As in svce, but withdrawn from svce & stored again London-Heathrow 12 Oct 58. Sold to The Babb Co 13 Mar 59. Del London-Newark, NJ 18 Mar 59. Tfd to Pacific Northern Airlines at Newark 20 Mar 59, regd N1554V, FN54V, G-regn canx 20 Mar 59. Crashed into the sheer face of Mount Gilbert, AK, at the 9,000 ft level at 04.47 hrs (AST) 14 Jun 60, killing all on board. Aircraft was flying the second sector of the Seattle-Tacoma-Cordova-Anchorage service, and was 28 nm to the right of its planned track. (TT: 30,562 hrs). Cause: failure of the crew to use all available navigation aids, and failure of Air Defense Radar, who had been tracking the aircraft, to notify either air traffic control or the crew that the aircraft was proceeding on a dangerous course.

2556 Laid down as 649-84-12 for Eastern Air Lines, then to 749-79-33 for KLM. LADD 24 Oct 47 as PH-TDD 'Delft', E-14761 dated 27 Oct 47, regd 3 Nov 47. To 749A. To LAC, as trade-in on Super Constellations, 12 Nov 53 and regd N90623. Official Dutch records give 9 Nov 53 as hand-over date. PH-regn canx 18 Dec 53. To Capital Airlines FN 864 (purchase date 18 Dec 53, dely date 11 Nov 53). Sold to BOAC 3 Dec 54 (TT: 18,554 hrs) and regd G-ANUX same day, CofA 8 Dec 54, dely to London-Heathrow 10 Dec 54 (E-21062, 3 Dec 54). Named 'Bala', in svce 15 Mar 55 & used as 60-Seater Tourist Class aircraft. CofA renewed 4 Jan 57. Last svce 27 Feb- 2 Mar 57. Stored London-Heathrow from 2 Mar 57, awaiting disposal from 21 Mar 57. Sold to The Babb Co 25 Apr 57, deld London-Newark, NJ 6 May 57. Tfd to Pacific Northern Airlines at Newark 6 May 57, regd N1593V, FN 93V, G-regn canx same day. Tfd to Western Airlines 1 Jul 67 FN 593. Withdrawn from svce 16 Dec 68 (TT: 45,700 hrs) and ferried to McCarran Fld, Las Vegas, NV, for storage. Sold to Concare Aircraft Leasing 11 Apr 69 and flown to Fort Lauderdale, FL, for storage May 69. Sold to Claude R. Soto 19 May 69. Used in bombing raid on presidential palace at Port au Prince, Haiti 4 Jun 69. Flew Great Exuma, Bahamas with crew of 10, plus fifty 33-gallon drums of JP-4 fuel & a number of 30-second mini-flares (to use as igniters), plus eight rifles, two sub-machine guns, automatic revolvers & hand grenades in the Speedpak. Carried out three bombing runs at 200-300 feet, but hit by ground fire about 32 times. No 2 engine damaged & also radio navigation equipment. Made emergency landing (low on fuel) at Grand Bahama Auxiliary Airfield, Freeport, Bahamas 4 Jun 69. Impounded by US Customs on arrival, as aircraft had numerous bullet holes. Aircraft released 6 Jun (or 7 Jun) and ret to Fort Lauderdale, FL. Remained at Fort Lauderdale until sold to Adventures in Dining Inc 25 Apr 70. Reregd N22CS (FAA records report regn painted on aircraft 21 Nov 69, but N1593V still carried at end Apr 70). Dep Fort Lauderdale Sep 70 (as N22CS), and on 23 Oct 70 a US customs alert was given that the aircraft had left New Orleans, LA, where it had been involved in some illegal dealings. By May 71, the aircraft was stored at Lima, Peru, and although sold to IDS Leasing Corp 29 Jul 71, the aircraft never left Lima. Rn Equico Leassors Inc 27 Dec 74. Continued in storage at Jorge Chavez Airport, Lima, very weatherbeaten by 1975, and derelict there, engines removed, wings half gone, roof broken open & fins missing by Oct 81. Believed scrapped shortly afterwards.

2557 Laid down as 649-84-12 for Eastern Air Lines, then to 749-79-33 for KLM. LADD 28 Oct 47 as PH-TDE 'Eindhoven', E-14762 same day, regd 7 Nov 47. Flew Amsterdam-Shannon-New York inaugural 17 May 49. To 749A. To LAC, as trade-in on Super Constellations, 11 Nov 53. Sold to Capital Airlines as N90625, FN 866, 16 Feb 54, and PH-regn canx 3 Mar 54. Sold to BOAC 28 Jan 55 (TT: 19,026 hrs), and regd G-ANUY same day, CofA 31 Jan 55, dely to London-Heathrow 2 Feb 55 (E-21063 dated 28 Feb 55).

Named 'Beaulieu', and in svce 23 Apr 55, used as 60-Seater Tourist Class aircraft. Damaged when the port undercarriage struck a ditch wall, bursting two tyres, on landing at Kai Tak, Hong Kong, in bad weather on 13 Jun 55. Repaired. CofA renewed 4 Feb 57. Last service 4-5 Mar 57 & stored at London-Heathrow. Awaiting disposal from 21 Mar 57, cocooned 6 Dec 57, CofA expiry 3 Feb 58. Sold to The Babb Co 13 May 59, and deld ex-London 12 May 59 to Newark, NJ. Reregd N6688N 13 May 59, G-regn canx & tfd to Avianca same day. Carried dual regn G-ANUY/N6688N to Windsor Locks, CT 13 May 59, for conversion to 74-80 Seater domestic Tourist layout for Avianca. Deld to Avianca (E-41602, dated 10 Jul 59) on 10 Jul 59 as N6688N via Newark, NJ, and reregd HK-651. Sold to Trans-Peruana 31 Oct 67 and regd OB-R-915. Withdrawn from use at Lima, Peru, by Sep 69 (bankruptcy of Trans-Peruana), and for sale by auction 8 Sep 70. Remained in storage at Lima, and scrapped by Apr 75.

2558 749-79-33 29 Oct 47 to KLM as PH-TDF 'Franeker', E-14763 same day. Regd 17 Nov 47. Flew inaugural Amsterdam-Batavia svce via Mauritius (after ban by India/Pakistan on overflights) 26 Jan 49. Crashed into a hillside at Ghatkopar, about three miles north of Santa Cruz Airport, Bombay, at approx 10.00 hrs (local) on 12 Jul 49, killing all on board. The aircraft had circled the airport for some time in monsoon weather, with low cloud and torrential rain, and had made several approaches to land before the accident. Was on a special charter flight from Batavia (Indonesia) to Amsterdam via Calcutta & New Delhi. TT: 3,381 hrs (immediately prior to crash flight). Regn canx 12 Jul 49.

2559 749-79-33 7 Nov 47 to KLM as PH-TDG 'Gouda', E-14764, same day. Regd 17 Nov 47, in svce 6 Dec 47. To 749A. First KLM Constellation to reach 10,000 hrs (on 30 Oct 51). To LAC as trade-in on Super Constellations, and on to Capital Airlines as N90621, FN 862, del 24 Sep 53, sold to Capital 25 Sep 53. PH-regn canx 26 Sep 53. Sold to BOAC and regd G-ANUZ 28 Feb 55, dely to London-Heathrow 5 Mar 55 (E-21064, dated 28 Feb 55). CofA 9 Mar 55. Named 'Belvedere', in svce 23 May 55, used as 60-Seater Tourist Class aircraft. Last svce 31 Jan 57. Stored at London-Heathrow from 1 Feb 57, later cocooned, CofA expiry 8 Mar 57, awaiting disposal from 21 Mar 57. Sold to The Babb Co 14 Mar 58, regd N9812F & deld ex-London 14 Mar 58, canx from G-register same day. Lsd to Transocean Airlines 8 Apr 58. Repossessed by The Babb Co Dec 58. Stored in the USA, probably at Oakland, CA, during 1959. Nominally repossessed by BOAC 12 Jun 59 & insured by BOAC from this date, ret to BOAC 29 Jun 59. Nominal tf date to BOAC 31 Jul 59. Remained in USA & with N-regn for sale by The Babb Co on behalf of BOAC. Title tfd back to The Babb Co/International Aircraft Services Inc 28 Jun 60. Lsd by The Babb Co to Miami Airlines 26 Jun 60 and named 'Mary H', possibly sold 29 Jun 60. Sub-lsd to Loftleidir-Icelandic Airlines for transatlantic services Britain-Iceland at least 29 Jul 60 to 6 Aug 60. To William M Weathers and immediately lsd World Wide Airlines 18 Jun-26 Aug 61. Ret William M Weathers and tfd to World Wide Airlines approx 18 Jul 62 (merely paper transaction), still owned by Weathers. Sold to California Airmotive Corp Inc on unknown date. Stored, no engines, at Fox Field, Lancaster, CA by Jan 65 in World Wide markings. Condition deteriorated until Nov 71, when fuselage only lying on ground. Scrapped shortly afterwards. Canx after request from California Airmotive from USCAR 12 Jul 70.

2560 749-79-34 26 Sep 47 to LAV as YV-C-AMA 'Jose Marti', E-14752, dated 29 Sep 47, deld Caracas 25 Oct 47. Received damage to elevator by another aircraft on ground at Maiquetia, Venezuela, 28 Jul 55. Repaired. Crashed into Mount Naiguata on approach to Maiquetia Airport, Caracas, shortly after 08.05 hrs (local) on 27 Nov 56, killing all on board. Aircraft hit south side of mountain at approx 6,000-ft level & 150ft below summit in area known as Boca Chica, in driving rain and low cloud. Was on flight from New York to Caracas. Cause: Apparently substantial errors had been reported in the aircraft's compasses.

2561 749-79-34 3 Oct 47 to LAV as YV-C-AMU 'Antonio Jose de Sucre', E-14753, dated 30 Sep 47. LAC reports lsd to KLM at one stage during LAV usage. Slightly damaged when hit by a truck 27 Oct 54. Repaired. Flown to LAS Idlewild, New York for storage by Aug 58. Sold to California Airmotive Corp for spares use as N9744Z (regn believed never carried), and stored at Idlewild, NY, until 1960, then flown to Hartford, CT, for storage. Last reported there Sep 62. Presumably scrapped there shortly afterwards.

2562 749-79-31 4 Oct 47 to Qantas as VH-EAA 'Ross Smith', E-14754, same day. Qantas dely date 10 Oct 47, arr in Sydney, Australia 14 Oct 47. Made first Qantas proving flight Sydney-London 15-21 Nov 47. Cvtd to 749A 27 Jan-28 Mar 52. Used for Royal flights Sydney-Brisbane-Townsville-Sydney for Queen Elizabeth II & Duke of Edinburgh Mar 54. Last svce dep Sydney 5 Feb 55 (to London & return). Sold to BOAC (TT: 18,798 hrs) and regd G-ANUP 'Branksome' 15 Feb 55 (CofA 9 Feb 55), deld to London-Heathrow 19 Feb 55. In svce 17 May 55 & used as 60-Seater Tourist Class aircraft. Last svce 14 Sep 57 was also last Constellation Colombo-London svce 13-14 Sep 57 and stored London-Heathrow from 21 Sep 57. Cocooned 10 Jan 58, prior to CofA expiry 29 Mar 58. CofA renewed 30 Mar 58, but remained in storage. De-cocooned mid-Jul 59 and del to Skyways 14 Sep 59, lsd to Skyways 25 Sep 59. Op as 65-Seater Tourist Class aircraft from 8 Apr 60, for use mainly on the London-Malta/Tunis route. Flew inaugural svce 26 Apr 60. Fitted with large rear cargo door by LAS, work completed Jul 61. Ret to BOAC Apr 62, CofA expired 22 Oct 62, stored London-Heathrow (TT: 30,435 hrs). Sold to Marian Kozuba-Kozubski/Aero-Transport (50% each) on lse-purchase 1 May 63 for £40,500 as OE- IFO and deld London-Heathrow to Luton 6 May 63, and to Vienna, Austria, 10 May 63. G-regn canx 14 May 63. Impounded by Vienna Customs authorities 16 Oct 63 at Vienna-Schwechat. Aero-Transport ceased ops Feb 64. Ownership tfd to Kozubski's guarantor Olof Herman Svensson 14 Feb 64. Deld to Luxembourg for Interocean Airways by 13 Jun 64. Austrian CofA renewal 1 Jul 64. Regd LX-IOK Jul 64 (OE-regn canx Aug 64), and used as all-cargo aircraft or as 86-Seater Tourist Class. Op an IT flight for Caledonian Airways from Manchester-Ringway on 13 Sep 64. Crashed landing at Addis Ababa, Ethiopia, on 2 Oct 64. Aircraft veered off the runway while landing and ran into soft mud, burying its nose and causing considerable damage. Was on a freight charter flight from Dublin, Ireland with cargo of cigarettes. One crew member subsequently died from injuries received. Cause: Aircraft attempted go-around at maximum power with blowers still in 'High' position, resulting in multiple engine failure.

2563 Laid down as 649-79-22 for Air France, updated to 749-79-22. Unallocated, and serial subsequently deleted.

2564 749-79-33 12 Nov 47 to KLM as PH-TDH 'Holland'. KLM dely date 13 Nov 47, E-14765 dated 14 Nov 47, and regd 26 Nov 47. Flew Amsterdam-Bangkok-Shanghai inaugural 28 Sep 48, retd 2 Oct 48. Flew first twice-weekly Amsterdam-Cairo-Damascus-Baghdad-Basra schedule 21 Apr 49. Suffered in-flight electrical emergency at 17,000ft over Atlantic en route Gander-Amsterdam 3 Aug 49, landed safely. To 749A. To LAC, as trade-in on Super Constellations, and on to Capital Airlines as N90608, FN 861, del 16 Jul 52 arr 17 Jul 52. PH-regn canx 17 Jul 52. Sold to BOAC on 22 May 55, E-21067 dated 27 May 55. Regd G-ANVA 28 May 55, CofA 31 May 55, deld to London-Heathrow 2 Jun 55. Named 'Blakeney', in svce 22 Aug 55 and used as 60-Seater Tourist Class aircraft. Last svce 1-3 Feb 57 and stored at London-Heathrow 4 Feb 57. Awaiting disposal from 21 Mar 57, CofA expired 18 Jul 57, cocooned 20 Dec 57. CofA renewed 28 May 58, but remained in storage, awaiting disposal. Sold to The Babb Co 29 Apr 59, and deld ex-London-Heathrow 28 Apr 59 to Newark, NJ. Reregd N6687N & tfd to Avianca 29 Apr 59, flown to Windsor Locks, CT, for conversion to 74-80 Seater Domestic Tourist layout for Avianca same day. Deld to Avianca (E-41601, dated 7 Jul 59) as N6687N, and regd HK-652. Fitted with large rear cargo door for use as freighter early in 1962 - probably cvtd by International Aircraft Services at Windsor Locks, CT. Sold to Trans-Peruana 31 Oct 67 and regd OB-R-916. Withdrawn from use by Sep 69 (bankruptcy of Trans-Peruana) and stored, possibly at Chiclayo, Peru. Up for sale by auction 8 Sep 70, but fate unknown - probably scrapped in Peru.

2565 Originally laid down as 749-79-33 for KLM, but completed as 749-79-31 for Qantas. LADD: 8 Oct 47 (9 Oct 47 also quoted by LAC), E-14755 dated 8 Oct 47, Qantas dely date 10 Oct 47 as VH-EAB 'Lawrence Hargrave'. Trng & acceptance flights Burbank 11-16 Oct 47, deld Burbank-Sydney 22-25 Oct 47, in svce 15 Dec 47. Operated several charters for Trans-Australian Airlines Nov 49. Cvtd to 749A 27 Oct-31 Dec 51. Right rudder damaged Karachi 11 Dec 52 in collision with KLM 749A PH-LDK. Repaired on site. Used on Royal flights for Queen Elizabeth II & Duke of Edinburgh Sydney-Adelaide-Kalgoorlie-Perth Mar 54. Last svce Sydey-Tokyo-Sydney 24-27 Feb 55. Sold to BOAC and regd G-ANUR 26 Feb 55, CofA 18 Feb 55. Deld Sydney-London- Heathrow 28 Feb-5 Mar 55 (QEA colours, G-regn), named 'Basildon'. In svce 12 Jul 55 and used as 60-Seater Tourist Class aircraft. Port undercarriage collapsed during maintenance at Heathrow 10 Sep 55. Repaired. Out of svce 17 Jul 57 with current CofA, stored London-Heathrow. Withdrawn from disposal pool Feb 58, and in svce again 28 Feb 58. CofA renewed 26 May 58, last flight on charter London-Khartoum-London 14-17 Jul 58. Withdrawn from svce & cocooned 17 Jul 58 at London-Heathrow, awaiting disposal. Lsd to Skyways 6 Jul 59, in svce 20 Jul 59 & flew inaugural London-Hong Kong Constellation cargo svce dep 22 Jul 59. Fitted with large rear cargo door by BOAC mid-Oct 59-22 Jan 60, in svce 13 Feb 60. Minor damage at Delhi 12 Sep 60. Repaired. Sold to Skyways 2 Jul 62, and taken over by Euravia (London) Ltd 1 Sep 62. Used as cargo aircraft or as 82-Seater for European ITs. Repainted in Euravia colours at Luton 15 Nov 63. Rn Britannia Airways & used as back-up to Britannias in use up to early summer 1965 (believed carried 'Britannia Airways' titling over pax door. Lsd to ACE Freighters and deld Luton-Gatwick 30 Jul 65, in svce 12 Aug 65 Gatwick-Lyneham, last svce Cairo-Gatwick 11 Sep 66. Ret to Euravia (Britannia Airways) on bankruptcy of ACE 14 Sep 66. Sold 17 Feb 67 to Nelson Puente & canx from G-register 23 Feb 67. Deld 18 Mar 67 (after ferry from Luton to Coventry for work prior to ferry flight over the Atlantic on 4 Mar 67) .Sold to Woodrow W Tilton 6 May 67, & regd 24 May 67 as N1949. Sold American National Bank of Jacksonville 25 May 67 and lsd Woodrow W Tilton same day. Reportedly tfd to Peru International Management Corp. Sold back to Woodrow W Tilton 6 Jan 68. Canx from US Register 29 Jan 68 (officially after an accident) but in fact sold to Laura Puente t/a Aerolineas Uruguayas as CX-BHC on 6 Jan 68. Believed deld ex-Miami in May 68, Aerolineas Uruguayas ceased operations in 1968 or 1969, and the aircraft was last reported stored at Montevideo in Jan 70. Presumably scrapped shortly afterwards.

2566 Laid down as 649-79-22 for Air France, updated to 749-79-22, and completed as 749-79-32 for Aerlinte as EI-ADE. LADD: 9 Oct 47, E-13439 dated 10 Oct 47 and deld same day. Named 'Saint Enda', later 'Saint Fintan'/'Fionntan'. CofRegn 24 Oct 47, in svce Nov 47 & flew pre-inaugural Dublin-Rome 28 Nov 47. Stored from Feb 48 until sale to BOAC on 15 Jun 48. Regd G-ALAO on 22 Jun 48, CofA (V353) 30 Jul 48 and named 'Braemar'. Cannibalized to service c/ns 2548 (G-ALAK) & 2549 (G-ALAL) 9 Dec 48-2 Mar 49. In svce 25 May 49. CofA no. changed to A1071 on renewal 16 Aug 50. Cvtd to 60-Seater Tourist class by 1955. Flew special pre-inaugural flt London-Tokyo, dep 2 May 55. Cvtd to 749A Aug-Oct 55. Damaged during engine run at Heathrow 20 Jan 56. Repaired. Last svce believed 24-25 Jun 58, one of last three BOAC 749As in svce. Carried out training flight 9 Jul 58, subsequently stored London-Heathrow. Cof A renewed 6 Aug 58 & sold via The Babb Co 26 Sep 58 to Capitol Airways as N4902C and del ex-London-Heathrow 27 Sep 58, G-regn canx 26 Sep 58. Ret to The Babb Co, taken over by International Aircraft Services Inc in 1959. CAB records show Capitol lsd the aircraft again from Mar 60 until 8 Feb 61. Lsd World Wide Airlines 16 Feb-16 Oct 61. Lsd Capitol Airways again (in svce Nov 62). Sold by International Aircraft Services to California Airmotive Corp (by 1965). Aircraft was stored at Long Beach, CA, from Sep to Nov 64 at least, and for reasons unknown was later owned by Canadair (a/o 28 Mar 65). Stored at Miami, FL, no airline titling, by Sep 65. Sold to Peru Internacional (COPISA) Dec 65 and deld Feb 66 as OB-R-802 'Ciudad de Iquitos', regd 15 Mar 66. Later named 'Lala'. Out of svce by late 1968 or 1969 and stored at Lima, Peru. Still whole in 1972, but condition deteriorated and derelict by 1975. Remains still at Lima in Sep 78. Scrapped by 1980.

2567 Laid down as 649-79-22 for Air France. To 749 and completed as c/n 2586.

2568 Laid down as 649-79-22 for Air France. To 749 and completed as c/n 2587.

2569 Laid down as 649-79-22 for Air France. To 749 and completed as c/n 2589.

2570 Laid down as 649-79-22 for Air France. To 749 and completed as c/n 2590.

2571 Laid down as 649/749 for unknown customer. Serial deleted, & completed as c/n 2600.

2572 749-79-31 11 Oct 47 to Qantas as VH-EAC 'Harry Hawker'. E-14758 dated 10 Oct 47. Used for trng at Burbank 13 Oct 47. Deld Burbank-Sydney 22-26 Oct 47, in svce 29 Dec 47. Flew first London-Sydney svce via Colombo & Bombay 20 Mar 50. Visited Christchurch, New Zealand 20 Dec 50 for airport opening. Wingtip damaged in collision with BOAC 749 G-ALAK 10 Feb 51. Repaired. All three blades of propeller of no.2 engine damaged when overran chocks on maintenance check and hit starter unit at Karachi 10 Jun 51. Blades replaced. Cvtd to 749A 24 Mar-29 Apr 52. Flew Qantas' first svce to Germany with stop at Frankfurt-Rhein Main 16 Oct 52 (first Australian airliner to make a scheduled flight to Germany since WW2), return inaugural 21 Oct 52 to Sydney. Starboard wingtip damaged in collision with floodlight pole Ciampino, Rome 10 May 53. Repaired. Flew the "Coronation Special" svce, painted with special emblem & royal coat of arms 2 Jun 53 (set London-Singapore record). Inaugurated Bangkok svce as stop on Sydney-London route 14 Nov 53. Inaugurated Qantas Tourist svce Sydney-London 29 Mar-1 Apr 54 & flew Tokyo inaugural from Sydney 3 Nov 54. Sold to Aerovias Guest SA 8 Oct 55 (TT: 19,820 hrs), deld 8 Oct 55 ex-Sydney with Speedpak. VH-regn canx 13 Oct 55, and regd XA-LIO. Wfs Dec 61. Sold to California Airmotive Corp (no regn known). Stripped for spares at Burbank, CA, during 1963 and broken up by Jul 63. (Nose survived in junk yard at Burbank for some time afterwards).

2573 749-79-31 18 Oct 47 to Qantas as VH-EAD 'Charles Kingsford Smith'. E-14759 dated 17 Oct 47. Qantas dely date 10 Oct 47. Deld Burbank-Sydney 25 Oct-27 Oct 47, in svce 6 Nov 47. Inaugurated Sydney-London svce (Flight 16Q1) 1-5 Dec 47, returned as Flt 15Q1 7 Dec 47 ex-London & flew first Sydney-London svce via Djakarta 30 Aug 50. Flew TEAL charter to Ohakea, New Zealand 20 Dec 47. Cvtd 749A 26 Feb-9 Mar 51. First proving flight Sydney-South Africa dep 25 Jul 52, retd to Sydney 7 Aug 52, followed by inaugural to Johannesburg 1-4 Sep 52, retd 6-9 Sep 52. Wingtip damaged in collision with Butler AT DC-3 at Sydney 2 Mar 53. Repaired. Port rudder damaged while aircraft was being towed at Cocos Island 26 Mar 55. Repaired. Flew last Qantas 749A schedule Sydney-Tokyo-Sydney 20-25 Oct 55. Sold to Aerovias Guest SA 30 Oct 55 (TT: 19,963 hrs) & deld 2-5 Nov 55. VH-regn canx 7 Nov 55, and regd XA-LIP. Wfs Jan 62. Sold to California Airmotive Corp approx mid-1962 and regd N9733Z. Stored at Burbank, CA, in Sep 62, and then at Long Beach, CA, by Aug 63. Flown to Fox Field, Lancaster, CA, for storage by Jan 65, engineless and derelict by Aug 66, and condition deteriorated until Nov 71, when fuselage only lying on ground. Scrapped shortly afterwards. Canx from USCAR 12 Jul 70 after request from California Airmotive.

2574 Serial deleted. Completed as c/n 2601.

2575 Serial deleted. Completed as c/n 2602.

2576 Serial deleted. Completed as c/n 2603.

2577 749-79-22 25 Mar 48 to Transcontinental & Western Air as NC91201 'Star of New York', FN 701. In svce 28 Mar 48. To

N91201. First intl svce Mar 49. Regd to Trans World Airlines Inc 29 May 50. Tfd to domestic network 14 Oct 50 & renamed 'Star of Portugal'. Fitted with new cabin layout for 57-seater (First class) at Fairfax, KS 7 Aug-29 Aug 55. Withdrawn from svce at Fairfax Airport, KS 29 Dec 66 (TT: 42,278 hrs). Stored until sale to Aero Tech Inc 20 Jun 68 and scrapped by them by Jul 68.

2578 749-79-22 2 Apr 48 to Transcontinental & Western Air Inc as NC91202 'Star of Pennsylvania', FN 702. In svce 4 Apr 48 on intl network. To N91202. Regd to Trans World Airlines Inc 29 May 50. Tfd to domestic network 28 Oct 50 (44-Seater) & renamed 'Star of Madrid'. Substantially damaged at Sky Harbor Airport, Phoenix, AZ, at 00.14 (MST) on 19 Mar 51 when aircraft landed with undercarriage fully retracted. On flight TW59 New York-Los Angeles. Cause: Captain failed to place landing gear operating lever in full-down position. No injuries. Repaired. Later modified to 57-Seater (First class) .Withdrawn from svce at Fairfax Airport, KS 31 Dec 66 (TT: 41,357 hrs) .Stored until sale to Aero Tech Inc 25 Jun 68 and scrapped by them by Ju168.

2579 749-79-22 21 Apr 48 to Transcontinental & Western Air Inc as NC91203 'Star of Ohio', FN 703. TWA dely date 22 Apr 48 (also another LAC source), and in svce 23 Apr 48 on intl network. To N91203. Regd to Trans World Airlines Inc 29 May 50. To domestic network 14 Jan 51 (44-Seater) & renamed 'Star of the Riviera'. Later modified to 57-Seater (First class). Stored for a short period from 22 Oct 61, and again from 23 Dec 62 (at Mid-Continent, Kansas City, MO). Withdrawn from svce at Fairfax Airport, KS 29 Dec 66 (TT: 40,780 hrs). Stored until sale to Aero Tech Inc 18 Jun 68 and scrapped by them by Jul 68.

2580 749-79-22 7 May 48 to Transcontinental & Western Air Inc as NC91204 'Star of Indiana', FN 704. In svce 9 May 48 on intl network. To N91204. Involved in accident (between 1948 & 1950) - no details. Regd to Trans World Airlines Inc 29 May 50. To domestic network 22 Oct 50 (44-Seater) & renamed 'Star of the Matterhorn'. Later modified to 57-Seater (First class) at Fairfax, KS 29 Aug-25 Sep 55. Substantial damage on landing at Louisville, KY at 20.31 hrs (CST) on 16 Jan 57. On approach, the crew was unable to get a "down-and-locked" indication on the port undercarriage. The approach was broken off, and the crew tried to get the undercarriage down by emergency extensions. When the gear appeared to be fully down, a landing was made, but when the aircraft had almost stopped on the landing roll, the port main undercarriage retracted. Repaired. Sustained fire damage while taking-off from Philadelphia, PA at 19.00 hrs (local) on 27 Dec 60. Repaired. Withdrawn from svce 22 Jul 65 at Mid-Continent Airport, Kansas City, MO (TT: 39,171 hrs) and stored until sale to Aero Tech Inc 13 May 68. Scrapped by them end May to early Jun 68.

2581 749-79-22 19 May 48 to Transcontinental & Western Air Inc as NC91205 'Star of Michigan', FN 705. TWA dely date 20 May 48, in svce 21 May 48 on intl network. To N91205. Regd to Trans World Airlines Inc 29 May 50. To domestic network 3 Dec 50 (44-Seater) & renamed 'Star of Italy'. Later modified to 57-Seater (First class) at Fairfax, KS 15 Nov-7 Dec 55. Involved in near-miss with Hycon Aerial Surveys Lockheed P-38 Lightning (N69902) on approach to Greater Pittsburgh Airport, PA on 23 Aug 57. The P-38 crashed killing the crew, the Constellation's captain put the aircraft into a climbing right turn to avoid the P-38 on approach, 1.5mls from the airport & landed safely, no injuries. Withdrawn from svce 28 Jun 65 at Mid-Continent Airport, Kansas City, MO (TT: 38,824 hrs) and stored until sale to Aero Tech Inc 11 Jun 68. Scrapped by them by Jul 68.

2582 749-79-22 28 May 48 to Transcontinental & Western Air Inc as NC91206 'Star of Illinois', FN 706. In svce 31 May 48 on intl network. To N91206. Regd to Trans World Airlines Inc 29 May 50. Last Model 749 on transatlantic network. To domestic network 24 Apr 51 (44-Seater) & renamed 'Star of Venice'. Later modified to 57-Seater (First class) at Fairfax, KS 22 Jan-20 Feb 56. Stored for a short period from 15 Apr 63 at Mid-Continent Airport, Kansas City, MO. Withdrawn from svce 31 Dec 66 and stored at Fairfax Airport, KS (TT: 40,319 hrs) until sale to Aero Tech Inc 19 Jun 68. Scrapped by them by Jul 68.

2583 749-79-22 Used for publicity shots as NC91207 prior to dely in Trans World Airline colours but with "Lockheed Constellation " on cabin roof. LADD: 10 Jun 48 to Transcontinental & Western Air Inc as NC91207 'Star of Missouri', FN 707. In svce on intl network 11 Jun 48. To N91207. Regd to Trans World Airlines Inc 29 May 50. To domestic network (44-Seater) 24 Sep 50 & renamed 'Star of Milan', re-entered svce 2 Oct 50. Later modified to 57-Seater (First class) at Fairfax, KS 21 Jul-6 Aug 55. Withdrawn from svce 13 Dec 66 at Mid-Continent Airport, Kansas City, MO (TT: 41,855 hrs) and stored there until sale to Aero Tech Inc 23 May 68. Scrapped by them during Jun 68.

2584 749-79-22 Used by LAC prior to dely to Transcontinental & Western Air Inc as NC91208. LADD: 25 Jun 48. TWA dely date 24 Jun 48 (TT: 220 hrs), in svce on intl network 26 Jun 48. Named 'Star of Massachusetts', FN 708. To N91208. Regd to Trans World Airlines Inc 29 May 50. To domestic network (44-Seater) 12 Nov 50, re-entered svce 20 Nov 50 & renamed 'Star of Athens'. Later modified to 57-Seater (First class) at Fairfax, KS 17 Oct -14 Nov 55. Withdrawn from svce 31 Dec 66 (TT: 41,525 hrs) and stored at Fairfax Airport, KS, until sale to Aero Tech Inc 21 Jun 68. Scrapped by them by Jul 68.

2585 749-79-22 19 Jul 48 to Transcontinental & Western Air Inc as NC91209 'Star of New Mexico, FN 709. In svce on intl network 25 Jul 48. To N91209. Regd to Trans World Airlines Inc 29 May 50. To domestic network (44-Seater) 29 Aug 50, in svce 16 Sep 50 (first domestic 749 conversion) & renamed 'Star of Israel'. Later modified to 57-Seater (First class) at Fairfax, KS 18 May-14 Jun 55. Sustained damage when the nose gear retracted during an emergency landing on a foam-covered runway at Boston-Logan Intl Airport, MA at 00.46 hrs (EST) on 9 Mar 64. After take-off from Washington, DC, on a flight from Dayton, OH, to Baltimore, MD, the crew heard a breaking sound as the undercarriage was retracted, although appearing to retract normally. On approach to land at Baltimore, however, the nose gear would not extend. For weather and other reasons, the aircraft was diverted to Boston. On landing on the foam-covered runway, only slight damage was caused to the nose structure and two propellers bent. No casualties. Cause: Stress corrosion and fatigue failure of the nose-gear actuating strut piston-rod-end clevis; the part had been in svce for about 5,200hrs. Repaired. Withdrawn from svce at Fairfax Airport, KS on 29 Dec 66 (TT: 40,665 hrs) and stored until sale to Aero Tech Inc 24 Jun 68. Scrapped by them by Jul 68.

2586 749-79-22 22 Jul 48 to Transcontinental & Western Air Inc as NC91210 'Star of Delaware', FN 710. In svce on intl network 24 Jul 48. To N91210. Regd to Trans World Airlines Inc 29 May 50. To domestic network (44-Seater) 16 Dec 50, re-entered svce 29 Dec 50 & renamed 'Star of Bombay'. Later modified to 57-Seater (First class) at Fairfax, KS 27 Dec 55-23 Jan 56. Stored from 2 Nov 61 for a period. (TT: 34,379 hrs a/o 30 Jun 61). Re-entered svce until 1 Apr 63. Stored Mid-Continent Airport, Kansas City, MO (TT: 36,283 hrs). Sold to the FAA 6th Region for spares use on 1 Apr 63. Deld to FAA 17 Apr 63. Broken up, presumably at Oklahoma City, OK, some time afterwards. (NB: The fuselage of an ex-TWA Constellation was still at the FAA facility at Oklahoma City as late as May 73. It may have been this aircraft).

2587 749-79-22 29 Jul 48 to Transcontinental & Western Air Inc as NC91211 'Star of Arizona', FN 711. TWA dely date 30 Jul 48, in svce on intl network same day. To N91211. Regd to Trans World Airlines Inc 29 May 50. To domestic network (44-Seater) 12 Sep 50 & renamed 'Star of the Suez'. Renamed 'Star of Illinois' for Adlai Stevenson's electioneering flights in 1953. Later modified to 57-Seater (First class) at Fairfax, KS 14 Jun-4 Jul 55. Repainted by mistake as N91211C sometime during 1962/63 & flew on TWA schedules until noticed as error! Withdrawn from svce at Fairfax Airport, KS 30 Dec 66 (TT: 40,878 hrs) and stored there until sale to Aero Tech Inc 26 Jun 68. Scrapped by them by Jul 68.

N91211C 749. An enthusiastic workman obviously thought all Trans World Constellation registrations should end in a "C" (as in fact many did). The photographer (unfortunately unknown) noticed the error as the aircraft taxied out from the terminal in about 1963. (PJM collection)

2588 749-79-22 21 Jun 48 to Transcontinental & Western Air Inc as NC91212 'Star of California', FN 712. In svce 21 Jun 48 on intl network. To N91212. Regd to Trans World Airlines Inc 29 May 50. To domestic network (44-Seater) 18 Nov 50, re-entered svce 30 Nov 50 & renamed 'Star of Baghdad'. Later modified to 57-Seater (First class) at Fairfax, KS 25 Sep-17 Oct 55. Withdrawn from svce at Fairfax Airport, KS 30 Dec 66 (TT: 41,755 hrs) and stored there until sale to Aero Tech Inc on 27 Jun 68. Scrapped by them by Jul 68.

2589 749-79-33, cvtd to 749A-79-33 prior to dely by LAC to KLM on 22 Oct 48 as PH-TDI 'Enschede'. KLM dely date 14 Oct 48, E-13755 dated 21 Oct 48, and regd 22 Oct 48. To LAC, as trade-in on Super Constellations, and on to Capital Airlines, official hand-over date 10 Dec 53, dely date 12 Dec 53, sold 14 Dec 53, as N90624, FN 865. PH-regn canx 18 Dec 53. Sold to BOAC 25 Mar 55 and regd 28 Mar 55 as G-ANVB, E-21065 dated 28 Mar 55, CofA 1 Apr 55 and deld to London-Heathrow 3 Apr 55. Named 'Blackrod', in svce 20 Jun 55 and used as 60-Seater (Tourist class). Damaged at Singapore 15 Feb 57. Repaired. Withdrawn from svce 15 Sep 57 & stored London-Heathrow in cocooning 2 Oct 57, two engines removed, CofA current until 31 Mar 58. Sold to The Babb Co 11 Mar 58, regd N9813F & del ex-London 12 Mar 58. G-regn canx 11 Mar 58. Lsd to Transocean Airlines 20 Mar 58, del 2 Apr 58. Repossessed by The Babb Co Dec 58. Nominally repossessed by BOAC 12 Jun 59 & insured by BOAC from this date, ret to BOAC 29 Jun 59. Nominal tf date to BOAC 31 Jul 59. Remained in storage at Oakland, CA, from 1959 & with N-regn for sale by The Babb Co on behalf of BOAC. Lsd to Miami Airlines approx Aug 60. Sold to California Airmotive Corp 15 Jan 62 for spares and broken up at Miami, FL, in 1963.

2590 749-79-33, cvtd to 749A-79-33 prior to dely by LAC to KLM on 9 Nov 48 as PH-TDK 'Amsterdam'. KLM dely date 19 Nov 48, E-13756 dated 9 Nov 48, officially regd 20 Feb 49(!). Reregd PH-LDK 3 Mar 54. Flew Amsterdam-Khartoum inaugural via Vienna, Athens & Cairo 26 Apr 56, retd 27 Apr 56. Lsd briefly to Air Ceylon Oct 58. Withdrawn from svce 8 Nov 59 at Schiphol, Amsterdam, and stored in cocooning awaiting sale. KLM quote as being used for spares 12 Aug 61. Aircraft out of cocooning and being scrapped in autumn 1962 and canx as broken up for spares 25 Jun 63, after PH-regn canx 24 Jun 63.

2591 to 2599 All these serials were deleted - not built.

2600 749-79. Modified on production line to VIP aircraft as 749-79-38/VC-121B for USAF as 48-608. This aircraft, in contrast to c/n 2601-2609, had no cargo door, an airline-type light floor, and fewer cabin windows. First flight 11 Oct 48, USAF acceptance date 12 Nov 48, LADD: 24 Nov 48. Dep Burbank 23 Nov 48 for dely to Washington, DC, and official handover 24 Nov 48. Used by 1254 ATS (SM) at Washington National. Used primarily by the following VIPs: W.S. Symington, Secretary of the Air Force (1948-50); George C. Marshall, Secretary of State (1948-49); back-up aircraft for President Truman's C-118 46-505 'Independence' (1948 onwards); John Foster Dulles, Secretary of State (1953-59), C.E. Wilson, Secretary of Defense (1953-57). (Secretary Wilson had the name 'Dewdrop' painted on the aircraft as a reminder of the fact that, if Thomas E. Dewey had been elected president in 1948, he would have preferred the Constellation to the C-118); Donald A.Quarles, Secretary of the Air Force (Aug 55-Mar 57). Secretary Quarles had the 30 flags painted on the aircraft's nose to represent the nations he visited in the aircraft during his term of office. 1254 ATS became 1254 ATG in 1952, 1254 ATW (SM) in 1960 and 89 MAW (SM) in Jan 66. To C-121A Aug 56. To 4435 ATS Apr 66 (in support of US Army command), and to 4 TFW 8 Mar 68 (US Army command). Withdrawn from svce Apr 68 and flown to MASDC, Davis Monthan, AZ, for storage Aug 68 after removal of interior furnishings. (TT: 12,763 hrs). Sold at DofD auction 17 Jun 71 to Kolar Inc. To Aero Tech Inc 23 Sep 71, and to Aviation Specialties Inc 26 Sep 72 for conversion to sprayer. Regd N608AS with Aircraft Specialties 26 Mar 73. Stored late 1976 to early 1979, flying again 1979, but then stored again in 1981 at Mesa, AZ, as no work available for it. Reregd to Globe Air Inc (CofRegn issued 28 Apr 81). Available, for sale at $84,000 in early 1982. Sold in Globe Air auction 24-26 Oct 85 to Tom Woodward t/a Silver Skies Inc, official tfd 23 Apr 86, regd 4 Jun 86. Ferried Mesa, AZ to Tucson-Ryan Fld 19 Jul 86. Planned use as sprayer at Roswell, NM fell through. Auctioned 8 Aug 87, unsold. Sold to Henry Oliver III 21 Feb 90, regd 2 Mar 90. Stored at Tucson-Ryan Fld, AZ used as source of spares during the 1990s & up to 2001 for c/n 2604, 4137 & other C-121As. Derelict by 1994, finally broken up for scrap Jan 2002.

2601 749A-79-36/C-121A 31 Dec 48 to USAF MATS Atlantic as 48-609. Flew Westover AFB, MA-Frankfurt Rhein-Main shuttle flights in support of Berlin Air Lift. Tfd to 1254 ATS(SM) in 1950 or 1951 and modified to VIP aircraft by Middletown AMA, PA, and LAS as VC-121A. To 1254 ATG in 1952, 1254 ATW (SM) in 1960 and 89 MAW (SM) in Jan 66. To C-121A Aug 56. Withdrawn from svce and transferred to MASDC, Davis Monthan, AZ, for storage 11 Mar 68 (TT: 16,063 hrs). Sold at DofD auction 5 May 70 to Christler Flying Service Inc and regd N9464 on 10 Jul 70. Cvtd to sprayer by Desert Air at Tucson, AZ. Sold 18 Apr 79 to Beaver Air Spray Inc, E-46044 (26 Apr 79). Regd to Les Arrosages Aériens Castor Inc as C-GXKO 8 May 79, CofA 1 Jun 79. Sold to Conifair Aviation Inc 30 Apr 80 after repaint in their colours Jan 80, FN 1. Stored at St Jean, PQ 1983 after last sprayer season. Sold to John Travolta t/a Star of Santa Barbara Inc 31 Aug 84 for $150,000 (TT: 16,781 hrs), canx from C-register 2 Oct 84, regd N494TW 15 Oct 84. Ferried St Jean-Green Bay, WI-Oshkosh, WI-La Crosse, KS-Santa Barbara, CA 14-18 Sep 84. Planned conversion to luxury private aircraft fell through after further expenditure of $50,000 & numerous problems, as also did plans for donating it to a museum. Inspected 21 May 87 onwards prior to ferry flight to Tucson-Ryan Fld. Sold to Vern L Raburn t/a The Constellation Group Inc 28 Jul 87, regd 24 Sep 91 after extensive overhaul & restoration in full USAF-MATS colour-scheme as "8609", completed Oct 91. Suffered in-flight cabin fire & made emergency landing Blythe, CA 5 Oct 91. Cause: Faulty wiring from former spray system. Repaired. Base tfd to Avra Valley, AZ. Flown regularly on airshow circuit 1992 onwards, first public appearance Oshkosh, WI Jul 92. Badly damaged 9 Aug 94 when lost brake pressure, overran taxiway & ran across 100yds of desert scrub at Avra Valley, AZ; seven prop blades bent & landing gear doors damaged. Repaired with propeller blades & engines from c/n 2603 in Santo Domingo Oct 94 onwards, test flown 3 Jun 95. Made extensive European tour 1 Jun 98 (dep Ft.Worth, TX), arr Woodford, England 3 Jun. Dep Shannon, Ireland 26 Sep, arr back Avra Valley, AZ 5 Oct 98. For sale for $1,200,000 (a/o May 2000). Sold to United Technologies Corp (Pratt and Whitney Division, regd 22 Feb 05, for donation to Korean Air as a static exhibit at their Flight Training Centre at Cheju Island, South Korea. Ferried Avra Valley, AZ – Oakland, CA – Anchorage, AK – Cold Bay, AK – Hakodate, Japan – Inchon, South Korea – Gimhae/Busan, South Korea (for repainting in Air Korea colours) 1 Apr-10Apr 05. Made last flight to Cheju Island 18 Apr 05. Marked as "HL4003". Preserved.

2602 749A-79-36/C-121A 22 Nov 48 to USAF MATS Atlantic as 48-610. (LAC also quote 3 Jan 49). USAF acceptance date 22 Dec 48, dely ex-Burbank 7 Jan 49. Not used by MATS, but bailed on contract to LAS Intl, MacArthur Fld, Long Island, NY, for flights in support of the Keflavik (Iceland) maintenance facility. Flew nine round trips per month 8 Jan 49-Nov 49 MacArthur-Keflavik. Ret to Burbank Nov 49 for conversion to VC- 121A (for presidential use). Deld to Washington National Feb 50 for 1254 ATS (SM). Used primarily by the Secretary of the Air Force, then by President Dwight D Eisenhower for his Far East trip in Nov 52. Retained by Eisenhower and named 'Columbine' (the second). Presidential aircraft until replaced by the VC-121E c/n 4151 on 24 Nov 54. To 1254 ATG in 1952, used as back-up aircraft for VC-121E until May 55. Tfd to USAF Department of National Defense as N9907F and op by Pan American as N9907E 'Clipper Fortuna' on special assignment for the Government of Thailand May-Jun 55. Ret to 48-610, with 1254 ATG; to C-121A in Aug 56. To 1254 ATW (SM) in 1960 and to 89 MAW (SM) in Jan 66. Withdrawn from svce and transferred to MASDC, Davis Monthan, AZ, 4 Apr 68. (TT: 14,072 hrs). Sold at DofD auction 5 May 70 to Christler Flying Service 10 Jul 70, regd N9463 12 Jul 70. Never cvtd to sprayer, but remained in storage with Desert Air Inc, at Tucson, for use for spares for Christler's other four aircraft. Tfd Christler Flying Service Inc 2 Jan 74. Regn never applied to aircraft, although a CofRegn was issued dated Mar 74. Stored in stripped condition at Desert Air Inc/Desert Aircraft Supplies, Tucson, AZ awaiting possible restoration. Moved to Allied Aircraft storage area by Jan 84, put back on nosewheel after resting on tail for many months 13 Feb 87. Ownership tfd to Melvin N & Francis Christler t/a Christler Flying Service & for sale a/o Mar 87. Auctioned 8 Aug 87. Restored to airworthy condition by Eisenhower Centennial Committee 1989-Apr 90, after 5 months & $200,000 project. Sold to Columbine II Inc 30 Jan 90, officially tfd 22 Feb 90, regd 5 Mar 90. First flight in 22 years 5 Apr 90 Davis Monthan-Ryan Fld, AZ. N521KE allotted 10 Apr 90, but ntu. Lsd Henry Oliver III May 90. After FAA certification work completed 9 Oct 90, flew to Abilene, KS 14 Oct 90 for Eisenhower's 100th Birthday anniversary celebrations. Flew to Santa Fe, NM 13 Oct 98 after storage & to Scottsdale, AZ 18 Oct 98 for sale by auction. Remained unsold & retd to Santa Fe, NM for further storage. Engines run up at intervals. Flew Santa Fe-Avra Valley, AZ 3 May 03. For sale at $3,200,000 in 2005. Current, but stored.

2603 749A-79-36/C-121A 31 Dec 48 to USAF MATS Atlantic as 48-611. Flew Westover AFB, MA-Frankfurt Rhein-Main shuttle flights in support of Berlin Air Lift. Tfd to 1254 ATS (SM) in 1950 or 1951 and modified to VIP aircraft by Middletown AMA, PA, and LAS as VC-121A. To 1254 ATG in 1952, 1254 ATW (SM) in 1960 and 89 MAW (SM) in Jan 66. To C-121A in Aug 56. Withdrawn from svce and transferred to MASDC, Davis Monthan, AZ, 4 Apr 68 for storage (TT: 16,307 hrs). Sold at DofD auction 17 Jun 71 to Kolar Inc. To Aero Tech Inc 23 Sep 71, and to Aviation Specialties Inc 6 Sep 72 for conversion to sprayer. Regd N611AS to Aircraft Specialties Inc 26 Mar 73. Stored at Mesa, AZ, from late 1976 in good condition. Reregd to Globe Air Inc (CofRegn issued 29 Apr 81). Sold via Rafael O Belliard 20 Nov 81 to Argo SA Nov 81, and deld through Miami, FL, 26-27 Nov 81. Reregd HI-393. N-regn canx 1 Dec 81. Argo ceased operations Feb 83. Stored at Santo Domingo, Dominican Republic, condition deteriorated 1985-86, but restored during 1987 to all-over polished metal condition with all engines fitted. Moved to operational ramp from storage area 29 Mar 88, but never flew owing to various problems with the aircraft. Reverted to "stored" status after ban on Dominican freight operators Mar 93. All propellers & engines sold to Vern L Raburn Oct 94 for c/n 2601 (qv). Remained stored at Santo Domingo until moved to edge of airfield by Nov 00. Dumped in bushes, on tail, no engines (a/o Mar 03).

2604 749-79-38/C-121A 18 Jan 49 to USAF MATS Atlantic as 48-612. Flew Westover AFB, MA-Frankfurt Rhein-Main shuttle flights in support of Berlin Air Lift. Tfd to 1254 ATS (SM) 25 Jul 50 and modified to VIP aircraft by Middletown AMA, PA, and LAS as VC-121A. Used by General Eisenhower, Supreme Commander, SHAPE Jan 51-c.Jun 51. To 1254 ATG in 1952, 1254 ATW (SM) in 1960. To C-121A in Aug 56. Tfd to USAF in Europe (Special Missions) on 14 Dec 62 and op by 7101 ABW. Withdrawn from svce and transferred to MASDC, Davis Monthan, AZ, 26 Oct 67 for storage (TT: 14,541 hrs). Sold at DofD auction 5 May 70 to Christler Flying Service Inc and regd N9465 on 10 Jul 70. Cvtd to sprayer by Desert Air at Tucson, AZ. Stored at San Juan, PR, after spraying season there Oct 77-Sep 78. Sold 18 Apr 79 to Beaver Air Spray Inc, E-46045. Regd Les Arrosages Aériens Castor Inc as C-GXKR in May 79. Sold to Conifair Aviation Inc Apr 80 after repaint in their colours Dec 79, FN2. Stored at St Jean, PQ after last sprayer season. Sold to Forest Industries Flying Tankers Ltd approx 1987 as engine/propeller spares source for Martin Mars flying boats. Sold to The Constellation Group Inc 30 Aug 93, regd N749VR 2 Sep 93 on behalf of the Stichting Constellation Club Nederland (Dutch Constellation Group). Ferried after 10 years storage from Mt Joli, PQ to Avra Valley, AZ via Presque Isle, ME, Dayton, OH & Ft.Smith Regional, AR 9-12 Sep 94. Tfd to Dutch Constellation Group 11 Oct 95, N749NL reserved 1 Dec 95, but ntu. Restored by Dutch Group & Constellation Group volunteers, working together with the Aviodome Dutch National Aviation Museum for planned transatlantic ferry flight. Fitted with short (non-radar) nose again Aug 01 (on loan from Le Bourget museum). Named 'Connie's Comeback' with 'The Blue Feeling.www.aviodome.nl' titling. On high power test run on No.4 engine Sep 01 metal particles were found in engine. Replacement engine found, but certification & other problems delayed flight to Europe to Sep 02. Flown USA to Amsterdam via Manston, UK, arr Amsterdam Sep 02. Propellers & engine returned to owners, repainting into 1950s style KLM colours undertaken during 2003 with 'last two' of regn letters "LE" only. Ownership tfd from Dutch National Aviation Museum Aviodome Inc to Aircraft Guaranty Trust LLC Trustee 15 Feb 03. Moved 20 May 03 from KLM hangar to old Fokker hangar at Schiphol. Flew to Aviodrome Museum (new name) at Lelystad 2 Jul 04. Preserved. Engines run up regularly.

2605 749A-79-38/C-121A 26 Jan 49 to USAF MATS Atlantic as 48-613. Flew Westover AFB, MA-Frankfurt Rhein-Main shuttle flights in support of Berlin Air Lift. Tfd to 1254 ATS (SM) 1 Jul 50 and modified to VIP aircraft by Middletown AMA, PA, and LAS as VC-121A. To LAC, Burbank 30 Jul 50. Became first C-121 to be fitted with APS-10 Weather Avoidance Radar. Also fitted with modified engines (believed YR3350-75) and short exhaust stacks, ("jet stacks"). Used by General MacArthur, named 'Bataan' painted over map of Philippines, later inscribed 'S.C.A.P' (Supreme Commander, Allied forces Pacific) over map of Japan, and used within Korea and between Korea and the USA from at least Sep 50 until his return to the USA in Apr 51. Then used by General Matt Ridgway in USA and Korea during 1952-53 (still named 'S.C.A.P'). Modified engines & jet stacks removed shortly after MacArthur's use of the aircraft. To C-121A Aug 56. Transferred to HQ, Pacific Air Command after Korean war until end 1965, when the aircraft was declared surplus to requirements. Arrived at MASDC, Davis Monthan, AZ, for storage 18 Jan 66. Tfd to NASA in Jun 66 and used at the Goddard Flight Test Center, Greenbelt, MD, as NASA422. VIP interior removed, and instrumentation for the Apollo space program installed. Became an Apollo spacecraft simulator, providing realistic training and operational testing of the worldwide network of ground stations, ships and ARIA aircraft, in preparation for the initial Apollo flights. After the flight of Apollo 11, a certificate was awarded to the aircraft by the crew of Apollo 11 for helping to put the first man on the moon. Later in NASA use named 'Bataan' again, and carried the flags of the countries visited by the aircraft below the cockpit on the port side. Regd N422NA by Apr 69, although official date of regn was 25 Jun 69. A cutback at NASA led to the aircraft's suspension from use, and the aircraft was tfd to the General Services Administration in late 1969(?). Flown to the US Army Aviation Museum at Fort Rucker, AL, 10 Mar 70 (TT: 12,788 hrs) and donated by the General Services Administration to the museum approx May 70. N-regn canx 11 May 70. Preserved at Fort Rucker, AL, in NASA colours, with name 'Bataan', but no regn carried until 1993, with condition deteriorating. Sold to The Air Museum & restored as N422NA 7 May 93, prepared for ferry flight & made first flight in just under 24 years on 23 Jun 93 from Ft Rucker, AL to Dothan, AL, where PEMCO stripped off NASA paint & repainted aircraft in USAF 'Bataan' colours as "8613". Flew to Addison,TX May 94 where Foster-Edwards Aircraft Co reproduced the MacArthur era VIP interior. Ferried Addison, TX-Avra Valley, AZ-Chino, CA 3-6 Dec 94. Flown to Grand Canyon Valle Airport, AZ for formal opening 17 Jun 95 & on display at Air Museum there. Not flown, but engines & systems tested approx every six months. Current.

48-613 C-121A of MATS Atlantic is seen on a flight at Frankfurt Rhein-Main in 1949 in support of the Berlin Air Lift. (Lockheed via John T Wible)

2606 749A-79-38/C-121A 6 Feb 49 (3 Feb also quoted) to USAF MATS Atlantic as 48-614. Used on Westover AFB, MA-Frankfurt Rhein-Main shuttle in support of Berlin Air Lift. Transferred to 1254 ATS (SM) 12 Dec 50. Modified to VC-121A by LAS. Used by General Eisenhower, Supreme Commander, SHAPE at Paris-Orly, named 'Columbine' (the first) Jun 51-Mar 52, then used by General Greunther (visited Merryfield, UK, Jul 54). To C-121A Aug 56. Ret to 1254 ATW (SM) about 1960 and then to USAF in Europe (Special Missions) approx 1962 and op by 7101 ABW. Tf to MASDC, Davis Monthan, AZ, for storage 19 Jan 67, and ferried there from Wiesbaden, Germany 13 Jun 67. Struck off USAF inventory Jan 68 and acquired by USAF Museum for loan to the Pima County Air Museum, Tucson, AZ. Stored at Pima County Museum and restored to display condition Mar 89-Aug 90. Placed on display as 'Columbine' in polished metal finish 28 Aug 90 after 3,000 man hours of restoration work. Current.

2607 749A-79-38/C-121A 16 Feb 49 to USAF MATS Atlantic as 48-615. Used on Westover AFB, MA, -Frankfurt Rhein-Main shuttle in support of Berlin Air Lift. Modified to VC-121A by LAS. Tfd to HQ, SHAPE, at Paris-Orly in 1953, and used by General Lauris Norstad, and believed also by General Vandenberg. To C-121A Aug 56. To USAF in Europe (Special Missions) approx 1962, and op by 7101 ABW. Tfd to 4435 ATS (TAC), and either this aircraft or c/n 2600 served Commanding General of the 6th Army (but retaining USAF markings). Tfd to ANG HQ 11 May 68 until ferried to MASDC, Davis Monthan, AZ, for storage 3 Jul 68 (TT: 13,865 hrs). Sold at DofD auction 5 May 70 to Christler Flying Service Inc and regd N9466 on 10 Jul 70. Cvtd to sprayer by Desert Air at Tucson, AZ. By Apr 71 cvtd to crop duster, with large plywood hopper in the cabin area and outlet ducts under each wing. Lsd to Tall-Mantz for motion-picture contract during 1976. Painted up with 'S.C.A.P' markings (see c/n 2605) and flew for several weeks in the making of the film 'MacArthur'. Damaged in hail & windstorm Casper, WY 20 Jul 78 (TT: 14,479 hrs). Temporarily repaired, then flown to Thermopolis, WY for permanent repairs. Retained 'SCAP' titling after film until sold by Christler to Sea Hound Intl Inc 6 Dec 78, and deld to Miami, FL, 26 Jan 79 for conversion to freighter configuration again. Sold to Argo SA Apr 79 & deld ex-Miami 19 May 79, regd HI-328, with N-regn canx 15 May 79. Crashed on final approach to Harry Truman Airport, St. Thomas, Virgin Islands, at 18.29 hrs (local) on 26 Oct 81. The aircraft was on a non-scheduled cargo flight carrying fruit and vegetables from Santo Domingo via San Juan, PR, to St. Thomas. There was torrential rain at the time. Three members of the crew were killed when the nose section severed on striking the sea three miles west of the airport. The aircraft remained afloat for 15 hrs and in one piece until towed away some time afterwards as it was causing an obstruction to shipping lanes. Wreck then sank 27 Oct 81 in 150 ft of water and 600 ft off coast in Fortuna Bay. Cause of the premature descent unknown, but believed to be the result of the wingtip striking the sea in an attempt to make a visual approach in marginal weather conditions.

2608 749A-79-36/C-121A 8 Mar 49 to USAF MATS Atlantic as 48-616. Used on Westover AFB, MA, -Frankfurt Rhein-Main shuttle in support of the Berlin Air Lift. Interior modified by LAS to VC-121A approx 1950, but interior different to other C-121As, as had 42-Seater airline coach configuration. To 1254 ATS (SM) in 1950 or 1951. To C-121A Aug 56. Declared surplus in Apr 57, and purchased from US Department of State with Export-Import Bank funds for Emperor Haile Selassie of Ethiopia. Cvtd to 48-Seater, and painted in Ethiopian Airlines colours, with flight crews and technical assistance by TWA. CofA & CofRegn issued 28 May 57. Deld 2-4 Jun 57 as ET-T-35 via New York-London-Frankfurt-Rome-Athens-Addis Ababa, in svce 10 Jun 57. Damaged beyond repair in forced-landing in desert approx 22 miles from Khartoum, Sudan at approx 06.20 (GMT) on 10 Jul 57. While en route Athens to Addis Ababa on Flight ET3 at approx 10,000 ft, fire broke out in no.2 engine and nacelle about 50 miles north of Khartoum. Within a few minutes, port wing was on fire and no. 1 engine caught fire shortly afterwards. The aircraft was put into a steep diving descent, no.2 engine dropped out about 1,000ft above the ground & a successful forced landing with the undercarriage up was made on a large flat cultivated area in the northern Gezira district, all the occupants escaping. The aircraft was subsequently burned out, except for the tailplane structure (TT: 8,499 hrs). The aircraft had flown only 41,285 revenue miles with the airline. Cause: Believed to be due to a dragging brake which became overheated during taxying and takeoff. Leaking hydraulic fluid then probably ignited and the tyre blew out, rupturing hydraulic and fuel lines in the no.2 engine area.

2609 749A-79-36/C-121A 24 Mar 49 to USAF MATS Atlantic as 48-617. Used on Westover AFB, MA, -Frankfurt Rhein-Main shuttle in support of the Berlin Air Lift. Interior modified by LAS (to VC-121A) approx 1950, but interior different to majority of C-121As, as had 42-Seater airline coach configuration. Tfd to 1254 ATS (SM) 1950 or 1951, to 1254 ATG in 1952 and to 1254 ATW (SM) in 1960. To C-121A in Aug 56. 1254 ATW became 89 MAW (SM) in Jan 66. Tfd to 1001 ABW, HQ Command 5 Jun 68, and two weeks later to ANG HQ. Retired from svce and flown to Davis Monthan AFB, AZ, for storage with MASDC on 23 Aug 68 (the last C-121A to be retired). TT: 15,698 hrs. Sold at DofD auction 5 May 70 to Christler Flying Service Inc and regd N9467 on 10 Jul 70. Cvtd to sprayer by Desert Air at Tucson, AZ. Parked on unused taxy strip at Casper, WY from Oct 74, out of svce. Damaged by severe hail & windstorm 20 Jul 78. No.2 engine had been removed previously, nose cone was not in place & the aircraft had been vandalized in approx Oct 77. Stored in damaged condition until shortly before sold to Les Arrosages Aeriens Castor Inc/Beaver Air Spray Inc 18 Apr 79, E-46046 (30 May 79). Regd to Les Arrosages Aériens Castor Inc/Beaver Air Spray Inc as C-GXKS 1 Jun 79, CofA 1 Jun 79. (TT: 15,903 hrs). Damaged beyond repair in landing accident at Rivière du Loup, PQ at 05.45 hrs (EST) on 21 Jun 79. About 20 minutes after take-off on the second spraying mission of the day to Matane, PQ a failure of the secondary hydraulic system occurred. The flight engineer discovered a ruptured hydraulic line in the forward baggage compartment. (The secondary system operates the landing gear, brakes, nosewheel steering, wing flaps & spray pumps). The crew dumped fuel and decided to return to base. The insecticide was not dumped due to the high cost (although in fact in contravention of the Restricted CofA). On approach the nos. 3 & 4 hydraulic pumps were turned on to lower & lock the undercarriage, then turned off again. The hydraulic reservoir was refilled and the same pumps turned on again to lower flaps; however at this moment the nosegear unlocked. The pumps were turned off and flaps raised to initiate a go-around. During the go-around, the hand pump selector was placed to "Emergency Gear", and the nosegear locked down again using the hand pump. The crew decided to try a flap-less landing and use the emergency system for braking. (Subsequent evidence indicated that vital actions had been omitted from the emergency check list, and the only action accomplished had been the placing of the brake selector valve into the "Emergency" position - tank and brake pressure had not been checked, nor had selector valve been re-selected to "Brake" position). The aircraft made the approach at 122kts and touched down approx 800 feet from the runway end, with maximum reverse power and brake applied after the nosewheel was lowered onto the runway. Emergency brake pressure was attempted by the co-pilot, but was lost approx half-way down the runway. The captain ordered the flight engineer to switch everything off, but he only managed to turn off the master switch before the aircraft began bouncing across the uneven ground past the end of the runway. The aircraft travelled approx 1,100 ft past the runway end, during which time the undercarriage collapsed and all four engines were torn from their mounts, then swung 120 degrees to port before coming to a stop. Minor injuries only. While the aircraft was being dismantled several days afterwards, however, sparks ignited residual fuel, and the resulting fire destroyed the aircraft except for the fins and outer wings. Value of aircraft at accident assessed at $150,000, salvage value $8,000. Canx from C-register 25 Jul 79. The remains were still extant at Rivière du Loup until at least Jun 81.

2610 749A-79-12 6 Feb 49 to Eastern Air Lines as N115A, FN 115 (4 Feb 49 also quoted). Used on South American demonstration flight 1 Aug -15 Aug 49, calling at Miami, FL, San Juan, PR, Belem, Sao Paulo & Rio (Brazil), Montevideo (Uruguay), Buenos Aires (Argentina), Santiago (Chile), Barranquilla, Cartagena & Bogota (Colombia), Lima (Peru), Caracas (Venezuela), Balboa (Canal Zone), Mexico City (Mexico) and back to the USA. Crew (Eastern Air Lines) was Captains Fred Davis, Frank Bennett and G T (Roy) Munoz and Flight Engineer E L Graham. Out of svce & stored Louisville, KY Oct 60, later Miami, FL. Sold to California Airmotive Corp 10 Jan 61. Sold to Great Lakes Airlines (lse-purchase) and cvtd to 98-Seater high-density Coach-class configuration. Lsd Paramount Airlines 7 Sep 61 (to early 1962), subsequently lsd to California Hawaiian and Admiral Airways (Sep 62), also unconf use with Great Lakes during 1962. In svce with Paramount Airlines again by Sep 62. Repossessed by California Airmotive Corp as regd owner (USCAR Jun 63). Lsd to Trans California Airlines from at least Apr 64, out of svce & stored Burbank, CA by Sep 64. Sold to Cadelair Properties Corp Jul 64, but continued in storage at Burbank, CA, in ex-Trans California markings until May 66. Sold by Great Lakes Inc 9 May 66 via American Aeronautical Exporters Corp 7 May 66 to RIPSA. Flown to Miami, FL & cvtd to Freighter with large rear cargo door. N-regn canx 18 Jul 66 & deld 3 Sep 66 as OB-R-833 'Santa Rosa de Lima I', regd 10 Oct 66 (although US Export Licence B6-728-34241 is dated 31 Jan 67). Impounded for smuggling (whisky or cigarettes) at either Trujillo or Piura, Peru, on a Miami-Iquitos, Peru flight. RIPSA bankrupt by May 68, and aircraft stored out of use at Lima, Peru, by Feb 69. Condition deteriorated, and derelict by 1972. Canx from OB-register 21 Nov 79. Derelict hulk still extant there Oct 81, but many parts missing, engines off, wings half gone, roof broken open & fins missing. Remains disappeared some time afterwards.

2611 749A-79-12 16 Feb 49 to Eastern Air Lines as N116A, FN 116 (purchased 10 Feb 49). Lsd to Federal Aeronautical Administration 6th Region 23 Aug 60, and sold to them 30 Jun 61. Re-registration to N116 ntu. Crashed while landing on a training flight at Topham Fld, Canton Island, Pacific Ocean at 12.13 hrs (local) on 26 Apr 62, killing five of crew. Aircraft touched down right wing low on the starboard main gear. As the right wing continued to drop, the aircraft was lifted off in a nose-high and wing-down attitude. Wing tip struck the ground, and the aircraft cartwheeled, coming to rest inverted in three feet of water. (TT: 41,486 hrs). Cause: No.4 propeller went into reverse pitch during final approach, but was undetected by crew. Fault in control wrongly diagnosed by captain as due to malfunction of flying controls, leading him to de-activate aileron and rudder boost, which in turn caused more difficulty in controlling the aircraft.

2612 749A-79-43/PO-lW 5 Apr 50 to U S Navy as 124437. To WV-l. Actual dely date 8 Dec 50, and to NADC Johnsville 10 Dec 50. Ret to Burbank 2 Aug 51 (R & D). To VX-4 Patuxent 21 Jan 52, became VW-2 Patuxent 11 Jul 52, coded XD-9. To VW-2 Detachment 1 Gardermoen 30 Aug 52. To VW-2 Patuxent 20 Nov 52. Later coded XD-7 'Woden'. To College Point (R & D) 9 Nov 53, ret VW-2 Patuxent 16 Apr 54. To VW-4 Jacksonville J 15 Dec 54. To NAV CIC Officers College Glenview 28 Sep 55, NAV CIC Officers College Glynco 22 Nov 55. To storage Litchfield Park, AZ, 8 Oct 57. Struck off Oct 57 (TT: 2,582 hrs). Sold as N7623C Feb 58 to CAA. Ferried to Lockheeds for modification, radomes & other radar removed. To Federal Aeronautical Administration later in 1958, reregd N119, & cvtd to calibration aircraft. Later Federal Aviation Agency. To Aircraft Services Base Oklahoma City spring 66 for storage & disposal. Reregd N1192 19 Mar (or May) 66. Tfd to USAF approx Aug 66 and stored at Davis Monthan AFB, AZ (DMA code CK002). For sale by DofD (Davis Monthan) 8 Jan 69 (TT: 8,502 hrs), presumably scrapped shortly afterwards.

2613 749A-79-43/PO-lW 12 Aug 49 to U S Navy as 124438. To WV-l. Navy acceptance date 11 Aug 49. To Burbank May 50 (R & D). To NATC Patuxent 30 Jun 50 (R & D). To VX-4 Patuxent 16 Oct 50, became VW-2 Patuxent 2 Jul 52, coded XD-10. To VW-2 Detachment 1 Gardermoen 30 Aug 52. To VW-2 Patuxent 29 Sep 52. To VW-l Barbers Point 19 Dec 52, coded TE-l, to VW-l San Diego Aug 53, and to College Point Nov 53 (R & D). Ret VW-l

Barbers Point 20 Apr 54. To FASRON 110 San Diego 7 Feb 55. To VW-4 Jacksonville 21 Feb 55. To NAV CIC Officers College, Glynco 23 Nov 55. To storage Litchfield Park, AZ, 20 Mar 57. Struck off 20 Aug 57 (TT: 2,876 hrs). Sold as N7624C Feb 1958 to CAA. Ferried to Lockheeds for modification, radomes & other radar removed. To Federal Aeronautical Administration 4 Jun 58 as N120, and cvtd to calibration aircraft. Later Federal Aviation Agency.To Aircraft Services Base Oklahoma City, OK spring 66 for storage & disposal. Reregd N1206 21 Jul 66. Sold to Kansas Surplus Property Section (of the FAA?) 29 Dec 66. To Schilling Institute Department of Aeronautical Technology at Salina, KS, 1 Feb 67. Used for technical training. Schilling Institute renamed Salina VoTech School. Poor condition when sold to Air International Inc (still as N1206), CofRegn issued 24 Aug 78. Slow restoration to flying condition at Salina. Engines being run up early in 1980. Impounded at Salina Jun 81 by Salina County Sheriff for non-payment of company taxes. Sold in auction to Express Airways Inc 24 Nov 81. Advertized for sale "not flyable, any bid in excess of $16,368" in Dec 81. Tfd to First National Bank of Dallas. Sold to International Society Vehicle Preservation/Gordon B Cole 15 Aug 85, regd Dec 85. Slow restoration work carried out at Salina, KS from time to time in open. To Kansas College of Technology/Gordon B Cole 12 Jan 89. Made first flight in 25 years 8 Nov 92 at 15.08 hrs (local) en route for Sherman-Grayson, TX, where Gordon Cole wanted to complete restoration under cover, but made emergency landing back at Salina, KS after suffered engine failure on take-off. Stored at Salina, KS. Current.

2614 749A-79-12 7 Sep 49 to Eastern Air Lines as N117A, FN 117. Sold to California Airmotive Corp 10 Jan 61 and lsd to Great Lakes Airlines 1961. Possibly cvtd to 98-Seater high-density Coach-class configuration. Lsd to Associated Air Transport 18 Nov 61 and still in svce Sep 62. Lsd to California Hawaiian 1962, then to Standard Airways, who bought it 7 Feb 63. Sold to California Airmotive Corp again 24 Sep 63, who sold to LANSA on lse-purchase 17 Dec 63, regn OB-WAA-732 allotted 16 Dec 63, deld ex-Oakland, CA, 27 Dec 63. N-regn canx 9 Apr 64. Re-regd OB-R-732 and named 'Ciudad de Cuzco' (officially regd 29 Mar 66!). Stored at Lima, Peru, mid-1966 undergoing a leisurely Check 4. Believed never flew again, derelict by Mar 68, and probably scrapped shortly afterwards.

2615 749A-79-12 27 Oct 49 to Eastern Air Lines as N118A, FN 118. Damaged when starboard wing-tip struck tree at New Orleans, LA, during ILS approach in bad visibility 13 Mar 56. Repaired. Damaged when port main undercarriage collapsed while taxying for take-off at La Guardia, New York, NY at 14.38 hrs (EST) on 9 Mar 60. Aircraft settled on to its left wing, port nacelles and left vertical stabilizer. Was en route Albany, NY-New Orleans, LA, and was leaving La Guardia for Washington, DC. Cause: Material failure of the left drag shock-strut piston shaft. Sold in a non-airworthy condition to California Airmotive Corp on 9 Jul 60. Repaired and believed lsd to Associated Air Transport in late 1960. Stored at La Guardia, NY Nov 60 with no titling. Sold to Airline Management & Investment Inc on unknown date (officially regd to them until 26 Sep 61), but in fact re-sold to Air Haiti International SA in Feb 61 and regd HH-ABA in Mar 61. Missing, presumed crashed, on a flight from San Juan, PR, to Managua, Nicaragua, on 11 Nov 61 (TT: 37,457 hrs approx). No trace ever found. The aircraft had taken off from San Juan at 14.10 hrs (GMT) to pick up a cargo of meat, with ETA at Managua 19.50 hrs (GMT), and enough fuel for 12 hours. No radio contact with the aircraft after take-off. Weather en route was bad. The aircraft was flying in violation of its CofA, the captain's medical certificate was not current, the co-pilot had no type- or multi-engine rating, and the flight engineer had no type- or multi-engine rating either!

2616 749A-79-12 11 Nov 49 to Eastern Air Lines as N119A, FN 119. Received substantial damage at Mount Richmond, VA 19 Jul 51. The aircraft on Flight EA601 Newark, NJ-Miami, FL & was flying through a storm area, encountering violent turbulence and hail, accompanied by severe buffeting of the aircraft. After breaking out of the storm, the buffeting became so severe that the crew believed the aircraft would disintegrate. Captain elected to make a forced landing at approx 15.59hrs (EST) with the wheels up on a farm field. The starboard wing hit a telephone pole on approach, but the aircraft settled in on the field at Curles Neck Farm, 8.75mls & at bearing of 162 degrees from Richard Byrd Airport, Richmond, VA and skidded to a stop. A small fire in no.4 engine was extinguished quickly by rain and a fire-engine. No injuries. Cause of the buffeting was subsequently discovered to be the opening of the hydraulic reservoir access door in flight. TT: 5,776 hrs. Repaired. Stalled from approx 60 feet shortly after take-off from Idlewild, NY, during take-off climb en route to San Juan, PR, on 19 Oct 53. Crashed and caught fire, killing two. On take-off, there were patches of fog and varying visibility. After take-off, the captain did not go on instruments on entering fog as he expected the visibility to improve. Shortly afterwards, the first officer saw the ground, but the aircraft hit before corrective action could be taken. A fire broke out in the port wing, quickly spreading and destroying the aircraft. TT: 13,725 hrs. Probable cause: Pilot's loss of visual reference & resultant inadvertent taking-up of a descending flight path.

2617 749A-79-12 22 Nov 49 to Eastern Air Lines as N120A, FN 120. Received substantial damage while landing at Washington Natl, DC at 04.18 hrs (EST) on 4 Jan 60. Loss of secondary hydraulic pressure and fluid experienced en route Miami, FL-New York, NY. Landing gear and flaps extended manually on approach to Washington, and although all indicators showed undercarriage down and locked, the starboard main undercarriage collapsed shortly after touchdown. Cause: Fatigue failure of the starboard landing gear strut cylinder. No injuries. Sold in a non-airworthy condition to California Airmotive Corp 14 Mar 60. Repaired. Lsd Standard Airways 12 Aug 60. Damaged when undercarriage retracted during maintenance 17 Aug 60. Repaired. Sold to them 29 Aug 61. Lsd to Associated Air Transport by Sep 62. Sold to Casino Operations Inc 6 Jun 63 and lsd back to Standard 21 Jun 63. Stored at Long Beach, CA, from at least Apr 64 to Mar 65. Sold to Trans World Insurance Brokers 1 Dec 64 and to Las Vegas Hacienda Inc same day. Believed not used, and aircraft remained at Long Beach, until sold to Carrier Aircraft Interiors 22 Aug 66 & on to Jovan Corp at Opa Locka, FL, 23 Aug 66. Sold to Santa Fe Inc on 26 Dec 67, and to Trans Southern Corp 27 Jun 69. Landed on a farm strip near Aracatuba, Sao Paulo, Brazil on 4 Aug 69. After unloading its cargo of smuggled cigarettes and tobacco goods, a take-off was attempted, but the aircraft porpoised down the airstrip & crashed at the end of a small field, incurring slight damage. No details published about the accident - presumably the aircraft was scrapped some time afterwards. Cause : pilot lost control of the aircraft.

2618 749A-79-12 7 Dec 49 to Eastern Air Lines as N121A, FN 121. Still in use for pilot training at Miami; FL, in Oct 60, but sold shortly afterwards to California Airmotive Corp. Stripped to bare hulk for spares at Burbank, CA, by Sep 62. At Lancaster, CA, with no tail or engines in Jan 65, and scrapped there shortly afterwards.

2619 749A-79-44 20 Oct 49 to Air-India Intl as VT-DAR 'Maratha Princess', E-13768 dated 18 Oct 49, in svce 30 Oct 49 and deld India 31 Oct 49. Flew inaugural svce Bombay to Tokyo 7 May 55. Damaged 3 Jan 58. Repaired. To LAC as trade-in on Super Constellations and sold to Aeronaves de Mexico as XA-MEW 'Acapulco' 28 Feb 58. Remained in svce until Dec 59, then sold to The Babb Co 1 Feb 60 and regd N5596A 16 May 60. Tfd to International Aircraft Services Inc 14 Jul 60, and lsd to Miami Airlines 1960. Cvtd to cargo aircraft, believed by Lockheed Aircraft Services in 1961, using the rear fuselage section and large cargo door of ex-Navy turbo-prop Super Constellation R7V-2 c/n 4131. Sold to California Airmotive Corp 30 Jan 64. N-regn canx 22 Sep 64. Sold to Aerolineas Carreras as LV-PBH 10 Jul 64, re-regd LV-IIC 11 Sep 64. Impounded for smuggling flight at Montevideo-Carrasco in approx 67 and stored there. Still there whole in 1980, but condition deteriorating. On 23 Jan 82 auctioned at Montevideo-Carrasco, but sold for scrap. Broken up during the second week of February 1982.

Section 12: Constellation Production List

LV-IIC 749A Freighter is caught on a one-off cattle charter at London (Gatwick) in September 1966. An RCAF Yukon and British United Britannia and VC-10 can be seen in the background. (PJM collection)

2620 749A-79-44 10 Jan 50 to Air-India Intl as VT-DAS 'Himalayan Princess', E-13773 dated 9 Jan 50, in svce 23 Jan 50 and deld India 24 Jan 50. Flew Bombay-Singapore inaugural 16 Jul 54, and also Bombay-Hong Kong inaugural svce 14 Aug 54. To LAC as trade-in on Super Constellations and sold to Aeronaves de Mexico as XA-MEU (unnamed?) 28 Feb 58. Remained in svce until 11 Dec 59, then sold to The Babb Co 15 Dec 59, tfd 27 Apr 60 to International Aircraft Services Inc, regd N5595A 18 May 60. Lsd to Miami Airlines 8 Aug 60, but ret to International Aircraft Services Inc by 1961. Damaged beyond repair at Oakland, CA 20 Jun 61. While being towed to a hangar, Overseas National Airways DC-7 N312A rolled into the Constellation while the engines were being revved up. The DC-7 broke the Constellation's tail unit off completely and severely damaged the rear fuselage and wing. Fuel tanks of both aircraft were ruptured, but no fire broke out. Remains still standing at Oakland, CA Oct 61, but scrapped shortly afterwards. N-regn canx 14 Sep 62.

2621 749A-79-33 19 Aug 49 to KLM as PH-TDN 'Vlaardingen', regd 9 Sep 49 and E-13766 same day. Reregd PH-LDN 12 Mar 54. Flew inaugural svce Amsterdam-Frankfurt-Tunis & Tripoli 16 Apr 59, retd 17 Apr 59. Withdrawn from use at Schiphol Airport, Amsterdam 2 Nov 59, and stored there in cocooning, awaiting sale. KLM quote as being used for spares 17 Aug 61. Aircraft out of cocooning and being scrapped in autumn 1962 and canx as broken up for spares 25 Jun 63, after PH-regn canx 24 Jun 63.

2622 749A-79-33 16 Sep 49 to KLM as PH-TDO 'Maastricht', E-13771 dated 17 Sep 49, but not officially regd until 1 Oct 49 and CofRegn shows 10 Jan 50! Reregd PH-LDO 17 Mar 54. Lsd to Plane Equipment Inc 6 Nov 56 to 2 Mar 57 who sub-lsd to Pacific Northern Airlines as N10403 from 6 Nov 56 to 28 Feb 57. Ret to KLM and restored to PH-LDO 4 Mar 57. US-regn canx 6 Mar 57. Withdrawn from use by KLM at Schiphol Airport, Amsterdam 6 Oct 59, and stored there in cocooning, awaiting sale. Used for spares 17 Aug 61. Aircraft out of cocooning and being broken up in autumn 1962 and canx as broken up for spares 25 Jun 63, after PH-regn canx 24 Jun 63.

2623 749A-79-50 24 Apr 50 to South African Government as ZS-DBR 'Capetown', E-22020 dated 20 Apr 50, first SAA Constellation to arrive in South Africa 8 May 50, and used by South African Airways. Flew 749A Johannesburg-London inaugural 26-27 Aug 50 and London-Johannesburg inaugural 28-29 Aug 50. Flew first Johannesburg-London svce via Rome 31 Oct-1 Nov 50 & London-Johannesburg via Rome return svce 2-3 Nov 50. Made last visit of SAA 749A to London, flying Johannesburg-London 24-25 Oct 58 (positioning), followed by special flight London-Johannesburg 26-27 Oct 58. Cvtd to 58-Seater after withdrawal from European schedules and subsequently cvtd to 84-Seater domestic Tourist class. Stored at Johannesburg from Jan 59 until Feb 62. Made test flights on 5 Feb 62 and 14 Feb 62 and destined for Mr. Perez de Jerez in part-payment for ex-Cubana Viscounts. (Dec 61) Sales to Israeli Defence Force, possibly as 4X-AOL, via Mr. Perez de Jerez, and also to Trans-European Airways (United Kingdom), of which company he was a director, in early 1962, both fell through. Stored again (TT: 18,867 hrs a/o Apr 64). Sold to Aviation Charter Enterprises Ltd (ACE) in Nov 64. Made test flight 24 Nov 64, regd G-ASYS 24 Nov 64, painted on aircraft 2 Dec 64, and dep Johannesburg on dely 12 Jan 65, arr London-Gatwick 14 Jan 65. Flew to Coventry-Baginton 26 Jan 65 but never entered svce. Stored at Baginton. Sold at auction after bankruptcy of ACE in Dec 66 and scrapped at Baginton between Jan 67 and 9 May 67. Canx from G-register 13 Feb 67 as "sold to West Germany" and also "withdrawn from use". LAC records show "sold to Svensson & Kuhler".

2624 749A-79-46 11 Jan 50 to Air France as F-BAZE, E-13772 dated 5 Jan 50, arr Orly 13 Jan 50, CofA 28 Jan 50, in svce 30 Jan 50. Inaugurated Paris-Cairo-Nairobi-Tananarive svce 3 May 50. Cvtd to 65-Seater Tourist class by 1956. Sold to CGTA-Air Algérie 15 Nov 55 (TT: 18,612 hrs), in svce 22 Dec 55. Stored after CofA expiry 16 Nov 60 at Maison Blanche Airport, Algiers. Blown up by bomb placed aboard by terrorists on the ground at Maison Blanche at 05.30 hrs (BST) on 26 Apr 62 and almost completely destroyed. No casualties. Canx from register 27 Sep 62.

2625 749A-79-46 20 Jan 50 to Air France as F-BAZF, E-13777 dated 20 Jan 50, arr Orly 23 Jan 50 (TT: 22hrs), CofA 9 Feb 50, in svce 10 Feb 50. Cvtd to 65-Seater European Tourist class by 1956. Withdrawn from svce 3 Oct 60 & stored at Orly, Paris, 7 Oct 60 until 8 May 61 (TT: 29,556 hrs). Re-entered svce after lse to Air Inter 1 May 61 until 24 Mar 62. Retd Air France & withdrawn from svce on CofA expiry 26 Jul 62 (TT: 30,266 hrs). Stored at Orly, Paris, until 27 Mar 63. Tfd to SGAC Apr 63 and modified to 12-Passenger (special) + 8-crew configuration for SAR use at Toulouse 17 Apr 63-21 Nov 64 (as replacement for c/n 2545). CofA issued 20 Jul 64. Sold SGAC 5 Dec 64. Used by EARS 99

Squadron, Armée de l'Air, with call-sign F-SSFF on SAR duties. Withdrawn from use on 19 Mar 69 (also listed as 1 Apr 69), (TT: 32,196 hrs). Stored at St.Yan. Canx from F-register 18 Apr 69. Auctioned by Domaines at Macon 26 Oct 71 and sold to unknown buyer. Flew to Corfu (Mediterranean island) and abandoned there by Aug 72. Auctioned again by Domaines in Oct 73, given as located at St. Yan, but unconf whether aircraft ever left Corfu. (Auction notices gave regn F-BAZF, but c/n 2528. The aircraft in question, however, must have been c/n 2625). Fate unknown.

2626 749A-79-46 31 Jan 50 to Air France as F-BAZG, E-13778 dated 1 Feb 50, deld Orly 2 Feb 50 (TT: 28hrs), CofA issued 17 Feb 50, in svce 21 Feb 50. Named 'Place Vendôme' temporarily from Oct 51 on S.American svces. Modified to 61-Seater transatlantic Tourist configuration, and in late 1955 to 65-Seater European Tourist class. Sold CGTA-Air Algérie 14 Dec 55. Destroyed by fire after heavy landing at Maison Blanche Airport, Algiers, on 17 Dec 55. During a training sortie, with an Air Algérie crew under training by Air France Constellation instructors, a full-flap landing was being practised but airspeed was lost. A heavy landing was made, during the course of which the main undercarriage was pushed up through the wings, resulting in the fuel escaping from the burst tanks. Flames quickly engulfed the aircraft, which was completely burnt out. One member of the crew was injured. (TT: 18,413 hrs). Aircraft was officially tfd to Air Algérie on 28 Dec 55! Canx from F-register 8 Mar 57.

2627 749A-79-46 8 Feb 50 to Air France as F-BAZH, E-22014 dated 8 Feb 50. TOC Burbank 6 Feb 50, deld Orly 12 Feb 50 (TT: 31hrs), CofA issued 23 Feb 50, in svce 27 Feb 50. Inaugurated Paris-Istanbul 749A svce 25 Apr 51. Named temporarily 'Rue de la Paix' from Oct 51 on S.American svces. Inaugurated Paris-Noumea svces via Saigon 9-10 Jan 53. Cvtd to 61-Seater transatlantic Tourist configuration, and by 1956 to 65-Seater European Tourist class. Sold to Royal Air Maroc 14 Jan 60 as CN-CCP (TT: 28,006 hrs), with official canx 13 Jan 60, deld Casablanca 18 Jan 60 and CofA issue 20 Jan 60. Inaugurated svce to Dakar-Yoff 26 May 60. Fitted with large forward cargo door by SALA at San Jose, Costa Rica, between 9 Feb 61 and 14 Jun 61. Last svce 1 May 67, wfu by Royal Air Maroc 1 Jun 67 (TT: 38,471 hrs) and sold same day to Nelson C. Puente t/a American Aeronautical Exports. Ferried to Miami, FL, and regd 8 Aug 67 to COPISA as OB-R-898. Still regd as CN-CCP according to FAA files in 1967 to American National Bank of Jacksonville and tfd 23 Mar 70(!), still as CN-CCP, to Six T Ranch. Aircraft used by COPISA until ops ceased approx Dec 71. Subsequently stored at Lima, Peru. Derelict there by Aug 73, and scrapped shortly afterwards.

2628 749A-79-46 17 Feb 50 to Air France as F-BAZS, E-22015 dated 18 Feb 50, deld Orly 23 Feb 50 (TT: 54hrs), CofA 15 Mar 50, in svce 18 Mar 50. Inaugurated svce Paris-Montreal via Shannon & Gander 2 Oct 50. Made belly landing at Orly Airport, Paris, date uk. Repaired. Force-landed in the Aegean Sea, near Fethiye on the south-east Turkish coast, 40 miles from the island of Castellorizo at approx 02.25 hrs (GMT) on 3 Aug 53, following the in-flight failure and subsequent fire in nos. 1 & 2 engines. No.2 engine fell out at 18,000ft. Aircraft stayed afloat for just over an hour, then sank at approx 03.50 hrs (GMT). Four of the 42 passengers & crew killed. Aircraft was en route Paris (Orly)-Rome-Beirut-Teheran. (TT: 10,065 hrs). Canx from F-register 21 Sep 53.

2629 749A-79-46 24 Feb 50 to Air France as F-BAZT, E-22017 dated 23 Feb 50, TOC Burbank 24 Feb 50, deld Orly 2 Mar 50 (TT: 20hrs). CofA issued 20 Mar 50, in svce 27 Mar 50. Inaugurated New York-Mexico City svce 27 Apr 52. First AF conversion to 59-Seater Atlantic Tourist configuration Apr 52, flew transatlantic Tourist inaugural Paris-Gander-Montreal-New York 1-2 May 52. Modified to 65-Seater European Tourist configuration by 1956. Inaugurated Air France svce Casablanca-Lyon-Geneva-Frankfurt 1 Nov 52. Withdrawn from svce 1 Mar 60 (TT: 28,416 hrs). Sold to SGAC 15 Sep 60 and modified to special 12-passenger + 8-crew configuration for SAR use at Toulouse, with official tf to SGAC 26 Sep 60, CofA same day. Used by EARS 99 Squadron, Armée de l'Air, with call-sign F-SSFT on SAR duties. Withdrawn from use on CofA expiry 31 Dec 69 (TT: 33,288 hrs). CofA renewed 6 Jan 70 for ferry flight to St.Yan only, for storage. Canx from F-register 2 Feb 70 as wfu. Auctioned by Domaines at Macon 26 Oct 71 and sold for scrap. Scrapped at St.Yan shortly afterwards.

2630 749A-79-50 7 Jun 50 to South African Government as ZS-DBS 'Johannesburg', Dely date of 3 Jun 50 also quoted. E-22023 9 Jun 50 and used by South African Airways. First visit to London on flight from Johannesburg 3-4 Oct 50, returning 5-6 Oct 50 to Johannesburg. Made first visit of SAA 749A to Hurn, UK (due fog at London) 26 Nov 50 & flew return schedule from Hurn to Johannesburg 27-28 Nov 50. Flew first Johannesburg-London Tourist svce via Athens 5-6 Oct 53, returning London-Johannesburg 8-10 Oct 53. Cvtd to 58-Seater after withdrawal from European routes. Stored at Johannesburg from 30 Apr 59 until Feb 60; test-flown 12 Feb 60 and re-entered svce. Wfu and stored again 30 Sep 60, at Johannesburg. Started crew-training for Trek Airways 11 Sep 61 and made last flight in South African Airways colours 20 Oct 61. Painted in Trek colours 13 Nov 61 as 70-Seater and named 'Louis Trichardt'. Lsd Trek Dec 60, in svce 12 Jun 62. Trek lse ended Aug 63. Wfu Nov 63 and ret to South African Airways. Offered for sale (TT: 19,824 hrs a/o Apr 64). Made test-flight 28 Apr 64 and re-entered svce with South African Airways 3 May 64 for first of series of special flights to Windhoek. Flew last South African Constellation svce 22 May 64 Windhoek-Johannesburg (Flight SACH 899), and stored again until sold to Aviation Charter Enterprises Ltd (ACE) in Nov 64. Test-flown 28 Oct 64, and regd G-ASYF 3 Nov 64, regn painted on 17 Nov 64, dely ex-Johannesburg 2 Dec 64, arr London-Gatwick 4 Dec 64. Dep Gatwick for storage at Woensdrecht, Holland, 7 Dec 64. Flown to Coventry-Baginton 16 Jul 65 and stored there until 5 Jan 66, when the aircraft was flown to Renfrew, Scotland, and on to Prestwick, Scotland, for overhaul the following day. Cvtd to 82-Seater for IT use with ACE Scotland (on lse from ACE). CofA issued 13 May 66 and deld to Abbotsinch 14 Jul 66. In svce Abbotsinch-Barcelona & Palma 16 Jul 66. Op IT flights during summer 1966, last svce London (Heathrow)-London(Gatwick) 12 Sep 66. Flew London-Gatwick to Coventry-Baginton 14 Sep 66 after bankruptcy of parent company for storage. Stored at Baginton and for sale by tender Dec 66. Sold to Peru Internacional Management Corp, dely as G-ASYF Baginton-Shannon-Gander-Miami 23-24 Jun 67. Canx from G-register 10 Aug 67, but remained at Miami, FL, in full ACE Scotland colours and British regn, in storage, until scrapped there during Jul 69. Regd N1939 in Jun 67 but never carried.

2631 749A-79-50 20 Jun 50 to South African Government as ZS-DBT 'Pretoria'. Dely date of 22 Jun 50 also quoted; E-22024 22 Jun 50 and used by South African Airways. Christened at Palmietfontein airport 22 Aug 50 with local spring water! Made first visit to London on Johannesburg flight via Nairobi, Khartoum, Cairo & Tripoli 17-18 Sep 50, ret London-Johannesburg 19-20 Sep 50. Flew inaugural SAA Tourist svce Johannesburg-London via Lusaka, Nairobi, Khartoum, Cairo & Rome 3-4 Oct 53, returning via Athens in addition but not Lusaka 5-6 Oct 53. Paid last visit to London on special flight Johannesburg-London 30-31 Mar 58, ret London-Johannesburg via Brindisi, Wadi Seidna, Nairobi & Salisbury 1-2 Apr 58. Cvtd to 58-Seater after withdrawal from European routes, and later to 84-Seater domestic Tourist class. Stored at Johannesburg from late 1958; test-flown 16 Jan 59, but stored again 17 Jan 59 onwards. Destined for Mr. Perez de Jerez in part-payment for ex-Cubana Viscounts (Dec 61). Sales to Israeli Defence Force, possibly as 4X-AOM, via Mr. Perez de Jerez, and also to Trans-European Airways (United Kingdom), of which company he was a director, in early 1962, both fell through. (TT a/o Apr 64:17,845 hrs). Sold to Aviation Charter Enterprises Ltd (ACE) Nov 64. Regd G-ASYT 24 Nov 64, painted up at Johannesburg 3 Dec 64, and deld some time after mid-Jan 65, arr Coventry-Baginton for storage 22 Feb 65. British CofA never issued, and used for spares at Baginton. ACE bankrupt Sep 66. Stripped for scrapping by 2 Jun 67 and broken up during Jul 67. Canx from G-register 30 May 69.

SECTION 12: CONSTELLATION PRODUCTION LIST

2632 749A-79-50 31 Jul 50 to South African Government as ZS-DBU 'Durban'. E-22027 dated 28 Jul 50 and used by South African Airways. Paid first visit to London on Johannesburg-London svce 28-29 Oct 50. Departed to Johannesburg 30 Oct, but had to return on 3 engines, then flew London-Johannesburg 31 Oct-1 Nov 50. Paid last visit to London on special flt from Johannesburg 22-23 Oct 58, ret London-Johannesburg via Rome, Khartoum, Nairobi & Salisbury 24-25 Oct 58. Cvtd to 58-Seater after withdrawal from European routes. Stored at Johannesburg from late 1958. Made test flight 3 Jul 59 and re-entered svce until wfu again 12 Sep 60. Stored at Johannesburg again until test-flown 22 Nov 61. Last flight in South African Airways colours 25 Nov 61, lsd to Trek Airways and named 'Andries Pretorius'. Repainted in Trek colours 28 Nov 61, lsd Trek 1 Dec 61, & in svce 1 Dec 61 as Trek's first 749A flight, number N148 for Meredith, to Dusseldorf, West Germany. Used as 70-Seater. Held for 24 hours in Niamey, Africa, due to the closure of air-space to ZS-regd aircraft, on 25 Aug 63, signalling the end for some time of Trek's svces to Europe. Lse to Trek ended Aug 63. Stored from Nov 63, and offered for sale Apr 64 (TT: 20,381 hrs). Sold to Aviation Charter Enterprises Ltd (ACE) Nov 64, and regd G-ASYU 24 Nov 64. Test-flown 5 Nov 64. Painted up as G-ASYU at Johannesburg 1 Dec 64, dep on dely flight 12 Dec 64 and arr London-Gatwick 14 Dec 64. Continued from Gatwick to Woensdrecht, Holland, 15 Dec 64 to unload cargo and for storage. Engines removed one by one for spares, and then scrapped at Woensdrecht late 1966-early 1967 (after ACE went bankrupt Sep 66) in lieu of money owed. Canx from G-register 17 Mar 67 as wfu.

2633 749A-79-52 24 Mar 50 to Transcontinental & Western Air Inc as N6001C 'Star of New Jersey', FN 801. TWA dely date 23 Mar 50, in svce 27 Mar 50 (domestic network). To intl network 8 Apr 50. Regd to Trans World Airlines Inc 29 May 50. Ret domestic network 7 Nov 54. To intl network again 16 Feb 55, ret domestic 4 Apr 56. Final use with intl network from 30 Apr 56, ret to domestic 4 May 57. Withdrawn from use at Mid-Continent Airport, Kansas City, MO 22 Sep 66, (TT: 37,591 hrs), and stored until sold to Aero Tech Inc on 28 May 68. Broken up by Aero Tech by Jul 68.

2634 749A-79-52 11 Apr 50 to Transcontinental & Western Air Inc as N6002C 'Star of Kansas', FN 802. Dely to Burbank same day and in svce 13 Apr 50 (domestic network). To intl network 14 Apr 50. Regd to Trans World Airlines Inc 29 May 50. Later FN 802-S as Intl sleeper Apr 51-Dec 55. Ferried Los Angeles to LAS Burbank for cabin mods for domestic use 13 Dec 55 and re-entered svce 19 Jan 56 (FN 802 again) & renamed 'Star of Crete'. Out of svce and stored at Mid-Continent Airport, Kansas City, MO 22 Jun 65. Sold to Charles E Bush t/a Bush Aviation 30 Dec 65 and deld 9 Feb 66. Lsd to All-American Engineering for use at their Flight Research Institute at Sanford, FL, by Dec 66. Also used by Hudson Institute at Fort Bragg, NC, for tests. Sold to Aviation Development Corp by Jan 69 and stored at Miami, FL. Semi-derelict by Aug 69, and last reported Apr 70. Scrapped shortly afterwards.

2635 749A-79-52 24 Apr 50 to Transcontinental & Western Air Inc as N6003C 'Star of Texas', FN 803. TWA dely date 21 Apr 50, in svce 26 Apr 50 (domestic network), 27 Apr 50 (intl network). Regd to Trans World Airlines Inc 29 May 50. To domestic network 29 Oct 51, ret intl network 30 May 52. Renamed 'Star of America' for Round-the-World survey flight Idlewild-New York back to Idlewild 11 Nov-14 Dec 52. To domestic network 18 Dec 52, ret intl network 29 May 53. Domestic again 23 Sep 53, ret intl 19 Mar 54. To domestic again 18 Dec 56, and to final intl season 23 May 57, ret domestic 7 Jun 57. Withdrawn from use and stored at Fairfax Airport, KS 31 Dec 66 (TT: 37,447 hrs). Stored there until sold to Aero Tech Inc 14 Aug 68. Flown to Tucson, AZ, for storage Aug 68 and sale. Remained unsold and eventually scrapped there between Mar 71 and Oct 73.

2636 749A-79-52 2 May 50 to Transcontinental & Western Air Inc as N6004C 'Star of Maryland', FN 804. TWA dely date 1 May 50, in svce 2 May 50 (intl network). Regd to Trans World Airlines Inc 29 May 50. Destroyed by fire after attempted forced-landing near Wadi Natrun, 48 miles north of Cairo, Egypt, at 00.03hrs (GMT) on 31 Aug 50, after no.3 engine caught fire and fell off. Acft was on Flight TW903 Bombay-New York, NY via Cairo & Rome. After take-off from Cairo, the rear master-rod failed on no.3 engine at the top of the climb. The crew possibly failed to notice the signs that always preceded a master-rod bearing failure, namely drop in oil pressure and rise in oil temperature, as such failures on the BD-series engine were comparatively rare. There was widespread disintegration of the aircraft at the crash site, followed by general fire. All passengers & crew killed. (TT: 1,100 hrs 45 mins).

2637 749A-79-52 19 May 50 to Trans World Airlines Inc as N6005C 'Star of New York', FN 805. TWA dely date 18 May 50, in svce 26 May 50 (domestic), 29 May 50 (Intl network). Ret to domestic network 2 Jan 55, then to intl 20 Jun 55 for final season, ret domestic network 18 Sep 56. Withdrawn from use at Fairfax Airport, KS 6 Apr 67 (TT: 38,214 hrs) and stored there until sold to Aero Tech Inc 17 Jun 68. Scrapped by them by Jul 68 at Fairfax, KS.

2638 749A-79-33 19 May 50 to KLM as PH-TDP 'Rotterdam', E-22021 and regd same day. Reregd PH-LDP 16 Feb 54. Lsd to Air Ceylon in a 12-Sleeper/35-Tourist class configuration 7 Feb 56 and named 'Mahadevi'. First svce in London-Heathrow 10 Mar 56. Ret to KLM 1 Nov 58, and withdrawn from use 3 Nov 58. Stored at Schiphol Airport, Amsterdam, in cocooning awaiting sale. Used for spares from 17 Aug 61 and broken up late 1962, canx 25 Jun 63, after PH-regn canx 31 May 63.

2639 749A-79-52 29 Jun 50 to Trans World Airlines Inc as N6006C 'Star of Pennsylvania', FN 806. TWA dely date 27 Jun 50, in svce 1 Jul 50 (domestic) and 2 Jul 50 (intl). To domestic network 28 Oct 57. Withdrawn from use at Mid-Continent Airport, Kansas City, MO 30 Apr 66 (TT:37,767 hrs) and stored until sold to Aero Tech Inc on 14 May 68. Scrapped by Aero Tech during Jun 68.

2640 749A-79-33 31 May 50 to KLM as PH-TFD 'Arnhem', E-22022 dated 26 May 50 and regd 31 May 50. Flew Amsterdam-Sydney inaugural svce 7 Dec 51. Reregd PH-LDD 14 Apr 54. Withdrawn from use 30 Mar 60 and stored in cocooning at Schiphol Airport, Amsterdam until sold to CAUSA on 8 Nov 63. PH-regn canx 15 Nov 63, deld as PH-LDD 21 Nov 63 and reregd CX-BCS. Stored at Montevideo, Uruguay after CAUSA ceased ops 9 May 67. Condition deteriorated by Mar 72 and scrapped by Sep 72.

2641 749A-79-33 29 Jun 50 to KLM as PH-TFE 'Utrecht'. E-22026 dated 5 Jul 50 and regd 28 Jul 50. Flew Amsterdam-Tokyo inaugural svce 4 Dec 51. Reregd PH-LDE 10 Mar 54. Damaged during ground engine run at Schiphol 17 Feb 55 when cowlings were sucked into the propeller during engine run with prop in reverse. Repaired. Withdrawn from use 3 Mar 60 and stored at Schiphol Airport, Amsterdam in cocooning (TT: 26,274 hrs). Sold to CAUSA 5 Feb 63. Deld shortly afterwards and regd CX-BBN. PH-regn canx 24 Jan 63. Overran the runway at Buenos Aires Aeroparque 29 Aug 64 due to nose-wheel flutter. Slight damage to aircraft. Believed repaired, but out of svce at Montevideo by Apr 67. CAUSA ceased ops 9 May 67. Condition deteriorated by Mar 72 and scrapped by Sep 72.

2642 649A-79-60 1 Aug 50 to Chicago & Southern as N86521 'City of Houston', FN 521. C&S dely date 12 Aug 50. Later named 'Ciudad Trujillo'. Merged with Delta Airlines 26 Feb 53, effective 1 May 53. Cvtd to 749A. Sold by Delta C&S to Trans World Airlines Inc & handed over at Chicago-Midway 1 Apr 54 (TT: 11,467 hrs). Flown to Fairfax Airport, KS same day for cockpit mods. Completed 10 Apr 54 and used for pilot training until 1 Jun 54. Ret to Fairfax for mods, including conversion to intl sleeper configuration 1 Jun 54. In svce 16 Aug 54 named 'Star of Oregon', FN 827-S, intl network. To LAS Burbank 28 Nov 55 for conversion to domestic configuration, and re-entered svce 8 Jan 56, FN 827, later named 'Star of Colombo'. Withdrawn from svce and stored at Mid-Continent Airport, Kansas City, MO 6 Dec 64. (TT: 33,730 hrs). Remained in storage there until sold to Aero Tech Inc 5 Jun 68 and scrapped by them during Jun 68.

2643 749A-79-52 18 Aug 50 to Trans World Airlines Inc as N6007C 'Star of Ohio', FN 807. In svce 20 Aug 50 (domestic network). To intl network 22 Aug 50. Ret to domestic 17 Feb 55, then final intl 21 Apr 55. To domestic network 14 Feb 58. Withdrawn from use 24 Feb 66 and stored at Mid-Continent Airport, Kansas City, MO (TT: 37,740 hrs), until sold to Aero Tech Inc 10 Jun 68. Scrapped by them during Jun 68.

2644 749A-79-52 7 Sep 50 to Trans World Airlines Inc as N6008C 'Star of Indiana', FN 808. In svce 9 Sep 50 (domestic network), to intl network 10 Sep 50. Ret to domestic network 3 May 57. Withdrawn from use 29 Nov 66 and stored at Mid-Continent Airport, Kansas City, MO (TT: 37,708 hrs) until sold to Aero Tech Inc 16 May 68. Scrapped by them during Jun 68.

2645 749A-79-52 11 Sep 50 to Trans World Airlines Inc as N6009C 'Star of Michigan', FN 809. TWA dely date 12 Sep 50, in svce 13 Sep 50 (domestic network) and 14 Sep 50 (intl network). Ret to domestic network 1 Nov 51, and to intl 1 Jun 52. To domestic 6 Nov 53. Slightly damaged when struck tractor at Boston, MA 20 Sep 53. Repaired. To intl network 28 Apr 54. Ret to domestic 21 Sep 54, and to intl 25 Apr 55. Ret to domestic 7 Jul 55 and to final intl season 26 Aug 55. Flew New York-Bermuda-New York svces for BOAC 3-4 Mar 56. To domestic network 28 Oct 56. Sold to Avianca 27 Oct 59 and deld to New York-Newark same day (TT: 26,265 hrs). Cvtd to 74-80 Seater for domestic Tourist class use. E-42300 dated 26 Oct 59 and regd HK-653. Damaged in belly-landing at Bogota International Airport 11.56hrs (local) on 20 Mar 62, when port undercarriage failed to lower (locked in 'up' position). Landed on foam-covered runway after circling airport for three & a half hours to use up fuel. Was on Flight AV689 Medellin-Bogota. No injuries. Repaired. Sold to Trans-Peruana 31 Oct 67 and regd OB-R-917. Withdrawn from use by Sep 69 (bankruptcy of Trans-Peruana) and stored at Lima, Peru. Up for sale by auction 8 Sep 70. Remained in storage at Lima until scrapped during summer/autumn 1975.

2646 749A-79-52 20 Sep 50 to Trans World Airlines Inc as N6010C 'Star of Illinois', FN 810. In svce 22 Sep 50 (domestic network) and 24 Sep 50 (intl network). Converted to intl sleeper, date uk, with FN 810-S. Severely damaged by fire at New York-Idlewild, NY, 21 Apr 52. (TT: 3,453 hrs). While parked on apron in front of Hangar 5, left wing tanks were being refuelled from a tank truck when refuelling hose burst, spilling out 150-200 gallons of fuel. Fire broke out immediately by left side of fuselage in front of leading edge of wing. Heat & flames fused the aluminium skin of the fuselage & continued to burn between the outer skin & the interior cabin sheathing. The interior of the aircraft was completely gutted and structural members warped & twisted by the heat. Damage was assessed at $700,000. Repaired by LAS, Idlewild during the next eight months, again with intl sleeper mods, and re-entered svce 19 Dec 52, first revenue flight 26 Dec 52, with FN 810-S. To LAS, Burbank 3 Oct 55 for cabin mods for domestic use, re-entered svce 28 Nov 55. Renamed 'Star of Germany' and reverted to FN 810. Withdrawn from use 31 Dec 66 (TT: 32,825 hrs) and stored at Fairfax Airport, Kansas City, KS until sold to Aero Tech Inc 14 Aug 68. Flown to Tucson, AZ, for storage and remained there until broken up between Mar 71 and Oct 73.

2647 749A-79-52 10 Oct 50 to Trans World Airlines Inc as N6011C 'Star of Missouri', FN 811. In svce 13 Oct 50 (domestic network) and 14 Oct 50 (intl network). To domestic network 6 Jul 51 and back to intl 31 Oct 51. To domestic again 31 Oct 52 and intl 30 Apr 53. To domestic network 9 Nov 53 and to intl for final period 6 May 54. To domestic network 2 Dec 56. Withdrawn from use 5 Apr 67 (TT: 35,983 hrs) and stored at Fairfax Airport, KS, until sale to Aero Tech Inc 4 Aug 68. Flown to Tucson, AZ, for storage and lsd or sold to unknown operator by Nov 69. Last reptd flight was 11 Nov 69. The aircraft, painted in an all-over green colour-scheme with a black registration on a white panel, was carrying colour TVs & radios from Panama to Asuncion, Paraguay when engine trouble developed. An emergency landing was made at Arica, Chile with one engine feathered. Officially regd to Aero Tech Inc 9 Mar 70. The aircraft was eventually abandoned & parked for years at Chacalluta Airport. The three good engines were run up periodically. N-regn canx 24 Apr 74. Sold for scrap 30 Jul 94 to ITACA Metal Works Co/Fabrica Perfiles Metalicos (Antonio & Darko Dekovic) for 7,140,000 escudos (approx US$ 7,515). The fuselage & engines were still in a metal recycling centre at Arica a/o late 1996, but by May 04 only small parts remained, the three engines having been sold for Aviodrome's 749A (c/n 2604) in 2003!

2648 749A-79-52 13 Oct 50 to Trans World Airlines Inc as N6012C 'Star of Massachusetts', FN 812. TWA dely date 16 Oct 50, in svce (domestic network) 18 Oct 50, intl network 20 Oct 50. Modified to intl sleeper configuration Mar 51, with FN 812-S, until Jan 56. To LAS, Burbank 9 Jan 56 for cabin mods for domestic use, re-entered svce 10 Feb 56. Reverted to FN 812 and later renamed 'Star of Spain'. Sold to FAA on 20 Jul 62 for $160,000 (TT: 29,196 hrs), and regd to them 9 Aug 62. Modified to calibration aircraft and reregd N65. Damaged beyond repair while performing an emergency landing on three engines at Tachikawa AFB, near Tokyo, Japan, at approx 11.00 hrs on 15 Aug 66. While cruising at 10,000 feet en route to Itazuke AB to check navigation aids, the low-pressure warning light for the no.2 engine-driven hydraulic pump came on. The shut-off valve was turned off and control boost disconnected, and subsequently the no. 1 shut-off valve. Shortly afterwards, hydraulic fluid started issuing from near no.1 engine on the leading edge of the wing, so no.1 engine was shut down. The approach & landing was carried out still without elevator and rudder boost. Just before touchdown, the aircraft swerved to the right, continuing after touchdown, off the runway and on to the grass. After rolling straight for a time, the aircraft swung to the left, skidded through two drainage ditches, which caused both main undercarriage legs to collapse and the nose landing gear to separate from the aircraft. The no.2 engine subsequently separated from the wing, with the aircraft coming to rest 2,000 feet from the runway threshold and 125 feet to the right of the runway centreline. No fire, and no injuries to the crew. Wreckage tfd to the USAF for disposal 17 Feb 67.

2649 749A-79-52 24 Oct 50 to Trans World Airlines Inc as N6013C 'Star of New Mexico', FN 813. TWA dely date 26 Oct 50, in svce (domestic network) 29 Oct 50, to intl network 30 Oct 50. Modified to intl sleeper configuration Apr 51, with FN 813-S, until Mar 56. Damaged at Reykjavik, Iceland, en route Frankfurt-New York 29 May 55, when starboard undercarriage caught fire on the ground. Repaired. To LAS, Burbank, 13 Feb 56 for cabin mods for domestic use. Re-entered svce 14 Mar 56. Reverted to FN 813 and later renamed 'Star of Majorca'. Slightly damaged 11.45 hrs (CST) on 14 Nov 64 when the aircraft encountered extreme in-flight turbulence shortly before reaching Wichita, KS, en route from Kansas City, MO, while on an ILS approach. Injuries to several passengers. Repaired. Withdrawn from use 3 Jan 66 (TT: 33,609 hrs) and stored at Mid-Continent Airport, Kansas City, MO until sold to Aero Tech Inc 27 May 68. Scrapped by them during Jun 68.

2650 749A-79-52 3 Nov 50 to Trans World Airlines Inc as N6014C 'Star of Delaware', FN 814. In svce (domestic network) 6 Nov 50, intl network 8 Nov 50. To domestic network 28 Oct 54 and ret to intl 2 Jun 55. Flew New York-Bermuda-New York svce for BOAC 5 Apr 56. To domestic network 23 Oct 57. (TT: 29,559 hrs a/o 30 Jun 61). Withdrawn from use 27 Mar 67 (TT: 37,331 hrs) and stored at Kansas City, MO, until sold to Central American Airways Flying Service 5 Oct 67. Reregd N273R 23 Oct 67. (TWA also give 31 Dec 67 as sale date, presumably this is the date the payments on the aircraft were completed). Sold to World Wide Leasing Inc 23 Mar 73, and lsd to World Citizens International (Travel Club) Jul 73 until 22 Oct 74 (canx of certificate), named 'Miss America'. Sold to CIM Associates Inc 16 Nov 74. Overran chocks at Fort Lauderdale, FL, during Feb 75, minor damage, but badly damaged the Ercoupe 415 it hit. Repaired. Lsd to Lanzair (CI) Ltd Feb 76 and deld Fort Lauderdale,FL, to Shannon, Ireland, arr 16 Feb 76 and stored until 10 Aug 76, when it re-entered svce. Impounded by authorities at Lome, Togo, when the aircraft landed with mechanical problems on 16 Nov 76. Crew abandoned the aircraft the following day. Aircraft remained standing at the airport at Lome. On 8 Apr 77, the airport authorities had the aircraft taxied on one engine to a hard standing. A representative from the owners (CIM Associates Inc) attempted to get the aircraft airworthy in order to fly it back to Florida during the period 10 Oct -18 Oct 77, but left to obtain further spares. On 22 Oct 77, a fire broke out on board the aircraft, causing severe damage -fuselage burnt out, aircraft's back broken, only fins, wings and undercarriage still basically intact. Apparently, the aircraft was set on fire because a certain A Voyna owed money to some undercover agents. The latter heard A Voyna was in W.Africa, so they set fire to what was assumed to be his aircraft (in fact his aircraft was a DC-4 N67147!). Derelict remains subsequently used for fire-training at Lome and main wreck plus tail unit were still extant in spring 1983.

2651 749A-79-52 17 Nov 50 to Trans World as N6015C 'Star of Arizona', FN 815. In svce 19 Nov 50 (domestic network), to intl network 21 Nov 50 until ret to domestic network 3 Jan 57. Withdrawn from use 26 Mar 65 and stored at Kansas City, MO. Sold to Charles E. Bush t/a Bush Aviation on 23 Mar 66 and deld to Fort Lauderdale, FL, by May 66. Stored there until at least Jan 67. Aircraft not paid for, retd to Mid-Continent Airport, Kansas City, MO for storage until sold to Aero Tech Inc on 23 May 68 (5 Apr 68 also quoted) (TT: 34,875 hrs), and broken up by them shortly afterwards at Mid-Continent Airport, Kansas City, MO.

2652 749A-79-33 12 Jul 50 to KLM as PH-TFF 'Venlo', E-22028, date unknown, and regd 28 Jul 50. On 22 Mar 52 at 21.11 hrs, the aircraft departed Karachi for Bangkok, en route Amsterdam, Holland, to Sydney, Australia. 54 kms from Don Muang Airport, Bangkok, considerable vibration of the control-wheel and instrument panel was noticed by the pilots. At a height of 500 metres on approach to Don Muang Airport on 23 Mar 52, a turn to the left was made on to the base leg. A loud noise was suddenly heard and the aircraft started vibrating severely; one of the propeller blades of no.3 engine had failed. Immediately afterwards, as the aircraft turned on to finals, the engine broke free of the aircraft and a fire broke out in the nacelle. The aircraft was landed normally on Runway 21-03, but after the aircraft stopped, the starboard main undercarriage collapsed and the fire spread from no.3 nacelle. Aircraft destroyed by fire. No casualties. Regn canx 25 Mar 52.

2653 649A-79-60 27 Sep 50 to Chicago & Southern as N86522, 'City of Memphis', FN 522. Merged with Delta Airlines 26 Feb 53, effective 1 May 53. Cvtd to 749A. Sold by Delta C&S to Trans World Airlines Inc and handed over at Chicago-Midway 1 Jun 54 (TT: 11,979 hrs). Flown to Fairfax Airport, KS, for conversion to TWA domestic standards. In svce 4 Jul 54, named 'Star of Washington', FN 829. Renamed 'Star of Madeira'. Damaged 20 Jul 54, when no.3 engine caught fire in flight and emergency landing made at Washington Natl, DC. (TT: 12,096 hrs). Provisionally repaired, and ferried to Fairfax, KS, on 26 Jul 54, where repairs were completed and the aircraft converted to intl sleeper configuration. Re-entered svce 27 Sep 54 (intl network), FN 829-S. To LAS, Burbank, for domestic conversion 22 Jan 56. Re-entered svce 22 Feb 56, to FN 829, later named 'Star of Dhahran'. Withdrawn from use 2 Nov 66 (TT: 36,241 hrs) and stored at Mid-Continent Airport, Kansas City, MO until sold to Aero Tech Inc on 2 Jun 68. Broken up by them during Jun 68.

2654 749A-79-52 12 Dec 50 to Trans World Airlines Inc as N6016C 'Star of California', FN 816. In svce 15 Dec 50 (domestic network), 17 Dec 50 (intl network). Ret to domestic network 5 Feb 58, (TT: 28,997 hrs a/o 30 Jun 61) and sold to FAA 6 Mar 63. (TT: 31,322 hrs). Deld 26 Mar 63. Reregd N121. Later regd to Department of Transportation. Suffered damage while undergoing maintenance Manila, Philippines early 64. Repaired. Damaged in hard landing Tachikawa Jan 68. Nose gear support structure cracked. Repaired again. Last flight for FAA 12 Feb 69 Tachikawa to Itazuke AB on flight aids checking mission. Withdrawn from svce, regn canx 21 Mar 69 and tfd to the USAF in an airworthy condition 22 Apr 69. Offered for sale by US Department of Defense at Tachikawa, Japan on 1 Oct 69 (TT: 34,321 hrs). Presumably remained unsold, as subsequently stored at Tachikawa AFB. Being used for fire practice there in early 1970s, and later scrapped.

2655 749A-79-52 21 Dec 50 to Trans World Airlines Inc as N6017C 'Star of the District of Columbia', FN 817. In svce (domestic network) 23 Dec 50, to intl network 27 Dec 50. Ret to domestic network 28 Oct 56. Lsd to Pacific Northern Airlines 17 Aug 60. (TT: 27,721 hrs). Sold to Connie Air Leasing Inc (also known as Connie Rentals Inc) on 24 Nov 61, lse to Pacific Northern continued until 30 Sep 63. Sold to Pacific Northern 1 Oct 63. Used as a 55-Seater, later as a 57-Seater, FN 17C. Tfd to Western Air Lines 1 Jul 67, FN later 517. Withdrawn from svce 8 Dec 68 and ferried to McCarran Fld, Las Vegas, NV, for storage (TT: 40,421 hrs). Sold to Concare Aircraft Leasing Inc, probably on 11 Apr 69, and to Vincent M. Castora later in 1969. Flying in full Western Airlines colours at Georgetown, Guyana 18 Oct 69. Probably used for illegal flight and stored at Panama-Tocumen Airport, Panama by Nov 71, in ex-Western colours, but with dark blue/green roof. Condition deteriorated, and moved to dump at Tocumen by late 1976, cowlings and parts of engines missing. Scrapped during 1978 or 1979.

2656 749A-79-52 29 Dec 50 to Trans World Airlines Inc as N6018C 'Star of Nevada', FN 818. In svce (domestic network) 1 Jan 51, to intl network 4 Jan 51. Ret to domestic network 25 Dec 56. Damaged at Greater Pittsburgh Airport, PA, 15 Jan 57 at 12.07 hrs (EST) when it collided with a Capital Airlines DC-3, causing damage to the wing nacelle and tail unit. Collision occurred at the inter-section of two taxiways, ice on them, DC-3's braking ineffective. (TT: 19,262 hrs). Repaired and re-entered svce 31 Jan 57. Withdrawn from use 6 Apr 67 (TT: 37,202 hrs) and stored at Fairfax Airport, KS, until sold to Aero Tech Inc 14 Aug 68. Flown to Tucson, AZ, for storage and broken up there between Mar 71 and Oct 73.

2657 749A-79-52 17 Jan 51 to Trans World Airlines Inc as N6019C 'Star of Minnesota', FN 819. In svce (domestic network) 21 Jan 51, to intl network 24 Jan 51. Ret to domestic 20 Oct 53. To intl again 1 Jun 54. Starboard wing-tip damaged when hit by BOAC 049 G-AMUR taxiying at Gander, Nfld 3 Jul 54. Repaired and ret to domestic 26 Sep 54. To intl network for final period 3 Mar 55, and ret to domestic 29 Oct 57. Withdrawn from use 16 Nov 66 (TT: 36,325 hrs) and stored at Mid-Continent Airport, Kansas City, MO until sold to Aero Tech Inc 22 May 68. Scrapped by them during Jun 68.

2658 749A-79-52 25 Jan 51 to Trans World Airlines Inc as N6020C 'Star of Kentucky', FN 820. In svce (domestic network) 29 Jan 51, to intl network 2 Feb 51. Damaged at Gander, Nfld, 29 Sep 51, when it taxied into a four-foot ditch at night. (TT: 1,958 hrs). Left wing, nos. 1 & 2 nacelles, left tail unit and main undercarriage damaged. Repaired by LAS and re-entered svce 25 Feb 52 (intl network). Tfd to domestic network 29 Oct 56. Three propellers were damaged by a ladder at Idlewild, NY, on 5 Dec 57. Repaired. First TWA 749/749A Connie to be radar-fitted. Made Trans World's last piston-engined passenger flight with large "Bye Bye Connie" inscription on rear fuselage on 6 Apr 67, TW 249 New York (J F Kennedy)-Philadelphia-Pittsburgh-Columbus-Louisville-St.Louis. Withdrawn from svce 7 Apr 67 (TT: 35,291 hrs) and stored at Fairfax Airport, KS, until sold to Aero Tech Inc 14 Aug 68. (25 Jun 68 also quoted). Flown to Tucson, AZ, for storage and broken up there between Mar 71 and Oct 73.

2659 649A-79-60 21 Nov 50 to Chicago & Southern as N86523 'City of Detroit', FN 523. C&S dely date 21 Oct 50. Later named 'City of Caracas Venezuela'. Merged with Delta Airlines 26 Feb 53, effective 1 May 53, with same name and FN. Cvtd to 749A. Lsd by Delta C&S to Pacific Northern Airlines Mar 55 (possibly Jan-Mar 55), and sold to them, probably on 2 Mar 56. Named 'Rendezvous Queen', FN 523. Sustained damage to wing during a heavy landing at Seattle, WA, 26 Sep 56. Repaired. Received substantial damage near Whittier, AK, 5 Dec 57, when the forward port cabin door blew out, resulting in explosive decompression,

N6020C 749A. Close-up taken on the sad occasion of Trans World's last Constellation flight on 6th April 1967. The four people were on the first, record-breaking, flight of a Constellation in TWA colours on 17th April 1944. From left to right they are: Ed Minser (meteorology department), Robert L Proctor (Flight Engineer), Lee Spruill (Director, Powerplant overhaul) and Captain Orville Olson (Co-pilot on first flight). (TWA via Ed Betts)

while climbing through 18,000 feet. Followed by power loss on no.2 engine, due to the ingestion of foreign material from the cabin through the carburetor air inlet. Engine feathered and successful emergency landing made at Anchorage, AK, with no injuries. Aircraft was en route Anchorage, AK, to Seattle, WA. Repaired. Damaged on making a hard landing at Kenai, AK, on 6 Jun 66. Fuselage sprung and skin wrinkled, due to nose-gear retraction scissors breaking. No injuries. Repair uneconomical, so withdrawn from use at Seattle, WA, 16 Jun 66. Canx 29 Jun 66 and scrapped at Seattle by late 1966.

2660 649A-79-60 7 Feb 51 to Chicago & Southern as N86524 'City of San Juan', FN 524. C&S dely date 6 Feb 51. Merged with Delta Airlines 26 Feb 53, effective 1 May 53, with same name and FN. Cvtd to 749A. Lsd by Delta C&S to Pacific Northern Airlines Mar 55 (possibly Jan-Mar 55), and sold to them 2 Mar 56, FN 524. Used as 55-Seater, later 57-Seater. Tfd to Western Air Lines 30 Jun 67 (1 Jul 67 also quoted), same FN. Withdrawn from svce 21 Dec 68 and ferried to McCarran Fld, Las Vegas, NV, for storage. (TT: 41,003 hrs). Sold to Concare Aircraft Leasing Corp 11 Apr 69 and flown to Fort Lauderdale, FL. Sold to US Turbine Corp 29 May 69, and to Stevens Enterprises Inc 30 May 69. Sold via US Turbine Corp (agents for Carolina Aircraft) 31 Oct 69 to Robert W. Cobaugh same day. Flown to Faro, Portugal, by Sep 69, and used on the Biafran airlift as part of the Phoenix Air Transport combine. Reregd 5N86H by Dec 69. Flew Biafran leader, Colonel Ojuwku, from Uli, Biafra 10 Jan 70 to exile in Abidjan, Ivory Coast. Dep Abidjan for Faro, Portugal 12 Jan 70 and stored there. Canx from USCAR 9 Dec 71 (failure to file). As the last owner, R.W. Cobaugh, was lease-purchasing the aircraft using income from the Biafran government, the fall of Biafra in Jan 70 resulted in the non-payment of the instalments, and the aircraft actually reverted to the ownership of Concare Aircraft Leasing. In late 1972, Jack A.Crosson took over ownership of the aircraft as payment for money owed to him by Concare, and also paid the parking fees owed to Faro Airport. Restored to the USCAR by Mar 73 as N86524. Work undertaken on an occasional basis on the restoration of the aircraft up till at least May 74. The aircraft was then abandoned and became Faro Airport property. In approx Dec 77, the aircraft was purchased by Air International Inc (L.W. Dreyer) and was scrapped for spares during the first few months of 1978. Fuselage sold to Jose Rodriques Catarno of Vale de America, Faro, on 6 Feb 78 for unknown use. Fuselage still extant at Faro in Jul 79, broken up by Nov 79.

2661 749A-79-33 11 Jan 51 to KLM as PH-TFG 'Friesland'. E-22035 dated 9 Feb 51, regd 5 Feb 51; dely date of 10 Feb 51 also quoted by LAC. Reregd PH-LDG on 25 Mar 54 (KLM quote 12 Mar 54). Lsd to Plane Equipment Inc, who sub-lsd to Pacific Northern Airlines as N10401 from 27 Oct 56 to 3 Apr 57. PH-regn canx 26 Oct 56. Ret to KLM and restored as PH-LDG 3 Apr 57. N-regn canx 8 Apr 57. Withdrawn from use by KLM at Schiphol Airport, Amsterdam, 14 Apr 60 (also given as 30 Mar 60), (TT: 25,061 hrs). Stored there in cocooning, awaiting sale. Sold to CAUSA on 26 Dec 62 and deld shortly afterwards. PH-regn canx 24 Jan 63. Reregd CX-BBM. Stored at Montevideo after CAUSA ceased ops on 9 May 67. Condition gradually deteriorated until aircraft was finally broken up during Nov 77.

2662 649A-79-60 1 Feb 51 to Chicago & Southern as N86525 'City of Kingston', FN 525. Dely date of 2 Feb 51 quoted by C&S; 14 Feb 51 may be in svce date (also quoted). Merged with Delta Airlines 26 Feb 53, effective 1 May 53, with same FN. Cvtd to 749A. Lsd by Delta C&S to Pacific Northern Airlines 15 Mar 55 (possibly Jan 55-Mar 55), sold to them, probably on 2 Mar 56, FN 525. Used as 55-Seater, later as 57-Seater. Tfd to Western Air Lines 1 Jul 67, same FN. Withdrawn from svce 10 Dec 68 (TT: 41,228 hrs) and ferried to McCarran Fld, Las Vegas, NV, for storage. Sold to Concare Aircraft Leasing Corp 11 Apr 69 and flown to Fort Lauderdale, FL. Sold Air Interamerica Inc (believed as agents of Carolina Aircraft) 27 May 69 and flown to Lisbon, Portugal, by Aug 69. Used on the Biafran airlift as part of the Phoenix Air Transport combine. Believed reregd 5N85H by late Nov 69. Crashed in mountainous country near the Algerian-Moroccan border, in Algeria, after the failure of three engines, on 28 Nov 69, killing all on board. En route Lisbon-Sao Tome-Uli, Biafra. Canx from USCAR 27 Jul 70.

2663 749A-79-74 18 May 51 to Avianca as HK-162, E-22039 same day, and arr Bogota on dely 22 Jun 51. Ret to LAC and lsd to Capitol Airways as N4900C by May 57, sold Nov 57 to Capitol. Ret to LAC approx Jan 60, believed in part-exchange for 1049G c/n 4619. Probably stored at Burbank, CA. Sold to West Coast Airmotive Corp early in 1964, unconf lse to Modern Air Transport 1964. Sold to LANSA, Peru, for spares in late 1964, and canx from USCAR by Jan 65. Flown to Lima, Peru, still as N4900C. Used for spares, and derelict by Apr 66. Last reported sitting on tail there in Mar 68, and presumably scrapped shortly afterwards.

2664 749A-79-74 31 May 51 to Avianca as HK-163, E-22040 same day, arr Bogota on dely together with c/n 2663 on 22 Jun 51. Crashed into Monte de Pico, five miles west-south-west of Lajes AB, Azores, shortly after take-off, at approx 02.40 hrs (local) on 9 Aug 54, killing all on board. Aircraft had been diverted to Lajes from Santa Maria because of fog, en route Hamburg, Germany-Bogota. Cause: Probably the failure of the pilot to carry out the normal climb-out procedure from Lajes en route to Bermuda, making a left instead of a right turn and thus flying into the mountain instead of out over the sea.

2665 749A-79-73 21 Mar 51 to Air-India Intl as VT-DEO 'Bengal Princess'. Regd Aug 50, E-22036 dated 19 Mar 51, dely in India 3 Apr 51, in svce 5 Apr 51. Damaged 3 Nov 54. Repaired. Ret to LAC as trade-in on Super Constellations, canx from VT-register 20 Feb 58. Sold to Aeronaves de Mexico 26 Feb 58 and regd XA-MEV. Crashed into the La Latilla Mountain peak, approx 8 miles from the radio beacon west of Guadalajara, on climb-out from Guadalajara, Mexico, at approx 22.06 hrs (local) on 2 Jun 58, killing all on board. Aircraft was en route Tijuana-Guadalajara-Mexico City. Cause: Probably pilot error - aircraft was about half a mile off course and flew into the 7,500ft mountain just below the peak. Pilot failed to follow the established climb-out procedure.

2666 749A-79-73 30 Mar 51 to Air-India Intl as VT-DEP 'Kashmir Princess'. Regd Aug 50, E-22037 dated 30 Mar 51, dely in USA 3 Apr 51, India 8 Apr 51, in svce 12 Apr 51. Blown up by time-bomb explosion while flying at 18,000 feet and ditched shortly after 09.00 hrs (GMT) on 11 Apr 55 approx 1.5 miles off the west coast of Great Natuna Islands, Sarawak, South China Sea (4 30' N, 180 20' E). Three survived of 18 on board the aircraft. The aircraft was carrying Chinese Communist officials and journalists from Hong Kong to Bandoeing, Indonesia. A time-bomb had been placed in a suitcase which was in the aircraft's under-floor baggage compartment - reportedly the work of Nationalist Chinese saboteurs. (Other reports suggest the explosion was in the wheel well).

2667 749A-79-52 17 Apr 51 to Trans World Airlines Inc as N6021C 'Star of West Virginia', FN 821. TWA dely date 16 Apr 51, in svce 19 Apr 51 (domestic network), to intl network 24 Apr 51. Ret to domestic network 30 Oct 54, and to intl for final period 31 May 55. To domestic network 13 Nov 57. Withdrawn from use 27 Mar 67 (TT: 36,491 hrs) and stored at Fairfax Airport, KS, until sold to Aero Tech Inc 26 Jun 68 (FAA records)/14 Aug 68 (TWA records). Sold to Discover America Corp (Travel Club) 31 Jul 68. Repossessed by Gulf Coast National Bank 28 Jul 70, and sold to Travis Leasing Inc same day. Sold to Unlimited Leasing Inc 9 Nov 70. Flew little during the years 1971-73, stored at Miami, FL. Used for 6-8 weeks in Jan-Feb 74 on US Government research work from Sanford, FL. Leased out to unknown persons & subsequently impounded Winder, GA Aug 74 after drug smuggling. Released back to Unlimited Lsg (L C McKindree) & lsd LBA Inc t/a Air Carga Inc 28 Apr 75. Lsd Inair, Panama, during Sep 77 & lsd Aeromar, Dominican Republic, during Oct 78. Sold to Carib Airways Inc 24 Jan 79. Dep Miami, FL, 13 Feb 79 and flew to Santa Marta, Colombia, to collect a cargo of dope. Impounded at Panama City, FL, three days later with approx 36,000 lbs of dope on board. Auctioned by US authorities at Panama City, FL, and sold to Paramount Petroleum Corp (L.W. Dreyer) on 24 Oct 79 for a reported $17,500. Sold to Transglobal Inc (A.Voyna) in early Feb 80 for a reported $70,000(!), official sale date 29 May 80. Cof Regn issued 10 Jul 80. Overhauled at Panama City, FL, Apr 80. Aircraft was unusual in that it flew for some years with two BD-l engines and two CB-1 engines (from a 1049). Owner was killed in May 80. Stored, good condition, Panama City, FL, 1981. Ownership of Transglobal passed to Mrs.Voyna on death of husband and aircraft for sale in 1982 for $75,000. Sold to AeroChago SA 10 May 83, N-regn canx Jul 83, reregd HI-422 & deld Miami, FL-Santo Domingo, Dominican Republic mid-Aug 83. Flew regularly on Santo Domingo, DR to San Juan, PR route until approx Feb 88. Suffered violent nosewheel shimmy problem on landing with a full load of cargo at Las Americas Airport, Santo Domingo, from San Juan, PR at unknown date in 1988. Forward fuselage structure overstressed, and subsequently withdrawn from use & stored at Santo Domingo, believed by late May 88. Used for spares for AeroChago SA's Super Constellations & scrapped by 1993.

2668 749A-79-52 30 Apr 51 to Trans World Airlines Inc as N6022C 'Star of Virginia', FN 822. In svce (domestic network) 2 May 51, intl network 6 May 51. To domestic again 11 Nov 54, and to intl network 1 Jun 55. Ret to domestic network 19 Sep 55. To intl for final period 25 Dec 55, then to domestic 4 Nov 57. (TT: 28,367 hrs a/o 30 Jun 61). Sold to Pacific Northern Airlines (replacement for c/n 2659) 30 Jun 66, tf 23 Jun 66, in svce 23 Jul 66, FN 22C. Used as a 55-Seater, later 57-Seater. Tfd to Western Air Lines 1 Jul 67, FN 22C, later 522. Withdrawn from svce 20 Dec 68 (TT: 38,352 hrs) and ferried to McCarran Fld, Las Vegas, NV, for storage. Sold to Concare Aircraft Leasing Corp 11 Apr 69 and flown to Fort Lauderdale. Sold to Leasing Consultants Inc, officially on 5 May 69. Painted up as 'CX-BGP' at Miami, FL, on or just prior to 12 May 69. New evidence suggests this aircraft was not in fact used on the Haiti bombing raid of 4 Jun 69 (see c/n 2556). Sold to persons unknown Jun 69 & ferried Miami, FL – Montevideo-Carrasco early Jul 69 for use in smuggling operations. Flew Panama 7 Jul 69 and loaded with consumer goods and cigarettes plus other items for smuggling into South America. Waited in Panama while airstrip was prepared on a cattle ranch at Sarandi in south-eastern Uruguay. In mid-Aug 69 flew from Panama to Antofagasta, Chile, then on 16 Aug 69 to Uruguay, (possibly landing at Asuncion, Paraguay en route) before landing on prepared airstrip at Sarandi de Gutierrez, Lavalleja just after midnight on 17 Aug 69. Aircraft was undamaged, but the nosewheel became bogged down in the mud and the aircraft was subsequently impounded. The crew and the contraband disappeared. Aircraft remained stored, visible from Route 8 highway until at least Jun 74 but parts were stolen and aircraft suffered general damage. At one stage reportedly bought by ARCO SA for the Colonia-Buenos Aires shuttle. Ntu, as the aircraft was cut up for scrap on site in late 1970s and remains transported to unknown location.

2669 749A-79-52 8 May 51 to Trans World Airlines Inc as N6023C 'Star of Iowa', FN 823. In svce (domestic network) 11 May 51, to intl network 12 May 51. Ground crewman struck by propeller & killed 9 Sep 54 at Basra, Iraq, en route Dhahran-New York. No damage to aircraft. Back to domestic 1 Nov 55, and to intl network for final period 28 Mar 56. To domestic network 28 Oct 57. Withdrawn from use 16 Jun 66 (TT: 35,174 hrs) and stored at Mid-Continent Airport, Kansas City, MO until sold to Aero Tech Inc 17 May 68. Scrapped by them during Jun 68.

2670 749A-79-52 29 May 51 to Trans World Airlines Inc as N6024C 'Star of Nebraska', FN 824. In svce (domestic network) 1 Jun 51, to intl network 4 Jun 51. Ret to domestic 30 Oct 55, and to intl network for final season 31 May 56. To domestic network 23 Dec 56. Withdrawn from use 6 Apr 67 (TT: 35,472 hrs) and stored at Fairfax Airport, KS, until sold to Aero Tech Inc 14 Aug 68. Flown to Tucson, AZ, for storage. Broken up there between Mar 71 and Oct 73.

2671 749A-79-52 25 Jun 51 to Howard Hughes as N6025C. Allotted 'Star of Colorado', FN 825 with Trans World, but never taken up or even carried by the aircraft. Did not undergo the customary production flight test pre-delivery, but just towed across the airfield. Kept stored in hangar at Burbank, CA, engines run up by Howard Hughes from time to time, but not flown. Released by Howard Hughes approx May 53, tfd back to Trans World (for whom it was originally ordered), overhauled by LAS, Burbank & put into flying condition. Not used by TWA. Sold to BOAC via LAC in Aug 54. CofA issued 25 Jul 54 and regd G-ANNT 13 Aug 54. E-27637 dated 17 Sep 54, deld in USA 27 Sep 54, arr London-Heathrow 28 Sep 54, all silver with small black regn. Modified to 60-Seater Tourist-class configuration at Heathrow and used for training only Nov 54, named 'Buckingham'. In svce & also first 749 svce to Colombo 7-8 Dec 54, ret 9-10 Dec 54. Damaged when it landed at London-Heathrow 11 Aug 57 with port main undercarriage retracted (en route from Singapore & Frankfurt). Previous problems with undercarriage had been experienced but not reported. Repaired, CofA renewed 25 Sep 57. Flew last svce 25-26 Oct 57, followed by charter London-Delhi-London 17-21 Nov 57. Withdrawn from svce & stored 27 Nov 57, cocooned 13 Dec 57. Sold to Capitol Airways 25 Mar 58 for $850,000, regd N4901C 25 Mar 58, G-regn canx same day. Del ex-London Heathrow 29 Mar 58. Believed lsd to Trans International in early 1960s, but stored at Long Beach, CA, in Capitol colours from at least Jul 64 to Jan 65. Flown to Wilmington, DE, but withdrawn from svce by Sep 66 (though kept airworthy). Stored at Wilmington. Reregd N6695C in 1968, but remained in storage carrying regn N4901C during 1969. Donated to Bradley Air Museum (Connecticut Aeronautical Historical Association Inc) and flown to Windsor Locks, CT on dely 16 Mar 70, carrying both N4901C and N6695C. (TT: 18,283 hrs). Preserved by museum in outdoor collection at edge of Bradley Intl Airport, in Capitol Airways colours. Damaged beyond repair by tornado that blew up just after 15.00 hrs (local) on 3 Oct 79. The aircraft was hurled across the road from the exhibits by the wind (velocity of 86 mph at edge, over 150 mph at centre of tornado), carried approx 100 feet and landed upside down, with its back broken. Believed some parts salvaged, but most of aircraft scrapped.

2672 749A-79-52 29 Jun 51 to Trans World Airlines Inc as N6026C 'Star of Connecticut', FN 826. In svce (domestic network) 3 Jul 51, to intl 6 Jul 51. Ret to domestic network 31 Oct 57. Withdrawn from svce 8 Oct 65 (TT: 34,753 hrs) and stored at Mid-Continent Airport, Kansas City, MO until sold to Aero Tech Inc 31 May 68. Scrapped by them by Jul 68.

2673 749A-79-60 17 May 51 to Chicago & Southern as N86535 'City of Port au Prince', FN 535. Merged with Delta Airlines 26 Feb 53; effective 1 May 53. Sold by Delta C&S and handed over to Trans World Airlines Inc at Chicago-Midway 20 Apr 54 (TT: 9,876 hrs). Ferried to Fairfax Airport, KS, for conversion to intl standards. In svce 1 Aug 54 as 'Star of Corsica', FN 828. To domestic network 8 Aug 54. To Fairfax Airport, KS, 18 Sep 54 for conversion to intl sleeper configuration. In svce 12 Nov 54, FN 828-S. To LAS, Burbank, 31 Oct 55 for conversion to domestic network configuration. Re-entered svce 12 Dec 55, reverted to FN 828, later named 'Star of Basra'. Possibly named 'Star of Wisconsin' at one time, early in TWA use. Damaged at New York-La Guardia 1 Nov 57 when the main undercarriage retracted suddenly while the aircraft was parked on the ramp. (TT: 19,713 hrs). The aircraft had been jacked up for a check after gear vibration had been reported. The gear handle had been placed in the 'UP' position during re-assembly of the gear struts and had been inadvertently left in this position as the aircraft was towed to the ramp for a test flight. The flight crew did not notice the 'UP' position of the handle during the reading of the check list prior to starting engines. As no.3 engine was started, the gear retracted, severely buckling the fuselage as the aircraft settled on the ground. (On a Constellation, the gear retraction hydraulics are normally powered by the pump on the no.3 engine). Repaired and re-entered svce early in 1958. Withdrawn from use 20 Dec 65 and stored at Mid-Continent Airport, Kansas City, MO (TT: 32,007 hrs) until sold to Aero Tech Inc 3 Jun 68. Scrapped by them during Jun 68. Canx USCAR 10 Sep 68.

2674 749A-79-46 18 Jul 51 to Air France as F-BAZZ, E-22044 dated 16 Jul 51, del Orly 21 Jul 51 (TT: 32hrs), CofA 3 Aug 51, in svce 6 Aug 51. Crashed into the 10,850 foot Mont Cemet in the French Basses Alpes at 22.33hrs (GMT) on 1 Sep 53, near Barcelonnette. Aircraft was en route Paris-Orly to Saigon, Vietnam, departing Orly at 20.50hrs (GMT) and was due to land at Nice at 22.55hrs. Hit mountain with starboard wing at the 9,750ft level near the Col des Cayottes, 140mls northeast of Nice, spun round and crashed, killing all on board. Cause: Probably pilot error, as aircraft was far off course. Canx from F-register 22 Sep 53. Engines & other wreckage still in situ in mid-1970s.

2675 749A-79-46 9 Aug 51 to Air France as F-BBDT, E-22046 1 Aug 51, TOC Burbank 1 Aug 51, del Orly 11 Aug 51 (TT: 30hrs), CofA 17 Aug 51, in svce 20 Aug 51. Carried name "Champs Elysées" temporarily from Oct 51 on South American svces. Modified to 61-Seater transatlantic Tourist-class. Operated BOAC flts BA631 London-Prestwick-Montreal 9-10 Jun 57 & London-Prestwick-Gander-Montreal 25-26 Jun 57. Sold to Royal Air Maroc 30 Jan 60 (TT: 24,431 hrs), F-regn canx 27 Jan 60. CofA issued 28 Jan 60 & regd as CN-CCN 30 Jan 60. Fitted with forward cargo door at San Jose, Costa Rica, by SALA between 26 Sep and 30 Nov 61. Withdrawn from svce 1 Jun 70 (TT: 39,508 hrs). Canx 2 Jun 70 and tfd to the Royal Air Maroc Centre de Formation Professionnelle at Casablanca-Anfa. In use there for training until 1982, but replaced by a Caravelle early 1982. Stored in open at Casablanca. By May 1990, the port side rear fuselage had been painted in camouflage colours for use in a film. Fully restored by Jan 06 & repainted in final Royal Air Maroc colours for Museum. Current.

2676 749A-79-46 31 Aug 51 to Air France as F-BBDU, E-22047 same day, del Orly 3 Sep 51 (TT: 28hrs), CofA 10 Sep 51, in svce 11 Sep 51. Flew first proving flight Paris-Bogota via Lisbon, Santa Maria & Fort de France 27 Dec 52 to 8 Jan 53. Modified to 61-Seater transatlantic Tourist class and then to 65-Seater European Tourist class by 1956. Withdrawn from svce 24 Jan 60 (TT: 24,335 hrs). Sold to Royal Air Maroc 24 Jan 60, F-regn canx 23 Jan 60. CofA issued 1 Feb 60 & regd as CN-CCO 24 Jan 60. Damaged nose-wheel undercarriage landing at Nouasseur Airport, Casablanca, 26 Oct 61, and withdrawn from svce (TT: 28,087 hrs). Provisionally repaired, regd F-BAVN and ferried to Toulouse-Montaudran 18 Jan 62 after sold back to Air France for spares use. Withdrawn from use same day (TT: 28,091 hrs). Used for spares at Montaudran. CofA suspended 29 Jan 62. Withdrawn from use 6 Nov 64 & scrapped at Toulouse, France. Canx 6 Nov 64.

2677 749A-79-46 17 Sep 51 to Air France as F-BBDV, E-22048 13 Sep 51. Del Orly 20 Sep 51 (TT: 31hrs), CofA issued 27 Sep 51, in svce 30 Sep 51. Inaugurated couchette svce Paris-Marseilles-Dakar 21 Jan 55. Modified to 65-Seater European Tourist class in 1955. Withdrawn from svce 4 Jan 56 (TT: 14,408 hrs). Sold to CGTA-Air Algérie 4 Jan 56 (as replacement for c/n 2626 which had been written off during training) and in svce 30 Jan 56. Flew last Air Algérie Constellation svce 12 Jan 61, and withdrawn from use after CofA expiry on 28 Jan 61 (TT: 23,693 hrs). Stored at Maison Blanche Airport, Algiers. Presumed destroyed in terrorist bomb attacks on airport 1963. Canx from F-register 6 Jan 64 as wfu, and remains probably scrapped about this time at Algiers.

3001 onwards. For details of cancelled Model 549 Constellations in this c/n range, see note after c/n 1980.

THE SUPER CONSTELLATIONS

1961S *For details of the prototype Super Constellation, see first aircraft in the Constellation production list.*

4001 1049-53-67 First flight Jul 51. Retained by LAC for type certification and development flying, regd N6201C. LADD: 18 Mar 52 to Eastern Air Lines, FN 201. Cvtd to 1049-54 by mid-53 and to 1049/ 02-54 by mid-56. Substantial damage on landing at Charlotte, NC, on 8 May 58 with nose-gear partially retracted. No injuries. After take-off, the crew were unable to fully retract or fully extend the nose-gear again. After circling the airport to burn off fuel, a successful landing was made on the main undercarriage only on a foam-covered runway. Repaired. Cvtd to 95-Seater by 1964/65. Withdrawn from svce 24 Jul 67 and stored at Miami, FL. Sold to Aviation Corporation of America 30 Sep 68 (TT: 39,657 hrs). Continued in storage, parts missing, until tfd to the George T Baker Aviation School at Miami, probably in 1971 or 1972. Derelict, sitting on tail by Sep 72 and partly burnt by Sep 73. Scrapped shortly afterwards.

4002 1049-53-67 Regd N6202C. Retained by LAC for type certification and development flying. LADD: 4 Apr 52 to Eastern Air Lines, FN 202. Cvtd to 1049-54 by mid-53 and to 1049/02-54 by mid-56. To 95-Seater by 1964/65. Withdrawn from svce 15 Feb 68 and stored at Opa Locka, FL. Sold to Aviation Corporation of America 30 Sep 68 but believed actually tfd Aug 68, (TT: 41,532 hrs). Sold to Donald L.Shepard Aircraft Leasing Co 31 Jul 69, and tfd to Donald L.Shepard 29 Dec 69. Sold Trans American Leasing Inc 21 Aug 70. Stored at West Palm Beach Intl, FL, by Apr 72. Sold to Hubert H Clements 31 Dec 72 and to James Ruscoe 25 Jan 73. Flown to Fort Lauderdale, FL, and repainted for the Happy Hours Air Travel Club in Apr 73, deld same month. Damaged beyond repair in forced-landing at Tamarac, FL, at 19:25 hrs (local) on 5 Aug 73. No injuries. En route Freeport, Bahamas to Fort Lauderdale via St. Petersburg, FL, and on approach to Fort Lauderdale, the aircraft suffered a partial power loss on all four engines due to fuel starvation, and a forced landing on open country was made. Cause: Improper transfer of fuel by crew, circuit breaker corroded and inadequate inspection of aircraft by maintenance personnel and crew. Aircraft subsequently scrapped on site.

4003 1049-53-67 26 Nov 51 to Eastern Air Lines as N6203C, FN 203. Flew New York-Newark to Miami Super Constellation inaugural 17 Dec 51. Cvtd to 1049-54 by mid-53 and to 1049/02-54 by mid-56. To 95-Seater by 1964/65. Withdrawn from svce 15 Feb 68 and stored at Opa Locka, FL. Sold to Aviation Corporation of America 30 Sep 68, (TT: 42,589 hrs). Sold to Donald L.Shepard Aircraft Leasing Co. Stored at West Palm Beach Intl by Dec 71. Condition deteriorated. By Jan 75, the radar had been removed from the nose and a small red maple leaf added to the aircraft's outer fins. Unconf report says sold to Downair Ltd for spares, but ntu. (Downair bankrupt spring 1975.) Still intact late Apr 75, but scrapped at West Palm Beach Intl shortly afterwards.

4004 1049-53-67 11 Dec 51 to Eastern Air Lines as N6204C, FN 204. Cvtd to 1049-54 by mid-53 and to 1049/02-54 by mid-56. To

95-Seater by 1964/65. Sold to International Aerodyne Inc on 3 May 67 after being stored at Miami, FL, since at least Dec 66. Broken up at Miami during May 67.

4005 1049-53-67 21 Dec 51 to Eastern Air Lines as N6205C, FN 205. Cvtd to 1049-54 by mid-53 and to 1049/02-54 by mid-56. Damaged at Atlanta, GA, 13 Jan 58. Repaired. To 95-Seater by 1964/65. Withdrawn from svce 18 Jan 68 and stored at Opa Locka, FL. Sold to Aviation Corporation of America 25 May 68 (TT: 42,135 hrs). Seized by Sheriff of Dade County 1969. Stored at Miami, FL from Oct 69 at least. Sold to Butler Aviation Miami Inc 22 Feb 71, but remained in storage. Sold to Bellomy Lawson Aviation Inc 30 Aug 74 on bankruptcy of previous owner. Derelict by 1975 and condition deteriorating. Miami Airport records give owner as 'Mr. Shepard' in Nov 75, but FAA have no mention. Scrapped at Miami 12 Mar 77-end Apr 77. Regn canx 22 Mar 77 at owner's request as 'scrapped'.

4006 1049-53-67 31 Dec 51 to Eastern Air Lines as N6206C, FN 206. Cvtd to 1049-54 by mid-53 and to 1049/02-54 by mid-56. To 95-Seater by 1964/65. Withdrawn from svce 18 Jan 68 and stored at Opa Locka, FL. Sold to Aviation Corporation of America 27 May 68 (TT: 41,886 hrs). Flying from Miami in red/green colour scheme from Aug 69. Stored at West Palm Beach Intl, FL, by Apr 72 and until at least Jul 74. Sold to Overseas Charter Intl, Panama Jan 75, but ntu. Flown to Fort Lauderdale, FL, by Feb 75 and named 'Nani'. Regn canx 7 May 75, and aircraft stored at Fort Lauderdale in good condition. Stripped down to bare metal and under overhaul during spring 1979. Restored to Hub Aviation Inc 6 Jul 79 as N6206C and sold to Aero Sacasa Inc on 26 Jul 79. Work almost completed when sale fell through and aircraft reverted to Hub Aviation Inc approx Oct 80. Sold for scrap for a reported $12,000, and scrapped at Fort Lauderdale between 14 Nov 80 and end of Dec 80, only bits left by Mar 81. Useable parts reclaimed and purchased by Aeroborne Enterprises.

4007 1049-53-67 8 Jan 52 to Eastern Air Lines as N6207C, FN 207. Cvtd to 1049-54 by mid-53 and to 1049/02-54 by mid-56. Damaged by fire on ground Atlanta, GA 15 Mar 54, en route Chicago-Miami. Repaired. To 95-Seater by 1964/65. Withdrawn from svce 15 Feb 68 and flown to Opa Locka, FL, for storage same day. Sold to Aviation Corporation of America 17 Apr 68 (TT: 41,126 hrs), but remained in storage at Opa Locka. Tfd to Air Fleets Intl 5 Jan 70 (believed not used). To Fort Lauderdale, FL, by Jul 72. Owned by Carolina Aircraft Corp (a/o Jul 72), but not in FAA file. In storage at Fort Lauderdale, sold to Aero Sacasa Inc 26 Nov 76, but remained in storage, with condition deteriorating, bad corrosion, etc. Sold to Hub Aviation Inc approx Oct 80. Sold for scrap same month for a reported $12,000, and scrapped at Fort Lauderdale between Nov 80 and 20 Dec 80, useable parts reclaimed and purchased by Aeroborne Enterprises. Officially sold to Bobby C.Rager 1 Dec 80 (for scrap).

4008 1049-53-67 21 Jan 52 to Eastern Air Lines as N6208C, FN 208. Cvtd to 1049-54 by mid-53 and to 1049/02-54 by mid-56. Slightly damaged Long Beach, CA 11 Sep 58. Repaired. To 95-Seater by 1964/65. Withdrawn from svce 18 Feb 67 and stored at Opa Locka, FL. Sold to Aviation Corporation of America 30 Sep 68 (TT: 39,543 hrs). Remained in storage at Opa Locka until scrapped there between Feb 72 and mid 73. USCAR shows 'Sale Reported' in Jul 73.

4009 1049-53-67 31 Jan 52 to Eastern Air Lines as N6209C, FN 209. Cvtd to 1049-54 by mid-53 and to 1049/02-54 by mid-56. To 95-Seater by 1964/65. Withdrawn from svce 18 Feb 67 and flown to Miami Intl for storage. Sold to Aviation Corporation of America 30 Sep 68 (TT: 39,776 hrs). Restored to use and painted in red/green trim by Apr 70. Stored at Boca Raton, FL, by Apr 72. Sold to James Ruscoe t/a Happy Hours Air Travel Club mid-73, but believed never flew for the company. Sold to Aerotours Dominicano C por A and deld ex-Fort Lauderdale 30 Jan 74 as HI-228. Damaged nose-wheel landing at St. Croix, VI 13 Mar 77. Repaired. Ban on carrying passengers by Dominican authorities Jan 78, but continued in use for cargo. (TT: 42,038 hrs a/o 23 Jan 80). Fitted with forward cargo door (from c/n 4536/HI-329) during Feb 82. Sold to Aero Chago SA by Nov 82, lsd to Aerotours (carried sticker 'Rentado a Aerotours'). Out of svce for periods from Nov 85. Withdrawn from use 1987 after mechanic inadvertently retracted the main gear on the ground at Las Americas Airport, Dominican Republic. Used for spares by Aero Chago from Jan 88, last reported Jan 91. Scrapped during early 1990s.

4010 1049-53-67 6 Feb 52 to Eastern Air Lines as N6210C, FN 210. cvtd to 1049-54 by mid-53 and to 1049/02-54 by mid-56. To 95-Seater by 1964/65. Withdrawn from svce 1 Dec 67 and flown to Miami Intl for storage. Sold to Aviation Corporation of America 30 Sep 68, believed actually tfd Aug 68, (TT: 41,661 hrs). Probably never flew again, but continued in storage at Miami. Derelict by May 72, condition deteriorated and believed scrapped at Miami late in 1974.

4011 1049-53-67 14 Feb 52 to Eastern Air Lines as N6211C, FN 211. Cvtd to 1049-54 by mid-53 and to 1049/02-54 by mid-56. To 95-Seater by 1964/65. Withdrawn from svce 4 Feb 68 and flown to Opa Locka, FL for storage. Sold to Aviation Corporation of America 30 Sep 68, believed actually tfd Aug 68, (TT: 41,493 hrs). Continued in storage at Opa Locka until scrapped during Mar 72.

4012 1049-53-67 20 Feb 52 to Eastern Air Lines as N6212C, FN 212. Cvtd to 1049-54 by mid-53 and to 1049/02-54 by mid-56. Lsd to Pan American (joint use with Eastern A/L) a/o Jun 57. Destroyed by fire on the ground at Miami Intl Airport, FL on 28 Jun 57. While Eastern Air Lines DC-7B (N808D) was being taxied to the gate, the pilot found the nose-wheel steering was ineffective. Propellers were reversed, but before the pilot could stop the DC-7B, the right wing struck the empennage of the parked Super Constellation. The DC-7B immediately swung to the right and the windshield struck the left wing of the Super Constellation, rupturing a fuel tank. Fuel spilled and immediately ignited, burning both aircraft. No injuries. Remains (complete forward fuselage, centre section and engines), still standing on undercarriage at Miami until 1958, then scrapped.

4013 1049-53-67 27 Feb 52 to Eastern Air Lines as N6213C, FN 213. Cvtd to 1049-54 by mid-53 and to 1049/02-54 by mid-56. Lsd

C/n 4007. A small plate that was affixed in the cockpit as an amendment to the original manufacturer's plate on the aircraft's conversion from a model 1049-53 to a 1049-54 with the fitting of updated engines.

N6212C 1049 Eastern Air Lines boards passengers at Miami Airport in 1952. A U S Airlines C-46 (N1912M) can be seen in the background. (Eastern Air Lines via John T Wible)

to Pan American Jun 55 named 'Clipper Climax' for brief period to allow Pan American to evaluate the 1049 Super Constellation against the DC-6B. Ret to Eastern Air Lines probably by 10 Nov 55. Lsd to Pan American again (joint use with Eastern A/L) a/o Jun 57. Received substantial damage during emergency landing on foam-covered runway at Idlewild Airport, New York, NY, at 22.30 hrs (EST) on 28 May 62. Aircraft was en route Washington, DC, to La Guardia-New York. Pilot was unable to lower the nosewheel and a visual inspection showed that the gear was hanging free. During the landing roll, the nose gear collapsed. No injuries. Cause: The bolt attaching the nose gear actuating cylinder piston rod to the nose gear drag strut was broken, caused probably by fatigue. Repaired and cvtd to 95-Seater by 1964/65. Withdrawn from svce and flown to Opa Locka, FL for storage 5 Feb 68. Sold to Aviation Corporation of America 30 Sep 68 (TT: 41,710 hrs). Remained in storage at Opa Locka until scrapped between Feb 71 and Feb 72.

4014 1049-53-67 8 Mar 52 to Eastern Air Lines as N6214C, FN 214. Received substantial damage landing at Chicago-Midway, IL, on 3 Mar 53 en route from Miami, FL. The aircraft made a bad approach and landed too far down the runway, bounced. After landing and during the landing roll, the entire landing gear retracted. No injuries. Undercarriage functioned normally on inspection after the accident. Cause: An improperly executed approach resulting in excessive speed to permit a normal landing. Repaired. Cvtd to 1049-54 by mid-53. Crashed and burned out during emergency landing at McChord AFB, Tacoma, WA 6 Sep 53, while on an interchange flight for Northwest Orient Airlines. No casualties. After take-off from Seattle-Tacoma at 02.06hrs (local), en route for Chicago, no.3 engine failed and the propeller feathered. This was followed by the shut down of no.4 engine. A GCA was made to McChord AFB as weather conditions there were more favourable, but on approach, the flaps could not be extended, and left undercarriage was not fully down. On touch-down, the nose gear and right main undercarriage collapsed as well as the left gear, the aircraft veered off the runway, tearing off the two port engines, and fire broke out. (TT: 4,509 hrs).

4015 1049-54-80 First flight Mar 52. Used by LAC for development flying at Burbank. LADD: 6 Aug 52 to Trans World as N6901C 'Star of the Thames', FN 901. Subsequently believed remained at Burbank for berth mods, with TWA dely date 8 Oct 52 (TT: 67 hrs). In svce 9 Oct 52. Badly damaged in wheels-up landing at 16.38 hrs (CST) on 17 Jan 59 at Olathe NAS, KS. No injuries. Aircraft was on Flight TW 125 from Washington, DC to Kansas City, MO via Indianapolis and St. Louis. On approach to St. Louis, the hydraulic system failed when the nosewheel was partially retracted, left gear jammed down and right gear retracted. Aircraft circled over St. Louis and then Kansas City for five hours. Leak in hydraulic system found and repaired temporarily with use of a one cent piece, and fluid topped up with mixture of coffee and water (!), enabling left main gear to be raised and a safe wheels-up landing on foam to be made. (TT: 17,706 hrs). Repaired. Sold to Airline Transport Carriers Inc dba California Hawaiian Airlines on lse-purchase agreement 28 Oct 60. Deld 14 Dec 60 (TT: 20,798 hrs), with official tf date 15 Dec 60. Reclaimed by Trans World at Los Angeles Intl due to default with payments 9 Apr 62, repossessed 26 Apr 62. Stored, probably at Mid-Continent Airport, Kansas City. Unconf lse to Modern Air Transport 1963. Sold to Florida State Tours Inc 22 Jun 63. Stored at Miami, FL, out of use by Nov 64, at which time had additional titling "BRT Special" & "Fun Special", until sale to Lineas Aereas Patagonicas Argentinas early in 1966. Crashed into sea southwest of Callao, Peru, 70 miles south of Lima, on 6 Mar 66, after one engine caught fire and two other engines had to be feathered. En route to Asuncion, Paraguay, on delivery flight with contraband aboard. One member of crew believed drowned.

4016 1049-54-80 21 May 52 to Trans World as N6902C 'Star of the Seine', FN 902. Remained at Burbank, CA, for berth mods & to Los Angeles, CA, 15 Aug 52. Used for pilot training, then in svce 10 Sep 52. Destroyed in mid-air collision with United Air Lines DC-7 (N6324C) at 10.31 hrs (PST) on 30 Jun 56 at about 21,000 feet over the Grand Canyon, AZ, killing all on board. Wreckage fell into the Canyon near the confluence of the Colorado and Little Colorado Rivers. (TT: 10,518 hrs). The Super Constellation was operating Flight TW 2 from Los Angeles to Kansas City. Initial impact occurred with the DC-7 moving from right to left, and the Super Constellation to the right and aft relative to the DC-7, with the left aileron tip striking the centre fin of the 1049. The lower surface of the DC-7 left wing then struck the upper aft fuselage of the Super Constellation with disintegrating force. This probably caused complete destruction of the 1049's aft fuselage and separation of the empennage. Probable cause: Failure of both flight crews to see one another in time, coupled with intervening clouds reducing time for visual separation and possibly preoccupation with giving passengers a more scenic view of the Grand Canyon area.

4017 1049-54-80 28 May 52 to Trans World as N6903C 'Star of the Tiber', FN 903. TWA dely date: 29 May 52. Remained at Burbank, CA, for berth mods and deld to Los Angeles, CA, 15 Aug 52. Used for pilot training, then in svce 10 Sep 52. Lsd to South Pacific Air Lines 1 Feb 60 and deld to Oakland, CA, same day (TT: 20,520 hrs). Modified for over-ocean use and painted by LAS,

SECTION 12: CONSTELLATION PRODUCTION LIST

Oakland, 15 Feb-28 Feb 60 (test-flight). In svce with South Pacific 2 Apr 60 named 'Bounty'. Sold to South Pacific 1 Jun 62. Withdrawn from use at Oakland, CA early in 1965. Scrapped during Oct 65, but fuselage section used with Trans-International Airlines for flight attendant evacuation training at Oakland until at least 1974. The fuselage section survived at Oakland out of use for a number of years & was last reported dumped there in Oct 99.

4018 1049-54-80 6 Jun 52 to Trans World as N6904C 'Star of the Ganges', FN 904. Remained at Burbank, CA, for berth mods and deld to Los Angeles, CA, 27 Aug 52. Used for maintenance training, then in svce 10 Sep 52. Received substantial damage in emergency landing at approx 18.53 (PST) on 7 Dec 52 at Fallon, NV. While cruising, no.3 engine failed, followed shortly afterwards by no.4 engine. During the landing at Fallon, the emergency braking system was not properly utilized and the crew had neither nose-wheel steering nor brakes during the landing. The aircraft veered off the runway, ran through a ditch and several piles of gravel and the starboard wing and undercarriage were torn from the fuselage. No injuries. (TT: 700 hrs). Cause: Improper use of the emergency braking system during the emergency landing necessitated by complete loss of power on nos.3 & 4 engines. The engine failure was caused by the failure of the teeth of the intermediate gears of both front cam gear trains. Because both engines lost were on the same side of the aircraft, the hydraulics on that side were also lost. After this accident, a switch valve was introduced making crossover feed of the hydraulics possible. Aircraft repaired by LAS at Fallon and ferried to Fairfax, KS on 10 Sep 53. Re-entered svce 24 Sep 53. Lsd to World Wide Airlines approx Sep 60, and possibly also to Modern Air Transport same year. Out of svce by Jun 61 and stored, probably at Mid-Continent Airport, Kansas City, MO, until lsd to South Pacific Air Lines on 7 Jun 62 (TT: 18,408 hrs). Repossessed by Trans World due to non-completion of payments at San Francisco, CA 29 Jan 64. Sold to Florida State Tours Inc 7 Aug 64 and deld to Miami, FL. Stored there in ex-South Pacific colours and "BRT Special" titling by Oct 64, derelict by May 68, and presumably scrapped shortly afterwards. (Last report Jul 68).

4019 1049-54-80 31 Jul 52 to Trans World as N6905C ' Star of the Rhone,' FN 905. TWA dely date 1 Oct 52 at Burbank: (TT: 33hrs), so presumably the aircraft had been at Burbank for berth mods and/or some test flying. In svce 2 Oct 52. To LAC at Burbank 23 Apr 54 for soundproofing tests and spinner afterbodies tests. Spinner afterbodies later installed as standard on the 1049-54. Ret to Trans World 1 Jul 54. Deld to Burbank for lease-purchase by Airline Transport Carriers Inc t/a California Hawaiian Airlines 6 Jan 60 (TT: 18,932 hrs). Officially tfd 11 Jun 60. This aircraft made the first transatlantic crossing by a 1049-53/54 Super Constellation, while with CHA early in Jun 60. Reclaimed by Trans World at New York-La Guardia 9 Apr 62 due to default of payments, and repossessed 7 May 62. Stored at Mid-Continent Airport, Kansas City, MO. Sold to Florida State Tours Inc 7 Aug 64, but aircraft never left Kansas City, and scrapped there approx Dec 64.

4020 1049-54-80 16 Jul 52 to Trans World as N6906C 'Star of the Rhine', FN 906. Remained at Burbank, CA, for berth mods until 13 Sep 52, then deld to Los Angeles same day, in svce 27 Sep 52. Withdrawn from svce 29 Sep 59 (TT: 19,812 hrs) and stored at Mid-Continent Airport, Kansas City, MO. Sold to California Airmotive 15 Feb 60 and deld same day to Burbank, CA, for overhaul by Flying Tiger Line. Deld 1 Apr 60. Lsd World Wide Airlines 17 Jun 60 to 17 Nov 60, lsd General Airways 21 Nov 60 to 23 Mar 61, lsd Paul Mantz Air Service 23 Mar 61 to 20 Apr 61, later Paramount Airlines (given as still current with them in Jul 61 fleet list). Lsd to Modern Air Transport briefly during 1961, and lsd to Admiral Airways by Nov 61. Lsd to California Hawaiian late 1961 until mid-62 approx, then stored at Long Beach, CA. Lsd to Standard Airways by Aug 63, and ret to California Airmotive 2 Jan 64, sold to Pasco-Aviation Inc 25 Aug 64, and to Henry J Heuer 31 Aug 64. Sold to Allied Leasing Corp 3 Mar 66, lsd to Hamm's Brewery for several short periods. Painted in Aeronaves de Panama colours at Miami, FL for a few days during Mar 66, but sale fell through. Used by Passaat Airlines (H J Heuer company) and in svce by Aug 66 until stored in Passaat titling at Miami by May 68. Sold to Pinellas Central Bank & Trust Co 17 Apr 68. Sold to Flying W Airways 18 Mar 69 and to William H Conrad 25 Aug 69. Sold to Jose A Balboa 5 Sep 69 and to Roy Renderer 6 Aug 70. Lsd to Santiago Sablon in Oct 71. Suffered hydraulic failure at Teterboro, NJ during Mar 72 after sale to Vortex Inc on 2 Feb 72, although still op by Jose Balboa. Repaired. Sold to Aircraft Airframe Inc 15 Dec 72 and lsd back to Vortex Inc in 1973. Substantially damaged at Miami International Airport on 3 Apr 73 when hydraulic pressure was too low while taxying to the ramp. Starboard undercarriage collapsed while being positioned into a parking space by the use of reverse thrust, damaging wing and propellers. Downlock assembly on the starboard undercarriage had been wrongly adjusted. Stored at Miami in damaged condition until broken up during 1974. Canx USCAR 7 May 75.

4021 1049-54-80 11 Aug 52 to Trans World as N6907C 'Star of Sicily', FN 907. Presumably remained at Burbank, CA, for berth mods, as TWA dely date is 16 Oct 52, in svce 18 Oct 52. Collided with United Air Lines DC-8 (N8013U) over Miller Fld, Staten Island, NY at 10.33 hrs (EST) on 16 Dec 60, killing all on board. The Super Constellation, en route Dayton, OH to La Guardia, NY on Flight TW 266 was under IFR descending to La Guardia, the DC-8 under IFR descending to New York Intl. Weather was overcast with poor visibility, light rain and fog. Cause: The DC-8 proceeded beyond its clearance limit to the Preston intersection by approx 11 miles and hit the Super Constellation at 90 degree converging tracks - the no.4 engine of the DC-8 was found embedded in the 1049's cockpit after the accident. A contributing factor was the high rate of speed (301 kts) of the DC-8 as it approached the intersection. The Super Constellation fell on to Miller Fld and surrounding area. (TT: 21,554 hrs).

4022 1049-54-80 25 Jul 52 to Trans World as N6908C 'Star of Britain', FN 908. Presumably remained at Burbank,,CA, for berth mods, as TWA dely date is 24 Sep 52, in svce 27 Sep 52. Withdrawn from use 31 Dec 60 (TT: 21,920 hrs) and stored at Mid-Continent Airport, Kansas City, MO. Sold to Florida State Tours Inc 7 Aug 64 under the condition the aircraft be removed within 90 days. Never deld and aircraft broken up at Mid-Continent in about Dec 64.

4023 1049-54-80 5 Sep 52 to Trans World as N6909C 'Star of Tipperary', FN 909. Remained at Burbank, CA, for berth mods until 22 Oct 52, deld to Los Angeles same day, in svce 26 Oct 52. Withdrawn from use 30 Dec 60 (TT: 21,328 hrs) and stored at Mid-Continent Airport, Kansas City, MO. Sold to Florida State Tours Inc 7 Aug 64 under the condition the aircraft be removed within 90 days. Never deld and aircraft broken up at Mid-Continent in about Dec 64.

4024 1049-54-80 22 Sep 52 to Trans World as N6910C 'Star of Frankfurt', FN 910. Remained at Burbank, CA, for berth mods until 31 Oct 52, deld to Los Angeles same day, in svce 3 Nov 52. Withdrawn from use 31 Dec 60 (TT: 22,264 hrs) and stored at Mid-Continent Airport, Kansas City, MO. Sold to Florida State Tours Inc 7 Aug 64 under the condition the aircraft be removed within 90 days. Never deld and aircraft broken up at Mid-Continent in about Dec 64.

4025 to 4100 not used.

4101 R7V-l/1049B-55-75 5 Nov 52 to U S Navy as 128434. R & D Burbank Nov 52. To MATS VR-7 Hickam 7 Mar 55. To Dallas (R & D) 30 Dec 55. Ret to VR-7 Hickam 13 Mar 56. To VR-7 Moffett 30 Jul 57. Struck off 15 Jun 58 (TT: 3,994 hrs). Tfd to U S Air Force as C-121G 54-4048 Jun 58 MATS WESTAF 'City of Calcutta'. Assigned to 8th TS Moffett 1 Jul 58. To Wyoming ANG 187th AMS Cheyenne 1 Aug 63 'City of Rock Springs'. To 153rd TG Cheyenne 7 Feb 64, 153rd MAG Cheyenne 2 Feb 66, 153rd AEA Gp Cheyenne 17 Oct 68. To MASDC Davis Monthan for storage 7 Mar 72. For sale by DofD (Davis Monthan) 30 Oct

74 (TT: 16,424 hrs). Sold to Helitec Inc 7 Jan 75. Scrapped, subsequent to Jan 79. NB. This aircraft reportedly started production as a Model 749A, with the fuselage lengthened on the production line. Subsequently used for test and certification purposes prior to acceptance by Navy; aircraft had 749A wings.

4102 R7V-l/1049B-55-75 23 Jun 53 to U S Navy as 128435. To MATS VR-8 Hickam 10 Sep 53. To MATS VR-7 Hickam 27 Apr 55. To NAS NART Spokane 31 Aug 55. To VR-8 Hickam I Oct 55. To VR-8 Moffett 7 Dec 57. Struck off 15 Jun 58 (TT: 4,949 hrs). Tfd to U S Air Force as C-121G 54-4049 Jun 58 MATS WESTAF 'City of Los Altos'. Assigned to 8th TS Moffett 1 Jul 58, 4406th MTC Wg Moffett 13 Jan 63, ret 8th TS Moffett 2 Jun 63. To Pennsylvania ANG 171st TG Greater Pittsburgh 16 Feb 64. To 171st MAG Gr Pittsburgh 1 Jan 66. To 171st AEA Gp Gr Pittsburgh 17 Feb 68, 375th AEA Wg (171st AAG) Scott 13 May 68. Ret 171st AEA Wg Gr Pittsburgh 11 Dec 68. To 553rd Recon Wg Korat 12 Feb 69. Ret 171st AEA Wg Gr Pittsburgh 2 Feb 70. To 171st ARF Gp Gr Pittsburgh 5 Oct 72. To MASDC Davis Monthan for storage 7 Oct 72, arr 8 Oct 72. For sale by DofD Davis Monthan 23 Mar 77 (TT: 17,932 hrs). Sold to Delcon 5 Apr 78. Scrapped shortly after.

4103 R7V-l/1049B-55-75 4 Dec 52 to U S Navy as 128436. R & D Burbank 5 Dec 52. To VR-1 LANT Patuxent 23 Sep 53 coded RP-436 'Scorpius'. To VR-8 MATS Hickam 29 Sep 54. To Dallas (R & D) 29 Feb 56. To VR-8 Hickam 25 Apr 56. To VR-8 Moffett 17 Sep 57. Struck off 15 Jun 58 (TT: 4,962 hrs). Tfd to U S Air Force as C-121G 54-4050 Jun 58 MATS WESTAF 'City of Karachi'. Assigned to 8th TS Moffett 1 Jul 58. To Wyoming ANG 187th AMS Cheyenne 29 Oct 63 'City of Sundance'. To 153rd TG Cheyenne 7 Feb 64, 153rd MAG Cheyenne 2 Feb 66. To MASDC Davis Monthan 12 May 67. Assigned 552nd AEW Wg McClellan 17 Oct 68. To MASDC Davis Monthan 29 Apr 71 for storage. Ret to 552nd AEW Wg 21 Sep 71. To Davis Monthan again 12 Mar 73, arr 13 Mar 73. For sale by DofD Davis Monthan 23 Mar 77 (TT: 18,697 hrs). Sold to Delcon 4 Apr 78. Scrapped shortly after.

4104 R7V-l/1049B-55-75 23 Dec 52 to U S Navy as 128437. VR-l LANT Patuxent 6 Mar 53 coded RP-437 'Polaris'. To VW-ll Patuxent 1 Aug 55. To VW-15 Patuxent 25 Nov 55. To AEW MATRON 2 Barbers Point 19 Oct 56. To VW-3 Agana 8 Dec 56. (TT: 2,780 hrs a/o 28 Feb 57). To VW-l Barbers Point 25 May 57. To AIR BARSRON 2 Barbers Point 27 Jun 57. To VW-11 Argentia 1 Sep 57. To VW-11 Patuxent 1 Dec 57. Crashed on training flight at Patuxent River, MD, at 08.30 on 14 Jan 58. Aircraft was being used to practise ILS landings & crashed on attempted instrument landing in fog & drizzle, missed runway & hit trees. Destroyed by fire after impact. All crew killed. Struck off 17 Jan 58 (TT: not given).

4105 R7V-l/1049B-55-75 24 Dec 52 to U S Navy as 128438. VR-8 MATS Hickam 10 Mar 53. To VR-8 Hickam 1 Oct 55. To VR-8 Moffett 26 Aug 57. Struck off 15 Jun 58 (TT: 5,456 hrs). Tfd to U S Air Force as C-121G 54-4051 Jun 58 MATS WESTAF 'City of Saigon'. Assigned to 8th TS Moffett 1 Jul 58, 4406th MTC Wg Moffett 12 Jan 62. Ret 8th TS Moffett 31 Jul 62. To West Virginia ANG 167th AMS Martinsburg 14 Nov 63. To 167th ATG Martinsburg 31 Dec 64, 167th MAG Martinsburg 2 Feb 66. To 551st AEW Wg Otis 21 Jul 67, tfd 552nd AEW Wg McClellan 27 Nov 67. Reptd to PAC AF 1970, but not in records. To MASDC Davis Monthan for storage 30 Jun 75. For sale by DofD (Davis Monthan) 7 Jun 78 (TT: 22,687 hrs). Sold to Southwestern Alloys 15 May 79. Scrapped shortly after.

4106 R7V-l/1049B-55-75 24 Jan 53 to U S Navy as 128439. To VR-8 MATS Hickam 6 Oct 53. To VR-8 Hickam 1 Oct 55. To VR-8 Moffett 17 Sep 57. Struck off 15 Jun 58 (TT: 5,333 hrs). Tfd to U S Air Force as C-121G 54-4052 Jun 58 MATS WESTAF 'City of Sunnyvale'. Assigned to 8th TS Moffett 1 Jul 58, 4406th MTC Wg Moffett 30 Jun 62. Ret 8th TS Moffett 17 Jun 62. To New Jersey ANG 150th AMS Newark 22 Nov 63. To 170th ATG Newark 18 Jan 64, 170th MAG McGuire 1 Jan 66. To 551st AEW Wg Otis 17 Mar 67, deployed McClellan 18 Nov 67. To 552nd AEW Wg McClellan 15 Jan 68, assigned 966th AEW Sq McCoy 2 Dec 68. Ret 552nd AEW Wg McClellan 13 Dec 68, to 966th AEW Sq 12 Feb 69, ret 552nd AEW Wg McClellan 7 Mar 69. Assigned AFRES 915th AEW Gp Homestead 2 Dec 76, to 79th AEW Sq Homestead 14 Nov 77. To MASDC Davis Monthan 10 Oct 78, arr 11 Oct 78 for storage. For sale by DofD (Davis Monthan) 15 Aug 84 (TT: 23,761 hrs), & again 20 Aug 85, poor condition. Sold to unknown dealer & scrapped.

4107 R7V-l/1049B-55-75 13 May 53 to U S Navy as 128440. To VR-l LANT Patuxent 14 May 53. Written-off in accident at Chestertown, MD, 7 Jul 53. Crashed on test flight when split flap condition was experienced (left flap retracted, right 97% extended). Aircraft's tail reportedly broke off in flight. Was flying from NATC at Patuxent. Struck off Jul 53 (TT: 215 hrs).

4108 R7V-l/1049B-55-75 23 May 53 to U S Navy as 128441. To VR-l LANT Patuxent 28 May 53. Missing, presumed crashed, in Atlantic Ocean 30 Oct 54 en route Patuxent, MD, to Port Lyautey, North Africa, via the Azores. Aircraft took off at 21.39 hrs (local) and last message received at 23.00 hrs, at which time the aircraft was 350 miles off the U S East Coast. No report received at 24.00 hrs. Large-scale search made by air and sea from 01.00 hrs on 31 Oct 54 until 15.00 hrs 3 Nov 54, and again on 6 Nov 54, from Bermuda to the Azores and on to the Mediterranean, but no trace was ever found of the aircraft or the 42 persons on board. The aircraft was on a scheduled Fleet Logistics Wing service, and probably crashed between Bermuda and the Azores late on 30 Oct 54. Struck off 31 Oct 54. (TT: 1,373 hrs).

4109 R7V-l/1049B-55-75 14 Jun 53 to U S Navy as 128442. To VR-8 MATS Hickam 15 Jun 53. To VR-8 Hickam 1 Oct 55. To VR-8 Moffett 16 Jan 58. (Report of use by North Island NAS not confirmed by Naval records). Struck off 15 Jun 58 (TT: 5,264 hrs). Tfd to U S Air Force as C-121G 54-4061 Jun 58 MATS WESTAF 'City of Bangkok'. Assigned to 8th TS Moffett 1 Jul 58. In use in support of "Operation Deep Freeze" Mar 59. To 4406th MTC Sq Moffett 4 Jan 62, ret 8th TS Moffett 31 Jul 62. To Pennsylvania ANG 147th AMS Gr Pittsburgh 30 Oct 63. To 171st TG Gr Pittsburgh 16 Feb 64, 171st MAG Gr Pittsburgh 1 Jan 66. To 171st AEA Gp Gr Pittsburgh 18 Feb 68. Assigned 375th AEA Wg Scott 12 May 68, ret to 171st AEA Gp Gr Pittsburgh 11 Dec 68. To MASDC Davis Monthan for storage 6 Sep 72, arr 7 Sep 72. For sale by DofD (Davis Monthan) 23 Mar 77 (TT: 18,590 hrs). Sold to Delcon 4 Apr 78. Scrapped shortly after.

4110 R7V-l/1049B-55-75 28 Jun 53 to U S Navy as 128443. To Pool BAR M&S Burbank 28 Jun 53. To VR-l LANT Patuxent coded RP-443 29 Jun 53. To VW-11 Patuxent 1 Aug 55, tfd VW-13 Patuxent 22 Feb 56. To AEW MATRON 2 Barbers Pt 6 Oct 56, VR-7 Hickam 30 May 57, tfd VR-7 Moffett 19 Aug 57. To AIRBARSRON 2 Barbers Pt 10 Sep 57, AEWBARRONPAC Barbers Pt 17 May 60. To VP-31 San Diego 14 Jun 61, VP-31 North Island 26 Feb 62. Redesignated C-121J 1 Nov 62. To COM NAV AIR PAC by 1963 (North Island), coded RP (op by VP-31 San Diego). Named in Japanese 'zinsoku Seishuku goka' ('Swift, Quiet, Graceful') from same period. To VC- 121J. Tfd NAS North Island 4 Feb 67 until 14 Sep 71. To MASDC Davis Monthan 14 Sep 71. Struck off (Davis Monthan) 31 Jan 72 (TT: 11,448 hrs). For sale by DofD 23 Mar 77 (TT: 11,450 hrs). Sold to Delcon 9 Feb 78. Scrapped shortly after.

4111 R7V-l/1049B-55-75 25 Jun 53 to U S Navy as 128444. To Pool BAR M&S Burbank 25 Jun 53. To VR-l LANT Patuxent 'Cygnus' coded RP-444 2 Oct 53. To VW-13 Patuxent 21 Jun 56, VW-14 Barbers Pt 2 Jul 56. Tfd AEW MATRON 2 Barbers Pt 26 Feb 57, AIR BARSRON 2 Barbers Pt 6 Jun 57. To VW-15 Patuxent Jun 57, tfd VW-15 Argentia 11 Dec 57, ret VW-11 Patuxent 9 Jan 58. Tfd VW-11 Argentia 12 May 58, ret VW-15 Patuxent 13 May 58. To VW-11 Argentia 26 Jul 58 & to AEWTRAUNIT Patuxent 31 Mar 60, renamed AEWTULANT. Redes- ignated C-121J 30 Nov 62. Coded MM-8. To OASU Patuxent Aug 65 and arr Andrews AFB 25 Aug 65. To LAS New York for conversion to NC-121J for "Project Jenny" Nov 65. 'Blue

Eagles II'. To VX-8, Det Jenny, Saigon, Jul 67 coded JB-444. TT: (a/o 4 Mar 68:8,592 hrs). To VXN-8, Det Jenny, Saigon (after rework) again 4 Mar 68 until 2 Mar 69. To VXN-8 Patuxent 2 Mar 69. To LAS New York 6 Jun 69 for upgrading. Ret VXN-8 Det West Pacific 11 May 70. Ret VXN-8 Patuxent 3 Oct 70. To MASDC Davis Monthan for storage 27 Jan 71. Struck off (Davis Monthan) 25 May 71 (TT: 10,869 hrs). Reclaimed for parts 1972-74. Sold to Sun Valley Aviation 25 May 76. Scrapped shortly after.

4112 Laid down as R7V-l/1049B-55. Mod on production line to carry radomes as 1049B-55-84 and cvtd to RC-121C for U S Air Force by LAS. LADD: 31 Dec 53 to U S Air Force as 51-3836. Acc 27 Sep 54, del 8 Oct 54. To 4701 AEW Sq McClellan 10 Oct 54, assigned 8th AD, ADC, McClellan 22 Dec 54. To 552nd AEW Wg McClellan 16 Jun 55. Redes TC-121C 27 Jul 58 (radomes removed by LAS). To 551st AEW Wg Otis 30 May 67, ret 552nd AEW Wg McClellan 26 Jun 67. To MASDC Davis Monthan 19 Jan 68. Dismantled by 1970. For sale by DofD (Davis Monthan) 17 Jun 71 (TT: 13,202 hrs). Scrapped.

4113 Laid down as R7V-l/1049B-55. Mod on production line to carry radomes as 1049B-55-84 and cvtd to RC-121C for U S Air Force by LAS. LADD: 26 Jan 53 to U S Air Force as 51-3837. Acc 28 Oct 54, del 15 Nov 54 to 4701 AEW Sq McClellan. To 8th Air Division, ADC, McClellan 22 Dec 54, 552nd AEW Wg McClellan 15 Jul 55. Redes EC-121C 10 Jan 56, ret RC-121C 15 Dec 56. To AMC Tinker 22 Mar 57, ret 552nd McClellan 11 Apr 57. To AMC Ontario 30 Dec 57 & Ontario/Downey AMC during 1958. Cvtd to JRC-121C Downey 25 Nov 58. To Downey/Idlewild/Davis, MO) AMC 1959-60. To TAC Langley 4440th AD Gp 6 Mar 61, AMC Idlewild 8 Mar 61 (radomes removed by LAS). Bailed to IBM, Binghamton 1961. To Systems Cmd 21 Mar 62, cvtd JC-121C Ontario 1 Mar 63 and AFSC Wright-Patterson 1 Apr 63. To Logistics Cmd Middletown 2 Dec 63, AFSC Wright-Patterson 8 Apr 64, Logistics Cmd Olmstead 21 Sep 64, ret AFSC Wright-Patterson 20 Feb 65, mod to "Project Leap Frog" aircraft. To MASDC Davis Monthan 8 Sep 69, dismantled by 1970. For sale by DofD (Davis Monthan) 17 Jun 71 (TT: 4,294 hrs). Scrapped.

4114 Laid down as R7V-l/1049B-55. Mod on production line to carry radomes as 1049B-55-84 and cvtd to RC-121C for U S Air Force by LAS. LADD: 27 Feb 53 to U S Air Force as 51-3838. Acc & del 20 Nov 53. Del to 4701 AEW Sq McClellan 21 Dec 53. Crashed into 5 ft of water San Pablo Bay, near San Francisco, CA at night 5 Feb 54. Was returning from flight over the Sierra Nevada Mountains & was attempting a GCA landing at McClellan AFB, CA. No casualties. Aircraft was salvaged, assigned 566th Air Defense Gp, ADC, Hamilton 8 Feb 54, AMC 10 Feb 54, but struck off 31 May 54.

4115 Laid down as R7V-l/1049B-55. Mod on production line to carry radomes as 1049B-55-84 and cvtd to RC-121C for U S Air Force by LAS. LADD: 27 Mar 53 to U S Air Force as 51-3839. Acc & del 28 Dec 53. Del to 4701 AEW Sq McClellan 28 Dec 53, assigned 8th AD, ADC, McClellan 8 Feb 54. To 552nd AEW Wg McClellan 16 Jul 55. Redes EC-121C 10 Jan 56, ret RC-121C 15 Dec 56. To TC-121C 28 Jul 57 (radomes removed by LAS). To 551st AEW Wg Otis 30 May 67, ret 552nd AEW Wg McClellan 19 Jun 67. To MASDC Davis Monthan 22 Jan 68, dismantled by 1970. For sale by DofD (Davis Monthan) 17 Jun 71 (TT: 12,983 hrs). Scrapped.

4116 Laid down as R7V-l/1049B-55. Mod on production line to carry radomes as 1049B-55-84 and cvtd to RC-121C for U S Air Force by LAS. LADD: 24 Apr 53 to U S Air Force as 51-3840. Acc & del 5 May 54. Del to 4701 AEW Sq McClellan 5 May 54, assigned 8th Air Division, ADC, McClellan 22 Dec 54. To 552nd AEW Wg McClellan 16 Jul 55. To 551st AEW Wg Otis 13 May 56, redes TC-121C 20 Jul 58 (radomes removed by LAS). Ret to 552nd AEW Wg McClellan 8 Aug 67. To MASDC Davis Monthan 21 Nov 67, but ret to 552nd AEW Wg McClellan 16 Dec 67. To MASDC Davis Monthan 22 Jan 68 & dismantled Nov-Dec 69. For sale by DofD (Davis Monthan) 17 Jun 71 (TT: 10,963 hrs). Scrapped.

4117 Laid down as R7V-l/1049B-55. Mod on production line to carry radomes as 1049B-55-84 and cvtd to RC-121C for U S Air Force by LAS. LADD: 12 May 53 to U S Air Force as 51-3841. Acc & del 10 May 54. Del to 4701 AEW Sq McClellan 10 May 54, assigned 8th Air Division, ADC, McClellan 22 Dec 54. To 552nd AEW Wg McClellan 16 Jul 55. Redes EC-121C 10 Jun 56, ret RC-121C 15 Dec 56. Assigned AMC Schenectady 22 Nov 57, but arr already at General Electric Schenectady FTC mid-57. Mod to prepare the acft for Atlas flight tests. All AEW eqpt removed, belly radome removed, upper radome removed, cut down to size & relocated in belly posn. Test installations completed early 58. Redes JC-121C 11 Oct 58, with upper fuselage extension and additional camera portholes (as c/n 4464). Used in Florida on Atlantic Missile Range tests & as far south as San Salvador (Bahamas) & other islands in Caribbean. Subsequently used nr Omaha, NE (based at Offutt) & at Vandenberg AFB, CA for Atlas project & other Pacific Missile Range projects (based at Santa Barbara) Officially tf to Norton 2 Dec 60, assigned Logistics Cmd, Ontario 11 Jun 61, then after completion of missile tests late 1963, to AFSC Wright Patterson 12 Dec 66 & AFSC St Louis 30 Oct 67. To MASDC Davis Monthan 25 Jul 68, and dismantled by 1970. For sale by DofD (Davis Monthan) 17 Jun 71 (TT: 7,504 hrs). Scrapped.

4118 Laid down as R7V-l/1049B-55. Mod on production line to carry radomes as 1049B-55-84 and cvtd to RC-121C for U S Air Force by LAS. LADD: 15 May 53 to U S Air Force as 51-3842. Acc 28 May 54, del 3 Jun 54. Del to 4701 AEW Sq McClellan 3 Jun 54, assigned 8th Air Division, ADC, McClellan 12 Dec 54. To 552nd AEW Wg McClellan 16 Jul 55. Redes EC-121C 9 Feb 56, ret RC-121C 8 Oct 56.To 551st AEW Wg Otis 31 Oct 56, redes TC-121C 27 Jul 58 (radomes removed by LAS). To 7310 Support Gp, AF Europe, Rhein-Main 29 Jul 59.To AMC McClellan 7 Sep 59. Crashed into a swamp in the Butte Sink area, near Marysville, CA 22 Mar 61, while on a test flight from McClellan AFB. Crew killed, cause of accident unknown.

4119 Laid down as R7V-l/1049B-55. Mod on production line to carry radomes as 1049B-55-84 and cvtd to RC-121C for U S Air Force by LAS. LADD: 25 May 53 to U S Air Force as 51-3843. Acc & del 10 Jun 54, but del to 4701 AEW Sq McClellan 9 Jun 54, assigned 8th Air Division, ADC, McClellan 22 Dec 54. To 552nd AEW Wg McClellan 16 Jul 55. Redes EC-121C 10 Jan 56, ret RC-121C 15 Dec 56. To 551st AEW Wg Otis 13 May 56, redes TC-121C 27 Jul 58 (radomes removed by LAS). Reported as "RC-121Q" (Prestwick 1964). To MASDC Davis Monthan 22 Jan 68. Dismantled by Dec 68. For sale by DofD (Davis Monthan) 17 Jun 71 (TT: not given). Scrapped.

4120 Laid down as R7V-l/1049B-55. Mod on production line to carry radomes as 1049B-55-84 and cvtd to RC-121C for U S Air Force by LAS. LADD: 3 Jun 53 to U S Air Force as 51-3844. Acc & del 30 Jun 54. Del to 4701 AEW Sq McClellan 30 Jun 54, assigned 8th Air Division, ADC, McClellan 22 Dec 54. To 552nd AEW Wg McClellan 16 Jul 55. Redes EC-121C 10 Jan 56, ret RC-121C 15 Dec 56, redes TC-121C 8 Feb 58 (radomes removed by LAS). To MASDC Davis Monthan 31 Jan 68. Dismantled by Nov 69. For sale by DofD (Davis Monthan) 17 Jun 71 (TT: 12,620 hrs). Scrapped.

4121 Laid down as R7V-l/1049B-55. Mod on production line to carry radomes as 1049B-55-84 and cvtd to RC-121C for U S Air Force by LAS. LADD: 14 Jul 53 to U S Air Force as 51-3845. Acc & del 12 Jul 54, but del to 4701 AEW Sq McClellan 9 Jul 54, assigned 8th Air Division ADC, McClellan 22 Dec 54. To 552nd AEW Wg McClellan 16 Jul 55. Redes EC-121C 10 Jan 55, ret RC-121C 17 Dec 55. To 551st AEW Wg Otis 4 Mar 56. Redes TC-121C 10 Jan 58 (radomes removed by LAS). Ret RC-121C 1 Sep 64 & TC-121C 24 Feb 65. Ret 552nd AEW Wg McClellan 22 Aug 67. To MASDC Davis Monthan 22 Jan 68 (mispainted as 0-03845). Dismantled by Nov 69. For sale by DofD (Davis Monthan) 17 Jun 71 (TT: 9,646 hrs). Scrapped.

4122 R7V-l/1049B-55-75 23 Jun 53 to U S Navy as 131621. To VR-8 MATS Hickam 15 Oct 53. To VR-8 Hickam 1 Oct 55. To

Dallas (R & D) 29 Feb 56. Ret to Hickam VR-8 8 Apr 56. To VR-7 Hickam 9 Apr 56. To VR-8 Hickam 11 Jul 56. To VR-8 Moffett 6 Sep 57. Struck off 15 Jun 58 (TT: 6,209 hrs). Tfd to U S Air Force as C-121G 54-4053 MATS WESTAF 'City of Agana'. Assigned to 8th TS Moffett 1 Jul 58, to 4406th MTC Wg Moffett 1 Feb 62, ret 8th TS Moffett 30 Jun 62. To Wyoming ANG 187th AMS Cheyenne 7 Nov 63 'City of Agonic'. Renamed 'City of Casper'. To 153rd TG Cheyenne 10 Mar 64, 153rd MAG Cheyenne 2 Feb 66.To 153rd AEA Gp Cheyenne 17 Oct 68. To MASDC Davis Monthan 28 Apr 72, arr 29 Apr 72. For sale by DofD (Davis Monthan) 30 Oct 74. Sold to Allied Aircraft 31 Dec 74. Scrapped, subsequent to Jan 79.

4123 R7V-l/1049B-55-75 23 Jun 53 to U S Navy as 131622. To VR-8 MATS Hickam 7 Oct 53. To VR-8 Hickam 1 Nov 55. To VR-8 Moffett 10 Sep 57. Struck off 15 Jun 58 (TT: 6,185 hrs). Tfd to U S Air Force as C-l21G 54-4054 MATS WESTAF 'City of Berkeley'. Assigned to 8th TS Moffett 1 Jul 58, to 4406th MTC Wg Moffett 17 Jan 62, ret 8th TS Moffett 31 Jul 62. To Wyoming ANG 187th AMS Cheyenne 13 Nov 63 'City of Cody'. To 153rd TG Cheyenne 7 Feb 64, 153rd MAG Cheyenne 2 Feb 66. To 153rd AEA Gp 17 Oct 68. To MASDC Davis Monthan 6 May 72. For sale by DofD (Davis Monthan) 30 Oct 74 (TT: 18,390 hrs). Sold to unknown scrap dealer. Scrapped, subsequent to Jan 79.

4124 R7V-l/1049B-55-75 8 May 53 to U S Navy as 131623. To BAR M&S Burbank 8 May 53. To VR-l LANT Patuxent 16 Oct 53, coded RP-623 'Aquila'. To VW-11 Patuxent 1 Aug 55, VW-13 Patuxent 8 Nov 55, VW-15 Patuxent 19 Jul 56. To VW-14 Barbers Pt 30 Jul 56, tfd AEW MATRON 2 Barbers Pt 26 Feb 57, AIR BARSRON 2 Barbers Pt 10 Sep 57, coded SH-65. To AEWBARRONPAC Barbers Pt 31 May 60. Redes C-121J 30 Nov 62. Tfd to AFASDG ADMCS Tucson (i.e. Davis Monthan) for storage 18 May 65. To NATTC Memphis 1966 until 27 Nov 67. To LAS New York 27 Nov 67 for painting and rework for Blue Angels (aerobatic team support aircraft). To NABTC Pensacola 6 Mar 68 'Blue Angels 8'. To MASDC Davis Monthan for storage 7 Dec 70. Struck off (Davis Monthan) 31 Jan 72 (TT: 10,245 hrs). For sale by DofD 23 Mar 77. Sold to Delcon 10 Feb 78. Scrapped shortly after.

4125 R7V-l/1049B-55-75 8 May 53 to U S Navy as 131624. To BAR M&S Burbank 8 May 53. To VR-8 MATS Hickam 27 Oct 53, VR-8 Hickam 1 Oct 55, & to VR-8 Moffett 17 Sep 57. To BAR FA Ontario for mods. Tfd to COM AIR LANT (VX-6 Quonset Point) 20 Aug 58 for Antarctic Operations, coded JD 'Phoenix'. Used on "Operation Deep Freeze" annually, and stationed at Wigram, New Zealand each summer from approx Sep to Mar. First visit New Zealand 20 Sep 58. Used on Wigram/Christchurch-McMurdo Sound, Antarctica flights. Mod by Nov 60 with trap on starboard side of nose to catch airborne plankton. Coded JD-6 from approx Aug 62. One penguin painted on side nosewheel doors for each completed mission. Mod to R7V-1P Quonset 4 Oct 61 for 1961-62 "Operation Deep Freeze". Ret R7V-1 8 Mar 62 & redes C-121J at McMurdo 30 Nov 62. To VX-6 Christchurch 19 Nov 63, VX-6 Quonset 31 May 64, VX-6 Christchurch 24 Nov 64 & VX-6 Quonset 22 May 65. Continued on annual Antarctic ops. VX-6 to VXE-6 by 1970. Left Christchurch, New Zealand 16 Mar 71 after final season of Antarctic ops, .and ferried via Quonset Point to Davis Monthan 17 Mar 71 for storage. Struck off (MASDC Davis Monthan) 25 May 71 (TT: 15,609 hrs, also quoted as 15,709 hrs). For sale by DofD 23 Mar 77. Sold to Delcon 10 Feb 78. Scrapped shortly after.

4126 R7V-l/1049B-55-75 8 May 53 to U S Navy as 131625. To VR-l LANT 28 Oct 53, coded RP-625 'Perseus'. To VW-13 Patuxent 1 Sep 55. To Dallas (R & D) 25 Feb 56. To VW-11 Patuxent 5 May 56. To VW-13 Patuxent 1 Oct 56. To VW-15 (?-card unclear) Argentia Aug 57. To VW-15(?) Patuxent Sep 57. To VW-11 Patuxent 7 Apr 58. To VW-11 Argentia 12 May 58. To VW-15 Patuxent 22 May 58. To AEW TRA UNIT Patuxent (AEWTULANT) 28 Mar 60. To C-121J 8 Oct 62. Coded MM-6 by Aug 64. Received substantial damage on 3 Nov 64 when the landing gear was raised on landing Patuxent River, MD on a training. flight. Struck off 14 Nov 64 (TT: 14,068 hrs). This total may be wrong as aircraft card has only 8,105 hrs on 31 Aug 64!

4127 R7V-l/1049B-55-75 8 May 53 to U S Navy as 131626. To VR-8 MATS Hickam 12 Nov 53. To VR-8 Hickam 1 Oct 55. To Dallas (R & D) 29 Feb 56. To VR-8 Hickam 12 Apr 56. To VR-8 Moffett 11 Oct 57. Struck off 15 Jun 58 (TT: 5,633 hrs). Tfd to US Air Force as C-121G 54-4056 MATS WESTAF 'City of Tokyo'. Assigned to 8th TS Moffett 1 Jul 58, 4406th MTC Wg Moffett 23 Jan 62, ret 8th TS Moffett 22 Jan 63. To West Virginia ANG (167th AMS Martinsburg) 27 Oct 63, to 167th MAG Martinsburg 2 Feb 66. To 551st AEW Wg Otis 31 May 67, Logistics Cmd Lake City 10 Jun 68, ret 551st AEW Wg Otis 25 Jul 68. To 553rd Recce Wg, PACAF, Korat 29 Dec 69, Logistics Cmd Lake City 6 Jul 70, deployed Korat RTAFB 30 Jul 70. To MASDC Davis Monthan 30 Oct 70, arr 3 Nov 70. Parts missing by May 71, and for sale by DofD (Davis Monthan) 30 Oct 74. To Allied Aircraft 30 Dec 74. Still extant Jan 79, scrapped subsequently.

4128 R7V-l/1049B-55-75 8 May 53 to U S Navy as 131627. To Pool BAR M&S Burbank 8 May 53, VR-l LANT Patuxent 5 Nov 53, coded RP-627 'Centaurus'. To VW-13 Patuxent 1 Sep 55. To AEW MATRON 2 Barbers Pt 8 Sep 56, VR-7 Hickam 14 Jul 57. To VW-15 Patuxent 23 Sep 57, tfd VW-15 Argentia 28 Feb 58. To VW-11 Patuxent 7 Mar 58, tfd VW-11 Argentia 12 May 58. Ret VW-15 Patuxent 14 May 58, to VW-13 Patuxent 30 Nov 58. To AEWTRAUNIT Patuxent 15 Mar 60 (AEWTULANT). Redes C-121J 27 Oct 62, coded MM-2 by 1964, also MM-7. To NATC Det 24 May 65 and cvtd to NC-121J for "Project Jenny" by LAS New York May 65-Aug 65. 'Blue Eagles I'. To OASU Jul 65, coded JB. To VX-8 Det Jenny, Saigon Jul 67. To VXN-8 Jan 69, coded JB-627. Ret from West Pacific to Patuxent via Shannon 28 Nov 70. To MASDC Davis Monthan Feb 71 (officially), but at LAS Ontario May 71 (DCASR Pasadena 31 May 71 "awaiting strike"). Arr Davis Monthan 2 Jul 71. Struck off (Davis Monthan) Jan 72. (TT: 13,855 hrs). Still stored at Davis Monthan Oct 75. Sold to Sun Valley Aviation 28 May 76, scrapped shortly after.

4129 R7V-l/1049B-55-75 13 May 53 to U S Navy as 131628. To VR-8 MATS Hickam 20 Nov 53. To VR-8 Hickam 7 Oct 55. To VR-8 Moffett 10 Sep 57. Struck off 15 Jun 58 (TT: 5,972 hrs). Tfd to U S Air Force as C-121G 54-4058 MATS WESTAF 'City of Alameda'. (Reportedly also named 'City of Redwood City' at one time). Assigned to 8th TS Moffett 1 Jul 58. To Pennsylvania ANG 140th AMS Middletown-Olmsted 4 Nov 63. To 168th TSH Gp Olmsted 10 Aug 64, 168th MAG Olmsted 2 Feb 66. Tfd to 551st AEW Wg Otis 31 May 67 & to 552nd AEW Wg McClellan 8 Jan 68. Tfd to 966th AEW Sq McCoy 21 Oct 68, ret 552nd AEW Wg McClellan 7 Nov 68. To 966th AEW Sq McCoy 24 Mar 69, ret 552nd AEW Wg McClellan 12 Apr 69. To 966th AEW Sq McCoy again 12 May 69, ret 552nd AEW Wg McClellan 27 May 69. To MASDC Davis Monthan for storage 27 Apr 71. For sale by DofD (Davis Monthan) 30 Oct 74. Sold to Allied Aircraft 31 Dec 74. Scrapped subsequent to Jan 79.

4130 R7V-l/1049B-55-75 18 May 53 to U S Navy as 131629. To VR-l LANT 23 Dec 53, coded RP-629 'Draco'. To VR-7 MATS Hickam 3 Aug 55. To VR-7 Hickam 1 Oct 55. To VR-7 Moffett 10 Sep 57. Struck off 15 Jun 58 (TT: 5,113 hrs). Tfd to U S Air Force as C-121G 54-4059 MATS WESTAF 'City of Mountain View'. Assigned 8th TS Moffett 1 Jul 58. Named 'City of Pittsburgh' on tf to Pennsylvania ANG 147th AMS Gr Pittsburgh 10 Jul 63, to 171st TG Gr Pittsburgh 16 Feb 64, 171st MAG Gr Pittsburgh 1 Jan 66. To 171st AEA Gp Gr Pittsburgh 18 Feb 68. To 375th AEA Wg Scott 12 May 68, ret 171st AEA Gp Gr Pittsburgh 11 Dec 68. To MASDC Davis Monthan for storage 15 Aug 72. Stored at Davis Monthan & for sale by DofD (Davis Monthan) 30 Oct 74. Sold to Allied Aircraft 9 Jan 75. Scrapped subsequent to Jan 79.

4131 Laid down as R7V-l/1049B-55. Mod on production line to turboprop test aircraft as R7V-2/1249A-95-75. Dec 53 to U S Navy as 131630. Navy acceptance date 10 Sep 54. To Burbank (R & D) Feb 55. To storage at Litchfield Park 20 Dec 56. Struck off (Litchfield Park) 17 Apr 59 (TT: 109 hrs). Remained in storage at

131631 R7V-2 nicknamed "The Elation" (ie Electra-Constellation) whilst it was fitted with four Allison 501-D13 engines (with the intake on the top of the cowlings in contrast to the military T-56, where the intake was on the bottom). The turbo-Super Constellation was used by Allison and Rohr Aircraft (who manufactured the propellers) to speed up the Electra flight-test programme. (Lockheed)

Litchfield, being cannibalized for spares. Rear cargo-door fuselage section cut out, probably in 1961, and used in conversion of c/n **749-2619** to all-cargo configuration (qv). Remains at Burbank in Jul 63.

4132 Laid down as R7V-1/1049B-55. Mod on production line to turboprop test aircraft as R7V-2/1249A-95-75. Jan 54 to US Navy as 131631. Navy acceptance date 30 Nov 54. To Burbank (R & D) 3 Dec 54. (TT: 120hrs prior tf to Rohr). Cvtd by Rohr Aircraft in late 1956 to the "Elation". Powered by four Allison 501 D-13s with Aeroproducts 606 four-bladed propellers for the engine flight test programme for the Lockheed 188 Electra. First flight Jul 57. Struck off (Burbank) 30 Jul 59 (TT: 882 hrs), after damaged in accident at Palmdale, CA. To Litchfield Park for storage. Sold in May 60 to California Airmotive Corp, and regd N7938C. Fuselage and other parts used in the rebuild of c/n **1049G-4648** during 1960. Remainder of aircraft scrapped at Litchfield. (see c/n 4648 for further details).

4133 R7V-1/1049B-55-75 3 Aug 53 to US Navy as 131632. Navy acceptance date 30 Aug 53. To VR-8 MATS Hickam Nov 53. To VR-8 Hickam 1 Oct 55. To Dallas (R & D) 29 Feb 56. To VR-8 Hickam 29 Feb 56. To VR-8 Moffett 10 Sep 57. Struck off 15 Jun 58 (TT: 5,754 hrs). Tfd to U S Air Force as C-121G 54-4060 MATS WESTAF 'City of Sacramento'. Assigned to 8th TS Moffett 1 Jul 58. To West Virginia ANG 167th AMS Martinsburg 25 Oct 63, to 167th ATG Martinsburg 19 Jun 65. To 167th MAG Martinsburg 2 Feb 66. Tfd to Wyoming ANG 153rd MAG Cheyenne 21 Apr 67 'City of Laramie'. To 153rd AEA Gp Cheyenne 17 Oct 68. To MASDC Davis Monthan 22 Apr 72. For sale by DofD (Davis Monthan) 30 Oct 74 (TT: 19,575 hrs). Sold to unknown scrap dealer. Scrapped subsequent to Jan 79.

4134 R7V-1/1049B-55-75 16 Sep 53 to US Navy as 131633. To VR-1 LANT Patuxent Nov 53, coded RP-633 'Hercules'. To VW-13 Patuxent 9 Sep 55. To VW-2 Patuxent 13 Feb 56, VW-15 Patuxent 2 Jul 56. To VR-7 Moffett 21 Dec 57. Struck off 15 Jun 58 (TT: 4,412 hrs). Tfd to U S Air Force as C-121G 54-4072 MATS WESTAF 'City of San Jose'. Assigned to 8th TS Moffett 1 Jul 58. To Pennsylvania ANG 147th AMS Gr Pittsburgh 4 Nov 63, to 171st TG Gr Pittsburgh 16 Feb 64. To 171st MAG Gr Pittsburgh 1 Jan 66. Tfd to 551st AEW Wg Otis 16 Mar 67, to 552nd AEW Wg McClellan 29 Dec 69. To AFRES 915th MAG Homestead 1 Jul 71, tfd 79th AEW Wg Homestead 30 Jul 71. To MASDC Davis Monthan for storage 25 May 72. For sale by DofD (Davis Monthan) 30 Oct 74. Scrapped subsequent to Jan 79.

4135 R7V-1/1049B-55-75 21 Sep 53 to US Navy as 131634. To VR-8 MATS Hickam Nov 53. To VR-8 Hickam 1 Oct 55. To VR-8 Moffett 10 Sep 57. Struck off 15 Jun 58 (TT: 6,384 hrs). Tfd to U S Air Force as C-121G 54-4055 MATS WESTAF 'City of Monterey'. Assigned to 8th TS Moffett 1 Jul 58. To West Virginia ANG 167th AMS Martinsburg 14 Nov 63, to 167th ATG Martinsburg 3 Sep 65. To 167th MAG Martinsburg 2 Feb 66. Tfd to Wyoming ANG 153rd MAG Cheyenne 12 Mar 67. Salvaged 28 Sep 67 due to excessive corrosion. To Kelly AFB, TX for dismantling, later to Brooks AFB, TX, and fuselage used for training of aero-medical personnel in crash procedures, wings cut off simulating crash. In use at Brooks 1968-1971 at least. Subsequent fate unknown.

4136 R7V-1/1049B-55-75 29 Aug 53 to US Navy as 131635. Pool BAR M&S Burbank (Used for static tests by Navy) 29 Aug 53. To VR-1 LANT Patuxent coded RP-635 'Crux' 20 Feb 54. To VW-13 Patuxent 16 Nov 55, tfd VW-14 Barbers Pt 28 Jul 56. To AEW MATRON 2 Barbers Pt 26 Feb 57, coded SH-66. To VW-4 Jacksonville 8 Oct 57. Tfd VW-15 Patuxent 11 Jun 59. Ret VW-4 Jacksonville 19 Jun 59. To AEW TRA UNIT Patuxent (AEWTULANT) 11 Mar 60, coded MM-635. To C-121J 1962. To FASRON 107 (NAS Keflavik) 16 Jun 61, coded FN-635 until 1 May 65. To NAS Keflavik, named 'City of Reykjavik'. Later unnamed. Named 'Tiny's Little Helper' by 1969. In use with NAS Keflavik until at least Nov 70. To LAS New York (a/o Mar 71). Rough air inspection showed damaged elevator hinge. To VXN-8 Patuxent by May 71, coded JB-635. To MASDC Davis Monthan for storage 7 Jul 71. Struck off (Davis Monthan) 12 Jul 72 (TT: 13,236 hrs). Remained in storage at Davis Monthan. For sale by DofD 23 Mar 77 (TT: 13,245 hrs given). Sold to Delcon 23 Mar 78, scrapped subsequently.

4137 R7V-1/1049B-55-75 28 Sep 53 to US Navy as 131636. To VR-8 MATS Hickam 3 Oct 53. To VR-8 Hickam 1 Oct 55. To VR-8 Moffett 10 Sep 57. Struck off 15 Jun 58 (TT: 5,248 hrs). Tfd to U S Air Force as C-121G 54-4062 MATS WESTAF 'City of

HI-583CT C-121G of Aero Chago SA, a Dominican cargo airline, at Miami International in 1990. (MAP)

Saratoga'. Assigned 8th TS Moffett 1 Jul 58. Used in support of "Operation Deep Freeze" Oct 61. To 4406th Maint Wg Moffett 6 Feb 62, ret 8th TS Moffett 31 Jul 62. To Wyoming ANG 187th AMS Cheyenne 1 Oct 63. To 153rd TG Cheyenne 7 Feb 64. To 153rd MAG Cheyenne 2 Feb 66. Named 'City of Jackson Hole'. To 153rd AEA Gp Cheyenne 17 Oct 68. Tfd AFRES 79th AEW Sq Homestead 26 May 72. To 552nd AEW Wg McClellan 14 Feb 73. Ret 79th AEW Sq Homestead 19 Mar 76. To 915th AEW Gp Homestead 2 Dec 76, ret 79th AEW Sq Homestead 30 Sep 77. To MASDC Davis Monthan 14 Nov 77 for storage. Withdrawn from storage 3 Feb 78 & assigned to 915th CAMS Homestead. Ret to MASDC Davis Monthan for storage 31 May 78. For sale by DofD (Davis Monthan) 15 Aug 84 (TT: 22,274hrs), unsold. For sale again in poor condition by DofD (Davis Monthan) 20 Aug 85. Sold to Ralph Payne by Jan 87 & stored with plans to be made airworthy. Allotted N2114Z as candidate for DMI Aviation Inc 16 Oct 89, regd 6 Nov 89. Canx 31 Jan 90 on sale to Aero Chago SA, regd HI-583CT. In svce, first visited Miami, FL Jun 90. Grounded Mar 93 with ban on Dominican cargo carriers. Stored Santo Domingo, Dominican Republic. Made test flt SDQ 7 Jun 94, subsequently flew little but engines run up on a regular basis. Made last flight 1997 with Aero Chago SA. Offered to Dutch Aviodome Museum 1999, but ntu. Sold to Francisco Agullo t/a (Swiss) Super Constellation Flyers Association 15 Sep 00, regd N105CF 24 Oct 00. Del Santo Domingo, DR to Opa Locka, FL for rework 7 Nov 00. Flew Opa Locka-Conroe, TX-Avra Valley, AZ 4 Jan 01-7 Jan 01. Was undergoing major overhaul & reconfiguration to passenger aircraft at Avra Valley with dely to Switzerland planned for spring 2003. All work ceased, however, on 30 Aug 02. Currently stored in partly dismantled state at Avra Valley, AZ; remaining engines shipped to SCFA in Switzerland early 2006.

4138 R7V-l/1049B-55-75 15 Oct 53 to US Navy as 131637. Navy acceptance date 8 Oct 53. To VR-l LANT Patuxent 15 Oct 53, coded RP-637 'Libra'. To VR-8 MATS Hickam 15 Aug 55. To VR-8 Hickam 1 Oct 55. To VR-8 Moffett 16 Jan 58. Struck off 15 Jun 58 (TT: 5,020 hrs). Tfd to U S Air Force as C-121G 54-4057 MATS WESTAF 'City of Santa Cruz'. Assigned to 8th TS Moffett 1 Jul 58. To 4406th Maint Wg Moffett 23 Jan 62. Ret 8th TS Moffett 31 Jul 62. Damaged beyond repair in ground accident at Oakland, CA in approx Aug 62. While undergoing engine run-up checks, the technician failed to set the brakes properly. On increasing the power on all 4 engines to 1,200-1,300 rpm, the aircraft started moving forward, rolling approx 30 feet, overran the ground power unit, causing the unit to explode and spray the centre section of the aircraft and the immediate area with burning fuel. No injuries, US $120,000 damage to the C-121G. Stricken Oakland 7 Nov 62. Derelict remains stored at Oakland for sometime, subsequently scrapped approx 1965/66.

4139 R7V-l/1049B-55-75 15 Oct 53 to US Navy as 131638. Navy acceptance date 4 Oct 53. To VR-8 MATS Hickam 15 Oct 53. To VR-8 Hickam 1 Oct 55. In 1956, while the aircraft was en route from the USA to Japan over the Pacific Ocean, an engine fire occurred. The engine burned off the mounts and the aircraft landed safely in Japan with the engine hanging merely by the cables and hoses. Repaired by LAS. To VR-8 Moffett 6 Nov 57. Struck off 15 Jun 58 (TT: 6,111 hrs). Tfd to U S Air Force as C-121G 54-4063 MATS WESTAF 'City of Santa Clara'. Assigned to 8th TS Moffett 1 Jul 58, to 4406th Maint Wg Moffett 25 Jan 62, ret 8th TS Moffett 31 Jul 62. To Wyoming ANG 187th AMS Cheyenne 11 Oct 63, 'City of Laramie', to 153rd TG Cheyenne 7 Feb 64 & 153rd MAG Cheyenne 2 Feb 66. To 553rd Reconnaissance Wing, Otis, Mar 67, tfd 551st AEW Wg Otis 31 May 67. Assigned 552nd AEW Wg McClellan 12 Nov 69. Tfd AFRES 459th MAW Wg McClellan 30 Jun 71 & to 915th MAG (AFRES) McClellan 1 Jul 71. Moved to Homestead same day. To AFRES 79th AEW Sq Homestead 30 Jul 71. To MASDC, Davis Monthan 15 Jul 72 for storage. For sale by DofD (Davis Monthan) 30 Oct 74. Scrapped subsequent to Jan 79.

4140 R7V-1/1049B-55-75 24 Oct 53 to US Navy as 131639. Navy acceptance date 19 Oct 53. To VR-l LANT Patuxent 24 Oct 53, coded RP-639 'Aries'. Crashed near Newfoundland, NS 17 Jan 55, with VR-1 squadron. The aircraft departed Harmon AFB, Stephenville, Nfld for Patuxent River at 03.52 hrs. At 05.45 pilot radioed one engine had failed, followed moments later by a second engine failure. Aircraft turned back to Harmon (approx 200 mls away), but crashed in the Gulf of St.Lawrence, 29 mls off the SW tip of Newfoundland. Crew lost. Struck off 17 Jan 55 (TT: 467 hrs).

4141 R7V-l/1049B-55-75 5 Nov 53 to US Navy as 131640. Navy acceptance date 24 Oct 53. To VR-8 MATS Hickam 5 Nov 53. Possibly to VR-l LANT Patuxent Nov 53 briefly, coded RP-640 'Phoenix' (see c/n 4142), and ret to VR-8 MATS Hickam Nov 53. To VR-8 Hickam 1 Oct 55. To VR-8 Moffett 10 Sep 57. Struck off 15 Jun 58 (TT: 5,719 hrs). Tfd to U S Air Force as C-121G 54-4064 MATS WESTAF 'City of Honolulu'. Assigned 8th TS Moffett 1 Jul 58, to 4406th Maint Wg Moffett 25 Jan 62, ret 8th TS Moffett 31 Jul 62. To Pennsylvania ANG 147th AMS Gr Pittsburgh 30 Oct 63. To 171st TG Gr Pittsburgh 16 Feb 64 & 171st MAG Gr Pittsburgh 1 Jan 66. Withdrawn from use at Greater Pittsburgh 1966 or 1967. Cannibalized remains there in May 68. Scrapped on site.

4142 R7V-l/1049B-55-75 31 Oct 53 to US Navy as 131641. To BAR M&S Burbank 31 Oct 53. To VR-l LANT Patuxent 12 Nov 53, coded RP-641 'Phoenix'. Tfd to VW-15 Patuxent 18 Nov 55, to VW-1 Barbers Pt 17 Nov 56, VR-8 Hickam 14 May 57. To AIRBARSRON 2 Barbers Point 9 Sep 57, coded SH-67. Tfd AEW BARRON PAC Barbers Point 21 May 60. To C-121J 30 Nov 62. To VP-31 N Island 7 May 65, to LAS New York for conversion to NC-121J 25 Aug 65 for "Project Jenny". 'Blue Eagles III'. To OASU coded JB. To VX-8, Det Jenny, Saigon, Jul 67, coded JB-641. To VXN-8 Jan 69. To MASDC Davis Monthan for storage 13 Jan 71. Struck off (Davis Monthan) 25 May 71 (TT: 13,315 hrs). Sold to Sun Valley Aviation 25 May 76, presumably scrapped subsequently.

4143 R7V-l/1049B-55-75 31 Oct 53 to US Navy as 131642. To VR-8 MATS Hickam 13 Nov 53. To VR-8 Hickam 18 Oct 55. To VR-8 Moffett 10 Sep 57. Struck off 15 Jun 58 (TT: 6,118 hrs). Tfd to U S Air Force as C-121G 54-4065 MATS WESTAF 'City of San Francisco'. Assigned 8th TS Moffett 22 Sep 59. Lsd to NASA Sep 63 and arr at Friendship Airport, Baltimore, MD mid-Aug 63 for conversion. Officially assigned to AFSC (NASA) at Friendship, Baltimore 2 Jul 64. Regd NASA 20 at Goddard Space Flight Center, Greenbelt, MD. Used for Mercury, Gemini and Agena evaluation and tracking tests at worldwide flight-tracking stations. Based at Northwest Cape Space Tracking Station, Australia May-Oct 66. Reregd NASA 420 on ret to Goddard (possibly 31 May 67). Reregd N420NA 25 Jun 69 (officially), NASA received notification of change 14 Aug 69. Withdrawn from use with NASA (TT: 18,667 hrs) and tfd to US Army, Aberdeen Proving Grounds, Aberdeen, MD 23 Jan 73, for use as target for testing explosive devices on aircraft structures. For sale by DofD (Aberdeen) 23 Aug 78. Presumed scrapped subsequently - last reptd in a New Jersey scrapyard, date unknown.

4144 R7V-l/1049B-55-75 8 Dec 53 to U S Navy as 131643. To BAR M&S Burbank 19 Nov 53. To VR-l LANT Patuxent 8 Dec 53, coded RP-643. To VW-15 Patuxent 2 Oct 55, VW-14 Barbers Pt 2(?) Jul 56. To AEW MATRON 2 Barbers Pt 26 Feb 57, tfd AIRBARSRON 2 Barbers Pt 15 Jun 57, coded SH-66. To VW-15 Patuxent 12 Jun 58, VW-2 Patuxent 9 Oct 58. Tfd Pacific Missile Range, Pt Mugu 13 Jun 59. To C-121J 31 Oct 62. Tfd Naval Missile Center, Pt Mugu 1 Aug 63, ret Pacific Missile Range, Pt Mugu 30 Nov 63. Later named 'Ole Blue from Point Mugu'. To MASDC Davis Monthan for storage 3 Oct 73. Struck off (PMR) 29 Jul 74 (TT: 14,234 hrs). For sale by DofD 11 Feb 81 (TT: given as 14,217 hrs only) at Davis Monthan. Sold to Northern Peninsula Fisheries 12 Mar 81 & regd N4247K May 81. Taken out of storage. On first attempt blew two engines on take-off & made forced landing alongside runway. Del to Arlington, WA Jun 81. Official sale date 1 Sep 81. Overhauled at Arlington. Had "Winky's Fish" titles by Sep 83. Problems with licensing caused aircraft to remain stored at Arlington. Ownership tf officially from US Government to William C Crawford dba Northern Peninsular Fisheries 11 May 87, regd 15 May 87. To World Fish & Agriculture Inc Oct 87. Ferried Arlington, WA to Palau Island, Pacific Ocean via Majuro Intl Airport 16 Nov 87. Entered svce one week later, lsd to Palau Intl Traders, & flown until early 1988. Impounded Manila, Philippines by Jun 88. Stored at Manila, engines run up regularly until 1989. Eventually abandoned at Manila. Later registers list owner as World Fish & Agricultural Inc. Parts missing by Feb 01, but still stored on edge of apron at Manila. Current.

4145 R7V-l/1049B-55-75 19 Dec 53 to US Navy as 131644. To BAR M&S Burbank 27 Nov 53. To VR-l LANT Patuxent 19 Dec 53, coded RP-644 'Taurus'. To VW-15 Patuxent 2 Oct 55. To AEW MATRON 2 Barbers Pt 5 Oct 56, tfd AIRBARSRON 2 Barbers Pt 10 Sep 57, coded SH-68, & to AEWBARRONPAC Barbers Pt 31 May 60. To C-121J 30 Nov 62. To VX-6 Quonset Pt 3 Sep 64, coded JD-5 'Pegasus'. Used on "Operation Deep Freeze" annually. One penguin painted on side nose-wheel doors for each completed mission. Coded JD-7 from at least Mar 66. Mod with new aerials under tail unit for airborne ice-sounding late 1967 & flight tested Dec 67. To VXE-6 by 1970. Damaged beyond repair landing at McMurdo (Williams Field), Antarctica at 20.10 hrs (local) on 8 Oct 70. The aircraft, with 80 on board, was flying from Christchurch, New Zealand, on its first flight of the 1970-71 "Operation Deep Freeze" season. After making six low passes over the field, the C-121J attempted to land in zero visibility, winds gusting to 40 mph in a snowstorm and in 90° crosswinds. The starboard wing was torn off completely and tail unit broken. There were only slight injuries to five on board. The bulk of the airframe was still present, covered in ice & snow and with dayglo and paintwork clearly visible, at McMurdo in 2001.

4146 R7V-l/1049B-55-75 19 Jan 54 to US Navy as 131645. Navy acceptance date 28 Nov 53. To VR-8 MATS Hickam 19 Jan 54. To VR-7 MATS Hickam 17 Mar 54. To VR-7 Hickam 1 Oct 55. To VR-7 Moffett 10 Sep 57. Struck off 15 Jun 58 (TT: 4,766 hrs). Tfd to U S Air Force as C-121G 54-4066 MATS WESTAF. Name 'City of Tachikawa' unconf. (see c/n 4149). Assigned 8th TS Moffett 27 Jun 58. Crashed at Guam 4 Dec 62, no details. Struck off 13 Dec 62 (Moffett).

4147 R7V-l/1049B-55-75 7 Jan 54 to US Navy as 131646. Navy acceptance date 6 Dec 53. To VR-7 MATS Hickam 6 Jan 54. To VR-7 Hickam 1 Oct 55. To VR-7 Moffett 7 Jan 58. Struck off 15 Jun 58 (TT: 5,519 hrs). Tfd to U S Air Force as C-121G 54-4067 MATS WESTAF 'City of Campbell' (also 'City of Santa Clara' unconf). Assigned to 8th TS Moffett 1 Jul 58. To 4406th Maint Wg Moffett 30 Jan 62, ret 8th TS Moffett 31 Jul 62. To Pennsylvania ANG 147 AMS Gr Pittsburgh 18 Sep 63. To 171st TG Gr Pittsburgh 16 Feb 64 & to 171st MAG Gr Pittsburgh 1 Jan 66. Tfd 168th MAG Olmsted 20 May 66, ret 171st MAG Gr Pittsburgh 31 May 67. To 171st AEA Gp Gr Pittsburgh 18 Feb 68. Tfd 375th AEA Wg Scott 12 May 68. Ret to 171st AEA Gp (ANG) 11 Dec 68. To MASDC Davis Monthan for storage 16 Aug 72. For sale by DofD (Davis Monthan) 30 Oct 74, scrapped sometime subsequently.

4148 R7V-1/1049B-55-75 19 Jan 54 to US Navy as 131647. Navy acceptance date 23 Dec 53. To VR-7 MATS Hickam 19 Jan 54. To VR-7 Hickam 1 Oct 55. To VR-7 Moffett 5 Aug 57. Struck off 15 Jun 58 (TT: 5283 hrs). Tfd to U S Air Force as C-121G 54-4068 MATS WESTAF 'City of New Delhi'. Assigned 8th TS Moffett 1 Jul 58. To West Virginia ANG 167th AMS Martinsburg 1 Jul 63. To 167th TG Martinsburg 7 Apr 64. To 167th MAG Martinsburg 2 Feb 66. Tfd Pennsylvania ANG 171st MAG Gr Pittsburgh 27 May 67. To 171st AEA Gp Gr Pittsburgh 18 Feb 68. Tfd 375th AEA Wg Scott 17 May 68. Ret to 171st MAG Gr Pittsburgh 17 Jan 69, & to 171st AEA Gp Gr Pittsburgh 1 Sep 71. To MASDC Davis Monthan for storage 1 Nov 72. On tail, no engines by Jun 76. For sale by DofD Davis Monthan 23 Mar 77 (TT: 17,867 hrs). Sold to Delcon for scrap 20 Mar 78, scrapped shortly afterwards.

4149 R7V-1/1049B-55-75 2 Feb 54 to US Navy as 131648. Navy acceptance date 29 Dec 53. To VR-7 MATS Hickam 2 Feb 54. To VR-7 Hickam 1 Oct 55. To VR-7 Moffett 18 Oct 57. Struck off 15 Jun 58 (TT: 6,138 hrs). Tfd to U S Air Force as C-121G 54-4069 MATS WESTAF 'City of Tachikawa'. Assigned 8th TS Moffett 19 Sep 58. Written-off at Prescott, AZ 28 Feb 59.

4150 R7V-1/1049B-55-75 11 Feb 54 to US Navy as 131649. Navy acceptance date 15 Jan 54. To VR-7 MATS Hickam 11 Feb 54. To VR-7 Hickam 1 Oct 55. To VR-7 Moffett 6 Sep 57. Struck off 15 Jun 58 (TT: 5,384 hrs). Tfd to U S Air Force as C-121G 54-4070 MATS WESTAF 'City of Los Gatos'. Assigned 8th TS Moffett 1 Jul 58. To West Virginia ANG 167th AMS Martinsburg 12 Sep 63. To 167th ATG Martinsburg 17 Dec 65. To 167th MAG Martinsburg 2 Feb 66. Tfd Pennsylvania ANG 171st MAG Gr Pittsburgh 11 Mar 67. To 171st AEA Wg Gr Pittsburgh 18 Feb 68. Tfd 375th AEA Wg Scott 12 May 68. Ret to 171st AEA Gp Gr Pittsburgh 11 Dec 68. To MASDC Davis Monthan for storage 2 Aug 72. For sale by DofD (Davis Monthan) 30 Oct 74. Scrapped, subsequent to Jan 79.

4151 Laid down on production line as R7V-1/1049B-55-75, serial 131650 (ntu). Mod to 1049B-55-97/VC-121E under "Project

Green Valley" as Presidential aircraft. LADD: 10 Sep 54 to U S Air Force as 53-7885. Air Force acceptance date 31 Aug 54. To 1254th ATG, 1298th TG Washington, DC 10 Sep 54. Christened 'Columbine III' 24 Nov 54. To 1254th ATW (SM) Washington 31 May 61, to 1254th ATW Andrews 10 Jul 61. Later unnamed, when replaced as Presidential aircraft by VC-137A. To 89th MAW (SM) Andrews 10 Jan 66. Retired and tfd to U S Air Force Museum at Dayton-Wright Patterson 20 Apr 66. Preserved there, as one of the 'walk-through' exhibits in the 'Presidential Aircraft' display hangar.

4152 R7V-1/1049B-55-75 4 Mar 54 to US Navy as 131651. Navy acceptance date 16 Feb 54. To VR-7 MATS Hickam 4 Mar 54. To VR-7 Hickam 1 Oct 55. To VR-7 Moffett 10 Sep 57. Struck off 15 Jun 58 (TT: 4,983 hrs). Tfd to U S Air Force as C-121G 54-4071 MATS WESTAF 'City of Hayward'. Assigned 8th TS Moffett 19 Oct 59. To West Virginia ANG 167th AMS Martinsburg 1 Nov 63. To 167th MAG Martinsburg 2 Feb 66. To MASDC Davis Monthan for storage 13 Jun 67. Withdrawn from storage & assigned 375th AEA Wg Scott 25 Sep 68. To 171st AEA Gp Pennsylvania ANG Gr Pittsburgh 11 Dec 1968. To MASDC Davis Monthan for storage again 22 Sep 72. On belly, no engines, by Jun 76. For sale by DofD 23 Mar 77 (TT: 17,042 hrs). Sold to Delcon 29 Mar 78 and scrapped subsequent to Jan 79.

4153 R7V-1/1049B-55-75 16 Mar 54 to US Navy as 131652. Navy acceptance date 27 Feb 54. To VR-7 MATS Hickam 16 Mar 54. To VR-7 Hickam 1 Oct 55. To VR-7 Moffett 12 Aug 57. Was to become C-121G 54-4072 with U S Air Force, MATS WESTAF, in Jun 58, but crashed while flying with US Navy on 11 May 58, five miles east of Taft, CA. Navy records report substantial damage 14 May 58 (often quoted as write-off date). Struck off 15 May 58 (TT: 4,952 hrs). Serial 54-4072 re-allocated to R7V-l/C-121G c/n 4134 (qv).

4154 R7V-l/1049B-55-75 24 Mar 54 to US Navy as 131653. Navy acceptance date 10 Mar 54. To VR-7 MATS Hickam 24 Mar 54. To VR-7 MATS 1 Oct 55. To VR-8 Hickam 13 Jan 56. Ret to VR-7 Hickam 2 Mar 56. To VR-7 Moffett 17 Oct 57. Struck off 15 Jun 58 (TT: 6,057 hrs) .Tfd to U S Air Force as C-121G 54-4073 MATS WESTAF 'City of Burlingame'. Assigned 8th TS Moffett 1 Jul 58. To Pennsylvania ANG 147th AMS Gr Pittsburgh 12 Nov 63. To 171st TG Gr Pittsburgh 16 Feb 64. Tfd 168th TG Pennsylvania ANG Olmsted 17 Apr 64. Ret 171st ATG Gr Pittsburgh 7 Jan 65. To 171st MAG Gr Pittsburgh 1 Jan 66. To 171st AEA Gp Gr Pittsburgh 18 Feb 68. Tfd 375th AEA Wg Scott 12 May 68. Ret to 171st AEA Gp Gr Pittsburgh 11 Dec 68. To MASDC Davis Monthan for storage 1 Nov 72. On tail, no engines by Jun 76. For sale by DofD Davis Monthan 23 Mar 77 (TT: 18,373 hrs). Sold to Delcon 28 Feb 78, subsequently scrapped.

4155 R7V-l/1049B-55-75 6 Apr 54 to US Navy as 131654. To BAR M&S Burbank 17 Mar 54. To VR-7 MATS Hickam 6 Apr 54. To VR-7 Hickam 1 Oct 55, BAR FA Ontario 30 Oct 57. To VR-7 Moffett 14 Feb 58. To VW-l Agana 1 Sep 58, coded TE-00 by Dec 59. To C-121J 11 Oct 62. Uncoded by 1968. To VQ-l Atsugi by 31 May 71, coded PR-60. To VQ-l Agana 1971. Coded PR-50 by Jan 74, named 'Victory Liner', and adorned with Playboy "bunny" on fins. Struck off (VQ-l) 3 Sep 74 (TT: 19,528 hrs). To MASDC Davis Monthan for storage 3 Sep 74. For sale by DofD (Davis Monthan) 11 Feb 81 (TT: 19,538 hrs). Moved to Southwest Alloys scrap compound, Davis Monthan, by Apr 81. Sold to Ascher Ward for $16,501 on 1 May 81, to Bill A Conner 2 May 82, regd N27189 3 May 82. Stored in Allied Acft Sales scrapyard until ferried to Van Nuys, CA 11 Jun 82. Lsd to Classic Air Inc 13 Nov 83. To Air Flora Aviation Corp 15 Jan 86, but sale not completed; canx 24 Jun 86. Offered at auction 12 Jan 87, but did not reach reserve of $116,000. Repossessed by Bill A Conner & sold to Darryl L Greenamyer Inc 6 Nov 87, regd 18 Dec 87. Flown to Opa Locka, FL Mar 88 & sold to Aero Chago SA 26 Mar 88, N-regn canx 5 Apr 88, but still being worked on for Dominican Republic as N27189 at Opa Locka 10 Apr 88. Regd HI-532 May 88, in svce 6 May 88. Reregd HI-532CT by Nov 88. DBR when nosewheel collapsed landing Santo Domingo, DR and strut pierced fuselage, approx Jun 90. Subsequently used for spares at Santo Domingo. Stored derelict at Santo Domingo after ban on Dominican cargo airlines Mar 93 & scrapped on unknown date.

4156 R7V-l/1049B-55-75 24 Apr 54 to U S Navy as 131655. To BAR M&S Burbank 31 Mar 54. To VR-7 MATS Hickam 24 Apr 54. To VR-7 Hickam 1 Oct 55. To VR-7 Moffett 15 Nov 56. Tfd VW-3 Agana 4 Jun 58, coded PM-10. To VW-13 Patuxent 19 Dec 59. To AEW TRA UNIT Patuxent (AEWTULANT) 24 Mar 60, coded MM-655. To C-121J 8 Oct 62. Later coded MM-5 'Prottning Keflavikur' by 1964. To OASU coded JB-655 after Feb 65. To LAS New York for conversion to NC-121J for "Project Jenny". Conversion completed Sep 66 as "Blue Eagles IV". To VX-8, Det. Jenny, Saigon Jul 67, coded JB-655. To VXN-8 in Jan 69. To MASDC Davis Monthan for storage 28 Mar 72. Struck off (Davis Monthan) 16 Jan 73 (TT: 15,469 hrs). Still complete Sep 77. For sale by DofD 11 Feb 81 (TT: 15,479 hrs). Sold to Allied Aircraft 4 Jun 81. Still stored at Davis Monthan Jan 87 (in bad condition), subsequently scrapped.

4157 R7V-l/1049B-55-75 13 May 54 to US Navy as 131656. Navy acceptance date 24 Apr 54. To VR-7 MATS Hickam 13 May 54. To VR-7 Hickam 1 Oct 55. To Dallas (R & D) 29 Feb 56. To VR-7 Hickam 13 Apr 56. To VR-7 Moffett 7 Aug 57. Struck off 15 Jun 58 (TT: 5,594 hrs). Tfd to U S Air Force as C-121G 54-4074 MATS WESTAF 'City of Menlo Park'. Assigned 8th TS Moffett 1 Jul 58. To 4406th Maint Wg Moffett 14 Jan 62. Ret 8th TS Moffett 31 Jul 62. To Wyoming ANG 187th AMS Cheyenne 4 Sep 63 'City of Sheridan'. To 153rd TG Cheyenne 7 Feb 64, 153rd MAG Cheyenne 2 Feb 66, to 153rd AEA Gp Cheyenne 17 Oct 68. To MASDC Davis Monthan for storage 7 Jul 72. For sale by DofD (Davis Monthan) 30 Oct 74. Scrapped subsequently, date unknown.

4158 R7V-l/1049B-55-75 28 May 54 to US Navy as 131657. Navy acceptance date 30 Apr 54. To VR-7 MATS Hickam 28 May 54. To VR-7 Hickam 1 Oct 55. To VR-7 Moffett 22 Aug 57. Struck off 15 Jun 58 (TT: 6,186 hrs). Tfd to U S Air Force as C-121G 54-4075 MATS Westaf, name unknown. Assigned 8th TS Moffett 1 Jul 58.To Pennsylvania ANG 147th AMS Gr Pittsburgh 22 Aug 63. To 171st TG Gr Pittsburgh 16 Feb 64, to 171st MAG Gr Pittsburgh 1 Jan 66. Assigned 112nd Fighter Gp ANG Gr Pittsburgh 25 Oct 66. To 171st AEA Gp Gr Pittsburgh 18 Feb 68. Tfd 375th AEA Wg Scott 25 May 68. Ret 171st AEA Gp Gr Pittsburgh 11 Dec 68. To Wyoming ANG 153rd AEA Gp Cheyenne 19 Jan 71 'City of Medicine Bow'. To MASDC Davis Monthan for storage 21 Mar 72. For sale by DofD (Davis Monthan) 30 Oct 74. Scrapped subsequent to Jan 79.

4159 R7V-l/1049B-55-75 12 Jul 54 to US Navy as 131658. Navy acceptance date 15 Jun 54. To VR-7 MATS Hickam 12 Jul 54. To VR-7 Hickam 1 Oct 55. To VR-7 Moffett 16 Aug 57. Struck off 15 Jun 58 (TT: 5,946 hrs). Tfd to U S Air Force as C-121G 54-4076 MATS WESTAF 'City of Manila'. Assigned to 8th TS Moffett 1 Jul 58. Lsd to NASA Sep 63 and arr Friendship Airport, Baltimore, MD same month for conversion. Tfd AFSC (NASA) Friendship 5 Jul 64. Regd NASA 21 at Goddard Space Flight Center, Greenbelt, MD. Used for Mercury, Gemini and Agena evaluation and tracking tests at world-wide flight-tracking stations. Reregd NASA 421 in 1966. Reregd N421NA 25 Jun 69 (officially), NASA received notification of change 14 Aug 69. Tfd back to U S Air Force with 552nd AEW Wg McClellan 2 Feb 73 for removal of instrumentation (TT: 18,834 hrs). To MASDC Davis Monthan for storage 15 Feb 73 (officially), arr 17 Feb 73. On belly, no engines by Jun 76. For sale by DofD 23 Mar 77 (TT: 18,848 hrs). To Delcon 30 Mar 78, subsequently scrapped. Canx from USCAR 27 May 04 (!)

4160 R7V-l/1049B-55-75 Jun 54 to US Navy as 131659. To BAR M&S Burbank 28 May 54. ToVR-l LANT Patuxent 24 Nov 54, VR-1 Patuxent 11 May 55. Tfd VW-15 Patuxent 21 May 55. To VW-14 Barbers Pt 9 Aug 56, tf AEW MATRON 2 Barbers Pt 20 Feb 57, coded RW-46 in 1956. To VR-8 Hickam 27 May 57, BAR FA Ontario 24 Sep 57. To AIR BARSRON 2 Barbers Pt 13 Jan 58, coded SH-69 by Jun 58. Tfd AEW BARRON PAC Barbers Pt 31

Section 12: Constellation Production List

N421NA C-121G of NASA at Baltimore (Friendship) Airport in November 1969. (John T Wible)

May 60. To C-121J 30 Nov 62. Tfd NAS Whidbey Island 19 May 65. To NAS Agana by Jun 69 until at least May 71. To MASDC Davis Monthan for storage. Struck off (Davis Monthan) 29 Jul 74 (TT: 15,546 hrs). For sale by DofD 11 Feb 81 (TT: 15,569 hrs). To Southwestern Alloys Corp 25 Mar 81. Scrapped subsequent to Oct 82.

4161 Laid down on production line as R7V-l/1049B-55-75. Mod on production line to turboprop test aircraft as YC-121F/1249A-94-75 for U S Air Force. LADD: 4 Mar 55 to U S Air Force as BuAer 131660. To 53-8157, acc 31 Mar 55, del 30 Dec 55. To 6515th Maint Gp Edwards 29 Dec 55. Assigned 17th Test Sq (Turboprop) MATS Continental Division, Kelly 1 Feb 56, arr 11 Feb 56 on dely from Edwards. Flew Kelly, TX-Burtonwood, UK 12 Nov 56. To 17th Field Maint Sq Kelly 28 May 58. To AMC McClellan 7 Jun 58. Carried 'Sacramento' on fin (a/o 1958). To AMC Davis Monthan for storage 17 Feb 59. Assigned 2704th (ASD) Gp, Davis Monthan 20 Aug 61 for reclamation & SOC. Sold to California Airmotive Corp and regd N9746Z. Sold to the Flying Tiger Line in 1963 and fuselage used in construction of 1049H aircraft (see c/n **4674**), remainder of aircraft scrapped.

4162 Laid down on production line as R7V-l/1049B-55-75. Mod on production line to turboprop test aircraft as YC-121F/1249A-94-75 for U S Air Force. LADD: 30 Mar 55 to U S Air Force as BuAer 131661. To 53-8158, acc 30 Mar 55, del 20 Feb 56. To 6515th Maint Gp Edwards 2 Feb 56. Assigned 17th Test Sq (turboprop) MATS Continental Division, Kelly 17 Apr 56, arr same day on dely from Edwards. To AMC McClellan 3 Jun 57. Carried 'Sacramento' on fin (a/o 1958). To AMC Davis Monthan for storage 17 Feb 59. Assigned 2704th (ASD) Gp 20 Aug 61 for reclamation & SOC. Sold to California Airmotive Corp and regd N9749Z. Sold to the Flying Tiger Line in 1963 and fuselage used in construction of 1049H aircraft (see c/n **4636**), remainder of aircraft scrapped.

4163 1049D-55-85, mod to 1049D-55-116, for Seaboard & Western Airlines. Sold prior dely to Seagull Air Transport Corp (CAB approval given 4 Jun 54) for lse back by Seaboard & Western for five years. LADD: 19 Aug 54 to Seaboard & Western Airlines as N6501C 'American Airtrader'. Seaboard dely date 7 Sep 54. Updated to 1049D/01-82 approx 1955. Lsd briefly to BOAC 8 Mar 55 (in svce) to 7 Apr 55 for North Atlantic pax services (until aircraft in BOAC colours deld - see c/n 4165/4166). Lsd BOAC for New York-Bermuda-New York flt 6 Apr 56. Mod to 1049H/03-82 summer 1956 by LAS. Renamed Seaboard World Airlines 1961. Damaged at Shannon, Ireland, 9 Sep 61. Repaired. Sold to Canadair Ltd 1962 and lsd back. Sub-lsd to Capitol Airways May 62. Sold to Capitol 30 Dec 65 (1 Mar 66 also quoted), but withdrawn from use already by mid-1964 at Wilmington, DE. Remained in storage at Wilmington, and used for spares. Scrapped there some time after Aug 67. Canx from USCAR 1967.

4164 1049D-55-85, mod to 1049D-55-116 for Seaboard & Western Airlines. LADD: 2 Sep 54 as N6502C 'Zurich Airtrader' to Seaboard. Sold to Aviation Equipment Corp and lsd by Seaboard. Lsd BOAC for New York-Bermuda-New York svce 19-20 Dec 55. Updated to 1049D/01-82 approx 1955. Mod to 1049H/03-82 summer 1956 by LAS. CAB approved purchase of Aviation Equipment Corp by Seaboard & Western 15 Jun 59. Renamed Seaboard World Airlines 1961. Sold to Canadair Ltd 1962 and lsd back. Sub-lsd to Capitol Airways May 62. Sold to Capitol 30 Dec 65 (1 Mar 66 also quoted), but withdrawn from use by mid-1963 at Wilmington, DE. Remained in storage at Wilmington, derelict, with parts missing, and used for spares. Scrapped there some time after Aug 67. Canx from USCAR 1967.

4165 1049D-55-85, mod to 1049D-55-116 21 Sep 54 to Seaboard & Western Airlines as N6503C 'Paris Airtrader'. Sold to Aviation Equipment Corp and lsd by Seaboard. Cvtd for use by BOAC by LAS Burbank early 1955 to 86-pax Tourist-class configuration, with provision for tip-tanks. To 1049D/01-82. Lsd to BOAC in full colours for North Atlantic pax services from 17 Mar 55 (first svce New York-Heathrow) until 30 Mar 56 (last svce Bermuda-New York). Ret to Seaboard & Western. Crashed on take-off at New York-Idlewild Airport, NY, 10 Nov 58. Just after take-off, the aircraft suffered a propeller reversal. The aircraft swerved sharply to the left, hit the ground, broke off an engine and then the wing. Subsequently, it careered out of control along 300 yards of runway, heading for the passenger terminal, then collided with a parked V.724 Viscount (CF-TGL) of Trans-Canada Air Lines and burst into flames. Destroyed by fire. No casualties. (Regd owner at crash was still Aviation Equipment Corp, on lse to Seaboard & Western Airlines).

4166 1049D-55-85, mod to 1049D-55-116 28 Sep 54 to Seaboard & Western Airlines as N6504C, 'Frankfurt Airtrader'. Probably sold to Aviation Equipment Corp and lsd back immediately to Seaboard. Cvtd for use by BOAC by LAS Burbank early 1955 to 86-pax Tourist-class configuration, with provision for tip-tanks. To 1049D/01-82. Lsd to BOAC in full colours for North Atlantic pax services 10 Mar 55 (first svce New York-Heathrow) until 12 Feb 56 (last svce Bermuda-New York). Ret to Seaboard & Western. Seaboard received CAB approval to purchase Aviation Equipment Corp 15 Jun 59. Conversion to 1049H/03-82 unconf but probable. Slightly damaged at New York, NY 7 Jun 58. Repaired. Seaboard & Western renamed Seaboard World Airlines 1961. Sold to Canadair Ltd 1962 and lsd back to Seaboard. Sub-lsd to Capitol Airways May 62 until at least Aug 64, then ret to Seaboard World and sold to LAPA-Lineas

Aereas Patagonias Argentinas SRL Nov 64. Painted up at New York-Idlewild same month as LV-PCQ. Deld 18 Dec 64 and reregd LV-ILW. Out of svce at Miami, FL, by Mar 66 and stored there until Mar 68. Sold to H Warton (North American Aircraft Trading Corp) on lse-purchase. Del as LV-ILW Miami-Lisbon (via Sal) 15 Mar 68. Overhauled by TAP at Lisbon for use on the Biafran airlift, regd 5T-TAC, in svce Lisbon by 22 May 68. Written off at Bissau (Portuguese Guinea) on the night of 4 Jun - 5 Jun 68, while en route Lisbon-Uli, Biafra, with a cargo of Fouga Magister wings for the Biafran Air Force. Aircraft blown up on the ground and destroyed, probably the result of sabotage by one of the crew. No casualties.

4167 R7V-l/1049B-55-75 7 Jan 55 to US Navy as 140311. Navy acceptance date 30 Nov 54. To VR-7 MATS Hickam 7 Jan 55. To VR-7 Hickam 1 Oct 55. To VR-7 Moffett 10 Sep 57. Struck off 15 Jun 58 (TT: 4,989 hrs). Tfd to U S Air Force as C-121G 54-4077 MATS WESTAF 'City of San Mateo'. Assigned to 8th TS Moffett 1 Jul 58. To Wyoming ANG 187th AMS Cheyenne 22 Jun 63 'City of Cheyenne'. To 153rd TG Cheyenne 10 Mar 64, 153rd MAG Cheyenne 2 Feb 66. To 153rd AEA Gp Cheyenne 17 Oct 68, 153rd TAG Cheyenne 14 Jul 72. To MASDC Davis Monthan for storage 3 Oct 72. For sale by DofD 23 Mar 77 (TT: 17,487 hrs). Sold Delcon 30 Mar 78, subsequently scrapped.

4168 R7V-l/1049B-55-75 11 Jan 55 to US Navy as 140312. Navy acceptance date 27 Dec 55. To VR-8 Hickam 11 Jan 56. To VR-6 Moffett 10 Sep 57. Struck off 15 Jun 58 (TT: 3,563 hrs). Tfd to U S Air Force as C-121G 54-4078 MATS WESTAF 'City of Palo Alto'. Assigned 8th TS Moffett 2 Oct 59. To West Virginia ANG 167th AMS Martinsburg 15 Aug 63. To 167th TG Martinsburg 17 Jun 64, 167th MAG Martinsburg 2 Feb 66. Tfd Wyoming ANG 153rd MAG Cheyenne 15 Feb 67 'City of Torrington'. Tfd Pennsylvania ANG 171st AEA Gp Gr Pittsburgh 10 May 68. To 375th AEA Wg Scott 12 May 68, ret Wyoming ANG 153rd MAG Cheyenne 8 Jun 68. To 153rd AEA Gp Cheyenne 8 Nov 68. To MASDC Davis Monthan for storage 27 Jun 72. For sale by DofD (Davis Monthan) 30 Oct 74 (TT: 16,831 hrs). Sold Allied Acft 6 Feb 75. Scrapped, subsequent to Apr 81.

4169 R7V-l/1049B-55-75 2 Feb 55 to US Navy as 140313. Navy acceptance date 28 Dec 54. To VR-7 MATS Hickam 2 Feb 55. To VR-7 Hickam 25 Nov 55. To VR-7 Moffett 10 Sep 57. Struck off 15 Jun 58 (TT: 5,051 hrs). Tfd to U S Air Force as C-121G 54-4079 MATS WESTAF 'City of Oakland'. Assigned 8th TS Moffett 1 Jul 58. To North Carolina ANG 145th AMG Douglas 22 Aug 63. To 145th TG Douglas 24 Jan 64, 145th MAG Douglas 1 Feb 66. Terminated in USAF 4 Apr 66 ('tf out'). Reinstated with US Navy May 66 as C-121J 140313. To OASU coded JB-313. To VX-8 Jul 67, still coded JB-313. To VXN-8 Jan 69, same code. "Snoopy" caricature painted on nose. To MASDC Davis Monthan for storage 9 Feb 71. Struck off (Davis Monthan) 31 Jan 72 (TT: 17,161 hrs). For sale by DofD 23 Mar 77 (TT quoted as 17,159 hrs). Sold to Delcon 23 Mar 78, scrapped subsequently.

4170 C-121C/1049F-55-96 22 Jun 55 to U S Air Force as 54-151. Del to MATS Atlantic, 41st TS Charleston 2 Dec 55. Assigned 1608th Maint Gp Charleston 1 Jan 56, 1608th FMS Charleston 1 Dec 56, 1608th Wg Charleston 15 Feb 58. Tfd Mississippi ANG 183rd AMS Hawkins 2 Jul 62. To 172nd TSG Jackson 11 Jan 64, 172nd MAG Jackson 1 Jan 66. Tfd West Virginia ANG 167th MAG Martinsburg 17 Apr 67 & to New Jersey ANG 170th MAG McGuire 29 Mar 68. Ret West Virginia ANG 167th AEA Gp Martinsburg 17 Jul 69, to 167th TAG Martinsburg 4 Jun 72. To MASDC Davis Monthan for storage 7 Jul 72. For sale by DofD (Davis Monthan) 30 Oct 74. Sold Allied Aircraft 10 Jan 75. Scrapped subsequent to Jan 79.

4171 C-121C/1049F-55-96 29 Jul 55 to U S Air Force as 54-152. Del to MATS Atlantic, 41st TS Charleston 22 Dec 55. Assigned 1608th Maint Gp Charleston 1 Nov 56, 1608th FMS Charleston 1 Dec 56, 1608th Wg Charleston 13 Feb 58. Tfd New Jersey ANG 150th AMS Newark 3 Oct 62. To 170th MAG McGuire 1 Jan 66, 170th AEA Gp McGuire 10 Jan 70. Named 'Lady Diane' by 1972. To MASDC Davis Monthan for storage 11 Apr 73. For sale by DofD 23 Mar 77 (TT: 12,623 hrs). Sold Delcon 30 Mar 78, subsequently scrapped.

4172 C-121C/1049F-55-96 16 Sep 55 to U S Air Force as 54-153. (USAF acceptance 26 Aug 55). Del to MATS Atlantic, 41st TS Charleston 16 Sep 55 'City of Charleston'. Assigned 1608th Maint Gp Charleston 1 Nov 56, 1608th FMS Charleston 1 Dec 56, 1608th Wg Charleston 21 Feb 58. Tfd New Jersey ANG 150th AMS Newark 5 Dec 62. To 170th ATG Newark 2 Jul 64, 170th MAG McGuire 5 Nov 67. To 170th AEA Gp McGuire 10 Jan 70. To MASDC Davis Monthan for storage 16 May 73. For sale by DofD 23 Mar 77 (TT: 15,460 hrs). On belly, no engines, by Jun 76. Sold Delcon for scrap 31 Mar 78. Scrapped subsequent to Jan 79.

4173 C-121C/1049F-55-96 24 Sep 55 to U S Air Force as 54-154. (USAF acceptance 13 Sep 55). Del to MATS Atlantic, 41st TS Charleston 24 Sep 55 'City of Winnipeg'. Assigned 1608th Maint Gp Charleston 1 Nov 56, 1608th FMS Charleston 1 Dec 56, 1608th Wg Charleston 18 Jun 58. Tfd North Carolina ANG 156th AMS Douglas 31 Jul 62. To 145th AMS Douglas 31 Dec 63, 145th MAG Douglas 1 Feb 66. Tf West Virginia ANG 167th MAG Martinsburg 29 Jan 67, 167th AEA Gp Martinsburg 1 Aug 68, 167th TAG Martinsburg 4 Jun 72. To MASDC Davis Monthan for storage 14 Jul 72. For sale by DofD (Davis Monthan) 30 Oct 74. Sold Allied Aircraft 10 Jan 75, scrapped subsequent to Jan 79.

4174 C-121C/1049F-55-96 20 Oct 55 to U S Air Force as 54-155. (USAF acceptance 20 Sep 55). Del to MATS Atlantic, 41st TS Charleston 20 Oct 55. Assigned 1608th Maint Gp Charleston 1 Nov 56, 1608th FMS Charleston 1 Jul 57, 1608th Wg Charleston 1 May 58. Tfd Pennsylvania ANG 140th AMS Olmsted 11 Dec 62. To 168th MAG Olmsted 2 Feb 66. To 193rd TEWG Olmsted 27 Oct 67. Cvtd EC-121S by LAS New York from 1967, redes EC-121S 5 Jun 69. Assigned 193rd SOG Olmsted 3 Nov 77, ret 193rd TEWG Olmsted 2 Apr 79. Withdrawn from use & flown to Kelly AFB Apr 79 for removal of equipment. To Lackland AFB, TX mid-1979 for museum, and placed on display in 193rd TEWS markings by Aug 79. Repainted in MATS colours there as '40155' by 1981. Preserved as part of Heritage Center collection (a/o 1983). Rn USAF History & Traditions Museum at San Antonio-Lackland.

4175 C-121C/1049F-55-96 1 Nov 55 to U S Air Force as 54-156. (USAF acceptance 21 Sep 55). Del to MATS Atlantic, 41st TS Charleston 1 Nov 55. Assigned 1608th Maint Gp Charleston 1 Nov 56, 1608th FMS Charleston 1 Dec 56, 1608th Wg Charleston 13 Feb 58. Tfd Mississippi ANG 183rd AMS Hawkins 17 Oct 62. To 172nd ATG Jackson 2 Apr 65, 172nd MAG Jackson 1 Jan 66. Tfd West Virginia ANG 167th MAG Martinsburg 1 Mar 67, 167th AEA Gp Martinsburg 1 Aug 68. To MASDC Davis Monthan for storage 18 Apr 72. Regd to NASM Smithsonian Institution, Washington, DC 14 Jun 72. Tfd to Aviation Specialties Inc 17 Aug 72 in exchange for the company's Boeing 307 Stratoliner (N19903) & flown to Mesa, AZ. Sold Aircraft Specialties Inc 22 Mar 73, regd N73544 on 26 Mar 73. Mod as insecticide sprayer by R E Packard of Mesa 24 Apr 73 with 4 sets of pairs of 830-USG tanks & wing-mounted full-span spray booms. Experimental CofA 8 Mar 73 for tests, restricted CofA 27 Apr 73 for agricultural work. In svce by May 73 as sprayer. Stored at Mesa from 1976 until approx Nov 78. Flying again from Goodyear, AZ, during 1979, and flown to Chandler Memorial Airport, AZ, early 1980. Made emergency landing with two engines u/s en route to spraying mission in Maine. Stored at Chandler. Reregd to Globe Air Inc 18 Feb 81, CofRegn issued 28 Apr 81. Regd to Mehrdad I Khoramian & Daryoush B Younesi 17 Jan 82. Planned dely to California end Feb 83, but blew engine & ret to Chandler. Del Chandler-Chino, CA 11 Mar 83 & Chino-Camarillo, CA 15 Jan 84 (on 3 engines after problems with a runaway prop). Planned use as passenger aircraft by Ascher Ward t/a Classic Air 1982-83 fell through, as did use by William Crawford ('Winky's Fish') for hauling tuna fish in 1984. Stored Camarillo. Further abortive sale to World Fish & Agriculture Inc Dec 87. Regd to Mehrdad I Khoramian (sole

Section 12: Constellation Production List

54-156 C-121C in MATS colours taken in the mid-1950s. This aircraft is now based in Europe with the Swiss Super Constellation Flyers Association. (Robert C Mikesh via John T Wible)

owner) 23 Mar 88. Sold to Daryoush B Younesi 29 Jan 92, regd 11 Feb 92. Restored at Camarillo for use by the Constellation Historical Society group 1992-1994. First flight after restoration 23 Jun 94, visited first airshow Pt Mugu, CA 24 Sep 94. Flew on airshow circuit in western USA. Painted in National Guard Bureau colours Apr 96, and named 'Camarillo Connie - Queen of the Skies' by Apr 97. Repainted with Presidential style 'United States of America' titling by Sep 00. Grounded by FAA mid-2001 and stored Camarillo, CA. For sale on internet in Jan 02, bid of $600,000 not accepted - $750,000 being asked. Sold to Super Constellation Flyers Association on lse-purchase agreement signed 17 Dec 03. Overhauled & painted with "Breitling Super Constellation" titles & fin logo Apr 04 (Breitling Swiss chronometers are sponsors). Ferried Camarillo-Omaha, NE-Manchester, NH-Stephenville, Nfld-Keflavik, Iceland-Prestwick, Scotland-Paris Le Bourget-Basel, Switzerland 26 Apr-8 May 04. Flown on European airshow circuit. HB-RSC rsvd 2007. Current.

4176 C-121C/1049F-55-96 6 Oct 55 to U S Air Force as 54-157. Del to MATS Atlantic 41st TS Charleston 7 Nov 55. Assigned to 1608th Maint Gp Charleston 1 Nov 56, to 1608th FMS Charleston 1 Dec 56. To 1608th Wg Charleston 5 Feb 58. Tfd Mississippi ANG 183rd AMS Hawkins 25 Jul 62, to 172nd MAG Jackson 1 Jan 66. Tf West Virginia ANG 167th MAG Martinsburg 15 Feb 67, to 167th AEA Gp Martinsburg 1 Aug 68. Tfd Pennsylvania ANG 193rd TEWG Olmsted 24 Mar 72. To MASDC Davis Monthan for storage 26 Mar 77. For sale by DofD (Davis Monthan) 16 Nov 83 (TT: 18452 hrs), unsold as only $9,000 offered. For sale again by DofD 15 Aug 84 & 26 Feb 85. Tfd to USAF Museum & accepted by Travis AFB Museum 8 Feb 85, awaiting engines to ferry to Travis, CA (a/o Apr 86). Never deld, remained in storage at Davis Monthan. Tfd by USAF Museum to NASM of Australia Nov 91 after inspection by HARS & swap with Bristol Beaufighter for USAF Museum. Moved to Pima Air Museum, Tucson, AZ for restoration 16 Apr 92. Originally painted with blue cheat line & small 'HARS' titles (a/o mid 94). Restoration continued & regd N4115Q to National Air & Space Museum of Australia 17 Aug 94. First flight in 17 years 21 Sep 94 Davis Monthan to Tucson Intl as N4115Q, regd VH-EAG (the second) 23 Sep 94. N4115Q canx 22 Sep 94 as 'sold in Australia'. Repainted in 1950s Qantas colour-scheme (without Qantas titles) mid Nov 94, named 'Southern Preservation' by Jan 95 and with 'Connie' titles by Sep 95. Fitted with tip-tanks. Del Tucson-Oakland, CA 24 Jan 96, & flew across Pacific Ocean via Honolulu, Pago Pago & Nadi to Sydney 25 Jan-3 Feb 96 (38:10 hrs flying over 12 days). Handed over by NASMA to the Historical Aircraft Restoration Society 21 Feb 97. Flies to airshows and other occasions throughout Australia. Current.

54-157 C-121C. Close-up of the miniscule serial on the Pennsylvania ANG 193rd TEWG aircraft. Photo taken at Greenham Common, England on 7th July 1974. (PJM)

4177 C-121C/1049F-55-96 10 Oct 55 to U S Air Force as 54-158. Del to MATS Atlantic 41st TS Charleston 7 Nov 55. Assigned to 1608th Maint Gp Charleston 1 Nov 55, to 1608th FMS Charleston 1 Dec 56. Ret 1608th Maint Gp Charleston 14 Jan 58. To 1608th Wg Charleston 8 Feb 58. Tfd New Jersey ANG 150th AMS Newark 15 Nov 62. To 170th ATG Newark 11 Feb 65, 170th MAG McGuire 1 Jan 66. To MASDC Davis Monthan 16 Feb 73 for storage. For sale by DofD 23 Mar 77 (TT: 15,432 hrs). Sold to Delcon 5 Apr 78, scrapped subsequent to Jan 79.

4178 C-121C/1049F-55-96 19 Nov 55 to U S Air Force as 54-159. (USAF acceptance 20 Oct 55). Del to MATS Atlantic 41st TS Charleston 19 Nov 55. Assigned to 1608th Maint Gp Charleston 1 Nov 56, to 1608th FMS Charleston 1 Dec 56. To 1608th Wg Charleston 13 Feb 58. Tfd MATS 1503th ATW, Det A, op by VR-7 (Navy), Det A Tachikawa 31 Jul 62. To 68th MAG, Det A, Tachikawa 1 Jan 66. Assigned Pennsylvania ANG 168th MAG Olmsted 31 May 67, to 193rd TEWG Olmsted 27 Oct 67. Cvtd to EC-121S by LAS New York, probably from 1967, redesignated EC-121S on 5 Jan 69. Deployed Korat 1 Aug 70, ret 193rd TEWG Olmsted 8 Jan 71. To MASDC, Davis Monthan for storage 16 Nov 77. For sale by DofD (Davis Monthan) 15 Aug 85 (TT: 18,649 hrs) & again 26 Feb 85 and 20 Aug 85. Sold to DMI Aviation Inc, but remained in storage in scrapyard. Sold to Save A Connie Inc for spare parts for c/n 4830 in 1986. Stripped for spares at Tucson scrapyard Jan-Mar 87, remainder subsequently scrapped.

4179 C-121C/1049F-55-96 24 Oct 55 to U S Air Force as 54-160. Del to MATS Atlantic 41st TS Charleston 22 Nov 55. Assigned 1608th Maint Gp Charleston 1 Nov 56, to 1608th FMS

54-160 JC-121C Air Force Systems Command (also referred to as a DC-121C) shows the whole aircraft (above) at Wright-Patterson AFB, Ohio on 18th May 1969 (Peter Russell-Smith) and a close up (below) of the gondola fitted. The two seats in the gondola were used by a test subject and a behavioral scientist, to test man against infrared and radar sensors. (United States Air Force)

Charleston 1 Dec 56. To 1608th Wg Charleston 3 Feb 58. Tfd MATS 1503rd ATW, Det A, op by VR-7 (Navy) Tachikawa 21 Nov 62. To AFSC Wright- Patterson 1 May 63. Cvtd to JC-121C for AFSC-ASD, with addition of dorsal and ventral radomes, redesignated JC-121C Wright-Patterson 25 Jul 63. Used in "Project Marcom Relay". To Logistics Cmd Lake City 11 Oct 66, ret AFSC Wright-Patterson 21 Dec 66. To DC-121C, with gondola under centre fuselage, Wright-Patterson, by May 69, but not officially designated as such. To MASDC Davis Monthan for storage (still as JC-121C) 15 Jul 71. For sale by DofD (Davis Monthan) 30 Oct 74 (TT: 12,448 hrs). Sold Allied Aircraft 10 Feb 75. Still present in scrapyard of Allied Aircraft Sales, Davis Monthan, in 1981 in ex-AFSC/ASD markings, nose & parts only left by Oct 82. Cockpit saved & on display Frankfurt Rhein-Main, Germany since 2003.

4180 C-121C/1049F-55-96 2 Nov 55 to U S Air Force as 54-161. Del to 41st TS MATS Atlantic Charleston 1 Dec 55. Assigned 1608th Maint Gp Charleston 1 Nov 56, to 1608th FMS Charleston 1 Dec 56. To 1608th Wg Charleston 13 Feb 58. Tfd New Jersey ANG 150th AMS Newark 22 Jan 63. To 170th MAG McGuire 1 Jan 66, 170th AEA Gp McGuire 10 Jan 70. To MASDC Davis Monthan for storage 23 Mar 73. For sale by DofD (Davis Monthan) 23 Mar 77 (TT: 15,035 hrs). Sold Delcon 6 Apr 78, scrapped subsequent to Jan 79.

4181 C-121C/1049F-55-96 4 Oct 55 to U S Air Force as 54-162. (USAF acceptance 7 Nov 55). Del to MATS Atlantic 41st TS Charleston 2 Dec 55. Assigned 1608th Maint Gp Charleston 1 Nov 56, to 1608th FMS Charleston 1 Dec 56, ret 1608th Maint Gp Charleston 20 Jan 58. To 1608th Wg Charleston 13 Feb 58. Tfd Mississippi ANG 183rd AMS Hawkins 28 May 62. To 172nd MAG Jackson 1 Jan 66. Tfd West Virginia ANG 167th MAG Martinsburg 11 Apr 67, to 167th AEA Gp Martinsburg 1 Aug 68, 167th TAG Martinsburg 4 Jun 72. To MASDC Davis Monthan for storage 23 Jun 72. For sale by DofD (Davis Monthan) 30 Oct 74. Sold Allied Aircraft 2 Jan 75. Scrapped subsequent to Jan 79.

4182 C-121C/1049F-55-96 10 Nov 55 to U S Air Force as 54-163. Del to MATS Atlantic 41st TS Charleston 2 Dec 55. Assigned 1608th Maint Gp Charleston 1 Nov 56, 1608th FMS Charleston 1 Dec 56, ret 1608th Maint Gp Charleston 7 Jan 58. To 1608th Wg Charleston 13 Feb 58. Tfd North Carolina ANG 156th AMS Douglas 28 Nov 62, to 145th AMG Douglas 31 Dec 65, to 145th MAG Douglas 1 Feb 66. Tfd West Virginia ANG 167th MAG Martinsburg 1 Feb 67, 167th AEA Gp Martinsburg 1 Aug 68, to 167th TAG Martinsburg 4 Jun 72. To MASDC Davis Monthan for storage 28 Jul 72. For sale by DofD (Davis Monthan) 30 Oct 74. Sold Allied Aircraft 2 Jan 75, scrapped subsequent to Jan 79.

4183 C-121C/1049F-55-96 17 Nov 55 to U S Air Force as 54-164. Del to MATS Atlantic 41st TS Charleston 26 Jan 56. Assigned 1608th FMS Charleston 27 Apr 57, 1608th Wg Charleston 22 Dec 58. Tfd Pennsylvania ANG 140th AMS Olmsted 20 Nov 62. To 168th MAG Olmsted 2 Feb 66. Allotted 193rd TEWS Olmsted 16 Sep 67, cvtd EC-121S by LAS Aug 67-1968. Tfd 193rd TEWG Olmsted 1 Aug 68. Deployed to Korat 1 Aug 70, ret Olmsted 3 Jan 71. To MASDC Davis Monthan for storage 14 May 79. For sale by DofD (Davis Monthan) 15 Aug 84 (TT: 16,717 hrs), again on 20 Aug 85 in poor condition. Sold to unknown scrap dealer, scrapped by Jan 87.

4184 C-121C/1049F-55-96 23 Nov 55 to U S Air Force as 54-165. Del to MATS Atlantic 41st TS Charleston 22 Dec 55. Assigned 1608th Maint Gp Charleston 1 Nov 56, to 1608th FMS Charleston 1 Dec 56. Crashed short of the runway on approach to Dhahran, Saudi Arabia, in thick fog at approx midnight 30-31 Dec 56, on regular MATS flight from McGuire AFB, NJ to Tripoli, Libya and Dhahran. The aircraft hit the sand approx 1,000 yards short of the threshold and burst into flames. The airport's GCA equipment was not operating at the time of the accident. 15 out of 41 on board killed.

4185 C-121C/1049F-55-96 28 Dec 55 to U S Air Force as 54-166. (USAF acceptance 9 Dec 55). Del to MATS Atlantic 41st TS Charleston 28 Dec 55 'City of Bogota'. Assigned 1608th Maint Gp Charleston 1 Nov 56, 1608th FMS Charleston 1 Dec 56. To 1608th Wg Charleston 1 Feb 58. Tfd North Carolina ANG 156th AMS Douglas 22 Oct 62, to 145th AMG Douglas 31 Dec 65, 145th MAG Douglas 1 Feb 66. Tf Pennsylvania ANG 168th MAG Olmsted 10 Apr 67, to 193rd TEWG Olmsted 27 Oct 67. Tfd New Jersey ANG 170th MAG McGuire 19 Mar 68, to 170th AEA Gp McGuire 10 Jan 70. To MASDC Davis Monthan for storage 27 Apr 73. For sale by DofD (Davis Monthan) 23 Mar 77 (TT: 15,433 hrs). Sold to Delcon 4 Apr 78. Scrapped subsequent to Jan 79.

4186 C-121C/1049F-55-96 28 Dec 55 to U S Air Force as 54-167. (USAF acceptance 20 Dec 55). Del to MATS Atlantic 41st TS Charleston 28 Dec 55. Assigned 1608th Maint Gp Charleston 1 Nov 56, 1608th FMS Charleston 1 Dec 56. To 1608th Wg Charleston 13 Feb 58. Tfd North Carolina ANG 156th AMS Douglas 2 Aug 62, 145th AMG Douglas 31 Dec 64, 145th ATG Douglas 28 Jan 65. To 145th MAG Douglas 1 Feb 66. Tfd Pennsylvania ANG 168th MAG Olmsted 26 Jan 67, to 193rd TEWG Olmsted 27 Oct 67. To MASDC Davis Monthan for storage 27 Jul 77. For sale by DofD (Davis Monthan) 16 Nov 83 (TT:19,711 hrs). Offer of $8,000 refused. For sale again by DofD 15 Aug 84, 26 Feb 85 & 20 Aug 85 in poor condition. Sold to Hangar 10 Inc dba Atkins Aviation for spares for c/n 4202. Regd N5510Y candidate 28 Oct 85, canx Mar 86. Stored with Southwestern Alloys, Tucson, for spares reclamation. Scrapped subsequent to Aug 88.

4187 C-121C/1049F-55-96 17 Jan 56 to U S Air Force as 54-168. (USAF acceptance 29 Dec 55). Del to MATS Atlantic 17 Jan 56. Assigned 1608th FMS Charleston 18 Jan 56. To 41st TS Charleston 26 Jan 56, 1608th FMS Charleston 29 Jan 56, 1608th

Maint Gp Charleston 1 Nov 56, ret 1608th FMS Charleston 1 Dec 56 & 1608th Maint Gp Charleston 13 Jan 58. To 1608th Wg Charleston 8 Feb 58. Tfd MATS 1503rd ATW, Det A, op by VR-7 (Navy), Det A, Tachikawa 18 May 62. To 7th TS Tachikawa 31 Jul 62, 68th MAG, Det A Tachikawa 1 Jan 66. Tfd to Mississippi ANG 172nd MAG Jackson 7 Feb 66. To Det 1, National Guard Bureau (709th HGA HQ) Andrews 1 Apr 67 District of Columbia ANG. Titling changed to 'National Guard Bureau' by Jun 67. To VC-121C Andrews 12 Jun 69. To MASDC Davis Monthan for storage 16 Jun 75. For sale by DofD (Davis Monthan) 23 Aug 78. (TT: 17,174 hrs). Sold to Allied Aircraft 1 Nov 78, but stored in South West Alloys scrapyard, Davis Monthan, by Oct 79, and in Allied Aircraft Sales scrapyard, Davis Monthan, by Apr 81. Scrapped subsequent to Jan 87, with only centre section & part of fuselage still extant by Aug 88.

4188 C-121C/1049F-55-96 13 Jan 56 to U S Air Force as 54-169. (USAF acceptance 4 Jan 56). Del to MATS Atlantic 41st TS Charleston 13 Jan 56. Assigned 1608th FMS Charleston 18 Jan 56. To 76th TS Charleston 29 Mar 56. To 1608th Maint Gp Charleston 1 Nov 56, ret 1608th FMS Charleston 1 Dec 56, 1608th Maint Gp Charleston 8 Jan 58. To 1608th Wg Charleston 13 Feb 58. Tfd New Jersey ANG 150th AMS Newark 21 Dec 62, 170th MAG McGuire 1 Jan 66. Named 'The Patrician' by 1970. To MASDC Davis Monthan for storage 22 Feb 73. For sale by DofD (Davis Monthan) 23 Mar 77 (TT: 15,791 hrs). Sold to Delcon 31 Mar 78, scrapped subsequent to Jan 79.

4189 C-121C/1049F-55-96 16 Jan 56 to U S Air Force as 54-170. (USAF acceptance 6 Jan 56). Del to MATS Atlantic 41st TS Charleston 16 Jan 56. Assigned 1608th FMS Charleston 18 Jan 56. To 76th TS Charleston 9 Apr 56. To 1608th Maint Gp 1 Nov 56, ret 1608th FMS Charleston 1 Dec 56. To 1608th Wg Charleston 13 Feb 58. Tfd North Carolina ANG 156th AMS Douglas 30 May 62, 145th AMG Douglas 31 Dec 63, 145th TG Douglas 17 Feb 64. To 145th MAG Douglas 1 Jan 66. Tfd Pennsylvania ANG 168th MAG Olmsted 6 Apr 67. To 193rd TEWG Olmsted 27 Oct 67. To MASDC, Davis Monthan, for storage 23 Mar 72. For sale by DofD (Davis Monthan) 30 Oct 74. Sold Allied Aircraft 2 Jan 75. Scrapped subsequent to Jan 79.

4190 C-121C/1049F-55-96 18 Jan 56 to U S Air Force as 54-171. (USAF acceptance 13 Jan 56). Del to MATS Atlantic 1608th FMS Charleston 18 Jan 56. Assigned 41st TS Charleston 26 Jan 56, to 76th TS Charleston 15 Feb 56. To 1608th Maint Gp Charleston 1 Nov 56, ret 1608th FMS Charleston 1 Dec 56, 1608th Maint Gp Charleston 11 Jan 58. To 1608th Wg Charleston 13 Feb 58. Tfd New Jersey ANG 150th AMS Newark 10 Jan 63. To 170th MAG McGuire 1 Jan 66. To 170th AEA Gp McGuire 10 Jan 70. To MASDC Davis Monthan for storage 27 Apr 73. No engines, on belly, by Jun 76. For sale by DofD (Davis Monthan) 23 Mar 77 (TT: 15,609 hrs). Sold Delcon for scrap 23 Mar 78, scrapped subsequent to Jan 79.

4191 C-121C/1049F-55-96 26 Jan 56 to U S Air Force as 54-172. (USAF acceptance 18 Jan 56). Del to MATS Atlantic 41st TS Charleston 30 Jan 56. Assigned 1608th FMS Charleston 2 Feb 56, to 76th TS Charleston 4 May 56, 1608th Maint Gp Charleston 1 Nov 56. Ret 1608th FMS Charleston 1 Dec 56. To 1608th Wg Charleston 13 Feb 58. Tfd Mississippi ANG 183rd AMS Hawkins 13 Aug 62. To 172nd MAG Jackson 1 Jan 66. Tfd West Virginia ANG 167th MAG Martinsburg 24 May 67, 167th AEA Gp Martinsburg 1 Aug 68. To MASDC Davis Monthan for storage 23 May. For sale by DofD (Davis Monthan) 30 Oct 74. Sold to Allied Aircraft 9 Jan 75, scrapped subsequent to Jan 79.

4192 C-121C/1049F-55-96 10 Feb 56 to U S Air Force as 54-173. Del to MATS Atlantic 76th TS Charleston 10 Feb 56 'City of San Juan'. Assigned 1608th Maint Gp Charleston 1 Nov 56, 1608th FMS Charleston 1 Dec 56. Ret 1608th Maint Gp Charleston 20 Jan 58. To 1608th Wg Charleston 3 Feb 58. Tfd Pennsylvania ANG 140th AMS Olmsted 9 Oct 62, 168th MAG Olmsted 17 Jun 66. Allotted 193rd TEWS Olmsted 16 Sep 67. Cvtd to EC-121S by LAS Sep 67-1968. To 193rd TEWG Olmsted 16 Jul 68, redesignated EC-121S same day. To 193rd SOG Olmsted 12 Dec 77. To MASDC Davis Monthan for storage 13 Apr 78. For sale by DofD (Davis Monthan) 15 Aug 84 (TT: 15,420 hrs), and again 20 Aug 85 in poor condition. Sold to DMI Aviation Inc 5 Mar 87, regd N88879 8 Apr 87. Overhauled at Tucson, AZ, sold to AMSA-Aerolineas Mundo SA 15 May 87, regd HI-515. N-regn canx Jun 87, in svce Santo Domingo, DR Aug 87. Named 'City of Santo Domingo' by Dec 88, reregd HI-515CT by Feb 89. Ditched off Levittown, Puerto Rico 5 Apr 90 on 3-engined ferry from San Juan, PR to Santo Domingo. Twenty minutes into flight, pilot reported a fire in no.2 engine. Aircraft turned back towards San Juan, but fire could not be extinguished & engine fell away. Shortly afterwards, no.1 engine also failed & pilot elected to ditch in sea off Puerto Rico, shutting down the one remaining engine just before impact. One killed, two injured in crash.

4193 C-121C/1049F-55-96 17 Feb 56 to U S Air Force as 54-174. Del to MATS Atlantic 76th TS Charleston 17 Feb 56. Assigned 1608th Maint Gp Charleston 1 Nov 56, to 1608th FMS Charleston 1 Dec 56. To 1608th Wg Charleston 13 Feb 58. To MATS 1503rd ATW, Det A, op by VR-7 (Navy), Det A, Tachikawa 1 Jun 62. To 7th TS Tachikawa 31 Jul 62. Tfd North Carolina ANG 145th MAG Douglas 1 Feb 66, tfd Pennsylvania ANG 168th MAG Olmsted 22 Mar 67. To 193rd TEWG Olmsted 27 Oct 67. Tfd New Jersey ANG 170th MAG McGuire 21 Aug 68, ret 193rd TEWG Olmsted 25 Jan 69. To AFRES 915th MAG Homestead 13 Jul 71, 79th AEW Sq Homestead 30 Jul 71. To Andrews AFB Aug 71 for use by Commanding General, HQ, Air Force Reserve (unmarked), assigned 459th TAW AFRES Andrews as VC-121C 20 Oct 71. To MASDC Davis Monthan for storage 13 Oct 72. For sale by DofD (Davis Monthan) 23 Mar 77 (TT: 16,883 hrs). Sold to Delcon 29 May 78, scrapped subsequent to Jan 79.

4194 C-121C/1049F-55-96 24 Feb 56 to U S Air Force as 54-175. Del to MATS Atlantic 76th TS Charleston 24 Feb 56. Assigned 1608th Maint Gp Charleston 1 Nov 56, to 1608th FMS Charleston 1 Dec 56. To 1608th Wg Charleston 13 Feb 58. Tfd North Carolina ANG 156th AMS Douglas 17 Aug 62, to 145th AMG Douglas 31 Dec 63, 145th ATG Douglas 28 Apr 65. To 145th MAG Douglas 1 Feb 66. Tfd New Jersey ANG 170th MAG McGuire 12 Jan 67, to 170th AEA Gp McGuire 10 Jan 70. To MASDC Davis Monthan for storage 8 Feb 73. For sale by DofD 23 Mar 77 (TT: 15,857 hrs). Sold to Delcon 29 May 78, scrapped subsequent to Jan 79.

4195 C-121C/1049F-55-96 9 Mar 56 to U S Air Force as 54-176. Del to MATS Atlantic 76th TS Charleston 9 Mar 56. Assigned 1608th Maint Gp Charleston 1 Nov 56, to 1608th FMS Charleston 1 Dec 56. Ret 1608th Maint Gp Charleston 4 Jan 58. To 1608th Wg Charleston 11 Feb 58. Tfd Mississippi ANG 183rd AMS Hawkins 11 Jan 63. To 172nd MAG Jackson 1 Jan 66. Tfd West Virginia ANG 167th MAG Martinsburg 3 Apr 67, to 167th AEA Gp Martinsburg 1 Aug 68. To MASDC Davis Monthan for storage 4 Aug 72. For sale by DofD (Davis Monthan) 30 Oct 74 (TT: 15,407 hrs). Sold Allied Aircraft 10 Jan 75, scrapped subsequent to Jan 79.

4196 C-121C/1049F-55-96 27 Mar 56 to U S Air Force as 54-177. (USAF acceptance 21 Mar 56). Del to MATS Atlantic 76th TS Charleston 27 Mar 56 'City of Prestwick'. Assigned 1608th Maint Gp Charleston 1 Nov 56, to 1608th FMS Charleston 1 Dec 56. Ret 1608th Maint Gp Charleston 22 Jan 58. To 1608th Wg Charleston 13 Feb 58. Tfd Mississippi ANG 183rd AMS Hawkins 30 Oct 62. To 172nd MAG Jackson 1 Jan 66. Tfd West Virginia ANG 167th MAG Martinsburg 3 Apr 67, to 167th AEA Gp Martinsburg 1 Aug 68. Tfd Pennsylvania ANG 193rd TEWG Olmsted 7 Apr 72. To MASDC Davis Monthan for storage 1 Nov 77. Still stored Jan 79. Withdrawn from storage on sale to Ascher Ward 14 Aug 81, regd N104W in Aug 81. Flown to Van Nuys, CA Aug 81. Cvtd to 105-Seater, named 'Connie is a Lady' by Dec 81. Reptd regd to R L Upstrom, but ret to Ascher Ward 5 Jan 82. Regd to Bill A Conner, lsd to Classic Air Inc 13 Nov 83. To Air Flora Aviation Corp 15 Jan 86, regd 21 Apr 86. Sale canx, ret to Classic Air Inc 24 Jun 86, regd 1 Aug 86. For sale by auction 12 Jan 87 at Van Nuys, but failed to reach reserve of $116,000. Regd to Darryl L Greenamyer Inc 18

Dec 87 (repossession), regd 13 May 88. Donated to NASM, Washington, DC & made last flight Van Nuys-Kansas City, MO-Dulles Intl Airport, Washington, DC 20-21 Feb 88. Darryl L Greenamyer tf officially to NASM 28 Nov 89, regd 1 Dec 89. Stored at Washington Dulles outside hangar, engineless (a/o Apr 96). To be preserved inside when new NASM facility at Dulles opens in Dec 2003.

4197 C-121C/1049F-55-96 23 Mar 56 to U S Air Force as 54-178. Del to MATS Atlantic 76th TS Charleston 23 Mar 56. Assigned 1608th Maint Gp Charleston 1 Nov 56, to 1608th FMS Charleston 1 Dec 56. To 1608th Wg Charleston 13 Feb 58. To MATS 7th TS Tachikawa 21 Nov 62. Tfd AFSC Wright-Patterson 7 May 63. Cvtd to JC-121C for AFSC-ASD by AFLC Lake City 1 Dec 66. Used in "Project Marcom Relay". Ret AFSC Wright-Patterson 25 Feb 67. To EC-121C (unconf in AF records), redesignated C-121C Wright-Patterson 1 Feb 70. To MASDC, Davis Monthan, for storage 3 Jan 72. For sale by DofD (Davis Monthan) 30 Oct 74. Sold to unknown scrap dealer. Still stored Jan 79, subsequently scrapped.

4198 C-121C/1049F-55-96 5 Apr 56 to U S Air Force as 54-179. (USAF acceptance 3 Apr 56). Del to MATS Atlantic 76th TS Charleston 'City of Munich' 5 Apr 56. Assigned 1608th Maint Gp Charleston 1 Nov 56, to 1608th FMS Charleston 1 Dec 56. To 1608th Wg Charleston 13 Feb 58. Tfd Pennsylvania ANG 140th AMS Olmsted 4 Jan 63. To 168th MAG Olmsted 2 Feb 66. Assigned 193rd MAG Olmsted 27 Oct 67, tfd 193rd TEWG Olmsted 18 Jul 68. To MASDC Davis Monthan for storage 16 Apr 73. For sale by DofD (Davis Monthan) 23 Mar 77 (TT: 14,516 hrs). Sold to Delcon 30 Mar 78, scrapped subsequent to Jan 79.

4199 C-121C/1049F-55-96 14 Apr 56 to U S Air Force as 54-180. (USAF acceptance 9 Apr 56). Del to MATS Atlantic 41st TS Charleston 14 Apr 56. Assigned 1608th Maint Gp Charleston 1 Nov 56, to 1608th FMS Charleston 1 Dec 56. To 1608th Wg Charleston 13 Feb 58. Tfd Pennsylvania ANG 140th AMS Olmsted 6 Nov 62. To 168th MAG Olmsted 2 Feb 66. To 193rd TEWG Olmsted 27 Oct 67. To MASDC Davis Monthan for storage 9 Nov 77, but arr Davis Monthan 28 Apr 77. For sale by DofD (Davis Monthan) 15 Nov 83 (TT: 18,810 hrs). Unsold as did not meet reserve of $7,000. For sale again DofD (Davis Monthan) 15 Aug 84 & 26 Feb 85. USAF Museum tfd rights on aircraft to Charleston AFB Museum Feb 85. Overhauled & on operational ramp 10 May 85. Flew Davis Monthan, AZ-Charleston, SC Jun 85. Restoration completed & on display at the Transport Aircraft Museum, Charleston, SC, painted as "54-153" by May 86, repainted in MATS colours as "4153" by May 98.

4200 C-121C/1049F-55-96 26 Apr 56 to U S Air Force as 54-181. (USAF acceptance 18 Apr 56). Del to MATS Atlantic 41st TS Charleston 26 Apr 56. Assigned 1608th Maint Gp Charleston 1 Nov 56, to 1608th FMS Charleston 1 Dec 56. Ret 1608th Maint Gp Charleston 29 Jan 58. To 1608th Wg Charleston 12 Feb 58. To MATS 1503rd ATW, Det A, op by VR-7 (Navy), Det A, Tachikawa 14 Jun 62. Tfd North Carolina ANG 145th MAG Douglas 3 Feb 66. Tfd District of Columbia ANG (121st TFS support aircraft), assigned 709th NG AHQ Andrews 21 Mar 67. To New Jersey ANG 170th MAG McGuire 29 Jul 68, ret NG AHQ Andrews 31 Jan 69 (National Guard Bureau). To VC-121C at Andrews 23 Dec 69. To MASDC Davis Monthan for storage 29 Jun 75. For sale by DofD (Davis Monthan) 24 May 78, and again 7 Jun 78 (TT: 17,008 hrs). Sold to Southwestern Alloys 15 May 79, but stored in Allied Aircraft Sales scrapyard, Davis Monthan, by Oct 79. Scrapped subsequent to Apr 81.

4201 C-121C/1049F-55-96 11 May 56 to U S Air Force as 54-182. (USAF acceptance 4 May 56). Del to MATS Atlantic 76th TS Charleston 'City of Port of Spain' 11 May 56. Assigned 1608th Maint Gp Charleston 1 Nov 56, to 1608th FMS Charleston 1 Dec 56. To 1608th Wg Charleston 13 Feb 58. Tfd New Jersey ANG 150th AMS Newark 10 Feb 63, 170th ATG McGuire 9 Jul 65. To 170th MAG McGuire 1 Jan 66, 170th AEA Gp McGuire 4 Mar 70. To MASDC Davis Monthan for storage 27 Apr 73. For sale by DofD (Davis Monthan) 23 Aug 78, and again on 11 Jul 79. (TT: 15,911 hrs). Sold to Southwestern Alloys 10 Sep 79, scrapped, date unknown.

4202 C-121C/1049F-55-96 23 May 56 to U S Air Force as 54-183. (USAF acceptance 14 May 56). Del to MATS Atlantic 76th TS Charleston 'City of Manchester' 23 May 56. Assigned 1608th Maint Gp Charleston 1 Nov 56, to 1608th FMS Charleston 1 Dec 56. To 1608th Wg Charleston 7 Feb 58. Tfd Pennsylvania ANG 140th AMS Olmsted 28 Feb 63. To 168th MAG Olmsted 2 Feb 66. To 193rd TEWG 27 Oct 67. To MASDC Davis Monthan for storage 28 Sep 77. For sale by DofD (Davis Monthan) 15 Nov 83 (TT: 19,543 hrs). $4,500 offered, but not enough, so for sale again by DofD (Davis Monthan) 15 Aug 84, 26 Feb 85 & 20 Aug 85 in poor condition. Sold to Hangar 10 Inc Oct 85, regd N515AC 28 Oct 85. In svce, t/a Atkins Aviation Inc, by Oct 86. Out of svce Mar 88 and stored McAllen, TX. Sold to Aero Chago SA, regd HI-548 3 Sep 88. N-regn canx 8 Sep 88. Reregd HI-548CT by Feb 89. Grounded at Santo Domingo, DR Mar 93, but in fact had not flown since early 1992. Damaged beyond repair 22 Sep 98 when Curtiss C-46 HI-503CT was blown on top of it by Hurricane George. Wings broken & fuselage was split mid-way. Subsequently scrapped at Santo Domingo, Dominican Republic, half gone by 30 Mar 99. Cockpit section saved by Francisco Agullo on behalf of SCFA & shipped to Engineering School at Geneva, Switzerland for restoration.

4203 to 4299 Not allotted

4300 Not allotted

4301 PO-2W=WV-2/1049A-55-70 29 Oct 53 to US Navy as 126512. Burbank (R & D). To NATC Patuxent 23 Dec 54. BIS (Board of Inspection & Survey) Trials. Burbank (R & D) 14 May 55. Cvtd to WV-2 Experimental 2 Feb 56. Re-designated WV-2E 2 Feb 56. Redeld to NADU South Weymouth 2 Mar 58, coded NADU-2. Burbank 15 Jul 59 (R & D, Testing & Evaluation). NMC Point Mugu 2 Dec 60. Fitted with prototype AMTI - Airborne Moving Target Indicator 1960. Programme terminated due to in-flight failure of the rotodome. To Storage Facility, Litchfield Park 5 Jun 62. Re-designated EC-121L 30 Nov 62. Struck off (Litchfield Park) 8 Jan 63 (TT: 965 hrs). For sale by DofD (Davis Monthan) 18 Feb 65. Scrapped.

4302 PO-2W=WV-2/1049A-55-70 22 Mar 55 to US Navy as 126513. Navy acceptance date 16 Apr 54. To BuAer Facility, Alameda (M & S) 22 Mar 55. To FAETULANT Norfolk 9 May 55, VW-11 Patuxent 15 Sep 55. Tfd VW-13 Patuxent 16 Feb 56, VW-15 Patuxent 11 Apr 56. Ret VW-11 Patuxent 21 Mar 57. To FASRON 102 Norfolk 13 Aug 58. Modified for Antarctic ops, upper & lower radomes deleted. Coded FJ, named 'El Paisano'. First visit to Christchurch, New Zealand 26 Sep 59. To NAS Patuxent 21 Jun 60, used for "Project Magnet", still named 'El Paisano'. Crashed landing at McMurdo Sound, Antarctica, 31 Oct 60. En route from Christchurch, New Zealand, the aircraft hit a snowbank on landing, the landing gear collapsed, port wing and one engine were sheared off. Fuselage broke into several parts. Eight injuries among the crew/pax. Electronic gear salvaged and much used in replacement aircraft 'Paisano Dos' (c/n **5506**). Struck off (Patuxent) 1 Nov 60 (TT: 3,100 hrs).

4303 PO-2W=WV-2/1049A-55-70 14 Apr 54 to US Navy as 128323. Navy acceptance date 31 Dec 53. To VW-1 Barbers Pt 14 Apr 54, coded TE-2. Burbank (M & S) 16 Dec 54. BuAer Facility Alameda 16 Aug 55. To VW-1 Barbers Pt 25 Sep 55, VW-1, Det A, Atsugi 1 Feb 56. Ret VW-1 Barbers Pt 15 May 56, VW-1, Det A, Cubi Pt 5 Sep 56, VW-1 Barbers Pt 9 Nov 56, VW-1, Det A, Cubi Pt 29 May 57. Tfd VW-1 Agana 14 Sep 57. To NAMTC Point Mugu (R & D) 6 Jan 58, NMC Point Mugu (R & D) 28 Feb 59, coded Point Mugu-8323. Tfd PMR Point Mugu 10 Jun 59. To Storage Facility, Litchfield Park, AZ 20 Jul 59. Re-designated EC-121K 30 Nov 62. Struck off (Litchfield Park) 21 Mar 63 (TT: 2,682 hrs) and cannibalized for parts. For sale by DofD (Davis Monthan) 18 Feb 65. Scrapped.

Section 12: Constellation Production List

4304 WV-2/1049A-55-70 23 Mar 54 to US Navy as 128324. Navy acceptance date 29 Jan 54. To BAR M&S Burbank 29 Jan 54, VW-2 Patuxent 24 Mar 54, coded XD-8. Tfd NADU South Weymouth 31 Jul 54, NATU Quonset Pt 1 Jul 56, NADU South Weymouth 1 Aug 56. To NATC R&D Patuxent 28 Aug 57, carried titles 'Naval Research Laboratory' Jan 59. To NATC RDT & E Patuxent 30 Dec 59. Used for Weapons System Tests, named 'Sundowner' by 1962. Redesignated YEC-121K 30 Nov 62, EC-121K 28 Apr 63 to NEC-121K 26 Jul 63. Ret to YEC-121K Mar 65 on installation of special APU by AiResearch at NATC Patuxent. Continued with Weapons System Test (NRL). To NEC-121K and upper radome deleted by Jun 65. Name later not carried. To NC-121K. Retired from NATC Patuxent (NRL) Jul 74. To MASDC Davis Monthan for storage 6 Aug 74. Struck off (Davis Monthan) 6 Aug 74 (TT: 6,711 hrs). For sale by DofD (Davis Monthan) 11 Feb 81 (TT quoted as 6,717 hrs). Sold to Allied Aircraft 18 Jun 81. Scrapped subsequent to Feb 84 (tail unit & rear fuselage sawn off in mechanical saw demonstration, probably in 1985).

4305 WV-2/1049A-55-70 7 Mar 55 to US Navy as 128325. Navy acceptance date 2 Feb 54. Used for pilot training at LAC prior to LADD. To BuAer Facility Alameda (M & S) 7 Mar 55, VW-2 Patuxent 17 Mar 55. Tfd VW-11 Patuxent 21 Nov 55, VW-13 Patuxent 20 Apr 56, VW-15 Patuxent 30 Aug 56. Ret VW-11 Patuxent 26 Feb 57. To VW-15 Patuxent 27 Jun 57, to VW-11 Argentia 26 Nov 57, ret VW-11 Patuxent 28 Feb 58. To Storage Facility, Litchfield Park 12 May 58. Redesignated EC-121K 30 Nov 62. Struck off (Litchfield Park) 21 Mar 63 (TT: 1,071 hrs), and cannibalized for parts. For sale by DofD (Davis Monthan) 18 Feb 65. Scrapped.

4306 WV-2/1049A-55-70 13 May 54 to US Navy as 128326. Navy acceptance date 30 Apr 54. To NATC Patuxent (R & D) 13 May 54. Used for BIS (Board of Inspection & Survey) Trials, Burbank 17 Jun 55. Ret NATC Patuxent (R & D) 15 Feb 56. To Storage Facility, Litchfield Park, 12 Jun 57. Redesignated EC-121K 30 Nov 62. Struck off (Litchfield Park) 21 Mar 63 (TT: 724 hrs), and cannibalized for parts. For sale by DofD (Davis Monthan) 18 Feb 65. Scrapped.

128326 WV-2 formerly of the Naval Air Test Center Patuxent is seen stored at Litchfield Park, Arizona in the late 1950s. (Brian R Baker)

4307 WV-2/1049A-55-91 17 Jul 54 to US Navy as 131387. Navy acceptance date 30 Jun 54. To NADU South Weymouth 17 Jul 54. Coded NADU-4 'Big Dipper'. Crashed on landing at NAS Johnsville, PA 9 Dec 54. Rolled for about 100 yards after hitting the landing strip, turned over and skidded a short distance before bursting into flames. No casualties. Struck off (NADU South Weymouth) 20 Dec 54 (TT: 227 hrs).

4308 WV-2/1049A-55-91 29 Jun 54 to US Navy as 131388. To BAR M&S Burbank 29 Jun 54. To VW-l Barbers Pt, believed coded TE-3 18 Oct 54. Tfd VW-15 Patuxent 4 Oct 56, to VW-11 Patuxent 26 Feb 57, ret VW-15 Patuxent 27 Jun 57. To VW-11 Argentia 26 Nov 57. Tfd NADU South Weymouth 24 Jan 58. To NATC RDT&E Patuxent 12 Sep 61, Coded NADU-1. Stored at Litchfield Park (a/o Apr 62), but not in records. To NADC Johnsville 10 Apr 62, EC-121K 30 Nov 62, to NAS Johnsville 30 Nov 62 & NAF Johnsville 31 Aug 63. Redesignated NC-121K 10 Jun 64. NAF Johnsville RDT&E 30 Nov 64. Upper radome deleted by 1969. To MASDC Davis Monthan for storage 21 Mar 74. Struck off (Davis Monthan) 22 Mar 74 (TT: 6,219 hrs). Still in storage (complete) Oct 75. Sold to Sun Valley Aviation 16 Sep 76, subsequently scrapped.

4309 WV-2/1049A-55-91 16 Jul 54 to US Navy as 131389. To VW-2 Patuxent 18 Aug 54, coded XD-9 'Brunhilde' (but see also c/n 4324). To VW-13 Patuxent 7 Oct 55, tfd VW-11 Patuxent 9 Nov 55. Ret to VW-2 Patuxent Sep 57 (possibly May 57- card unclear). To VW-4 Jacksonville 17 Dec 57. To Storage Facility, Litchfield Park 24 Feb 59. Redesignated EC-121K 30 Nov 62. Struck off (Litchfield Park) 21 Mar 63 (TT: 1,499 hrs), and cannibalized for parts. For sale by DofD (Davis Monthan) 18 Feb 65. Scrapped.

4310 WV-2/1049A-55-91 16 Jul 54 to US Navy as 131390. To VW-l Barbers Pt 18 Oct 54. Tf VW-2 Patuxent 24 May 56. Ret VW-l Barbers Pt 4 Jan 57, VW-l, Det A, Cubi Pt 10 Feb 57, VW-l Barbers Pt 7 May 57. Tfd VW-l Agana 15 Aug 57. To Storage Facility, Litchfield Park, 26 Mar 58. Withdrawn from storage and flown to LAS Ontario 24 Sep 58. Cvtd to WV-2Q 9 Jan 59. To NATC Patuxent (R & D) 17 Nov 59. VQ-2 Rota 9 Sep 60, VW-2 Patuxent 17 Feb 61 (error?), ret VQ-2 Rota 20 Feb 61, coded '15'. Crashed nr Fuerstenfeldbruck, 14 miles east of Munich, West Germany, shortly after 11.00 hrs (local) on 22 May 62, killing all on board. The aircraft, on a training flight from Rhein-Main, Frankfurt, was on approach to Fuerstenfeldbruck for an emergency landing, when it rolled over in the air several times and crashed into a field 1.25 miles from the village of Markt Schwaben, followed by explosion and fire. The tail empennage had torn off in flight, cause unknown. All 26 crew killed. (TT: 2,755 hrs). Struck off same day.

4311 WV-2/1049A-55-91 16 Jul 54 to U S Navy as 131391. To BAR M&S Burbank 16 Jul 54. To VW-2 Patuxent 24 Nov 54, believed coded XD-10. To VW-11 Patuxent 11 Nov 55, VW-13 Patuxent 20 Apr 56. Tfd VW-4 Jacksonville 19 Jun 57, believed coded MH-4. To Storage Facility, Litchfield Park 14 Feb 58. Withdrawn from storage 27 Nov 58, to BAR M&S Ontario 28 Nov 58, cvtd to WV-2Q by LAS Ontario, redesignated WV-2Q 8 Jan 59. To BAR M&S Baltimore 6 May 59. To VQ-2 Rota 21 Mar 60, coded 13, later 10 (unconf). Redesignated EC-121M 6 Oct 62. By 1972 named 'Ajax Airlines'. Last flight from Europe Mildenhall-Lajes 4 May 72. To MASDC, Davis Monthan, for storage 9 May 72. Struck off (Davis Monthan) 29 Jul 74 (TT: 12,146 hrs). Sold to Sun Valley Aviation 28 May 76, subsequently scrapped.

4312 WV-2/1049A-55-91 26 Jul 54 to US Navy as 131392. To BAR M&S Burbank 26 Jul 54. To VW-1 Barbers Pt 22 Nov 54, VW-1, Det A Atsugi 26 Aug 55, ret VW-1 Barbers Pt 9 Oct 55. To VW-1, Det A Atsugi 3 Jan 56, ret VW-1 Barbers Pt 25 Jan 56. Tfd VW-11 Patuxent 14 Feb 56, VW-13 Patuxent 24 Apr 56. Ret VW-1 Barbers Pt 22 Mar 57, VW-1, Det A Cubi Pt 5 Apr 57, ret VW-1 Barbers Pt 11 Jun 57. To VW-1 Agana 1 Sep 57. To Storage Facility, Litchfield Park, 24 Mar 58. Withdrawn from storage 24 Oct 58. To BAR M&S Ontario 25 Oct 58, cvtd to WV-2Q by LAS Ontario, redesignated WV-2Q 8 Jan 59. To BAR M&S Baltimore 2 Mar 59. To VQ-2 Rota 23 Feb 60, coded 12. Redesignated EC-121M 5 Oct 62. Coded 11 by May 70. By 1972 named 'Lakeys Loafers', recoded 31 after Mar 72. To MASDC, Davis Monthan, for storage 19 Aug 74. Struck off (VQ-2) 19 Aug 74 (TT: 12,917 hrs). Still stored whole Sep 77. For sale by DofD (Davis Monthan) 11 Feb 81 (TT quoted as 12,891 hrs). Sold to Allied Aircraft 5 Jun 81, subsequently scrapped. Nose & parts only by Oct 82.

4313 WV-2/1049A-55-86 5 Aug 54 to US Navy as 135746. To VW-2 Patuxent 25 Nov 54, VW-2, Det B Capodichino 15 Aug 56. Ret VW-2 Patuxent 15 Nov 56, VW-2, Det B Capodichino, 29 Aug 57. Ret VW-2 Patuxent 28 Mar(?) 58 (card unclear). To Storage Facility, Litchfield Park, 16 Jan 59. Redesignated EC-121K 30 Nov 62. Struck off (Litchfield Park) 21 Mar 63, (TT: 1,453 hrs), and cannibalized for parts. For sale by DofD 18 Feb 65. Scrapped.

4314 WV-2/1049A-55-86 13 Aug 54 to US Navy as 135747. To BAR M&S Burbank 13 Aug 54. To VW-2 Patuxent 29 Nov 54, coded XD-6 'Hugin', later TF-6 'Hugin'. To VW-4 Jacksonville 16 Oct 57. To BAR M&S Ontario 25 Feb 59. Cvtd to WV-2Q by LAS Ontario, redesignated WV-2Q 25 Feb 59. To BAR M&S Baltimore 10 Aug 59. To VQ-l Iwakuni 16 Jun 60 coded PR-24, tfd VQ-1 Atsugi 31 Aug 60, coded PR-25. Redesignated EC-121M 30 Nov 62. Written-off after undercarriage collapsed landing at Atsugi 20 Aug 65. During touch & go landings, the port main undercarriage hydraulic cylinder failed, causing the port wheels & inner cylinder to drop off the aircraft. A two-wheel landing was executed, the aircraft slid off the runway upon settling on to its radome & ran into a navigation aids building. One crewman injured. Severely damaged by fire later, and scrapped. Struck off Jan 66. (TT: 5,600 hrs).

4315 WV-2/1049A-55-86 2 Sep 54 to US Navy as 135748. To VW-2 Patuxent 17 Dec 54, coded XD-4. BAR Facility Norfolk 14 Feb 56, BAR Facility Corpus Christi 19 Oct 56. Ret to VW-2 Patuxent 18(?) Apr 57 (card unclear). To VW-4 Jacksonville 18 Oct 57, coded MH-7. To VW-15 Patuxent 9 Jul 59, coded ML-748. To Storage Facility, Litchfield Park, 27 Apr 60. Redesignated EC-121K 30 Nov 62. Struck off (Litchfield Park) 21 Mar 63 (TT: 2,391 hrs), and cannibalized for parts. For sale by DofD (Davis Monthan) 18 Feb 65. Scrapped.

4316 WV-2/1049A-55-86 3 Sep 54 to US Navy as 135749. To BAR M&S Burbank 3 Sep 54. To VW-l Barbers Pt 21 Dec 54, VW-1 Det A Atsugi 4 May 55, ret VW-1 Barbers Pt 1 Aug 55. To VW-1 Det A Atsugi 3 Mar 56, ret VW-1 Barbers Pt 2 Jun 56. To VW-1 Det A Cubi Pt 31 Aug 56, ret VW-1 Barbers Pt 9 Nov 56. To VW-1 Det A 11 Mar 57, ret VW-1 Barbers Pt 29 May 57, tfd VW-1 Agana 31 Jul 57. To Storage Facility, Litchfield Park 3 May 58. To BAR M&S Ontario 6 Nov 58, cvtd to WV-2Q 8 Jan 59. To BAR M&S Baltimore 31 Mar 59. To VQ-1 Iwakuni 11 Feb 60, tf VQ-1 Atsugi 1 Aug 60. Redesignated EC-121M 4 Nov 62. Coded PR-21. Damaged in rocket attack Da Nang 15 Jul 67, repaired & ret to svce 12 Sep 67. Shot down by two North Korean MiG fighter aircraft at 13.50 hrs (local) on 14 Apr 69, and crashed in the Sea of Japan, approx 170 kms SE of Chongjin, with the loss of all on board. (TT: 10,980 hrs). The aircraft was on a reconnaissance flight from Atsugi, Japan, and had just been warned to abort mission and was setting course back to Atsugi when the MiGs attacked.

4317 WV-2/1049A-55-86 7 Sep 54 to US Navy as 135750. To VW-2 Patuxent 4 Dec 54, coded XD-5 'Munin'. VW-4 Jacksonville 25 Oct 57. To VW-13 Patuxent 19 Aug 59, VW-11 Argentia 14 Jun 60. To NAS Patuxent (Research Lab?) 6 Feb 61. Redesignated EC-121K 30 Nov 62. To Storage Facility, Litchfield Park 25 Jan 63. Struck off (Litchfield Park) 21 May 65 (TT: 4,274 hrs, also quoted as 4,297 hrs). Scrapped at Litchfield Park approx Oct 65.

4318 WV-2/1049A-55-86 13 Sep 54 to US Navy as 135751. To BAR M&S Burbank 13 Sep 54. To VW-l Barbers Pt 21 Dec 54. To VW-1 Det A Atsugi 3 Jul 55, ret VW-1 Barbers Pt 7 Aug 55. To VW-1 Det A Atsugi 2 Dec 55, ret VW-1 Barbers Pt 8 Mar 56. To M&S Corpus Christi 7 Aug 56. To VW-3 Agana 1 Nov 57. To Storage Facility, Litchfield Park 10 Apr 58. To BAR M&S Ontario 7 Jan 59, cvtd to WV-2Q 8 Jan 59. To BAR M&S Baltimore 6 May 59. To VQ-1 Iwakuni 30 Apr 60, tf VQ-1 Atsugi 31 Aug 60, coded PR-22. Redesignated EC-121M 30 Nov 62. Written-off after accident and fire on the ground at Atsugi, Japan 27 Jan 66. DBR when fire started when heat lamps being used to cure the radome were blown against it by the wind. Struck off (VQ-l Atsugi) 3 Mar 66. (TT: 6,555 hrs). Stored in damaged state at Atsugi post strike for some time afterwards (at least till Nov 68), and used for parts.

4319 WV-2/1049A-55-86 29 Nov 54 to US Navy as 135752. To BAR M&S Burbank 29 Nov 54. To VW-l Barbers Pt 14 Jan 55. To VW-1 Det A Atsugi 4 May 55, ret VW-1 Barbers Pt 3 Jul 55. To VW-1 Det A Atsugi 6 Aug 55, ret VW-1 Barbers Pt 5 Nov 55. To VW-1 Det A Atsugi 2 Apr 56, ret VW-1 Barbers Pt 15 Nov 56. Tfd VW-1 Det A Cubi Pt 24 Nov 56, ret VW-1 Barbers Pt 9 Jan 57. To VW-1 Agana 29 Aug 57. To Storage Facility, Litchfield Park 7 May 58. To BAR M&S Ontario 23 Jan 59, cvtd to WV-2Q 23 Jan 59. To BAR M&S Baltimore 5 Jun 59. To VQ-1 Iwakuni 27 May 60, tfd VQ-1 Atsugi 31 Aug 60, coded PR-23. Redesignated EC-121M 30 Nov 62. Damaged in rocket attack Da Nang 15 Jul 67, repaired & ret to svce 5 Aug 67. To VQ-2 Rota 24 Nov 70, coded 12. Tf to MASDC, Davis Monthan for storage 24 Nov 70. Struck off (Davis Monthan) 25 May 71 (TT: 12,185 hrs). Sold to Sun Valley Aviation 13 Sep 76, subsequently scrapped.

4320 WV-2/1049A-55-86 4 Jan 55 to US Navy as 135753. Navy acceptance date 30 Nov 54. To BAR M&S Burbank 30 Nov 54. To VW-2 Patuxent 5 Jan 55, coded XD-2, later TF-2 'Fricka'. To VW-4 Jacksonville 15(?) Nov 57. To NATC Patuxent (R&D) 12 Feb 58 and cvtd to research laboratory, NATC RDT&E Patuxent 29 Feb 60. Reportedly cvtd to EC-121N by Oct 63 and to EC-121P by Sep 64, but neither appears in Navy records. Re-designated EC-121K 26 Nov 62. Used for Weapons System Test, NATC Patuxent. To NRL Patuxent until tfd to MASDC Davis Monthan for storage 16 Dec 75. Struck off Jun 76. For sale by DofD (Davis Monthan) 11 Feb 81 (TT: 8,362 hrs). Sold to Allied Aircraft 18 Jun 81, subsequently scrapped (nose & parts only in Allied's scrapyard Oct 82).

4321 WV-2/1049A-55-86 8 Jan 55 to US Navy as 135754. Navy acceptance date 30 Nov 54. To NADU, South Weymouth 9 Jan 55, later coded NADU-3 (until wfu). Flew across Atlantic & back in support of Navy's ZPG-2 airship 'Snowbird' during record-breaking endurance flt 4-15 Mar 57. To Storage Facility, Litchfield Park 7 Sep 61. Redesignated EC-121K 30 Nov 62. Struck off (Litchfield Park) 21 Mar 63 (TT: 2,887 hrs), cannibalized for parts. For sale by DofD (Davis Monthan) 18 Feb 65. Scrapped.

4322 WV-2/1049A-55-86 21 Dec 54 to US Navy as 135755. Navy acceptance date 16 Nov 54. To VW-l Barbers Pt 20 Dec 54. To VW-l Det A Atsugi 5 Oct 55. Ret VW-1 Barbers Pt 10 Jan 56. To VW-l Det A Atsugi 20 Jun 56, ret VW-1 Barbers Pt 10 Jul 56. Tfd VW-l Det A Cubi Pt 5 Jan 57. Ret VW-l Barbers Pt 20 Mar 57, tfd VW-l Agana 9 Sep 57. To VW-3 Agana 15 Feb 58. To Storage Facility, Litchfield Park 14 Feb 59. Redesignated EC-121K 30 Nov 62. Struck off (Litchfield Park) 21 Mar 63 (TT: 2,301 hrs), cannibalized for parts. For sale by DofD (Davis Monthan) 18 Feb 65. Scrapped, probably same year.

4323 WV-2/1049A-55-86 15 Jan 55 to US Navy as 135756. Navy acceptance date 28 Dec 54. To BAR M&S Burbank 28 Dec 54. To VW-l Barbers Pt 15 Jan 55. To VW-1 Det A Atsugi 1 Nov 55, ret VW-1 Barbers Pt 5 Feb 56. Tfd VW-1 Det A Atsugi 5 Jul 56, ret VW-1 Barbers Pt 10 Sep 56. To VW-1 Det A Cubi Pt 3 Nov 56, ret VW-1 Barbers Pt 21 Jan 57. To VW-1 Det A Cubi Pt 10 Jun 57. Tfd VW-1 Agana 14 Sep 57. To VW-1 Dep A Cubi Pt 8 Oct 57, ret VW-1 Agana 13 Dec 57. Tfd VW-3 Agana 12 Jan 58. To NAMTC R&D Pt Mugu 15 Oct 58, to Pacific Missile Range Pt Mugu 10 Jun 59. Fitted with two extra lower radomes by 1961. Redesignated EC-121K 30 Nov 62. To Naval Missile Center Pt Mugu 1 Aug 63, ret PMR Pt Mugu 13 Sep 63. To VAQ-33 NAS Norfolk by Jun 70, coded GD-10. To MASDC, Davis Monthan, for storage 7 Jan 71. Struck off (Davis Monthan) 12 Jul 72 (TT: 7,588 hrs). Sold to Sun Valley Aviation 13 Sep 76, subsequently scrapped.

4324 WV-2/1049A-55-86 10 Feb 55 to US Navy as 135757. Navy acceptance date 28 Dec 54. To BAR M&S Burbank 28 Dec 54. To O&R BAR M&S Alameda 10 Feb 55. To VW-2 Patuxent, coded TF-9 'Brunhilde', 10 Mar 55. To VW-2 Det B Capodichino 3 Sep 56, ret VW-2 Patuxent 5 Dec 56. Coded MG-9, later MG-757. To Storage Facility Litchfield Park 10 Feb 58. To BAR M&S Ontario 16 Jan 59, cvtd to WV-2Q 16 Jan 59. To BAR M&S Baltimore 25 May 59. To VQ-2 Rota, coded 14, 28 Apr 60. Redesignated EC-121M 30 Oct 62. TDY VQ-1 Det B Jul 67, ret VQ-2 Rota Sep 67. Later coded 757. To MASDC, Davis Monthan, for storage 14 Nov 72 (en route at Mildenhall 27 Jul-26 Aug 72). Struck off (Davis Monthan) 29 Jul 74 (TT: 11,217 hrs). Sold to Sun Valley Aviation 16 Sep 76, subsequently scrapped.

4325 WV-2/1049A-55-86 3 Feb 55 to US Navy as 135758. Navy acceptance date 10 Jan 55. To BAR M&S Burbank 10 Jan 55. To VW-l Barbers Pt 3 Feb 55. To VW-1 Det A Atsugi 4 May 55, ret

One of the early USAF RC-121Ds makes an impressive sight in this take-off view from underneath. (United States Air Force)

VW-1 Barbers Pt 1 Aug 55. Tfd VW-1 Det A Atsugi 26 Aug 55, ret VW-1 Barbers Pt 15 Dec 55. To VW-1 Det A Atsugi 4 May 56, ret VW-1 Barbers Pt 3 Jul 56. To VW-1 Det A Cubi Pt 6 Oct 56, ret VW-1 Barbers Pt 7 Dec 56. Possibly to VW-2 Patuxent briefly Feb 57, but unlikely, ret VW-1 Barbers Pt 12 Feb 57. To VW-1 Det A Cubi Pt 4 May 57. ToVW-1 Agana 26 Sep 57. Tfd NAMTC R&D Pt Mugu 30 Dec 57. To Naval Missile Center R&D Pt Mugu 28 Feb 59, tfd Pacific Missile Range Pt Mugu 10 Jun 59. Fitted with two extra lower radomes by Nov 61. Redesignated EC-121K 30 Nov 62. To General Electric Schenectady Flight Test Center early 63 for installation of their 'Mod III' (Missile tracking test system) & new radome forward of the belly radome to house the Mod III antennae & a tracking light. Completed late 63. To NMC Pt Mugu 1 Aug 63, ret PMR Pt Mugu 17 Sep 63. To MASDC, Davis Monthan, for storage 3 Sep 70. Struck off (Davis Monthan) 31 Dec 70 (TT: 7,579 hrs). Sold to Kolar Inc 10 Oct 74, subsequently scrapped.

4326 WV-2/1049A-55-86 18 Feb 55 to US Navy as 135759. Navy acceptance date 17 Jan 55. To VW-2 Patuxent 21 Feb 55, coded XD-3 'Vidar'. To VW-2 Det B Capodichino 9 Jan 57, ret VW-2 Patuxent 6 Feb 57. Tfd VW-4 Jacksonville 16 Nov(?) 57 (card unclear). To VW-ll Argentia 27 May 59. Ret VW-2 Patuxent 22 Oct 60. Tfd VW-11 Argentia 25 Oct 60. To Storage Facility, Litchfield Park, 26 Jun 61. Redesignated EC-121K 30 Nov 62. Struck off (Litchfield Park) 21 Mar 63 (TT: 4,991 hrs), cannibalized for parts. For sale by DofD (Davis Monthan) 18 Feb 65. Scrapped, probably same year.

4327 WV-2/1049A-55-86 17 Feb 55 to US Navy as 135760. Navy acceptance date 9 Feb 55. To VW-2 Patuxent 17 Feb 55, coded XD-l 'Woden'. To VW-2 Det B Capodichino 15 Aug 56. Recoded TF-l 'Woden'. Ret VW-2 Patuxent 1 Oct 56. Tfd VW-4 Jacksonville 4 Sep 58, to VW-4 Roosevelt Roads 30 Nov 60. Tfd NAS Patuxent 13 Dec 60. To Storage Facility, Litchfield Park, 9 Feb 61. Redesignated EC-121K 30 Nov 62. Struck off (Litchfield Park) 21 May 65 (TT: 2,721 hrs). Scrapped approx Oct 65.

4328 WV-2/1049A-55-86 1 Mar 55 to US Navy as 135761. Navy acceptance date 10 Feb 55. To BAR Alameda (M & S) 10 Mar 55. To VW-2 Patuxent 12 Mar 55, coded TF-8 'Thor' by May 56. Tfd VW-4 Jacksonville 25 Oct 57, coded MH-8. To VW-13 Patuxent 23 Apr 59, coded MK-761. To Storage Facility, Litchfield Park 22 Jun 60. Redesignated EC-121K 30 Nov 62. Struck off (Litchfield Park) 21 May 65 (TT: 3,264 hrs). Scrapped approx Oct 65.

4329 RC-121D/1049A-55-86 10 Sep 54 to U S Air Force as 52-3411. Del 4701st AEW Sq McClellan 10 Sep 54. Assigned 8th AD (ADC) McClellan 22 Dec 54, to 552nd AEW Wg McClellan 19 Jul 55. Redesignated EC-121D 2 Dec 55, ret RC-121D 29 Feb 56. Assigned 551st AEW Wg McCoy 28 Nov 62, ret 552nd AEW Wg McClellan 6 Feb 63. Redesignated EC-121D 30 Sep 63, to 966th AEW Sq McCoy 22 Apr 64, ret 552nd AEW Wg McClellan 18 May 67. To 966th AEW Sq McCoy 27 Jun 67, ret 552nd AEW Wg McClellan 29 Aug 68. Later EC-121D/T, redesignated EC-121T 20 Apr 70. Deployed Tainan 20 Feb 71, Kwangju 19 Jun 71, Tainan 16 Sep 71, Kwangju 3 Dec 71, Korat 19 May 73. Ret McClellan 28 May 74. To MASDC, Davis Monthan for storage 25 Oct 74, arr 26 Oct 74 (TT: 21,231 hrs). For sale by DofD (Davis Monthan) 24 May 78 & again 7 Jun 78. Derelict, on tail, by Nov 78. Sold Southwestern Alloys 25 Oct 79, subsequently scrapped.

4330 RC-121D/1049A-55-86 25 Aug 54 to U S Air Force as 52-3412. USAF acceptance & dely 26 Aug 54. Del to 4701st AEW Sq McClellan 25 Aug 54. Assigned 8th AD (ADC) McClellan 22 Dec 54, to 552nd AEW Wg McClellan 19 Jul 55. Redesignated EC-121D 1 Oct 55, ret RC-121D 9 Feb 56. Assigned 551st AEW Wg McCoy 19 Oct 62, ret 55nd AEW Wg McClellan 17 Nov 62. Redesignated EC-121D by 19 May 64. Later EC-121D/T. Deployed Tainan 11 Sep 66, ret McClellan 5 May 67. Deployed

Tainan 19 Oct 67, ret McClellan 2 Feb 68. Deployed Tainan 9 Feb 68, ret McClellan 16 Feb 68. Assigned 966th AEW Sq McCoy 11 Aug 68, ret 55nd AEW Wg McClellan 24 Aug 68. Redesignated EC-121T 30 Apr 70, deployed Tainan 3 Nov 70, Kwangju 19 Jun 71, Korat 15 May 73, ret McClellan 18 May 74. Deployed Korat several times 1975. Tf 79th AEW Sq AFRES Homestead 2 Apr 76, assigned 915th AEW Gp AFRES Keflavik 2 Dec 76, ret 79th AEW Sq AFRES Homestead 8 Oct 77. To MASDC Davis Monthan for storage 25 Sep 78. For sale by DofD (Davis Monthan) 15 Nov 83 (TT: 22,997 hrs). Sold to DMI Aviation for $10,500, subsequently scrapped.

4331 RC-121D/1049A-55-86 18 Sep 54 to U S Air Force as 52-3413. USAF acceptance & dely 15 Sep 54. Del to 4701st AEW Sq McClellan 18 Sep 54. To 6520th Test Wg Hanscom 12 Oct 54. Redesignated JC-121D 1 Dec 56, JRC-121D 20 Dec 56, JEC-121D 28 Jan 57 & ret JRC-121D 6 May 57 (all at Hanscom). Assigned 552nd AEW Wg McClellan as RC-121D again 26 Apr 58, redesignated EC-121D 30 Sep 63. Deployed McCoy 4 Apr 64, ret McClellan 28 Feb 65. To McCoy 13 May 65, ret McClellan 16 Apr 66. Assigned 966th AEW Sq McCoy 17 Jan 67, ret 552nd AEW Wg McClellan 2 Mar 67. Deployed Tainan 7 Nov 67, ret McClellan 12 Jun 68. Deployed Tainan 5 Aug 68, ret McClellan 13 Apr 69. Deployed Tainan 28 Jul 69, ret McClellan 5 Jul 70. Deployed McCoy 14 Sep 70, ret McClellan 12 Oct 70. To MASDC Davis Monthan for storage 24 Nov 70. Scrapped subsequent to Jul 74.

4332 RC-121D/1049A-55-86 11 Aug 54 to U S Air Force as 52-3414. USAF acceptance date 10 Aug 54, dely 11 Aug 54. Del to AMC Wright-Patterson 11 Aug 54. Assigned 8th AD McClellan 27 Feb 55. To 552nd AEW Wg McClellan 19 Jul 55. Tfd 551st AEW Wg McCoy 23 Jan 62, ret 552nd AEW Wg McClellan 4 Mar 62. Redesignated EC-121D 30 Sep 63. Deployed Tainan 15 Sep 65, ret McClellan 7 Nov 65. Later EC-121D/T. Deployed Tainan 17 Oct 66, ret McClellan 4 Apr 67. Deployed Tainan 24 Aug 67, ret McClellan 12 Jan 68. Deployed Tainan 30 Mar 68, ret McClellan 20 Aug 68. Redesignated EC-121T 24 May 70. Deployed Tainan 26 Jan 71, Kwangju 19 Jun 71, Korat 15 May 73, ret McClellan 22 May 74. Tfd 79th AEW Sq AFRES Homestead 2 Apr 76, assigned 915th AEW Gp Keflavik 2 Dec 76, ret 79th AEW Sq Homestead 20 Aug 77, tf Keflavik 30 Sep 77. To MASDC Davis Monthan 3 Oct 78 for storage. For sale by DofD (Davis Monthan) 15 Nov 83 (TT: 22,739 hrs). Sold to DMI Aviation for $9,500, subsequently scrapped.

4333 RC-121D/1049A-55-86 20 Aug 54 to U S Air Force as 52-3415. Del 4701st AEW Sq McClellan 20 Aug 54. Assigned 8th AD (ADC) McClellan 22 Dec 54, to 552nd AEW Wg McClellan 19 Jul 55. Redesignated EC-121D 30 Nov 55, ret RC-121D 15 Dec 55. Redesignated EC-121D again 30 Sep 63. Deployed McCoy 17 May 66, ret McClellan 29 Jun 66. Deployed Tainan 13 Sep 68, ret McClellan 9 Jun 69. Deployed Tainan 7 Jul 69, Itazuke 24 Jul 70, Tainan 27 Aug 70, ret McClellan 11 Jun 71. To Davis Monthan for storage 29 Jun 71. Struck off 13 Apr 72. Scrapped subsequent to Jul 74.

4334 RC-121D/1049A-55-86 14 Sep 54 to U S Air Force as 52-3416. USAF acceptance & dely 15 Sep 54. Del 4701st AEW Sq McClellan 15 Sep 54. Assigned 8th AD (ADC) McClellan 22 Dec 54, to 552nd AEW Wg McClellan 19 Jul 55. Assigned 966th AEW Sq McCoy 10 Oct 63. Redesignated EC-121D 10 Oct 63, ret 552nd AEW Wg McClellan 16 May 66. To 966th AEW Sq McCoy 20 Jun 66, ret 552nd AEW Wg McClellan 11 Apr 67. To 966th AEW Sq McCoy 5 Dec 67, ret 552nd AEW Wg McClellan 27 May 69. To 966th AEW Sq McCoy 7 Jun 69, ret 552nd AEW Wg McClellan 8 Jul 69, deployed Keflavik 9 Aug 70, ret McClellan 23 Sep 70. To MASDC Davis Monthan for storage 14 Oct 70. Scrapped subsequent to Jul 74.

4335 RC-121D/1049A-55-86 28 Sep 54 to U S Air Force as 52-3417. Del 4701st AEW Sq McClellan 29 Sep 54. Assigned 8th AD (ADC) McClellan 22 Dec 54. Tfd 551st AEW Sq Otis 1 Mar 55, 551st AEW Wg Otis 17 Apr 55. Technical Order dated 1 Apr 62 gives "cvtd to EC-121H", but not cvtd. TDY 551st AEW Wg McCoy 21 Sep 62, ret 551st AEW Wg 5 Dec 62. TDY 551st AEW Wg McCoy 23 Dec 62, ret 551st AEW Wg Otis 24 Feb 63. Assigned 966th AEW Sq McCoy 25 Apr 63. Redesignated EC-121D 10 Oct 63, later EC-121D/T. Tfd 552nd AEW Wg McClellan 15 Sep 68, assigned 966th AEW Sq McCoy 27 Sep 68. Ret 552nd AEW Wg McClellan 30 Jun 70. Re- designated EC- 121T 30 Jun 70 (after mods by LTV Electrosystems Inc), but upper radome never removed. Deployed Keflavik 16 May 71, ret McClellan 29 Jun 71. Deployed Keflavik 9 Aug 71, ret McClellan 27 Sep 71. Deployed Keflavik further periods 1972-73. Tfd AFRES 79th AEW Sq Homestead 20 Jun 74. To MASDC Davis Monthan for storage 23 Mar 76. Sold to Helena Vocational Tech Center, MT, regd N4257L 11 Mar 81. Withdrawn from storage Jun 81 & ferried to Helena in early Jul 81. Preserved there in good condition. Used for teaching of pressurization & heating controls, cooling & airconditioning, also used by local fire-training school (but never set alight!). Engines run up regularly until early 1990s, three engines still ok, but no.4 has broken cylinder after a student forgot his check-list.

4336 RC-121D/1049A-55-86 16 Oct 54 to U S Air Force as 52-3418. USAF acceptance & dely 18 Oct 54. Del 4701st AEW Sq McClellan 16 Oct 54. Assigned 8th AD(ADC) McClellan 22 Dec 54.To 551st AEW Sq Otis 2 Mar 55, 551st AEW Wg Otis 1 May 55. Assigned 33rd MSG Otis 19 Jul 57, ret 551st AEW Wg Otis 1 Sep 57. Technical Order dated 1 Apr 62 gives "cvtd to EC-121H", but not cvtd. Tfd 966th AEW Sq McCoy 1 Mar 63. Redesignated EC-121D 10 Oct 63. Tfd 552nd AEW Wg McClellan 12 Nov 68. To 966th AEW Sq McCoy 27 Nov 68, ret 552nd AEW Wg McClellan 1 Jun 69. To 966th AEW Sq McCoy 15 Jun 69, ret 552nd AEW Wg McClellan 14 Aug 69. Re- designated EC-121T 22 Aug 70. Deployed Tainan 1 Jun 71, Kwangju 19 Jun 71, Korat 15 May 73. Ret McClellan 17 May 74. Assigned AFRES 79th AEW Sq Homestead 21 Jun 74. To MASDC Davis Monthan for storage 7 Apr 76, arr 8 Apr 76. Sold to Combat Air Museum Inc, Topeka, KS, regd N4257U Mar 81. Withdrawn from storage Jun 81 for delivery to Topeka. Preserved at Topeka.

4337 RC-121D/1049A-55-86 2 Nov 54 to U S Air Force as 52-3419. USAF acceptance 20 Oct 54, dely 4 Nov 54. Del 4701st AEW Sq McClellan 2 Nov 54. Assigned 8th AD(ADC) McClellan 22 Dec 54. To 551st AEW Sq Otis 9 Mar 55, 551st AEW Wg Otis 18 Apr 55. Assigned 33rd MSG Otis 19 Jul 57, ret 551st AEW Wg Otis 1 Sep 57. Technical Order dated 1 Apr 62 gives "cvtd to EC-121H", but not cvtd. Tfd 966th AEW Sq McCoy 6 Mar 63. Redesignated EC-121D McClellan 3 Oct 63. To 966th AEW Sq McCoy 7 Nov 63. To 552nd AEW Wg McClellan 25 Jun 64. To 966th AEW Sq McCoy 27 Jun 66, ret 552nd AEW Wg McClellan 18 Aug 68. To 966th AEW Sq McCoy 1 Sep 68, ret 552nd AEW Wg McClellan 21 Apr 69. Later EC-121D/T. To 966th AEW Sq McCoy 1 Jun 69, ret 552nd AEW Wg McClellan 28 Sep 69. Deployed Keflavik 12 Jul 70, ret McClellan 15 Jul 70. To MASDC Davis Monthan for storage 14 Oct 70. Still stored Jul 74, scrapped subsequently.

4338 RC-121D/1049A-55-86 26 Nov 54 to U S Air Force as 52-3420. USAF acceptance 29 Oct 54. Del 4701st AEW Sq McClellan 26 Nov 54. Assigned 8th AD (ADC) McClellan 22 Dec 54. To 551st AEW Sq Otis 2 Mar 55, 551st AEW Wg Otis 22 Apr 55. Assigned 33rd MSG Otis 19 Jul 57, ret 551st AEW Wg Otis 6 Sep 57. Redesignated EC-121H 8 Dec 62. To MASDC Davis Monthan for storage 28 Nov 69. Scrapped subsequent to Mar 71.

4339 RC-121D/1049A-55-86 30 Dec 54 to U S Air Force as 52-3421. USAF acceptance 29 Nov 54, dely 30 Nov 54. Del McClellan 30 Dec 54 (no unit given). Assigned 8th AD (ADC) McClellan 30 Dec 54. To 551st AEW Sq Otis 1 Mar 55, 551st AEW Wg Otis 18 Apr 55. Assigned 33rd MSG Otis 19 Jul 57, 551st MSG Otis 18 Aug 57, ret 551st AEW Wg Otis 1 Sep 57. Technical Order dated 1 Apr 62 gives "cvtd to EC-121H", but not cvtd. Tfd 966th AEW Sq McCoy 6 Mar 63. Redesignated EC-121D 10 Oct 63. To 966th AEW Sq McClellan 17 May 65, ret 966th AEW Sq McCoy 26 Jul 65. To 552nd AEW Wg McClellan

SECTION 12: CONSTELLATION PRODUCTION LIST   485

11 Oct 65, assigned 966th AEW Sq McCoy 6 Feb 66. Ret 552nd AEW Wg McClellan 17 Mar 66, deployed Tainan 4 Jan 68. Ret McClellan 18 Jul 68, to 966th AEW Sq McCoy 18 Apr 69, ret 552nd AEW Wg McClellan 20 Aug 69. Deployed Keflavik 26 Jul 70. Flew direct to MASDC Davis Monthan for storage 17 Sep 70. Scrapped subsequent to Jul 74.

4340 RC-121D/1049A-55-86 7 Jan 55 to U S Air Force as 52-3422. USAF acceptance 13 Dec 54, dely 10 Jan 55. Del McClellan 7 Jan 55 (no unit given). Assigned 8th AD (ADC) McClellan 12 Jan 55. To 551st AEW Sq Otis 3 Mar 56, 551st AEW Wg Otis 30 Apr 56. Redesignated EC-121D 18 Oct 56, ret RC-121D Otis 15 Dec 56. To 551st MSG Otis 18 Aug 57, ret 551st AEW Wg Otis 1 Sep 57. Bailed to Burroughs Corp, Dayton, OH, 1962-63, for development work for EC-121H mods. Redesignated EC-121H Otis 11 Jan 63. With 551st AEW Wg Otis until to MASDC Davis Monthan for storage 10 Nov 69. Scrapped subsequent to Mar 71.

4341 RC-121D/1049A-55-86 12 Jan 55 to U S Air Force as 52-3423. USAF acceptance 7 Dec 54, dely 13 Jan 55. Del McClellan 12 Jan 55 (no unit given). Assigned 8th AD (ADC) McClellan 12 Jan 55. To 551st AEW Sq Otis 7 Mar 56, 551st AEW Wg Otis 27 Apr 56.Tfd 33rd MSG Otis 19 Jul 57, 551st MSG Otis 18 Aug 57, ret 551st AEW Wg Otis 1 Sep 57. Technical Order dated 1 Apr 62 gives "cvtd to EC-121H", but not cvtd. Tfd 966th AEW Sq McCoy 25 Mar 63. Redesignated EC-121D 10 Oct 63. Tf 552nd AEW Wg McClellan 8 Mar 66, assigned 966th AEW Sq McCoy 19 Mar 66. Ret 552nd AEW Wg McClellan 1 Sep 68. To 966th AEW Sq McCoy 17 Sep 68. Ret 552nd AEW Wg McClellan 8 Jun 69. Later EC-121D/T. Redesignated EC-121T 18 Apr 70. Deployed Tainan 21 May 71, Kwangju 19 Jun 71, ret McClellan 10 Aug 71. Deployed Kwangju 8 Apr 72, Korat 15 May 73, ret McClellan 26 Oct 73. Deployed Keflavik 26 Dec 73, ret McClellan 23 Feb 74. Assigned AFRES 79th AEW Sq Homestead 30 Jun 74. To MASDC Davis Monthan for storage 23 Mar 76. For sale by DofD (Davis Monthan) 15 Nov 83. (TT: 19,711 hrs). Sold to DMI Aviation for $9,500. Subsequently scrapped.

4342 RC-121D/1049A-55-86 12 Jan 55 to U S Air Force as 52-3424. USAF acceptance 17 Dec 54, del 13 Jan 55. Del McClellan 12 Jan 55 (no unit given). Assigned 8th AD (ADC) McClellan 12 Jan 55. To 551st AEW Sq Otis 3 Mar 56, 551st AEW Wg Otis 22 Apr 56. Technical Order dated 1 Apr 62 gives "cvtd to EC-121H", but not cvtd. Tfd 966th AEW Sq McCoy 21 Mar 63. Redesignated EC-121D 10 Oct 63. Tfd 552nd AEW Wg McClellan 25 Jun 67, assigned 966th AEW Sq McCoy 31 Jul 67. Later EC-121D/T. Redesignated EC-121T 2 Apr 70, but upper radome not removed. Tfd McClellan 31 Mar 71, assigned 552nd AEW Wg McClellan 20 Jun 71. Deployed Keflavik 21 Feb 72, ret McClellan 6 Apr 72. Deployed McCoy 26 Oct 72, ret McClellan 10 Dec 72. Deployed Keflavik 11 Jan 73, ret McClellan 20 Feb 73. Further deployments to Keflavik 1973-74. Assigned AFRES 79th AEW Sq Homestead 2 Aug 76, to 915th AEW Gp AFRES Keflavik 2 Dec 76, ret Homestead 28 Sep 77, to 79th AEW Sq Homestead 8 Oct 77. To MASDC Davis Monthan for storage 12 Sep 78. For sale by DofD (Davis Monthan) 15 Nov 83 (TT: 20,230 hrs). Sold to DMI Aviation for $10,000. Scrapped subsequent to May 84.

4343 RC-121D/1049A-55-86 17 Jan 55 to U S Air Force as 52-3425. USAF acceptance 27 Dec 54, del 17 Jan 55. Del McClellan 17 Jan 55 (no unit given). Assigned 8th AD (ADC) McClellan 18 Jan 55. To 551st AEW Sq Otis 7 Mar 56, 551st AEW Wg Otis 11 Apr 56. Tfd 33rd MSG Otis 19 Jul 57, 551st MSG Otis 18 Aug 57, ret 551st AEW Wg Otis 1 Sep 57. Technical Order dated 1 Apr 62 gives "cvtd to EC-121H", but not cvtd. Tfd to 966th AEW Sq McCoy 11 Mar 63. Redesignated EC-121D 10 Oct 63. Tfd 552nd AEW Wg McClellan 9 Aug 64, to 966th AEW Sq McCoy 31 May 66. Deployed McClellan 26 May 67, ret McCoy 9 Jul 67. Later EC-121D/T. Redesignated EC-121T 7 Apr 70, but upper radome not removed. Assigned 552nd AEW Wg McClellan 13 Apr 70, deployed McCoy 17 Jun 71. Ret McClellan 1 Jul 71. Deployed Keflavik 12 Dec 71, ret McClellan 28 Jan 72. Deployed Singapore 26 Feb 72, ret McClellan 6 Jul 72. Deployed Kwangju 8 Jul 72, ret McClellan 27 Mar 73. Various deployments 1974-75. Assigned AFRES 79th AEW Sq Homestead 19 Mar 76. To 79th AEW Sq AFRES 30 Sep 78 (special activity, non-operational). WFU Oct 78 and flown to Peterson AFB, CO late Oct 78 for preservation. Preserved on display at Peterson Air & Space Museum, good condition (a/o Oct 02).

4344 WV-2/1049A-55-86 4 Mar 55 to US Navy as 137887. To VW-l Barbers Pt 6 May 55, VW-l Det A Cubi Pt 12 Aug 56. Ret VW-l Barbers Pt 10 Oct 56. To VW-l Det A Cubi Pt 15 Jan 57. Ret VW-l Barbers Pt 8 Apr 57. To VW-l Agana 12 Jul 57. To Storage Facility, Litchfield Park 6 Feb 59. Redesignated EC-121K 30 Nov 62. Struck off (Litchfield Park) 21 Mar 63 (TT: 2,418 hrs) & cannibalized for parts. For sale by DofD (Davis Monthan) 18 Feb 65. Scrapped, probably same year.

4345 WV-2/1049A-55-86 4 Mar 55 to US Navy as 137888. To VW-l Barbers Pt 7 May 55, VW-l Det A Atsugi 15 Jan 56. Ret VW-l Barbers Pt 7 Apr 56. To VW-l Det A Atsugi 29 Jun 56, ret VW-l Barbers Pt 13 Sep 56. To VW-l Det A Cubi Pt 5 Nov 56. Ret VW-l Barbers Pt 19 Feb 57. To VW-l Agana 5 Sep 57. To Storage Facility, Litchfield Park 20(?) Jan 59. Redesignated EC- 121K 30 Nov 62. Struck off (Litchfield Park) 21 Mar 63 (TT: 2,370 hrs) & cannibalized for parts. For sale by DofD (Davis Monthan) 18 Feb 65. Scrapped, probably same year.

4346 WV-2/1049A-55-86 19 May 55 to US Navy as 137889. To M&S Burbank 21 Apr 55. To FAETUPAC San Diego 19 May 55, tfd FAETUPAC North Island 31 Aug 55, coded FP-1. To VW-11 Patuxent 15 Nov 55, tfd VW-13 Patuxent 27 Apr 56. To O&R BAR Corpus Christi 6 Sep 56. Tfd NADC Johnsville 5 Apr 58, coded NADC 889. Tfd NAS Johnsville 30 Nov 62. Redesignated EC-121K 30 Nov 62. To NAF Johnsville 3 Sep 63, RDT & E Johnsville 30 Nov 64. To Davis Monthan for storage 19 Jan 66. Struck off (AFASDC-ADMCS, Davis Monthan) 8 Feb 67 (TT: 3,418 hrs). Stored at Davis Monthan, derelict by Dec 69, and reported scrapped by Mar 71. Sale date to Kolar Inc, however, was 17 Oct 74.

4347 WV-2/1049A-55-86 7 Mar 55 to US Navy as 137890. Navy acceptance 7 Apr 55. To M&S Burbank 7 Apr 55, BAR R&D Burbank 8 Apr 55. To VW-2 Patuxent 7 Jun 56. To VW-2 Det B Capodichino 23 Sep 56. Ret VW-2 Patuxent 5 Dec 56. To VW-2 Det B Capodichino 14 Aug 57, ret VW-2 Patuxent 6 Dec 57. Coded MG-4 by 1958. To storage Litchfield Park 27 Jan 59. Withdrawn from storage & to Pacific Missile Range Pt Mugu 24 Jul 59. Redesignated EC-121K 30 Nov 62. Tfd NMC Pt Mugu 1 Aug 63, ret PMR Pt Mugu 30 Nov 63. Mod by late 1960s, with two additional small radomes on upper fuselage in front of large radome, and two additional small radomes on lower fuselage to rear of large radome (no change in designation). To Pacific Missile Test Center Pt Mugu 25 Apr 75. (TT: 9,809 hrs, a/o Jun 75). Named "Baa Baa" (by Nov 77). To MASDC Davis Monthan for storage 7 May 79. Withdrawn from storage May 85 & tfd from Navy to Air Force inventory at Davis Monthan 9 May 85. Ferried to Tinker AFB, OK 1 Oct 85 for preservation at base museum. Preserved there in USAF mks as "0-30552" (a/o Apr 94).

4348 RC-121D/1049A-55-86, mod to 1049A-55-137 1 Feb 55 to U S Air Force as 53-533. USAF acceptance 13 Jan 55, del 2 Feb 55. Del 8th AD McClellan 3 Feb 55. Assigned 551st AEW Wg Otis 7 May 55. Redesignated EC-121D 15 Nov 55, ret RC-121D 15 Dec 55. Assigned 33rd MSG Otis 16 Jul 57, ret 551st AEW Wg Otis 1 Sep 57. Redesignated EC-l21H 13 Dec 62. (although records show ret RC-121D 10 Sep 64, EC-121H again 24 Feb 65). Assigned 966th AEW Sq McCoy 11 Aug 69. To MASDC Davis Monthan for storage 25 Nov 69. Scrapped subsequent to Feb 72.

4349 RC-121D/1049A-55-86, mod to 1049A-55-137 17 Feb 55 to U S Air Force as 53-534. USAF acceptance 26 Jan 55, del 17 Feb 55 (no unit given). Assigned 551st AEW Wg Otis 9 Jul 55. Technical Order dated 1 Apr 62 gives "cvtd to EC-121H", but not cvtd. Redesignated EC-121D 31 Oct 55, ret RC-121D 16 Dec 55. Assigned 33rd MSG Otis 19 Jul 57, 551st MSG Otis 18 Aug 57, ret 551st AEW Wg Otis 1 Sep 57. Deployed McCoy 4 Apr 62, ret

Otis 28 May 62. Redesignated EC-121D again 30 Sep 63. Tfd 552nd AEW Wg McClellan 15 Feb 65. Deployed Tainan 5 Jan 66, Tan Son Nhut 11 Jan 66, Tainan 28 Feb 66, ret McClellan 29 Apr 66. Deployed Tan Son Nhut 31 Mar 67, ret McClellan 29 Apr 67. Deployed Tainan 10 May 67, ret McClellan 25 Feb 68. Deployed Tainan 9 Jun 68, ret McClellan 23 Oct 68. Deployed Tainan 11 Dec 68, ret McClellan 8 May 70. Deployed Tainan 27 May 70, ret McClellan 25 Nov 70. Deployed Keflavik 14 Dec 70, ret McClellan 10 Jan 71. To MASDC Davis Monthan for storage 28 Jan 71. Parts missing by Feb 72, scrapped subsequent to May 74.

4350 RC-121D/1049A-55-86, mod to 1049A-55-137 16 Mar 55 to U S Air Force as 53-535. USAF acceptance 25 Feb 55, del 16 Mar 55 (no unit given). Assigned 551st AEW & Wg Otis 21 Jul 55. Redesignated EC-121D 1 Oct 55, ret RC-121D 25 Nov 55. Assigned 33rd MSG Otis 19 Jul 57, 551st MSG Otis 18 Aug 57, ret 551st AEW Wg Otis 1 Sep 57. Redesignated EC-121H 27 Nov 63. To MASDC Davis Monthan for storage 29 Dec 69. Donated to Pima County Air Museum, Tucson, AZ by Oct 73. Preserved there, poor condition, until 28 Oct 81, when tfd back to Davis Monthan (Pima Co Museum received a better EC-121 in lieu). Stored at Davis Monthan Museum (on display near main gate to MASDC). Sold to Leonard Parker & stored in his leased area near Allied Aircraft scrapyard a/o 25 Apr 89. Regd N51006 as candidate for P Regina & Janet S Shepardson 6 Jun 92, regd Janet S Shepardson 28 Dec 92. Sold to Vern L Raburn t/a The Constellation Group Feb 96. Stripped for spares. Derelict hulk sold to Urs V Lauppi Jul 01, who donated the aircraft to the (Swiss) Super Constellation Flyers Association to use for spares for c/n 4137 in same month. Derelict at the Minden Air Corp scrapyard, still marked as 0-30535 (a/o Aug 02).

4351 RC-121D/1049A-55-86, mod to 1049A-55-137 24 Mar 55 to U S Air Force as 53-536. USAF acceptance 25 Feb 55, del 24 Mar 55. Del 8th AD (ADC) McClellan 24 Mar 55. Assigned 551st AEW Wg Otis 1 Jun 55. Redesignated EC-121D 1 Oct 55, ret RC-121D 15 Dec 55. Assigned 33rd MSG Otis 19 Jul 57, 551st MSG Otis 18 Aug 57, ret 551st AEW Wg Otis 1 Sep 57. Technical Order dated 1 Apr 62 gives "cvtd to EC-121H", but not cvtd. Redesignated EC-121D again 30 Sep 63. Tfd 552nd AEW Wg McClellan 26 Jun 65. Assigned 966th AEW Sq McCoy 26 Sep 65, ret 552nd AEW Wg McClellan 1 Apr 66. Deployed Tainan 28 Sep 67, ret McClellan 6 May 68. Deployed Tainan 28 Jun 68, ret McClellan 27 Feb 69. Deployed Tainan 19 Jun 69, ret McClellan 27 Aug 69. Deployed Tainan 28 Oct 69, ret McClellan 5 Jul 70. Deployed Keflavik 26 Aug 70, ret McClellan 6 Oct 70. To MASDC Davis Monthan for storage 24 Nov 70. Scrapped subsequent to May 74.

4352 RC-121D/1049A-55-86, mod to 1049A-55-137 4 Mar 55 to U S Air Force as 53-537. USAF acceptance 10 Mar 55, del 6 Apr 55. Del 8th AD (ADC) McClellan 6 Apr 55. Assigned 551st AEW & Wg Otis 17 Jul 55. Redes-ignated EC-121D 1 Oct 55, ret RC-121D 15 Dec 55. Assigned 33rd MSG Otis 19 Jul 57, 551st MSG Otis 18 Aug 57, ret 551st AEW Wg Otis 1 Sep 57. Technical Order dated 1 Apr 62 gives "cvtd to EC-121H", but not cvtd. Tfd 552nd AEW Wg McClellan 13 Jan 65. Redesignated EC-121D 24 Sep 65. Deployed Tainan 29 Nov 65, ret McClellan 30 May 66. Deployed Tainan 23 Aug 68, ret McClellan 19 Dec 68. Deployed Tainan 5 Mar 69, ret McClellan 19 May 70. Deployed Tainan 13 Aug 70, ret McClellan 10 Jan 71. To MASDC Davis Monthan for storage 28 Jan 71. Withdrawn from storage & assigned to AFRES 79th AEW Sq Homestead 29 Jul 72. Ret to MASDC Davis Monthan for storage 11 Jun 74. For sale by DofD (Davis Monthan) 24 May 78 (TT: 19,040 hrs), and again 7 Jun 78. Sold Southwestern Alloys 10 Apr 79, subsequently scrapped.

4353 RC-121D/1049A-55-86, mod to 1049A-55-137 28 Feb 55 to U S Air Force as 53-538. USAF acceptance 31 Mar 55, del 15 Jun 55. Del 8th AD (ADC) McClellan 15 Jun 55, assigned 552nd AEW Wg McClellan 19 Jul 55. Tfd 551st AEW Wg Otis 21 Jul 55. Redesignated EC-121D 1 Oct 55, ret RC-121D 15 Dec 55. Assigned 33rd MSG Otis 19 Jul 57, 551st MSG Otis 18 Aug 57. Redesignated EC-121H 9 Dec 62. Ret 551st AEW Wg Otis 18 Apr 65. Tfd 552nd AEW Wg McClellan 31 Oct 66, ret 551st AEW Wg Otis 29 May 67. To MASDC Davis Monthan for storage 10 Nov 69. Scrapped subsequent to May 74.

4354 RC-121D/1049A-55-86, mod to 1049A-55-137 early 1955 to U S Air Force as 53-539. USAF acceptance 26 Apr 55, del 13 May 55. Del 8th AD (ADC) McClellan 12 May 55. Assigned 551st AEW Wg Otis 11 Aug 55. Re- designated EC-121D 1 Oct 55, ret RC-121D 22 Feb 56. Assigned 33rd MSG Otis 19 Jul 57, ret 551st AEW Wg Otis 20 Aug 57. Redesignated EC-121H 20 Oct 63. Mispainted as 0-50539 (a/o May 68), corrected to 0-30539 by 1970. Tfd 966th AEW Sq McCoy 2 Sep 69. To MASDC Davis Monthan for storage 2 Dec 69. Scrapped subsequent to May 74.

4355 RC-121D/1049A-55-86, mod to 1049A-55-137 18 May 55 to U S Air Force as 53-540. USAF acceptance 28 Apr 55, del 19 May 55. Del 8th AD (ADC) McClellan 9 Jun 55. Assigned 552nd AEW Wg McClellan 19 Jul 55, tfd 551st AEW Wg Otis 4 Aug 55. Redesignated EC-121D 1 Oct 55, ret RC-121D 15 Dec 55. Assigned 33rd MSG Otis 19 Jul 57, 551st MSG Otis 18 Aug 57, ret 551st AEW Wg Otis 8 Sep 57. Redesignated EC-121H 13 Sep 63. To MASDC Davis Monthan for storage 10 Dec 69. Scrapped subsequent to Apr 71.

4356 RC-121D/1049A-55-86, mod to 1049A-55-137 8 Jun 55 to U S Air Force as 53-541. USAF acceptance 18 May 55, del 9 Jun 55. Del 8th AD (ADC) McClellan 8 Jun 55. Assigned 552nd AEW Wg McClellan 19 Jul 55, tfd ARDC Wright-Patterson 7 Sep 55. Redesignated JRC-121D 1 Dec 55, ret RC-121D 18 Jun 56. Ret 552nd AEW Wg McClellan 27 Jun 56. Redesignated EC-121D 30 Sep 63. Deployed McCoy 13 Aug 64, ret McClellan (966th AEW Sq) 24 Feb 65. Deployed Tainan 30 Oct 65, Tan Son Nhut 23 Oct 65, Tainan 29 Oct 65, Tan Son Nhut 5 Nov 65, ret McClellan (552nd AEW Wg) 24 Jan 66. Deployed Tainan 16 Jun 66, ret McClellan 15 Dec 66. Deployed Jamaica 26 Sep 67, ret McClellan 22 Nov 67. Deployed Tainan 13 Dec 67, ret McClellan 8 Jul 68. Deployed Tainan 25 Sep 68, ret McClellan 1 Jul 69. Deployed Tainan 19 Aug 69, tf AFLC Jamaica 25 Nov 69, ret McClellan 16 Jan 70. Deployed Tainan 25 Jan 70, Itazuke 14 Jul 70, ret Tainan 24 Jul 70, McClellan 10 Aug 70. Deployed Keflavik 21 Aug 70, ret McClellan 26 Aug 70. Deployed McCoy 12 Oct 70, ret McClellan 21 Oct 70. Deployed McCoy 4 Dec 70, ret McClellan 15 Jan 71. To MASDC Davis Monthan for storage 22 Jan 71. Tfd AFLC Lake City 12 Oct 72, ret 552nd AEW Wg McClellan 26 Jan 73. Redesignated EC-121Q 3 Apr 73. Deployed McCoy 14 May 73, ret McClellan 27 Jul 73. Deployed McCoy 10 Aug 73, Homestead 13 Aug 73, ret McClellan 28 Oct 73. Deployed Homestead 16 Nov 73, ret McClellan 22 Nov 73. Deployed Homestead 28 Nov 73, ret McClellan 28 Jan 74. Deployed Homestead 10 Feb 74, ret McClellan 2 May 74. Deployed Homestead 30 May 74, ret McClellan 6 Sep 74. Deployed Homestead 19 Sep 74, ret McClellan 6 Jan 75. To MASDC Davis Monthan for storage 23 Jan 75, arr 24 Jan 75. For sale by DofD (Davis Monthan) 24 May 78 (TT: 19,858 hrs), and again 7 Jun 78. Derelict, on tail by Dec 78. Sold Southwestern Alloys 20 Feb 79, subsequently scrapped.

4357 RC-121D/1049-A-55-86, mod to 1049A-55-137 27 Apr 55 to U S Air Force as 53-542. USAF acceptance 27 Apr 55, del 1 Sep 55. Del to AMC (Lockheed plant) 1 Jul 55. Assigned Air Proving Ground Cmd, Eglin 5 Dec 55. Tfd ARDC Wright-Patterson 5 Dec 55. Assigned 552nd AEW Wg McClellan 22 Mar 56. Tfd 966th AEW Sq McCoy 11 Jun 63. Redesignated EC-121D 10 Oct 63, cvtd to EC-121Q McClellan 21 Jan 65 (still 966th AEW Sq McCoy 7 Apr 65). Ret 552nd AEW Wg McClellan 11 May 69, tfd 966th AEW Sq McCoy 25 May 69. Ret 552nd AEW Wg McClellan 21 Dec 69. Deployed McCoy 3 Jan 70, ret McClellan 31 Jan 70. Deployed McCoy 10 Feb 70, ret McClellan 5 Jul 70. Deployed McCoy 11 Jul 70, ret McClellan 1 Dec 70. Deployed McCoy 14 Dec 70, ret McClellan 16 Feb 71. Further five deployments to McCoy during 1971, last 5 Dec 71. Ret McClellan 14 Feb 72. Several further deployments to McCoy 1972. To MASDC Davis Monthan for storage 30 May 73. Sold Sun Valley Avn 27 May 76, subsequently scrapped.

Section 12: Constellation Production List

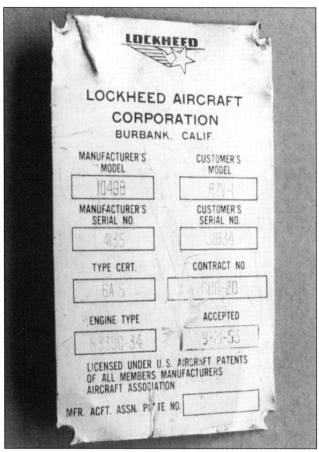

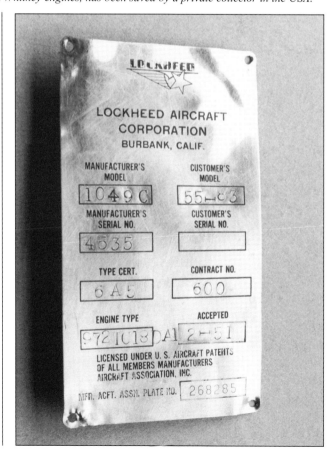

Three examples of Super Constellation manufacturer's plates from the author's collection. The plates were made basically to the same format throughout Constellation production and were affixed in the cockpit. They show the Lockheed and customer's model, Lockheed and customer's serial number, civil type certificate, contract number, engine type and acceptance date. The photos show (left) 1049B/R7V-1 c/n 4135, (right) 1049A-55-85/WV-2 c/n 4497 and (below) 1049C-55-83 c/n 4535. The 'plate number' entry is blank on the R7V-1 plate, the 'civil type certificate' on the WV-2 plate and the 'customer's serial number' on the 1049C plate. Note that although the engine-type is identical, the R7V-1 & WV-2 show the military designation and the Eastern Air Lines 1049C the civil designation. Interestingly, the plate from the prototype Constellation 'Old 1961', showing the modification with four Pratt & Whitney engines, has been saved by a private collector in the USA.

4358 RC-121D/1049A-55-86, mod to 1049A-55-137 21 Jul 55 to U S Air Force as 53-543. USAF acceptance 5 Jul 55. Del to 552nd AEW Wg McClellan 21 Jul 55. Redesignated EC-121D 1 Oct 55, ret RC-121D 15 Dec 55. Tfd 551st AEW Wg McCoy 14 Jan 62, ret 552nd AEW Wg McClellan 30 Apr 62. Assigned 551st AEW Wg McCoy 19 Oct 62, ret 552nd AEW Wg McClellan 28 Nov 62. Redesignated EC-121D 30 Sep 63. Deployed Tainan 15 Dec 65, ret McClellan 27 Jun 66. Deployed Tainan 6 Mar 67, ret McClellan 27 Aug 67. To Tainan 21 May 68, ret McClellan 12 Sep 68. To Tainan 26 Nov 68, ret McClellan 4 Mar 70. Deployed Tainan 9 Apr 70, ret McClellan 27 Nov 70. Deployed Keflavik 26 Dec 70, ret McClellan 13 Feb 71. Deployed Keflavik 21 Feb 71, ret McClellan 19 Mar 71. To MASDC Davis Monthan for storage 25 Jun 71. Assigned AFRES 79th AEW Sq Homestead 3 Dec 71. Ret to MASDC Davis Monthan for storage 6 Aug 74. For sale by DofD (Davis Monthan) 24 May 78 (TT: 22,103 hrs) & again 7 Jun 78. Sold Southwestern Alloys 21 Feb 79, subsequently scrapped.

4359 RC-121D/1049A-55-86, mod to 1049A-55-137 1 Jul 55 to U S Air Force as 53-544. USAF acceptance 17 Jun 55. Del to 8th AD (ADC) McClellan 1 Jul 55. Assigned 552nd AEW Wg McClellan 19 Jul 55, tfd 551st AEW Wg Otis 5 Aug 55. Redesignated EC-121D 1 Oct 55, ret RC-121D 15 Dec 55. Assigned 33rd MSG Otis 19 Jul 57, ret 551st AEW Wg Otis 29 Jul 57. TDY McCoy 27 May 62, ret Otis 28 Jul 62. TDY McCoy 14 Aug 62, ret Otis 20 Sep 62. Redesignated EC-121H 29 Apr 63. To 966th AEW Sq McCoy 18 Aug 69. To MASDC Davis Monthan for storage 25 Nov 69. Scrapped subsequent to Apr 71.

4360 RC-121D/1049A-55-86, mod to 1049A-55-137 15 Jul 55 to U S Air Force as 53-545. USAF acceptance 30 Jun 55. Del to 8th AD (ADC) McClellan 15 Jul 55. Assigned 552nd AEW Wg

McClellan 19 Jul 55. Redesignated EC-121D 1 Oct 55, ret RC-121D 15 Dec 55. Assigned 551st AEW Wg McCoy 27 Mar 62, tfd Otis 20 May 62. Deployed TDY McCoy 6 Jun 62, ret 551st AEW Wg Otis 28 Apr 63. Tfd 552nd AEW Wg McClellan 28 Apr 63. Redesignated EC-121D 30 Sep 63. Deployed McCoy 2 Feb 65. Ret McClellan 15 Feb 65. Deployed Tainan 22 Aug 66, ret McClellan 13 Mar 67. Deployed Tainan 16 Jul 67, ret McClellan 25 Jun 68. To Tainan again 7 Nov 68, ret McClellan 4 May 69. To Tainan 10 Jul 69, ret McClellan 4 Jul 70. Deployed Keflavik 18 Sep 70, ret McClellan 3 Nov 70. Deployed Keflavik 29 Nov 70, ret McClellan 23 Jan 71. To Keflavik 7 Feb 71, ret McClellan 24 Feb 71. To MASDC Davis Monthan for storage 16 Mar 71. Scrapped subsequent to May 74.

4361 RC-121D/1049A-55-86, mod to 1049A-55-137 22 Jul 55 to U S Air Force as 53-546. USAF acceptance 12 Jul 55. Del to 552nd AEW Wg McClellan 22 Jul 55. Redesignated EC-121D 1 Oct 55, ret RC-121D 15 Dec 55. Redesignated EC-121D again 30 Sep 63. Deployed Tainan 16 Nov 65, ret McClellan 14 Jul 66. Assigned 966th AEW Sq McCoy 21 May 67, ret 552nd AEW Wg McClellan 10 Jun 67. Deployed Tainan 2 May 68, ret McClellan 13 Jan 69. To Tainan 16 Mar 69, ret McClellan 2 Dec 69. Deployed Tainan again 23 Mar 70, ret McClellan 3 Oct 70. Deployed Keflavik 21 Oct 70, ret McClellan 2 Dec 70. To MASDC Davis Monthan for storage 10 Dec 70. Still at MASDC 31 Mar 71. No further dets on card. However, reportedly to AFRES 79th AEW Sq Homestead, date unknown, until at least Jul 74. Ret to MASDC Davis Monthan for storage again by Oct 74. Scrapped.

4362 RC-121D/1049A-55-86, mod to 1049A-55-137 28 Sep 55 to U S Air Force as 53-547. USAF acceptance 14 Sep 55, del 29 Sep 55. Del to 552nd AEW Wg McClellan 28 Sep 55. Redesignated EC-121D 1 Oct 55, ret RC-121D 22 Dec 55. Assigned 551st AEW Wg McCoy 29 Dec 62. Ret 552nd AEW Wg McClellan 14 Feb 63, assigned 966th AEW Sq McCoy 31 May 63. Redesignated EC-121D 10 Oct 63, to EC-121Q 17 Feb 65 (still 966th AEW Sq McCoy). Assigned 552nd AEW Wg McClellan 18 Dec 68, tfd 966th AEW Sq McCoy 10 Apr 69. Ret 552nd AEW Wg McClellan 27 Nov 69. Deployed McCoy 15 Dec 69, ret McClellan 15 Feb 70. TDY McCoy 22 Feb 70, ret McClellan 30 Apr 70. To McCoy 10 May 70, ret McClellan 12 Jul 70. Deployed McCoy again 22 Jul 70, ret McClellan 28 Sep 70. TDY McCoy 11 Oct 70, ret McClellan 16 Dec 70. Deployed McCoy 22 Dec 70, additional deployments to McCoy during 1973. Ret McClellan 5 Sep 73. To MASDC Davis Monthan for storage 6 Sep 73. Sold Sun Valley Avn 28 May 76, subsequently scrapped.

4363 RC-121D/1049A-55-86, mod to 1049A-55-137 18 Aug 55 to U S Air Force as 53-548. USAF acceptance 5 Aug 55, del 19 Aug 55. Del to 552nd AEW Wg McClellan 18 Aug 55. Redesignated EC-121D 1 Oct 55, ret RC-121D 15 Dec 55. Assigned 551st AEW Wg McCoy 5 Jan 62, ret 552nd AEW Wg McClellan 9 Feb 62. To 551st AEW Wg McCoy 2 Dec 62, ret 552nd AEW Wg McClellan 5 Dec 62. Redesignated EC-121D again 30 Sep 63. Deployed Tainan 5 Jan 67, ret McClellan 7 Jun 67. Later EC-121D/T, redesignated EC-121T 18 May 70. Deployed Tainan 30 Nov 70, Kwangju 6 Aug 71, ret McClellan 8 Jul 72. Deployed Kwangju 26 Jul 72, ret McClellan 5 Sep 72. Tfd AFRES 79th AEW Sq Homestead 23 Mar 76, assigned 915th AEW Gp Keflavik 2 Dec 76, tfd 79th AEW Sq Keflavik 7 Oct 77. Last 79th AEW Sq EC-121T to be retired. Del Homestead-Bergstrom 14 Oct 78, flown to MASDC Davis Monthan for storage 15 Oct 78, arr 16 Oct 78. Withdrawn from storage & tfd to Pima County Museum, Tucson, AZ 30 Sep 81, rn Tucson Air Museum Foundation. Sold to Waynes Aviation Inc 29 Dec 94, preparation for ferry flt began 18 Jan 95. Official tf date to Waynes Avn Inc t/a Global Aeronautical Foundation 4 Apr 95, regd N548GF 7 Apr 95. First flight in nearly 17 yrs on 14 Apr 95 (ferried Davis Monthan-Tucson Intl), ferried Tucson–Camarillo, CA 15 Apr 95 (TT: 24,018hrs). Flown regularly to airshows as 0-30548/N548GF until 2000. Grounded with outer wing corrosion Jun 00. Stored Camarillo, CA with wing-tips removed (a/o Mar 01). For sale $595,000 (Trade-a-Plane Mar 02), also Jun 02 (no price mentioned). To be made airworthy again for ferry flight to museum at Chino, CA 2006, after sale to the Yanks Air Museum 22 Dec 05, CofRegn 24 Jan 06.

4364 RC-121D/1049A-55-86, mod to 1049A-55-137 26 Aug 55 to U S Air Force as 53-549. USAF acceptance 16 Aug 55, del 27 Aug 55. Del to 552nd AEW Wg McClellan 27 Aug 55. Assigned 551st AEW Wg Otis 3 Sep 55. Redesignated EC-121D 1 Oct 55, ret RC-121D 15 Dec 55. Assigned 33rd MSG Otis 19 Jul 57, 551st MSG Otis 18 Aug 57. Ret 551st AEW Wg Otis 1 Sep 57. Redesignated EC-121H 14 Sep 63. Crashed into the Atlantic Ocean about one mile south of Nantucket Island, MA on the evening of 25 Apr 67. The aircraft had taken off from Otis AFB at 18.30 hrs (local). Approx eight minutes after take-off, when the aircraft was at 2,000 feet, there was a small explosion and fire on the starboard side after an engine caught fire. The aircraft went into a dive, levelled off at 300 feet above a line of cottages on the island and then headed out to sea, exploding on impact with the water. One survivor among crew. Crash led to temporary grounding of the EC-121H by Otis as this was the third fatal accident to the type in 22 months. (See c/ns 4409 & 4413).

4365 RC-121D/1049A-55-86, mod to 1049A-55-137 14 Aug 55 to U S Air Force as 53-550. USAF acceptance 29 Aug 55, del 14 Sep 55. Del to 552nd AEW Wg McClellan 14 Sep 55. Redesignated EC-121D 3 Oct 55, ret RC-121D 19 Dec 55. To EC-121D again 30 Sep 63. Deployed Tan Son Nhut 26 Aug 65, Tainan 29 Nov 65, ret McClellan 27 Feb 66. Assigned 966th AEW Sq McCoy 3 Apr 66, ret 552nd AEW Wg McClellan 22 Aug 66. Deployed Tainan 6 Nov 66, ret McClellan 3 Jul 67. Later EC-121D/T, redesignated EC-121T 8 May 70. Deployed Kwangju 28 Nov 71, ret McClellan 29 Nov 71. Deployed Kwangju 15 Jun 72, Korat 15 May 73, ret McClellan 19 May 74. To MASDC Davis Monthan for storage 2 Jul 74. Sold by DofD (Davis Monthan) 20 May 82 (TT: 21,737 hrs). Subsequently scrapped.

4366 RC-121D/1049A-55-86, mod to 1049A-55-137 29 Sep 55 to U S Air Force as 53-551. USAF acceptance 6 Sep 55, del 30 Sep 55. Del to 552nd AEW Wg McClellan 29 Sep 55. Redesignated EC-121D 1 Oct 55, assigned 551st AEW Wg Otis 1 Oct 55, ret RC-121D 15 Dec 55. Assigned 33rd MSG Otis 19 Jul 57, 551st MSG Otis 18 Aug 57, ret 551st AEW Wg Otis 1 Sep 57. Bailed to Burroughs Corp, Dayton, OH 1962-63, as one of the EC-121H development aircraft. Ret to 551st AEW Wg Otis, redesignated EC-121H 25 Jan 63. To MASDC Davis Monthan for storage 20 Nov 69. Scrapped subsequent to Apr 71.

4367 RC-121D/1049A-55-86, mod to 1049A-55-137 14 Oct 55 to U S Air Force as 53-552. USAF acceptance 27 Sep 55. Del to 552nd AEW Wg McClellan 14 Oct 55. Redesignated EC-121D 14 Oct 55. Assigned 551st AEW Wg Otis 19 Oct 55. Ret RC-121D 17 Dec 55. Assigned 33rd MSG Otis 19 Jul 57, 551st MSG Otis 29 Aug 57, ret 551st AEW Wg Otis 1 Sep 57. Deployed TDY McCoy 18 Sep 62, ret Otis 1 Dec 62. Redesignated EC-121D 30 Sep 63. Tf 552nd AEW Wg McClellan 25 Jun 65. Deployed Tainan 16 Apr 66, ret McClellan 4 Aug 66. Deployed Tainan 16 Mar 68, ret McClellan 19 Aug 68. Assigned 966th AEW Sq McCoy 14 Jan 69, ret 552nd AEW Wg McClellan 17 Jun 69. Tfd AFSC Edwards AFB 30 Aug 70, ret 552nd AEW Wg McClellan 9 Oct 70. Deployed Keflavik 14 Mar 71, ret McClellan 6 Apr 71. To MASDC Davis Monthan for storage 25 Jun 71. Assigned AFRES 79th AEW Sq Homestead 9 Sep 71. Ret to MASDC Davis Monthan for storage 29 May 74. On tail, no engines, by Jun 76. For sale by DofD (Davis Monthan) 24 May 78 (TT: 19,163 hrs), and again 7 Jun 78. Sold to Southwestern Alloys 11 Apr 79, subsequently scrapped.

4368 RC-121D/1049A-55-86, mod to 1049A-55-137 12 Oct 55 to U S Air Force as 53-553. USAF acceptance 23 Sep 55. Del to 552nd AEW Wg McClellan 12 Oct 55. Tfd to NADU, South Weymouth for use on Project ADC-4C-440 (nfd). Redesignated EC-121D 22 Oct 55, ret RC-121D 15 Dec 55. Assigned 551st AEW Wg Otis 19 Jul 56. To 33rd MSG Otis 19 Jul 57, ret 551st AEW Wg Otis 1 Sep 57. Redesignated EC-121H 18 Jun 63. To MASDC Davis Monthan for storage 12 Nov 69. Scrapped subsequent to Oct 75.

4369 RC-121D/1049A-55-86, mod to 1049A-55-137 14 Oct 55 to U S Air Force as 53-554. USAF acceptance 29 Sep 55. Del to 552nd

SECTION 12: CONSTELLATION PRODUCTION LIST

AEW Wg McClellan 14 Oct 55. Redesignated EC-121D 14 Oct 55, ret RC-121D 1 Jan 56. Assigned 966th AEW Sq McCoy 20 Mar 63, ret 552nd AEW Wg McClellan 25 Mar 63. Redesignated EC-121D again 30 Sep 63, assigned 966th AEW Sq McCoy 18 Apr 66. Ret 552nd AEW Wg McClellan 12 Nov 67. Later EC-121D/T. Reached 20,000 hrs in Mar 68, first USAF Super Constellation to do so, having used up 54 engines in the process! Redesignated EC-121T 10 Sep 70, but upper radome not removed. Deployed Keflavik 30 May 71, ret McClellan 13 Jul 71. To Keflavik 4 Oct 71, ret McClellan 1 Dec 71. Several further deployments to Keflavik 1972 & 1973. To AFRES 79th AEW Sq Homestead 27 Oct 74. To MASDC Davis Monthan for storage 26 Feb 76. Still stored there Apr 81. Tfd during 1981 to Pima County Museum, Tucson, AZ. Preserved there as 0-30554. Rn Tucson Air Museum Foundation. Current.

4370 RC-121D/1049A-55-86, mod to 1049A-55-137 16 Nov 55 to U S Air Force as 53-555. USAF acceptance 31 Oct 55. Del to 552nd AEW Wg McClellan 16 Nov 55. Assigned 551st AEW Wg McCoy 16 Feb 62, ret 552nd AEW Wg McClellan 29 Mar 62. Redesignated EC-121D 30 Sep 63. Deployed Tainan 19 Oct 65, Tan Son Nhut 10 Nov 65, ret McClellan 25 Nov 65. Deployed Tainan 25 Jul 66, ret McClellan 25 Feb 67. To Tainan 1 Jul 67, ret McClellan 3 Apr 68. To Tainan again 16 Oct 68, ret McClellan 19 Aug 70. Deployed Tainan 18 Sep 70, ret McClellan 26 May 71. Tfd to 'inactive training' McClellan 10 Aug 71. In fact donated to the USAF Museum, and deld McClellan, CA to Wright-Patterson, OH 9 Aug 71. Nicknamed "Triple Nickel". Subsequently named 'City of Sacramento'. Preserved at Wright-Patterson in open storage as 0-30555.

4371 RC-121D/1049A-55-86, mod to 1049A-55-137 19 Oct 55 to U S Air Force as 53-556. USAF acceptance 6 Oct 55. Del to 552nd AEW Wg McClellan 19 Oct 55. Redesignated EC-121D 19 Oct 55, ret RC-121D 30 Nov 55. Assigned 551st AEW Wg McCoy 20 Oct 62, ret 552nd AEW Wg McClellan 5 Jun 63. Redesignated EC-121D again 30 Sep 63. Deployed Tainan 8 May 66, ret McClellan 25 Oct 66. Deployed Tainan 8 Sep 67, ret McClellan 26 Oct 67. To Tainan 19 Feb 68, ret McClellan 22 Jul 68. Assigned 966th AEW Sq McCoy 1 Dec 68, ret 552nd AEW Wg McClellan 21 May 69. Deployed Keflavik 12 Jul 70, ret McClellan 14 Aug 70. Deployed Keflavik 5 Sep 70, ret McClellan 23 Oct 70. To MASDC Davis Monthan for storage 29 Jan 71. Ret to 552nd AEW Wg, deployed McCoy 24 Sep 72. Ret McClellan 1 Nov 72 (carried Arctic red markings, presumably special assignment). Redesignated EC-121Q 24 Sep 73. Ret to MASDC Davis Monthan for storage 25 Mar 75. For sale by DofD (Davis Monthan) 24 May 78 (TT: 22,409 hrs), and again on 7 Jun 78. Sold Southwestern Alloys 20 Feb 79, subsequently scrapped.

4372 RC-121D/1049A-55-86, mod to 1049A-55-137 16 Nov 55 to U S Air Force as 53-3398. USAF acceptance 25 Oct 55. Del to 552nd AEW Wg McClellan 16 Nov 55. Assigned 551st AEW Wg McCoy 25 Jan 63, ret 552nd AEW Wg McClellan 7 Mar 63. On record as EC-121D 4 Aug 64. Deployed Tainan 2 Aug 65, ret McClellan 27 Sep 65. Carried 28 'mission completed' symbols on nose (a/o Oct 65). Updated to EC-121D/T. To MASDC Davis Monthan for storage 10 Sep 70. Scrapped subsequent to May 74.

4373 RC-121D/1049A-55-86, mod to 1049A-55-137 7 Oct 55 to U S Air Force as 53-3399. USAF acceptance 7 Mar 56. Del to 552nd AEW Wg McClellan 7 Mar 56. On record as EC-121D 2 Jun 64. Deployed Tainan 1 Apr 66, ret McClellan 4 Oct 66. Deployed Tainan 29 May 67, ret McClellan 18 Mar 68. To Tainan 6 Jul 68, ret McClellan 13 Nov 68. To Tainan again 25 Jan 69, ret McClellan 20 May 70. Deployed Keflavik 12 Jul 70, ret McClellan 28 Jul 70. Deployed McCoy 10 Aug 70, ret McClellan 12 Oct 70. Deployed Keflavik 2 Nov 70, ret McClellan 15 Dec 70. To Keflavik 7 Jan 71, ret McClellan 10 Mar 71. To Keflavik again 17 Mar 71, ret McClellan 5 May 71. To AFRES 915th MAG Homestead 1 Jul 71, assigned 79th AEW Sq Homestead 30 Jul 71. To MASDC Davis Monthan for storage 7 May 74. For sale by DofD (Davis Monthan) 24 May 78 (TT: 24,067 hrs), and again 7 Jun 78. Sold to Southwestern Alloys 16 May 79, subsequently scrapped.

4374 RC-121D/1049A-55-86, mod to 1049A-55-137 12 Oct 55 to U S Air Force as 53-3400. USAF acceptance 20 Mar 56. Del to 552nd AEW Wg McClellan 20 Mar 56. Assigned 966th AEW Sq McCoy 20 Aug 64, ret 552nd AEW Wg McClellan 1 Feb 65. Redesignated EC-121D 29 Jul 65. Named 'Canella City 49er' by mid-1960s, but later unnamed. Deployed Tainan 24 Sep 66, ret McClellan 18 May 67. Assigned 966th AEW Sq McCoy 18 Oct 67, ret 552nd AEW Wg McClellan 21 Oct 67. Deployed Tainan 28 Nov 67, ret McClellan 2 Jun 68. Deployed Tainan 13 Jul 68, ret McClellan 13 Mar 69. To Tainan again 25 May 69, ret McClellan 26 Aug 70. Deployed Keflavik 2 Oct 70, ret McClellan 20 Nov 70. To MASDC Davis Monthan for storage 1 Dec 70. Scrapped subsequent to May 74.

4375 RC-121D/1049A-55-86, mod to 1049A-55-137 9 Feb 56 to U S Air Force as 53-3401. USAF acceptance 30 Mar 56. Del to 552nd AEW Wg McClellan 3 Apr 56. Assigned 551st AEW Wg McCoy 11 Apr 62, tfd 551st AEW Wg Otis 6 Jun 62. Ret 552nd AEW Wg McClellan 8 Aug 63. On record as EC-121D 2 May 64. Deployed Tainan 24 Oct 68, ret McClellan 5 Dec 68. Updated to EC-121D/T. Redesignated EC-121T 4 Aug 70. Deployed Keflavik 3 May 72, ret McClellan 1 Jun 72. Deployed Kwangju 17 Sep 72, ret McClellan 13 Nov 72. Deployed Kwangju 8 Jan 73, Korat 15 May 73, ret McClellan 22 May 74. To MASDC Davis Monthan for storage 26 Mar 75. Withdrawn from storage 15 Dec 79 on tf to 355th CSG Davis Monthan. Acft was derelict, no engines at this stage. Still stored Davis Monthan in May 82, subsequently scrapped.

4376 RC-121D/1049A-55-86, mod to 1049A-55-137 9 Feb 56 to U S Air Force as 53-3402. USAF acceptance 30 Apr 56. Del to 552nd AEW Wg McClellan 8 May 56. Assigned 551st AEW Wg Otis 18 May 56. On record as EC-121H 5 Jan 65. Assigned 966th AEW Sq McCoy 6 Aug 69. To MASDC Davis Monthan for storage 2 Dec 69. Scrapped subsequent to Oct 74.

4377 RC-121D/1049A-55-86, mod to 1049A-55-137 9 Feb 56 to U S Air Force as 53-3403. USAF acceptance 27 Apr 56. Del to 551st AEW Wg Otis 1 May 56. Redesignated EC-121H 9 Mar 65. Assigned 966th AEW Sq McCoy 10 Jul 69. Ret 551st AEW Wg Otis 1 Oct 69. To MASDC Davis Monthan for storage 28 Nov 69. Scrapped subsequent to Jul 74.

4378 WV-3/1049A-55-95 29 Apr 56 to US Navy as 137891. Navy acceptance date 24 Mar 55. Burbank (R&D) 29 Jun 55 as WV-3 development aircraft. To VW-4 Jacksonville 3 Mar 59, coded TH-1. Tfd VW-4 Roosevelt Roads 1 Nov 60, coded MH-1 by Dec 61. Redesignated WC-121N 28 Oct 62. Coded MH-00 (a/o Feb 63). Fitted with elongated 'canoe-type' radome on upper forward fuselage, in front of large radome (unique to this aircraft and c/n 5522). Recoded MH-l by 1964. Written-off after hurricane damage when flying from Guantanamo 23 Aug 64. Upon initial penetration of the storm eye of hurricane "Cleo", the port wing-tip fuel-tank & a portion of the wing were torn away by extreme updraft turbulence. On trying to exit the storm, the starboard tip-tank & a larger portion of the starboard wing were torn away by extreme downdraft turbulence. The aircraft returned to base for an emergency landing at Roosevelt Roads, PR safely - proof of the extraordinary strength of the Super Constellation. Injuries to crew, but no casualties. On inspection, the aircraft was found to be so torque-twisted, with major wing & fuselage damage, that it was grounded and never flew again. Struck off (Roosevelt Roads VW-4) 14 Oct 64 (TT: 4,353 hrs). Used for crash-crew fire training at Roosevelt Roads and later scrapped on site.

4379 WV-3/1049A-55-95 8 Apr 55 to US Navy as 137892. BAR M&S Burbank 8 Apr 55. To VW-4 Jacksonville 2 Sep 55, coded TH-2, recoded MH-2 by Mar 58. Tfd to VW-4 Roosevelt Roads 4 Nov 60. Redesignated WC-121N 30 Nov 62. To VW-4 Jacksonville 1 Jun 65. To MASDC Davis Monthan for storage. Struck off (Davis Monthan) 16 Jan 73 (TT: 11,032 hrs). Scrapped subsequent to Oct 75.

4380 WV-3/1049A-55-95 8 Apr 55 to US Navy as 137893. Navy acceptance date 13 Apr 55. To VW-3 Agana (Guam) 30

Sep 55, coded PM-1. Written-off after forced landing in the Pacific Ocean, 100 miles south of Guam on 17 Sep 56. Cause: Fuel starvation due to fuel mismanagement. Struck off 17 Sep 56 (VW-3), (TT: 723 hrs). Aircraft would not sink, drifted into shipping lanes & became a hazard to shipping. US jets from Anderson AFB, Guam, were sent to shoot at it, filling it with holes so that it eventually sank.

4381 WV-3/1049A-55-95 18 Apr 55 to US Navy as 137894. To BAR M&S Burbank 18 Apr 55, to VW-4 Jacksonville 19 Oct 55, coded TH-7, later coded TH-3. Later coded MH-l (by Apr 58). Tfd VW-4 Roosevelt Roads 30 Nov 60, coded MH-4 by Dec 61. Redesignated WC-121N 24 Oct 62. Ret VW-4 Jacksonville 29 May 65. Named 'Betsy', later 'Camille'. To MASDC Davis Monthan for storage 29 Dec 71. Struck off (Davis Monthan) 12 Jul 72 (TT: 11,097 hrs). Sold Sun Valley Avn 21 May 76, subsequently scrapped.

4382 WV-3/1049A-55-95 26 Apr 55 to US Navy as 137895. To BAR M&S Burbank 26 Apr 55. To VW-3 Agana 16 Nov 55, coded PM-2. Tfd VW-4 Jacksonville 24 Mar 58, coded MH-3 by Apr 58. To VW-4 Roosevelt Roads 13 Nov 60, re-coded MH-5 by Dec 61. Redesignated WC-121N 3 Nov 62. Ret VW-4 Jacksonville 7 May 65, named 'Blanche'. To Davis Monthan for storage and struck off (VW-4) 26 Jan 67 (TT: 8,056 hrs). Tfd to U S Air Force, Burbank 10 Apr 67. Flown to Ontario, CA 30 Jun 67 and cvtd to EC-121R by LAS for U S Air Force as 67-21471. Del to 551st AEW Wg Otis 22 Dec 67. Deployed McCoy 8 Jan 68, ret Otis 6 Feb 68. Assigned 552nd AEW Wg McClellan 21 Dec 69. To MASDC Davis Monthan for storage 29 Jun 71, TOC 30 Jun 71. Sold Sun Valley Avn 20 Sep 76, subsequently scrapped.

4383 WV-3/1049A-55-95 26 Apr 55 to US Navy as 137896. WV-3 development aircraft. To BAR M&S Burbank 26 May 55, NATC R&D Patuxent 5 Nov 55, used for electronic tests. To VW-4 Jacksonville 28 Jun 56, ret NATC R&D Patuxent 29 Jun 56. To VW-4 Jacksonville 29 Oct 56, FAETUPAC Nth Island 3 Jan 57, tfd VW-3 Agana 15 Feb 57, coded PM-3. Ret VW-4 Jacksonville 23 Apr 58, tfd VW-4 Roosevelt Roads 1 Nov 60, coded MH-6 by Dec 61. Redesignated WC-121N 30 Nov 62. Ret VW-4 Jacksonville 4 Jun 65. Re-coded MH-5 by May 67. Later named 'Blanche'. Coded MH-6 again by 1971. To MASDC Davis Monthan for storage 16 Jul 71. Struck off (Davis Monthan) 12 Jul 72 (TT: 10,007 hrs). Sold to Sun Valley Avn 13 Sep 76, subsequently scrapped.

4384 WV-3/1049A-55-95 2 Jun 55 to US Navy as 137897. To VW-4 Jacksonville 21 Nov 55, coded TH-l. Tfd VW-4 Roosevelt Roads 4 Nov 60, coded MH-7. Ran into a drainage ditch on aborted take-off Jacksonville, FL 7 Oct 57. Slid 400ft off runway into a sewage pipe. Repaired & ret to svce, but apparently never flew properly after the accident, so the acft was flown into storage. To Storage Facility, Litchfield Park 17 Nov 61. Redesignated WC-121N 30 Nov 62. Struck off (Litchfield Park) 21 Mar 63, and cannibalized for parts. Weather equipment tfd to Bu 141323 (c/n 4447). For sale by DofD (Davis Monthan) 18 Feb 65 (TT: 2,644 hrs) and again 22 Apr 65. Scrapped, probably same year.

4385 WV-3/1049A-55-95 8 Jun 55 to US Navy as 137898. To BAR M&S Burbank 8 Jun 55. To VW-3 Agana. 23 Nov 55, coded PM-4. To VW-4 Jacksonville27 Jan 58, tfd VW-4 Roosevelt Roads 9 Nov 60, coded MH-l, re-coded MH-7 by Dec 61. Redesignated WC-121N 30 Nov 62. Ret VW-4 Jacksonville 29 Jun 65, named 'Dora'. Tf to Davis Monthan for storage. Struck off (VW-4) 26 Jan 67, (TT: 8,175 hrs). Tfd to US Air Force, Burbank 10 Apr 67. Flown to Ontario, CA 1967 and cvtd to EC-121R by LAS for U S Air Force as 67-21472. USAF acceptance 10 Apr 57, del 29 Apr 67. On roll-out, this aircraft appeared in U S Navy-style colours (white top, midnight blue lower surfaces, fins, tip-tanks, etc) with U S Air Force in large letters on nose and 'last-five' of serial on fin; later repainted in tactical camouflage colours, as other EC-121Rs. Del to 553rd Recon Wg Otis 29 Apr 67. Deployed McCoy 9 Jan 68. Assigned 551st AEW Wg Otis 8 Feb 68, tfd 552nd AEW Wg McClellan 30 Nov 69. To MASDC Davis Monthan for storage 14

67-21472 EC-121R is seen on roll-out at Lockheed's facility in April 1967 after conversion from a Navy WC-121N and still basically in the former Navy midnite blue with white top colours. Prior to service, all the EC-121Rs were painted in a tactical camouflage scheme. (Lockheed)

May 71, TOC 15 May 71. Sold Sun Valley Avn 17 Aug 76, scrapped subsequent to Sep 76.

4386 RC-121D/1049A-55-86, mod to 1049A-55-137 9 Feb 56 to U S Air Force as 54-2304. USAF acceptance 31 May 56. Del to 552nd AEW Wg McClellan 5 Jun 56. Assigned 551st AEW Wg Otis 20 Apr 57, ret 552nd AEW Wg McClellan 23 Apr 57. To 551st AEW Wg McCoy 19 Oct 62, ret 552nd AEW Wg McClellan 20 Nov 62. To 551st AEW Wg McCoy 29 Dec 62, ret 552nd AEW Wg McClellan 31 Jan 63. Assigned 966th AEW Sq McCoy 15 Mar 63, ret 552nd AEW Wg McClellan 25 Mar 63. Deployed Tainan 7 Oct 65, Tan Son Nhut 28 Oct 65, Tainan 7 Nov 65. Ret McClellan & redesignated EC-121D 9 Feb 66. Deployed Tainan 6 Jul 66, ret McClellan 27 Dec 67. To Tainan 28 Jan 68, ret McClellan 15 Jul 68. Updated to EC-121D/T. To 966th AEW Sq McCoy 18 Apr 69, ret 552nd AEW Wg McClellan 6 Aug 69. Deployed Keflavik 12 Jul 70, ret McClellan 21 Oct 70. Deployed McCoy 10 Nov 70, ret McClellan 5 Dec 70. To MASDC Davis Monthan for storage 10 Dec 70. Scrapped subsequent to Jul 74.

4387 RC-121D/1049A-55-86, mod to 1049A-55-137 9 Feb 56 to U S Air Force as 54-2305. USAF acceptance 26 Jun 56. Del 551st AEW Wg Otis 28 Jun 56. Assigned 33rd MSG Otis 19 Jul 57, 551st MSG Otis 29 Aug 57, ret 551st AEW Wg Otis 1 Sep 57. Redesignated EC-121H 4 Mar 62. To 966th AEW Sq McCoy 25 Aug 69. To MASDC Davis Monthan for storage 25 Nov 69, TOC 1 Dec 69. Scrapped subsequent to Jul 74.

4388 RC-121D/1049A-55-86, mod to 1049A-55-137 9 Feb 56 to U S Air Force as 54-2306. USAF acceptance 29 Jun 56, del 12 Jul 56. Del to 552nd AEW Wg McClellan 27 Sep 56. Assigned 551st AEW Wg (966th AEW Sq) McCoy 31 Jan 63. Ret 552nd AEW Wg McClellan 25 Mar 63. Redesignated EC-121D 30 Sep 63. Deployed Tainan 1 Nov 65, Tan Son Nhut 6 Nov 65. Ret McClellan 18 May 66. Updated to EC-121D/T. Assigned 966th AEW Sq McCoy 15 Sep 68. Ret 552nd AEW Wg McClellan 25 Jan 69, to 966th AEW Sq McCoy 4 May 69, ret McClellan 28 Jul 69. To MASDC Davis Monthan 10 Sep 70 for storage. Still stored Sep 72, subsequently scrapped.

4389 RC-121D/1049A-55-86, mod to 1049A-55-137 9 Feb 56 to U S Air Force as 54-2307. USAF acceptance 29 Jun 56. Del to AF Plant 10 Jul 56. Assigned 552nd AEW Wg McClellan 27 Oct 56. Assigned 551st AEW Wg McCoy 12 Mar 62, tfd 551st AEW Wg Otis 11 May 62. Deployed McCoy 20 Jun 62, ret Otis 15 Aug 62. To McCoy 12 Sep 62, ret Otis 17 Nov 62. Deployed McCoy again 30 Nov 62, ret Otis 15 Apr 63. Tfd 552nd AEW Wg McClellan 15 Apr 63. Redesignated EC-121D 30 Sep 63. Deployed Tan Son Nhut 3 Oct 65, Tainan 9 Oct 65, ret McClellan 18 Oct 65. Updated to EC-121D/T. Assigned 966th AEW Sq McCoy 23 May 68, ret 552nd AEW Wg McClellan 1 Dec 68. To 966th AEW Sq McCoy 15 Dec 68. Redesignated EC-121T McClellan 1 Oct 70, ret 552nd AEW Wg McClellan 7 Oct 70.

55-121 RC-121D modified with a 'canoe' radome and small under-fuselage radome at an unknown Air Force plant. The aircraft was used in an unknown special test programme in 1956-57. (John T Wible collection)

Deployed McCoy 31 May 71, ret McClellan 17 Jun 71. Deployed Keflavik 12 Jul 71. Many short deployments to Keflavik 1972-73 & 1974-75. Tfd to AFRES 79th AEW Sq Homestead 22 Aug 76. Assigned 915th AEW Gp AFRES Homestead 2 Dec 76, ret 79th AEW Sq Homestead 30 Sep 77. To MASDC Davis Monthan for storage 18 Sep 78, TOC 19 Sep 78. For sale by DofD (Davis Monthan) 15 Nov 83 (TT: 23,132 hrs). Sold to DMI Aviation for $9,500, subsequently scrapped.

4390 RC-121D/1049A-55-86, mod to 1049A-55-137 9 Feb 56 to U S Air Force as 54-2308. USAF acceptance 31 Jul 56. Del to 552nd AEW Wg McClellan 3 Aug 56. Written-off after engine fire and crash nr McClellan AFB, CA, 22 Mar 58. The acft had taken off on a radar mission from McClellan AFB, when one engine failed. The RC-121D crashed six minutes later between Sacramento & Roseville, CA. No casualties.

4391 RC-121D/1049A-55-86, mod to 1049A-55-137 1 Mar 56 to U S Air Force as 55-118. USAF acceptance 1 Mar 56. Del to 552nd AEW Wg McClellan 1 Mar 56. Assigned 551st AEW Wg Otis 25 Oct 60, 551st Det McCoy 11 Dec 61, ret 551st Otis 21 Jan 62. Deployed McCoy 26 Jul 62, ret Otis 23 Dec 62. Assigned 552nd AEW Wg McClellan 7 Mar 65. Redesignated EC-121D 25 Mar 65. Deployed Tainan 25 Apr 67, ret McClellan 24 Jul 67. Updated to EC-121D/T. Redesignated EC-121T 1 Jun 70. Deployed Tainan 6 Jun 71, Kwangju 19 Jun 71, Korat 15 May 73. Ret McClellan 15 Jun 73. Deployed Korat 21 Oct 73, ret McClellan 17 May 74. Deployed Keflavik 6 Dec 74, additional deployments 1974-75. Tfd to AFRES 915th AEW Gp Homestead 3 Jan 77. Assigned 79th AEW Sq AFRES Homestead 30 Sep 77. Deld Homestead-Davis Monthan 12 Oct 78 on tf to MASDC Davis Monthan for storage, TOC 13 Oct 78. For sale by DofD (Davis Monthan) 15 Nov 83 (TT: 21,957 hrs). Sold to DMI Aviation for $9,750, subsequently scrapped.

4392 RC-121D/1049A-55-86, mod to 1049A-55-137 24 Feb 56 to U S Air Force as 55-119. USAF acceptance 31 Aug 56, del 6 Sep 56. Del to 551st AEW Wg Otis 5 Sep 56. Assigned 33rd MSG Otis 12 Aug 57, 551st MSG Otis 18 Aug 57, ret 551st AEW Wg Otis 1 Sep 57. Redesignated EC-121H 15 Jan 63. To 966th AEW Sq McCoy 15 Jul 69. To MASDC Davis Monthan for storage 2 Dec 69. Scrapped subsequent to Oct 74.

4393 RC-121D/1049A-55-86, mod to 1049A-55-138 5 Nov 56 to U S Air Force as 55-120. USAF acceptance 29 Oct 56. Del to 552nd AEW Wg McClellan 5 Nov 56. Assigned 966th AEW Sq McCoy 1 Aug 63. Redesignated EC-121D 10 Oct 63. Cvtd to EC-121Q with 966th AEW Sq McClellan 16 Sep 64. To 966th AEW Sq McCoy 19 Apr 66, ret 552nd AEW Wg McClellan 12 Sep 68. To 966th AEW Sq McCoy 4 Oct 68, ret 552nd AEW Wg McClellan 3 Jan 70. Deployed McCoy 22 Jan 70, ret McClellan 8 Mar 70. To McCoy 23 Mar 70, ret McClellan 18 May 70. To McCoy again 2 Jun 70, ret McClellan 6 Aug 70. TDY McCoy 21 Oct 70, ret McClellan 26 Dec 70. Deployed McCoy 7 Jan 71, followed by similar deployments to McCoy 1971-72, ret McClellan. Deployed to Homestead 31 Aug 73, ret McClellan 8 Jan 74. TDY Homestead 31 Jan 74, ret McClellan 19 Apr 74. Last deployment Homestead 29 Apr 74, ret McClellan 22 Jun 74. To MASDC Davis Monthan for storage 27 Jun 74. Engines removed by Jun 76. For sale by DofD (Davis Monthan) 24 May 78 & again 7 Jun 78 (TT: 20,791 hrs). Sold Southwestern Alloys 10 Apr 79, subsequently scrapped.

4394 RC-121D/1049A-55-86, mod to 1049A-55-138 3 Jul 56 to U S Air Force as 55-121. USAF acceptance 27 Jul 56. Del to AF Plant/AMC-6C-607 (BLMT) 27 Jul 56 (presumed for special test program). Mod with canoe radome forward of upper large radome, and additional small radome immediately aft of lower large radome, purpose unknown. To 552nd AEW Wg McClellan 4 Mar 58. Redesignated EC-121D 30 Sep 63. Deployed Tainan 29 Mar 67. Assigned 551st AEW Wg Otis 23 May 67, ret 552nd AEW Wg McClellan 10 Oct 67. Updated to EC-121D/T. To 966th AEW Sq McCoy 9 Aug 68. Redesignated EC-121T (McCoy) 5 Mar 70. Ret 552nd AEW Wg McClellan 9 Mar 70. Deployed Keflavik 3 Apr 71, ret McClellan 19 May 71. TDY Keflavik 14 Jun 71, ret McClellan 27 Jul 71. To Keflavik 23 Aug 71, ret McClellan 23 Sep 71. To Keflavik again 1 Nov 71, ret McClellan 17 Dec 71. Further short deployments to Keflavik 1972-1973. Assigned AFRES 79th AEW Sq Homestead 14 Jun 74. Tfd 915th AEW Gp AFRES Homestead 2 Dec 76. Ret 79th AEW Sq Homestead 30 Sep 77. Written-off at Keflavik, Iceland, 15 Mar 78. Starboard undercarriage collapsed while taxying out for take-off, aircraft swerved and port undercarriage collapsed as well. Fuel caught fire and the aircraft was burnt out. No casualties. SOC 15 Mar 78. Remains on fire dump at Keflavik until removed to local scrapyard at Reykjavik by Oct 83.

4395 RC-121D/1049A-55-86, mod to 1049A-55-138 4 May 56 to U S Air Force as 55-122. USAF acceptance 30 Apr 56, del 7 May 56. Del to 552nd AEW Wg McClellan 4 May 56. Assigned 551st AEW Wg (deployed McCoy) 28 Feb 62. Ret to home base Otis 14 Apr 62. Deployed McCoy 1 May 62, ret Otis 10 Jul 62. TDY McCoy 23 Jul 62, ret Otis 30 Sep 62. Assigned 552nd AEW Wg McClellan 2 Jan 63. Redesignated EC-121D 30 Sep 63. Deployed Tainan 7 Dec 66, ret McClellan 2 Feb 67. Deployed Tainan 2 May 67, ret McClellan 4 Dec 67. Updated to EC-121D/T. Assigned 966th AEW Sq McCoy 29 Jul 69. Redesignated EC-121T 13 Apr 70. Ret 552nd AEW Wg McClellan 17 Apr 70. Deployed Tainan 15 Oct 70, Kwangju 19 Jun 71, ret McClellan 2 Dec 71. Additional deployments to SE Asia 1972-75. Assigned AFRES 79th AEW Sq Homestead 22 Feb 76. To 915th AEW Gp AFRES Homestead 2 Dec 76. Ret 79th AEW Sq Homestead 30 Sep 77. To MASDC Davis Monthan for storage 11 Oct 78, TOC 12 Oct 78. Reportedly to be flown to Ent AFB, CO for open display

55-126 RC-121D of the 551st AEW & CW was photographed at Andrews AFB, Maryland on 12th May 1962 just prior to conversion to an EC-121H. The unit badge can be seen on the rear fuselage. (R F Besecker via John T Wible)

at HQ, Aerospace Defense Command (ADC), but still stored (complete) at MASDC Davis Monthan in May 82 & Apr 83. For sale by DofD (Davis Monthan) 15 Nov 83. (TT: 21,957 hrs). Sold to DMI Aviation for $9,500. Subsequently scrapped.

4396 RC-121D/1049A-55-86, mod to 1049A-55-138 8 May 56 to U S Air Force as 55-123. USAF acceptance 30 Apr 56. Del to 552nd AEW Wg McClellan 8 May 56. Assigned 551st AEW Wg Otis 18 May 56. To 551st MSG Otis 20 Aug 57, ret 551st AEW Wg Otis 1 Sep 57. Written-off at Otis AFB, MA 25 May 58. Explosion followed by fire on ground while aircraft was preparing for take-off, destroying aircraft. No casualties.

4397 RC-121D/1049A-55-86, mod to 1049A-55-138 14 May 56 to U S Air Force as 55-124. USAF acceptance 11 May 56. Del to 552nd AEW Wg McClellan 14 May 56. Assigned 551st AEW Wg (deployed McCoy) 24 Feb 63, tfd 966th AEW Sq McCoy 20 Mar 63. Ret 552nd AEW Wg McClellan 25 Mar 63. Redesignated EC-121D 30 Sep 63. Deployed Tainan 19 Sep 65, Tan Son Nhut 9 Oct 65, Tainan 5 Nov 65, ret McClellan 10 Dec 65. Deployed Tainan 4 May 66, ret McClellan 23 Sep 66. To Tainan 27 May 67, ret McClellan 18 Dec 67. Updated to EC-121D/T. Assigned 966th AEW Sq McCoy 10 Aug 68. Redesignated EC-121T 7 Jun 70. Ret 552nd AEW Wg McClellan 15 Jun 70. Deployed McCoy 26 Jan 71, ret McClellan 7 Feb 71. Deployed Keflavik 2 May 71, ret McClellan 16 Jun 71. Deployed McCoy 18 Jun 71, ret McClellan 24 Jun 71. Deployed Keflavik 26 Jul 71, additional deployments to Keflavik during 1972. Ret McClellan 18 Feb 73. Deployments to Keflavik 1973-1974. Assigned AFRES 915th AEW Gp Homestead 2 Dec 76. Tfd 79th AEW Sq AFRES Homestead 30 Sep 77. To MASDC Davis Monthan for storage 19 Jun 78, TOC 21 Jun 78. Still stored (complete) Davis Monthan Mar 83. For sale by DofD (Davis Monthan) 15 Nov 83 (TT: 22,558 hrs). Sold to DMI Aviation for $9,500. Subsequently scrapped.

4398 RC-121D/1049A-55-86, mod to 1049A-55-138 15 May 56 to U S Air Force as 55-125. USAF acceptance 30 Apr 56. Del to 552nd AEW Wg McClellan 15 May 56. Assigned 551st AEW Wg Otis 6 Jun 56. To 33rd MSG Otis 19 Jul 57, 551st MSG Otis 18 Aug 57. Ret 551st AEW Wg Otis 1 Sep 57. Redesignated EC-121H 7 Oct 62. To 966th AEW Sq McCoy 18 Jul 69. Assigned 552nd AEW Wg McCoy 20 Nov 69. To MASDC Davis Monthan for storage 2 Dec 69. Scrapped subsequent to Oct 74.

4399 RC-121D/1049A-55-86, mod to 1049A-55-138 28 May 56 to U S Air Force as 55-126. USAF acceptance 25 May 56. Del to 552nd AEW Wg McClellan 28 May 56. Assigned 551st AEW Wg Otis 6 Jun 56. To 33rd MSG Otis 19 Jul 57, 551st MSG Otis 18 Aug 57. Ret 551st AEW Wg Otis 1 Sep 57. Redesignated EC-121H 30 May 63. To MASDC Davis Monthan for storage 12 Nov 69. Scrapped subsequent to Oct 74.

4400 RC-121D/1049A-55-86, mod to 1049A-55-138 19 May 56 to U S Air Force as 55-127. USAF acceptance 16 May 56, del 21 May 56. Del to 552nd AEW Wg McClellan 19 May 56. Tfd 551st AEW Wg Otis 12 Nov 62, deployed McCoy 22 Nov 62. Ret Otis 16 Jan 63. Deployed McCoy 20 Feb 63, ret Otis 12 Apr 63. Redesignated EC-121D 30 Sep 63. Ret 552nd AEW Wg McClellan 22 May 64, assigned 966th AEW Sq McCoy 23 Jan 65. Ret 552nd AEW Wg McClellan 17 May 65. Deployed Tainan 17 Jan 66, ret McClellan 11 Apr 66. Assigned 966th AEW Sq McCoy again 13 Apr 67, ret 552nd AEW Wg McClellan 25 Jun 67. To 966th AEW Sq McCoy 21 Jul 67, ret 552nd AEW Wg McClellan 15 Aug 67. Deployed Tainan 19 Jun 68, ret McClellan 2 Feb 69. Deployed Tainan 23 Apr 69, ret McClellan 12 May 70. TDY Tainan again 14 Jun 70, ret McClellan 7 Jun 71. Assigned AFRES 915th MAG Homestead 22 Jul 71, tfd 79th AEW Sq Homestead 30 Jul 71. To MASDC Davis Monthan for storage 6 Aug 74. On tail, no engines, by Jun 76. For sale by DofD (Davis Monthan) 24 May 78, and again 7 Jun 78 (TT: 21,351 hrs). Sold Southwestern Alloys 21 Feb 79, subsequently scrapped.

4401 RC-121D/1049A-55-86, mod to 1049A-55-138 9 Jun 56 to U S Air Force as 55-128. USAF acceptance 31 May 56, del 11 Jun 56. Del to 552nd AEW Wg McClellan 31 Aug 56. Assigned 966th AEW Sq McCoy 27 Jun 63. Redesignated EC-121D 10 Oct 63. Deployed McClellan 23 Apr 65, ret McCoy 26 Jun 65. Recorded as EC-121Q 12 May 66 (McCoy). Ret to 552nd AEW Wg McClellan 26 Oct 68. Assigned 966th AEW Sq McCoy 6 Nov 68, ret 552nd AEW Wg McClellan 27 Apr 69. To 966th AEW Sq McCoy 10 May 69, assigned 552nd AEW Wg McCoy 31 Dec 69. Ret McClellan 21 Jan 70. Deployed McCoy 30 Jan 70, ret McClellan 3 Apr 70. TDY McCoy 10 Apr 70, ret McClellan 15 Jun 70. To McCoy 25 Jun 70, ret McClellan 26 Aug 70. To McCoy again 6 Sep 70, ret McClellan 10 Nov 70. Deployed McCoy 26 Nov 70, additional deployments McCoy during 1972-1974. Det Homestead, by early 1974. Data plate carried "EC-121S" (a/o Jul 74), but mispaint for EC-121Q (not in USAF records). To MASDC Davis Monthan for storage 24 Mar 75. For sale by DofD (Davis Monthan) 24 May 78 & again 7 Jun 78 (TT: 20,615 hrs). Sold Southwestern Alloys 21 Feb 79, subsequently scrapped.

4402 RC-121D/1049A-55-86, mod to 1049A-55-138 12 Jun 56 to U S Air Force as 55-129. USAF acceptance 31 May 56. Del to 551st AEW Wg Otis 12 Jun 56. Assigned 33rd MSG Otis 19 Jul 57, 551st MSG Otis 18 Aug 57, ret 551st AEW Wg Otis 1 Sep 57.

Redesignated EC-121H 24 Jan 63. To MASDC Davis Monthan for storage 10 Nov 69. Scrapped subsequent to Jul 74.

4403 RC-121D/1049A-55-86, mod to 1049A-55-138 18 Jun 56 to U S Air Force as 55-130. USAF acceptance 31 May 56. Del to 551st AEW Wg Otis 18 Jun 56. Assigned 33rd MSG Otis 19 Jul 57, 551st MSG Otis 20 Sep 57, ret 551st AEW Wg Otis 20 Sep 57. Deployed McCoy 30 Jul 62, ret Otis 26 Sep 62. Redesignated EC-121H 2 Apr 63. Assigned 966th AEW Sq McCoy 21 Jul 69. To MASDC Davis Monthan for storage 25 Nov 69. Scrapped subsequent to Jul 74.

4404 RC-121D/1049A-55-86, mod to 1049A-55-138 13 Jul 56 to U S Air Force as 55-131.USAF acceptance 29 Jun 56, del 12 Jul 56. Del to 551st AEW Wg Otis 11 Jul 56. Assigned 33rd MSG Otis 19 Jul 57, ret 551st Wg Otis 15 Dec 57. Redesignated EC-121H 20 Dec 63. To MASDC Davis Monthan for storage 20 Nov 69. Scrapped subsequent to Jul 74.

4405 RC-121D/1049A-55-86, mod to 1049A-55-138 10 Aug 56 to U S Air Force as 55-132. USAF acceptance 27 Jul 56. Del to 551st AEW Wg Otis 10 Aug 56. Redesignated EC-121H 23 Mar 63. In use with 960th AEW Sq Otis (a/o Jun 66). To MASDC Davis Monthan for storage 20 Nov 69. Scrapped subsequent to Jul 74.

4406 RC-121D/1049A-55-86, mod to 1049A-55-138 13 Jul 56 to U S Air Force as 55-133. USAF acceptance 29 Jun 56. Del to 552nd AEW Wg McClellan 13 Jul 56. Assigned 551st AEW Wg McCoy 16 Nov 62, ret 552nd AEW Wg McClellan 5 Dec 62. Assigned 966th AEW Sq McCoy 31 May 63, ret 552nd AEW Wg McClellan 2 Aug 63. Redesignated EC-121D 30 Sep 63. Assigned 966th AEW Sq McCoy 14 Jan 65, ret 552nd AEW Wg McClellan 29 Mar 65. Deployed Tainan 17 Sep 65, Tan Son Nhut 9 Nov 65, ret McClellan 27 Jan 66. To 966th AEW Sq McCoy 26 Jun 66, ret 552nd AEW Wg McClellan 12 Apr 69. To 966th AEW Sq McCoy again 24 May 69, ret 552nd AEW Wg McClellan 28 Sep 69. Redesignated EC-121T 6 Aug 70. Deployed Kwangju 31 Jul 71, ret McClellan 20 Sep 72. Deployed Kwangju 25 Nov 72, Korat 15 May 73, ret McClellan 28 May 74. To MASDC Davis Monthan for storage 28 Mar 75. Sold by DofD (Davis Monthan) 20 May 82 (TT: 23,278hrs). Subsequently scrapped.

4407 RC-121D/1049A-55-86, mod to 1049A-55-138 9 Aug 56 to U S Air Force as 55-134. USAF acceptance 31 Jul 56. Del to 551st AEW Wg Otis 9 Aug 56. Assigned 33rd MSG Otis 29 Jul 57, ret 551st AEW Wg Otis 28 Sep 57. Deployed 551st AEW Det McCoy 9 Dec 61, ret Otis 11 Dec 61. Redesignated EC-121H 3 Jul 63.Assigned 966th AEW Sq McCoy 27 Jul 69. To MASDC Davis Monthan for storage 2 Dec 69. Parts missing by Feb 72, scrapped subsequent to Jul 74.

4408 RC-121D/1049A-55-86, mod to 1049A-55-138 14 Aug 56 to U S Air Force as 55-135. USAF acceptance 31 Jul 56, del 15 Aug 56. Del to 552nd AEW Wg McClellan 14 Aug 56. Assigned 551st AEW Wg McCoy 4 Jan 62, ret 552nd AEW Wg McClellan 15 Dec 62. Assigned 966th AEW Sq McCoy 29 Jul 63, ret 552nd AEW Wg McClellan 14 Aug 63. Redesignated EC-121D 30 Sep 63. Deployed Tainan 23 May 66, ret McClellan 15 Nov 66. To Tainan 22 Jul 68, ret McClellan 1 Dec 68. Deployed Tainan again 15 Feb 69, ret McClellan 29 Jul 70. To Tainan 22 Aug 70, ret McClellan 7 Feb 71. Deployed Keflavik 7 Mar 71, ret McClellan 20 Apr 71.To MASDC Davis Monthan for storage 25 Jun 71. Withdrawn from storage & assigned AFRES 79th AEW Sq Homestead 5 Nov 71. Ret to MASDC Davis Monthan for storage 19 Jun 74. Stored, less engines, on tail, by Feb 77. For sale by DofD (Davis Monthan) 24 May 78, and again 7 Jun 78 (TT: 22,242 hrs). Sold Southwestern Alloys 16 Feb 79, subsequently scrapped.

4409 RC-121D/1049A-55-86, mod to 1049A-55-138 10 Aug 56 to U S Air Force as 55-136. USAF acceptance 31 Jul 56. Del to 551st AEW Wg Otis 10 Aug 56. Assigned 33rd MSG Otis 19 Jul 57, ret 551st AEW Wg Otis 4 Oct 57. Deployed McCoy 4 Aug 62, ret Otis 12 Oct 62. Redesignated EC-121H 27 Sep 63. Written-off 11 Jul 65. Acft ditched in the Atlantic Ocean approx 145 mls north-east of Nantucket Island, with one engine on fire and a second engine feathered, shortly after 22.20 hrs (local). The aircraft had taken off from Otis AFB, MA at 21.13 hrs (EDT). Weather was foggy with thunderstorms. No.2 engine failed to shift from low to high blower during climb at 11,000 ft, and was left in low blower. Aircraft reached on-station for tie-in with SAGE at 22.07 hrs. Three minutes later no.3 engine caught fire and an emergency declared, followed by failure of no.2 engine two minutes later. The decision was made to ditch and a rapid descent (1,660 ft/min) made from 15,000 ft. Fuselage broke into three parts on striking the water. 3 survivors.

4410 RC-121D/1049A-55-86, mod to 1049A-55-138 28 Aug 56 to U S Air Force as 55-137. USAF acceptance 24 Aug 56, del 28 Aug 56. Del to 552nd AEW Wg McClellan 16 Nov 56. Assigned 551st AEW Wg McCoy 20 Oct 62, ret 552nd AEW Wg McClellan 24 Nov 62. To 551st AEW Wg McCoy again 29 Dec 62, ret AEW Wg McClellan 26 Feb 63. Redesignated EC-121D 30 Sep 63. Deployed Tainan 30 Jul 67, ret McClellan 25 May 68. Assigned 966th AEW Sq McCoy 24 Apr 69, ret 552nd AEW Wg McClellan 17 Jul 69. Redesignated EC-121T 26 Aug 70. To MASDC Davis Monthan for storage 27 Mar 75. For sale by DofD (Davis Monthan) 24 May 78, and again 7 Jun 78 (TT: 22,139 hrs). Sold Southwestern Alloys 11 Apr 79, subsequently scrapped.

4411 RC-121D/1049A-55-86, mod to 1049A-55 138 28 Aug 56 to U S Air Force as 55-138. USAF acceptance 24 Aug 56, del 28 Aug 56. Del to 552nd AEW Wg McClellan 13 Nov 56.

55-137 EC-121T of 552nd AEW & CW is posed in 1972 with a new EC-137D AWACS (71-1408) that will replace it, at Boeing Field, Seattle. (Lockheed)

Redesignated EC-121D 30 Sep 63. Deployed Tainan 1 Feb 66. Ret McClellan 6 Sep 66. Updated to EC-l21D/T. Assigned 966th AEW Sq McCoy 10 May 68, ret 552nd AEW Wg McClellan 27 Jul 70. Redesignated EC-121T 22 Jul 70 (McCoy). Deployed McCoy 15 Mar 71, ret McClellan 26 Mar 71. Deployed Keflavik 18 Apr 71, additional short deployments during 1971, ret McClellan 29 Dec 71. Additional deployments to Keflavik during 1972-73. Assigned AFRES 79th AEW Sq Homestead 30 Jun 74. To MASDC Davis Monthan for storage 25 Feb 76. For sale by DofD (Davis Monthan) 15 Nov 83 (TT: 20,320 hrs). Sold to DMI Aviation for $9,750, subsequently scrapped.

4412 RC-121D/1049A-55-86, mod to 1049A-55-138 26 Oct 56 to U S Air Force as 55-139. USAF acceptance 22 Oct 56. Del to 551st AEW Wg Otis 26 Oct 56, assigned 33rd MSG Otis 19 Jul 57, 551st MSG Otis 18 Aug 57, ret 551st AEW Wg Otis 28 Oct 57. Tfd 552nd AEW Wg McClellan 30 Dec 60. Redesignated EC-121D 30 Sep 63. Deployed Tainan 2 Jun 68, ret McClellan 2 Oct 68. Deployed Tainan 8 Jan 69, ret McClellan 21 Mar 70. To Tainan 7 May 70 again, ret McClellan 16 Dec 70. Deployed Keflavik 20 Jan 71, ret McClellan 16 Mar 71. Assigned AFRES 915th MAG Homestead 9 Jul 71, tf AFRES 79th AEW Sq Homestead 30 Jul 71. Ret 552nd AEW Wg McClellan 21 Oct 73. To MASDC Davis Monthan for storage 6 Jun 74. Engines, parts missing by Feb 77. For sale by DofD (Davis Monthan) 24 May 78 & again on 7 Jun 78 (TT: 21,642 hrs). Derelict, on tail by Dec 78. Sold to Southwestern Alloys 11 Apr 79, subsequently scrapped.

4413 WV-2/1049A-55-86, mod to 1049A-55-137 24 Feb 56 to US Navy as 141289. To VW-13 Patuxent 5 Jul 56, tfd VW-13 Argentia 11 Jul 57. To VW-15 Patuxent 13 Sep 57. To VW-2 Patuxent 3 Oct 57, tfd VW-2 Det B Malta 5 Sep 59, coded MG-5 'Munin'. Ret VW-2 Patuxent 31 Aug(?) 59. To VW-15 Patuxent 30 Jun 60 & to VW-4 Roosevelt Roads 15 Apr 61. To Storage Facility, Litchfield Park 5 Dec 61. Struck off (Litchfield Park) 3 May 62. (TT: 3,216 hrs). Tfd to BUWEPS 4 May 62. Cvtd to EC-121H for U S Air Force as 55-5262. Assigned 551st AEW Wg Otis 31 May 63. Redesignated EC-121K Otis 1 Jun 63, but ret to EC-121H Otis a/o 23 Mar 65. Written-off 11 Nov 66. Crashed into the Atlantic Ocean, approx 120 miles east of Nantucket Island, MA with the loss of all on board. Aircraft had taken off from Otis AFB, MA at 00.35 hrs (local) on a routine air-defence mission. The last radio report was at 01.22 hrs. The aircraft made a rapid descent into water at approx 01.30 hrs (55 minutes after take-off) for unknown reasons. Weather foggy at time, only eyewitnesses were in a fishing boat near the crash site.

4414 WV-2/1049A-55-86, mod to 1049A-55-137 24 Feb 56 to US Navy as 141290. To VW-13 Patuxent Jul 56, tfd VW-13 Argentia May 57. To VW-15 Patuxent Sep 57. To VW-2 Patuxent 31 Oct 57, tfd VW-2 Det B Chinco -teague Dec 58, coded MG-6 'Hugin'. Ret VW-2 Patuxent (date unclear on card). To VW-2 Det B Chincoteague 5(?) Apr 59. Ret VW-2 Patuxent 13 Jun 59. To VW-2 Det B Malta 7 Aug 59, ret VW-2 Patuxent 3 Oct 59. Tfd VW-13 Patuxent 30 Jun 60. To Storage Facility, Litchfield Park 26 Jun 61. Redesignated EC-121K 30 Nov 62. Struck off (Litchfield Park) 21 May 65 (TT: 4,398 hrs). Scrapped approx Oct 65.

4415 WV-2/1049A-55-86, mod to 1049A-55-137 24 Feb 56 to US Navy as 141291. To VW-15 Patuxent 3 Oct 56, tfd VW-15 Argentia 26 Jan 58. Ret VW-15 Patuxent 10 May 58. To VW-13 Patuxent 17 Sep 58, coded MK-291. To VW-13 Argentia 20 Jul 61. To Storage Facility, Litchfield Park 5 Aug 61. Struck off (Litchfield Park) May 62 (TT: 5,674 hrs). Tfd to BUWEPS 19 May 62. Cvtd to EC-121H for U S Air Force as 55-5263. Redesignated EC-121K Olmsted 28 Sep 63. Assigned 551st AEW Wg Otis as EC-121H 9 Apr 65. To MASDC Davis Monthan for storage 10 Dec 69. Scrapped subsequent to Jul 74.

4416 WV-2/1049A-55-86, mod to 1049A-55-137 24 Feb 56 to US Navy as 141292. To BAR FA Burbank 29 Feb 56. To VW-11 Patuxent Oct 56, tfd VW-11 Argentia 31 Aug 57, ret VW-11 Patuxent Dec 57. To VW-11 Argentia again 14 Jun 58. Tfd AEWTRAUNIT Patuxent 8 Jun 62. To VW-13 at some stage (unconf from Navy records). Redesignated EC-121K 4 Dec 62. Cvtd to EC-121P. To NAS Glynco (NATTU) 5 May 64, coded 4B-502. (TT: 9,293 hrs a/o 21 Oct 67). To Patuxent, unit unknown 1969, uncoded. Modified to NC-121K by LAS Ontario for VAQ-33 Jun 72-Nov 72. Redesignated NC-121K 9 Nov 72. To Dynalectron for check 16 Nov 72, del to VAQ-33 Norfolk end Nov 72. Highly modified, with canoe radomes on upper and lower fuselage in front of large radomes, small radome aft of large lower radome; aerials on lower & upper parts of rear fuselage; slab-sided "tip-tanks" with ECM mods & chaff-dispensing tube at extreme end of tail. Coded GD-10 (a/o Apr 73), GD-11 (a/o Oct 75) & GD-12 by May 76. To VAQ-33 Key West Feb 80. Was the last EC-121 Warning Star Constellation in service with the US armed forces. Last operational flights with US Navy 8 Jun-11 Jun 82 Key West-Oceana- Atlantic Fleet electronic warfare mission -Oceana-Key West. Made final landing at Key West, FL 14.07 hrs (local) 11 Jun 82. Stripped of all sensitive & useable equipment & flown to the Florence Air & Missile Museum, Florence, SC 25 Jun 82. Struck off 25 Jun 82 (VAQ-33). Preserved at Florence as 'walk-through' exhibit until museum closed Sep 97. After being damaged in a grass fire summer 97, the acft was cannibalized by various sources during 1998; on belly without tip-tanks or engines or cargo door (a/o Dec 98) & by Aug 99 only parts of rear fuselage remained. The cockpit & forward fuselage (front 53ft of aircraft) was acquired by Brian Hicks and trucked to Stanley, NC. Slowly being restored in 2005 as static exhibit complete with trailer to be taken to airshows.

4417 WV-2/1049A-55-86, mod to 1049A-55-137 24 Feb 56 to US Navy as 141293. To BAR FA Burbank 24 Feb 56. To VW-11 Patuxent Oct 56, tfd VW-11 Argentia 8 Sep 57, ret VW-11 Patuxent Dec 57. To VW-11 Argentia 30 Jun 58, coded MJ-293 "Bamboo Clipper". Tfd AEWTRAUNIT/AEWTULANT Patuxent 4 Jun 62. Redesignated EC-121K 15 Oct 62, coded MM-3, later MM-l by Jun 63. To VW-13 Argentia 8 Jun 63, coded MK-293. Believed cvtd to EC-121P, but not in Navy records. To AFASDG, Davis Monthan, 23 Feb 65. Struck off (Davis Monthan) 22 May 70 (TT: 9,137 hrs). Sold to Kolar Inc 15 Oct 74, subsequently scrapped.

4418 WV-2/1049A-55-86, mod to 1049A-55-137 24 Feb 56 to US Navy as 141294. To VW-11 Patuxent 9 Nov 56, tfd VW-11 Argentia 18 Oct 57. Ret VW-11 Patuxent 28 Feb 58. To VW-15 Patuxent 1 May 58. Written-off 18 Oct 58 (VW-15). While making a GCA instrument approach to Argentia, Newfoundland, the aircraft crashed into the sea into Placentia Bay, 1000ft short of the runway, killing 11 of the 29 crew. The pilots were trying to get in to Argentia under the weather en route from Patuxent. Struck off 18 Oct 58 (TT: 1,592 hrs).

4419 WV-2/1049A-55-86, mod to 1049A-55-137 24 Feb 56 to US Navy as 141295. To AEW MATRON 2 Barbers Pt Dec 56. To VW-11 Patuxent Jun (?)57, tfd VW-11 Argentia Jul (?)57. To VW-15 Argentia Feb 58, tfd VW-15 Patuxent 17 May 58. To VW-13 Patuxent 10 Apr 61. To Storage Facility, Litchfield Park, 5 Jul 61. Redesignated EC-121K 30 Nov 62. Struck off (Litchfield Park) 21 Mar 63 (TT: 4,817 hrs). Used for spares. For sale by DofD (Davis Monthan) 18 Feb 65. Scrapped. (Note: LAC records show Quonset Pt prior to VW-15, but not in Navy records).

4420 WV-2/1049A-55-86, mod to 1049A-55-137 24 Feb 56 to US Navy as 141296. To BAR FA Burbank 24 Feb 56. To AEW MATRON 2 Barbers Pt 4 Dec 56. To VW-13 Patuxent Feb(?)57, tfd VW-13 Argentia 1 Jun 57. To VW-15 Patuxent 13 Sep 57, tfd VW-2 Patuxent 9 Oct 57, ret VW-13 Patuxent 14 Nov 58, coded MK-296. To VW-13 Argentia 16 Jul 61, tfd VW-4 Roosevelt Roads 7 Aug 61. To Storage Facility, Litchfield Park, by Apr 62. To AEWTRAUNIT/AEWTULANT Patuxent 7 Sep 62, coded MM-1. Redesignated EC-121K 6 Dec 62 & EC-121P 24 Feb 64. To Davis Monthan for storage 21 Jun 65. Struck off (AFASDG) 19 Jan 67 (TT: 7,410 hrs). Flown to Ontario, CA 10 Apr 67 for conversion to EC-121R by LAS for U S Air Force as 67-21473. USAF acceptance 10 Apr 67, del to 553rd Reconnaissance Wing, Korat 13 Dec 67. Deployed U-Tapao 31 Jan 69, ret Korat 1 Mar

69. Assigned 388th TFW Korat 15 Dec 70. To MASDC Davis Monthan for storage 4 Dec 71. Scrapped subsequent to May 74.

4421 WV-2/1049A-55-86, mod to 1049A-55-137 24 Feb 56 to US Navy as 141297. To BAR FA Burbank 24 Feb 56, R&D Burbank Aug 56 (?). To NADU South Weymouth 2 Dec 56, coded 4 (a/o Feb 58), recoded 2. To Naval Research Laboratory Patuxent (RDT&E) 8 Sep 61. Redesignated EC-121K 26 Oct 62. Used for Weapons System Test, NATC Patuxent. Cvtd to YEC-121K with installation of special APU by AiResearch Mar 65. Ret to EC-121K by Jul 66, still with NATC, Weapons System Test. (TT: 3,753 hrs a/o 28 Nov 67). With NRL Patuxent until 1 Aug 79, when the aircraft dep Patuxent on tf to MASDC Davis Monthan for storage. (TT: a/o Jun 75 was 6,654 hrs). TOC Davis Monthan 2 Aug 79. Prepared by DMI Aviation for flight to Warner Robins summer 87. Del to Warner Robins AFB, GA 20 Nov 87 by Save-A Connie crew. Preserved at the Warner Robins Museum of Aviation, GA in USAF mks, serial 141297 (a/o 1996), but with no serial (a/o Oct 00).

4422 WV-2/1049A-55-86, mod to 1049A-55-137 24 Feb 56 to US Navy as 141298. To VW-13 Patuxent 27 Jul 56. Tfd VW-11 Patuxent 28 Jul 56, ret VW-13 Patuxent 1 Oct 56. To VW-15 Patuxent '57, tfd VW-15 Argentia Dec 57. Ret to VW-11 Patuxent 19 Feb 58. To VW-15 Patuxent 1 May 58, tfd VW-13 Patuxent 18 Sep 58, coded MK-298. To VW-13 Argentia 21 Jul 61. To Storage Facility, Litchfield Park 13 Aug 61. Redesignated EC-121K 1962. Struck off (Litchfield Park) 21 May 65 (TT: 6,427 hrs). Scrapped approx Oct 65.

4423 WV-2/1049A-55-86, mod to 1049A-55-137 24 Feb 56 to US Navy as 141299. To BAR FA Burbank 24 Feb 56, R&D Burbank 13 Sep 56. To VW-13 Patuxent Mar 57, tfd VW-13 Argentia 1 Jun 57. Tfd VW-11 Argentia 17 Sep 57. To VW-11 Patuxent 28 Feb 58, ret VW-11 Argentia 25 May 58. To VW-13 Patuxent 29 Jun 61, tfd VW-13 Argentia 16 Jul 61, coded MK-299. Redesignated EC-121K 18 Oct 62 & EC-121P 7 Jan 64. To AFASDG Davis Monthan for storage 14 Jun 65 (TT: 10,372 hrs). Struck off (Davis Monthan) 22 May 70. Used for spares. Sold Kolar Inc 23 Oct 74, subsequently scrapped.

141299 WV-2 photographed prior to delivery at Burbank in 1956. This aircraft was used at the factory for various tests. (Lockheed)

4424 WV-2/1049A-55-86, mod to 1049A-55-137 24 Feb 56 to US Navy as 141300. To VW-11 Patuxent 27 Apr 56. Tfd VW-13 Patuxent 1 Oct 56, coded TK-300. To VW-15 Patuxent 13 Sep 57, tfd VW-15 Argentia 11 Dec 57. Ret VW-15 Patuxent 12 May 58, coded ML-3. Damaged when port undercarriage collapsed taxying, date uk. Repaired. To VW-13 Patuxent 11 Apr 61, tfd VW-13 Argentia 20 Jul 61. To Storage Facility, Litchfield Park, 3 Aug 61. Struck off (Litchfield Park) 11 May 62 (TT: 5,217 hrs). Tfd to BUWEPS 14 May 62. Redesignated EC-121K Olmsted 31 Aug 63. Cvtd for U S Air Force use as 55-5264. Assigned to 551st AEW Wg Otis 27 Apr 65 as EC-121H. To MASDC Davis Monthan for storage 20 Nov 69. Scrapped subsequent to Jul 74.

4425 WV-2/1049A-55-86, mod to 1049A-55-137 24 Feb 56 to US Navy as 141301. To VW-11 Patuxent 27 Apr 56, tfd VW-11 Argentia 19 Jul 57(?). To VW-15 Argentia 5 Feb 58, to VW-15 Patuxent 12 Jul 58. Tfd VW-13 Patuxent 5 Sep 58, coded MK-301 "Surprise" (a/o Feb 60). To Storage Facility, Litchfield Park 5 Jul 61. Redesignated EC-121K 30 Nov 62. Struck off (Litchfield Park) 21 Mar 63 (TT: 6,041 hrs). Cannibalized for spares at Litchfield Park. For sale by DofD (Davis Monthan) 18 Feb 65 and again 22 Apr 65. Scrapped.

4426 WV-2/1049A-55-86, mod to 1049A-55-137 24 Feb 56 to US Navy as 141302. To VW-11 Patuxent 27 Apr 56, tfd VW-11 Argentia 10 Aug 57, ret VW-11 Patuxent 2 Dec 57. To VW-11 Argentia again 21 May 58. To Storage Facility, Litchfield Park 18 Oct 61. Struck off May 62 (TT: 4,668 hrs). Tfd to BUWEPS 16 May 62. Cvtd to EC-121H for U S Air Force as 55-5265. Assigned 551st AEW Wg Otis 20 Nov 63. Redesignated EC-121K Otis 7 Dec 63, ret to EC-121H Otis 11 May 65. To MASDC Davis Monthan for storage 12 Nov 69. Scrapped subsequent to Jul 74.

4427 WV-2/1049A-55-86, mod to 1049A-55-137 25 May 56 to US Navy as 141303. Navy acceptance date 17 May 56. To VW-11 Patuxent 25 May 56. To VAH-11 Sanford 10 Apr 57, ret VW-11 Patuxent 11 Apr 57. Tfd VW-11 Argentia 27 Aug 57, ret VW-11 Patuxent 12 Dec 57. To VW-15 Argentia 1 Feb 58, tfd VW-15 Patuxent 3 May 58. To VW-13 Patuxent 15 Sep 58, coded MK-6. Written-off Argentia, Nfld 2 Apr 59. Developed engine problems 35 minutes after take-off from Argentia on a barrier patrol mission. Returned to Argentia & made a three-engined instrument approach in fog. Landing was hard & starboard wing broke off during landing impact, causing aircraft to flip upside down. Acft slid along runway upside down & burned. One crew member killed. Struck off Jun 59 (VW-13), TT: 3,158 hrs.

4428 WV-2/1049A-55-86, mod to 1049A-55-137 25 May 56 to US Navy as 141304. Navy acceptance date 21 May 56. To BAR FA Burbank 21 May 56. To VW-11 Patuxent 25 May 56, tfd VW-11 Argentia 14 Sep 57, ret VW-11 Patuxent 7 Dec 57. To VW-15 Argentia 29 Jan 58, tfd VW-15 Patuxent 28 Jun 58. To VW-13 Patuxent 7 Oct 58, tfd VW-13 Argentia 17 Jul 61. To Pacific Missile Range, Point Mugu 15 Aug 61. Redesignated EC-121K 30 Nov 62. To Naval Missile Center, Pt Mugu 1 Aug 63, ret PMR Pt Mugu 11 Sep 63. Mod by May 65 with two additional small radomes on upper fuselage in front of large radome, and two additional small radomes on lower fuselage to rear of large radome (no change in designation). All four radomes removed between Oct 71 & Oct 73. Struck off (PMR) 13 Dec 73 (TT: 11,274 hrs). To storage at MASDC Davis Monthan 12 Dec 73. (Reportedly remained at Pt Mugu in storage until Oct 74). Sold at Davis Monthan to Sun Valley Aviation 13 Sep 76, subsequently scrapped.

4429 WV-2/1049A-55-86, mod to 1049A-55-137 19 Jun 56 to US Navy as 141305. Navy acceptance date 11 Jun 56. To VW-11 Patuxent Jun 56, tfd VW-11 Argentia 57. Ret VW-11 Patuxent 28 Feb 58. To VW-11 Argentia 1 May 58. Damaged on 9 Mar 60, when starboard undercarriage drag strut broke during a practice landing. Aircraft landed again 90 minutes later, damaged undercarriage collapsed, but additional damage minimal. (TT: 4,391 hrs). Repaired, but flown to Storage Facility, Litchfield Park 8 Jun 61. Redesignated EC-121K 30 Nov 62. Struck off (Litchfield Park) 21 May 65 (TT: 4,435 hrs). Scrapped approx Oct 65.

4430 WV-2/1049A-55-86, mod to 1049A-55-137 22 Jun 56 to US Navy as 141306. To BAR FA Burbank 19 Jun 56. To VW-11 Patuxent 22 Jun 56, tfd VW-11 Argentia Aug 57. Ret VW-11 Patuxent 28 Feb 58. To VW-11 Argentia 18 Aug 58, coded MJ-306 by Jun 62. To AEWTRAUNIT/AEWTULANT Patuxent 5 Jul 62, coded MM-3. Redesignated EC-121K 30 Nov 62 & EC-121P 31 May 64. To Davis Monthan for storage. Struck off (AFASDG) Davis Monthan 19 Jan 67 (TT: 9,112 hrs). Flown to Ontario, CA 10 Apr 67 for conversion to EC-121R for U S Air Force by LAS as 67-21474. USAF acceptance 10 Apr 67. Del 553rd Reconnaissance Wing Otis 22 Sep 67. Deployed Korat 6 Nov 67, U-Tapao 30 Jan 69, ret Korat 2 Mar 69. To MASDC Davis Monthan for storage 14 May 70. Sold to Kolar & Co 1 Aug 74, subsequently scrapped. (Note: it is possible that c/ns 4430 & 4480 were mixed up at the time of their conversion to EC-121R as AF records show an anomaly with their respective origins. AF EC-121R manuals, however, show the two aircraft as listed.)

4431 WV-2/1049A-55-86, mod to 1049A-55-137 2 Jul 56 to US Navy as 141307. To BAR FA Burbank 22 Jun 56. To VW-13 Patuxent Jul 56, tfd VW-11 Patuxent Jul 56. Ret VW-13 Patuxent 1 Oct 56, tfd VW-13 Argentia Aug 57. Ret VW-13 Patuxent 12 Sep 57. To VW-15 Patuxent 13 Sep 57. Tfd to VW-2 Patuxent 28 Feb 58, coded MG-10. To VW-2 Dep B Chincoteague 19 Jan 59, ret VW-2 Patuxent 18 Mar 59. To VW-2 Det B Sigonella 21 Jan 60, coded MG-307. To VW-11 Argentia 18 May 60, tfd VW-13 Argentia 18 Aug 61, coded MK-307. Redesignated EC-121K 27 Oct 62 & EC-121P 28 Feb 64. To AFASDG (Davis Monthan) for storage 24 Jun 65. (TT: 9,568 hrs). Struck off (Davis Monthan) 22 May 70. Sold to Kolar Inc 9 Oct 74, subsequently scrapped.

4432 WV-2/1049A-55-86, mod to 1049A-55-137 2 Aug 56 to US Navy as 141308. Navy acceptance date 20 Jul 56. To VW-13 Patuxent 3 Aug(?) 56. To VW-15 Patuxent 24 Apr 57, tfd VW-15 Argentia 15 Feb 58. To VW-11 Patuxent 6 Mar 58, coded MJ-308 "Tradewind". To Storage Facility, Litchfield Park 23 Jun 61. Redesignated EC-121K 30 Nov 62. Struck off (Litchfield Park) 21 Mar 63 (TT: 6,190 hrs). Cannibalized for spares. For sale by DofD (Davis Monthan) 18 Feb 65 and again 22 Apr 65. Scrapped shortly afterwards.

4433 WV-2/1049A-55-86, mod to 1049A-55-137 1 Aug 56 to US Navy as 141309. Navy acceptance date 20 Jul 56, to BAR FA Burbank same day. To VW-13 Patuxent 1 Aug 56, tfd VW-13 Argentia 1 Jun 57. To VW-15 Patuxent 13 Sep 57. To VW-2 Patuxent 11 Oct 57, coded MG-11. To VW-15 Patuxent 6 Jun 58, to VW-13 Patuxent 10 Sep 58, coded MK-309 by Feb 60. Tfd VW-13 Argentia 17 Jul 61. To Pacific Missile Range, Point Mugu 18 Aug 61. Redesignated EC-121K 16 Oct 62. To Naval Missile Center, Pt Mugu 1 Aug 63, ret PMR Pt Mugu 1 Nov 63. Mod by Apr 65 with two additional small radomes on upper fuselage in front of large radome, and two additional small radomes on lower fuselage to rear of large radome (no change of designation). To Pacific Missile Test Center Pt Mugu 25 Apr 75. (TT: 11,646 hrs a/o Jun 75). All four additional radomes removed by 1974. To MASDC Davis Monthan for storage 6 Mar 78. Withdrawn from storage by 12 Mar 83. Flown to McClellan AFB, CA 8 Apr 83, tfd to McClellan Aviation Museum 8 Apr 83. Repainted in USAF markings as '53-552' (to represent the resident AEW Wing (the 552nd AEW & CW) by Nov 85. Subsequently repainted as '30552' (a/o 1986), & then as '03-0552' (by Mar 88). Interior restored as USAF AEW EC-121 for Sep 90 reunion of 552nd AEW Wg personnel. Preserved at the McClellan Aviation Museum, Sacramento, CA.

4434 WV-2/1049A-55-86, mod to 1049A-55-137 5 Sep 56 to US Navy as 141310. Navy acceptance date 22 Aug 56. To VW-15 Patuxent 5 Sep 56, coded TL-1. Tfd VW-15 Argentia 24 Jan 58. Missing approx 110 mls west of Corvo Island, Azores between checkpoints "Mahogany" & "Pendulum", presumed crashed in the North Atlantic Ocean in the early hours of 20 Feb 58. The aircraft had taken off from Argentia NAS,Nfld on a routine barrier patrol at 08.53 hrs (EST) on 19 Feb 58 and was due back the following day at 11.00 hrs. Last radio contact was made with the aircraft at 02.59 hrs (20 Feb 58). All 22 crew presumed killed. Struck off 28 Feb 58 (TT: 1,693 hrs approx). No trace has ever been found of the aircraft or her crew.

4435 WV-2/1049A-55-86, mod to 1049A-55-137 20 Aug 56 to US Navy as 141311. Navy acceptance date 8 Aug 56. To BAR FA Burbank Aug 56. To VW-13 Patuxent 20 Aug 56, tfd VW-13 Argentia 18 Mar 57. To VW-15 Patuxent 13 Sep 57. To VW-2 Patuxent 7 Oct 57. Tfd VW-2 Det B Capodichino 20 Oct 57, ret VW-2 Patuxent 6 Dec 57. To VW-15 Patuxent 7 May 58, tfd VW-13 Patuxent 25 Nov 58. To VW-13 Argentia 18 Jul 61. To Pacific Missile Range, Point Mugu 11 Aug 61. Redesignated EC-121K 4 Nov 62. Tfd Naval Missile Center, Pt Mugu 1 Aug 63, ret PMR Pt Mugu 7 Oct 63. Mod with two additional small radomes on upper fuselage in front of large radome, and two additional small radomes on lower fuselage to rear of large radome (no change in designation). Removed by 1973. To PMR Hawaii Facilities, Kaneohe 1971-73. Ret PMR Pt Mugu 1973. To PMR Alameda 23 Apr 75 & to Pacific Missile Test Center, Pt Mugu 25 Apr 75. (TT: 12,347 hrs a/o Jun 75). To MASDC Davis Monthan for storage 7 May 79. Struck off May 79. Withdrawn from storage by 12 Mar 83. Flown to Chanute AFB, IL approx Apr 83, no.2 prop feathered prior landing. Preserved there at the Octave Chanute Aerospace Museum, Rantoul, IL. Still in PMTC markings (Jun 83-Aug 89). Purchased by the NASM of Australia in early 1992, in particular for the engines (as spares for c/n 4176, qv). Plans to fly the EC-121K to Australia appear to have been dropped, & the aircraft is still on display at Chanute. Repainted in midnite blue overall Navy colour-scheme, coded SH-15 (a/o Jul 03).

4436 WV-2/1049A-55-86, mod to 1049A-55-137 20 Aug 56 to US Navy as 141312. To BAR FA Burbank Aug 56. To VW-13 Patuxent 20 Aug 56. Rear fuselage twisted by approx 15 degrees and rivets popped out of upper wing surfaces in rough weather GCA landing at Argentia, Nfld 16 Jan 57. Flown to LAS New York for overhaul. Ret to VW-13 Apr 57, tfd VW-15 Patuxent 13 Sep 57. To VW-2 Patuxent 4 Oct 57. To VW-2 Det B Chincoteague 1 Dec 58, possibly coded MG-l, later MG-7. Ret VW-2 Patuxent 10 Apr 59. To VW-2 Det B Chincoteague 9 Jun 59, ret VW-2 Patuxent 14 Aug 59. To VW-11 Argentia 5 May 60 'Surprise', coded MJ-312 by Apr 62. Redesignated EC-121K 6 Oct 62 & EC-121P 4 Dec 63. To Davis Monthan for storage by Aug 65. Struck off (AFASDG) 19 Jan 67 (TT: 9,352 hrs). Flown to Ontario, CA approx 10 Apr 67, USAF acceptance 10 Apr 67. Cvtd to EC-121R by LAS for U S Air Force as 67-21475. Del 551st AEW Wg Otis 30 Nov 67. Deployed McCoy 15 Jan 68, ret Otis 6 Feb 68. Assigned 552nd AEW Wg McClellan 25 Nov 69. Believed also used by AFSC-ADTC at Eglin, FL 1969/70, but not on card. To MASDC Davis Monthan for storage 29 Jun 71, TOC 30 Jun 71. Sold Sun Valley Aviation 17 Sep 76, subsequently scrapped.

4437 WV-2/1049A-55-86, mod to 1049A-55-137 21 Aug 56 to US Navy as 141313. Navy acceptance date 13 Aug 56. To VW-13 Patuxent Aug 56, tfd VW-15 Patuxent 13 May 57. To VW-2 Patuxent 7 Oct 57, coded MG-l by May 58, named 'Woden'. Recoded MG-313 by Jul 59. To VW-2 Det B Sigonella 27 Nov 59. Ret VW-2 Patuxent 22 Feb 60. To VW-13 Patuxent Apr 60. To Storage Facility, Litchfield Park 30 Jun 61. Redesignated EC-121K 30 Nov 62. Struck off (Litchfield Park) 21 Mar 63 (TT: 4,800 hrs). Cannibalized for spares. For sale by DofD (Davis Monthan) 18 Feb 65. Scrapped shortly afterwards

4438 WV-2/1049A-55-86, mod to 1049A-55-137 19 Sep 56 to US Navy as 141314. Navy acceptance date 5 Sep 56. To VW-15 Patuxent 19 Sep 56. Written-off 17 Apr 57 at Argentia, Nfld. Crashed at 09.33 hrs (local) in a wheels-up landing as a result of an in-flight fire. After take-off from Argentia on a barrier patrol flight, there was a fire in the area of no.2 nacelle and engine, probably after a dragging brake which became overheated ignited hydraulic fluid causing the tyre to blow out and rupture hydraulic and fuel lines. No 2 engine subsequently fell off in flight. The aircraft returned for a crash landing & burned on the runway. Only injury was a sprained ankle. Struck off (VW-15) 30 Apr 57, (TT: 558 hrs).

4439 WV-2/1049A-55-86, mod to 1049A-55-137 19 Sep 56 to US Navy as 141315. Navy acceptance date 7 Sep 56. To VW-15 Patuxent 19 Sep 56, tfd VW-15 Argentia Jan 58. Ret VW-15 Patuxent 1 Jul 58. To VW-13 Patuxent 8 Apr 61 & to VW-13 Argentia 16 Jul 61. To Storage Facility, Litchfield Park 16 Aug 61. Redesignated EC-121K 30 Nov 62. Struck off (Litchfield Park) 21 May 65, (TT: 6,013 hrs). Scrapped approx Oct 65.

4440 WV-2/1049A-55-86, mod to 1049A-55-137 27 Sep 56 to US Navy as 141316. Navy acceptance date 12 Sep 56, to BAR FA Burbank same day. To VW-2 Patuxent 26 Sep 56. Tfd VW-15 Patuxent 11 Feb 57, coded TL-5. To VW-13 Patuxent 26 Sep 58. To VW-11 Argentia 5 Feb 61, ret VW-13 Patuxent 28 Jun 61. To VW-13 Argentia 17 Jul 61, coded MK-316. Redesignated EC-121K 25 Sep 62 & to EC-121P 10 May 64. To AFASDG Davis Monthan for storage 15 Apr 65, (TT: 9,512 hrs). Struck off (Davis Monthan) 22 May 70. Sold to Kolar Inc 11 Oct 74, subsequently scrapped.

Section 12: Constellation Production List

4441 WV-2/1049A-55-86, mod to 1049A-55-137 26 Sep 56 to US Navy as 141317. To BAR FA Burbank 11 Sep 56. To VW-15 Patuxent 26 Sep 56, tfd VW-15 Argentia 11 Dec 57. Ret VW-15 Patuxent 20 Jun 58. To VW-11 Argentia 14 Apr 61, tfd VW-13 Argentia 16 Jul 61, coded MK-317. Redesignated EC-121K 19 Oct 62 & to EC-121P 22 Dec 63. Still with VW-13 Argentia (a/o 28 Feb 65). To Davis Monthan for storage by Aug 65. Struck off (AFASDG) 19 Jan 67, (TT: 10,463 hrs). Flown to Ontario, CA approx 10 Apr 67. Cvtd to EC-121R by LAS for U S Air Force as 67-21476. USAF acceptance 1 Oct 67, del to 553rd Reconnaissance Wg Otis 1 Oct 67. Tfd 551st AEW Wg Otis 22 Nov 67. Possibly used by AFSC-ADTC Eglin 1968/69, but not on card. Written-off in landing accident 20 Jan 69 probably at Eglin AFB, FL. Struck off 24 Jan 69 (Otis).

4442 WV-2/1049A-55-86, mod to 1049A-55-137 8 Oct 56 to US Navy as 141318. Navy acceptance date 21 Sep 56. To VW-11 Patuxent 6 Oct 56. To VAH-11 Sanford 10 Apr 57, ret VW-11 Patuxent 11 Apr 57. To VW-11 Argentia 19 Aug 57. Tfd VW-15 Argentia 30 Jan 58 & to VW-15 Patuxent 5 Jul 58. To Storage Facility, Litchfield Park 15 Jun 60. Struck off (Litchfield Park) May 62, (TT: 4,391 hrs). Tfd to BUWEPS 25 May 62. Cvtd to EC-121H for U S Air Force as 55-5267. Assigned 551st AEW Wg Otis as EC-121H 30 Sep 63. Redesignated EC-121K Otis 12 Oct 63, ret to EC-121H Otis (a/o 8 Mar 65). To MASDC Davis Monthan for storage 12 Nov 69, TOC 13 Nov 69. Sold Sun Valley Aviation 20 Sep 76, subsequently scrapped.

4443 WV-2/1049A-55-86, mod to 1049A-55-137 4 Dec 56 to US Navy as 141319. Navy acceptance date 21 Nov 56, to BAR FA Burbank same day. To AEW MATRON 2 Barbers Pt 4 Dec 56. Tfd VW-11 Patuxent 1 May 57. To VW-15 Patuxent 12 May 57, tfd VW-15 Argentia 27 Jan 58. Ret VW-15 Patuxent 3 May 58. To VW-11 Argentia 14 Apr 61, tfd VW-13 Argentia 18 Jul 61, coded MK-319. Redesignated EC-121K 10 Oct 62 & to EC-121P 4 Feb 64. Remained with VW-13 Argentia. To Davis Monthan for storage 7 Jul 65 (TT: 10,440 hrs). Struck off (Davis Monthan) 22 May 70. Sold to Kolar Inc 15 Oct 74, subsequently scrapped.

4444 WV-2/1049A-55-86, mod to 1049A-55-137 23 Oct 56 to US Navy as 141320. To BAR FA Burbank 21 Nov 56. To VW-2 Patuxent 24 Oct 56, tfd VW-2 Det B Capodichino 21 Dec 56, coded TF-2 "Fricka II". To VW-15 Patuxent 20(?) Feb 57, tfd VW-15 Argentia 28 Dec 57. Ret VW-15 Patuxent 26 May 58. To VW-11 Argentia 14 Apr 61, coded MJ-320. Redesignated EC-121K 3 Oct 62 & to EC-121P 22 Aug 63 (VW-11's first EC-121P). Remained with VW-11 Argentia. To Davis Monthan for storage by Aug 65. Struck off (AFASDG) Davis Monthan 19 Jan 67 (TT: 9,868 hrs). Flown to Ontario, CA approx 10 Apr 67. Cvtd to EC-121R by LAS for U S Air Force as 67-21477. USAF del 30 Jun 67. Del to 553rd Reconnaissance Wing Otis 30 Jun 67. Deployed to Korat 6 Nov 67, U-Tapao 31 Jan 69, ret to Korat 2 Mar 69. To MASDC Davis Monthan for storage 13 Nov 70. Scrapped subsequent to Jul 74.

4445 WV-2/1049A-55-86, mod to 1049A-55-137 23 Oct 56 to US Navy as 141321. Navy acceptance date 11 Oct 56. To VW-15 Patuxent Oct 56, tfd VW-15 Argentia 10 Jan 58. Ret VW-15 Patuxent 17 Jul 58. Tfd VW-11 Argentia 13 Apr 61. To VW-13 Argentia 4 Aug 61, coded MK-321. Redesignated EC-121K 6 Nov 62 & to EC-121P 4 Dec 63. Damaged beyond repair in landing gear failure at Keflavik, Iceland, 11 Jun 65. The aircraft was parked on the ramp with engines off & no hydraulic system pressure. A ground crewman attempting to install a ground downlock safety-pin inadvertently released the down-lock mechanism, whereupon the landing gear collapsed, fatally injuring the crewman, who was trapped in the wheel-well. Struck off (VW-13) 21 Jun 65, (TT: 10,440 hrs). Scrapped on site.

4446 WV-2/1049A-55-86, mod to 1049A-55-137 30 Oct 56 to US Navy as 141322. Navy acceptance date 16 Oct 56, to BAR FA Burbank same day. To VW-15 Patuxent Oct 56, tfd VW-15 Argentia 10 Jan 58. Ret VW-15 Patuxent 1 May 58. To VW-11 Argentia 13 Apr 61, coded MJ-322. Redesignated EC-121K 18 Oct 62 & to EC-121P 19 Mar 64. Remained with VW-11 Argentia. To AFASDG (Davis Monthan) for storage 11 Mar 65. (TT: 10,009 hrs). Struck off (Davis Monthan) 22 May 70. Sold to Kolar Inc 10 Oct 74, subsequently scrapped.

4447 WV-2/1049A-55-86, mod to 1049A-55-137 30 Oct 56 to US Navy as 141323. Navy acceptance date 18 Oct 56, to BAR FA Burbank same day. To VW-15 Patuxent Oct 56. Tfd VW-13 Patuxent 10 Nov 56 & to VW-13 Argentia 16 Jun 57. Ret to VW-15 Patuxent 13 Sep 57. To VW-2 Patuxent 10 Oct 57, tfd VW-15 Patuxent 28 Mar 60. To VW-13 Patuxent 13 Apr 61. To Storage Facility, Litchfield Park 17 Aug 61. Weather eqpt from BuAer 137897 (c/n 4384) tfd to c/n 4447 at Litchfield Park. Flown to Ontario, CA for conversion to WV-3 by LAS. To BWR FR Burbank 22 Sep 61, redesignated WV-3X 23 Sep 61 & then WV-3 22 Nov 61. Deld to VW-4 Roosevelt Roads 15 Dec 61 as replacement aircraft for c/n 4384, coded MH-3. Damaged Feb 62 when hit by a truck on the ramp at Roosevelt Roads, PR. Sailor driving a pick-up truck at night on the ramp fell asleep & drove into the nose-gear, severely twisting the airframe. The acft was shored & braced, then flown at low altitude with gear down to Long Island for repair by LAS, New York. Ret to VW-4 later in 1962. Redesignated WC-121N 8 Dec 62. Served as test-bed for DALS (Data Acquisition Logging System). Fitted with rocket sonde modification on port side of fuselage immediately forward of aft entry door by Sep 64. Named 'Camille' by 1966. To MASDC Davis Monthan for storage 1 Apr 71. Struck off (Davis Monthan) 12 Jul 72, (TT: 9,534 hrs). Sold to Sun Valley Avn 19 May 76, subsequently scrapped.

4448 WV-2/1049A-55-86, mod to 1049A-55-137 8 Nov 56 to US Navy as 141324. Navy acceptance date 29 Oct 56. To AEW MATRON 2 Barbers Pt 6 Nov 56. Tfd to AIR BARSRON 2 Barbers Pt 5 Sep 57. To VW-11 Patuxent 19 Feb 58, tfd VW-11 Argentia 8 Jul 58. To AEWTRAUNIT/AEWTULANT Patuxent 27 Jun 62, coded MM-4. Crashed at Patuxent River, MD 9 Aug 62. On returning to Patuxent from Corpus Christi, TX, where the acft had been on static display, the aircraft crashed attempting to land in a heavy rainstorm at 16.35 hrs (local). The acft cleared pond no.2 at Patuxent, but mushroomed into the incline behind the pond, crashed & burned. 14 of 19 crew survived. Struck off 9 Aug 62 (AEWTRAUNIT/LANT), (TT: 6,480 hrs).

4449 WV-2/1049A-55-86, mod to 1049A-55-137 9 Nov 56 to US Navy as 141325. Navy acceptance date 30 Oct 56, to BAR FA Burbank same day. To AEW MATRON 2 Barbers Pt Nov 56, tf AIR BARSRON 2 Barbers Pt 14 Jul 57. To VW-11 Patuxent 14 Dec 57, tf VW-11 Argentia 14 May 58. To VW-13 Argentia 2 Aug 61. Tf to Storage Facility, Litchfield Park by Apr 62 (briefly, not in Navy records). Redesignated EC-121K 1 Nov 62. Ret to VW-13 Argentia by 1963, coded MK-325. Believed cvtd to EC-121P (not in records). Used for Project Birdseye & cvtd to Polar Ice Reconnaissance aircraft 1964/65. To OASU Patuxent 1 Jul 65, coded JB-325. Upper radome removed, redesignated NC-121K Aug 65. To VX-8 Patuxent, still coded JB-325 Jul 67, named 'The Arctic Fox', with fox on snow emblem on forward fuselage. To VXN-8 Patuxent Jan 69, still coded JB-325. Used on Project Birdseye until tf to MASDC Davis Monthan for storage 3 Oct 73. Struck off (Davis Monthan) 29 Jul 74 (TT: 16,044 hrs). Sold to Sun Valley Avn 16 Sep 76, subsequently scrapped.

4450 WV-2/1049A-55-86, mod to 1049A-55-137 9 Nov 56 to US Navy as 141326. Navy acceptance date 2 Nov 56, to BAR FA Burbank same day. To AEW MATRON 2 Barbers Pt Nov 56, tfd AIR BARSRON 2 Barbers Pt 11 Jun 57. To VW-11 Patuxent 28 Feb 58, tfd VW-11 Argentia 6 May 58, coded MJ-326 by Sep 61. Redesignated EC-121K 2 Oct 62. Tfd VW-13 Argentia by Apr 63 (but not in records), coded MK-326. Ret to VW-11 Argentia by Jan 64. Redesignated EC-121P 9 Apr 64. To AFASDG (Davis Monthan) for storage 22 Mar 65. Struck off (Davis Monthan) 22 May 70 (TT: 10,032 hrs). Sold to Kolar Inc 10 Oct 74, subsequently scrapped.

4451 WV-2/1049A-55-86, mod to 1049A-55-137 20 Nov 56 to US Navy as 141327. Navy acceptance date 6 Nov 56. To AEW MATRON 2 Barbers Pt 20 Nov 56, tfd AIR BARSRON 2 Barbers Pt 5 Sep 57. To VW-11 Patuxent 13 Jan 58, tfd VW-11 Argentia 26 Jun 58. To Storage Facility, Litchfield Park 20 Aug 61. Struck off 9 May 62 (Litchfield Park), (TT: 3,281 hrs). Tfd to BUWEPS 10 May 62. Cvtd to EC-121H for U S Air Force as 55-5268. Assigned 551st AEW Wg Otis as EC-121H 24 May 63, redesignated EC-121K Otis 14 Jun 63, ret EC-121H Otis (a/o 20 Feb 65). To MASDC Davis Monthan for storage 10 Nov 69. Scrapped subsequent to May 73.

4452 WV-2/1049A-55-86, mod to 1049A-55-137 23 Nov 56 to US Navy as 141328. To BAR FA Burbank 13 Nov 56. To AEW MATRON 2 Barbers Pt 23 Nov 56, tfd AIR BARSRON 2 Barbers Pt 12 Aug 57. To VW-11 Patuxent 21 Jan 58, tfd VW-11 Argentia 13 May 58. To VW-13 Argentia 25 Jul 61, coded MK-328. Redesignated EC-121K 4 Oct 62 & EC-121P 29 Mar 64, still with VW-13 Argentia. To Davis Monthan for storage by Aug 65. Struck off (AFASDG) Davis Monthan 19 Jan 67 (TT: 9,753 hrs). Flown to Ontario, CA approx 10 Apr 67 and cvtd to EC-121R for U S Air Force by LAS as 67-21478. USAF acceptance 10 Apr 67, del 16 Nov 67. To 553rd Reconnaissance Wg Otis 16 Nov 67. Deployed Korat 30 Nov 67, U-Tapao 31 Jan 69, ret Korat 3 Mar 69. Assigned 388th TFW Korat 15 Dec 70. To MASDC Davis Monthan for storage 6 Dec 71. Scrapped subsequent to May 74.

4453 WV-2/1049A-55-86, mod to 1049A-55-137 5 Dec 56 to US Navy as 141329. Navy acceptance date 23 Nov 56. To AEW MATRON 2 Barbers Pt 15 Dec 56, tfd AIR BARSRON 2 Barbers Pt 11 Jul 57. To VW-11 Patuxent 14 Dec 57, tfd VW-11 Argentia 1 May 58. To VW-13 Patuxent 3 Jun 59, ret VW-11 Argentia 4 Jun 59. To VW-13 Argentia 4 Aug 61, coded MK-329. Redesignated EC-121K 1 Nov 62. Written-off Gander, Nfld 30 Jul 63. On a crew training flight from Argentia, the crew were practising ILS approaches at Gander. Upon touchdown, a misunderstanding arose in the cockpit as to whether a 'full stop' or 'touch & go' was being carried out. In fact power was added too late to take off again, but the aircraft was travelling too fast to stop on the remaining runway, so the aircraft overran the end of the runway into the mud, demolishing the ILS transmitter building & causing strike damage to the aircraft (fuselage broken in front of wing near the galley). No injuries. Struck off (VW-13) 30 Jul 63, (TT: 8,444 hrs). NB: date has also been given as 31 Jul 63.

4454 WV-2/1049A-55-86, mod to 1049A-55-137 12 Dec 56 to US Navy as 141330. To BAR FA Burbank 28 Nov 56. To AEW MATRON 2 Barbers Pt 12 Dec 56, tfd AIR BARSRON 2 Barbers Pt 5 Sep 57. To VW-ll Patuxent 13 Jan 58, tfd VW-11 Argentia 31 May 58. To VW-13 Argentia 23 Jul 61, coded MK-330. Redesignated EC-121K 25 Sep 62 & EC-121P 6 Feb 64, still with VW-13 Argentia. To Davis Monthan for storage by Aug 65. Struck off (AFASDG) Davis Monthan Jan 67 (TT: 10,078 hrs). Flown to Ontario, CA approx 10 Apr 67 and cvtd to EC-121R for U S Air Force by LAS as 67-21479. USAF acceptance 10 Apr 67, del 1 Dec 67. To 553rd Reconnaissance Wg Korat 1 Dec 67. Deployed U-Tapao 31 Jan 69, ret Korat 10 Feb 69. Assigned 388th TFW Korat 15 Dec 70. To MASDC Davis Monthan for storage 24 Nov 71. Scrapped subsequent to Jul 74.

4455 WV-2/1049A-55-86, mod to 1049A-55-137 17 Dec 56 to US Navy as 141331. Navy acceptance date 6 Dec 56, to BAR FA Burbank same day. To NavCicOffsCol Glynco 17 Dec 56, later NAS Glynco 3 Oct 61 & used for radar training. Coded 4B-331 by Aug 62. Redesignated EC-121K 18 Oct 62. To NATTU Glynco 6 Nov 62 To VW-13 Argentia 8 Nov 62, coded MK-331. Redesignated EC-121P 30 Dec 63. To Davis Monthan for storage 12 Jul 65 (TT: 6,914 hrs). Withdrawn from storage and transitted Scott AFB 12 Apr 69 in VW-13 markings en route rework. Cvtd to WC-121N by LAS, New York 1969. To VW-l Guam, coded TE-11. With VW-1 until at least Apr 71. To VW-4, coded MH- (number uk). Ret to MASDC Davis Monthan for storage 12 Jul 72. Struck off (VW-4) 16 Jan 73, (TT: 8,922 hrs). Sold to Sun Valley Aviation 16 Sep 76, subsequently scrapped.

141331 EC-121P, still in VW-13 squadron markings and looking very much the worse for wear, was photographed transitting Scott AFB, Illinois on 12th April 1969 en route from storage at Davis-Monthan to a rework facility. (via John T Wible)

4456 WV-2/1049A-55-86, mod to 1049A-55-137 2 Jan 57 to US Navy as 141332. Navy acceptance date 12 Dec 56. To AEW MATRON 2 Barbers Pt 2 Jan 57, coded RW-11. Tfd AIR BARSRON 2 Barbers Pt 14 Jun 57, coded SH-11. To VW-11 Patuxent 21 Feb 58, coded MJ-17, tfd VW-11 Argentia 6 Jun 58. Written-off at Argentia, Nfld 29 Mar 59. The aircraft crashed on landing after an operational mission, due to icy runway conditions, severe crosswinds and turbulence, and caught fire. No casualties. Struck off (VW-11) 29 Mar 59, (TT: 2,315 hrs).

4457 WV-2/1049A-55-86, mod to 1049A-55-137 4 Jan 57 to US Navy as 141333. Navy acceptance date 20 Dec 56. To NavCicOffsColl NAS Glynco 4 Jan 57, tfd NAS Glynco 1 Oct 61. To Storage Facility, Litchfield Park 3 Apr 62. Struck off (Litchfield Park) 8 Jun 62 (TT: 2,904 hrs). Tfd to BUWEPS 8 Jun 62. Cvtd to EC-121H for U S Air Force as 55-5266. Assigned 551st AEW Wg Otis as EC-121H 1 Nov 63. Redesignated EC-121K Otis 22 Nov 63, ret EC-121H Otis (a/o 18 May 65). To MASDC Davis Monthan for storage 20 Nov 69, TOC 21 Nov 69. Sold to Sun Valley Aviation 17 Sep 76, subsequently scrapped.

4458 WV-2/1049A-55-137 20 Feb 57 to US Navy as 143184. Navy acceptance date 7 Feb 57, to BAR FA Burbank same day. To NavCicOffsColl Glynco 20 Feb 57 & used for radar training, tfd NAS Glynco 1 Oct 61. Redesignated EC-121K 1 Oct 62. To NATTU Glynco 1 Nov 62, tfd NAS Glynco 30 Nov 62, coded 4B-184. To storage at Litchfield Park 1 Feb 63. To AEWTRAUNIT/AEWTULANT Patuxent 19 Nov 63, coded MM-2. To Davis Monthan for storage 21 Jan 66 (TT: 4,593 hrs). Struck off 21 Jan 66 (AFASDG) and tfd to U S Air Force same day (AFLC Davis Monthan) as EC-121K, serial 57-143184 but acft carried '0-43184' only. To AFLC Greenville 28 Feb 66, 15th TFG Wg MacDill 22 May 67, 4500th AB Wg (TAC) Langley 15 Feb 69, ret AFLC Greenville 13 Aug 69. To 4500th AB Wg Langley again 25 Jan 70. Ret to MASDC Davis Monthan for storage 24 Aug 70. Scrapped subsequent to May 74.

4459 WV-2/1049A-55-137 25 Jan 57 to US Navy as 143185. Navy acceptance date 15 Jan 57, to BAR FA Burbank same day. To AEW MATRON 2 Barbers Pt 25 Jan 57, tfd AIR BARSRON 2 Barbers Pt 7 Jun 57, coded SH-12. Tfd AEW BARRON PAC Barbers Pt 17 May 60. Redesignated EC-121K 1 Oct 62. With AEW BARRON PAC until 28 Feb 65. To Davis Monthan (AFASDG-ADMCS) for storage 2 Mar 65. Struck off (AFASDG) Davis Monthan 19 Jan 67 (TT: 10,773 hrs). Tfd to USAF from US Navy 19 Jan 67, to AFLC Ontario 10 Apr 67. Flown to Ontario, CA approx 10 Apr 67 and cvtd to EC-121R by LAS for U S Air Force as 67-21480. USAF acceptance 10 Apr 67, del 8 Aug 67. To 553rd Reconnaissance Wing Otis 8 Aug 67. Deployed to Korat 30 Nov 67, U-Tapao 31 Jan 69, ret Korat 1 Mar 69. Assigned 388th TFW Korat 15 Dec 70. To MASDC Davis Monthan for storage 30 Sep 71, TOC 4 Oct 71. Sold Kolar Inc 31 Jul 74, subsequently scrapped.

4460 WV-2/1049A-55-137 29 Jan 57 to US Navy as 143186. Navy acceptance date 17 Jan 57, to BAR FA Burbank same day. To AEW MATRON 2 Barbers Pt 29 Jan 57, tfd AIR BARSRON 2 Barbers Pt 20 Jul 57, coded SH-13. To AEW BARRON PAC Barbers Pt 13 May 60, coded SH-13. Redesignated EC-121K 15 Nov 62. Possibly cvtd to EC-121P, but not on card. To Davis Monthan (AFASDG-ADMCS) for storage 11 Mar 65. Stricken AFASDG Tucson 6 Apr 66. To NASC Dallas 9 Nov 66 for repair/rework (TT: 11,079 hrs a/o 13 Feb 67), probably cvtd to EC-121M at this stage. To VQ-1 Atsugi spring 67, coded PR-27 'Al's Pearl of the Orient'. To VQ-1 Agana 1971. Retired 4 Apr 74 & to MASDC Davis Monthan for storage 25 Sep 74. Struck off (Davis Monthan) 26 Sep 74 (TT: 17,732 hrs). For sale by DofD (Davis Monthan) 11 Feb 81 (TT given as 17,706 hrs). Sold Kolar Inc 21 May 81, subsequently scrapped.

4461 WV-2/1049A-55-137 31 Jan 57 to US Navy as 143187. Navy acceptance date 18 Jan 57. To AEW MATRON 2 Barbers Pt 31 Jan 57, tfd AIR BARSRON 2 Barbers Pt 8 Aug 57. To VW-1 Agana 9 Nov 57. To Storage Facility, Litchfield Park 30 Jan 59. To BAR Burbank (M & S) 21 Jun 59 & BWR FR Burbank 2 Feb 60. Ret to Storage Facility, Litchfield Park 5 Feb 60. Redesignated EC-121K 30 Nov 62. Struck off (Litchfield Park) 21 May 65 (TT: 2,018 hrs). Scrapped approx Oct 65.

4462 WV-2/1049A-55-137 31 Jan 57 to US Navy as 143188. Navy acceptance date 22 Jan 57, to BAR FA Burbank same day. To AEW MATRON 2 Barbers Pt 31 Jan 57, coded RW-15. Tfd AIR BARSRON 2 Barbers Pt 10 Jun 57, coded SH-15 & to AEW BARRON PAC Barbers Pt 31 May 60, still coded SH-15. Redesignated EC-121K 30 Nov 62 & EC-121P 15 May 64. To AFASDG/ADMCS Davis Monthan for storage 29 Apr 65. Struck off (AFASDG) 19 Jan 67, (TT: 11,102 hrs). Tfd to USAF from US Navy as 57-143188 at Davis Monthan 19 Jan 67. To AFLC Ontario 16 Feb 67 for conversion to EC-121R by LAS for U S Air Force as 67-21481. Serial changed Ontario 10 Apr 67, USAF acceptance 10 Apr 67, del 8 Dec 67. To 553rd Reconnaissance Wing Korat 8 Dec 67. Deployed U-Tapao 31 Jan 69, ret Korat 1 Mar 69. Assigned 388th TFW Korat 15 Dec 70. To MASDC Davis Monthan for storage 28 Nov 71. Scrapped subsequent to Sep 72.

4463 WV-2/1049A-55-137 13 Feb 57 to US Navy as 143189. To BAR FA Burbank 31 Jan 57. To VW-2 Patuxent 13 Feb 57, tfd VW-11 Patuxent 20(?) Mar 57. To AEW MATRON 2 Barbers Pt Mar 57, tfd AIR BARSRON 2 Barbers Pt 17 Jun 57, coded SH-4. To AEW BARRON PAC Barbers Pt 5 Jul 60. Redesignated EC-121K 30 Nov 62 & EC-121P 19 Mar 64. To AFASDG/ADMCS Davis Monthan for storage 28 Apr 65. Struck off (no details) Mar 66. Tfd to U S Air Force as EC-121P 57-143189, but aircraft carried '43189' only. To AFLC Jamaica, NY 21 Apr 66 & to AFSC Martin-Baltimore 28 Jul 66. Believed cvtd to JEC-121P, but not on card. Tfd AFSC Friendship 31 May 67. Use with AF unknown. Ret to storage at MASDC Davis Monthan 1 Dec 67. In storage MASDC 6 Jun 69 & 15 Jan 70. Scrapped by Mar 71.

4464 WV-2/1049A-55-137 13 Feb 57 to US Navy as 143190. Navy acceptance date 31 Jan 57, to BAR FA Burbank same day. To VW-2 Patuxent 13 Feb 57, tfd VW-11 Patuxent 27 Feb 57. To AEW MATRON 2 Barbers Pt 1 May 57, tfd AIR BARSRON 2 Barbers Pt 5 Aug 57, coded SH-23. To AEW BARRON PAC Barbers Pt 5 May 60, coded SH-23. Redesignated EC-121K 22 Oct 62. To AFASDG/ADMCS Davis Monthan for storage 9 Mar 65. (TT: 10,918 hrs). Struck off (AFASDG) 19 Jan 67, but reinstated 2 Feb 67 MASDC Tucson. Struck off (Davis Monthan) May 70 again. Preserved as representative EC-121K/P aircraft for museum until at least Jul 74, but then sold to Kolar Inc 9 Oct 74, subsequently scrapped when U S Navy museum at Pensacola acquired aircraft c/n 4495 (143221) in same year.

4465 WV-2/1049A-55-137 5 Mar 57 to US Navy as 143191. Navy acceptance date 13 Feb 57, to BAR FA Burbank same day. To AEW MATRON 2 Barbers Pt Mar 57, tfd AIR BARSRON 2 Barbers Pt 8 Jun 57, coded SH-7. To AEW BARRON PAC 31 May 60, coded SH-7. Redesignated EC-121K 22 Oct 62. To AFASDG/ADMCS Davis Monthan for storage 2 Mar 65 (TT; 11,343 hrs). Struck off (AFASDG) 19 Jan 67. Tfd to USAF from US Navy as 57-143191 Davis Monthan 19 Jan 67. To AFLC Ontario, CA 15 Feb 67 for conversion to EC-121R by LAS for U S Air Force as 67-21482. Serial changed Jamaica, NY 10 Apr 67, USAF acceptance 10 Apr 67, del 1 Dec 67. To Ontario 20 Aug 67, del 553rd Reconnaissance Wing Korat 1 Dec 67. Deployed U-Tapao 31 Jan 69, ret Korat 1 Mar 69. To MASDC Davis Monthan for storage 23 May 70. Scrapped subsequent to Jul 74.

4466 WV-2/1049A-55-137 7 Mar 57 to US Navy as 143192. Navy acceptance date 15 Feb 57, to BAR FA Burbank same day. To NavCicOffsColl Glynco Mar 57 and used for radar training, tfd NAS Glynco 1 Oct 61. Redesignated EC-121K 4 Oct 62, coded 4B-501 by 1965. Rework Lake City, FL 18-25 Apr 72, ret NAS Glynco 25 Apr 72. To TRARON 86 (VT-86) Glynco 7 Feb 73, still coded 4B-501. To MASDC Davis Monthan 3 Oct 73, TOC 4 Oct 73. Struck off (Davis Monthan) 29 Jul 74. (TT: 7,663 hrs). Sold to Sun Valley Aviation 16 Sep 76, subsequently scrapped.

4467 WV-2/1049A-55-137 13 Mar 57 to US Navy as 143193. Navy acceptance date 28 Feb 57. To AEW MATRON 2 Barbers Pt 13 Mar 57, tfd AIR BARSRON 2 Barbers Pt 22 Jul 57, coded SH-16. To AEW BARRON PAC Barbers Pt 12 May 60, coded SH-16. Written-off at Midway Island, Pacific Ocean 22 Jan 61. Aircraft took off from Midway on a radar patrol mission, the mission was aborted & the acft was returning to Midway when it landed short of the runway, hit seawall debris at the end of the runway while landing, sheared off the main undercarriage, cartwheeled onto its back, slid into the crash-crew truck, exploded & burned. 6 of 22 crew killed plus three in the truck. Struck off (AEW BARRON PAC) 22 Jan 61, (TT: 4,632 hrs).

4468 WV-2/1049A-55-137 1 Mar 57 to US Navy as 143194. To AEW MATRON 2 Barbers Pt 20 Mar 57, tfd AIR BARSRON 2 Barbers Pt 16 Jul 57, coded SH-17. To Storage Facility, Litchfield Park 28 Jan 60. Redesignated EC-121K 30 Nov 62. Struck off (Litchfield Park) 21 May 65, (TT: 3,145 hrs). Scrapped approx Oct 65.

4469 WV-2/1049A-55-137 1 Mar 57 to US Navy as 143195. To BAR FA Burbank 1 Mar 57. To AEW MATRON 2 Barbers Pt 29 Mar 57, tfd AIR BARSRON 2 Barbers Pt 5 Sep 57, coded SH-18. To AEW BARRON PAC Barbers Pt 17 May 60, coded SH-18. Redesignated EC-121K 8 Nov 62. To AFASDG/ADMCS Davis Monthan for storage 4 Mar 65. Struck off (AFASDG) 19 Jan 67 (TT: 11,048 hrs). Tfd to USAF from US Navy as 57-143195 Davis Monthan 19 Jan 67. To AFLC Ontario 10 Apr 67 for conversion to EC-121R for U S Air Force by LAS as 67-21483. USAF acceptance 10 Apr 67, del 20 Jun 67. To 553rd Reconnaissance Wing Otis 20 Jun 67. Deployed Korat 30 Nov 67, U-Tapao 31 Jan 69, ret Korat 2 Mar 69. Assigned 388th TFW Korat 15 Dec 70. To MASDC Davis Monthan 25 Dec 70, TOC 29 Dec 70. Sold Sun Valley Aviation 17 Sep 76, subsequently scrapped.

4470 WV-2/1049A-55-137 1 Mar 57 to US Navy as 143196. To BAR FA Burbank 1 Mar 57. To AEW MATRON 2 Barbers Pt 28 May 57, tfd AIR BARSRON 2 Barbers Pt 24 Aug 57. To VW-1 Agana 5 Sep 57. To Storage Facility, Litchfield Park 6 Feb 59. To BAR (M&S) Burbank 24 Sep 59. Ret to storage Litchfield Park 13 Jan 60. Withdrawn from storage 31 May 61. Tfd to U S Army 10 Aug 61 (bailment to Bell Telephone Laboratory, New York, NY) & cvtd to unpressurized camera platform for U S Army, Kwajalein. Radomes removed, elongated dome on upper fuselage fitted, with cine cameras and other equipment in this and in the rear cargo-doorway. BuAer number retained, records show designation as EC-121K 30 Nov 62, but also referred to as a JC-121K. Named 'Younger's Mistress'. Retired from Army use and to MASDC Davis Monthan 19 Dec 67. Struck off by Navy (Davis Monthan) 22 May 70, no TT given. Derelict, parts missing by Jan 72. Sold to Kolar Inc 23 Oct 74 and subsequently scrapped.

4471 WV-2/1049A-55-137 1 Mar 57 to US Navy as 143197. To AEW MATRON 2 Barbers Pt 3 Apr 57, tfd AIR BARSRON 2

Barbers Pt 12 Jul 57, coded SH-17. Written-off 23 Dec 57, after the aircraft ditched in the Pacific Ocean 25 mls NW of Oahu, HI. Acft was on a routine training mission & sent radio message at 15.20 hrs (Hawaii time), due back at Barbers Pt 18.09 hrs. The acft was being tracked by land radar when it disappeared from the screen at 15.50 hrs. Cause of crash unknown, four crew rescued, remaining 19 missing. Struck off (AIR BARSRON 2) 23 Dec 57, (TT: 663 hrs).

4472 WV-2/1049A-55-137 1 Mar 57 to US Navy as 143198. To BAR FA Burbank 1 Mar 57. To AEW MATRON 2 Barbers Pt Apr 57, tfd AIR BARSRON 2 Barbers Pt 28 Jun 57, coded SH-20. To AEW BARRON PAC Barbers Pt 4 May 60. Redesignated EC-121K 4 Oct 62. To VW-4 Roosevelt Roads 24 Jun 63, coded MH-8. To VP-10 Brunswick 7 Aug 63 (possibly in error). Redesignated WC-121N 8 Aug 63. Tfd VW-4 Jacksonville 21 Apr 65, re-coded MH-l and later named 'Dora'. At Seletar, Singapore Sep 71, no unit markings (possibly brief usage with VW-l/VQ-l). With VW-4 Jacksonville a/o Oct 71. To MASDC Davis Monthan for storage 19 Jul 72. Struck off (Davis Monthan) 16 Jan 73, (TT: 14,664 hrs). Sold to Sun Valley Aviation 16 Sep 76, subsequently scrapped.

4473 WV-2/1049A-55-137 1 Mar 57 to US Navy as 143199. To BAR FA Burbank 1 Mar 57. To AEW MATRON 2 Barbers Pt 11 Apr(?) 57, tfd AIR BARSRON 2 Barbers Pt 5 Sep 57, coded SH-21. To AEW BARRON PAC Barbers Pt 21 May 60, coded SH-21. Redesignated EC-121K 28 Nov 62. Cvtd to EC-121P, but no details. To AFASDG/ADMCS Davis Monthan for storage 4 May 65. Struck off (no details) Apr 66. Tfd to USAF from US Navy as 57-143199 Davis Monthan 12 Apr 66, aircraft carried '43199' only. To AFLC Jamaica, NY 31 May 66, tfd AFSC JFK-New York 1 Jun 66. To AFSC Martin-Baltimore 13 Jul 66, tfd AFSC Friendship, MD 31 May 67. Cvtd to JEC-121P, no dets of use. To storage at MASDC Davis Monthan 12 Feb 68. Withdrawn from storage, to AFSC Hughes Aircraft Co 1 May 68. Ret to storage Davis Monthan 11 Feb 69. At MASDC 15 Jan 70. Scrapped, early 70s, no dets.

4474 WV-2/1049A-55-137 1 Mar 57 to US Navy as 143200. To BAR FA Burbank 1 Mar 57. To AEW MATRON 2 Barbers Pt 2 May 57, tfd AIR BARSRON 2 Barbers Pt 4 Sep 57, coded SH-22. Lost upper radome in flight 28 Jan 58 en route Midway Island, knocking off centre fin. Safe landing made at Barbers Pt. Repaired. To AEW BARRON PAC Barbers Pt 17 May 60. Redesignated EC-121K 15 Oct 62 & EC-121P 1 Jun 64. To AFASDG/ADMCS Davis Monthan for storage 5 May 65. Struck off (no details) Jan 66. Tfd to USAF from US Navy as 57-143200 Davis Monthan 3 Jan 66, aircraft carried '43200' only.To AFLC Jamaica, NY 15 Feb 66. To AFSC Martin-Baltimore 6 Jul 66, tfd AFSC Friendship, MD 31 May 67. Cvtd to JEC-121P, no dets of use. Ret to storage at Davis Monthan 21 Feb 68. At MASDC 15 Jan 70. Scrapped, early 70s, no dets.

4475 WV-2/1049A-55-137 1 May 57 to US Navy as 143201. Navy acceptance date 22 Apr 57, to BAR FA Burbank same day. To AEW MATRON 2 Barbers Pt 1 May 57, tfd AIR BARSRON 2 Barbers Pt 5 Sep 57, coded SH-8. To AEW BARRON PAC Barbers Pt 31 May 60, coded SH-8. Redesignated EC-121K 30 Nov 62. To AFASDG/ADMCS Davis Monthan for storage 7 May 65. Tfd NASA 21 May 65. NASA lsd from Navy 3 Nov 65 as EC-

143200 EC-121K of AEWBARRONPAC was the 775th aircraft delivered after rework from the Lockheed Aircraft Service base at Honolulu in the period 1957-65 to Barbers Point NAS. (Lockheed Aircraft Service via John T Wible)

Section 12: Constellation Production List

121P NASA 671 for use at Wallops Island, VA. Reregn to N671NA requested by NASA 17 Apr 69. Reregd 25 Jun 69 (officially), NASA notified 14 Aug 69. Aircraft carried both BuAer serial and NASA regn. Ret to MASDC Davis Monthan for storage 3 May 71. Struck off by Navy (Davis Monthan) 19 May 71. No TT given. Sold to Kolar Inc 23 Oct 74, subsequently scrapped.

4476 WV-2/1049A-55-137 9 May 57 to US Navy as 143202. Navy acceptance date 30 Apr 57, to BAR FA Burbank same day. To AEW MATRON 2 Barbers Pt 9 May 57, tfd AIR BARSRON 2 Barbers Pt 5 Sep 57, coded SH-24. To AEW BARRON PAC Barbers Pt 17 May 60, coded SH-24. Redesignated EC-121K 4 Dec 62. To AFASDG/ADMCS Davis Monthan for storage 5 May 65. Struck off (AFASDG) 19 Jan 67, (TT: 10,821 hrs). U S Air Force received from Navy as 57-143202 Ontario 5 Feb 67. To AFLC Jamaica, NY 8 Mar 67. Cvtd to EC-121R by LAS for U S Air Force as 67-21484 Jamaica 10 Apr 67. USAF acceptance 10 Apr 67, del 23 Sep 67. To Ontario 26 Jun 67, del 553rd Reconnaissance Wing Otis 23 Sep 67. Deployed to Korat 6 Nov 67, U-Tapao 30 Jan 69, ret Korat 1 Mar 69. To MASDC Davis Monthan for storage 1 Jun 70, TOC 4 Jun 70. Derelict, parts missing, on belly by May 74. Sold to Kolar Inc 1 Aug 74, subsequently scrapped.

4477 WV-2/1049A-55-137 20 May 57 to US Navy as 143203. Navy acceptance date 7 May 57, to BAR FA Burbank same day. To AEW MATRON 2 Barbers Pt 20 May 57, tfd AIR BARSRON 2 Barbers Pt 3 Sep 57, coded SH-25. To AEW BARRON PAC Barbers Pt 6 May 60, coded SH-25. Redesignated EC-121K 30 Nov 62. To AFASDG/ADMCS Davis Monthan for storage 24 Feb 65, TOC (AFASDG) 15 Aug 65. Struck off (AFASDG) 19 Jan 67, (TT: 10,746 hrs). U S Air Force received from Navy as 57-143203 Davis Monthan 18 Jan 67. To AFLC Ontario 28 Jan 67. Cvtd to EC-121R by LAS for U S Air Force as 67-21485 Ontario 10 Apr 67. USAF acceptance 10 Apr 67, del 16 Jun 67. Del to 553rd Reconnaissance Wing Otis 16 Jun 67. Deployed to Korat 19 Oct 67, U-Tapao 30 Jan 69, ret Korat 22 Feb 69. To MASDC Davis Monthan for storage 16 Nov 70. Scrapped subsequent to May 73.

4478 WV-2/1049A-55-137 29 May 57 to US Navy as 143204. Navy acceptance date 16 May 57, to BAR FA Burbank same day. To AIR BARSRON 2 Barbers Pt 29 May 57, coded SH-27, & to AEW BARRON PAC Barbers Pt 17 May 60, still coded SH-27. Redesignated EC-121K 8 Oct 62. To AFASDG/ADMCS Davis Monthan for storage 3 Mar 65. Struck off (AFASDG) 19 Jan 67, (TT: 10,203 hrs). U S Air Force received from Navy as 57-143204 & to AFLC Ontario 30 Jan 67. Cvtd to EC-121R by LAS for U S Air Force as 67-21486 Ontario 10 Apr 67. USAF acceptance 10 Apr 67, del 11 Jun 67. Del to 553rd Reconnaissance Wing Otis 11 Jun 67. Deployed to Korat 8 Nov 67, U-Tapao 30 Jan 69, ret Korat 21 Feb 69. Assigned 388th TFW Korat 15 Dec 70. To MASDC Davis Monthan for storage 17 Dec 70. Scrapped subsequent to May 73.

4479 WV-2/1049A-55-137 7 Jun 57 to US Navy as 143205. Navy acceptance date 27 May 57, to BAR FA Burbank same day. To AIR BARSRON 2 Barbers Pt Jun 57, coded SH-28 & to AEW BARRON PAC Barbers Pt 11 May 60, still coded SH-28. Redesignated EC-121K 1 Nov 62. To AFASDG/ADMCS Davis Monthan for storage 9 Mar 65. (TT: 10,704 hrs). Withdrawn from storage 21 Apr 69 and flown to New York for conversion by LAS to WC-121N. Cvtd 29 Jul 69. To VW-1 Agana, coded TE-12. Tfd VQ-1 Agana 5 May 71. To VQ-1 Weather Agana 10 May 71, coded PR-52. Ret MASDC Davis Monthan for storage 24 Nov 71. Struck off (Davis Monthan) 12 Jul 72, (TT: 12,503 hrs). Sold Sun Valley Aviation 24 May 76, subsequently scrapped.

4480 WV-2/1049A-55-137 28 Jun 57 to US Navy as 143206. Navy acceptance date 17 Jun 57, to BAR FA Burbank same day. To AIR BARSRON 2 Barbers Pt 2(?) Jun 57, coded SH-29. To AEW BARRON PAC Barbers Pt 31 May 60. Redesignated EC-121K 30 Nov 62 & EC-121P 9 May 64. To AFASDG/ADMCS Davis Monthan for storage 7 May 65. Struck off (AFASDG) 19 Jan 67, (TT: 10,490 hrs). U S Air Force received from Navy as 57-143206 & to AFLC Ontario 3 Feb 67. Cvtd to EC-121R by LAS for U S Air Force as 67-21487 Ontario 10 Apr 67. USAF acceptance 10 Apr 67, del 1 Sep 67. Del to 553rd Reconnaissance Wing Otis 1 Sep 67. Deployed to Korat 18 Oct 67, U-Tapao 30 Jan 69, ret Korat 3 Mar 69. Deployed to 366th TFW Da Nang 27 Jun 69, ret Korat 31 Aug 69. Ret to MASDC Davis Monthan for storage 16 May 70, TOC 21 May 70. Sold to Kolar Inc 1 Aug 74, subsequently scrapped. (Note: It is possible that c/ns 4430 & 4480 were mixed up at the time of their conversion to EC-121R as AF records show an anomaly with their respective origins).

4481 WV-2/1049A-55-137 2 Jul 57 to US Navy as 143207. Navy acceptance date 20 Jun 57, to BAR FA Burbank same day. To AIR BARSRON 2 Barbers Pt 2 Jul 57, coded SH-30. To AEW BARRON PAC Barbers Pt 11 May 60. Redesignated EC-121K 30 Nov 62. To AFASDG/ADMCS Davis Monthan for storage 29 Apr 65. Struck off (AFASDG) 19 Jan 67, (TT: 11,089 hrs). U S Air Force received from Navy as 57-143207 Ontario 1 Feb 67. To AFLC Jamaica, NY 14 Mar 67. Cvtd to EC-121R by LAS for U S Air Force as 67-21488 Jamaica 10 Apr 67. USAF acceptance 10 Apr 67. To Ontario 8 Jul 67. Del 553rd Reconnaissance Wing Otis 9 Nov 67. Deployed to Korat 30 Nov 67, U-Tapao 30 Jan 69, ret Korat 1 Mar 69. Assigned 388th TFW Korat 15 Dec 70. Ret to MASDC Davis Monthan for storage 2 Dec 71. Scrapped subsequent to Jul 74.

4482 WV-2/1049A-55-137 12 Jul 57 to US Navy as 143208. Navy acceptance date 26 Jun 57, to BAR FA Burbank same day. To AIR BARSRON 2 Barbers Pt 12 Jul 57, coded SH-31. To AEW BARRON PAC Barbers Pt 19 May 60. Redesignated EC-121K 18 Oct 62. To AFASDG/ADMCS Davis Monthan for storage 10 Mar 65. Struck off (AFASDG) 19 Jan 67, (TT: 10,322 hrs). U S Air Force received from Navy as 57-143208 Ontario 1 Feb 67. To AFLC Jamaica, NY 1 Mar 67. Cvtd to EC-121R by LAS for U S Air Force 67-21489 Jamaica 10 Apr 67. To Ontario 8 Jun 67. Del to 553rd Reconnaissance Wing Otis 11 Sep 67. Deployed to Korat 19 Oct 67, U-Tapao 7 Feb 69, ret Korat 1 Mar 69. Assigned 388th TFW Korat 15 Dec 70. Ret to MASDC Davis Monthan for storage 18 Dec 70. Scrapped subsequent to Jul 74.

4483 WV-2/1049A-55-137 17 Jul 57 to US Navy as 143209. Navy acceptance date 3 Jul 57, to BAR FA Burbank same day. To AIR BARSRON 2 Barbers Pt 17 Jul 57, coded SH-32. To AEW BARRON PAC Barbers Pt 6 May 60. Redesignated EC-121K 14 Nov 62. To AFASDG/ADMCS Davis Monthan for storage 17 Mar 65. (TT: 10,077 hrs). Withdrawn from storage Mar 66 and to VQ-1 Atsugi. Cvtd to EC-121M 27 Apr 66, coded PR-22. To VQ-2 Rota 18 Dec 69, NARF Jacksonville 15 Jul 70 & NAVAIR SYSCOM Lake City (O&R) 19 Nov 70. Ret to VQ-2 Rota 7 Feb 71, coded 14. Recoded 32 by Oct 72. Retired 1 Mar 74. Struck off (VQ-2 Rota) at Jacksonville 25 Jun 74, (TT: 16,884 hrs). Scrapped on site.

4484 WV-2/1049A-55-137 8 Aug 57 to US Navy as 143210. Navy acceptance date 25 Jul 57, to BAR FA Burbank same day. To AIR BARSRON 2 Barbers Pt 8 Aug 57, coded SH-33. To AEW BARRON PAC Barbers Pt 17 May 60. Redesignated EC-121K 30 Nov 62. To AFASDG/ADMCS Davis Monthan for storage 30 Apr 65, TOC 1 May 65. Struck off (AFASDG) 19 Jan 67, (TT: 10,835 hrs). U S Air Force received from Navy as 57-143210 Davis Monthan 19 Jan 67. To AFLC Jamaica, NY 21 Feb 67. Cvtd to EC-121R by LAS for U S Air Force as 67-21490 Jamaica 10 Apr 67. To Ontario 12 Jun 67. Del 553rd Reconnaissance Wing Otis 30 Aug 67. Deployed to Korat 18 Oct 67, U-Tapao 21 Feb 69, ret Korat 2 Mar 69. To MASDC Davis Monthan for storage 6 Dec 70. Scrapped subsequent to May 74.

4485 WV-2/1049A-55-137 31 Jul 57 to US Navy as 143211. Navy acceptance date 19 Jul 57, to BAR FA Burbank same day. To AIR BARSRON 2 Barbers Pt 31 Jul 57, coded SH-34. To AEW BARRON PAC Barbers Point 13(?) May 60. On 28 Aug 60 the aircraft received strike damage at Midway Island. On take off, the right main gear came loose, bounced off the runway & up into the tail unit, breaking off the starboard fin, rudder & elevator. The acft flew around for one hour & 42 minutes to use up fuel, the pilot then

143211 WV-2 of AEWBARRONPAC made a safe emergency landing at Midway Island, Pacific Ocean late in 1960. The right main gear came loose on take-off, bouncing off the runway on to the tail-unit and taking with it the starboard fin, rudder and elevator. The "Willie Victor" flew for an hour and 42 minutes dumping and using up fuel before making a wheels-up landing. There were no injuries, but the aircraft received sufficient damage that it was provisionally repaired and flown for spares reclamation to Litchfield Park, Arizona. (United States Navy via John T Wible)

returned to Midway & made a safe wheels-up landing on the runway. The aircraft was provisionally repaired by 12 Jan 61 and then flown to Storage Facility, Litchfield Park 30 Jan 61 for spares reclamation. Redesignated EC-121K 30 Nov 62. Struck off (Litchfield Park) 21 May 65, (TT: 3,655 hrs). Scrapped approx Oct 65.

4486 WV-2/1049A-55-137 7 Aug 57 to US Navy as 143212. Navy acceptance date 25 Jul 57, to BAR FA Burbank same day. To AIR BARSRON 2 Barbers Pt 7 Aug 57, coded SH-1. To AEW BARRON PAC Barbers Pt 31 May 60. Redesignated EC-121K 30 Nov 62. To Storage Facility, Litchfield Park 12 Jun 63, presumably after damage in accident, but details uk. Struck off (Litchfield Park) 21 May 65, (TT: 7,885 hrs). Scrapped approx Oct 65.

4487 WV-2/1049A-55-137 21 Aug 57 to US Navy as 143213. Navy acceptance date 12 Aug 57, to BAR FA same day. To AIR BARSRON 2 Barbers Pt 21 Aug 57, coded SH-11. To AEW BARRON PAC Barbers Pt 31 May 60. Redesignated EC-121K 30 Nov 62. To AFASDG/ADMCS Davis Monthan 4 Mar 65. Struck off (AFASDG) 19 Jan 67, (TT: 10,602 hrs). U S Air Force received from Navy as 57-143213 Ontario 5 Feb 67. Cvtd to EC-121R by LAS for U S Air Force as 67-21491 Ontario 10 Apr 67. To AF Plant 14 on 4 Sep 67. Del to USAF & 553rd Reconnaissance Wing Otis 25 Oct 67. Deployed to Korat 30 Nov 67, U-Tapao 31 Jan 69, ret Korat 1 Mar 69. Assigned 388th TFW Korat 15 Dec 70. To MASDC Davis Monthan for storage 3 Oct 71. Scrapped subsequent to Jul 74.

4488 WV-2/1049A-55-137 26 Aug 57 to US Navy as 143214. Navy acceptance date 9 Aug 57, to BAR FA Burbank same day. To AIR BARSRON 2 Barbers Pt 26 Aug 57, coded SH-5. To AEW BARRON PAC Barbers Pt 31 May 60. Redesignated EC-121K 9 Oct 62. To AFASDG/ADMCS Davis Monthan for storage 24 Feb 65. Struck off (AFASDG) 19 Jan 67, (TT: 10,432 hrs). U S Air Force received from Navy as 57-143214 Ontario 1 Feb 67. Cvtd to EC-121R by LAS for U S Air Force as 67-21492 Ontario 10 Apr 67. Del to USAF & 553rd Reconnaissance Wing Otis 15 Jul 67. Deployed to Korat 19 Oct 67. Ret Otis 31 Oct 67. Deployed Korat 9 Nov 67, U-Tapao 30 Jan 69, ret Korat 1 Mar 69. Ret to MASDC Davis Monthan for storage 11 Dec 70. Scrapped subsequent to Oct 73.

4489 WV-2/1049A-55-137 29 Aug 57 to US Navy as 143215. Navy acceptance date 15 Aug 57, to BAR FA Burbank same day. To AIR BARSRON 2 Barbers Pt 29 Aug 57, coded SH-10. To AEW BARRON PAC Barbers Pt 6(?) May 60. Redesignated EC-121K 29 Oct 62 & EC-121P 10 Jun 64. To AFASDG/ADMCS Davis Monthan for storage 4 May 65. Struck off (AFASDG) 19 Jan 67, (TT: 10,289 hrs). Tfd to U S Air Force & cvtd to EC-121R by LAS at Ontario as 67-21493 10 Apr 67. Del to USAF & 553rd Reconnaissance Wing Otis 8 Jul 67. Deployed to Korat 19 Oct 67, U-Tapao 31 Jan 69, ret Korat 27 Feb 69. Written-off 25 Apr 69. Crashed shortly after take-off from Korat AFB, Thailand at 10.25 hrs (CET) into a rice field, three miles northwest of the base, killing all of the crew. The aircraft was on a combat mission from Korat. Struck off same day.

4490 WV-2/1049A-55-137 4 Sep 57 to US Navy as 143216. Navy acceptance date 22 Aug 57, to BAR FA Burbank same day. To AIR BARSRON 2 Barbers Pt Sep 57, coded SH-26. To AEW BARRON PAC Barbers Pt 17 May 60. Redesignated EC-121K 30 Nov 62. To AFASDG/ADMCS Davis Monthan for storage 23 Feb 65. Struck off (AFASDG) 19 Jan 67, (TT: 10,911 hrs). U S Air Force received from Navy as 57-143216 Ontario 3 Feb 67. Cvtd to EC-121R by LAS for U S Air Force as 67-21494 Ontario 10 Apr 67. USAF del & to 553rd Reconnaissance Wing Otis 22 Jul 67. Assigned 551st AEW Wg Otis 15 Nov 67, deployed McCoy 5 Jan 68. Ret Otis 6 Feb 68. Tfd 553rd Reconnaissance Wg Korat 5 Apr 69. Assigned 552nd AEW Wg McClellan 11 Jun 70. To MASDC Davis Monthan for storage 16 Nov 70. Scrapped subsequent to Oct 73.

4491 WV-2/1049A-55-137 Sep 57 to US Navy as 143217. Navy acceptance date 26 Aug 57, to BAR FA Burbank same day. To AIR BARSRON 2 Barbers Pt Sep 57, coded SH-19. To AEW BARRON PAC Barbers Pt 4 May 60. Redesignated EC-121K 2 Oct 62. To AFASDG/ADMCS Davis Monthan 3 Mar 65. Struck off (AFASDG) 19 Jan 67, (TT: 10,684 hrs). Tfd from Navy to U S Air Force Ontario 10 Apr 67. Cvtd to EC-121R by LAS for U S Air Force as 67-21495. Del to USAF & to 553rd Reconnaissance Wing Otis 5 Sep 67. Deployed to Korat 6 Nov 67, U-Tapao 30 Jan 69, ret Korat 2 Mar 69. Written-off on combat mission 6 Sep 69. Crashed while landing in a heavy rainstorm at Korat AFB, Thailand. Hit the ground at the end of runway, killing four of the crew and four on the ground.

4492 WV-2/1049A-55-137 19 Sep 57 to US Navy as 143218. Navy acceptance date 5 Sep 57, to BAR FA Burbank same day. To AIRBARSRON 2 Barbers Pt 19 Sep 57, coded SH-2. To AEW BARRON PAC Barbers Pt 31 May 60, coded SH-2. Redesignated EC-121K 20 Nov 62. To AFASDG/ADMCS Davis Monthan for storage 23 Feb 65, TOC by AFASDG Davis Monthan 15 Aug 65. Struck off (AFASDG) 19 Jan 67, (TT: 10,197 hrs). U S Air Force received from Navy as 57-143218 Ontario 8 Feb 67. Cvtd to EC-121R by LAS for U S Air Force as 67-21496 Ontario 10 Apr 67. USAF del & to 553rd Reconnaissance Wing Otis 11 Sep 67. Deployed to Korat 19 Oct 67, U-Tapao 31 Jan 69, ret Korat 2 Mar 69. To MASDC Davis Monthan for storage 21 Nov 70. Scrapped subsequent to Jul 74.

4493 WV-2/1049A-55-137 19 Sep 57 to US Navy as 143219. Navy acceptance date 10 Sep 57, to BAR FA Burbank same day. To AIR BARSRON 2 Barbers Pt Sep 57, coded SH-9. To AEW BARRON PAC Barbers Pt 25 May 60. Redesignated EC-121K 30 Nov 62. To AFASDG/ADMCS Davis Monthan for storage 28 Apr 65. Struck off (AFASDG) 19 Jan 67, (TT: 10,629 hrs). U S Air Force received from Navy Jamaica, NY 10 Apr 67. Cvtd to EC-121R by LAS for U S Air Force as 67-21497 Ontario 11 Apr 67. USAF del & to 553rd Reconnaissance Wing Otis 16 Jun 67. Deployed to Korat 19 Oct 67, U-Tapao 10 Feb 69, ret Korat 1 Mar 69. Ret to MASDC Davis Monthan for storage 10 Dec 70, TOC 11 Dec 70. Derelict, no engines, on belly by May 74. Sold to Kolar Inc 1 Aug 74, subsequently scrapped.

4494 WV-2/1049A-55-137 3 Oct 57 to US Navy as 143220. Navy acceptance date 18 Sep 57, to BAR FA Burbank same day. To NAVCICOFFSCOLL Glynco Oct 57 and used for radar training, tfd NAS Glynco 1 Oct 61. Redesignated EC-121K 1 Oct 62. To NATTU Glynco 1 Nov 62, ret NAS Glynco 1 Dec 62. To Davis Monthan for storage Aug 65, TOC

(AFASDG) 3 Sep 65, (TT: 4,146 hrs). Withdrawn from storage 21 Jul 67, to NPRO Burbank 21 Jul 67. Cvtd to NEC-121K 13 May 69. Ret to MASDC Davis Monthan 14 May 69. Cvtd to NC-121K 8 Nov 69. Reason for redesignations uk. Struck off (Davis Monthan) 30 Dec 70, (TT: 4,146 hrs still!). Sold to Kolar Inc 9 Oct 74, subsequently scrapped.

4495 WV-2/1049A-55-137 10 Oct 57 to US Navy as 143221. Navy acceptance date 27 Sep 57, to BAR FA Burbank same day. To NAVCICOFFSCOLL Glynco 16(?) Oct 57 and used for radar training, tfd NAS Glynco 1 Oct 61. Redesignated EC-121K 18 Oct 62. To NATTU Glynco 1 Nov 62, ret NAS Glynco 1 Dec 62. Coded 4B-2 by 1966. To OASU Oceanographic Jun 66, named 'Arctic Fox' (still carried NAS Glynco code). Ret to NAS Glynco 31 Aug 66. Recoded 4B-502 with NATTC, Glynco, by Nov 71. To TRARON 86 Glynco (VT-86) 28 Feb 73, tfd TRARON 86 Pensacola 28 Feb 73. Struck off (TRARON-NAS Glynco) 19 Oct 73. Tfd to U S Navy Museum, Pensacola, FL, (TT: 7,445 hrs). Stored there in open, still carrying VT-86 markings, coded 4B-502. By 1998 had been repainted in VW-4 markings, coded MH-3 'Brenda' with 'Weather Reconnaissance Squadron Four' titling.

4496 WV-2/1049A-55-137 23 Oct 57 to US Navy as 143222. Navy acceptance date 10 Oct 57, to BAR FA Burbank same day. To AIR BARSRON 2 Barbers Pt 23 Oct 57, coded SH-6. To AEW BARRON PAC Barbers Pt 18 May 60, coded SH-6. Redesignated EC-121K 30 Nov 62. To AFASDG/ADMCS Davis Monthan for storage 10 Mar 65. Struck off (AFASDG) 19 Jan 67, (TT: 10,404 hrs). U S Air Force received from Navy as 57-143222 Ontario 8 Feb 67. To AFLC Jamaica, NY 22 Mar 67. Cvtd to EC-121R by LAS for U S Air Force as 67-21498 Jamaica 10 Apr 67. To Ontario 25 Jul 67. Del & to 553rd Reconnaissance Wing Korat 4 Dec 67. Deployed U-Tapao 31 Jan 69, ret Korat 1 Mar 69. Assigned 388th TFW Korat 15 Dec 70. To MASDC Davis Monthan for storage 26 Nov 71. Scrapped subsequent to Oct 73.

4497 WV-2/1049A-55-137 4 Nov 57 to US Navy as 143223. Navy acceptance date 17 Oct 57, to BAR FA Burbank same day. To AIR BARSRON 2 Barbers Pt 4 Nov 57, coded SH-3. To AEW BARRON PAC Barbers Pt 31 May 60. Redesignated EC-121K 22 Oct 62. To AFASDG/ADMCS Davis Monthan for storage 11 Mar 65. Struck off (AFASDG) 19 Jan 67, (TT: 10,733 hrs). U S Air Force received from Navy Jamaica, NY 10 Apr 67. Cvtd to EC-121R by LAS for U S Air Force as 67-21499. To Ontario 17 May 67. Del & to 553rd Reconnaissance Wing Otis 30 Jul 67. Deployed to Korat 30 Nov 67, U-Tapao 30 Jan 69, ret Korat 1 Mar 69. Assigned 388th TFW Korat 15 Dec 70. To MASDC Davis Monthan for storage 4 Oct 71, TOC 1 Dec 71. Sold to Sun Valley Aviation 17 Sep 76, subsequently scrapped.

4498 WV-2/1049A-55-137 13 Nov 57 to US Navy as 143224. Navy acceptance date 18 Oct 57, to BAR FA Burbank same day. To AIR BARSRON 2 Barbers Pt 13(?) Nov 57, coded SH-14. To AEW BARRON PAC Barbers Pt 31 May 60, coded SH-14. Redesignated EC-121K 30 Nov 62. To AFASDG/ADMCS Davis Monthan for storage 17 Mar 65. Struck off (AFASDG) 19 Jan 67, (TT: 10,983 hrs). U S Air Force received from Navy as 57-143224 Ontario 9 Feb 67. Cvtd to EC-121R by LAS for U S Air Force as 67-21500 Ontario 10 Apr 67. To Jamaica, NY 13 Apr 67, ret Ontario 15 Aug 67. Del & to 553rd Reconnaissance Wing Otis 18 Nov 67. Deployed to Korat 30 Nov 67, U-Tapao 18 Feb 69, ret Korat 2 Mar 69. To MASDC Davis Monthan for storage 14 May 70. Scrapped subsequent to Jul 74.

4499 WV-2/1049A-55-137 2 Dec 57 to US Navy as 143225. Navy acceptance date 31 Oct 57, to BAR FA Burbank same day. To VW-3 Agana 2 Dec 57, tfd VW-1 Agana 11 Feb 59. To Storage Facility, Litchfield Park 20 Jun 60. Redesignated EC-121K 30 Nov 62. Struck off (Litchfield Park) 21 May 65, (TT: 2,046 hrs). Scrapped approx Oct 65.

WV-2/1049A series continues with c/n **5500** - see later.

4500 not used.

4501 1049C-55-81 First flight 17 Feb 53 - the first commercial passenger Turbo-Compound powered Super Constellation. Remained at Burbank for test and development flying as PH-TFP in all-metal scheme. LADD: 20 Dec 53 to KLM as PH-TFP 'Atoom', E-22268 18 Dec 53. KLM dely date 12 Dec 53 and officially regd 20 Dec 53. Re-regd PH-LKP 8 Mar 54. Flew Amsterdam-Tokyo inaugural 1049C schedule 1 Nov 54. To 1049E/01 4 May 56, later 1049G/02-82. Flew BOAC charters London-Havana 9-10 Apr 59, Kingston-London (immigrant charter) 12-13 Apr 59. Set up a 3-engined flight record for KLM Super Constellations 12 May 59 (New York back to New York 9 hrs 20 mins!). Flew Amsterdam-Tunis-Lagos-Accra inaugural 1 Nov 60. Withdrawn from svce 17 Dec 60 and stored at Schiphol Airport, Amsterdam, in cocooning. Canx as broken up 1 Oct 65, after PH-regn canx 22 Jun 65.

4502 1049C-55-81 Used for development flying for Turbo-Compound Super Constellation at Burbank prior dely. 10 Jun 53 to KLM as PH-TFR 'Electron', regd same day. E-22260, dated 9 Jun 53 and KLM dely date 11 Jun 53. Reregd PH-LKR 24 Feb 54. To 1049E/01 in 1955, later 1049G/02-82. Flew last Amsterdam-Djakarta svce 2 Dec 57. Flew Amsterdam-Bangkok-Saigon inaugural 31 Mar 59, ret 2 Apr 59. Withdrawn from svce 24 Jul 61 and cocooned at Schiphol Airport, Amsterdam, in storage. Used for spares 5 Aug 62 and broken up. Regn canx 24 Jun 63.

PH-TFU 1049C of KLM was the first airline Super Constellation ever to visit London (Heathrow) Airport when it landed on 3rd September 1953 to give a demonstration flight to the British press. (PJM collection)

4503 1049C-55-81 23 Jun 53 to KLM as PH-TFS 'Proton', regd same day. E-22261 dated 19 Jun 53 and KLM dely date 23 Jun 53. Reregd PH-LKS 17 Mar 54. Updated to 1049E/01 in 1955/56. Flew Benghazi-Tripoli-Amsterdam inaugural 16 Jul 60. Withdrawn from svce 11 Oct 60 and stored at Schiphol Airport, Amsterdam, in cocooning. Hulk stored near end of runway at Schiphol a/o May 64. Canx as broken up 12 Jul 65, after regn canx 22 Jun 65.

4504 1049C-55-81 30 Jun 53 to KLM as PH-TFT 'Neutron', regd same day. E-22262 same day and also KLM dely date. Reregd PH-LKT 18 Mar 54. Updated to 1049E/01 in 1955/56. Crashed into the sea shortly after take-off from Biak, Dutch New Guinea, five miles from the airport at 03.36 hrs (local) on 16 Jul 57 (18.06 hrs GMT 15 Jul 57), with heavy loss of life. One of the aircraft's engines caught fire shortly after take-off and exploded shortly afterwards, when a fuel tank ignited. The pilot had intended to make a low pass over the airport for the benefit of the passengers before setting course for Manila. The aircraft was heading back towards the airport when the engine caught fire & exploded. The pilot attempted a forced landing in the sea one kilometre from the shore, but the aircraft's tail unit broke off on contact with the water on ditching, the aircraft burst into flames & sank immediately. En route Biak to Amsterdam via Manila, Djakarta, Bangkok, Rangoon, Karachi, Beirut and Rome. Regn canx 28 Aug 57.

4505 1049C-55-81 17 Jul 53 to KLM as PH-TFU 'Photon', regd same day. E-22263 dated 14 Jul 53 and KLM dely date 17 Jul 53. Made first visit to England of commercial Super Constellation with demonstration flights at London-Heathrow 3 Sep 53. Reregd PH-LKU 16 Feb 54. To 1049E/01 Dec 56, & to 1049G/02-82 winter 1958/59. Withdrawn from svce 11 Nov 61 and stored at Schiphol Airport, Amsterdam, in cocooning. Canx as broken up 25 Jun 63, after regn canx 24 Jun 63.

4506 1049C-55-81 26 Jul 53 to KLM as PH-TFV 'Meson', regd same day. E-22264 dated 25 Jul 53, and KLM dely date 27 Jul 53. Reregd PH-LKV 6 Apr 54. Updated to 1049E/01 3 Sep 56 onwards. Lsd briefly to Air Ceylon 6-9 Feb 59 & Jul 60. Withdrawn from svce 25 Nov 60 and stored at Schiphol Airport, Amsterdam, in cocooning. Canx as broken up 1 Oct 65, after regn canx 22 Jun 65.

4507 1049C-55-81 31 Jul 53 to KLM as PH-TFW 'Deuteron', regd same day. E-22265 dated 30 Jul 53 and KLM dely date 1 Aug 53. Reregd PH-LKW 4 Mar 54. Damaged when it hit another aircraft at Shannon Airport, Eire 12 Aug 54. Repaired. Updated to 1049E/01 winter 1956/57. Withdrawn from svce 20 Sep 60 and stored at Schiphol Airport, Amsterdam, in cocooning. Canx as broken up 9 Jun 65, regn canx 22 Jun 65.

4508 1049C-55-81 5 Aug 53 to KLM as PH-TFX 'Nucleon', regd same day. E-22266 dated 4 Aug 53, KLM dely date 6 Aug 53. Reregd PH-LKX 25 Feb 54. To 1049E/01 winter 1956/57 & to 1049G/02-82 in 1958/59. Withdrawn from svce 31 Oct 61 and stored at Schiphol Airport, Amsterdam, in cocooning. Canx as broken up 25 Jun 63, after regn canx 24 Jun 63. Reportedly still extant in derelict state a/o end Apr 64.

4509 1049C-55-81 26 Aug 53 to KLM as PH-TFY 'Triton', regd same day. E-22267 dated 22 Aug 53, KLM dely date 27 Aug 53. Reregd PH-LKY 23 Mar 54. Crashed into the shallow water of the River Shannon estuary, immediately after take-off from Shannon Airport, Ireland, and only two miles from the runway end at 03.40 hrs (local) on 5 Sep 54. Aircraft only slightly damaged, but 28 of the 56 on board drowned after being overcome by petrol fumes. Fuselage subsequently submerged by the rapidly rising tide. Alarm not given until two and a half hours later when co-pilot and navigator swam and waded through mud two miles to the shore. Aircraft was en route Amsterdam-Shannon-New York. Cause: Failure of the captain to correlate and interpret his instrument readings during flap retraction on the climb out, coupled with the loss of aircraft performance due to the inadvertent re-extension of the undercarriage. Aircraft was therefore in a near-stalled condition during the initial climb; reduction in power plus flap raising plus partially re-extended undercarriage caused the aircraft to lose height and "mush in" to the river. Regn canx 5 Sep 54. (TT on departure Amsterdam for Shannon: 2,498 hrs).

4510 1049C-55-81 20 Jun 53 to Air France as F-BGNA. E-22269 dated 19 Jun 53, del Burbank-New York-Paris (Orly) 27-28

F-BGNA 1049C of Air France was the first Super Constellation to visit the Paris Airshow. It is seen in June 1953 with the original small Air France titles and makes an interesting comparison to the French competition, a Sud-Est SE2010 Armagnac, behind it. (Stephen Piercey collection)

SECTION 12: CONSTELLATION PRODUCTION LIST

Jun 53 (TT: 102 hrs). C of A issued 15 Jul 53. Inaugurated Super Constellation svce to New York 16-17 Jul 53, also in svce date. Damaged beyond repair in forced-landing in a field at Preston City, CT, shortly after 08.29 hrs (EST) on 3 Aug 54. No casualties. Aircraft was en route Paris (Orly)-New York (Idlewild) & Mexico City via Shannon. After arrival over the Scotland intersection (15 miles from Idlewild) at 07.30 (EST), the flight received clearance for an ILS approach, which was discontinued due to unexpected heavy turbulence, heavy rain and low ceiling. Clearance subsequently given for a diversion to Boston, MA, at 07.50. No radio contact with the flight from 08.01 until 08.22, when the captain declared an emergency and asked for instructions to land at Providence, RI. At 08.29, the flight announced it was not landing at Providence (only 15 minutes fuel approx remaining). Aircraft descended, propellers feathered on final approach to the field, brushed tree-tops and skidded across the field and a small ravine with undercarriage up and flaps down. Struck three trees and a garage and came to a stop 1,153 feet from first contact with the ground. Nos 1 & 2 engines torn away, also no 3 nacelle and outer section of starboard wing. Fire after impact destroyed a major portion of the aircraft. Cause: Inadequate in-flight planning, particularly as regards the low fuel state and suitable alternate airfields after the initial missed approach at New York. (TT: 2,479 hrs). Canx from F-register 23 Sep 54.

4511 1049C-55-81 27 Jul 53 to Air France as F-BGNB. E-22270 dated 26 Jul 53, del Burbank-New York-Paris (Orly) 28-29 Aug 53 (TT: 55 hrs). C of A issued 9 Sep 53, in svce 10 Sep 53 (to New York). To 1049E/01-55, later 1049G/02-82 on 12 Nov 55. Damaged Paris-Orly 1 Mar 60. Repaired. Mod to 91-Seater high-density European Tourist class configuration, re-entered svce 1 Apr 60. Stored at Paris (Orly) for a period during 1961 (presumably after the aircraft was damaged by fire while undergoing work at Paris-Orly on 27 Jul 61). Re-entered svce (1962) and withdrawn from svce 3 May 63 at Paris (Orly). CofA renewed 25 Jun 63 at Orly for ferry flight to Toulouse only. Ferried Orly-Toulouse-Montaudran 1 Jul 63 & wfu there after suspension of CofA 9 Jul 63 (TT: 24,996 hrs). Canx as wfu 2 Nov 66. Sold to A Bertin t/a Aviasol in Feb 67 (possibly Feb 68). Preserved as tourist attraction, less engines, at entrance to zoo, St.Vincent de Tyrosse, Landes, France, until broken up there in the spring of 1979.

4512 1049C-55-81 23 Aug 53 to Air France as F-BGNC. E-22271 dated 22 Aug 53, del Paris-Orly 3 Sep 53 (TT: 33 hrs). CofA issued 16 Sep 53, in svce 19 Sep 53. Lost propeller in flight on 26 Aug 55, en route Douala, Cameroons, to Paris. Landed safely at Algiers & ferried to Orly on 3 engines. To 1049E/01-55, later to 1049G/02-82 24 Dec 55. Slightly damaged landing at Munich, Germany, 7 Feb 60. Repaired. Mod to 91-Seater high-density European Tourist-class configuration, re-entered svce 1 Apr 60. Cvtd to cargo configuration with rear cargo door by SALA at San Jose, Costa Rica, between 8 Oct 60 and Mar 61, ret to svce 18 Apr 61 (TT: 22,333 hrs). Flew Paris (Orly)-New York cargo inaugural 23 Apr 61. Withdrawn from svce 2 Oct 67 (TT: 33,539 hrs). Sold to Le Gouvello de la Porte, Nantes, 11 Jun 68 and to CATAIR 13 Nov 68. Crashed into high ground on approach to Douala, Cameroons, on 9 Aug 69, while on a non-scheduled cargo flight. Crew killed.

4513 1049C-55-81 4 Sep 53 to Air France as F-BGND. E-22272 dated 31 Aug 53, del Burbank-New York-Gander-Paris (Orly) 6-7 Sep 53. (TT: 32 hrs). CofA issued 24 Sep 53, in svce 2 Oct 53 (to New York). Badly damaged in heavy landing 13 Oct 53. Repaired. To 1049E/01-55, later to 1049G/02-82 in 1956. Cvtd to cargo configuration by Air France at Toulouse, France, with rear cargo door, between Sep 62 and Dec 62. First flight after conversion 14 Dec 62 (TT: 23.902 hrs). Withdrawn from svce 22 Aug 65, ferried to Toulouse-Montaudran 9 Sep 65 & wfu there after CofA expiry 14 Sep 65 (TT: 28,490 hrs). Stored at Toulouse-Montaudran, canx as wfu 9 Aug 67. Presumably remained in storage until late 1969/early 1970. Restored to CATAIR as F-BRNH in a 102-pax/cargo convertible configuration, with CofA issued 16 Jan 70 at Chateauroux, France. Believed tfd to René Meyer in Apr 70 and back to CATAIR 9 Mar 71. Withdrawn from use after CofA expiry 31 Mar 72 at Cormeilles-Pontoise, France, and stored there. Derelict by Jun 73, slowly scrapped between Jul 73 and Feb 74. Canx from F-register as wfu 12 Oct 73.

4514 1049C-55-81 17 Sep 53 to Air France as F-BGNE. E-22273 dated 16 Sep 53, del Burbank-New York-Paris (Orly) 22-23 Sep 53 (TT: 29 hrs). CofA issued 24 Sep 53, in svce 26 Sep 53. Damaged landing Bogota, Colombia, 23 Feb 55. Repaired. To 1049E/01-55, later to 1049G/02-82 in 1956. One pax killed when a window failed at 17,500 feet on night of 20-21 Apr 57 while the aircraft was en route Baghdad-Istanbul, about 25 miles south of Kirkuk, Iraq, over the Turkish-Persian border. Repaired. Stored at Paris (Orly) for period during winter 1961-62. Mod to 91-Seater high-density European Tourist-class configuration, re-entered svce 13 Feb 60. Withdrawn from svce 1 Oct 63 (TT: 23,610 hrs) & stored at Orly after CofA expiry 4 Oct 63. Remained in storage at Paris (Orly) until 27 Jul 67. Restored and sold to Etablissements Jean Gaudet as F-BGNE 9 Aug 67. Del Orly - Lisbon 10 Aug 67 & Lisbon - Enugu, Biafra 17 Aug 67 and reregd 5N-07G. Nicknamed 'The Grey Ghost'. Reportedly owned by Rhodesian Airlines, then Transportader do Ar, but used by Biafran Government on the Portugal-Biafra airlift. Hit by anti-aircraft fire on approach to Enugu in dark during last week of Sep 67. Made a go-around and landed safely second time. Aircraft damaged, re-entered svce just over a week later. Canx from F-register as 'Sold to Portugal' 2 Feb 68. Stored at Lisbon, Portugal Jan 70. Derelict by Aug 70 and broken up by Jun 71.

4515 1049C-55-81 20 Sep 53 to Air France as F-BGNF. E-22274 dated 19 Sep 53, del Paris-Orly 26 Sep 53 (TT: 29 hrs). CofA 1 Oct 53, in svce 12 Oct 53. To 1049E/01-55 by Mar 56, to 1049G/02-82 by late 56. Stored at Paris (Orly) 2 Aug 61 for a period. Re-entered svce until withdrawn from svce 2 Aug 64 (TT: 25,722 hrs). Ferried to Toulouse-Montaudran 10 Dec 64, and stored there after CofA expiry 16 Dec 64. Withdrawn from use 2 Nov 66 & canx on 24 Nov 66. Dismantled and sold to A Bertin t/a Aviasol in Feb 67 (possibly Feb 68). Transported to Berck-sur-Mer, northern France, and preserved in the "Parc d'Attractions de Bagatelle" on the edge of Berck airport, with 'Bagatelle' titling. Moved in mid-1976 to new site on edge of the Nl road on hilltop north of Marquise, northern France. At Marquise by Aug 76, used as the "Discothèque-Bar Tango Charly", with red cheatline. Still there in 1981, but condition deteriorating. Repainted with blue trim by May 82, but scrapped due to corrosion by end Dec 84.

4516 1049C-55-81 2 Oct 53 to Air France as F-BGNG. E-22275 dated 29 Sep 53, del Burbank-New York-Paris (Orly) 3-6 Oct 53. CofA 9 Oct 53, in svce 23 Oct 53. To 1049E/01-55 to 1049G/02-82 14 Jan 56. Mod to 91-Seater high-density European Tourist-class configuration, re-entered svce 1 Apr 60. Cvtd to cargo configuration by SALA at San Jose, Costa Rica, with rear cargo door, between Dec 60 and May 61. Re-entered svce May 61. Withdrawn from svce 2 Oct 67 (TT: 33,918 hrs). Sold to Ets Le Gouvello de la Porte, Nantes, 23 Nov 67 & to René Meyer 12 Jun 68, del for CATAIR use same day. Painted in CATAIR colours by early 1969 and in a 102-pax/cargo convertible configuration by Apr 69, but remained regd to René Meyer. Withdrawn from use at Cormeilles-Pontoise after CofA expiry 19 Nov 72. Stored until sale to Air Fret in late 73. Flown to Nîmes-Garons for use as spares aircraft. Canx from register in Jul 76. Stored at Nîmes, two propellers, one engine & part of tail unit missing by May 77, and last reported Jun 78 with two engines and other parts missing. Believed scrapped during 1979 after Air Fret's airworthy Super Constellation was sold.

4517 1049-55-81 23 Oct 53 to Air France as F-BGNH. E-22276 dated 23 Oct 53, del Paris (Orly) 27 Oct 53 (TT: 34 hrs). CofA 29 Oct 53, in svce 1 Nov 53 (to Rio de Janeiro). To 1049E/01-55 & to 1049G/02-82 in 1956. Withdrawn from svce 21 Jan 65 at Paris (Orly), with CofA expiry 1 Feb 65. Stored there until wfu 15 Apr 66 & broken up during 1967. Canx from F-register as wfu 27 Apr 66.

F-BGNI 1049G Freighter/combi of Air Cameroun was photographed in service at Douala, Cameroon on 17th November 1967. (R Caratini)

4518 1049C-55-81 24 Oct 53 to Air France as F-BGNI. E-22277 dated 23 Oct 53, del Paris (Orly) 29 Oct 53. CofA 3 Nov 53, in svce 12 Nov 53 (to Rio de Janeiro). Damaged when collided with 749A F-BAZI at Orly 25 Feb 54. Repaired. To 1049E/01-55 & to 1049G/02-82 on 9 Jun 56. Damaged when it ran off runway landing at Bogota, Colombia, 18 May 56. Repaired. Mod to 91-seater high-density European Tourist-class configuration, re-entered svce 1 Apr 60. Cvtd to cargo configuration by Air France at Toulouse, with rear cargo door, ferried to Toulouse 30 Jan 62, completed 12 Sep 62. First flight after conversion 13 Sep 62. Withdrawn from svce at Paris (Orly) 31 Dec 66 (TT: 29,072 hrs), after CofA expiry 23 Dec 66. Stored until lease to Air Cameroun as F-BGNI 3 Jun 67. Used as pax/cargo convertible aircraft until CofA renewal 17 Dec 70, when permitted to carry cargo only. Withdrawn from use at Douala, Cameroons, in late 1971, and CofA validated 22 Jan 72 for ferry-flight to Nîmes-Garons, France, only. Stored at Nîmes in Air Cameroun colours, and used for spares by Air Fret. Canx from F-register 10 Apr 73 as wfu. Scrapped at Nîmes during the winter of 1975-76.

4519 1049C-55-81 4 Nov 53 to Air France as F-BGNJ. E-22278 dated 4 Nov 53, del Burbank-Pittsburgh-New York-Paris (Orly) 6-8 Nov 53 (TT: 35hrs). CofA 10 Nov 53, in svce 15 Nov 53. Damaged when struck concrete island taxying at Mexico City 1 Aug 54. Repaired. To 1049E/01-55 & to 1049G/02-82 in 1956. Damaged at Paris (Orly) on 20 Jul 60. Repaired. Cvtd to 91-seater high-density European Tourist-class configuration, re-entered svce 7 Jan 61. Damaged at Nice 11 Jul 61. Repaired. Withdrawn from svce 30 Oct 63 (TT: 24,282 hrs) and stored at Paris (Orly) after CofA expiry 13 Nov 63. Sold to TAE in Sep 66 and regd EC-BEN. Fully painted in TAE colours, but never deld. Remained in storage at Paris (Orly) until 4 Jul 67 (CofA renewal). Restored to Air France in Aug 67 as F-BGNJ. Sold to Gesto Finance, Panama 8 Aug 67 & canx from F-register 18 Aug 67. Seized at Paris (Orly) 13 Nov 67, the doors were sealed and a court order requested to prevent the aircraft leaving by a M. Arnould, acting for unnamed parties, who said a considerable sum of money was owed. Remained in storage at Orly in a modified TAE colour scheme (white with red/blue trim). Sold to Air Fret 14 Mar 68, restored to F-register on 5 Sep 68 as F-BRAD. In svce on Biafran airlift between France, Libreville and Sao Tome/Uli, first flight 7 Sep 68 Orly-Luqa (Malta)-Douala-Libreville. Repainted in Biafran camouflage scheme with dark blue roof by Nov 69. Sold to CATAIR 31 Dec 69. Withdrawn from svce with CATAIR by early 1973. CofA renewed for one month only at Cormeilles-Pontoise 22 May 73. Sold back to Air Fret 24 May 73 and ferried to Nîmes-Garons during May 73. Withdrawn from use at Nîmes prior to CofA expiry on 22 Jun 73. Engines used to keep c/n 4671 flying. Canx from F-register 17 May 74 as wfu, but taken to Château Bougon Airport, Nantes, for use as a tourist attraction. Painted in the colours of the prototype Super Constellation (c/n 1961-S) by mid-75 & preserved in good condition on edge of airfield. Repainted in old Air France livery Nov 85 as 'Lockheed Super G'. Moved from car-park location at Nantes to new site 500m away next to preserved Noratlas late 1997. Seen on display at Nantes Apr 07, restored to immaculate condition and in full Air France 1950s colours as F-BGNJ, its original French registration.

4520 1049C-55-81, modified to 1049C-55-103 1 Feb 54 to Government of Pakistan for use by Pakistan International Airlines Corp as AP-AFQ. E-27600 dated 29 Jan 54. Inaugurated Karachi-Dacca svce 7 Jun 54 & Karachi-London svce via Cairo 1 Feb 55. Believed updated to 1049E/01 or 02-82. Tfd to Pakistan Intl ownership in 1958. Damaged in accident 29 Jun 59. Repaired. Withdrawn from use and cannibalized for spares at Karachi Airport in 1964. Subsequently used for cabin-staff training at Karachi. Painted in brown sand camouflage colours during Indo-Pakistan war Dec 71. Fuselage still stored behind the PIA-KLM Midway Airport Hotel, Karachi in Nov 73, but believed sold for scrap mid-1983.

4521 1049C-55-81, modified to 1049C-55-103 18 Mar 54 to Government of Pakistan for use by Pakistan International Airlines Corp as AP-AFR. E-27602 dated 10 Mar 54. Believed updated to 1049E/01 or 02-82. Tfd to Pakistan Intl ownership in 1958. Sold to Lebanese Air Transport Charter Co S A L in early 1967, painted up by Mar 67, but never deld. Stored at Karachi Airport. Re-entered svce with Pakistan Intl until withdrawn from use after CofA expiry 28 Feb 69. Donated to AURI-Indonesian Air Force shortly afterwards, probably as T-1043, coded 43. Last report based Halim, Indonesia late in 1970. Fate unknown, probably scrapped.

4522 1049C-55-81, modified to 1049C-55-104 Apr 54 to Government of Pakistan for use by Pakistan International Airlines Corp as AP-AFS. E-27603 dated 7 Apr 54. Starboard undercarriage retracted accidentally on 21 Jun 55, while the aircraft was being serviced in a hangar at Karachi, Pakistan. Badly damaged. Repaired. Believed updated to 1049E/01 or 02-82. Tfd to Pakistan Intl ownership in 1958. Sold to Lebanese Air Transport Charter Co S A L in early 1967, painted up by Mar 67, but never deld. Stored at Karachi Airport. Canx from AP-register prior to 1968, so presumably used for spares. Remains of a Super Constellation in Lebanese colours reported on far side of airfield at Karachi in Jul 70 was probably this aircraft. Exact fate unknown, presumably scrapped.

4523 1049C-55-83 25 Nov 53 to Eastern Air Lines as N6215C, FN 215. FN to be changed to 261 approx 1960 on conversion to 95-pax configuration, but remained as FN 215. Engines updated to QEC DA-3/4 type. Withdrawn from svce 16 Aug 67 and stored at Miami Intl Airport, FL until scrapped during May 68.

4524 1049C-55-83 7 Nov 53 to Eastern Air Lines as N6216C, FN to be changed to 262 approx 1960 on conversion to 95-pax configuration, but remained as FN 216. Engines updated to QEC DA-3/4 type. Withdrawn from svce 11 Dec 67 and stored at Opa Locka, FL. Sold to California Airmotive Corp 30 Sep 68 and flown to Fox Fld, Lancaster, CA for storage. Canx from USCAR 12 Jul 70. Last reported Fox Fld Mar 71, fuselage only. Scrapped shortly afterwards.

4525 1049C-55-83 16 Nov 53 to Eastern Air Lines as N6217C, FN 217. FN to be changed to 263 approx 1960 on conversion to 95-pax configuration, but remained as FN 217. Engines updated to QEC DA-3/4 type. Withdrawn from svce 7 Sep 67 and stored at Opa Locka, FL. Sold to California Airmotive Corp 30 Sep 68 and flown to Fox Fld, Lancaster, CA for storage. Canx from USCAR 12 Jul 70. Last reported Fox Fld Nov 69. Scrapped by early 1971.

4526 1049C-55-83 20 Nov 53 to Eastern Air Lines as N6218C, FN 218. FN to be changed to 264 in 1960 on conversion to 95-pax configuration, but remained as FN 218. Engines updated to QEC DA-3/4 type. Destroyed in forced-landing on a hillside near North Salem, NY, after a mid-air collision with TWA Boeing 707 (N748TW) over the Carmel, NY Vortac at approx 16.19 hrs (EST) on 4 Dec 65. The Super Constellation was operating Flight EA853 shuttle service from Boston, MA to Newark, NJ and was flying southwest at 11,000 feet when evasive action was taken to avoid the Boeing 707,

N6226C 1049C Freighter of Eastern Air Lines, with cargo fleet no.253, shows the titling used with the broad red-band scheme, "Ship Eastern". (John T Wible)

whose crew took similar action on seeing the Constellation. The port wing of the Boeing 707, outboard of the no.1 engine, struck the starboard horizontal stabilizer of the 1049C. As the 707 passed under and towards the rear of the 1049C, the no.1 engine cowling struck the underside of the 1049C's fuselage, tearing out the hydraulic boost package and the control cables to the rear empennage of the 1049C, rendering elevator and rudder controls inoperative. The Super Constellation then entered a tight left spiral into the clouds, recovering below the clouds by the use of throttles only to make a forced landing in the twilight, 4.2 mls north of the collision area. The Super Constellation hit two trees on approach, the second tree causing the port wing to separate from the fuselage. The aircraft came to rest 700 feet up a slope with the fuselage separating into three pieces and all engines separated from the nacelles. Most of the aircraft was consumed by fire on the ground. Thanks to the remarkable flying skill of the Captain of the Super Constellation, with the use of the throttle controls only, 50 of the 54 people on board the Super Constellation survived the accident, the Captain however losing his life in the blazing wreckage while trying to save the last of the passengers. (TT: 32,883 hrs). Cause: Probably misjudgement of altitude separation due to an optical illusion created by the up-slope effect of cloud tops resulting in an evasive manoeuvre.

4527 1049C-55-83 30 Nov 53 to Eastern Air Lines as N6219C, FN 219. FN to be changed to 265 approx 1960 on conversion to 95-pax configuration, but remained as FN 219. Engines updated to QEC DA-3/4 type. Damaged beyond repair at Miami Intl Airport, FL on 18 Oct 66. Withdrawn from use 11 Nov 66, used for spares and derelict by Apr 67. Scrapped at Miami during Jun 67, probably by Thomas E Chatlos.

4528 1049C-55-83 13 Dec 53 to Eastern Air Lines as N6220C, FN 220. Engines updated to QEC DA-3/4 type. Cvtd to all-cargo configuration by LAS during Mar-Apr 60, with FN 251, front and rear cargo doors. Damaged beyond repair when starboard main undercarriage collapsed and aircraft burst into flames while taxying to take-off at Idlewild Airport, NY at 22.45 hrs (EST) on 3 Aug 61. When the undercarriage collapsed, a fire broke out in the vicinity of the no.3 engine, destroying part of the fuselage and the starboard wing. Cause: Probably fatigue failure at the root of the weld joining the upper extension cap to the top of the main undercarriage shock-strut cylinder on the starboard side. No casualties.

4529 1049C-55-83 19 Dec 53 to Eastern Air Lines as N6221C, FN 221. FN to be changed to 266 approx 1960 on conversion to 95-pax configuration, but remained as FN 221. Engines updated to QEC DA-3/4 type. Withdrawn from svce 7 Aug 67 and stored at Miami Intl Airport, FL. Broken up there during May-Jun 68.

4530 1049-55-83 23 Dec 53 to Eastern Air Lines as N6222C, FN 222. FN to be changed to 267 in 1960 on conversion to 95-pax configuration, but remained as FN 222. Engines updated to QEC DA-3/4 type. Cvtd to all-cargo configuration with front and rear cargo doors by LAS between Jun and Jul 63, FN 256. Sold to California Airmotive Corp 19 Jan 66 (29 Apr 66 also reported) and flown to Fox Fld, Lancaster, CA for storage. Canx from USCAR 12 Jul 70. Last reported Nov 71, believed scrapped by early in 1972.

4531 1049C-55-83 31 Dec 53 to Eastern Air Lines as N6223C, FN 223. FN to be changed to 268 approx 1960 on conversion to 95-pax configuration, but remained as FN 223. Engines updated to QEC DA-3/4 type. Withdrawn from svce 28 Jan 68 and stored at Opa Locka, FL. Sold to California Airmotive Corp 30 Sep 68 and ferried to Fox Fld, Lancaster, CA for storage. Canx from USCAR 12 Jul 70. Last reported Fox Fld Mar 71, fuselage only. Scrapped shortly afterwards.

4532 1049C-55-83 10 Jan 54 to Eastern Air Lines as N6224C, FN 224. Received substantial damage at Islip, NY on 9 Jan 58 when the aircraft collided with a snow-bank during the landing approach. During the flare-out, the crew tried unsuccessfully to pull up over a snowbank across the runway threshold. The port main undercarriage became detached on contact with the runway and the aircraft veered into a large snowbank. As the aircraft was turning through the snow, the left wing separated from the fuselage and the nose gear failed. On a training flight, no casualties. Repaired. FN to be changed to 269 approx 1960 on conversion to 95-pax configuration, but remained as FN 224. Engines updated to QEC DA-3/4 type. Withdrawn from svce 15 Feb 68 and stored at Opa Locka, FL. Sold to California Airmotive Corp 30 Sep 68 and ferried to Fox Fld, Lancaster, CA for storage. Canx from USCAR 12 Jul 70. Scrapped during early 1971.

4533 1049C-55-83 22 Jan 54 to Eastern Air Lines as N6225C, FN 225. Engines updated to QEC DA-3/4 type. Cvtd to all-cargo configuration with front and rear cargo doors by LAS between Apr and May 60, FN 252. Sold to California Airmotive Corp 29 Apr 66 (20 Jan 66 also reported) and flown to Fox Fld, Lancaster, CA for storage. Canx from USCAR 12 Jul 70. Last reported Nov 71, believed scrapped by early in 1972.

4534 1049C-55-83 24 Jan 54 to Eastern Air Lines as N6226C, FN 226. Engines updated to QEC DA-3/4 type. Cvtd to all-cargo configuration with front and rear cargo doors by LAS between Mar and Apr 60, FN 253. Withdrawn from svce 18 Feb 67 and stored at Opa Locka, FL. Sold to California Airmotive Corp (TT: 33,923 hrs) on 30 Sep 68 and ferried to Fox Fld, Lancaster, CA for storage. Sold to Aviation Corporation of America in approx Jul 69 and ferried to Miami, FL by Aug 69. Regn canx from USCAR on request of California Airmotive 12 Jul 70. However, aircraft was stored at Fort Lauderdale, FL by Sep 70 and subsequently withdrawn from use there. Still whole in Jun 72, but derelict & on tail by Aug 73. Scrapped during winter 1973/74 at Fort Lauderdale.

4535 1049C-55-83 11 Feb 54 to Eastern Air Lines as N6227C, FN 227 (FAA records give 18 Feb 54). Engines updated to QEC DA-3/4 type. Cvtd to all-cargo configuration with front and rear cargo doors by LAS between Mar and Apr 60. Re-certified as cargo aircraft 2 May 60 (TT: 19,740 hrs), FN 254. After withdrawal of Eastern's last Super Constellations from scheduled svce on 14 Feb 68, this aircraft was retained for non-revenue flying, especially as an engine carrier. By late 1969, the aircraft had been painted white overall, though still used by Eastern. Nicknamed "Casper the Ghost" (night-time operations & all-white paint scheme). Remained in svce until mid-1971, then stored at Miami Intl, FL (TT: 33,750 hrs). Sold to Wade Trading Corp 20 Sep 71. Planned use of aircraft by Southern Cross Intl Airways (Australia), same owner as Wade Trading, fell through. To Continental Aircraft Leasing Inc 7 Jul 72, and stored at Miami 1972-73. Ret to Wade Trading Co Nov 72. To Diablo Enterprises Inc (FN 227 again) Nov 73, regd 5 Dec 73. Sold to Air Cargo Support Inc 29 Jul 74 and used until autumn 1976. (TT: a/o 11 Sep 76 was 35,595 hrs). Made last flight 7 Oct 76. Engine failed on take-off from Miami Intl. Remaining three engines kept on maximum take-off power on the go-around until the downwind leg, suffering internal damage. The aircraft was subsequently withdrawn from use at Miami (had been en route to Ramey, PR, on a cattle charter). Regn revoked 22 Oct 76 (failure to file, 1973). Aircraft sold to Proimex International Ltd 10 Feb 77, but never used. Remained withdrawn at Miami and used for spares. Parts missing by mid-77 at which time aircraft moved off active ramp to Miami Port Authority ramp. Sold to Ed Ramsey for scrapping and scrapped between 30 Aug 78 and end Oct 78 at Miami Intl. Canx from USCAR 1981.

4536 1049C-55-83 19 Feb 54 to Eastern Air Lines as N6228C, FN 228. Engines updated to QEC DA-3/4 type. Cvtd to all-cargo configuration with front and rear cargo doors by LAS between Apr and May 60, FN 255. Withdrawn from svce 3 Jul 67 and stored at Opa Locka, FL. Sold to California Airmotive Corp 30 Sep 68 (FAA give 29 Aug 68) and flown to Fox Fld, Lancaster, CA for storage (TT: 34,122 hrs). Sold to Aviation Corporation of America 13 Feb 69. Sold to Air Fleets International Inc 5 Jan 70. Stored at Miami, FL by Sep 70. Regn canx from USCAR on request of California Airmotive 12 Jul 70. Sold to Butler Aviation (Miami) Inc at sheriff's sale 17 Feb 71. Remained in storage at Miami until sold back to Air Fleets Intl Inc 2 Jan 73. Sold to Aviation Specialties Inc 20 Mar 73 and cvtd to sprayer with fuselage tanks and overwing spray booms. Tfd to Aircraft Specialties Inc 10 Apr 73. Stored at Mesa, AZ after 1975 spraying season until sold via Jet Engine Support Inc 2 Apr 79 to Aerotours Dominicana C por A 8 Apr 79. Prepared for dely at Miami, and dely ex-Miami 8 Apr 79. Reregd HI-329. Used as cargo aircraft during 1979, but stored out of svce & minus two engines at Santo Domingo, Dominican Republic, by Oct 79. (TT: 34,352 hrs a/o 23 Jan 80). Aerotours titling painted out by Oct 80 for sale. Flying again by Nov 81, after two years in storage, in use for crew-training. Forward cargo door removed & used for HI-228 (c/n 4009) in Feb 82. Gap covered up with sheet metal & made one flight to San Juan as freighter (rear cargo door only). Found to be too heavy for regular use, withdrawn from use again Feb 83 & two engines removed. Sold to AeroChago SA for spares 1983. Lost parts gradually at Santo Domingo, derelict & on tail by Aug 87. Scrapped sometime after May 88 at Santo Domingo, DR.

4537 1049C-55-83 25 Feb 54 to Eastern Air Lines as N6229C, FN 229. FN to be changed to 270 on conversion to 95-pax configuration approx 1960, but remained as FN 229. Received substantial damage when it skidded off the runway after an aborted take-off at Washington, DC at 14.08 hrs (EST) on 13 Feb 60. Failure of the exhaust manifold caused a fire-warning on take-off in a snowstorm. Take-off was abandoned, and the aircraft went into a ground loop after braking was ineffective on the wet and slushy runway. Side loads imposed during the ground loop to the right caused the port main undercarriage to collapse. Repaired. Engines updated to QEC DA-3/4 type. Withdrawn from svce 3 Jan 68 and stored at Opa Locka, FL. Sold to California Airmotive Corp 30 Sep 68 and ferried to Fox Fld, Lancaster, CA for storage. Last reported there Nov 69. Canx from USCAR 12 Jul 70. Scrapped by early 1971.

4538 1049C-55-83 28 Feb 54 to Eastern Air Lines as N6230C, FN 230. Starboard undercarriage collapsed on landing at Washington National Airport, DC while on a flight from Newark, NJ to Houston, TX on 14 Jul 55. Received damage. Repaired. FN to be changed to 271 on conversion to 95-pax configuration approx 1960, but remained as FN 230. Engines updated to QEC DA-3/4 type. Sold to International Aerodyne Inc 26 Jan 67. Stored at Miami Intl, FL until scrapped there during Jun 67 by Thomas E Chatlos dba AAA Scrap Metals.

4539 1049C-55-81 29 Mar 54 to Qantas as VH-EAG 'Southern Constellation'. CofRegn 9 Feb 54, first flight 18 Mar 54. E-27609 dated 26 Mar 54, Qantas acceptance 28 Mar 54 (TT: 14hrs). Used for training flts in USA & Canada 6-10 Apr 54. Del Burbank-San Francisco-Honolulu-Nadi-Sydney 12-15 Apr 54. Used for training flts on arrival 15 Apr 54. Inaugurated Qantas' Super Constellation services 15 May 54 with a Sydney-Nadi-Canton Is-Honolulu-San Francisco flight, arr San Francisco 17 May 54 (with 51 pax). Continued San Francisco-Vancouver & ret Sydney 20 May 54. Op three courtesy flts from Sydney 29 May 54. First Sydney-London svce 9-12 Aug 54, ret London-Sydney 13-18 Aug 54. Flew Sydney-Singapore Super Constellation inaugural 4 Feb 55, Sydney-Manila & Tokyo Super Constellation inaugural 3 May 55 & Sydney-Christchurch, NZ inaugural with Super Constellation 19 Nov 55. To 1049E/01-55. Overhaul & radar nose fitted 23 Sep-20 Oct 57. Lsd Malayan Airways during Mar 60. Flew last Super Constellation svce to Port Moresby 7 Jul 60 (ex-Sydney). Lsd Tasman Empire Airways Ltd 16 Dec 60 (first TEAL charter to Christchurch, New Zealand), and from Jan 61 to Mar 61. Ret Qantas. Based Perth 22 Jul-30 Aug 61 and based Singapore 21 Oct-18 Nov 61. Departed Sydney on the last Qantas Super Constellation svce 7 Apr 63 (migrant charter to Malta), ret Sydney 15 Apr 63. Was first Qantas Super Constellation to arrive in Australia & last to leave. Painted up with sign "<u>V</u>ery good performer/<u>H</u>eld her reputation/<u>E</u>ntered service first/<u>A</u>lways reliable/<u>G</u>oing out last" (VH-EAG). Sold to Boeing Aircraft Corp (trade-in on Boeing 707s) 3 May 63 and tfd to Airmotive Inc 6 May 63. Del Sydney-Burbank via Nadi, Honolulu & San Francisco 6-8 May 63 (TT: 21,872 hrs). Believed never regd in the USA. Stored at Burbank, CA for spares use. In parking lot near Burbank by Dec 64 (minus outer wings & tail, awaiting scrapping). Scrapped in early 1965.

4540 1049C-55-94 26 Feb 54 to Trans-Canada Air Lines as CF-TGA, FN 401. E-27604 dated 26 Feb 54. Made first visit of a TCA Super Constellation to Prestwick, Scotland, on 12 May 54. Updated to 1049E/01. Withdrawn from svce (TT: 17,457 hrs) and sold to Douglas Aircraft Corp (trade-in on DC-8s) 9 Jan 63, and tf to Airmotive Inc. Stored at Burbank, CA for spares use. In parking lot near Burbank by Dec 64, minus outer wings, tail and engines, awaiting scrapping. Still there, derelict, in Aug 66, but scrapped shortly afterwards. Believed never regd in the USA.

SECTION 12: CONSTELLATION PRODUCTION LIST

Transport Canada / Transports Canada

NON-CERTIFICATE OF AIRWORTHINESS / CERTIFICAT DE NAVIGABILITÉ

1. Nationality and Registration Marks / Marques de nationalité et d'immatriculation: **CF-TGE**
2. Aircraft Manufacturer and Model - Constructeur et modèle de l'aéronef: **LOCKHEED AIRCRAFT CORPORATION 1049C-55**
3. Aircraft Serial Number / Numéro de série de l'aéronef: **1049C-4544**
4. Category – Catégorie: **STATIC DISPLAY**

5. Authority and basis for issuance
This Certificate of Airworthiness is issued pursuant to the **Aeronautics Act** and certifies that, as of the date of issuance, the aircraft to which it was issued has been inspected and found to conform to the type certificate therefor, to be in a condition for safe operation, and has been shown to meet the requirements of the comprehensive and detailed airworthiness code as provided by Annex 8 to the Convention on International Civil Aviation.

6. Terms and Conditions
Unless suspended or cancelled in accordance with the **Aeronautics Act**, this certificate shall remain in force so long as the aircraft identified above is maintained and certified in accordance with the applicable requirements of the Canadian Aviation Regulations.

7. In respect of Part II of Annex 16 (aircraft noise) to the Convention on International Civil Aviation and the **Aeronautics Act**, this aircraft:
- ☐ complies with the requirements / satisfait aux exigences
- ☒ does not comply with the requirements / ne satisfait pas aux exigences
- ☐ is not required to comply / n'est pas obligé de satisfaire aux exigences

DECEMBER 11, 1998 — Date of Issue – Date de délivrance
WAYNE JUNIPER — For the Minister of Transport – Pour le ministre des Transports

Seal / Sceau

24-0073 (96-06)

Canada

C/n 4544. An unusual twist to the normal "CofA" certificate is this Transport Canada Certificate of non-airworthiness issued for 1049G CF-TGE in December 1998 for static use (as a restaurant). (via Phil Yull).

4541 1049C-55-94 17 Mar 54 to Trans-Canada Air Lines as CF-TGB, FN 402. E-27605 dated 18 Mar 54. Flew Trans-Canada's Super Constellation inaugural to London (Heathrow) 14 May 54, from Toronto. Flew Trans-Canada's Super Constellation transcontinental inaugural Montreal-Toronto-Winnipeg-Vancouver 26 Sep 54. To 1049E/01-55, later to 1049G/02-82 in 1958. Flew Trans-Canada's non-stop trans-continental inaugural Toronto-Vancouver 1 Jun 57. Radar nose fitted by 1959. Propeller blade on no.2 engine snapped when aircraft was flying over Atlantic Ocean, 1,200 miles out from Goose Bay, Labrador, en route Toronto-London, on 28 Feb 60, striking the cowling of the engine. Aircraft landed safely at London-Heathrow on three engines. Repaired. Withdrawn from svce with TCA (TT: 17,000 hrs), sold to California Airmotive Corp 17 Mar 62, and reregd N9739Z. Lsd to Standard Airways 31 May 62. Reregd N189S and in svce 3 Aug 62. Later sold to Standard Airways. Undershot on approach to Manhattan Municipal Airport, KS on 29 May 63 after in-flight reversal of the no.3 propeller when the aircraft was just about to touch down, crashed and broke into three pieces. Aircraft caught fire and was burnt out. En route from California with US Army personnel (TT: 19,804 hrs). Cause: Propeller unit malfunction resulting from improper maintenance practices and inspection procedure. No casualties.

4542 1049C-55-94 9 Apr 54 to Trans-Canada Air Lines as CF-TGC, FN 403. E-27606 dated 9 Apr 54. Flew pre-inaugural transatlantic demonstration tour to London (Heathrow) 10 May 54, including press flights from London. To 1049E/01-55. Received damage to lower left rudder on 1 Nov 57 when hit by taxying BOAC Stratocruiser (G-AKGI) at London (Heathrow), repaired. Cvtd to 1049G/02-82 (tip-tanks fitted) in 1958. Radar nose fitted by Jun 59. Withdrawn from svce with TCA (TT: 18,566 hrs) and sold to California Airmotive Corp 18 Mar 62 for spares use only. Major components used in the rebuild of c/n **4851** (qv). Fuselage used for spares by World Wide Airways and parked outside World Wide Airways' hangar at Montreal Airport until at least Aug 65 (bankruptcy). Presumably scrapped some time afterwards.

4543 1049C-55-94 1 May 54 to Trans-Canada Air Lines as CF-TGD, FN 404. E-27607 dated 1 May 54. To 1049E/02, later to 1049G/02-82 (tip-tanks fitted), probably in 1958. Remained in use with TCA until 1963, (TT: 17,227 hrs on withdrawal from TCA svce). Sold to C Newhall, Dorval, t/a Newhall Ltd, 16 Nov 63. Immediately resold to Capitol Airways (sale date to Capitol given as 14 Nov 63, TCA records give 16 Nov 63) and regd N8743R. Reregd N4715G. Stored at Wilmington, DE from 22 Jan 64, but ret to svce for summer 1964. Rn Capitol International Airways. Op Mediterranean IT flights for British United Airways ex-London Gatwick 24-26 Jul 65. Withdrawn from use at Wilmington by 1967, no engines by Aug 67, and used for spares. In bad condition by Jul 69 and scrapped shortly afterwards. Canx from USCAR 1970.

4544 1049C-55-94 10 May 54 to Trans-Canada Air Lines as CF-TGE, FN 405. E-27608 dated 7 May 54. To 1049E/01 or 02, later to 1049G/02-82 (tip-tanks fitted) by Dec 57. Flew inaugural svce to Zurich 18 May 58. Radar nose fitted autumn 1958. Withdrawn from svce with TCA believed 7 Jan 62 (TT: approx 19,273 hrs). Sold to Aircraft Radio Industries, CT as N8742R on 16 Oct 63. Canadian regn canx 12 Nov 63. Aircraft believed never left Montreal. Sold to Montreal Air Services (D McVicar) Aug 64 (TT: 19,993 hrs) & regd CF-RNR 11 Sep 64, N-regn canx 25 Aug 64. Lsd to World Wide Airways Inc Sep 1964, first pax flt 30 Oct 64. Tfd to World-Wide Airways Inc 3 Mar 65. Op Mediterranean IT flights for British United Airways ex-London (Gatwick) 10-11 Jul 65 (LGW-Palma-LGW, followed by LGW-Barcelona-LGW). Last svce with World Wide 27 Jul 65. Impounded at Montreal on bankruptcy of World Wide Aug 65. The aircraft was in a hangar undergoing overhaul due to a cracked wing spar at the time. Acft grounded, and stripped of engines, electronics and useable spares at Montreal 1965-66. Sale for use as restaurant 1967 fell through. Canx from C-register 29 Aug 67 as 'presumed wfu'. Stored at Montreal until Dec 68, when it was sold to M Ferrand, dismantled and moved to a location near Quebec City at St.Marc (alongside the St. Lawrence River) for use as a coffee-shop and lounge, but permission refused. Sold to Bertrand Camiraud for C$15,000 in Jun 85. Moved by road St. Marc-St. Jean Port Joli, PQ 1-5 Jul 85. Reassembled 9-12 Jul 85 at Musée des Retrouvailles (mainly agricultural machinery) & opened to public from 20 Jun 87, interior slowly restored. Owner died 1990 & widow put land and

PH-LKA 1049G of KLM, but used in Iberia's colours after return off lease, is seen at Prestwick, Scotland in the summer of 1962. This aircraft was used on 18th August of that year to operate KLM's last Super Constellation passenger service to Prestwick. Note how close the spectators in the public enclosure are to the apron! (PJM collection)

acft up for sale at C$225,000, Super Constellation in poor condition, no starboard outer wing, engines or nose-wheel undercarriage. Partly repainted in Trans-Canada Air Lines scheme by Oct 92. Purchase sponsored by Phil Yull in May 96 & moved to site near Toronto-Pearson Intl Airport. Aircraft restored externally, then to site outside the Regal Constellation Hotel (near airport) on 10 Jun 96. Interior cvtd to cocktail lounge & conference centre. Opened 5 Aug 96, official opening 22 Aug 96. Closed down by owners of the hotel after two years as it gave them too much competition. Disassembled & transported back to Toronto Intl Airport, where it was reassembled 24-26 Jun 98. Opened for business 15 Oct 98 as the "Super Connie Restaurant & Bar". Closed down again 1999 and moved to another part of the international airport for storage. Still in good condition 2001. Ownership transferred to Catherine Scott and offered for sale on e-Bay for minimum C$200,000 in May 04. Dismantled winter 2005/6 for transport to a museum. Both the Toronto Aerospace Museum and the Seattle Museum of Flight made bids for the aircraft in Feb 06.

4545 1049C 55-81 25 Apr 54 to Qantas as VH-EAH 'Southern Sky'. CofRegn 9 Feb 54, first flt 22 Apr 54. Accepted by Qantas at Burbank 25 Apr 54. E-27610 dated 26 Apr 54, del Burbank-Honolulu-Nadi-Sydney 26-28 Apr 54. Flew training flts 28 Apr 54 after arrival & courtesy flts 11 May 54. In svce 13 May 54 (to Vancouver). Flew to Melbourne-Essendon 30 Jul 54 for courtesy flts. Made first Qantas flight with Super Constellation Sydney-London 2-8 Aug 54 (late arrival due cylinder change Singapore, fire in engine no.2 Calcutta, turbine change Karachi), ret Super Constellation inaugural London-Sydney, dep 9 Aug (three days late), arr Sydney 13 Aug 54. Dep Sydney for Tokyo 2 Jun 55, but ret after 10 hrs with no.2 engine shut down. To 1049E/01-55 in Sep 56. No.3 propeller blades damaged when slid forward on engine test run-up London (Heathrow) and collided with CO_2 trolley 8 Dec 56, repaired. Flew Sydney-Hong Kong Super Constellation inaugural 6 Jan 57. Overhauled & radar nose fitted 21 Oct-17 Nov 57. Dep Sydney on last svce 14 Oct 59 (to London via Melbourne). Sold to Lockheed Aircraft Corp (trade-in on L-188 Electras) 3 Nov 59. VH-regn canx & regd N9716C 3 Nov 59 (TT: 15,581 hrs). Dep Sydney for Ontario, CA 4 Nov 59. Stored at Burbank, CA, then lsd to Twentieth Century Airlines Inc from early 1960, probably until Mar 61. Lsd Capitol Airways Mar 61, sold to them Dec 61. Withdrawn from svce by Aug 64 and stored at Wilmington, DE. Used for spares. Derelict by Aug 67 and scrapped shortly afterwards. Canx from USCAR 27 Dec 67.

4546 1049C-55-81 20 May 54 to Qantas as VH-EAI. CofRegn 9 Feb 54, first flt 14 May 54. Accepted by Qantas at Burbank 20 May 54 & christened 'Southern Melody' by MGM film-star Ann Miller (to promote world premiere of "Interrupted Melody" in Melbourne). E-27611 dated 20 May 54, del Burbank-Honolulu-Nadi-Sydney 22-24 May 54. Renamed 'Southern Sun' on dely 24 May 54. In svce 29 May 54 (to Vancouver). First Sydney-London svce 6-9 Sep 54, ret London-Sydney dep 10 Sep 54. To 1049E/01-55 30 Jun-24 Jul 56. Flew Royal Flight Sydney-Darwin-Momote with Duke of Edinburgh. Overhauled & radar nose fitted 25 Feb-30 Mar 57. Dep Sydney on last Super Constellation svce to San Francisco 7 Sep 59. Last svce (to Nadi) 4 Nov 59. Sold to Lockheed Aircraft Corp (trade-in on L-188 Electras) 30 Nov 59 (TT: 15,739 hrs). VH-regn canx & regd N9717C 1 Dec 59. Dep Sydney for Burbank 1 Dec 59. Stored at Burbank, CA, then lsd to Twentieth Century Airlines Inc from early 1960. 20th Century flew c1,300 hrs with the acft. Lsd back to Qantas & del Portland-Honolulu-Canton-Nadi-Sydney 25-28 Oct 60. Regd VH EAI again 1 Nov 60, named 'Southern Boomerang'. In svce again 16 Nov 60 (to Nadi). Sub-lsd to Tasman Empire Airways Ltd 20 Dec 60 until 1 Mar 61. Dep Sydney on last svce (again!) to Nadi 1 Mar 61. Ret to Lockheed 27 Mar 61, dep Sydney for Ontario 28 Mar 61. VH-regn canx & regd N9717C again 1 Apr 61 (officially restored 29 Jun 61). Lsd to Twentieth Century Airlines Inc again 5 Apr 61. Lsd Trans International 20 May 62. Sold to LANSA and allotted OB-R-742 29 Feb 64, painted up but never deld. Regn canx 9 Oct 64. Sold to West Coast Airmotive Corp 1964 (possibly prior LANSA sale?). Sold to American Flyers Airline Corp 18 Oct 64. Sold to California Airmotive Corp by Nov 68 and ferried to Fox Fld, Lancaster, CA for storage. Canx from USCAR 12 Jul 70. Scrapped there by May 71, fuselage only still extant by Nov 71.

4547 1049C-55-87 26 Apr 54 to Air-India International as VT-DGL (regd Feb 53). Named 'Empress Nurjehan', E-27612 dated 26 Apr 54, at London-Heathrow 7 May 54, on dely flight, deld to

India 6 Jun 54 (after fitting out of galley by KLM at Amsterdam). In svce 19 Jun 54 on Air-India Super Constellation Bombay-London First-class inaugural svce. To 1049E/01, and later named 'Rani of Jhansi'. Flew inaugural Air-India Super Constellation svce to Tokyo 10 Jan 57. Damaged 27 Nov 57. Repaired. Sold to Indian Air Force 2 Apr 62, serialled BG-581 (believed coded 'E') and used by No.6 Squadron. Canx from VT-register 12 Apr 62. Tfd to Indian Navy 18 Nov 76 as IN-318. Cvtd for maritime reconnaissance; completed and awaiting painting, at Bombay May 77. Withdrawn from use Nov 81 at Goa. Derelict by Jan 84, subsequently scrapped.

4548 1049C-55-87 18 Jun 54 to Air-India International as VT-DGM (regd Feb 53). Named 'Rani of Ind', E-27613 dated 17 Jun 54, deld to India 30 Jul 54 (after fitting out of galley by KLM at Amsterdam). In svce 10 Aug .54. Flew Air-India inaugural svce to Beirut & Zurich 4 Jul 55. To 1049E/01. Damaged while being towed to run-up bay on 27 Jan 56. Repaired. Received damage to port wing when hit by another aircraft at Nairobi, Kenya, on 3 Mar 56. Repaired. Damaged again on 30 Oct 57. Repaired. Flew Air-India inaugural svce to Bahrein & Kuwait 4 Oct 60. Sold to Indian Air Force 5 Apr 62, serialled BG-582 coded 'F' and used by No.6 Squadron. Canx from VT-register 19 Apr 62. Tfd to Indian Navy 18 Nov 76 as IN-319. Cvtd for maritime reconnaissance; completed and in svce by May 77. Withdrawn from use late 1982 at Goa. Derelict by Jan 84, subsequently scrapped.

4549 Originally ordered by Braathens SAFE as 1049E-55-89. Order canx. To 1049E-55-81 for Qantas. CofRegn 9 Feb 54, first flight 4 Jun 54, LADD: 26 Jun 54 as VH-EAJ 'Southern Star'. E-27617 dated 18 Jun 54, Del Burbank-Honolulu-Nadi-Sydney 2-5 Jul 54 (TT: 84hrs). In svce 24 Jul 54 (to Vancouver). Starboard fin damaged when hit by BOAC 749 G-ANUZ taxying Darwin, NT 12 Feb 56. Repaired. Overhauled & mod to 1049E/01-55 22 Jul-8 Aug 56, later to 1049E/01-82. Overhauled & radar nose fitted 6 Mar-7 Apr 57. Damaged when wingtip hit wingtip of 1049H VH-EAM taxying out at Sydney for flight to Hong Kong 16 Dec 57. Repaired with only 7 hrs delay to flight. Flew inaugural London-Sydney svce via Brisbane 5-9 Apr 58. Last svce with Qantas 26 Nov 59 Sydney-Port Moresby, withdrawn from svce on return. Overhauled 2 Dec 59 (TT: 15,607 hrs). Sold to Lockheed Aircraft Corp 2 Jan 60 (trade-in on L-188 Electras). Del ex-Sydney to Ontario, CA 5 Jan 60, VH-regn canx 8 Jan 60 after arrival & regd N9718C 13 Jan 60. Lsd to Twentieth Century Airlines Inc, then lsd to Capitol Airways 6 Feb 61, sold to Capitol 19 May 61. Used in 108-Seater configuration. Later named Capitol International Airways. Op for Berliner Flug Ring on European IT flights during the summers of 1966 and 1967. (TT: 22,976 hrs a/o 12 Jul 67, of which 579 hrs were by Capitol). Stored at Wilmington, DE by end of summer 1967. Flown to Sebring, FL for storage Mar or Apr 70 (TT: 23,554 hrs) and for sale at $25,000. Sold to California Airmotive Corp 5 Jul 72, but remained in storage at Sebring. Sold to Midair Inc 13 Apr 73 for conversion to sprayer and deld to Barstow, CA. Midair went bankrupt and conversion never undertaken. Stored at Barstow, derelict by Sep 75, being broken up. Still there Mar 77, partly broken up, but scrapped shortly after. Still regd to Midair in USCAR 1981. Canx from USCAR Apr 82.

4550 1049E-55-81, mod to 1049E-55-99 6 Jun 54 to Iberia as EC-AIN 'Santa Maria'. E-27616 dated 28 May 54. Christened at Idlewild, NY, on dely flight 23 Jun 54, regd Jul 54. Later updated to 1049G/02-82 (with tip-tanks) and given FN 201. Lsd to Aviaco for European IT flights during summers of 1963 & 1964, in 80-seater configuration. Fitted with rear cargo door by Air France at Toulouse mid-63 - first flight after conversion 23 Aug 63. Crashed on third attempt to land at Los Rodeos Airport, Tenerife, in fog at 21.17 hrs (local) on 5 May 65, killing six crew and 25 pax. Aircraft made missed approach at 21.06 hrs (local) after warning from tower that weather conditions were below minima (visibility 100-500m reducing to zero in bar of 6/8 cover stratus cloud 0-30m above ground). Pilot made a second approach as he could see the beginning of Runway 30. Aircraft entered cloud on second go-around, struck a bulldozer & tractor 50m from runway edge with one undercarriage leg & lower aft fuselage, then crashed on western edge of a diversion canal of the Rodeo Gorge at 21.17 (local), slid 100m across farmland & burst into flames, aircraft destroyed. Was on scheduled flight IB401 from Madrid. (TT: approx 25,000 hrs).

4551 1049E-55-81, mod to 1049E-55-99 30 Jun 54 to Iberia as EC-AIO 'Nina'. E-27619 dated 30 Jun 54, regd Jul 54, deld via Idlewild, NY 23 Jul 54. Later updated to 1049G/02-82 (with tip-tanks) and given FN 202. Lsd to Aviaco for European IT flights during summers of 1963-1965, in 80-seater configuration. Fitted with rear cargo door by Air France at Toulouse early 64 - first flight after conversion 17 May 64. Sold to International Aerodyne Inc in May 67 and regd N8023. Stored at Miami, FL until sold to Compania Interamericana Export-Import, believed in Mar 68 and transferred to RAPSA as HP-475. Canx from USCAR Mar/Apr 68. Ret to International Aerodyne Inc at Miami in full RAPSA titling 16 Aug 68. Lsd by Phoenix Group & flown to Lisbon in Sep 68. Used on the Biafra airlift by the Phoenix group, lsd to the Biafran government, for arms flights. Named 'Angel of Peace'. Flown to Abidjan, Ivory Coast, at end of Biafran war in Jan 70 and impounded there Mar 70. Stored at Abidjan until broken up there between 1 Jan & 12 Jan 71.

4552 1049E-55-81, mod to 1049E-55-99 21 Jul 54 to Iberia as EC-AIP 'Pinta'. E-27635 dated 21 Jul 54, regd Aug 54. Starboard undercarriage failed to lower, made belly landing on foam-covered runway at Kindley AFB, Bermuda, on 25 Sep 55, en route Havana, Cuba, to Madrid, Spain. Damaged, but no injuries. Received further damage on 26 Sep 55, while the aircraft was being lifted free of the runway. Repaired by LAS and renamed 'Santa Clara'. Updated to 1049G/02-82 (with tip-tanks) and given FN 203. Damaged at Barajas, Madrid, on 3 Oct 58. Repaired. Lost altitude on approach to Sao Paulo Airport, Brazil, struck wall at the end of the runway, tearing off part of the undercarriage, rest of undercarriage collapsed on touchdown and aircraft skidded off the runway, crashed into a concrete barricade, caught fire and burnt out at 13.37 hrs (local) 6 Mar 61. No casualties. Aircraft was en route Madrid to Buenos Aires.

4553 1049E-55-81, mod to 1049E-55-108 25 May 54 to KLM as PH-LKA 'Isotoop'. (Regn PH-TFZ reserved only, but ntu). E-27614 and regn date both 25 May 54, KLM dely date 26 May 54. Updating to 1049G/02-82 (with tip-tanks) completed 16 Mar 56, type changed 20 Jun 56. Lsd to Air Ceylon 1 Nov 58 and named 'Somadevi'. In svce 12 Nov 58. Reregd 4R-ACH 29 Nov 58 (regd to KLM still, with note 'Op by Air Ceylon'). PH-regn canx 27 Nov 58. Ret to KLM 1 Nov 60 and restored as PH-LKA 15 Nov 60. Lsd to Iberia and regd EC-AQL 'La Confiada' from 1 Apr 61 to 28 May 62. PH-regn canx 4 Apr 61. Restored as PH-LKA 7 Jun 62 after ret to KLM on 28 May 62. In svce in Iberia colours, but KLM titles. Lsd Iberia again 26 Jun-22 Jul 62. Ret to KLM & op repatriation shuttle flights 7 Aug 62 onwards. Last scheduled svce 18 Aug 62. Withdrawn from svce 9 Dec 62 and stored at Schiphol Airport, Amsterdam, in cocooning. Taken out of cocooning and used for spares from mid-1963 until canx as broken up 22 Jul 64. PH-regn canx 25 Jun 64.

4554 1049E-55-92 Regd HK-175X to Lockheed Aircraft Corp for tests. LADD: 24 Aug 54 to AVIANCA as HK-175. E-27641 dated 23 Aug 54. Believed updated to 1049G/02-82. Tfd to Aerotaxi 1968, and withdrawn from use at Bogota same year. Believed broken up by Feb 69. Canx from HK-register by 1969.

4555 1049E-55-92 Regd HK-176X to Lockheed Aircraft Corp for tests. LADD: 10 Sep 54 to AVIANCA as HK-176. E-27643 dated 8 Sep 54. Believed updated to 1049G/02-82. Lsd to Aerotaxi in 1966 and used in 84-seater configuration for domestic Tourist-class services. Ret to AVIANCA by 1968, and withdrawn from svce late 1968 at Bogota. Stored at Bogota in Feb 69 and reportedly donated to a children's playground at Bogota shortly afterwards. Subsequently scrapped.

4556 1049E-55-92 Regd HK-177X to Lockheed Aircraft Corp for tests. LADD: 29 Sep 54 to AVIANCA as HK-177. E-27646 dated 28 Sep 54. Believed updated to 1049G/02-82. Crashed landing at Montego Bay Airport, Jamaica at 02.24 hrs (local) on 21 Jan 60. Nine survived from the 46 crew & pax on board. The aircraft had left Idlewild, NY at 10.35 hrs the previous day on Flight AV671 to Bogota, Colombia. A non-scheduled landing had been made at Miami, FL after no.3 engine was feathered 30 mins beyond Wilmington, NC and the aircraft had been at Miami for 6 hrs and 33 mins for rectification of no.3 engine and a defect in no.2 engine. Weather at Jamaica was overcast with intermittent rain. The approach was too high, so a very high rate of descent (1,200 ft/min) used, resulting in a heavy landing causing major structural damage. The aircraft bounced back into the air, then re-alighted on the runway, with the left wing breaking away from the fuselage causing fire to break out as no.2 fuel tank was ruptured. The undercarriage subsequently collapsed, and the fuselage finally came to rest 1,900 ft from the runway threshold, 200 ft to the left of the centreline on a heading of 130 degrees to the runway and completely inverted with fires burning almost all around it. Cause: Pilot error, probably the result of fatigue and nervous strain.

4557 Originally ordered by Braathens SAFE as 1049E-55-89, but canx. To 1049E-55-93, reserved for Jorge Pasquel, but mod to 1049E-55-115 & sold prior delivery to Cubana. LADD: 8 Nov 54 to Cubana as CU-P573, E-27648 dated 2 Nov 54. Sold to International Aviation Corp 28 Mar 56, lsd to Seaboard & Western Airlines Mar 56 and regd N1005C 'Geneva Airtrader'. Sub-lsd to BOAC 1 Apr-30 Apr 56, in svce New York-Bermuda 2 Apr 56, last svce New York-Bermuda-New York 29-30 Apr 56. Cvtd to 1049E/01-82 and in svce by Jul 56. Sub-lsd to Eastern Air Lines Jan 57-Jun 57. Sub-lsd to Aerlinte Eireann May 58 in 95-seater Economy-class configuration, named 'Brigid', arr Dublin 2 Jun 58. Sold to Seaboard & Western Airlines 31 Oct 60. Lse to Aerlinte continued. Last svce with Aerlinte/Irish Air Lines 22 Dec 60. Ret Seaboard & Western Airlines & flew for some time after in ex-Aerlinte colours, no titling. S&W renamed Seaboard World Airlines Apr 61, regd 11 May 61, but titling never carried. Lsd to TAP as CS-TLH Dec 61 until approx Apr 62, ret SWA as N1005C by 23 Apr 62. Sold to Canadair Ltd (trade-in on Canadair CL-44s) in 1962, and immediately lsd back. Sub-lsd to Intercontinental US Inc by Jun 62. Reported damaged in the Congo 30 Dec 62. Repaired. Painted in Transtate Airlines colours at Idlewild, NY Oct 63 as 84-seater for planned domestic scheduled services, but permission refused. Stored at Idlewild until ret to Seaboard World Airlines Jan 64. Lsd to Capitol Airways Inc 1 Jun 65, sold to them 6 May 66, regd 8 Jun 66 as 1049E/01-55. Withdrawn from svce and stored at Wilmington, DE by mid-67. To Capitol Intl Airways Inc 4 Aug 67. Sold to J Flannery 20 Aug 67. Dismantled and transported to Penndel, PA for use as restaurant. Mounted on top of restaurant in ex-Capitol colours, completed Aug 68. "Jim Flannery's" later painted on the blue cheat line and "Spirit of 76" insignia added in 1976. Sold to Margaret Loeffler 4 Nov 81, still as restaurant trading under name "Amelia's", manageress Mrs Virginia Giles. Repainted in brown & pink scheme, interior refurbished with much of cockpit instrumentation intact. Restaurant closed 1986 after building underneath was in danger of collapsing. Sold again in 1991 to Ghassan & Karen Dabbour, re-opened in Jan 92 as "The Airplane Family Restaurant & Diner" & used especially for children's parties. Closed again in 1997 to make way for an AMOCO gas station & convenience store. Dismantled Jul-Oct 97, with main dismantling taking place 14 Jul 97 in front of TV companies. AMOCO Oil Co donated aircraft to the USAF Air Mobility Command Museum at Dover, DE 10 Sep 97. Transported to Dover AFB for AMC Museum (120 mls away) Oct 97 by A&A Machinery Co of Tullytown, PA. To be used as static exhibit in USAF C-121C markings & as classroom for schoolparties. By Jan 03 fuselage interior was stripped in preparation for restoration & by Jul 03 was standing on undercarriage again with wings and tail unit fitted, in overall grey scheme. Restoration still in progress Jan 06.

4558 1049E-55-90, mod to 1049E-55-107 11 Aug 54 to KLM as PH-LKB 'Positon', (presumably a mis-painting of 'Positron'). (Regn PH-TGK reserved only, but ntu). E-27640 12 Aug 54 and also KLM dely date. Regd 11 Aug 54. Flew inaugural svce Amsterdam-Zurich-Kano-Johannesburg 7 Oct 54. Updating to 1049G/02-82 (with tip-tanks) completed 17 Apr 56, type changed 20 Jun 56. Lsd briefly to Air Ceylon Apr 58. Op KLM's last scheduled Super Constellation svce Amsterdam-Prestwick, Scotland-Amsterdam 25 Aug 62. Withdrawn from svce 10 Nov 62 and stored at Amsterdam (Schiphol) in cocooning. Taken out of cocooning and used for spares from mid-63 until canx as broken up 22 Jul 64. PH-regn canx 4 Aug 64.

4559 1049E-55-90, mod to 1049E-55-107 23 Sep 54 to KLM as PH-LKC 'Negaton'. (Regn PH-TGL reserved only, but ntu). E-27644 and regn date 23 Sep 54, KLM dely date 24 Sep 54. Updating to 1049G/02-82 (with tip-tanks) completed 17 May 56, type changed 20 Jun 56. Flew last revenue svce 10 Nov 61. Used for instructional flights 11 Nov 61-2 Apr 62. Withdrawn from svce 4 Apr 62 and stored at Schiphol Airport, Amsterdam. (TT: 21,969 hrs a/o 22 Aug 62). Canx as broken up 22 Jul 64. PH-regn canx 25 Jun 64.

4560 1049E-55-90, mod to 1049E-55-107 21 Oct 54 to KLM as PH-LKD 'Ion'. (Regn PH-TGM reserved only, but ntu). E-27645 dated 24 Sep 54. Regd 21 Oct 54 and KLM dely date 22 Oct 54. Updating to 1049G/02-82 (with tip-tanks) completed 17 Jun 56, type changed 20 Jun 56. Lsd briefly to Air Ceylon Dec 59. Withdrawn from svce 1 Sep 61 and stored at Schiphol Airport, Amsterdam, until canx as broken up 25 Jun 63. PH-regn canx 24 Jun 63.

4561 1049E-55-81 23 Oct 54 to LAV as YV-C-AMS 'Rafael Urdaneta'. Originally allocated YV-C-AMR but reregd pre-dely (E-27647 dated 22 Oct 54). Mod to 1049E/01-55. Crashed into the Atlantic Ocean approx 40 miles south of New York City off Asbury Park, NJ at approx 01.32 hrs (EDT) on 20 Jun 56, killing all on board. The aircraft had left Idlewild, NY at 23.18 hrs (19 Jun) en route for Caracas. Approx 1 hour and six mins after take-off the propeller on no.2 engine started over-speeding and could not be feathered. The aircraft turned back to New York at 00.46 hrs and when 50 miles from there, permission was received to start dumping fuel in order to bring the aircraft's weight down to the maximum permissible for landing. A few seconds after this, the fuel being dumped ignited, the port wing exploded and the aircraft dived out of control from 8,500 ft into the sea. Probable cause: Failure of the no.2 propeller coupled with the vibration from the faulty propeller causing one of the inside wing attachments to loosen or break between the fuel tank and the fuel dump chute; possibly also non-maintenance of the fuel-dump system.

4562 1049E-55-81 11 Nov 54 to LAV as YV-C-AMT 'Simon Bolivar'. E-27649 same day. Mod to 1049E/01-55. Badly damaged when the undercarriage failed landing at Maiquetia Airport, Caracas, Venezuela on 11 May 57. Rebuilt, cvtd to 1049G/02-82 and reregd YV-C-ANF in Jun 58. Op for VIASA during 1961 (last report Idlewild Dec 61). Sold to California Airmotive Corp end 1961 and regd N58921 (believed never carried). Ferried to Fox Fld, Lancaster, CA for storage, still carrying YV-C-ANF. Derelict there by Aug 66, still in full LAV old colours with Venezuelan regn, and scrapped some time afterwards.

YV-C-ANF 1049G of LAV was photographed on arrival at California Airmotive's Fox Field, Lancaster, storage area in 1962 or 1963. (For an aerial view, see Section 1.29) (PJM collection)

Section 12: Constellation Production List

4563 1049E-55-94, mod to 1049E-55-109 23 Jun 64 to Trans-Canada Air Lines as CF-TGF, FN 406. E-27618 and TCA dely date both 22 Jun 54. Mod to 1049G/02-82 (tip-tanks fitted) by Dec 57. Radar nose fitted winter 1958/59. Inaugurated TCA svce to Vienna 1 May 59. Withdrawn from svce with TCA (TT: 20,131 hrs) and sold to California Airmotive Corp 1 May 62, and regd N9742Z. Lsd Capitol Airways by Jul 62. In storage at Burbank, CA end Sep 62. Lsd Standard Airways 26 Oct 62, sold to them 26 Jan 64. Ret to California Airmotive Corp and sold to American Flyers Airline Corp 8 Apr 64 (9 Apr also quoted). Damaged on landing at Des Moines, IA on 8 Mar 65 when the aircraft skidded on the icy runway, yawed and struck a snow bank. (TT: 22,498 hrs). Repaired. Sold to California Airmotive Corp 1968 and ferried to Fox Fld, Lancaster, CA for storage by Sep 68. Scrapped there by 1970 and canx from USCAR 12 Jul 70.

4564 1049E-55-94, mod to 1049E-55-109 20 Jul 54 to Trans-Canada Air Lines as CF-TGG, FN 407. E-27636 dated 16 Jul 54. Crashed while circling for ILS approach at Malton Airport, Toronto, Canada in fog and rain at 21.32 hrs on 17 Dec 54. En route Tampa, FL to Toronto. Engine caught fire, the aircraft hit the ground 12 mls short of the runway end and 3 mls NW of Brampton,Ont, bounced, tore through a clump of trees and slithered to a stop in a field and caught fire after fuel ignited. No casualties. (TT: 763 hrs). Cause: Pilot negligence in descending below minimum altitude for an approach to the airport while flying on instruments, probably also crew fatigue; aircraft was dead in line with the runway at the time of the crash, but ADF needles and altimeters must have been ignored.

4565 1049E-55-94, mod to 1049E-55-109 31 Aug 54 to Trans-Canada Air Lines as CF-TGH, FN 408. E-27642 dated 31 Aug 54. Radar nose fitted early 1958. Mod to 1049G/02-82 (tip-tanks fitted) in 1958. Sold to Douglas Aircraft Corp 10 Feb 62 (trade-in for DC-8s) and ferried to Las Vegas, NV for storage. Regd N9639Z. Sold to California Airmotive Corp by Jan 64 and to American Flyers Airline Corp on 31 Jul 64. Sold back to California Airmotive Corp 1968 and ferried to Fox Fld, Lancaster, CA for storage. Canx from USCAR 12 Jul 70. Last reported stored, derelict, in May 71, subsequently scrapped.

4566 1049C-55-83 for Eastern Air Lines. Order canx. Not built.

4567 1049C-55-83 for Eastern Air Lines. Order canx. Not built.

4568 1049C-55-83 for Eastern Air Lines. Order canx. Not built.

4569 1049C-55-83 for Eastern Air Lines. Order.canx. Not built.

4570 1049C-55-83 for Eastern Air Lines. Order canx. Not built.

4571 1049C-55-83 for Eastern Air Lines. Order canx. Not built.

4572 1049E-55-102, but updated to become the first 1049G "Super G" on the production line. Rolled off the assembly line in Nov 54 as 1049G-82-102 for Northwest Orient Airlines as N5172V. First commercial airliner to be fitted with wing-tip fuel tanks. First flight 12 Dec 54. Remained at Burbank, CA for tests with LAC. Originally to be named 'Hawaiian Express', but dely unnamed. LADD: 19 Apr 55, in svce 26 Apr 55. Stored at Minneapolis, MN Jul 57. Sold to LAV as YV-C-ANB 31 Aug 57, E-22756 dated 4 Sep 57. Withdrawn from svce by Dec 60 and stored at LAS, Idlewild, NY. Sold to International Aircraft Services in Oct 62 and to California Airmotive Corp shortly afterwards. Regd N9747Z for ferry flight to Burbank, but believed never carried. Stored at Burbank until Jul 63. Stored at Fox Fld, Lancaster, CA by Aug 63, still in full later LAV colour-scheme with Venezuelan regn. Derelict by Aug 66 and scrapped there shortly afterwards.

4573 Laid down on production line as 1049E-55 for Northwest Orient Airlines, but released to Qantas Empire Airways. Completed as 1049E-55-118 for Qantas. Cof Regn 24 Sep 54 as VH-EAK. Originally to be named 'Southern Moon' (on production line 3 Nov 54), but renamed 'Southern Mist' by 14 Jan 55. First flight 4 Jan 55, LADD: 12 Jan 55 & E-27659 11 Jan 55. Del Burbank-Honolulu-Nadi-Sydney 15-17 Jan 55. In svce 2 Feb 55 (to San Francisco). Updated to 1049E/01-55 in 1956. Overhauled & radar nose fitted 4 Apr-5 May 57. Flew Sydney-Port Moresby 20 Jan 59 on courtesy flt, first Super Constellation to land there. Lsd to Malayan Airways in Mar 60. Op first Malayan Airways svce Hong Kong-Singapore-Djakarta on 6 Mar 60. Flew inaugural Super Constellation svce Sydney-Noumea 18 Mar 60. Op special charter 25 Aug 60 ex-Sydney to fetch pax from crashed VH-EAC at Mauritius. Lsd to Tasman Empire Airways Ltd 23 Dec 60 until Mar 61. Based Perth 10 Jun-26 Jul 61. (TT: 20,499 hrs a/o 1 Jan 63). Flew last svce 15 Jan 63 ex-Sydney on migrant charter. Sold to Boeing Aircraft Co (trade-in on Boeing 707s) 2 Feb 63 & VH-regn canx same day. Possibly reregd N93163 or N9712C (although FAA records do not show any N-regn for this aircraft) for dely Sydney-Nadi-Honolulu-San Jose-San Francisco-Burbank (arr 4 Feb 63), (TT: 20,680 hrs). Sold to Airmotive Inc. Used for spares at Burbank, CA in 1963. Stored near Burbank in a parking lot, minus outer wings, tail, etc by Dec 64, awaiting scrapping. Still there late 69, but disappeared shortly afterwards, presumably scrapped. (California Airmotive canx Super Constellation "N9712C" from USCAR 12 Jul 70).

4574 Laid down on production line as 1049E-55 for Northwest Orient Airlines, but released to Qantas Empire Airways. Completed as 1049E-55-118 for Qantas. CofRegn 24 Sep 54 as VH-EAL. Originally to be named 'Southern Mist', but renamed 'Southern Breeze'by 26 Jan 55 (acceptance date). First flight 22 Jan 55, LADD: 27 Jan 55 & E-27661 dated 27 Jan 55. Del Burbank-Honolulu-Nadi-Sydney 29-31 Jan 55. First svce 16 Feb 55 (to London). Updated to 1049E/01-55 in 1956. Overhauled & radar nose fitted 17 Apr 57 onwards. Last svce with Qantas 15 Oct 59 ex-Sydney to Port Moresby. Sold to Lockheed Aircraft Corp 9 Nov 59 (trade-in on L-188 Electras) & VH-regn canx 10 Nov 59 (TT: 13,990 hrs). Re-regd N9719C. Del Sydney 11 Nov 59 to Ontario, CA. Stored at Burbank, CA then lsd to Twentieth Century Airlines Inc from unknown date. Lsd Trans International Airlines 1 Jun 62. Sold to LANSA and allotted OB-R-741 29 Feb 64. Painted up and prepared for dely at Long Beach, CA by Apr 64, but never deld. N-regn canx 3 Aug 64. OB-regn canx 9 Oct 64. Ret to N9719C, but not restored officially until 15 Oct 68! Sold to West Coast Airmotive Corp 1964 (possibly prior LANSA sale?) & to California Airmotive Corp 1964 who sold to American Flyers Airline Corp 31 Oct 64. Received substantial damage landing at Ardmore, OK at 00.40 hrs (local) 20 Sep 65. After a three-engined ferry flight, the aircraft overshot the runway during the landing at Ardmore in rain and collided with ditches. Cause: Captain made a poorly-planned approach, failed to use flaps and unable to use reverse thrust on touchdown. Aircraft hydroplaned on the wet runway. Aircraft declared a total loss and believed used for spares at Ardmore after the accident. Aircraft last reported there in Aug 66 out of svce. Presumably scrapped there subsequently. Canx from USCAR 13 Jan 72.

4575 1049E-55-102, mod to 1049G-82-102 22 Jan 55 to Northwest Orient Airlines as N5173V (fitted with tip-tanks), in svce 6 Mar 55. Sold to LAV 31 Aug 57 and regd YV-C-ANC after storage at Minncapolis, MN since Jul 57. E-22758 dated 15 Sep 57. Crashed into the Alto del Cedro Mountain, in the Sierra de Perija, 48 nmls northwest of Maracaibo, just after 00.22 hrs (local) on 14 Oct 58, killing all on board. The aircraft was flying from Panama and was on the approach route from Riohacha, Colombia to Maracaibo, Venezuela along the Colombia-Venezuela border. It had struck very high tree-tops on the high hills of the Sierra de Perija at a height of approx 1,800ft, with the final impact against the rocky wall of a ravine at a height of 1,500ft. Cause: The premature descent caused by the pilot's failure to allow a suitable margin for an altered flight course, coupled with the shortage of navigational aids in the area.

4576 1049E-55-102, mod to 1049G-82-102 31 Jan 55 to Northwest Orient Airlines as N5174V (fitted with tip-tanks), in svce 2 Mar 55. Stored at Minneapolis, MN by Jul 57. Sold to LAV 31 Aug 57 and regd YV-C-AND. E-22757 dated 9 Sep 57. Withdrawn from svce and stored at LAS Idlewild, NY by Dec 60.

ENGINE INSTALLED IN AIRCRAFT—Type 1049 G   VH- EAE   Position #2

(1) HOURS BROUGHT FORWARD	Time Since New—Hours 7005 Mins.
	Time Since Last Complete Overhaul—Hours 538 Mins. 49

Date	Time in Air (2) Hrs.	Min.	(3) *Enter full details of Inspections, Minor Repairs and Maintenance Release Certificates issued hereunder
3/8/60	7	08	From Sydney to Nadi
3/8/60	5	02	" Nadi to Canton Island
3/8/60	7	12	" Canton Island to Honolulu
3/10/60	8	48	" Honolulu to Los Angeles LAX
3/10/60		26	" LAX to Ontario California
	28	36	
			Periodic aircraft inspection accomplished 2/25/60 by G Merta A/E 12423
			Last FAA AD note accomplished was AD 59-12-2 G Merta A/E 12423
Page Total	557	25	

*A signature under or in line with the entry in this page will be taken as a certification that the entry is correct

C/n 4578. A source for extra details on a particular aircraft can often be from a pilot's or flight engineer's log-book, but also, as here, from the Engine Log for Wright Turbo Compound TC18-DA series number 700114. The details given are for the Qantas 1049G VH-EAE's ferry flight to the USA on sale to become N9720C. This engine ended its days in "Corrosion Corner" at Miami International, Florida.

Sold to International Aircraft Services in Oct 62 and to California Airmotive Corp shortly afterwards. Regd N9745Z for ferry flight to Burbank, but believed never carried. Stored at Burbank until Jul 63. Stored at Fox Fld, Lancaster, CA by Aug 63, still in full old LAV colours with Venezuelan regn. Derelict by Aug 66 and scrapped there shortly afterwards.

4577 1049E-55-102, mod to 1049G-82-102 12 Feb 55 to Northwest Orient Airlines as N5175V (fitted with tip-tanks), in svce 15 Feb 55. Stored at Minneapolis, MN by Jul 57. Sold to LAV 31 Aug 57 and regd YV-C-ANE. E-22759 dated 19 Sep 57. Withdrawn from svce and stored at LAS, Idlewild, NY by Dec 60. Sold to International Aircraft Services in Oct 62 and to California Airmotive Corp shortly afterwards. Regd N9748Z for ferry flight to Burbank, but believed never carried. Stored at Burbank until Jul 63. Stored at Fox Fld, Lancaster, CA by Aug 63, still in full old LAV colours with Venezuelan regn. Scrapped there by 1966.

4578 1049E-55-81, mod to 1049E-55-118 6 Feb 55 to Qantas. Originally allotted VH-EAM 'Southern Sea'. CofRegn as VH-EAE 24 Sep 54, named 'Southern Moon'. First flight 1 Feb 55, E-27662 dated 4 Feb 55. Del Burbank-Honolulu-Nadi-Sydney 6-8 Feb 55. First svce 26 Feb 55 (to London). Updated to 1049E/01-55 in 1956. Overhauled & mod to 1049G/02-82 with radar nose & tip-tanks 8 Feb-21 Mar 58. Flew Royal flight Canberra-Bangkok with Princess Alexandra 25 Sep 59. Last svce 9 Feb 60 Sydney-Nadi. Sold to Lockheed Aircraft Corp 2 Mar 60 (trade-in on L-188 Electras) & VH-regn canx. (TT: 14,744 hrs). Re-regd N9720C. Del Sydney-Nadi-Canton Is-Honolulu-Los Angeles-Ontario 8-10 Mar 60. Lsd to Capitol Airways at least from Jul-Aug 60, and again from May 61. Used as 108-seater. Sold to Capitol Airways in Dec 61, later named Capitol International Airways. Op for Berliner Flug Ring on European IT flights during the summers of 1966 and 1967. Withdrawn from svce and stored at Wilmington, DE by mid-1968. Last reported there Jul 69, presumably scrapped there in 1970. Canx from USCAR 24 Jun 70.

4579 1049E-55-118 19 Feb 55 to Qantas. Originally allotted VH-EAN 'Southern Horizon'. CofRegn as VH-EAF 24 Sep 54, named 'Southern Wind'. First flight 12 Feb 55, E-27664 dated 18 Feb 55. Del Burbank-Honolulu-Canton Is-Nadi-Sydney 20-23 Feb 55. First svce 5 Mar 55 (to London). Flew Sydney-Auckland, NZ 2 Oct 55 for courtesy flights, six in Auckland, three in Wellington & six in Christchurch, ret Sydney 8 Oct 55. Updated to 1049E/01-55 in 1956. Flew Sydney-Hong Kong inaugural 6 Jan 57. Overhauled & radar nose fitted 3 May-4 Jul 57. Lsd to Tasman Empire Airways Ltd Jan 61-Mar 61. Flew last svce 13-16 Apr 63 Sydney-Johannesburg. Sold to Boeing Aircraft Co (trade-in on Boeing 707s) 23 Apr 63. Del Sydney-Nadi-Honolulu-San Francisco-Burbank 23-25 Apr 63. (TT on arrival: 20,705 hrs). VH-regn canx 25 Apr 63. Sold to Airmotive Inc. Used for spares at Burbank, CA in 1963. Stored near Burbank in a parking lot, minus outer wings and tail, awaiting scrapping, Dec 64. Presumably scrapped shortly afterwards.

Section 12: Constellation Production List

CF-PXX 1049G Freighter, but in passenger charter use with the Canadian airline World Wide Airways. The aircraft is seen in the original colour-scheme with the full titles and a green arrow at Amsterdam (Schiphol) on 19th December 1964. (Stephen Piercey collection)

4580 1049E-55-81, mod to 1049E/01-82-119 28 Feb55 to Qantas. Originally allotted VH-EAO 'Southern Mist'. CofRegn as VH-EAA 24 Feb 55, named 'Southern Sea'. First flight 22 Feb 55, E-27666 dated 28 Feb 55. Del Burbank-Honolulu-Canton Is-Sydney 1-4 Mar 55. First svce 22 Mar 55 (to San Francisco). Flew inaugural Sydney-Johannesburg with Super Constellation 5 Nov 55. Fitted with radar nose 16 Jun-13 Jul 57. Updated to 1049G/02-82 & fitted with tip-tanks 8-24 Jan 58. Op Royal Flight Christchurch-Colombo 14 Feb 58, also Royal Flight with Queen Mother Adelaide-London via Cocos Islands & Johannesburg, del 5 Mar 58, but extensive delay at Mauritius with engine trouble. Flew inaugural Super Constellation svce to Port Moresby 23 Jan 59. Flew Sydney-Ontario, CA 29-31 Jan 60 for fitting with rear cargo door by LAS, for use as cargo aircraft or convertible. Del Ontario-Sydney after conversion 29 Mar-4 Apr 60. Withdrawn from svce Apr 61. Test-flown 21 Dec 61 & re-entered svce. Flew last svce 15 Dec 62 ex-Sydney to London via Hong Kong. Sold to Lockheed Aircraft Corp 22 Jan 63 (presumably as trade-in on L-188 Electras) & VH-regn canx. Reregd N9714C & dep Sydney for Burbank 23 Jan 63 (TT: 17,709 hrs). Sold to Eagle Aircraft Inc Jan 63. Sold to D M McVicar/World-Wide Airways Inc on lease-purchase 16 Mar 64, E-46958 (17 Mar 64), with TT:17,710 hrs, regd CF-PXX 20 Mar 64. Del Long Beach, CA-Toronto 21 Mar 64 in svce late Mar 64 on cattle flights to Cuba. N-regn canx 25 Mar 64. Cvtd from cargo to pax 17 Dec 64 and in svce as pax acft Dec 64. Repossessed by Eagle Aircraft Inc 13 Aug 65, but "escaped" briefly to Buffalo, NY early in the morning of the day World-Wide ceased ops on 15 Aug 65. Eagle Aircraft Inc merged with International Aerodyne Aug 65. Canx from C-register 17 Sep 65 and restored as N9714C 23 Sep 65. Sold to International Aerodyne Inc May 66. Lsd to Cincinnati Symphony orchestra for world tour Aug-Nov 66. Lsd to Aerotransportes Entre Rios Apr 67. Regd LV-IXZ 12 Apr 67, but aircraft still flying as N9714C for AER on charter to London-Gatwick 14 Apr 67. N-regn canx 4 May 67. Withdrawn from use at Buenos Aires-Ezeiza by Apr 70. Stored there for some time and scrapped there at unknown date.

4581 1049E-55-81, mod to 1049E/01-82-119 4 Mar 55 to Qantas. Originally allotted VH-EAP 'Southern Breeze'. CofRegn as VH-EAB 24 Feb 55, named 'Southern Horizon'. First flight 26 Feb 55, E-27667 dated 4 Mar 55. Del Burbank-Honolulu-Canton Is-Nadi-Sydney 5-8 Mar 55. First svce 2 Apr 55 (to Vancouver). Flew to Paya Lebar, Singapore 20 Aug 55 for opening of new airport. Departed Athens, Greece 3 Nov 56 carrying the Olympic Flame for the Melbourne Games, arr Darwin 5 Nov 56. Overhauled & radar nose fitted 15 Jul-11 Aug 57. Updated to 1049G/02-82 & fitted with tip-tanks 23 Jan-6 Feb 58. Flew inaugural svce Brisbane to London 3-5 Apr 58. Stripped 26 May 60 for conversion to freighter. Flew Sydney-Ontario, CA 3 Jun 60 for fitting with rear cargo door by LAS, for use as cargo aircraft or convertible. Del Ontario-Portland, OR-Sydney after conversion 16-21 Aug 60. First svce as freighter dep Sydney 13 Sep 60 for London. Last svce dep Sydney for London 19 Jun 61, wfs after return. Test flown 26 Aug 61, then flew replacement engine Sydney-Hong Kong for VH-EAO. Wfs again & used by Qantas as static classroom, minus engines, at Sydney, during 1962. Re-entered svce, last svce for Qantas dep Sydney 24 Mar 63 on horse-charter to Christchurch, NZ-Nadi-Honolulu-San Francisco. Flew to Burbank 25 Mar 63. Sold to Boeing Aircraft Co (trade-in on Boeing 707s) 27 Mar 63, VH-regn canx same day (TT: 18,070 hrs). Sold to Airmotive Inc & regd N9715C 27 Mar 63. Lsd briefly to Flying Tiger Line. Sold to West Coast Airmotive Corp Inc 5 Aug 64 (FAA records say by Qantas), with TT now 18,104 hrs. N9715C canx 14 Aug 64. Reregd N93164 to West Coast Airmotive Corp on 31 Jul 64, tfd to California Airmotive Corp shortly afterwards. At Miami, FL with no titling Sep-Oct 65. Lsd to Galaxy Trading Corp and named 'San Patricio' (at Lima Apr 66). Ret to California Airmotive Corp and reregd N4192A 7 Sep 66 (N93164 not canx until 28 Sep 66). Sold to Lee J Matherne 27 Feb 68 and flew to Lisbon, Portugal, 17 Mar 68 as ZP-TBV (unofficial regn) in 'Transcontinental Airlines SA' titling (fictitious company) and Panamanian flag, for attempted use on Biafran airlift. Ret to Miami by 13 Jun 68 and stored there in Transcontinental titling but no regn. Reregd N442LM 23 Aug 68 and painted up in Wings Inc titling. Lsd to Bolivian Airways-TABSA as N442LM during the early part of 1969. For sale in Sep 69 by Atlantic Airways and stored at Opa Locka, FL. Sold to Lance W Dreyer 15 Dec 69 and reregd N11SR 24 Sep 70 on ret to Miami from flights in Europe. Tfd to Transnational Cargo Inc 15 Oct 70 and to Unum Inc 30 Jul 71 (both Dreyer companies). Stored at Port of Spain, Trinidad, for some time up to at least Feb 73. Reported sale to a Brazilian company fell through. Sold to Trans Global Leasing Inc 26 Oct 73 and ferried to Fort Lauderdale, FL for overhaul and repaint. Sold to PM Leasing Inc 11 Oct 74 (Duncan Baker) and named 'Janet' (after Duncan Baker's wife) by Mar 75. Lsd to Lanzair (CI) Ltd from 28 Mar 75 and op in Europe. PM Leasing flew acft from Miami to London, England, during 1975. No.2 engine ran away just after take-off from Shannon, Ireland, on 15 Nov 75. Emergency landing made at Shannon. Repaired. Impounded at Casablanca, Morocco, Feb 76 with cargo of arms for Angola. Released and ret to Shannon 29 Mar 76. Arrived Kuwait on last flight 18 Jun 76 from Athens with cargo of pre-fabricated fiberglass buildings. Reportedly nose-wheel tyres broke up on take-off from Athens, landed 9.5 hrs later at Kuwait in sandstorm. Because of alleged irregularities with the acft's clearance, the aircraft was impounded & a large fine was imposed on Lanzair. Lanzair was unable to pay or otherwise secure the acft's release. Note in FAA file states 'Violations throughout Europe and Middle East'. Aircraft subsequently abandoned at Kuwait International Airport and stored there, near Kuwaiti Air Force base until approx Nov 80, when the aircraft was towed to the edge of the airfield, abandoned. In Jul 81, a Kuwait Airways Engineer inspected N11SR with a view to preserving the aircraft with Qantas in Australia, but reported the acft could not possibly be made airworthy again. Still stored with engines missing in Dec 81. Canx from USCAR Apr 82. Auctioned by Director of Civil Aviation, Kuwait on 2 May 82. The only registered bidders were Ron Cuskelly (on behalf of Qantas) & Stephen Piercey (Editor of "Propliner" magazine on behalf of Aces High). Reserve price was 12,000 Kuwaiti dinars (to pay for landing fees, etc). Reported buyer (for approx £24,000) was a Kuwaiti who wanted to convert it into a beach-hut/cafe. Presumably this idea was abandoned & sold to Kuwaiti Ministry of Defence Jun 83 for training purposes. Used for firefighting drills at the military base, in derelict condition, until most of aircraft destroyed by bombing in the Gulf War in 1991. Remains still extant Jan 06.

"ZP-TBV" 1049G Freighter of the fictitious Transcontinental Airlines SA and with a Panamanian flag on the nose. The aircraft was photographed at Miami International in March 1968 prior to appearing on the Biafran airlift at Lisbon. (K Folkersma)

N7102C 1049G – the beginning: a publicity shot of Trans World's flagship "Super G" named "The United States" which was used for a European tour in April 1955. (Trans World Airlines via Louis Barr)

4582 Laid down on production line as 1049E-55 for VARIG as PP-VDA. Dely delayed for later model. To 1049G-82-110 for Trans World Airlines as N7101C, FN 101, 'Star of Balmoral'. Remained with LAC for development flying and deld to TWA 19 Sep 55 (TT: 176 hrs 54 mins), in svce 21 Sep 55 (domestic network). Fitted with tip-tanks. Damaged beyond repair when drag-strut failed and starboard main undercarriage collapsed rearward while taxying for take-off over very rough packed snow at Chicago-Midway Airport, IL at 11.59 hrs (CST) on 29 Feb 60. Aircraft was en route Chicago-Phoenix, AZ. (TT: 15,294 hrs). No casualties. Cause: Fatigue failure of starboard main gear drag-strut. Declared unrepairable by TWA 31 May 60 and sold to California Airmotive Corp, date unknown. Salvaged for spare parts.

4583 Laid down on production line as 1049E-55 for VARIG as PP-VDB. Dely delayed for later model. To 1049G-82-101 for Trans World Airlines as N7102C, FN 102, 'Star of Windsor'. Renamed 'The United States' by end Mar 55. LADD: 16 Mar 55 (TT: 36 hrs). Used for pilot training by TWA 16-29 Mar 55. First passenger flight 30 Mar 55. Non-revenue charter on route-proving trials to Europe 1 Apr 55, ret USA 11 Apr 55. Flew New York-Dublin (arr 2 Apr after 9:52 non-stop flight)-Shannon (3 Apr)-Cairo (non-stop)-Rome-Madrid-New York. First TWA "Super G" in Europe. In svce (revenue flying) 13 Apr 55. Tip-tanks re-installed 28 Jul 55 and to intl network for special flights - carried the United States delegation returning from a conference at Geneva, Switzerland; made first visit of a TWA "Super G" at London-Heathrow 12 Oct 55. Reverted to 'Star of Windsor' May 56. (TT: 13,651 hrs a/o 31 May 59). Withdrawn from use at Mid-Continent Airport, Kansas City, MO on 4 Feb 64 and cannibalized for parts (TT: 23,407 hrs). Hull sold to Normandie Iron & Metals 8 Feb 65. Scrapped.

4584 Laid down on production line as 1049E-55 for VARIG as PP-VDC. Dely delayed for later model. To 1049G-82-110 for Trans World Airlines as N7103C, FN 103, 'Star of Buckingham'. LADD: 14 Mar 55 - first TWA "Super G" to be delivered. Used for pilot training 14 Mar-2 Apr 55. First revenue flight 3 Apr 55. Inaugurated "Super G" schedules to London-Heathrow arr 6 Nov 55 (tip-tanks fitted). Used on intl schedules, later on domestic network. Cvtd to 92-pax domestic Coach-class aircraft, in svce 1 May 62. Withdrawn from use at Kansas City, MO 31 Dec 64 (TT: 25,868 hrs). Sold to Aaron Ferer & Sons Inc 3 May 65. To Arizona Aircraft Parts & Sales 13 Feb 67, Meyer Rabin Co 14 Mar 67 and Oxnard Aviation Corp 12 May 67. Sold to Eileen Golden 13 Mar 68 & to E Fay Co 10 Sep 69. To Gerald L. Schulman 10 Sep 69. Scrapped at Tucson, AZ 1970. Canx from USCAR 1971. Unconf whether any of owners after TWA actually used the aircraft.

4585 1049G-82-110 16 Mar 55 to Trans World Airlines as N7104C, FN 104, 'Star of Blarney Castle'. Used for pilot training 17 Mar-28 Mar 55. In svce 1 Apr 55. Used on intl schedules (fitted with tip-tanks), later on domestic network. (TT: 14,125 hrs a/o 31 May 59). Withdrawn from use at Kansas City, MO 2 Oct 64 (TT: 24,976 hrs). Sold to Aaron Ferer & Sons Inc 1 Sep 65 and broken up for spares (possibly at Tucson, AZ). Canx from USCAR 1970.

4586 1049G-82-110 14 Mar 55 to Trans World Airlines as N7105C, FN 105, 'Star of Chambord'. Used for pilot and maintenance training 14 Mar-31 Mar 55. In svce 2 Apr 55. Used on intl schedules (fitted with tip-tanks), later on domestic network. Cvtd to 92-pax domestic Coach-class aircraft (replacing 049s) and in svce 14 Dec 61 (TT: 23,730 hrs a/o 30 Apr 63). Withdrawn from use at Kansas City, MO 20 Sep 66. Sold to California Airmotive Corp 12 Dec 66 and del to Fox Fld, Lancaster, CA for storage Dec 66. Canx from USCAR 12 Jul 70. Derelict by May 71 and scrapped during 1971.

4587 1049G-82-110 21 Apr 55 to Trans World Airlines as N7106C, FN 106, 'Star of Ceylon'. Dely at Burbank, CA same day (TT: 51 hrs 46 mins). In svce 23 Apr 55. Used on intl schedules (fitted with tip-tanks), later on domestic network. Cvtd to 92-pax domestic Coach-class aircraft (replacing 049s), in svce 26 Dec 61. (TT: 23,450 hrs a/o 30 Apr 63). Sold to California Airmotive Corp 14 Jan 67 and deld to Fox Fld, Lancaster, CA for storage. Derelict by May 68. Canx from USCAR 12 Jul 70. Scrapped during 1971.

4588 1049G-82-110 31 Mar 55 to Trans World Airlines as N7107C, FN 107, 'Star of Carcassonne'. In svce 4 Apr 55. Used on intl schedules (fitted with tip-tanks), later on domestic network. (TT: 19,478 hrs a/o 30 Jun 61). Cvtd to 92-pax domestic Coach-class aircraft (replacing 049s), in svce 19 Dec 61. Withdrawn from use at Kansas City, MO 7 Nov 63 (TT: 24,634 hrs) and broken up for spares. Hull sold to Normandie Iron & Metals 8 Feb 65. Scrapped.

4589 1049G-82-110 30 Mar 55 to Trans World Airlines as N7108C, FN 108, 'Star of Segovia'. In svce 1 Apr 55. Used on intl schedules (fitted with tip-tanks), later on domestic network. (TT: 19,001 hrs a/o 30 Jun 61). Withdrawn from use at Kansas City, MO 31 Dec 64 (TT: 24,279 hrs). Sold to Aaron Ferer & Sons Inc 25 Jun 65, to Meyer Rabin Co 14 Mar 67 & to Oxnard Aviation Corp 12 May 67. Sold to Eileen Golden 13 Mar 68 and to E Fay Co 10 Sep 69. To Gerald L. Schulman 10 Sep 69. Believed scrapped at Tucson, AZ in 1970. Canx from USCAR 1971. Unconf whether any of owners after TWA actually used the aircraft.

4590 1049G-82-110 19 Apr 55 to Trans World Airlines as N7109C, FN 109, 'Star of Granada' .Deld Burbank, CA same day (TT: 19 hrs). In svce 22 Apr 55. Used on intl schedules (fitted with tip-tanks). Made emergency landing at Southend, England, 12 Jul 57 en route Frankfurt-London (Heathrow) on Flight TW863 at 17.57hrs (GMT) with No.4 engine on fire. No injuries. Repaired & ret to Heathrow from Southend at 23.59hrs on 13 Jul 57. Tfd to domestic network. Believed damaged in ground fire in 1961 and sold to California Airmotive Corp for spares 10 Nov 61. Deld to Burbank, CA (TT: 19,767 hrs). Stored at Burbank. Used for ground tests of an unknown turbo-prop engine in no.3 position at Burbank between Nov 61 and mid-1962. Scrapped at Burbank between Sep 62 and mid-1963 (nose only left there by Jul 63).

N7109C 1049G – the end: a once immaculate Trans World "Super G" stands forlornly on the edge of Burbank Airport, California in September 1962 awaiting scrapping. The reason for the turbo-prop engine mounting in no.3 position has still not been ascertained. (Harry Sievers)

4591 1049G-82-110 6 May 55 to Trans World Airlines as N7110C, FN 110, 'Star of the Escorial' .Deld at Burbank,CA same day (TT: 18 hrs). In svce 8 May 55. Used on intl schedules (fitted with tip-tanks), later on domestic network. (TT: 19,397 hrs a/o 30 Jun 61). Cvtd to 92-pax domestic Coach-class aircraft (replacing 049s), in svce 3 Dec 61. Withdrawn from use at Mid-Continent Airport, Kansas City, MO 14 Apr 64 (TT: 24,979 hrs) and broken up there for spares. Hull sold to Normandie Iron & Metals 8 Feb 65. Scrapped.

4592 1049G-82-110 6 May 55 to Trans World Airlines as N7111C, FN 111, 'Star of Toledo' .Deld at Burbank, CA same day (TT: 15 hrs). In svce 10 May 55. Used on intl schedules (fitted with tip-tanks), later on domestic network. (TT: 20,425 hrs a/o 30 Apr 63). Withdrawn from svce 31 Dec 66 and sold to California Airmotive Corp 4 Jan 67. Stored at Fox Fld, Lancaster, CA by Sep 68. Last reported there Nov 69 and scrapped during 1970. Canx from USCAR 12 Jul 70.

4593 1049G-82-110 9 May 55 to Trans World Airlines as N7112C, FN 112, 'Star of Versailles'. In svce 11 May 55. Used on intl schedules (fitted with tip-tanks), later on domestic network. (TT: 21,174 hrs a/o 30 Apr 63). Withdrawn from svce 8 Sep 66 and sold to California Airmotive Corp 5 Dec 66. Stored at Fox Fld, Lancaster, CA by Sep 68. Canx from USCAR 12 Jul 70. Derelict by May 71 and scrapped during 1971.

4594 1049G-82-110 10 May 55 to Trans World Airlines as N7113C, FN 113, 'Star of Fontainebleau'. Deld at Burbank, CA same day (TT: 14 hrs). In svce 11 May 55. Used on intl schedules (fitted with tip-tanks), later on domestic network. (TT: 20,533 hrs a/o 30 Apr 63). Withdrawn from use 14 Mar 66 and sold to California Airmotive Corp 15 Feb 67. Stored at Fox Fld, Lancaster, CA by Sep 68. Canx from USCAR 12 Jul 70. Derelict there by May 71 and scrapped during 1971.

4595 1049G-82-110 31 May 55 to Trans World Airlines as N7114C, FN 114, 'Star of Mont St.Michel'. Deld at Burbank same day (TT: 13 hrs). In svce 2 Jun 55. Used almost solely on domestic network. (TT: 18,230 hrs a/o 30 Jun 61). Withdrawn from svce 31 Oct 64 and sold to Aaron Ferer & Sons Inc 13 Jul 65. Used for spares and believed scrapped at Tucson, AZ. Canx from USCAR 1965.

4596 1049G-82-110 27 May 55 to Trans World Airlines as N7115C, FN 115, 'Star of Chillon'. Deld at Burbank, CA, same day (TT: 13 hrs). In svce 29 May 55. Used on domestic network. Damaged when no.3 tyre failed on take-off from St.Louis,MO on 23 Aug 56, en route from Washington, DC to Los Angeles, CA. Repaired. Lsd Avianca 27 Apr-26 May 60. Cvtd to 92-pax domestic Coach-class aircraft (replacing 049s), in svce 14 Apr 62. TT: 22,105 hrs a/o 30 Apr 63). Nosewheel failed while being towed at New York-JFK Airport, NY 26 Jan 66 and aircraft received substantial damage as the nose undercarriage collapsed. Not repaired. Stored in ex-TWA colours at JFK, used for spares & derelict with no engines by Jul 67. Sold as scrap to the Grater Co 31 Jul 67 & broken up at New York-JFK Oct 67.

4597 1049G-82-110 2 Jun 55 to Trans World Airlines as N7116C, FN 116, 'Star of Heidelberg'. Deld at Burbank, CA, same day (TT: 14 hrs). In svce 4 Jun 55. Used mainly on domestic network. TT: 18,676 hrs a/o 30 Jun 61). Withdrawn from use 8 Apr 64 and used for spares at Mid-Continent Airport, Kansas City, MO 30 Sep 64 (TT: 22,995 hrs). Hull sold to Normandie Iron & Metals 8 Feb 65. Scrapped.

4598 1049G-82-110 3 Jun 55 to Trans World Airlines as N7117C, FN 117, 'Star of Kenilworth'.Deld at Burbank, CA same day (TT: 15 hrs 51 mins). In svce 5 Jun 55. Used on domestic network. (TT: 18,869 hrs a/o 30 Jun 61). Withdrawn from svce 8 Oct 64 and sold to Aaron Ferer & Sons Inc 1 Oct 65, (TT: 24,052 hrs). Sold to Arizona Aircraft Parts & Sales 13 Feb 67, to Meyer Rabin Co 14 Mar 67 and to Oxnard Aviation Corp 12 May 67. Sold to Eileen Golden 13 Mar 68, to E Fay Co 10 Sep 69 & to Gerald L Schulman 10 Sep 69. Believed scrapped at Tucson, AZ in 1970. Canx from USCAR 1971. Unconf whether any of owners after TWA actually used the aircraft.

4599 1049G-82-110 7 Jun 55 to Trans World Airlines as N7118C, FN 118, 'Star of Capri' In svce 9 Sep 55. Used almost solely on domestic network. (TT: 19,038 hrs a/o 30 Jun 61). Withdrawn from use 11 Jan 64 and used for spares at Mid-Continent Airport, Kansas City, MO 30 Sep 64 (TT: 23,131 hrs). Hull sold to Normandie Iron & Metals 8 Feb 65. Scrapped.

4600 1049G-82-110 30 Jun 55 to Trans World Airlines as N7119C, FN 119, 'Star of Rialto'. Deld at Burbank, CA same day (TT: 28 hrs). In svce 1 Jul 55. Used on domestic network. (TT: 18,929 hrs a/o 30 Jun 61). Withdrawn from use 10 Jun 64 and used for spares at Mid-Continent Airport, Kansas City, MO 30 Sep 64 (TT: 23,715 hrs). Hull sold to Normandie Iron & Metals 8 Feb 65. Scrapped.

4601 1049G-82-110 16 Jun 55 to Trans World Airlines as N7120C, FN 120, 'Star of Heliopolis'. Deld Burbank, CA same day (TT: 12 hrs). In svce 17 Jun 55. Renamed 'Star of California' and used on California-Europe preview flight 23 Oct-3 Nov 55, routeing Los Angeles-New York-London-Frankfurt-Bonn-Zurich-Milan-Rome-Paris- Shannon-New York-Los Angeles, flying 14,024 mls in 49hrs 25min flying time (tip-tanks fitted for this flight, later removed). Used almost solely on domestic network. (TT: 18,587 hrs a/o 30 Jun 61). Cvtd to 92-pax domestic Coach-class aircraft (replacing 049s), in svce 31 Dec 61. Withdrawn from svce 25 Nov 63 and used for spares at Mid-Continent Airport, Kansas City, MO 30 Sep 64 (TT: 24,044 hrs). Hull sold to Normandie Iron & Metals 8 Feb 65. Scrapped.

4602 1049G-82-105 29 Mar 55 to Lufthansa as D-ALAK (regn allocated 22 Mar 55). First flight 24 Mar 55, E-27668 dated 29 Mar 55, Permit to Fly issued 1 Apr 55 and deld to Hamburg, Germany, 15 Apr 55 (with tip-tanks). First Lufthansa Super Constellation to land at Munich-Riem 24 Apr 55 (on training flight). Full CofA issued 7 Jun 55. Sold to Seaboard & Western Airlines (with option to repurchase after 6 months) 17 May 58, D-regn canx 16 May 58. Lsd to Aerlinte Eireann as 95-seater Economy-class aircraft 17 May 58 and regd N611C named 'Breandan'. In svce Dublin, Ireland, 4 Jun 58. Ret to Seaboard & Western 17 Nov 58, and sold back to Lufthansa. Restored to register as D-ALAK 24 Nov 58. Crashed and burst into flames approx half a mile from the runway end on Tubiacanga Beach, by Galeao Airport, Rio de Janeiro, Brazil at 11.25 hrs (local) on 11 Jan 59 after extended nose-wheel undercarriage caught the water on approach in bad weather. 36 killed, three survivors. Aircraft almost completely destroyed by fire after impact. Cause: Believed crew fatigue, pilot error in altitude on approach, possibly the additional distraction of military aircraft activity in the area. En route Hamburg to Rio de Janeiro.

4603 1049G-82-105 19 Apr 55 to Lufthansa as D-ALEM (regn allocated 22 Mar 55 & Lufthansa acceptance 18 Apr 55), E-27675 dated 19 Apr 55, Permit to Fly issued 1 Apr 55 and deld to Hamburg, Germany, 19 Apr 55 (with tip-tanks). Full CofA issued 4 May 55. First svce & also inaugural transatlantic flight Düsseldorf-Hamburg-New York 8-9 Jun 55. Cvtd to 86-seater domestic Tourist-class aircraft 1963. Made last flight 9 Mar 67, withdrawn from use 13 Mar 67 at Hamburg, Germany. Canx from D-register 20 Mar 67. Sold to A Roehrs for scrap and completely broken up at Hamburg 1 Apr 67.

4604 1049G-82-105 29 Apr 55 to Lufthansa as D-ALIN (regn allocated 22 Mar 55 & Lufthansa acceptance 28 Apr 55), E-27676 dated 29 Apr 55, Permit to Fly issued 1 Apr 55 and deld to Hamburg, Germany, 29 Apr 55 (with tip-tanks). Full CofA issued 7 Jun 55. In svce 13 Jun 55 (on transatlantic route). Made first visit to London of Lufthansa "Super G" 19 Jun 55. Used by Chancellor Adenauer for Moscow visit 8 Sep 55. Used on Manchester-Chicago inaugural flight 23 Apr 56, and also on re-opening of Manchester service (to New York) 3 Apr 59. Cvtd to 86-seater domestic Tourist-class aircraft 1963 and inaugurated AIRBUS services Frankfurt-Hamburg 1 Apr 63. Withdrawn from svce 10 Jul 67 and canx from D-register same day. Donated to Flughafen Hamburg GmbH 7 Sep 67 and preserved at Hamburg Airport for public relations duties as model showroom until May 80, when the aircraft was sold to Leo Junior for his museum at Hermeskeil, Mosel, Germany. Aircraft dismantled for transportation & dep Hamburg early Jul 80. Placed on display at Hermeskeil 1981. Still preserved there in good condition.

4605 1049G-82-105 28 May 55 to Lufthansa as D-ALOP (regn allocated 22 Mar 55 & Lufthansa acceptance 27 May 55), E-27678 dated 27 May 55, Permit to Fly issued 1 Apr 55 and deld to Hamburg, Germany 30 May 55 (with tip-tanks). Full CofA issued 7 Jun 55. In svce 11-12 Jun 55, inaugurated Hamburg-Frankfurt-Shannon-New York flights. Cvtd to 86-seater domestic Tourist-class aircraft 1963. Withdrawn from svce 6 Jun 67 & wfu 9 Jun 67. Canx from D-register as wfu 19 Jun 67. Sold to Siegfried Karas 2 Aug 67 and transported to Neu-Wulmstorf, Germany, for conversion to the "Flug-Cafe" cafe-restaurant there. Remained in use until 1975, then scrapped on site Apr 75.

4606 Laid down as 1049E-55 for Thai Airways, but updated to 1049E-82-140 on production line for Qantas. LADD: 20 Oct 55 to Qantas as VH-EAC 'Southern Wave'. First flight 8 Oct 55, CofRegn 14 Oct 55 & E-27697 dated 20 Oct 55. Del Burbank-Honolulu-Nadi-Sydney 22-25 Oct 55. First svce 22 Nov 55 (to Tokyo). Fitted with radar nose 2-29 Apr 56 & mod to 1049E/01. Updated to 1049G/02 & fitted with tip-tanks 16 Nov-11 Dec 57. Carried out Royal Flights with Princess Alexandra 8 Aug 59 Vancouver-Canberra & 25 Sep 59 Canberra-Bangkok. Flew Australian Prime Minister (R G Menzies) on tour 30 Nov-14 Dec 59 Sydney-Brisbane-Darwin-Djakarta-Kuala Lumpur-Singapore-Butterworth-Kuala Lumpur-Cocos Islands-Perth-Canberra. Op a Trans-Australian Airlines charter 22 May 60 Sydney-Brisbane. Dep Sydney 20 Aug 60 for Johannesburg. Crashed into an obstruction at the end of the runway at Plaisance Airport, Mauritius, Indian Ocean, at night on 24 Aug 60. No.3 engine failed during the take-off run, pilot braked, but the aircraft skidded off the wet runway, the undercarriage was torn off, and the aircraft caught fire, with flames and smoke spreading throughout the aircraft within a few seconds. Aircraft was completely destroyed except for the tail unit. En route Johannesburg, South Africa to Sydney, Australia on Flight EM 632/126. No casualties.

4607 Laid down as 1049E-55 for Thai Airways, but updated to 1049E-82-140 on production line for Qantas. LADD: 18 Nov 55 to Qantas as VH-EAD 'Southern Dawn'. First flight 14 Nov 55, CofRegn 14 Nov 55 & E-27699 dated 22 Nov 55. Del Burbank-Honolulu-Nadi-Sydney 23-26 Nov 55. First svce 4 Jan 56 (to Tokyo). First Super Constellation to land at Adelaide when flew from Sydney 24 Feb 56 to operate six courtesy flights. Flew inaugural "Express Service" Sydney-London via Darwin, Singapore, Calcutta, Karachi, Cairo & Rome in reduced flying time (54 hrs 30 mins) & in 43 First-class pax configuration 2 Mar 56. Fitted with radar nose 12 May-9 Jun 57 & mod to 1049E/01. Updated to 1049G/02 & fitted with tip-tanks 1-22 Dec 57. Flew last Qantas svce from Darwin 8 Feb 60. Withdrawn from svce & VH-regn canx 10 Feb 60. Sold to Lockheed Aircraft Corp (trade-in on L-188 Electras) 8 Mar 60 & reregd N9721C. LAC acceptance flt 14 Mar 60 (TT: 12,505 hrs). Del Sydney-Burbank 15-16 Mar 60. Lsd to Twentieth Century Airlines 1960-61 as N9721C. Stored at LAS, Ontario, CA in late 1961. Sold to Trans-International Airlines Inc 20 May 62. N9721C canx 16 Aug 62, reregd N9751C. Lsd to Standard Airways from 19 Jun 63 to Sep 63, ret to Trans-International by Oct 63. Unconf brief lse to Capitol Airways. Withdrawn from svce and stored at Oakland, CA by Aug 68. Sold to California Airmotive Corp, probably in Jul 68, but remained in storage at Oakland until at least Apr 69. Flown to Fox Fld, Lancaster, CA for storage by Nov 69. Canx from USCAR 12 Mar 71. Fuselage only remaining by May 71, scrapped shortly after at Lancaster.

4608 Serial number canx. No details - not built.

4609 Serial number canx. No details - not built.

4610 1049G-82-81 3 May 55 to VARIG as PP-VDA, E-27677 dated 29 Apr 55. Ditched into sea near Cabarete, off-shore the Dominican Republic at approx 15.34 hrs (GMT) on 16 Aug 57. One crew missing, presumed drowned. Aircraft had left Brazil on Flight RG850 for New York. After leaving Belem, trouble with no.2 engine was experienced and the aircraft flew to Ciudad Trujillo, Dominican Republic, where it was discovered that no.2 engine's no.10 cylinder head had swallowed an exhaust valve. Captain decided to ferry the aircraft empty to New York for an engine change. Aircraft took off from Ciudad Trujillo at 15.16 hrs (GMT), but no.4 propeller ran away. The propeller was eventually feathered but then flew off, striking no.3 engine, which was immediately shut down. With only one engine left, the captain decided to return to the Dominican Republic and ditched the aircraft approx 500 metres off the coast near Gaspar Hernandez, the fuselage breaking in two on impact.

4611 1049G-82-81 18 Jun 55 to VARIG as PP-VDB, E-27679 dated 17 Jun 55. Used for Brazilian Presidential visit to Great Britain and arr London-Heathrow 11 Jan 56. Continued in svce with VARIG until CofA expiry 21 Mar 66. Stored at Porto Alegre, Brazil, until broken up there during Jun 67. Regn canx 27 Jun 67.

4612 1049G-82-81 27 Jun 55 to VARIG as PP-VDC, E-27686 dated 20 Jun 55. Withdrawn from use after CofA expiry on 26 Feb 64. Stored at Porto Alegre, Brazil, until broken up there during Jun 67. Regn canx 27 Jun 67.

4613 1049E-55-87 mod to 1049E/02-55-106 28 Jan 55 to Air-India International as VT-DHL 'Rani of Ajanta'. E-27660 dated 26 Jan 55, deld to India after storage at Prestwick 17 Feb-5 Mar 55 and fitting-out of galley by KLM at Amsterdam 3 Apr 55, in svce 2 Apr 55. Slightly damaged when struck by a bird after take-off from Damascus, Syria, on 4 Jun 56. Landed safely. Mod probably to 1049G/02-82. Sold to Indian Air Force 11 Jun 62 and serialled BG-580 coded 'H'. Canx from VT-register 22 Jun 62. Used by No.6 Squadron. Tfd to Indian Navy as IN-317/H 18 Nov 76. Cvtd for maritime reconnaissance. Retained AF blue cheat-line colour-scheme. Last Indian Navy Super Constellation to fly (Bombay-Goa 20 Dec 83). Stored at Goa 1984. Scrapped, date unknown.

4614 1049E-55-87 mod to 1049E/02-55-106 17 Feb 55 to Air-India International as VT-DHM 'Rani of Ellora'. E-27663 dated 18 Feb 55, deld to India 29 Apr 55, after dely via Prestwick to Amsterdam 5 Mar 55 and fitting out of galley by KLM at Amsterdam. In svce 8 May 55. Mod probably to 1049G/02-82. Sold to Indian Air Force 30 Oct 61 and serialled BG-575 believed coded 'A'. Canx from VT-register 30 Oct 61. Used by No.6 Squadron. Tfd to Indian Navy as IN-315 18 Nov 76. Cvtd for maritime reconnaissance & coded DAB-15. Grounded at Dabolim, Goa May 83 & stored there, condition deteriorating. Later preserved for Naval Air Museum at Dabolim, in outside storage. Museum opened to public Oct 98 & IN-315 restored as a 'walk-through' exhibit in 2000. Current, in good condition.

4615 1049E-55-87 mod to 1049E/02-55-106 25 Feb 55 to Air-India International as VT-DHN 'Rani of Chittor'. E-27665 dated 25 Feb 55, deld to India 20 Mar 55, after fitting out of galley by KLM at Amsterdam. In svce 31 Mar 55. Mod probably to 1049G/02-82. Sold to Indian Air Force Dec 61 and serialled BG-577, coded 'C'. Canx from VT-register Dec 61. Used by No.6 Squadron. Last flight with Air Force 29 Sep 72. Withdrawn from svce Jan 76 and used for spares at Lohegaon, Pune AF Station, India. Derelict, engines & parts removed by Jul 83, subsequently scrapped.

4616 1049G-82-81 mod to 1049G-82-123 15 Jul 55 to Transportes Aereos Portugueses (TAP) as CS-TLA. E-27688 dated 15 Jul 55. Del to Lisbon 8 Aug 55. Flew Lisbon-London (Heathrow) inaugural with "Super Gs" 8 Oct 57. Named 'Vasco de Gama' in 1960s. Withdrawn from svce in Sep 67 (TT: 23,485 hrs) and regn canx 23 Nov 67. Sold 25 Sep 67 to International Aerodyne Inc and flown to Miami, FL for storage, still regd CS-TLA. Regd N8338 to International Aerodyne in Jul 68 and sold to Jack A Crosson on 21 Nov 68 (FAA records). However, the aircraft was already in use on the Biafran airlift on 7 Nov 68 at Lisbon, reportedly regd N-53H. Later used with the Phoenix Air Transport combine and named 'Endeavour'. Reregd 5N-83H by Nov 69 and withdrawn from use at Faro, Portugal, by 13 Nov 69. Stored at Faro, Portugal, and officially canx from USCAR 22 Jun 71 (failure to file 1973). Aircraft derelict at Faro by 1975, and interior stripped during spring 1977. Moved to the edge of the airport, near runway end in mid-1978, and stored there, derelict. Sold by Faro Airport to scrap-metal dealer for approx £350. Subsequently sold to Hohbert brothers who renovated acft for use as a restaurant May-Sep 81 near Faro Airport. Fitted with engines & spinners, using engine cowlings from 5T-TAK (c/n 4640) & some round window sections & undercarriage doors from 5N-86H (c/n 2660) and repainted in smart red/white/blue colours with "Super G" inscription. Starboard emergency exit converted into passenger exit door to wing terrace & another door cut into the port side aft of rear entry door for use as main entrance. Moved by summer 1988 to location near Faro on

DIPARTIMENT TA' L-AVJAZZJONI ĊIVILI	DEPARTMENT OF CIVIL AVIATION
Bejgħ bi Rkant	**Sale by Auction**
B'DIGRIET mogħti fis-6 ta' April, 1972, fuq l-applikazzjoni tal-Avukat Ġenerali tal-Kuruna, il-Qorti tal-Maġistrati tal-Pulizija Ġudizzjarja għall-Gżira ta' Malta ordnat il-bejgħ bi rkant ta' **Super Constellation Aircraft Reg. No. 5T-TAF** li għandu jsir fl-Ajrudrom ta' Ħal Luqa.	BY DECREE given on the 6th April, 1972 on the application of the Crown Advocate General, the Court of Magistrates of Judicial Police for the Island of Malta has ordered the sale by auction of Super Constellation Aircraft Reg. No. 5T-TAF to be held at Luqa Airfield.
1. Il-bejgħ għandu jsir nhar it-Tnejn, is-6 ta' Novembru, 1972 fl-10 ta' filgħodu Ħin Lokali (0900 GMT) fl-Ajruport ta' Ħal Luqa.	1. The sale will take place on Monday, 6th November, 1972 at 10.00 a.m. Local Time (0900 GMT) at Luqa Airport, Malta.
2. L-ajruplan se jinbiegħ "tale quale".	2. The aircraft will be sold "tale quale".
3. Ix-xerrej ma jitħalliex jieħu pussess ta' l-ajruplan jew parti minnu qabel ma jsir il-ħlas kollu għal dan l-ajruplan.	3. The buyer shall not be allowed to take possession of the aircraft or part thereof before payment in full has been effected for the said aircraft.
4. Ix-xerrej ma jħallas ebda dazju tad-dwana fuq l-ajruplan.	4. No customs duty on the aircraft will be charged to the buyer.
5. Ix-xerrej għandu jieħu l-ajruplan mill-post fi żmien xahar mid-data tal-bejgħ; jekk ix-xerrej jonqos li jieħu l-ajruplan mill-post fiż-żmien preskritt, huwa jkun soġġett li jħallas £M10 kull jum lill-Gvern ta' Malta għall-perijodu li matulu l-ajruplan jew parti minnu jitħallew fl-ajruport wara li jgħaddi xahar mid-data tal-bejgħ sakemm jittieħed mill-post għal kollox.	5. The buyer shall remove the aircraft within one month from the date of sale; if the buyer fails to remove the aircraft within the prescribed time limit, he shall be liable to the payment of £M10 per diem to the Government of Malta for the period during which the aircraft or part thereof are left at the airport after the lapse of one month from date of sale until totally removed.
6. Ix-xerrej għandu dejjem ifittex l-awtorità tad-Direttur ta' l-Avjazzjoni Ċivili biex jidħol fl-Ajruport biex jieħu mill-post l-ajruplan jew partijiet minnu.	6. The buyer shall at all times seek the authority of the Director of Civil Aviation to enter the Airport area in connection with the removal of the aircraft or parts thereof.
7. Ix-xerrej għandu jinżamm responsabbli għal xi ħsarat u/jew korrimenti li jistgħu jsiru lil proprjetà jew persuni waqt li jkun qiegħed jittieħed l-ajruplan mill-post u għandu jżomm lill-Gvern ta' Malta indennizzat dwar xi talbiet li jistgħu jinqalgħu rigward ħsarat bħal dawn.	7. The buyer shall be held responsible for any damages and/or injuries whatsoever which may be caused to property or persons during the removal operation of the aircraft and shall keep indemnified the Government of Malta in respect of any claims which may arise in respect of such damages.
8. Irkantatur pubbliku jiġi mogħti l-inkarigu li jbiegħ l-ajruplan imsemmi fil-ħin u l-post imsemmijin hawn fuq.	8. A public auctioneer shall be designated to sell the aircraft referred to herein on the appointed time and place.
9. Għal aktar tagħrif u kondizzjonijiet oħra dwar il-bejgħ ta' l-ajruplan, xerrejja prospettivi għandhom japplikaw lid-Direttur ta' l-Avjazzjoni Ċivili, Bini ta' l-Ajruport Ċivili, Ħal Luqa, Malta.	9. For any further information and ancillary conditions regarding the sale of the aircraft, prospective buyers should apply to the Director of Civil Aviation, Civil Airport Building, Luqa, Malta.
Il-15 ta' Settembru, 1972.	15th September, 1972.

C/n 4618. The Sale by Auction notice in Maltese and English served on Hank Warton's 1049G "5T-TAF" to take place on 6th November 1972, four years after the aircraft's arrival there. The Super Constellation was bought for use as a restaurant and remained part of the scenery for many years afterwards.

Faro-Porto de Maio road. By late 1991 was out of use & stored dismantled alongside the Faro-Albufeira motorway. Fuselage was badly damaged in an arson attack & burnt out hulk plus other pieces were removed Oct-Nov 99 to a scrapyard outside the Algarve area of Portugal.

4617 1049G-82-81 mod to 1049G-82-123 29 Jul 55 to Transportes Aereos Portugueses (TAP) as CS-TLB. E-27690 dated 28 Jul 55. Del to Lisbon 8 Aug 55. Damaged when it collided with TAP 1049G CS-TLC at Lisbon on 25 Feb 59. Repaired. Named 'Inf-D.Henrique' in 1960s. Withdrawn from svce mid-1967 and regn canx 14 Jul 67. Sold to International Aerodyne Inc Sep 67 and flown to Miami, FL for storage, still regd CS-TLB. Regd approx Apr 69 as N4624 to International Aerodyne. Sold to Air Cargo Operations Inc approx Jun 69, and to Leasing Consultants Inc same month. Never flew with US-regn, but used for spares at Miami. Dismantled during Oct 69, still carrying CS-regn. By Sep 71, the aircraft had been transported by road to the Everglades, FL and placed atop a restaurant at Dade Collier Airfield/Oasis Airport, Tamiami Trail, FL. Forecourt of building later used as a garage, and the aircraft remained there until early Feb 78. When the garage closed, the Super Constellation was taken about a mile away and cut up for scrap by the end of Feb 78.

F-BHBB 1049G of Air France is seen in a pre-delivery air-to-air photo sortie from Burbank. Air France's "Super Gs" were seldom seen with tip-tanks fitted when in service. (Lockheed)

4618 1049G-82-81 15 Sep 55 to Transportes Aereos Portugueses (TAP) as CS-TLC. E-27691 undated. Used as Presidential aircraft for visit to Great Britain, arr London (Heathrow) 27 Oct 55. Damaged when it collided with TAP 1049G CS-TLB at Lisbon on 25 Feb 59. Repaired. Named 'Cago Coutinho' in the 1960s. Became the first aircraft to land at the new airport at Funchal, Madeira on 8 Jul 64. Made TAP's final Super Constellation flight when it landed at Lisbon on 13 Sep 67 from Rio de Janeiro. Withdrawn from svce (TT: 23,064 hrs). Stored at Lisbon and sold to International Aerodyne Inc in Sep 67 (official change of ownership in FAA files 3 Nov 67). Sold (officially) to North American Aircraft Trading Co (H Warton) 8 Nov 67, though taken over at Lisbon Oct 67. CS-regn canx 23 Nov 67. Reregd 5T-TAF (unofficial regn) in early Nov 67 and used on Biafran airlift. Impounded at Luqa, Malta, with a load of aircraft tyres 16 Feb 68. Stored at Luqa, Malta. Official history:- FAA files state 'the aircraft was not flown by H Warton until May 70 and that he had tried to put the aircraft on the Mauretanian register'. Regd N51517 in Jun or Jul 70. Sold to Lance W Dreyer on 28 Aug 70, & to Transnational Cargo Inc (a Dreyer company) on 28 Sep 70. Tfd to Unum Inc (a Dreyer company) on 12 Mar 71. Canx from USCAR 1976. Actual history:- remained in storage at Luqa, Malta. Sold by auction by Crown Advocate General, the Court of Magistrates of Judicial Police, Malta on 6 Nov 72 for £M3,000 to Salvatore Bezzina & Sons Ltd. Ownership tfd 10 Jan 73, after aircraft was towed off the airfield on 9 Jan 73 to a site on the edge of the village of Kirkop. Resold to Messrs B F B Ltd (C Bajjada, C Fajenza & A Bajjada) and cvtd into a restaurant bar at a cost of over £M10,000. Named the "Super Constellation Bar & restaurant". Cockpit, engines & instruments kept intact, and repainted in Maltese colours with Maltese cross on each of the triple fins. Kept in good condition during the 1970s. In 1980s, business slackened off & aircraft hired out to a series of managers as a bar/snack bar, still at Kirkop/Safi, near Luqa Airport, Malta. Condition deteriorated, though still in occasional use until 1990, despite vandalism. Most of aircraft destroyed in arson attack 30 Jan 97. Four engines complete in cowlings plus a few small parts donated to the Malta Aviation Museum Foundation at Ta Qali 1997.

4619 1049G-82-1l0 24 Feb 56 to Hughes Tool Co, unregistered. Remained in storage in a hangar near the Lockheed Engineering Flight Test facility at Burbank, CA and not flown. Sold back to Lockheed Aircraft Corp, who sold to Capitol Airways Jan 60 and regd N4903C. Flew a BOAC immigrant charter Kingston, Jamaica-London (Heathrow) 4-5 Jun 60. Later renamed Capitol International Airways. Used by Berliner Flug Ring for European IT flights as 108-seater during summers 1966-67. Stored at Wilmington, DE by mid-1968. Reregd N6696C 1968, but believed never painted on aircraft. Proposed sale to North Slope Supply Co in 1969 not taken up. Used for spares and believed scrapped at Wilmington in 1970 (last report Jul 69). Canx from USCAR 1970.

4620 1049G-82-98 7 Jul 55 to Air France as F-BHBA. E-27687 same day, CofA issued 6 Jul 55, del Burbank-New York-Paris(Orly) 13-14 Jul 55 with tip-tanks (TT: 40hrs). Flew low-level all-day "Super G introduction to the public" flight 15 Aug 55 Paris-Channel coast beaches-Atlantic coast beaches-Bordeaux-Côte d'Azur beaches-Nice. In svce 17 Aug 55. Mod to 91-seater Tourist-class configuration. Withdrawn from svce 29 Mar 63. Ferried Orly-Toulouse 18 Apr 63 for storage, CofA expiry 18 Apr 63. (TT: 18,974 hrs). Wfu 2 Nov 66, F-regn canx 24 Nov 66. Stored at Toulouse until sold to A Bertin t/a Aviasol in Feb 67 (possibly Feb 68). Dismantled and transported to Castelnaudary (Aude), France, for use in a children's playground by Jun 68. Condition deteriorated until the aircraft was scrapped between Aug 75 and Dec 76.

4621 1049G-82-98 29 Jul 55 to Air France as F-BHBB. E-27689 same day, CofA issued 6 Jul 55, del Burbank-New York-Shannon-Paris (Orly) 30-31 Jul 55 with tip-tanks (TT: 34hrs). In svce 22 Aug 55. Flew first South Atlantic svce Paris-Lima (extended from Caracas) 12 Sep 57. Mod to 91-seater Tourist class configuration, then to 99-seater European high-density Tourist-class configuration 3-30 Sep 60. Withdrawn from svce 2 Oct 67 (TT: 24,621 hrs), CofA expiry 10 Feb 68. Sold to Ets Le Gouvello de la Porte 23 Nov 67 & to Air Fret 11 Jun 68. Flown to Nîmes-Garons and used for spares there. Derelict by Aug 69, canx from F-register 28 Jan 70 as wfu. Scrapped during Jun 73 at Nîmes-Garons.

4622 1049G-82-98 9 Aug 55 to Air France as F-BHBC. E-27692 same day, del Burbank-Shannon (direct, in 20hrs 50mins)-Paris (Orly) 12-13 Aug 55 (TT: 31hrs), CofA issued 19 Aug 55. In svce 31 Aug 55. Flew President Vincent Auriol on official visit to Rio de Janeiro Mar 56. Used as test acft for Doppler radar prior introduction into Boeing 707 fleet. Crashed into the sea about one mile off-shore and three miles southwest of Dakar-Yoff Airport on bad weather approach to Dakar, Senegal, at 06.48 hrs (GMT) on 29 Aug 60, killing all on board. The aircraft arrived over Dakar at 06.35 hrs, and after making two approaches to the runway towards the sea, on the third approach over the airport, in a tornado-like rainstorm, low cloud and almost zero visibility, the aircraft overshot the runway and shortly afterwards struck the surface of the sea, exploding on impact. Aircraft sank into 65 feet of water. En route Paris-Dakar-Abidjan. (TT: 16,452 hrs). Canx from F-register 11 Oct 60.

4623 1049G-82-98 22 Aug 55 to Air France as F-BHBD. E-27693 same day, del Paris (Orly) 24 Aug 55 (TT: 30hrs), CofA issued 1 Sep 55. In svce 11 Sep 55 (to New York). Flew Paris-Moscow inaugural 3 Aug 58. Mod to 91-seater European high-density Tourist-class configuration, re-entered svce 20 Nov 60. Damaged at Paris (Orly) 25 Sep 62. Repaired. Withdrawn from svce 1 Jan 66 (TT: 23,297 hrs) & stored at Orly until ferried to Toulouse 7 Jan 66, CofA expiry 7 Jan 66. Stored at Toulouse. Wfu 10 May 67, canx from F-register 9 Jun 67, scrapped.

4624 1049G-82-98 31 Aug 55 to Air France as F-BHBE. E-27694 dated 30 Aug 55, del Burbank-New York-Paris (Orly) 2-3 Sep 55 (TT: 34hrs). Del in max 90-seater configuration. In svce 26 Sep 55 (to New York). Named 'Chicago Parisien' on inauguration flight to new runway at Chicago O'Hare 29 Oct 55 (on regular Paris-Chicago flt). Mod to 91-seater Tourist-class configuration. Stored at Paris (Orly) during 1961. Re-entered svce, then withdrawn from svce 29 Oct 63. Stored at Toulouse from 9 Dec 63 until 28 Jul 65. Re-entered svce in modified colour-scheme. Withdrawn from svce 15 Jan 67 (TT: 19,335 hrs), & stored at Orly. Sold to Ets Le Gouvello de la Porte 23 Nov 67 and to René Meyer 15 Dec 68. Flown to Cormeilles-Pontoise and stored there (CofA expiry also 15 Dec 68). Used for spares by CATAIR at Cormeilles-Pontoise and tfd to CATAIR May 71. Derelict by Feb 71, fuselage only left in May 73 and completely broken up during Jun 73. Wfu 9 Mar 71, canx from F-register 28 Jun 72, scrapped.

4625 1049G-82-98 3 Oct 55 to Air France as F-BHBF. E-27695 dated 1 Oct 55, del Burbank-New York-Paris (Orly) 5-7 Oct 55 (TT: 29 hrs). CofA issued 17 Oct 55, in svce 28 Oct 55. Inaugurated Super Constellation svce Paris-Copenhagen-Stockholm 31 Oct 55. First Air France "Super G" to visit London-Heathrow with tip-tanks fitted (probably on inaugural "Eastern Epicurean" direct London-Tokyo svce 18 Jan 56). Flew President Guy Mollet to New York on official visit 24 Feb 57. Inaugurated Super Constellation svce Paris-Tel Aviv 4 Jun 57. Made proving flight Paris-Moscow 16 Jul 58. Named '12 Mai 1930-Jean Mermoz-Jean Dabry-Leo Gimie' from 12 May 60 (commemorating flight across South Atlantic by famous French aviation pioneers). Mod to 91-seater European high-density Tourist-class configuration, re-entered svce 6 Nov 60. Damaged at Paris (Orly) 25 Aug 61. Repaired. Withdrawn from svce 24 Sep 62, CofA expiry 4 Oct 62. (TT:19,436 hrs). Stored at Orly until broken up there during Jun 67. Wfu 15 Apr 66, canx from F-register 24 Sep 66.

4626 1049G-82-98 10 Oct 55 to Air France as F-BHBG. E-27696 same day. Del Paris (Orly) 20 Oct 55 (TT: 27hrs), CofA issued 28 Oct 55. In svce 4 Nov 55. First Super Constellation to be repainted with the large Air France cabin roof titling (1956). Had a runaway propeller on no.3 engine approx 04.00hrs 19 Sep 59 over the North Atlantic en route New York-Paris. Propeller eventually broke away when the acft crossed a weather front at low level & embedded itself in the fuselage/wing-root. Made an emergency landing at Shannon, Eire. Repaired. Damaged Paris (Orly) 17 Jun 60. Repaired. Inaugurated Super Constellation svce Paris-Barcelona 2 Sep 60. Mod to 91-seater Tourist class configuration. Stored at Orly during 1961. Re-entered svce, then withdrawn from svce again 14 Dec 62. Withdrawn from use at Toulouse after CofA expiry 18 Apr 63 (TT: 18,908 hrs). Later stored at Paris (Orly). Wfu 7 Nov 66, canx from F-register 24 Nov 66. Sold to A Bertin t/a Aviasol in Feb 67 (possibly Feb 68). Dismantled and transported to La Roche-Bernard, Morbihan, France as tourist attraction. Moved to new site at Vannes, France, by Dec 73 and repainted from Air France colours to green cheatline and 'Super Constellation' titling. Moved again, to Quimper (Bretagne), France, by Aug 76, using some parts from F-BHBA. Painted in light blue trim, same titling. Preserved in good condition during the 1970s at Le Moulin night-club, half way between Douarnenez and Quimper on the D765 road, one mile west of Orles Ploneis. Condition deteriorated by 1984. The acft still stands at the same site, but has only one fin, no engines and other parts missing by 2002.

4627 1049G-82-98 5 Dec 55 to Air France as F-BHBH. E-28700 same day. Del Burbank-New York-Bretigny-Paris (Orly) 7-9 Dec 55 (TT: 36hrs). CofA issued 16 Dec 55, in svce 14 Jan 56. Used tip-tanks for short period. Mod to 91-seater Tourist-class configuration. Withdrawn from svce 26 Nov 62, CofA expiry 4 Dec 62 (TT: 18,133 hrs) and stored at Paris (Orly). Wfu 5 May 66, canx from F-register 8 Jun 66. Continued in storage at Orly until scrapped Jun-Jul 67.

4628 1049G-82-92 27 Oct 55 to Avianca as HK-184X. E-27698 dated 26 Oct 55. To HK-184 after dely. Fitted with tip-tanks, but not used much. Named 'Santa Fe de Bogota' for brief period approx 1957. Lsd Aerotaxi 1966, and mod to 84-seater domestic Tourist-class configuration. Ret to Avianca. Withdrawn from use at Barranquilla, Colombia, by Aug 69. Subsequently scrapped there at unknown date.

4629 1049G-82-132 22 Dec 55 to KLM as PH-LKE 'Pegasus'. E-28701 same day, regd 22 Dec 55, KLM dely date 23 Dec 55. First KLM 1049G to be deld with tip-tanks. Slightly damaged Rome 18 May 57. Repaired. Lsd briefly to Air Ceylon Mar 58 & Dec 59. (TT 18,400 hrs a/o 21 Dec 61). Used on repatriation shuttle flights Bangkok-Biak 7 Aug 62 onwards. Withdrawn from svce 10 Nov 62 and stored at Amsterdam-Schiphol in cocooning. Out of cocooning by mid-1963 and canx as broken up 22 Jul 64. PH-regn canx 4 Aug 64.

4630 1049G-82-132 4 Jan 56 to KLM as PH-LKF 'Phoenix'. E-28702 same day, regd 4 Jan 56, KLM dely date 5 Jan 56 (fitted with tip-tanks). Damaged in heavy landing at Lisbon, Portugal, 13 Mar 56. Returned to Amsterdam-Schiphol 19 Mar 56 for repairs (TT: 567 hrs). Slightly damaged Schiphol 25 Nov 57. Repaired. Flew inaugural svce Amsterdam-Tunis-Lagos-Accra 17 Jan 61. Withdrawn from svce 1 Jun 61 and stored at Schiphol in cocooning. Out of cocooning by mid 1963, and canx as broken up 15 Mar 66, after PH-regn canx 5 Nov 65.

PH-LKF 1049G of KLM "Phoenix" with tip-tanks, but prior to the fitting of weather-radar, at Amsterdam (Schiphol) in 1956. (KLM)

4631 1049G-82-132 20 Jan 56 to KLM as PH-LKG 'Griffioen'. E-28703 dated 19 Jan 56, regd 20 Jan 56, KLM dely date 21 Jan 56 (fitted with tip-tanks). Withdrawn from svce 8 Apr 61 and stored at Amsterdam-Schiphol in cocooning. Canx as broken up 25 Jun 63, after PH-regn canx 24 Jun 63.

4632 1049G-82-112 20 Feb 56 to Cubana as CU-T601. E-28708 same day. Reregd CU-C601 by 1960. Withdrawn from use, probably in 1961, because of lack of spares, and stored at Jose Marti Airport, Havana. Broken up there by mid-1960s.

4633 1049G-82-112 15 Mar 56 to Cubana as CU-T602. E-28709 same day. Reregd CU-C602 by 1960. Withdrawn from use, probably in 1961, because of lack of spares, and stored at Jose Marti Airport, Havana. Broken up there by mid-1960s.

4634 1049G-82-98 23 Feb 56 to Air France as F-BHBI. E-28707 same day. Del Burbank-New York-Paris (Orly) 27-28 Feb 56. CofA issued 15 Mar 56, in svce same day. Inaugurated express svce Paris-Mauritius the "Etoile des Iles" 3-4 Apr 56. Mod to 91-seater European high-density Tourist-class configuration, re-entered svce 21 Apr 60. Withdrawn from svce 2 Oct 67 (TT: 22,254 hrs). Sold to Ets Le Gouvello de la Porte 23 Nov 67 & to Societe Air Fret 5 Apr 68. CofA expired 31 Mar 69 but used until stored at Nîmes-Garons with Air Fret titling in May 69. Flew subsequently on Biafran airlift until at least Nov 69, probably op by the Phoenix Air Transport combine and lsd to Biafran government, but still regd F-BHBI. Canx from F-register on 12 Nov 69 as 'Sold in Switzerland'. At end of Biafran airlift in Jan 70, the aircraft was stored at Lanzarote, Canary Islands. Still stored there in 1976 complete, and in good condition. Condition deteriorated subsequently, but still stored just outside the airport on the outskirts of new holiday village Playa Honda in derelict condition in mid-1981 (regn painted over as 'P-BHBI'). Destroyed in arson attack in late 1983 & remains removed by Jan 84.

4635 1049G-82-132 1 Feb 56 to KLM as PH-LKH 'Roc'. E-28704 same day, regd 1 Feb 56, KLM dely date 2 Feb 56 (fitted with tip-tanks). Radar nose installed 1-8 Aug 56. Slightly damaged Amsterdam-Schiphol 3 Nov 57. Repaired. Withdrawn from svce 5 May 61 and stored at Schiphol in cocooning. Used for spares and canx 5 Aug 62 as broken up. PH-regn canx 24 Jun 63.

4636 1049G-82-134 17 Feb 56 to LAV as YV-C-AME. E-28705 dated 16 Feb 56. Fitted with tip-tanks. Believed op by VIASA during 1961. YV-regn canx Feb 63. Sold to California Airmotive Corp, date unknown and regd N9749Z. Sold to the Flying Tiger Line 14 Mar 63 (30 Jun 63 also quoted) and rebuilt during mid-1963 into all-cargo aircraft. Wings, centre-section and tail of c/n 4636 used, fuselage taken from YC-121F turboprop Super Constellation c/n **4162** (BuAer 131661/AF 53-8158). Re-designated Model 1049H/06-03 on completion with c/n 4636, regd N9749Z. Reregd N174W 19 Sep 63. First flight as 1049H early Oct 63, in svce 6 Nov 63 with the Flying Tiger Line FN 817. Cvtd to bulk fuel-oil carrier by Flying Tiger for Jim Magoffin (Interior Airways), completed Jan 65 (66?). Sold to Interior Airways Inc 21 Jan 66. Lsd back to Flying Tiger 1 Jul 66, re-entered svce 27 Jul 66 (as all-cargo aircraft again), bt back by Flying Tiger 17 Oct 66. Tfd to Flying Tiger Air Services 14 Nov 66 and named 'City of Naha', FN 74W. Ret to Flying Tiger 1 Jan 68, but still at Taipei, China end Mar 68 in Flying Tiger Air Services titling, possibly stored. Sold to Murphree Air International Inc t/a Nusantara Airways 29 Jan 69 and painted up awaiting dely at Los Angeles Intl Airport in Jan 69. Ntu. Lsd to Interior Airways Inc for several periods between 17 Feb 68 and 22 May 69. Sold to North Slope Supply Co Inc 29 Apr 69. Undershot on landing at Milne Point Air Strip, nr Barrow, AK at 03.40 hrs (local) on 5 May 70 and destroyed in ensuing fire. No injuries to crew. Aircraft was on flight from Fairbanks, AK and on final approach to the airstrip, the aircraft collided with a snowbank, striking the port undercarriage, wing and tail unit, in blowing snow and visibility of half a mile or less, and crashed. Cause: Misjudgement of distance, speed and altitude by pilot combined with poor weather conditions. Remains sold to Lance W Dreyer (after bankruptcy of North Slope).

4637 1049G-82-105 for Lufthansa. Regn D-ACED allocated 22 Jul 55, changed to D-ALAB 8 Aug 55 and finally to D-ALAP on issue of Permit to Fly on 27 Jan 56. LADD: 20 Feb 56 to Lufthansa, E-28706 dated 20 Feb 56. Del Burbank-Stavanger (non-stop, 9,060 kms with tip-tanks), after diversion from Hamburg due to fog, arr Hamburg 25 Feb 56. CofA 6 Apr 56, in svce 18 Apr 56. Inaugurated Hamburg-Bangkok svce 1 Nov 59. Cvtd to 86-seater domestic Tourist-class aircraft in 1963. Withdrawn from svce at Frankfurt-Rhein Main 15 Nov 66 & sold to Karl Schmitz for scrap Dec 66. Canx from D-register 20 Dec 66. Scrapped at Frankfurt during Feb 67, completely broken up by 27 Feb 67.

4638 Serial number canx. No details - not built.

4639 1049G-82-98 4 May 56 to Air France as F-BHBJ. E-28712 same day. Del Burbank-New York-Paris (Orly) 7-9 May 56. Del in max 90-seater configuration. Tip-tanks used occasionally. CofA issued 22 May 56, in svce 23 May 56. Mod to 91-seater European high-density Tourist-class configuration, re-entered svce 24 Sep 60. Withdrawn from svce 3 Oct 62, CofA expiry 19 Oct 62 (TT: 16,881 hrs). Stored at Paris (Orly). Canx from F-register 8 Jan 66, wfu 5 May 66 & broken up at Orly 14 Jun 67.

4640 1049G-82-105 for Lufthansa. Regn D-ACID allocated 22 Jul 55, changed to D-ALEC 8 Aug 55. Permit to fly issued 27 Jan 56. LADD: 28 Mar 56 to Lufthansa, E-28710 undated, del Hamburg 1 Apr 56 with tip-tanks. CofA issued 28 Apr 56, in svce 5 May 56. Used for inaugural svce on South Atlantic to Sao Paulo, Rio de Janeiro & Buenos Aires 15-16 Aug 56. Cvtd to 86-seater domestic Tourist-class aircraft in 1963. Op last scheduled Lufthansa Super Constellation flight into Munich-Riem 30 Jul 67. Withdrawn from svce 5 Oct 67. Sold to North American Aircraft Trading Corp (H Warton) 8 Mar 68, canx from D-register 9 Mar 68 on issue of export permit to Portugal same day. Regd 5T-TAK (unofficial regn) and used on Biafran airlift. Also regd N8025 (unofficially) as required Jul-Sep 68. Flown to Lisbon in damaged condition and on three engines between 20 Sep and 23 Sep 68 and withdrawn from use there. Stored at Lisbon, carrying regn 5T-TAK and remains of N8025. Condition deteriorated, but still at Lisbon in derelict condition in Jan 81. Broken up at Lisbon by Apr 81, forward fuselage preserved at the TAP-Air Portugal Museum at Lisbon Airport. Still there 2004.

4641 1049G-82-109 22 Apr 56 to Trans-Canada Air Lines as CF-TEU, FN 409. E-28711 dated 20 Apr 56, TCA dely date 21 Apr 56. (Replacement aircraft for c/n 4564). Fitted with tip-tanks & radar nose 1958. Withdrawn from svce (TT: 16,183 hrs), sold to Douglas Aircraft Corp 26 Feb 62 (trade-in on DC-8s) and regd N9640Z. Stored at Las Vegas, NV. Sold to California Airmotive Corp 1963 and flown to Fox Fld, Lancaster, CA for storage by mid-1963. Derelict at Fox Fld by Aug 66 and scrapped there shortly afterwards. Canx from USCAR 1965.

4642 1049G-82-105 for Lufthansa. Allocated D-ALOF on 18 Aug 55 (this regn had previously been allocated to c/n 4649, qv). Permit to fly issued 4 May 56. Believed used by LAC prior dely for fuel-vent tests after crash of c/n 4561 (qv). LADD: 25 Jul 56, del Hamburg 28 Jul 56 (with tip-tanks). E-28717 dated 7 Aug 56, CofA issued 14 Aug 56. In svce 18 Aug 56. Cvtd to 86-seater domestic Tourist-class aircraft in 1963. Withdrawn from svce 6 Oct 67 after flying the last Lufthansa Super Constellation schedule (Copenhagen-Hamburg) 6 Oct 67. Sold to North American Aircraft Trading Corp (H Warton) 8 Dec 67, canx from D-register 13 Dec 67 on issue of export permit to Mauretania same day. Regd 5T-TAG (unofficial regn) and used on Biafran airlift. Also regd N8025 (unofficially) Jun 68. Crashed on approach to the airstrip at Uli-Ihiala, Biafra, while on charter to the International Red Cross,

N174W 1049H of Flying Tiger Air Services "City of Naha". The round windows on this Super Constellation stem from the fact that it was rebuilt into an all-cargo aircraft by Flying Tiger using the fuselage of a turbo-prop YC-121F. (The YC-121F can be seen in its former glory on the back cover). The photo was taken at Hong Kong on 1st November 1967. (P R Keating)

approx 2 miles from the runway end at about 02.00 hrs (local) on 1 Jul 68, killing the four on board. Aircraft en route Lisbon-Fernando Poo-Uli with medical supplies. Weather bad at the time, with tropical rainstorms.

4643 1049G-82-109 15 May 56 to Trans-Canada Air Lines as CF-TEV, FN 410. E-28713 same day. Fitted with radar nose 1957 & tip-tanks Jan 58. Flew inaugural TCA svce to Brussels, Belgium 2 Apr 58. Withdrawn from svce (TT: 15,243 hrs), sold to Douglas Aircraft Corp 20 Feb 62 (trade-in on DC-8s) and regd N9641Z. Stored at Las Vegas, NV. Sold to California Airmotive Corp 1963 and flown to Fox Fld, Lancaster, CA for storage by mid-1963. Derelict at Fox Fld by Aug 66 and scrapped there shortly afterwards. Canx from USCAR 1965.

4644 Originally ordered by Thai Airways Co as 1049G-82-124 regd HS-TCA. Released to KLM and mod on production line to 1049G-82-151. LADD: 20 Jul 56 to KLM as PH-LKI 'Wyvern', regd and KLM dely date same day (tip-tanks fitted). E-28716 20 Jul 56 also. Lsd to Air Ceylon Mar-Apr 59. Lsd to Iberia 12 Mar 61 & regd EC-AQM, FN 214 15 Mar 61. PH-regn canx 16 Mar 61. Purchased by Iberia 15 Aug 62 and named 'La Garza'. Lsd to Aviaco during the summers for European IT flights as an 80-seater. Damaged when it brushed trees on Russ Hill on approach to London-Gatwick at 01.55 hrs (GMT) on 2 Sep 63, 1.75 nautical miles from the runway threshold. Aircraft landed safely, no injuries, with damaged port wing landing light, six inches broken from the tip of no.3 propeller, no.3 engine nacelle dented, and a hydraulic line on the starboard landing gear strut broken. Low cloud, poor visibility and drizzle at the time. Cause: descent below safe approach path without glide path at night in low cloud. Repaired. Fitted with rear cargo door and cargo mods by Air France at Toulouse, France, from late 1963 to Jan 64. First flight after conversion 19 Jan 64. Continued in use with Iberia/Aviaco until sold to International Aerodyne Inc in May 67. Ferried to Miami, FL and regd N8024. Wfu & stored at Miami. Derelict by May 68 & broken up there between Sep 70 and Feb 71.

4645 Originally ordered by Thai Airways Co as 1049G-82-124 regd HS-TCB. Released to KLM and mod on production line to 1049G-82-151. LADD: 28 Jun 56 to KLM as PH-LKK 'Centaurus'. Regd 28 Jun 56, KLM dely date 29 Jun 56, E-28715 28 Jun 56 (tip-tanks fitted). Lsd to Iberia 12 Mar 61 & regd EC-AQN, FN 215 15 Mar 61. PH-regn canx 16 Mar 61. Purchased by Iberia 15 Aug 62 and named 'La Rabida'. Lsd to Aviaco during the summers for European IT flights as an 80-seater. Fitted with rear cargo door and cargo mods by Air France at Toulouse, France, from mid-1963 to Oct 63. First flight after conversion 27 Oct 63. Continued in use with Iberia/Aviaco until sold to International Aerodyne Inc in May 67, and regd N8025. In use with the North American Aircraft Trading Corp (H Warton) at Lisbon, on the Biafran airlift, by 29 Jun 67 and officially regd to the company 8 Aug 67. Repainted with blue cheat line at Lisbon 12 Aug 67 and reregd 5T-TAC early Sep 67 (unofficial regn). Canx from USCAR Oct 67. Crashed on landing at Port Harcourt, Biafra, in early Feb 68 when the port wingtip reportedly struck the runway on a tight turn on final approach. Aircraft rolled over and destroyed by fire. No casualties. En route from Lisbon, reportedly on charter to Caritas with medical supplies. Remains at Port Harcourt in May 68.

4646 1049G-82-106 5 Jun 56 to Air-India International as VT-DIL 'Rani of Nilgiris'. E-28714 dated 5 Jun 56, dep USA 8 Jun 56, dely India 11 Jun 56. In svce 3 Aug 56. Inaugurated Sydney-London through service via India 5 Oct 56. Sold to Indian Air Force 5 May 62 and serialled BG-578 coded 'J'. Canx from VT-register 16 May 62. Used by No.6 Squadron. Last flight 9 Jan 75. Wfu & used for spares Jan 76 at Lohegaon, Pune IAF Station, India. In poor condition, with engines & parts removed by Jul 83. Scrapped sometime after Jan 84.

4647 1049G-82-105 for Lufthansa. Regn D-ACOD allocated 22 Jul 55, changed to D-ALID 8 Aug 55. Permit to fly issued 4 May 56. LADD: 8 Aug 56 to Lufthansa, E-28718 dated 7 Aug 56, Lufthansa dely date 7 Aug 56, del to Hamburg 9 Aug 56 (with tip-tanks), CofA issued 31 Aug 56. In svce 5 Sep 56. Flew inaugural svce Hamburg-Teheran 12 Sep 56, and inaugural svce Hamburg-Cairo 5 Jan 59. Cvtd to 86-seater domestic Tourist-class aircraft in 1963. Last flight for Lufthansa 29 Sep 67, wfu 30 Sep 67 and canx from D-register 4 Oct 67 'to be broken up'. Restored to Lufthansa as D-ALID 21 Feb 68 for ferry flight only Hamburg-Lisbon, Portugal. Sold to North American Aircraft Trading Corp (H Warton) 23 Feb 68. Canx from D-register 29 Feb 68 on issue of export permit to Portugal same day. Reregd 5T-TAH (unofficial regn) on arrival at Lisbon, and used on Biafran airlift. Also regd N8025 (unofficially) as required Jul-Sep 68. Damaged while landing at Uli strip, Biafra, in early Aug 68. Ferried to Sao Tome 14 Aug 68, used for spares for a fortnight, then made flyable for last flight, ferried to Abidjan, Ivory Coast 28 Sep 68 with no.2 propeller feathered. Withdrawn from use there on arrival. Stored at Abidjan, carrying regn 5T-TAH and remains of N8025. Condition deteriorated, but still there, derelict in long grass, less engines, in Apr 78. Subsequently scrapped.

4648 1049G-82-114, mod to 1049G-82-144 21 Jun 56 to Hughes Tool Co, lsd to Trans World Airlines same day as N7121C, FN121, 'Star of Edinburgh' (TT: 21 hrs 59 mins). In svce 23 Jun 56, used on domestic network. Sold to TWA 11 Jun 57. Seam on front fuselage burst with explosive force in accidental gross over-pressurization (dump valves wired shut) while the aircraft was undergoing pressurisation leak test in a hangar at Idlewild Airport, New York, NY at 11.45 hrs (local) on 25 Jun 59. Severe damage to whole of front fuselage forward of wing (TT: 10,883 hrs). Damaged aircraft sold to California Airmotive Corp 28 Sep 59, officially 27 Nov 59. (Deld 16 Mar 60?) Rebuilt into cargo convertible aircraft by California Airmotive Corp at Burbank from mid-1960 to early 1961, using the wings, aft fuselage and tail unit of the 1049G and the fuselage of Navy turboprop Super Constellation c/n **4132** (R7V-2 BuAer 131631). Completed as 1049H/06-82, mod to 1049H/06-03, still regd N7121C, and lsd to Trans-International Airlines Inc, in svce 23 Apr 61. Sold to Bill Murphy-Buick Inc 11 Jul 62. Lsd to Standard Airways late 1962 until mid-1963. Lsd to the Flying Tiger Line Inc 1 May 64 until 28 Jun 65, FN 821 (used as pax aircraft). Sold to International Aerodyne Inc 1966 (no official record). Lsd to LEBCA (Venezuela) from at least 24 Nov 66 to 18 Dec 66, and again from 1 Jan 67 onwards for unknown period. Aircraft then stored at Miami, FL. The aircraft was sold by Bill Murphy-Buick Inc to Aerolessors Inc on 27 Mar 68 (although the aircraft carried Aerolessors titling by Apr 67), but there were irregularities in the paperwork, and the tf of regn to Aerolessors was never completed; legally the aircraft remained the property of Bill Murphy. Used by Aerolessors for some time. Withdrawn from use at Miami by Sep 70, and stored there, condition deteriorating. Slowly cannibalized for spares from Mar 72 onwards and derelict by Aug 73. Scrapped shortly afterwards (last report Sep 73) at Miami. Regn canx 2 Apr 79.

N7121C 1049H of Trans-International in a non-standard colour-scheme at Oakland, California. This Super Constellation was rebuilt into a convertible passenger/cargo aircraft after severe structural damage was suffered during pressure testing in 1959. Most of the fuselage of a turbo-prop R7V-2 was used. (D Olson via Jennifer M Gradidge)

4649 Laid down as 1049G-82-105 for Lufthansa. Regn D-ACUD allocated 22 Jul 55, changed to D-ALOF 8 Aug 55. D-ALOF transferred to c/n 4642 on 18 Aug 55. Completed as 1049G-82-114, mod to 1049G-82-144 for Trans World Airlines as N7122C, FN 122, 'Star of Gibraltar'. LADD: 29 Jun 56, deld Burbank same day (TT: 16 hrs); in svce 1 Jul 56. Used on domestic network. (TT 16,168 hrs a/o 30 Jun 61). Withdrawn from svce 30 Jun 64 and sold to Aaron Ferer & Sons Inc 9 Dec 65. (TT: 21,080 hrs). Sold to Consolidated Aircraft Sales Inc, probably in 1966. Believed scrapped at Tucson, AZ.

4650 1049G-82-114, mod to 1049G-82-144 20 Jul 56 to Trans World Airlines as N7123C, FN 123, 'Star of Stirling Castle'. Deld Burbank, CA same day (TT: 25hrs 28mins), in svce 21 Jul 56. Used on domestic network. (TT: 15,743 hrs a/o 30 Jun 61). Withdrawn from svce 16 Oct 64. Sold to Aaron Ferer & Sons Inc 20 Jul 65. (TT: 21,214 hrs). Sold to Oxnard Aviation Corp 3 Apr 67, reregd N137X with Oxnard Aviation in 1967 (no official record) and then N137XR on 5 Oct 67. Fate unknown, probably scrapped. Canx from USCAR 23 Nov 70.

4651 1049G-82-114, mod to 1049G-82-144 31 Jul 56 to Trans World Airlines as N7124C, FN 124, 'Star of Amboise'. Deld Burbank, CA same day (TT: 12 hrs), in svce 1 Aug 56. Used on domestic network. (TT: 11,802 hrs a/o 30 Apr 63). Withdrawn from use 26 Nov 66 and sold to California Airmotive Corp 29 Nov 66. Stored at Fox Fld, Lancaster, CA by May 68, derelict. Canx from USCAR 12 Jul 70. Scrapped during 1971.

4652 1049G-82-114, mod to 1049G-82-144 27 Aug 56 to Trans World Airlines as N7125C, FN 125, 'Star of Chenonceaux'. Deld Burbank, CA same day (TT: 17 hrs), in svce 29 Aug 56. Used on Domestic network. Received minor damage at Los Angeles, CA 16 Dec 58. Aircraft was incorrectly parked with wing extending into the taxi area. TWA 1649A N7311C struck the right wing-tip of the 1049G with its left wing-tip. Repaired. (TT: 10,343 hrs a/o 31 May 59). Damaged when supercharger of no.2 engine failed in flight over Goffs, CA on 6 Jul 59. Repaired. Withdrawn from svce 4 Mar 60. Lsd to Iberia and del ex-Idlewind, NY 14 Mar 60 (TT: 12,748 hrs) arr Madrid 15 Mar 60 and lse effective that day. Crashed on landing Runway 17 at 16.00 hrs (local) on 8 Nov 60 at Muntadas Airport, Barcelona, while flying a Madrid-Barcelona svce for Iberia. No casualties. Aircraft hit a small heap of rubbish with the port main gear approx 35 metres short of the runway, tearing off the port main-wheels. The aircraft continued along the runway for 170 metres, running on the starboard main-wheels & the stub of the port undercarriage leg. The Super Constellation swerved to the left off the runway and veered into mud at the side of the runway. Caught fire immediately; the fuselage was burnt out except for the radar nose & fuselage aft of the rear entrance door, the nose-wheel leg had a broken axle & one wheel torn off, as was no.3 engine. Probable cause: Pilot error in estimating the height of the aircraft immediately prior to landing. (TT: 14,413 hrs).

4653 1049G-03-142 SPECIAL 26 Oct 56 to Eastern Air Lines as N6231G, FN 231. Cvtd to 95-seater by 1964/65. Withdrawn from svce 18 Jan 68 and stored at Opa Locka, FL. Sold to California Airmotive Corp 30 Sep 68 and flown to Fox Fld, Lancaster, CA for storage. Canx from USCAR 12 Jul 70. Derelict by May 71 and scrapped later same year.

4654 1049G-82-114, mod to 1049G-82-144 30 Aug 56 to Trans World Airlines as N7126C, FN 126, 'Star of Inverness'. Deld Burbank, CA 31 Aug 56 (TT: 15 hrs), in svce 1 Sep 56. Used on domestic network. (TT: 17,154 hrs a/o 30 Apr 63). Withdrawn from use 16 Jan 66 and sold to California Airmotive Corp 20 Jan 67. Stored at Fox Fld, Lancaster, CA by May 68, derelict. Canx from USCAR 12 Jul 70. Scrapped during 1971.

4655 1049G-03-142 SPECIAL 14 Sep 56 to Eastern Air Lines as N6232G, FN 232. Cvtd to 95-seater by 1964/65. Flew Eastern's last pax Constellation service New York (Newark)-Washington 14 Feb 68. Withdrawn from svce 15 Feb 68 and stored at Opa Locka, FL. Sold to California Airmotive Corp 30 Sep 68 and flown to Fox Fld, Lancaster, CA for storage, same month. Canx from USCAR 12 Jul 70. Derelict by May 71 and scrapped later same year.

4656 1049G-82-114, mod to 1049G-82-144 26 Sep 56 to Trans World Airlines as N7127C, FN 127, 'Star of Aberdeen'. Deld Burbank, CA 26 Sep 56 (TT: 19 hrs), in svce 27 Sep 56. Used on domestic network. Made emergency landing at Atlanta, GA at 11.35 hrs (EST) on 5 Dec 60 after loss of power on no.4 engine and fire in no.3 engine shortly after take-off. No injuries. After the first power reduction was made after take-off, the Flight Engineer informed the pilot that no.4 engine was losing power, and a yaw to the right felt. No.4 was feathered and the aircraft turned back for a landing. At that moment, no.3 propeller oversped and no.3 engine was observed to be on fire. The fire was extinguished, and no.4 restarted for the landing, which was accomplished without incident. No fault subsequently found with no.4 engine, fire on no.3 caused by hole in no.2 cylinder and failure of the piston land or ring on no.2 piston. Repaired. (TT:17,949 hrs a/o 30 Apr 63). Withdrawn from use 12 Dec 66 and sold to California Airmotive Corp 14 Dec 66. Stored at Fox Fld, Lancaster, CA by May 68. Canx from USCAR 12 Jul 70. No engines, and parts missing by May 71 and scrapped during 1971.

4657 1049G-03-142 SPECIAL 1 Oct 56 to Eastern Air Lines as N6233G, FN 233. Cvtd to 95-seater by 1964/65. Withdrawn from svce 8 Jan 68 and stored at Opa Locka, FL. Sold to California Airmotive Corp 30 Sep 68 and flown to Fox Fld, Lancaster, CA for storage. Canx from USCAR 12 Jul 70. Derelict by May 71 and scrapped same year.

4658 1049G-82-114, mod to 1049G-82-144 28 Sep 56 to Trans World Airlines as N7128C, FN 128, 'Star of Rheinstein Castle'. Deld at Burbank same day. In svce 29 Sep 56. Used on domestic network. (TT: 15,591 hrs a/o 30 Jun 61). Withdrawn from svce 20 Oct 64. (TT: 21,025 hrs). Sold to Aaron Ferer & Sons Inc 11 Aug 65, to Meyer Rabin Co 14 Mar 67 and to Oxnard Aviation Corp by Nov 67. Sold to Eileen Golden 13 Mar 68 and to E Fay Co 10 Sep 69. Sold to Gerald L Schulman 10 Sep 69. Canx from USCAR 1971. Unconf whether any of owners after TWA actually used the aircraft. Believed scrapped at Tucson, AZ in 1970/71.

4659 1049G-03-142 SPECIAL 12 Oct 56 to Eastern Air Lines as N6234G, FN 234. Cvtd to 95-seater by 1964/65. Withdrawn from svce 15 Feb 68 and stored at Opa Locka, FL. Sold to California Airmotive Corp 30 Sep 68 and flown to Fox Fld, Lancaster, CA for storage same month. Canx from USCAR 12 Jul 70. Dismantled by May 71 and scrapped shortly afterwards.

4660 1049G-03-142 SPECIAL 18 Oct 56 to Eastern Air Lines as N6235G, FN 235. Cvtd to 95-seater by 1964/65. Withdrawn from svce 28 Nov 67 and stored at Miami, FL. Sold to California Airmotive Corp 30 Sep 68 and flown to storage at Fox Fld, Lancaster, CA. Canx from USCAR 12 Jul 70. Dismantled by May 71 and scrapped shortly afterwards.

4661 1049G-03-142 SPECIAL 29 Oct 56 to Eastern Air Lines as N6236G, FN 236. Cvtd to 95-seater by 1964/65. Withdrawn from svce 1 Feb 68 and stored at Opa Locka, FL. Sold to California Airmotive Corp 30 Sep 68 and flown to storage at Fox Fld, Lancaster, CA. Last reported there Nov 69, scrapped, probably during 1970. Canx from USCAR 12 Jul 70.

4662 1049G-03-142 SPECIAL 2 Nov 56 to Eastern Air Lines as N6237G, FN 237. Cvtd to 95-seater by 1964/65. Withdrawn from svce 26 Jan 68 and stored at Opa Locka, FL. Sold to California Airmotive Corp 30 Sep 68 and flown to Fox Fld, Lancaster, CA. Canx from USCAR 12 Jul 70. Derelict by May 71, scrapped later same year.

4663 1049G-03-142 SPECIAL 9 Nov 56 to Eastern Air Lines as N6238G, FN 238. Cvtd to 95-seater by 1964/65. Withdrawn from svce 15 Feb 68 and stored at Opa Locka, FL. Sold to California Airmotive Corp 30 Sep 68 and flown to Fox Fld, Lancaster, CA. Last reported there Nov 69, scrapped, probably during 1970. Canx from USCAR 12 Jul 70.

4664 1049G-03-142 SPECIAL 15 Nov 56 to Eastern Air Lines as N6239G, FN 239. Cvtd to 95-seater by 1964/65. Withdrawn from svce and stored at Miami, FL from at least 24 Aug 66. EAL markings painted over and two engines missing by 24 Nov 66. Sold to International Aerodyne Inc 12 Jan 67. Cannibalized for spares and hulk sold for scrap to Thos E Chatlos dba AAA Scrap Metals. Broken up at Miami, FL Jun 67. Canx from USCAR 12 Jul 70 (by California Airmotive, in error, as they did not own it!).

4665 1049G-03-142 SPECIAL 30 Nov 56 to Eastern Air Lines as N6240G, FN 240. Eastern del date 8 Dec 56. Received substantial damage at 16.23 hrs (EST) on 17 Jan 59 when an engine caught fire on take-off from Miami Intl, FL and the starboard main gear collapsed on landing. Immediately after take-off, when the aircraft was 150 ft above the runway, no.3 engine showed a fluctuation in rpm and the propeller was feathered. Shortly afterwards, no.3 engine caught fire and could not be extinguished. On landing, the braking system became ineffective, and reverse thrust was only partially effective as no.4 engine stopped during the roll. The runway was overrun by 75 feet and the starboard main gear collapsed as the aircraft came to a halt. No injuries, but the fire was not extinguished for 30 minutes due to a lack of fire-fighting equipment and capability (the airport firemen ran out of foam). (TT: 7,309 hrs). Repaired. Cvtd to 95-seater by 1964/65. Collided on ground at Newark Airport, NJ at 17.38 hrs (EST) on 14 Mar 67, with New York Airways Vertol 107 (N6676D). Left wing-tip of Super Constellation hit rear rotor of the helicopter. No injuries. Repaired. Withdrawn from svce 3 Feb 68 and stored at Opa Locka, FL. Sold to California Airmotive Corp 30 Sep 68 and flown to Fox Fld, Lancaster, CA for storage. Canx from USCAR 12 Jul 70. Derelict by May 71, scrapped shortly afterwards.

4666 1049G-82-106 6 Dec 56 to Air-India International as VT-DIM 'Rani of Ayodhya'. E-28721 dated 5 Dec 56, dely in USA 7 Dec 56, via London-Heathrow 10 Dec 56 & arr India 11 Dec 56. Tip-tanks used on dely flight, but not afterwards. In svce 21 Dec 56. Tfd to Indian Air Force 2 Dec 61 and canx from VT-register same day. Serialled BG-576, believed coded 'B'. Used by No.6 Squadron. Tfd to Indian Navy 18 Nov 76 and re-serialled IN-316, coded DAB-16. Written-off in taxying accident Santa Cruz, Bombay 11 Jan 83. Remained stored at Bombay, with fuselage propped up, but broken in two, until at least Jan 87. Subsequently scrapped.

4667 1049G-82-106 13 Dec 56 to Air-India International as VT-DIN 'Rani of Agra'. E-28722 dated 11 Dec 56, dely in USA 14 Dec 56, via London-Heathrow, arr India 19 Dec 56. Tip-tanks used on dely flight, but not afterwards. In svce 22 Jan 57. Swung off runway landing in heavy monsoon weather at 17.07 hrs (GMT) on 19 Jul 59 at Santa Cruz Airport, Bombay. Skidded into swampy ground, broke off landing-gear and caught fire. Acft burnt out. No casualties. En route Tokyo-Bombay.

4668 1049G-82-98 26 Dec 56 to Air France as F-BHMI. E-28723 dated 24 Dec 56. Del Paris (Orly) 31 Dec 56, in svce 9 Jan 57. Flew inaugural svce on route Paris to Lima via Quito, Ecuador 13 Mar 58. Mod to 91-seater Tourist configuration. Withdrawn from svce 21 Jan 61, and stored at Orly from 25 Jan 61 until CofA renewal 31 Jul 63. Withdrawn from svce 22 Nov 66 (TT: 15,750 hrs). Sold to Ets Le Gouvello de la Porte 23 Nov 67, and to René Meyer 14 Dec 67. Tf to CATAIR 1 Jul 68. Withdrawn from svce and stored at Cormeilles-Pontoise by Nov 71 prior to CofA expiry 6 Jan 72. Used for spares from Oct 72 approx, and canx as wfu 12 Oct 73. Broken up at Cormeilles between Oct 74 and early 1975. (aircraft on belly, many parts missing and no engines by Dec 74).

4669 1049G-82-98 27 Dec 56 to Air France as F-BHMJ. E-28724 dated 24 Dec 56. Del Paris (Orly) 4 Jan 57, in svce 11 Jan 57. CofA issued 24 Jan 57. Mod to 91-seater Tourist configuration, then to 99-seater European high-density Tourist configuration 16 Oct 60. Withdrawn from svce 21 Jan 61 & stored at Orly for a period. Withdrawn from svce 30 Nov 62 & stored at Toulouse-Montaudran. CofA expired 18 Apr 63 (TT: 14,996 hrs). Flown back to Orly at some stage. Canx as wfu 2 Nov 66. Stored at Paris (Orly) until Jun 67, when the aircraft was dismantled. Sold to A Bertin t/a Aviasol Feb 68 (67?) and sold again in 1969 for use as restaurant-bar at Strasbourg, Bas-Rhin, France. Conversion to the "Super Club" completed mid-1969. In Air France colours, no regn, only telephone number 36.65.19 on rear fuselage. By 1976, called the "Stella Artois Super Club Bar". Caught fire in late 1978 & badly damaged, after which it was towed away from its site by the Pont-du-Rhin (close to the Franco-German border) and the remains scrapped.

4670 1049G-82-98 22 Jan 57 to Air France as F-BHMK. E-28725 dated 21 Jan 57. Del Burbank-New York-Paris (Orly) 23-25 Jan 57. CofA issued 31 Jan 57, in svce 8 Feb 57. Crashed on landing at Paris (Orly) at 18.00 hrs (GMT) on 6 Dec 57 at the end of a training flight. (TT: 3,078 hrs). No casualties. The crew had been practising ILS approaches and the fourth and final landing was being carried out at night at Orly on runway 26 Left using an ILS GCA approach with a cloud ceiling of 200 feet and visibility of approx one mile. After making a normal approach, the aircraft banked sharply to the left, touched the ground approx 430 yards beyond the runway entry with the left wingtip and climbed a few feet. At this moment a fire developed on board the aircraft and spread rapidly. The aircraft struck the ground to the right and left successively and crashed approx 750 yards beyond the runway threshold, the left wing and the right wing-tip became detached from the aircraft, and the main body of the wreckage came to a halt approx 1,245 yards from the entry and 75 yards away from the edge of the runway. Cause: excessive corrective manoeuvres performed by the crew at the time of contact with the runway, with possible icing reducing the aircraft's aerodynamic qualities. Canx from F-register 24 Jan 58.

4671 1049G-82-98 4 Feb 57 to Air France as F-BHML. E-28726 dated 1 Feb 57, del Paris (Orly) 7 Feb 57, in svce 8 Feb 57. CofA issued 14 Feb 57. In use with the SFP (Service de Formation des Pilotes) a/o 1 Mar 57. Damaged 23 Jan 59. Repaired. Named 'Maurice Nogues' by Nov 60. Mod to 91-seater Tourist configuration. Lsd to Tunis Air summer 1961-Sep 61. Ret to Air France, withdrawn from svce 4 Sep 61 (?) and stored at Paris (Orly) from 22 Sep 61. Restored to svce at unknown date and wfu again at Orly on CofA expiry 16 Oct 63 (TT: 13,546 hrs). Stored at Orly until 12 Jul 65, then mod to European high-density Tourist-class configuration 15 Oct 65 & re-entered svce. Withdrawn from svce 2 Oct 67 (TT: 15,568 hrs). Sold to Ets Le Gouvello de la Porte 23 Nov 67, then to Compagnie Air Fret 8 Mar 68. Wfu at Nîmes-Garons in Aug 76 and stored there. Sold to Air Classic approx Nov 77, made airworthy, CofA issued 1 Jun 78 limited ferry flight Nîmes-Düsseldorf, West Germany. Ferried to Düsseldorf 27 Jun 78 & painted in Air Classic titles with false regn "D-ADAM". Proposed sale to a company in Panama via Euroworld in Oct 78 fell through. Preserved at Düsseldorf Airport. Canx from F-register Feb 80. Air Classic collection at Düsseldorf dissolved in first half of 1985 when space needed for new car-park. Acft sold to the Frankfurt Airport authorities & transported by road to Frankfurt 1985. Planned use as restaurant fell through. Painted as "D-ALAP" in Lufthansa colours by 1987. Moved to the new Munich Airport 18 Aug 93 & displayed by Albatros Airport Service GmbH (Werner Dubrovolny) in spectators' area. Sold to Flughafen Muenchen GmbH 1 Mar 00. Renovated in original Lufthansa colours as "D-ALEM" complete with tip-tanks by team of Lufthansa technicians 29 Jan-16 May 01 (representing the aircraft used on Lufthansa's first post-war scheduled flight Hamburg-New York). Vandalised night of 10-11 Apr 01, but repaired. Restoration, costing approx. DM100,000, financed jointly by Lufthansa & Munich Airport authorities. Officially re-opened 16 May 01 by Business Director of Munich Airport (Willi Hermsen) & opened to public next day.

4672 1049G-03-124 22 Jul 57 to Thai Airways as HS-TCA. E-28728 dated 19 Jul 57. In svce for short time only, then stored from early 1958 at Bangkok, Thailand, until sold to Guest Aerovias Mexico 15 Sep 59 via Scandinavian Airlines System and regd XA-NAC. Overhauled by Flying Tiger & del Dec 59 (tip-tanks fitted).

Regn canx 25 Apr 61 on sale to Southern Aircraft Holdings Ltd. Lsd immediately to Transportes Aereos Portugueses as CS-TLF, regd May 61. Named 'Mousinho D'Albuquerque'. Withdrawn from svce with TAP approx Jul 67 and ferried to Shannon, Ireland, 6 Jul 67 (as CS-TLF) for D McCarthy. Regn EI-ARS reserved but ntu Jul 67. D McCarthy acting as broker for TAP on sale to Air Trans Africa. Aircraft dep Shannon approx one week later and ferried to Salisbury, Rhodesia, for use as spares. Stored at Salisbury. CS-regn canx 2 Oct 67. Last reported Jul 69 at Salisbury, Rhodesia, being stripped for useable spares. Subsequently scrapped.

4673 1049G-82-99 8 Jul 57 to Iberia as EC-AMP 'San Juan', FN 211. E-28727 same day. Del with tip-tanks. Lsd to Aviaco for European IT work as 80-seater during summers of 1963-65. Fitted with rear cargo door and cargo mods by Air France at Toulouse spring 64-Jul 64. First flight after conversion 12 Jul 64. Sold to International Aerodyne Inc May 67 and ferried to Miami, FL for storage. Regd N8021. Still stored Aug 69, but sold or lsd some time afterwards to unknown operator. Damaged slightly on landing at La Antigua, 60 kilometres northeast of La Rioja, Argentina, on 6 Jun 70, when undercarriage collapsed. When aircraft was found by the authorities, however, it was 95% destroyed by fire and no trace of the crew. Aircraft had presumably been used on smuggling flight. Canx from USCAR 10 Jul 70.

4674 1049G-82-134 21 Aug 57 to Linea Aeropostal Venezolana-LAV as YV-C-AMI. E-28730 dated 19 Aug 57. Del with tip-tanks. Op by VIASA during 1961. Sold to California Airmotive Corp, date unknown and regd N9746Z. Sold to the Flying Tiger Line 14 Mar 63 and rebuilt into all-cargo aircraft. Wings, centre-section and tail of c/n 4674 used, fuselage taken from YC-121F turboprop Super Constellation c/n **4161** (BuAer 131660/AF 53-8157). Redesignated Model 1049H/06-03 on completion, with c/n 4674, regd N9746Z. First flight as 1049H 5 Jul 63, in svce same day, with the Flying Tiger Line FN 816, reregd N173W 20 Sep 63. Used as all-cargo aircraft only. To Mercury General Aviation 1966, lsd to Flying Tiger Air Services 1 Jun 66-31 Dec 67. Sold to Etablissements Jean Godet (or Gaudet), Agencia Anglo Portuguesa, Lisbon (for use on Biafran airlift) Nov 67, E-65719 (6 Nov 67), but export CofA canx. Ret to Flying Tiger Line 1 Jan 68. Stored at Kingman, AZ during 1968. Sold to Murphree Air International Inc 19 Dec 68 (officially 28 Feb 69) & painted up in Nusantara Airways colours, but never used. Lsd to Interior Airways during Feb 69. Sold to North Slope Supply Co 29 Apr 69, unconf lse to Kodiak Airways 1970. Stored at Anchorage, AK from at least Sep 70 until ferried to Miami, FL via Seattle, WA, Kingman, AZ & New Orleans, LA Dec 71 after sale to Unum Inc on 2 Feb 71 via Small Business Administration. (TT: 18,162 hrs a/o Jan 72). Sold to John Stivers dba Stivers Aviation 4 May 72: Ret to Unum Inc 22 Sep 72 and sold to Aviation Specialties 8 Mar 73 and to Aircraft Specialties 23 Apr 73. Cvtd to sprayer. Crashed shortly after take-off from Casey Airport, PQ at 06.11 hrs (EST) on 9 Jun 73 into tree-covered, hilly terrain, one and three-quarter miles southwest of runway 23, killing the crew. The aircraft had taken off on a tree-spraying mission at 06.10 hrs. At approx 200 feet, the aircraft levelled off momentarily, then descended in a wing level, nose-high attitude into the trees. The aircraft was destroyed by explosion and fire. Cause: Take-off flaps inadvertently retracted at low altitude before zero-flap flying speed was reached, also crew fatigue, with possible contributory factor of exposure to chemical spray (Fenitrothion). In addition, the aircraft was carrying a greater load of spraying liquid than usual.

4675 1049G-82-112 27 Jul 57 to Cubana as CU-T-631. E-28729 dated 26 Jul 57. Lsd Iberia (date unknown). Withdrawn from use at Jose Marti International Airport, Havana, probably in 1961, due to lack of spares. Sold to World-Wide Airways Inc Jun 64 and regn CF-PZZ allotted Jun 64, but sale fell through and regn canx Nov 64 as aircraft not imported. Probably scrapped by the mid-1960s at Havana.

4676 1049G-82-99 12 Aug 57 to Iberia as EC-AMQ 'Palos de Moguer', FN 212. E-28731 same day. Del with tip-tanks. Lsd to Aviaco for European IT work as 80-seater during summers 1963-65. Fitted with rear cargo door and cargo mods by Air France at Toulouse late 1963 to Mar 64. First flight after conversion 15 Mar 64. Sold to International Aerodyne Inc May 67 and ferried to Miami, FL for storage. Regd N8022. Stored there until broken up during Sep 70. Canx from USCAR 1971.

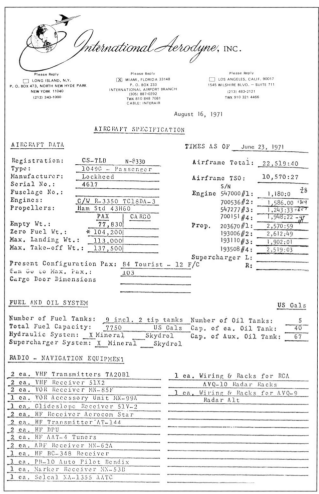

C/n 4677. An illustration to show that you cannot always believe official-looking documents. This Aircraft Sale Specification dated 16th August 1971 from one of the well-known dealers in Constellations in the 1960s and 1970s shows the aircraft as "c/n 4617 CS-TLB/N833D". Only the last-mentioned detail is correct, as c/n 4617/CS-TLB had long since been erected atop a restaurant in the Everglades. The aircraft in question was the former TAP CS-TLE c/n 4677, which was sold on as N833D shortly after this date.

4677 1049G-03-124 29 Aug 57 to Thai Airways as HS-TCB. E-28732 dated 27 Aug 57. In svce for short time only, then stored from early 1958 at Bangkok, Thailand, until sold to Guest Aerovias Mexico 15 Sep 59 via Scandinavian Airlines System and regd XA-NAD. Overhauled by Flying Tiger & del Nov 59 (tip-tanks fitted). Lsd to Aerovias Panama Airways SA as HP-281 Dec 59-Feb 60. HP-regn canx 9 Feb 60. Ret to Guest as XA-NAD Feb 60. Inaugurated Mexico City-Paris Super G svce 1 Mar 60. Regn canx 25 Apr 61 on sale to Southern Aircraft Holdings Ltd. Lsd immediately to Transportes Aereos Portugueses as CS-TLE, regd May 61, in svce May 61. Named 'Salvador Correia'. Withdrawn from svce with TAP Jun 67 and ferried to Miami, FL, arr approx 2 Jul 67 as CS-TLE. Sold to International Aerodyne Inc 10 Jul 67. CS-regn canx 17 Jul 67, but stored at Miami as CS-TLE. Regd N833D 5 Jul 68 (date of application for regn) to International Aerodyne Inc. Sold to Air Cargo Operations Inc 6 Mar 69, and to Leasing Consultants Inc 5 Jun 69. Remained in storage at Miami, believed non-airworthy, and still carried CS-TLE (and N833D). Restored to International Aerodyne Inc 24 May 71 (bankruptcy sale) and up for sale Aug 71 (TT: 22,519 hrs) as 1049G-82 with 103 pax seats, for $25,000 (including four spare QEC engines), plus $5,000 for annual inspection. Tfd to International Air Leases 29 Nov 71, but remained in store at Miami. In official records, Leasing Consultants Inc ownership was canx 8 Mar 72 (failure to file), but restored 2 May 72. Made airworthy during first six months of 1972 and given new paint scheme. Sold to Constellation Air Leasing Inc 16 Mar 72. Owner/operator L 'Ticky' Hernandez (a/o Aug 72), flew to Buffalo, NY Aug 72 & stored there by Jan 73. Repossessed by Manufacturers & Traders Trust Co 23 Mar 73. Sold to Ronald A Adimey, Robert L Shere & John L Jurgens 15 Nov 73 (no regn papers or bill of sale filed with FAA). Made one flight from Buffalo in Jun 74, but two engines reportedly caught fire and the aircraft made only a short circuit and an emergency landing. Remained in storage at Buffalo. Sold to Air Cargo Support Inc approx late 1974/early 1975 (USCAR Jan 75 gives 'Sale Reported'). Stripped for spares Dec 76 & parts flown to Miami, FL in 1049H N1007C. All useable parts missing by Oct 77, hulk presumably broken up shortly afterwards.

4678 1049G-03-124 24 Sep 57 to Thai Airways as HS-TCC. E-28733 dated 19 Sep 57. In svce for short time only, then stored from early 1958 at Bangkok, Thailand, until sold to Guest Aerovias Mexico 15 Sep 59 via Scandinavian Airlines System and regd XA-NAF. Overhauled by Flying Tiger & del Oct 59 (tip-tanks fitted). Lsd to Aerovias Panama Airways SA as HP-280 Dec 59-Feb 60. HP-regn canx 9 Feb 60. Ret to Guest as XA-NAF Feb 60 & in use with Guest on crew training flts at Miami, FL a/o 17 Mar 60. Regn canx 17 Nov 61. Sold to Iberia by Feb 62 and regd EC-WRN, later EC-ARN 'Santiago', FN 217. Lsd to Aviaco for European IT work as 80-seater summers 1963-65. Fitted with rear cargo door and cargo mods by Air France at Toulouse mid 64-Oct 64. First flight after conversion 31 Oct 64. Sold to International Aerodyne Inc May 67 and regd N8026. Ferried to Miami for storage. Lsd to Compania Interamericana Export-Import early 1968 and op by RAPSA-Panama as HP-467. Crashed after take-off from Tocumen Intl Airport, Panama City, at 20.25 hrs on 30 Mar 68. No.3 engine caught fire on take-off. Aircraft destroyed after impact explosion. Crew killed.

4679 1049G-82-153 25 Oct 57 to Qantas as VH-EAO 'Southern Aurora'. First flight 24 Oct 57, CofRegn 25 Oct 57, E-28734 dated 25 Oct 57. Del Burbank-Honolulu-Sydney 26-28 Oct 57, with tip-tanks (first time an airliner had flown Honolulu-Sydney non-stop). Test flown 30 Nov 57, in svce 2 Dec 57 (to Hong Kong). Painted up with names of cities on Qantas' round-the-world route on cabin roof by Dec 57. Flew Round-the-World proving flt Sydney-Sydney 20 Dec 57-8 Jan 58. Inaugurated Qantas Round-the-World scheduled services (with c/n 4680) 14-20 Jan 58, flying eastbound Melbourne-San Francisco, then via London-Singapore back to Sydney (flying time 128hrs). En route San Francisco-New York 12 Aug 59 on RTW schedule, vibration in no.4 propeller experienced during cruise at 13,000ft. Prop could not be feathered, acft diverted to Lovelock, NV after dumping fuel. Engine seized & shortly after, at 1,500ft on base leg, the prop separated from the engine. Landed safely. Wfs & VH-regn canx 19 Sep 59. Sold to Lockheed Aircraft Corp (buy-back program) 13 Oct 59 (TT: 5,874 hrs) and regd N9722C same day. Del ex-Sydney to USA 14 Oct 59. Lsd back to Qantas 18 Aug 60 (TT: 5,903 hrs), del Portland-Honolulu-Nadi-Sydney 19-21 Aug 60. Regd VH-EAO again 23 Aug 60 & named 'Southern Prodigal'. Re-entered svce 24 Aug 60 (to Melbourne, Auckland, Nadi & Sydney). Bought from LAC 31 Mar 61. Based Perth 29 Apr-16 Jun 61 & 23 Dec 61-11 Feb 62. Flew last svce 13 Feb 62 (migrant charter) & last flt (training, Sydney-Narromine) 25 Feb 62. Sold on 5 Mar 63 to California Airmotive Corp, VH-regn canx, and reregd N86682 5 Mar 63. Del ex-Sydney 5 Mar 63 to Burbank (TT:10,299 hrs). To American Flyers Airline Corp, believed on lse-purchase 1965. Sold to California Airmotive Corp Nov 68 and flown to Fox Fld, Lancaster, CA for storage. Canx from USCAR 12 Jul 70. Fuselage only left by Nov 71, scrapped shortly afterwards.

4680 1049G-82-153 20 Nov 57 to Qantas as VH-EAP 'Southern Zephyr'. First flight 8 Nov 57, CofRegn 20 Nov 57, E-28735 dated 20 Nov 57. Del Burbank-San Francisco 21 Nov 57 (with tip-tanks). Made proving flt San Francisco-New York-Gander-London & return in preparation for Round-the-World svces. Del San Francisco-Honolulu-Sydney 3-5 Dec 57. (TT: 107hrs on arrival). In svce 30 Dec 57 (to Hong Kong). Inaugurated Qantas Round-the-World scheduled services (with c/n 4679) 14-20 Jan 58 flying westbound Melbourne-Singapore, then via London-San Francisco back to Sydney (128hrs flying time). Damaged in landing accident at Nadi Airport, Fiji, on 14 Nov 58. Aircraft landed short of the runway & hit four-foot high bank and acacia bushes 29 feet from runway end, landed heavily on runway, bounced back into the air and then landed again. Severe rippling and buckling of the skin and sprung rivets found on both upper and lower surfaces of both mainplanes and the fuselage. En route San Francisco-Sydney. Flown to Sydney for repairs. Test-flt 15 Dec 58 & re-entered svce. Flew last svce 3 Oct 59 (to Johannesburg). Sold to Lockheed Aircraft Corp (buy-back program) 23 Oct 59 (TT: 5,765 hrs). Del Sydney-Ontario, CA 25-27 Oct 59. VH-regn canx 5 Nov 59, re-regd N9723C same day. Lsd Resort Airlines late 59-Jun 60 when the company ceased ops. Stored at Oakland, CA Jul 60 in Resort colours. Lsd Twentieth Century Airlines by Aug 60 until sometime in 1961. Stored at LAS Ontario, CA by late 1961 in Twentieth Century colours. Unconf lse to Capitol Airways 1962. Ret to Lockheed Aircraft Corp by Jun 63 and used as company aircraft until approx 1970. Up for sale by LAC Apr 70. Sold to California Airmotive Corp/American Jet Industries 12 Dec 70 and stored at Fox Fld, Lancaster, CA by May 71. Repainted with 'California Airmotive Inc' titling and named 'Red Baron' with racing number 64c by Jul 71 and flown to San Diego Brown Fld (see Section 9). Ret to Burbank, CA and stored. Sold to Stereo Vision International Inc 27 Sep 71. Mod to represent a Supersonic Transport aircraft at Burbank, CA Nov 71-Jan 72. Fitted with pointed nose (similar to Concorde) and windows in forward fuselage mod to become small, round ones. Carried Global (Airlines) titling in small letters on forward fuselage and also the inscription 'The Condor-A Product of Great Britain' by May 72. Regd to Stereo Vision International Inc 2 Oct 72 and made several short flights, including one to Long Beach, CA around 1 Nov 72 in connection with the film work. Piloted by H.R."Fish" Salmon. The filming idea was, however, eventually given up due to the problems involved, and the aircraft ret to California Airmotive. Scrapped at Burbank, CA Jul 74. Canx from USCAR Jan 75 at request of California Airmotive Inc as scrapped. Tip-tanks acquired by Duncan Baker in 1975 for N11SR (c/n 4581).

4681 1049G-82 Believed originally ordered by Aerolineas Argentinas in 1956, but order canx, subsequently for Qantas as VH-EAQ, but order also canx. Updated to 1049G/01-03-158. LADD: 18 Nov 57 to VARIG as PP-VDD (in lieu of 1649A). E-28745 dated 18 Nov 57 (tip-tanks fitted). Damaged by another aircraft on ground Porto Alegre, Brazil 19 Sep 59. Repaired. Flew VARIG's last scheduled pax svce New York-Rio de Janeiro with Super Constellations 20 Jul 60. CofA expired 15 Jun 62 and stored at Sao Paulo-Congonhas, Brazil. Withdrawn from use there and derelict by Feb 64. Broken up Jun 67 at Sao Paulo.

4682 1049G-82 Believed originally ordered by Aerolineas Argentinas in 1956, but order canx, subsequently for Qantas as VH-EAR, but order also canx. 1049G-82-109, mod to 1049G-82-161. LADD: 22 Nov 57 to Trans-Canada Air Lines as CF-TEW, FN 411. E-28746 dated 22 Nov 57 (tip-tanks fitted). Flew the 'Hudson Bay' inaugural svce London-Gander-Winnipeg-Vancouver 28 May 58. Withdrawn from svce with TCA (TT: 11,571 hrs) and sold to A Paulson (t/a California Airmotive Corp) 28 Jun 62. Regd N7772C. Flown to Burbank, CA and stripped for spares Jul 62-autumn 1962. Fuselage lying on ground in junk yard at north end of Burbank late Sep 62. Subsequently scrapped.

4683 1049G-82 Believed originally ordered by Aerolineas Argentinas in 1956, but order canx, subsequently for Qantas as VH-EAS, but order also canx. 1049G-82-109, mod to 1049G-82-161. LADD: 20 Dec 57 to Trans-Canada Air Lines as CF-TEX, FN 412. E-28751 dated 20 Dec 57 (tip-tanks fitted). Withdrawn from svce with TCA (TT: 11,437 hrs?) and sold to Douglas Aircraft Corp 1 Mar 62 (trade-in on DC-8s). Regd N9642Z. Stored at Las Vegas, NV. Sold to California Airmotive Corp 10 Jul 63 and flown

N1006C 1049H of Intercontinental (US) Inc was photographed on a transatlantic passenger charter at Shannon, Ireland in 1963. (Stephen Piercey collection)

to Fox Fld, Lancaster, CA for storage. Sold to Walter R von der Ahe, dba Van Nuys Skyways, 1 Feb 64, and to Continental Counselors 18 Feb 64 (believed same owner, as regd to Continental Counselors and Walter R von der Ahe on 6 Mar 64). Carried 'Townsend' insignia on rear fuselage mid-64. Ret to Van Nuys Skyways 11 Jun 64. Lsd to United States Airways-USAIR by Jul 64. Stored Frankfurt Rhein-Main Sep-Dec 64. Impounded at London-Gatwick 20 Jan 65, released 2 Feb 65. Officially sold to USAIR 20 Jan 65. Flown to Beek, Holland, 2 Feb 65, regn N9642Z overpainted and false regn 9G-28 painted on aircraft. Flown by Vincent Frans Burger & Lucien Pickett to Prague, Czechoslovakia, to collect cargo of arms for Algeria. Dep Prague 3 Feb 65 en route for Benina, Libya, but made emergency landing at Luqa, Malta, 4 Feb 65 and aircraft plus cargo impounded. Repossessed by the Estate of Walter R von der Ahe 10 Mar 65, aircraft regn changed on aircraft at Malta to N964. Ownership changed to Gene S Mulkey-Conservatore 1965. Aircraft released by Malta (after legal battle between Lucien Pickett and the aircraft's owners) on 29 Jan 66. Sold to California Airmotive Corp 10 Jan 66. Painted in Soli Transocean titles. Projected lse to Cyprus Airways as 5B-CAJ 'Archbishop Makarios III' fell through. Ret to California Airmotive Corp 26 Jan 67 and regd N9642Z again (officially). Deld Malta-London(Gatwick)-Los Angeles 25/26 Jan 67, still in Soli Transocean titles and with Cypriot name 'Makarios' still on nose. To Fox Fld, Lancaster, CA for storage. Parts missing by Apr 69. Canx from USCAR 12 Jul 70. Last reported Mar 71, fuselage only, on belly. Scrapped shortly after.

4684 1049G-82 Believed originally ordered by Aerolineas Argentinas in 1956, but order canx, subsequently for Qantas as VH-EAT, but order also canx. Updated to 1049G/01-03-158. LADD: 11 Dec 57 to VARIG as PP-VDE. (in lieu of 1649A). E-28748 dated 11 Dec 57 (tip-tanks fitted). Stored at Porto Alegre, Brazil, after CofA expiry on 11 Oct 63, wfu there by Nov 65 and broken up at Porto Alegre in Jun 67.

4685 1049G-82 Believed originally ordered by Aerolineas Argentinas in 1956, but order canx, subsequently for Qantas as VH-EAU, but order also canx. Updated to 1049G/01-03-158. LADD: 17 Jan 58 to VARIG as PP-VDF. (in lieu of 1649A). E-28754 dated 17 Jan 58 (tip-tanks fitted). Withdrawn from use by VARIG by Nov 65 and stored until sold to Norte Importadora Limitida in Mar 67. Sold to Air Trans Africa 1 Mar 67 and regd VP-WAW. Regd ZS-FAA to Protea Airways 12 May 67, but ntu. Reverted to VP-WAW and regd 27 Jul 67 to Air Trans Africa. Used on Biafran airlift (see Section 9). Reregd TR-LNY in Sep 68 (still to Air Trans Africa). Tfd to Afro-Continental Airways in 1970 and regd VP-WAW again. In svce by Sep 70. Withdrawn from use after last flight 28 Sep 74 from Salisbury Airport, Salisbury, Rhodesia, to Charles Prince Airport, Salisbury, Rhodesia, arriving at 08.25 hrs (local). Preserved at Charles Prince Airport, and used as clubhouse for the Air Traffic Control Flying Club. Named 'Proud Mary' by late 1980. Still used from time to time in early 1980s. Salisbury, Rhodesia renamed Harare, Zimbabwe. For sale by tender 30 Dec 89 by the Director of National Museums & Monuments of Zimbabwe. No buyer found, so scrapped on site some time afterwards.

4686 1049G-82-106 18 Jul 58 to Air-India International as VT-DJW 'Rani of Bijapur', E-27680 dated 18 Jul 58. Deld Burbank-London (Heathrow) 25 Jul 58-India 26 Jul 58. In svce 8 Aug 58. Inaugurated svce India to Moscow 14 Aug 58. Fitted with rear cargo door as freighter/convertible by LAS May-Jul 60. Called 'The Flying Sherpa'. Tfd to Indian Air Force 2 Apr 62 and serialled BG583, coded 'G'. Canx from VT-register 12 Apr 62. Used by 6 Squadron, call-sign VU-QLG, later VU-QGG. In camouflage Jan 72, later reverted to normal colours. In use by IAF as combi pax/cargo acft, last flight 11 Nov 83. Stored outside at Agra Air Base for Indian Air Force Museum. Still awaiting restoration, condition deteriorating (a/o 2002).

4687 1049G-82-106 13 Aug 58 to Air-India International as VT-DJX 'Rani of Sagurai', E-27681 dated 12 Aug 58. Deld in USA 12 Aug 58, via London (Heathrow) 17 Aug 58, arr India 18 Aug 58. In svce 30 Aug 58. Fitted with rear cargo door as freighter/convertible by LAS Aug-Oct 60. Inaugurated Air-India all-cargo services London (Heathrow)-India 14-15 Nov 60. Called 'The Flying Sherpa'. Tfd to Indian Air Force 16 Jan 62 and serialled BG579, coded 'D'. Canx from VT-register 23 Jan 62. Used by 6 Squadron, callsign VU-QLD, later VU-QGD. Involved in 'near-miss' with Olympic Airways Boeing 727 (SX-CBB) over Greenford, England, on missed approach to London-Northolt Airport at 17.41 hrs (GMT) on 9 Jan 70. In use by IAF as combi pax/cargo acft, grounded by 31 Mar 84. Stored at Lohegaon Air Base, condition deteriorating a/o 1998, but scrapped by 2002.

4688 to **4799** not used. **4800** not used.

4801 1049H-82-133 Prototype Model 1049H 'Husky' convertible pax/cargo aircraft. First flight 20 Sep 56 as VH-EAM (CofRegn issued 13 Oct 56). LADD: 13 Oct 56 to Qantas 'Southern Spray', E-28719 dated 13 Oct 56. Dep Burbank on dely 13 Oct 56, but ret, dep again 15 Oct via Honolulu-Nadi to Sydney, arr 17 Oct 56, Qantas dely date 18 Oct 56. In svce 2 Nov 56 (to San

Francisco). First Qantas Super Constellation to be fitted with radar nose (27 Dec 56-26 Jan 57). Op a TAA charter flt 21 Mar 57. Wing tip damaged by departing VH-EAJ at Mascot, Sydney 16 Dec 57. Repaired. Last svce 11 Jun 62. Dep Sydney 11 Jul 62 via Nadi & Honolulu to Ontario, arr 13 Jul 62. (TT: 13,922 hrs). Sold to Air New-Mex Inc 24 Jul 62. VH-regn canx & regd N7776C 24 Jul 62. Stored at Burbank, CA and under overhaul there end Sep 62. Cvtd to 1049H/06. Lsd to Intercontinental US Inc by Jan 63. Damaged at Miami, FL 24 Jan 63 when left undercarriage collapsed. Repaired. Lsd to Alaska Airlines 23 Apr 64. Ownership tf to International Aerodyne Inc 31 Dec 64 (lse to Alaska continued). Last reported with Alaska Jul 66. Lsd to Trans International by Dec 66 (in Alaska colours) until at least May 67. Lsd to Aerotransportes Entre Rios at Miami as N7776C 23 Jun 68, N-regn canx 24 Jun 68 and reregd LV-PJU. Reregd LV-JHF 23 Aug 68, with Aerotransportes Entre Rios (no titling carried), but regn carried prior to this date. Ret to Miami by Sep 68 and lsd to Bolivian Airways as CP-797 'Carmen'. Canx from LV-register 11 Dec 68 & from CP-register 9 Jan 69, latter on sale to USA. Restored to US-register 10 Jan 69 as N7776C to International Aerodyne Inc. To Air Cargo Operations Inc 6 Mar 69 and to Leasing Consultants Inc 5 Jun 69. In use on Biafran airlift by Aug 69 until Jan 70. Stored at Faro, Portugal until at least Mar 70, then flown to Fort Lauderdale, FL by Sep 70. Stored at Fort Lauderdale until Jul 72. Sold to L & H International Airmotive Inc 26 Jan 71, CofRegn issued 5 Mar 71. Flown to Columbus, OH in Jul 72, and broken up for spares some time afterwards for Aircraft Specialties. Also reported as sold for spares use to Century Airfreight 23 Feb 73. Believed scrapped at Columbus after being stripped for spares.

4802 1049H-82-147 5 Dec 56 to Air World Leases Inc and lsd to Seaboard & Western Airlines as N1006C 'Prestwick Airtrader'. Sub-lsd to Eastern Air Lines Jan-Jun 57. Ret to S & W Jun 57. Sub-lsd to Sabena in full Sabena colours for Brussels World Fair May-Oct 58. Ret S & W. S & W renamed Seaboard World Airlines Apr 61, regd 11 May 61. Lsd Capitol Airways 17 Mar 62 to 15 Jun 63, then to Intercontinental US Inc from Jul 63. Mortgaged to Canadair Ltd 15 Jun 63, but remained under Seaboard World ownership. Intercontinental lse continued until Jan 64, but parked out of use at New York-Idlewild in Intercontinental colours from Sep 63 until at least 31 Dec 65. Sold to Capitol Airways probably on 31 Dec 65, and in use as 108-seater. Capitol renamed Capitol International Airways. Lsd to Berliner Flug Ring during summer 1967 for European IT work. Stored at Wilmington, DE by Mar 68, then flown to Sebring, FL for storage in Mar/Apr 70 (TT: 19,758 hrs). Sold to California Airmotive Corp 5 Jul 72, and to Midair Inc Apr 73, but ntu, and aircraft remained in storage at Sebring. Sold to R B Bergstresser at Sheriff's sale 12 Aug 74, tfd officially 20 Dec 74 and broken up for spares at Sebring late 1974/early 1975 by R B Bergstresser. Canx from USCAR 21 Jan 75 as "reduced to produce-engines removed and rest scrapped".

4803 1049H-82-133 15 Nov 56 to Qantas as VH-EAN 'Southern Tide'. First flight 8 Nov 56, CofRegn 12 Nov 56, E-28720 dated 12 Nov 56. Del Burbank-Honolulu-Canton Island-Nadi-Sydney 18-20 Nov 56. In svce 1 Dec 56 (to Singapore). Damaged at Biak 7 Dec 56 during unloading of R-3350 engine for stranded KLM Super Constellation, tipped on tail, damaging rudders. Repaired. Fitted with radar nose 28 Jan-2 Mar 57. Withdrawn from svce 28 Oct 59, pax fittings stripped & ret to svce as pure freighter 3 Nov 59 (to London). Last svce dep Sydney (to London) 25 Oct 61. During overhaul after return to Sydney, port undercarriage retracted 28 Nov 61 & no.1 fuel tank pierced by wing jack. Test flown after repairs 8 Jul 62. Dep Sydney 11 Jul 62 via Nadi & Honolulu to Ontario, arr 13 Jul 62. (TT: 13,320 hrs). Sold to Air New-Mex Inc 24 Jul 62. VH-regn canx & regd N7777C 24 Jul 62. Stored at Burbank, CA. Cvtd to 1049H/04. Unconf lse to Alaska Airlines Mar 63-Apr 63. Stored at Burbank, CA again by Jul 63. Lsd to Alaska Airlines 19 May 64. Ownership tfd to International Aerodyne Inc 31 Dec 64 (lse to Alaska continued). Damaged beyond repair at Kotzebue, AK 17 Apr 67 while on a freight flight. Undercarriage failed to extend completely on approach and subsequently collapsed on landing. No injuries. Cannibalized for useable spares at Kotzebue and aircraft then sold to Jay Snort for use as a clubhouse/bar. Erected just beyond the city limits, still in Alaska A/L colours with "The Flying Martini Inc" titling. On day before official opening, however, the city council moved the city limits an extra 50 yards. As Kotzebue was a "dry" town, this halted the project & the owner abandoned the Super Constellation. Remained in position, on a mound of earth, with wings & tail unit in place until 1978, but then vandalized & fell derelict. In 1980, a fire broke out in the fuselage & the interior was gutted. Broken up at Kotzebue during Sep 80 & remains to city tip. Canx from USCAR 8 Jul 70.

4804 1049H-03-148, mod to 1049H-03-156 1 Feb 57 to Flying Tiger Line as N6911C, FN 801. Cvtd to 1049H/0l-03. Mortgaged to Chase Manhattan Bank and Canadair Ltd 1 Jun 59-24 Jan 62. Damaged when starboard main undercarriage collapsed taxying at 11.34 hrs (CST) on 1 Dec 61 at Grand Island, NE. Aircraft was taxying for take-off when the starboard undercarriage broke through the concrete, due to lack of reinforcement in the concrete. En route Chicago, IL-Burbank, CA on all-cargo flight. No injuries. Repaired. Undershot and crashed on approach to Adak NAS, Aleutian Islands, AK at 01.14 hrs (EST) 15 Mar 62. One of crew killed. During a precision radar approach to land on runway 23, the aircraft touched down 328 feet short of the threshold lights and four feet below the runway elevation, striking rocks. The aircraft slid approx 3,000 feet, the main gear & one wing separated from the aircraft, & caught fire. The crew had been advised several times during the talk-down that the aircraft was below the glide-slope, and one and three-quarter miles from touch-down had been advised to execute a missed approach. The captain then reported field in sight and the crew continued a visual approach. Just before the crash, the captain warned the co-pilot he was too low, and as the latter applied power, the captain pulled back on the yoke, but at the same instant the right main landing-gear struck the rocks short of the runway. Cause: Probably misjudgement of distance and altitude during the approach. Aircraft was on an international military contract cargo flight Travis AFB, CA-Okinawa, Japan. The crew had reported nose-heaviness during two previous landings on the flight, due to an open access door, and then the cargo loading (at the last stop before Adak, at Cold Bay, AK). (TT: 16,038 hrs).

4805 1049H-82-147 10 Jan 57 to Air World Leases Inc as N1007C for op by Seaboard & Western Airlines. Lsd immediately to Eastern Air Lines (in full EAL colours) Jan-Jun 57. To Seaboard & Western Jun 57 and named 'Brussels Airtrader'. Lsd to Sabena in full Sabena colours for Brussels World Fair May-Oct 58. Ret S & W. Cvtd to 1049H-03. Renamed Seaboard World Airlines Apr 61, regd 11 May 61. Mortgaged to Canadair Ltd 17 Jan 62, but remained under Seaboard World ownership. Lsd Intercontinental US Inc, then lsd to Capitol Airways 17 Mar 62. Sold to Capitol Airways, later Capitol International Airways 31 Dec 65. (CAB records show 30 Dec 65 and 1 Mar 66). Had reverted to 1049H-82 with Curtiss Electric 858FE props for increased weights when stored at Wilmington, DE 2 Nov 62-2 May 67. Withdrawn from storage & used for military cargo contract 2 May-16 Aug 67. Stored again 17 Aug 67-3 Oct 69. Overhauled & flown to Sebring, FL in Mar/Apr 70. (TT: 17,369 hrs). Sold to California Airmotive Corp 5 Jul 72, official tf 12 Jul 72, and to Midair Inc 13 Apr 73, but ntu and remained in storage at Sebring. Sold to R.B. Bergstresser 12 Aug 74 at sheriff's sale, tfd officially 20 Dec 74. Flown to Miami, FL for overhaul Oct 74. Canx from USCAR 21 Jan 75 as "reduced to produce", but restored to use Mar 75. Fitted with cargo-restraining bulkhead by Aeronautical Engineers Inc at Miami 1975. Was to be lsd to Bolivian (International?) Airways Mar 75, possibly as CP-998 (reported May 75), but lse fell through. Op by Air Cargo Support (R B Bergstresser). Ownership tfd to Gordon R Maddox 1 Feb 76, but continued to be op by Air Cargo Support. Damaged at Miami Intl early Nov 75, when the aircraft tipped up on its tail. Repaired. Ownership tfd to Air Cargo Support Inc 16 Feb 77. Lsd to Aeromar (Dominica) for several periods during 1977-1979 (final contract expired Jul 79). Appeared in TV commercial for Goodyear Tyres and flew four circuits at Miami Intl for the company Jan 79. (TT: 20,166 hrs a/o 18 Apr 78). Last commercial flt 20 Feb 81. Flown from Miami Intl to Opa

N1010C 1049H of Seaboard & Western Airlines (second from right), with N1006C on the right, and making an interesting comparison with a 1049D N6503C (c/n 4165) seen third from the right, plus two further 1049Hs on the far left. The photo was probably taken in 1957. (Seaboard & Western via John T Wible)

Locka, FL on 7 Feb 82 for storage. Sold to Antonio Perez Dec 83. Sale to Belizean company fell through. Remained in storage with no.4 engine seized & no.2 with problems, condition deteriorating, until scrapped Nov-Dec 87 at Opa Locka.

4806 1049H-82-147 28 Jan 57 to Seaboard & Western Airlines as N1008C 'London Airtrader'. Lsd to Eastern Air Lines immediately (in full EAL colours) Jan-Jun 57. Lsd to Sabena in full Sabena colours for Brussels World Fair May-Oct 58. Ret to S & W. Cvtd to 1049H-03. Lsd to Aerlinte as 95-seater, named 'Breandan'. First svce 3 Jun 59, last svce 27 Sep 60. Mortgaged to Canadair Ltd 1962. S& W renamed Seaboard World Airlines Apr 61, regd 11 May 61. Lsd to Capitol Airways Mar 62 for unknown period & in use as 108-seater. Ret Seaboard World. Lsd Intercontinental US Inc (a/o Jul 63). Lsd Capitol Airways again 5 Jun 64 and stored at Newcastle, DE, being used for spares by Aug 64. Capitol renamed Capitol International Airways. Flown for further storage at Wilmington, DE by Jun 65. Reverted to 1049H-82 with Curtiss Electric 858FE props for increased weights. Believed sold to Capitol early 1966 (Seaboard still owned 31 Dec 65). In use with Capitol again 14 Jun-21 Jul 67. Ret to storage at Wilmington Aug 67. Flown to Sebring, FL for storage Mar/Apr 70 (TT: 20,149 hrs). Sold to California Airmotive Corp 5 Jul 72, and to Midair Inc Apr 73, but ntu and remained in storage at Sebring. Sold to R B Bergstresser at sheriff's sale 12 Aug 74, officially tfd 20 Dec 74. Broken up for spares at Sebring late 1974-early 1975 by R B Bergstresser. Canx from USCAR 21 Jan 75 as "reduced to produce - engines removed and rest scrapped".

4807 1049H-82-147 13 Feb 57 to Seaboard & Western Airlines as N1009C 'Shannon Airtrader'. Lsd to Eastern Air Lines immediately (in full EAL colours) Feb 57-6 May 57. Cvtd to 1049H-03. Lsd to Aerlinte as 95-seater, named 'Padraig'. First svce 24 Apr 58 (Aerlinte's pre-inaugural eastbound flt, ex-New York). Diverted to Gander, Nfld with engine failure, ferried back to New York for engine change & eventually arrived at Dublin 26 Apr 58. Flew Aerlinte's westbound inaugural Dublin-Shannon-Gander-New York 28-29 Apr 58. Slightly damaged taxying New York, NY 14 Dec 58. Repaired. Last Aerlinte svce 21 Oct 60. In S & W use when not required by Aerlinte, winter 1958/59 and winter 1959/60. S & W renamed Seaboard World Airlines Apr 61. Mortgaged to Canadair Ltd 1962. Unconf lse to Capitol Airways 1962. Lsd to Intercontinental US Inc by Jun 62 until Jan 64. Sub-lsd to Transtate Airlines as 84-seater Nov 63, but never entered svce and stored at New York-Idlewild. Ret to Seaboard World early 1964, but believed not used. Sold to LEBCA May 65 and deld to New York-JFK early May 65, in svce Nov 65(?), regd YV-C-LBP.

Stored at Miami, FL after LEBCA ceased ops spring 1968. Tfd nominally to Transcarga, who canx regn 13 Jun 68. Sold to International Aerodyne Inc Jun 68. Lsd to Bolivian Airways as CP-797 'Carmen' Sep 68, although regd officially 10 Nov 67. Ret to International Aerodyne Inc Nov 68 (and replaced by c/n 4801). Lsd to Aerotransportes Entre Rios as LV-PKW in Oct 68 (officially), but not deld until Jan 69. Reregd LV-JJO 19 Feb 69. Ret to International Aerodyne Inc and stored at Miami from at least Oct 70, as LV-JJO, in ex-AER colours. Derelict by early 1972. Reported sale to Peter C Shortell t/a Southern Cross International Airways Dec 72 fell through. Last reported derelict, many parts missing at Miami Sep 73 and broken up by end of 1973.

4808 1049H-82-147 18 Feb 57 to Seaboard & Western Airlines as N1010C. Lsd immediately to Eastern Air Lines (in full EAL colours) Feb-May/Jun 57. To S & W spring 1957 and named 'Munich Airtrader'. Cvtd to 1049H-03. Lsd to Transportes Aereos Portugueses Jun 58 and regd CS-TLD to Seatern Corp. Deld via London-Heathrow to Lisbon 24 Jun 58. Ret to Seaboard & Western Jun 59 and in svce as N1010C again by 18 Jun 59. S & W renamed Seaboard World Airlines Apr 61. Mortgaged to Canadair Ltd 1962. Lsd to Capitol Airways Mar 62 until at least May 64. Ret to Seaboard World, but believed not used. Stored silver overall at Newcastle, DE a/o Aug 64. Sold to LEBCA as YV-C-LBI Jun 65, in svce Nov 65 (?). Stored at Miami, FL after LEBCA ceased ops spring 1968. Tf nominally to Transcarga, who canx regn 13 Jun 68. Sold to International Aerodyne Inc Jun 68. Sold to Aerotransportes Entre Rios Oct 68 and del Oct 68 as LV-JIO (no LV-Pxx regn allotted). Officially regd 12 Dec 68. Ret to International Aerodyne Inc and stored at Miami from at least May 71, as LV-JIO, in ex-AER colours. Derelict by early 1972 and last reported May 72. Broken up at Miami during 1972.

4809 1049H/01-03-149 25 Mar 57 to Flying Tiger Line as N6912C, FN 802 (cargo non-convertible). Entered svce on scheduled domestic cargo flts. Damaged 27 Jan 58 at uk location. Repaired. Mortgaged to Chase Manhattan Bank and Canadair Ltd 1 Jun 59-24 Jan 62. Lsd to Mercury General Aviation Mar-May 66. Ret to Flying Tiger (in use Oct 66). Tfd to Flying Tiger Air Services with FN 12C 1966(?) until 31 Dec 67. Ret Flying Tiger 1 Jan 68 and stored at Kingman, AZ until sold to Bluebell Inc 25 Feb 69, in svce by end Feb 69. Carried "Wrangler Jeans & Sportswear" titling by Oct 70. Last flight 14 Dec 73. Sold to James Downey/Downair Ltd (TT: 34,579 hrs), E-119638 (4 Feb 74) and del Greensboro, NC to Stephenville, Nfld 7 Feb 74. Regd C-FBDB (allotted 28 Dec 73 but CofR never issued). N-regn canx 11 Feb 74. Never flew with Downair and stored at Stephenville, Nfld (TT:

34,584 hrs). To Dunwoody Ltd (Receiver for Downair Ltd) Mar 75. Sold to Lance W Dreyer t/a Paramount Petroleum Corp approx Dec 78 and broken up for spares at Stephenville, Nfld Jan-Apr 79. Canx from C-register 15 Feb 79.. Remains of fuselage still extant Feb 80.

4810 1049H/01-03-149 4 Mar 57 to Flying Tiger Line as N6913C, FN 803 (cargo non-convertible). Entered svce on scheduled domestic cargo flts. Mortgaged to Chase Manhattan Bank and Canadair Ltd 1 Jun 59-24 Jan 62. Crashed into a residential/industrial area in the San Fernando Valley 1.25 miles west of Burbank Airport, CA at 22.12 hrs (PST) on 14 Dec 62, killing all on board. The aircraft was on a scheduled domestic cargo svce en route from Chicago to Burbank, and was destroyed by fire and impact. The airport was shrouded in fog and the crew were making an ILS approach to runway 07. Position was acknowledged 2 miles from the runway end and 20 seconds before the crash. Probable cause: Incapacitation of the captain (severe coronary artery disease) during a critical situation, resulting in loss of control, from which the co-pilot was unable to recover (the co-pilot had been written up for an unsatisfactory instrument approach one month before the accident).

4811 1049H/01-03-149 8 Mar 57 to Flying Tiger Line as N6914C, FN 804 (cargo non-convertible). Entered svce on scheduled domestic cargo flts. Mortgaged to Chase Manhattan Bank and Canadair Ltd 1 Jun 59-24 Jun 62. In Quicktrans markings (a/o Oct 65). Crashed at the 13,000-foot level on the southwest face of Blanca Peak, CO, 22 nautical miles out on the 039 radial from the Alamosa, CO, VOR at 01.30 hrs (PST) on 15 Dec 65, killing the crew. The aircraft was on a scheduled domestic cargo svce en route Los Angeles-Chicago. Destroyed by fire and impact. (TT: 25,617 hrs). Aircraft was at normal cruise in low cloud and snow. Cause: Pilot probably became disorientated and failed to turn to airway V-210 outbound heading at Alamosa VORTAC.

4812 1049H/01-03-149 15 Mar 57 to Flying Tiger Line as N6915C, FN 805 (cargo non-convertible). Entered svce on scheduled domestic cargo flts. Damaged in accident Burbank, CA 15 May 57. Repaired. Mortgaged to Chase Manhattan Bank and Canadair Ltd 1 Jun 59-24 Jan 62. Cvtd to 1049H/05 or 06. Damaged when port main undercarriage failed while taxying at Detroit, MI on 4 Mar 60. Repaired. Crashed on Sweeney's Ridge, CA on the 860-foot level during the initial climb out from San Francisco Intl Airport at 00.31 hrs (PST) on 24 Dec 64, killing the crew. The aircraft was flying a scheduled domestic cargo svce Flight 282 from San Francisco to New York-JFK, NY. The flight took off from Runway 28L at 00.28 hrs and was 27 lbs below the maximum AUW. Weather was scattered clouds at 400 ft and wind gusting to 28 knots. Immediately after take-off the crew was advised they were left of course, but within seconds the aircraft had hit the ridge in the San Bruno mountains and was destroyed by fire and impact. Cause: Deviation from departure course into an area of rising terrain where downdraft activity and turbulence affected the climb capability of the aircraft.

4813 1049H/01-03-148 18 Apr 57 to California Eastern Aviation as N6931C, FN 931C (tip-tanks fitted). Lsd to Hughes Tool Co 18 Dec 57 and del from Oakland to Mid-Continent Airport, Kansas City 30 Jan 58 (TT: 2,251 hrs). Lsd to Trans World Airlines same day. Mods from 1 Feb 58 to 10 Mar 58, In svce with Trans World 13 Mar 58, FN 1253. Used on intl cargo and MATS flights until Aug 59. (TT: 7,041 hrs a/o 31 Aug 59). Used also on pax flights until ret to California Eastern 18 Jan 61. CEA renamed Dynalectron Corp. Lsd to World Airways 19 Jan 61, then to Slick Airways from Sep 63 until end of 1965. Ownership tfd to Bank of America National Trust & Savings 29 Apr 64, lsd Dynalectron, sub-lse to Slick continued. After Slick ceased ops, sub-lsd to Airlift International 1 Jul 66 and later named 'Ilha Taiwan'. Airlift ret to Dynalectron Corp Dec 67 and stored at Cheyenne, WY until at least May 68. Sold to Charlotte Aircraft Corp 12 Jul 68 and to Jack Richards Aircraft Co Inc 14 Mar 69. Lsd to Skyways Inc and in svce by May 69 (at London-Heathrow). Lsd to Dynalectron Corp, sold to them 20 Jul 71. Stored at Vero Beach, FL 1971/72 and for sale, unlicensed, Jan 72 by Dynalectron Corp. Stored at Miami, FL by May 72, and sold to Ronald K Saulan 29 Mar 72. Stored at Fort Lauderdale, FL by Oct 73. Lsd to D Mylo Beam t/a Sky Truck International 20 Apr 74 and in svce, named 'Fort Lauderdale'. Lsd to Bernie & Laura Watson t/a Laura Sales & Leasing Inc 1 Dec 74, who reportedly took over Sky Truck International Inc in 1975. Carried Air Lauderdale titling by May 75. Aircraft continued in use with Sky Truck until 3 Sep 75. On this day, the aircraft flew from Fort Lauderdale to Guadeloupe & Martinique. On the return flight, with a full load of fuel and cargo, no.1 engine was lost on take-off from Martinique. The crew prepared to make a three-engined ferry flight to Fort Lauderdale via San Juan, PR but no.3 engine was lost on take-off. The aircraft turned back to Guadeloupe, but suffered a power loss on no.2 engine on the approach, and landed on no.4 engine only at Guadeloupe. Repairs commenced at Guadeloupe, but the aircraft was subsequently abandoned there due to lack of finance (for three new engines). After storage at Point-a-Pitre, Guadeloupe, until Jun 79, the aircraft was reportedly scrapped there during the latter part of 1979. During its final period of use, the Super Constellation was nicknamed "The Green Goblin" (presumably partly because of its green colour-scheme), but did not have this name painted on. Cockpit section bought by French Air Force Warrant Officer Lombard for preservation at the Musee de l'Air, Paris 1985. Parts survive in private collection in France, but current location unknown.

4814 1049H/01-03-156 4 Apr 57 to Flying Tiger Line as N6916C, FN 806. Entered svce on transatlantic pax charters. Mortgaged to Chase Manhattan Bank and Canadair Ltd 1 Jun 59-24 Jan 62. In Quicktrans markings Oct 65. Lsd to Mercury General Aviation Mar-May 66, subsequently lsd to Flying Tiger Air Services FN 16C, name unknown, until 30 Nov 67. Ret to use with Flying Tiger Line. Stored at Kingman, AZ by mid-1968. Sold to Murphree Air International Inc 28 Feb 69, to North Slope Supply Co Inc 29 Apr 69 and to R.C.Wheatley 24 Dec 69. Resold to Dean E Finkbeiner 26 Jan 70, and ret to North Slope Supply Co Inc 12 Jul 70. Aircraft remained in storage at Kingman, however, with full Flying Tiger Line markings 1969-70. Probably sold to Unum Inc via Small Business Administration 2 Feb 71. Remained in storage at Kingman. No engines by Apr 73 & last reported Sep 73. Presumably scrapped there for spares late 1973 or early 1974.

4815 1049H/01-03-156 9 Apr 57 to Flying Tiger Line as N6917C, FN 807. CofA issued 8 Apr 57 (to LAC). FTL dely date 11 Apr 57. Entered svce on transatlantic pax charters. Cvtd to 1049H/06-03. Mortgaged to Chase Manhattan Bank and Canadair Ltd 1 Jun 59-24 Jan 62. The co-pilot, who was flying the aircraft, died at the controls as he landed at Prestwick Airport, Scotland, on 14 Jul 62, on arrival from New York, NY at night. The captain brought the aircraft to a stop safely. In Quicktrans markings late 1965. Lsd to Mercury General Aviation Mar-May 66, then lsd to Flying Tiger Air Services, with FN 17C, until 14 Nov 66. Subsequently lsd out again (probably to Flying Tiger Air Services) until 1 Jan 68, but stored at Kingman, AZ from Sep 67. Sold to Murphree Air International Inc 28 Feb 69 and to North Slope Supply Co Inc 29 Apr 69, but aircraft remained in storage at Kingman. Sold to Sandy L Murphree 2 Jan 70 & to Trademark Leasors Inc (F Jorge Areces) 26 Jan 70, officially 10 Feb 70. Ferried to Miami, FL 10 Feb 70. Damaged tail while unloading cattle at San Juan, PR in spring 1970. Repaired. According to the FAA, the aircraft was legally owned by North Slope Supply Co Inc a/o 30 Jun 70, and was canx from USCAR Aug 70 on sale in Panama. By 10 Sep 70, the aircraft was regd HP-526 with AFISA. Panamanian CofA issued 18 Jul 71 to Trademark Leasors t/a AFISA (Aerofletes Internacionales SA). Named 'Urula' but later renamed 'Orula'. Damaged when the landing strut collapsed on 9 Apr 72, location unknown. Repaired. Continued in use with AFISA until HP-regn canx 6 Jul 73 on sale to Aircraft Pool Leasing Corp same day.

Ret to N6917C, and continued to carry name 'Orula'. (TT: 28,905 hrs a/o 16 Aug 73). Crashed on take-off from Miami International Airport, FL at 23.53 hrs (EST) on 15 Dec 73, killing the crew and several on the ground. The aircraft was on a non- scheduled cargo flight on lse to ANDES (of Ecuador) with a load of Christmas trees for Maiquitia, Caracas, Venezuela. On take-off from runway 9L at Miami, the aircraft became airborne abruptly 4,800 feet from the start of the take-off run and assumed an unusually high (20°-30°) nose-up attitude, and a maximum altitude of 100 to 120 feet, before striking high-tension wires and a tree 1.25 miles east of the airport, then crashing into a parking lot and several houses, cars, and other property before stopping on NW 30th Street between NW 32nd & NW 31st Avenues, Miami. The aircraft was destroyed by impact and fire post-impact. Probable casue: Over-rotation at take-off resulting in a semi-stall, probably caused by improper loading & rearward movement of unsecured cargo which resulted in a shift of gravity aft of the allowable limit, and deficient crew coordination.

4816 1049H/01-03-156 15 Apr 57 to Flying Tiger Line as N6918C, FN 808. Entered svce on transatlantic pax charters. Damaged when struck jet barrier on take-off from Kadena AFB, Okinawa 20 Sep 58. Repaired. Mortgaged to Chase Manhattan Bank and Canadair Ltd 1 Jun 59-24 Jan 62. Lsd to Mercury General Aviation Mar-May 66, subsequently lsd to Flying Tiger Air Services, FN 18C, name unknown, until 2 Jan 67. Ret to Flying Tiger Line 2 Jan 67 and lsd to Korean Air Lines as HL4006 Feb 67 until 4 Dec 67 (FTL report quotes HL4005). Ret to Flying Tiger as N6918C 4 Dec 67. Lsd to Murphree Air International Inc 7 Aug 68 and sub-lsd Nusantara Airways 6 Sep 68. Impounded at Singapore-Paya Lebar 21 Sep 68 on dely flight. Sold Murphree 28 Feb 69. Aircraft released May 69 and then impounded at Hong Kong-Kai Tak immediately afterwards. Sold to North Slope Supply Co Inc 5 Jun 69, and flown from Hong Kong to Anchorage, AK late 1969. Stored at Anchorage, still in Nusantara Airways colours. Probably sold to Unum Inc via Small Business Administration 2 Feb 71. Remained in storage at Anchorage. No engines by Jun 72 (last report) and probably broken up there for spares late 1972 or 1973.

4817 1049H/01-03-143 for United States Overseas Airlines, regn unknown. Order canx, and mod to 1049H/01-03-148 for Air Finance Corp. LADD: 27 May 57 as N6921C, lsd same day to Flying Tiger Line, FN 811. Entered svce on transatlantic pax charters. Sold to Flying Tiger 1 Jun 59. Mortgaged to Chase Manhattan Bank & Canadair Ltd 1 Jun 59-24 Jan 62. Lsd to Lufthansa (in full Lufthansa colours) for cargo svces as N6921C 1 Nov 59-31 Mar 60. At San Francisco, still in Lufthansa colours 27 Apr 60, but ret shortly afterwards to Flying Tiger markings. Missing, presumed crashed in Pacific Ocean between Guam and Philippine Islands 15 Mar 62, with 96 pax and 11 crew on board. The aircraft took off from Agana NAS, Guam, at 12.56 hrs (GMT) on a MATS charter flight to Clark AFB, Philippines and Saigon, Vietnam and was last heard at latitude 13 14'N/longitude 144 00'E at 14.22 hrs (GMT). At 15.30 hrs (GMT) the crew of a surface vessel witnessed what appeared to be a midair explosion. The position and time of this observation coincided very nearly with the time and position given by the pilot for his next position report (13 44'N/134 49'E). A widespread search (involving 1,300 people, 48 aircraft flying 3,417 hours & 8 ships) failed to reveal any evidence that could definitely be connected with the missing Super Constellation. (TT: 17,224 hrs), at time of presumed crash. (See c/n 4804 for the other FTL 1049H accident on 15 Mar 62).

4818 1049H/0l-03-148 1 May 57 to Resort Airlines as N101R. Lsd to Hughes Tool Co for Trans World Airlines 14 Aug 57 and del Fairfax, Kansas City, same day (TT: 582 hrs). Mods at Fairfax until 9 Sep 57, then used for pilot training 10 Sep-9 Dec 57. To Mid-Continent Airport, Kansas City, MO 9 Dec 57 for mods for intl cargo ops. In svce with TWA in Resort colours 24 Dec 57 (possibly 14 Dec). Tfd to domestic network 4 Apr 58. Ownership tfd to California Eastern Aviation 1 May 58 (TWA lse continued). Ret to intl network shortly afterwards in Trans World colours with FN 1251. Used on intl cargo ops and MATS contract flights until Aug 59. (TT: 6,043 hrs a/o 31 Aug 59). With TWA, used also on pax svces until 1 May 61. Ret to California Eastern 1 May 61. CEA renamed Dynalectron Corp. Lsd to World Airways from 3 May 61 for unknown period (tip-tanks fitted). Ret to Dynalectron Corp and lsd to Flying Tiger Line, FN 820, 16 May 64. Ret to Dynalectron Corp 6 Oct 64. Lsd to CAUSA Jun 66 and regd CX-BEM to Brycol SA. E-46033 dated 10 Jun 66, canx USCAR same day. Ownership in Uruguay tfd to ONDA - Organizacion Nacional de Autobuses SA. Ret to Dynalectron Corp 3 Mar 67, and stored at Cheyenne, WY as CX-BEM in ex-CAUSA colours. Restored to US Register as N7023C. Sold to Jack Richards Aircraft Co Inc 7 Apr

N101R 1049H of Resort Airlines, probably taken on the aircraft's first visit to London (Heathrow) Airport in December 1957, while leased to Trans World Airlines for all-cargo flights. (Brian Stainer, APN)

Section 12: Constellation Production List

69 & lsd to Sky Lines International Inc 27 Jun 69. CofRegn issued to Dynalectron Corp 15 Sep 69. Ret to Jack Richards Aircraft Co Inc and stored at Vero Beach, FL by Jul 71. For sale, unlicensed, in Jan 72 at Vero Beach. Repossessed by Dynalectron Corp 2 Feb 72 and sold to Ronald K Saulan 29 May 72. Stored at Miami, FL by May 72 and derelict there by Apr 73. Broken up at Miami Intl, FL, probably in late 1974. Canx from USCAR 16 Aug 74.
NB: CX-BEN was reported at Miami, FL on 23 Dec 66. It is almost certain this was a mis-reading of CX-BEM, transitting Miami after CAUSA use en route to storage at Cheyenne, WY.

4819 1049H/01-03-150 20 May 57 to Flying Tiger Line as N6919C, FN 809. Entered svce on transatlantic pax charters. Mortgaged to Chase Manhattan Bank and Canadair Ltd 1 Jun 59-24 Jan 62. Lsd to Korean Airlines as HL4002 14 Apr 66 to 22 Mar 67. Ret to Flying Tiger Line. Lsd to Murphree Air International Inc 6 Dec 68. Sold to Murphree 25 Feb 69. In AMCO International markings May 69 in Alaska. Sold to North Slope Supply Co Inc approx Aug 69. Stored at Anchorage, AK by Aug 70. Probably sold to Unum Inc via Small Business Administration 2 Feb 71. Remained in storage at Anchorage, minus engines by Jun 72. Used for spares, and derelict hulk only by Jul 74. Used for fire-fighting practice at Anchorage. Fins, nose and other charred remains still extant in Oct 78.

4820 1049H/01-03-148 16 May 57 to Dollar Associates as N1880, CofRegn 22 May 57. Painted up in full Dollar Lines colours (tip-tanks fitted). Sold to 1880 Corp 3 Jul 57, Cof Regn 10 Jul 57. Mortgaged by Bank of America National Trust & Savings Association. Lsd to Transocean Airlines 9 Jul 57. Sub-lsd to Lufthansa as N1880 in full Lufthansa colours with tip-tanks Mar-Oct 59. Flew transatlantic all-cargo Super Constellation inaugural Frankfurt-New York 5 Mar 59. (TT: 6,151 hrs a/o 14 Oct 59). Aircraft transitted Prestwick, Scotland 22 Nov 59, still in Lufthansa colours, but titles painted out, at end of lse. Ret to Oakland, CA, where the aircraft was subsequently stored, and by Jul 60 was missing three engines and undercarriage doors. Lsd to South Pacific Air Lines for brief period in 1960. Lsd to World Airways 1 Jan 61 for unknown period. Lsd to Air New-Mex Inc 25 May 64 and sub-lsd to Alaska Airlines 5 Jun 64 (5 May also quoted). Sub-lsd to World Wide Airways briefly from 12 Aug 64. Sub-lsd again to Alaska Airlines. Air New-Mex taken over by International Aerodyne 31 Dec 64, lse to Alaska continued until Jun 65. Lse-purchased to Montreal Air Services Ltd 2 Jun 65, del Seattle, WA-Long Beach, CA 10 Jun 65, E-65922 (25 May 65). Regd CF-WWH and del to Canada 13 Jun 65. CofR to Montreal Air Services Ltd 17 Jun 65, CofA 17 Jun 65, lsd World-Wide Airways Inc Jun 65. N-regn canx 14 Jul 65. Op by World-Wide until ceased ops mid-Aug 65, then lse tfd to Nordair mid-Aug 65. Ret to Burbank, CA as CF-WWH on expiry of lse 7 Oct 65. CF-regn canx 12 Oct 65 & restored to International Aerodyne Inc as N1880 13 Oct 65. Cvtd to 1049H/01-06. Reportedly lsd Dynalectron Corp, then lsd to Alaska Airlines again approx 9 Jan-31 Oct 66, then lsd to Slick Airways from 1 Nov 66 until Mar 67, lsd Airlift International by Apr 67 until Dec 67. Ret International Aerodyne Inc Dec 67 (and reportedly also Dynalectron Corp same date, but in USCAR aircraft regd to International Aerodyne 1966-1971). Lsd or sold to Aero Lessors Inc by Nov 68 after a period of storage at Miami, FL. In svce with Aero Lessors until at least Feb 69, and flying for unknown company at Miami in Sep 70. Ret to International Aerodyne Inc, then sold to F A Conner 26 Oct 71. Unconf lse to Carib West Airways Jan-Feb 75. Continued in svce with F A Conner until damaged at Ramey AFB, PR during early Nov 75. Grating in taxiway collapsed while the aircraft was taxying and the aircraft received damage to no.1 engine and propeller, undercarriage and fin. Remained in damaged condition at Ramey until ferried back to Miami on about 4 Apr 77, with no propeller on no.1 engine. Never flew again, and remained in storage in the Conner area at Miami International Airport, condition deteriorating, until donated to the Dade County Aviation Department on 6 Oct 80 for fire-training at Miami Airport. Miami Airport Fire Dept informed FAA 14 Oct 81 that acft was in use "for fire-training only". Canx from USCAR 17 Nov 81 as destroyed. Derelict hulk remained at Miami Intl in use especially for non-destructive smoke-evacuation training work. Condition deteriorated until scrapped in late 2001.

4821 1049H/01-03-154 17 Jul 57 to Air Finance Corp as N1927H. Lsd same day to Transocean Airlines. Slightly damaged at Oakland, CA 30 Dec 57. Repaired. Tfd to The Babb Co Inc 1959. Lsd by Apr 59 to Capitol Airways & op in Transocean colours with Capitol titles (at LGW Aug 59), later painted in full Capitol colours. Sold to Capitol Airways on unknown date, renamed Capitol International Airways in 1964. In storage at Wilmington, DE by Mar 68, until sold to Nordair Ltd Nov 69 on behalf of CanRelief Air Ltd, E-83185 (7 Nov 69). TT (a/o 10 Nov 69) 12,456 hrs. Canx from USCAR 7 Nov 69, reregd CF-AEN (allotted 29 Oct 69). Del 9 Nov 69 to Dorval, PQ, CofA 9 Nov 69, sold CanRelief Air Ltd 12 Nov 69, but CofR not issued until 15 Dec 69 (after Canadian receipt of US de-registration 8 Dec 69). Del via London-Heathrow & Amsterdam (15 Nov) to Sao Tome, carrying Joint Church Aid titling and also "operated by Canairelief" and used on Biafran airlift in blue-top jungle camouflage scheme. Ret from Sao Tome to Downsview, Toronto, Ont 25 Jan 70. Stored at Downsview, Toronto, then at Dorval, Montreal, PQ from approx Sep 70, when the aircraft was sold to Hellenic Air Importing-Exporting Ltd and painted up in Hellenic Air Ltd titles. CofA expired 8 Nov 70. Flown to St.Hubert, PQ for storage 24 Apr 71. Hellenic Air ran into legal problems in 1972. Stored at St.Hubert, PQ, engines removed by Jan 73. Condition deteriorated until eventually broken up at St.Hubert in about Jun 74. Nothing left by end of summer 1974. Canx from C-register 26 Apr 79.

4822 1049H/01-03-150 31 May 57 to Flying Tiger Line as N6920C, FN 810. Entered svce on transatlantic pax charters & MATS charters. Crashed into Mount Oyama, Atsugi, Japan at 23.55 hrs (GMT) on 9 Sep 58, killing the crew and two pax on board. The aircraft was on a MATS cargo charter flight from Travis AFB, CA via Guam to Tachikawa, Tokyo. The flight had been cleared for a GCA approach, which was not acknowledged by the crew. The aircraft hit the mountain-side 10 miles west of Atsugi at the northern end of Sagami Bay, at relatively high speed while under instrument flying conditions. Destroyed by impact and fire. Cause: Possibly malfunction of directional instrument as the aircraft's maintenance record showed a number of such malfunctions; no evidence of engine or airframe malfunction.

4823 1049H/01-03-148 7 Jun 57 to California Eastern Aviation as N6932C, FN 932C (tip-tanks fitted). Lsd to Hughes Tool Co 18 Dec 57 and del Oakland, CA to Mid-Continent Airport, Kansas City, MO 1 Feb 58 (TT: 1,895 hrs). Mods at Mid-Continent 2 Feb-8 Mar 58. In svce with Trans World Airlines, FN 1254, 11 Mar 58 on intl cargo and MATS contract flights until Aug 59. (TT: 6,579 hrs a/o 31 Aug 59), later also for pax flights. Ret from TWA lse to California Eastern 10 Jan 61. Lsd to World Airways 13 Jan 61. CEA renamed Dynalectron Corp 19 Apr 62, lse to World continued for unknown period. Lsd to Slick Airways from 27 Apr 64 until end 1965. Ownership tfd to Bank of America National Trust & Savings 10 Jan 64. Lsd to Airlift International by Dynalectron Corp 27 Aug 66 until at least Oct 67. Ret to Dynalectron Corp and in storage at Cheyenne, WY by May 68. (NB: FAA records do not mention Dynalectron after 1964). Sold to Charlotte Aircraft Corp 12 Jul 68 and to Hemisphere Aircraft Leasing Corp 20 Mar 69. Lsd to unknown person(s) and in svce on charter flight at London-Heathrow Oct 69. Ret to Dynalectron Corp 29 Jan 70. Sold to Balair Inc (Jose Balboa) 22 Jun 70. Lsd Aviateca Mar-May 72 at least. Lsd to Agro Air on several occasions 1972 onwards. Lsd to J McKendry t/a Unlimited Leasing Oct 74, lsd to Jose Balboa Nov 74-Feb 75, lsd to Carib West Airways Jan or Feb 75 (for one flight to Barbados). N-regn canx 17 Sep 74 (failure to file), but in use from Miami, FL until Mar 75. Proposed lease to

Dominican company in Jul 75 fell through. Regd HI-254 19 Jul 75. Reports disagree on this proposed sale - either Aerotours Dominicano, who refused dely after the aircraft lost an engine on its dely flight from Miami to Santo Domingo - or Aerovias Quisqueyana, who refused to take up the aircraft as it was not legally regd in the USA at the time. At Miami in storage from Jul 75, owned by Jose Balboa, restored to N6932C with Balair Inc (Jose Balboa) 11 Sep 75. Impounded by Dade County Aviation Department, believed mid-Jun 76, for non-payment of airport fees. For sale to highest bidder, but remained in storage at Miami, unsold. Canx from USCAR 1976. Used for spares from 1977. On 1 Mar 79, all airworthiness was suspended by the FAA, and the aircraft was sold to Ed Ramsey for scrapping. Scrapped at Miami during the period 14 Mar-14 May 79.

4824 1049H/01-03-148 10 Jun 57 to Resort Airlines as N102R. Lsd to Hughes Tool Co for Trans World Airlines and del to Mid-Continent Airport, Kansas City, MO 30 Nov 57 (TT: 139 hrs). Mods at Mid-Continent 30 Nov-11 Dec 57. In svce with Trans World 12 Dec 57, FN 1252. Used on pax flights on domestic network, then to intl network 28 Jan 58, ret to domestic 31 Mar 58, and to intl network again 28 Apr 58. Ownership tf to California Eastern Aviation 1 May 58, lse to TWA continued. Used on pax, cargo and MATS contract flights until Aug 59. (TT: 5,058 hrs a/o 31 Aug 59). Used on domestic cargo flights. Crashed while turning onto final approach after a three- engined go-around at Chicago Midway Airport, IL at 05.35 hrs (CST) on 24 Nov 59. Crew killed. (TT: 5,624 hrs). The aircraft had taken off from Midway on scheduled all-cargo flight TW 595 en route to Los Angeles, CA at 05.31 hrs. As the aircraft began a left turn, the crew received a fire warning in no.2 engine, which was shut down. The aircraft proceeded in a continuing left turn around the airport in an elliptical pattern and below the clouds (cloud base 500-600 feet). In the turn to final approach, to land on Runway 31, the aircraft banked in excess of 45 degrees and developed an excessive rate of sink which could not be halted. The aircraft crashed into a residential area about a quarter of a mile southeast of the airport, caught fire on impact and was destroyed. Cause: Probably the manoeuvring of the aircraft in a manner causing an excessive rate of sink to develop.

4825 1049H/01-03-143 for United States Overseas Airlines, regn unknown. Order canx, and mod to 1049H/01-03-148 for Air Finance Corp. LADD: 24 Jun 57 as N6922C, via Aero-Hil Venture same day, Cof Regn 27 Jun 57. Lsd to Flying Tiger Line, FN 812, 24 Jun 57. Entered svce on transatlantic pax charters & MATS charters. Cvtd to 1049H/06-03. Mortgaged to Chase Manhattan Bank and Canadair Ltd 1 Jun 59-24 Jan 62. Bought by Flying Tiger 30 Jun 59, CofRegn 1 Jun 59 & official tf Aero Hil to FTL same day. Sold to Air America Inc (George A Doole, Jr.) for $472,850 on 7 Jul 63, officially tfd 11 Jul 63, regd 16 Jul 63. Dry-lsd to LAC immediately for 5 years, del 16 Jul 63. Used most of the time by LAC, but also for CIA operations, including uprising against the president of Bolivia Nov 64 to carry arms, and operations from Tainan, Taiwan from time to time. Sold to Lockheed Aircraft Corp 26 Mar 69, regd 23 Apr 69. Sold to American Jet Industries (Allen Paulson) 22 Dec 70. (TT: 8,517 hrs), on sale to Pederson Enterprises Inc 11 Jan 71. Flew to New Zealand 19 Jan 71 in an abortive attempt to land at the South Pole. Ret to USA 23 Jan 71. Believed stored until sold to Blue Bell Inc 19 Oct 71 and carried Wrangler titling. Major structural flight damage on trim tab & elevator found same day, caused by excessive wear between connection of trim-tab actuator push-pull rods & trim-tab brackets. Repaired. Blue Bell regd 21 Oct 71. Sold to James Downey & J W Earl Crane (Crane Aviation Ltd) 11 Jun 73, amended 22 Jun 73. Del Greensboro, NC to Stephenville, Nfld 24 Jun 73 (TT: 21,908 hrs). N-regn canx 29 Jun 73, E-119627 (20 Jun 73). CF-BFN (2) allotted 15 Jun 73 to Crane Aviation Ltd, sold to James Downey (in trust for Downair Ltd) 30 Aug 73, sold to Downair Ltd same day, CofR 10 Sep 73. Made last flight with Downair 30 Sep 74 (TT: 22,005 hrs) and stored at Stephenville, Nfld prior to CofA expiry on 2 Aug 75. To Dunwoody Ltd (Receiver for Downair Ltd) 1975. Sold to Lance Dreyer t/a Paramount Petroleum 28 Nov 78, officially 2 Dec 78, del to Miami, FL 15 Dec 78. C-regn canx 2 Feb 79 and restored to N6922C 5 Feb 79. Tfd to Air Cargo International Inc 19 Mar 79. Overhauled at Miami,FL and made test flight 17 Oct 79, in svce 9 May 80 (first revenue flight), op for Air International Inc. (TT: 26,868 hrs a/o 4 Apr 80). For sale for $225,000 in 1980. Painted up in full Iberia colours 28 May 80 (on port side only) with regn EC-ARN. Flew to Opa Locka, FL 30 May 80 for film work for Bank of America/Iberia advertizing. Titling and regn removed immediately afterwards and regd N6922C again on 30 May 80. Flew occasionally, i/c one flight late May 81 Miami-San Diego, CA & return, when 3 engine shut-downs were experienced! Sold by auction 23 Nov 81 and flown to Sanford, FL for Harry H Delno, t/a Express Airways Inc on 1 Dec 81. Stored Sanford, FL. Sold United Texas Petroleum Corp 5 Sep 85, regd 27 Sep 85, but remained at Sanford. Sold back to Harry H Delno t/a Express Airways 19 Jan 88, regd 28 Jan 88. N-regn canx 9 Jun 88 on sale to AMSA-Aerolineas Mundo SA. Del Sanford-Opa Locka 26 Jul 88 as HI-542. Named 'City of Miami'. Reregd HI-542CT by Feb 89. AMSA quoted TT as 11,762hrs (a/o 10 Jul 90), but see above! Damaged beyond repair 3 Feb 92 when hit by runaway DC-4 N74AF while parked overnight at Borinquen, PR. The DC-4 suffered complete hydraulic failure while being taxied by non-qualified personnel & struck the Super Constellation outboard of no.4 engine, damaging the main spar. Planned repair with starboard wing of N1880 (c/n 4820) late 1992 fell through with grounding of all Dominican airlines Mar 93. Stored in damaged state, condition deteriorating, at Rafael Hernandez Airport, Aguadilla, Borinquen. Still there 2006 for eventual restoration as USAF C-121C.

4826 1049H/01-03-148 9 Jul 57 to California Eastern Aviation as N6933C, FN 933C (tip-tanks fitted). Lsd to Hughes Tool Co 18 Dec 57 and del Oakland, CA to Mid-Continent Airport, Kansas City, MO on 28 Jan 58 for Trans World (TT: 1,614 hrs). Mods at Mid-Continent 28 Jan-28 Feb 58. In svce 6 Mar 58, FN 1255, on intl cargo and MATS contract flights until Aug 59. (TT: 6,429 hrs a/o 30 Aug 59). Slightly damaged New York-Idlewild 9 Jun 59. Repaired. Later used also on intl pax flights. Ret to California Eastern 17 Jan 61, CEA later renamed Dynalectron Corp. Lsd to World Airways 19 Jan 61 for unknown period (tip-tanks fitted). Lsd to Slick Airways Sep 63. ownership tfd to Bank of America National Trust & Savings 1964, lsd Dynalectron Corp, sub-lsd to Slick until end 1965, then stored at San Francisco, CA. Sub-lsd to Airlift International 1 Jul 66-Dec 67. Ret to Dynalectron Corp and stored at Cheyenne, WY. Sold to Charlotte Aircraft Corp 12 Jul 68 who sold to Bal Trade Inc 6 Feb 69. Stored at Miami, FL from 1970. Condition deteriorated and last reported there in Oct 75. Believed used for spares by R.B. Bergstresser in late 1975 and then scrapped at Miami.

4827 Laid down as 1049H-03-148. Manufactured 20 Feb 58 and regd to Lockheed Aircraft Corp as N5409V. Canx order for unknown company, possibly Dollar Lines. Updated to 1049H/01-03-156 and sold to Flying Tiger Line 1 May 58. LADD: 1 May 58 as N6923C, FN 813. (TT: 6.6 hrs on dely). Cvtd to 1049H/02-03. In Sep 62, the aircraft had two EA-3 and two EA-6 engines. Successfully ditched in the North Atlantic while on a MATS pax contract flight from McGuire AFB, NJ to Rhein-Main, Frankfurt, West Germany at 22.12 hrs (GMT) on 23 Sep 62 at position 54 13'N/24 5'W. Approx three hours flying time east of Gander, Nfld a fire developed in the no.3 engine after a PRT blew its oil seal. This engine was shut down and the propeller feathered. About six or seven minutes later the propeller of no.1 engine oversped when the Flight Engineer inadvertently closed the fire-wall shut-off valve to no.1 engine (instead of no.3). No.1 engine was shut down and no.1 propeller feathered. Attempts to restart no.1 engine were unsuccessful. The captain altered course for Shannon, Ireland, but after approx one hour of flying on two engines, the fire warning for no.2 engine came on (nos.2 & 4 were operating at METO power). Successive power reductions were made on no.2 engine, but after the fire warning on no.2 engine came on for a fourth time, this engine also failed, by which time the aircraft was down to

3,000 feet. The Captain, John Murray, ditched the aircraft approx 560 nautical miles west of Shannon, Ireland, in darkness, a 30-knot wind and an eight- to twelve-foot swell. All 76 on board were successfully evacuated from the aircraft before it sank (the port wing had failed on the forced landing) within ten minutes. 28, however, subsequently died in the heavy seas before rescue arrived. (TT: approx 15,800 hrs, was 15,791 hrs up to the last flight). Cause: The failure of two engines and improper action of the Flight Engineer which disabled a third engine, thus necessitating a ditching in the open sea.

4828 1049H-03-152 11 Sep 57 to National Airlines as N7131C (tip-tanks fitted). Stored at Miami, FL from mid-1963 until sold to International Aviation Co 3 Dec 64. Sold to Nordair Ltd 6 Dec 64, E-64953 (10 Dec 64). Regd as CF-NAJ 7 Jun 65, CofA 7 Jun 65. Updated to 1049H/02-03. Used as 110-seater. Stored at Dorval, PQ in late 1968, then sold to CanRelief Air Ltd 13 Dec 68. CofR to Oxfam of Canada Inc 8 Jan 69 TT (a/o 3 Jan 69) 12,699 hrs. Deld ex-Toronto to Sao Tome 17 Jan 69. Used on Biafran airlift. Damaged on ground at Uli, Biafra, early Feb 69, when the aircraft received shrapnel holes in the fuselage. Ferried to Luton, England, 12 Feb 69, for repairs. Refused permission to stay by British authorities and continued to Paris for repairs. Ret 27 Feb 69 to Sao Tome. Crashed on 3 Aug 69 at Uli, Biafra. Flew into a hillside while turning on to final approach to land at Uli at night, approx two miles from the runway end. En route from Sao Tome. Crew killed. Canx from C-register 4 Jun 70.

4829 1049H-03-152 16 Sep 57 to National Airlines as N7132C (tip-tanks fitted). Stored at Miami, FL from mid-1963 until sold to International Aviation Co 16 Dec 64. Sold to Nordair Ltd 19 Dec 64, E-64955 (10 Dec 64). Regd as CF-NAK 15 Apr 65, CofA 15 Apr 65. Updated to 1049H/06-03. Used as 110-seater. Remained in svce until at least late Mar 69. Sold to CanRelief Air Ltd 24 Apr 69, CofR 28 Apr 69, and deld Montreal, Canada to Sao Tome 2 May 69. Used on Biafran airlift TT (a/o 3 Sep 69) 14,246hrs. Destroyed on the ground in a bomb attack by the Federal Nigerian forces on the airstrip at Uli 17 Dec 69. Aircraft had just arrived from Sao Tome with 16 tons of food. Crew escaped unhurt. Canx from C-register 10 Apr 70.

4830 Laid down as 1049H-03-148. Canx order for unknown company, possibly Dollar Lines. Cvtd to 1049H-03-152 and updated to 1049H/01-03-152 at factory. Regd N5400V to Lockheed Aircraft Corp. Sold to Slick Airways 6 Aug 59. LADD: 17 Sep 59 as N6937C. In svce 1 Oct 59. Updated to 1049H/01-06. Ownership tf to The Slick Corp t/a Slick Airways 30 Aug 62. In svce until at least 31 Dec 65, then lsd to Airlift International on 29 Jun 66. Ret to The Slick Corp 12 Nov 68. Sold to Bal Trade Inc 14 Nov 68. Stored at Miami, FL from approx Oct 70. Seized by IRS at Miami 18 Jun 71 and sold by auction to Aircraft Airframe Inc same day. Lsd to Vortex Inc a/o Oct 71 and possibly also spring 1972. Lsd to Sky Truck International Inc 12 Sep 72. Sold to Aircraft Specialties Inc 12 Feb 73 and cvtd to sprayer configuration at Mesa, AZ with four tanks in fuselage 30 Apr 73 & overwing spray-booms 4 May 74. Flew last mission Jun 75 spraying in Canada. Made emergency 3-engined landing at Phoenix-Sky Harbor, then ferried for storage at Mesa Jun 75. Sale to Science Museum, London, England fell through Oct 79. Sale to Air Traders International in Mar 80 also fell through after loss of the company's other aircraft in Jun 80. Reregd to Globe Air Inc 18 Feb 81. Stored at Mesa in good condition except for no.3 engine. Sold in Globe Air auction 24 Oct 85 to Paul Pristo t/a Princess Land & Development Co for $4,000, official sale date to Paul Pristo 26 Nov 85. Work began on restoring the aircraft for the Save-A-Connie Group 5 May 86, regd Paul Pristo 7 May 86. Test flown Mesa 11 Jul 86 after 3,000+ man hrs. Flown non-stop to Kansas City-Downtown 15 Jul 86 in 5 hrs 3 mins. (TT: 24,042 hrs). Restoration continued at Kansas City. Paul Pristo donated to Save-A-Connie Inc, tfd officially 20 Dec 86. Rolled out at Kansas City-Downtown as 'Star of America' with tip-tanks & TWA colours but SAC titles 9 Jul 88 after 125,000 man hours. Standard Airworthiness Certificate issued 7 Nov 89. Fitted with radar nose during annual inspection Dec 90-Jan 91 & painted with Trans World Airlines titles Apr 96 (for planned European tour 1 Apr-25 May 96, canx after crash of TWA Boeing 747 into the Atlantic). Flown regularly to airshows throughout the USA, also to Canada & the Caribbean; took part in New York-JFK celebrations 13 Jun 00. SAC renamed the Airline History Museum in 2000, but the acft remains regd to Save-A-Connie Inc. Current.

4831 1049H-03-152 28 Oct 57 to National Airlines as N7133C (tip-tanks fitted). Stored at Miami, FL from mid-1963 until sold to International Aviation Co 10 Dec 64. (Canadian records show National Airlines to International Aviation Corp 10 Dec 64, then to International Aviation Export Corp 9 Dec 64). Sold to Nordair Ltd 9 Dec 64, E-64954 (10 Dec 64). Regd CF-NAL 5 Mar 65 (allotted 1 Dec 64). CofA Mar 65. Updated to 1049H/02-03. In svce Mar 65 as 110-seater. Lsd to Eastern Provincial Airways in late 1968 briefly. Sold to CanRelief Air Ltd 24 Apr 69. CofR 26 Jun 65 and del Montreal, PQ to Sao Tome 30 Jul 69. Used on Biafran airlift, with 'Kebec' insignia and titling on nose. Stored at Sao Tome from Jan 70, for sale. CofA expired 12 Aug 70. Sale to Canadian freight charter company in 1974 fell through when Canadian Government refused export permit for onward sale to Air Trans Africa (Rhodesia). Canx from C-register 29 Feb 80. Still stored at Sao Tome, in Biafran camouflage with blue top and "Canairelief" titling overpainted, but condition very poor with considerable corrosion.

4832 1049H-03-152 28 Oct 57 to National Airlines as N7134C (tip-tanks fitted). Stored at Miami, FL from mid-1963 until sold to International Aviation Co 18 Dec 64. (Canadian records show National Airlines to International Aviation Corp 17 Dec 64, then to International Aviation Export Corp 18 Dec 64). Sold to Nordair Ltd 18 Dec 64, E-64936 (18 Dec 64). Allotted regn CF-NAM 1 Dec 64. Did not enter svce, but stored at Dorval Airport, Montreal, PQ in ex-National A/L markings, and used for spares. Restored, updated to 1049H/06-03 , CofR 23 Feb 66 as CF-NAM to Nordair Ltd, CofA 23 Feb 66 (TT: 10,434 hrs) and entered svce with Nordair spring 1966, as 110-seater. Lsd to Sudair 23 Feb 66, suspended 2 Mar 66. Suspension of lse canx 26 May 66 to uk date. TT (a/o 28 Dec 68) 12,407 hrs. Sold to CanRelief Air Ltd 24 Apr 69 (16 May 69 in Canadian records), CofR 20 May 69 and del Montreal to Sao Tome 2 Jun 69. Used on Biafran airlift, with 'Kebec' insignia and titling on nose. Later also carried "Jointchurchaid" titling on cabin roof. Damaged when a bomb exploded in front of the aircraft's nose while landing at Uli on 5 Dec or 6 Dec 69. Splinters damaged the aircraft's skin in front of the nose-wheel doors. Repaired, but stored at Sao Tome from Jan 70, for sale. CofA expired 19 Jan 70. Sale to Canadian freight charter company in 1974 fell through when Canadian Government refused export permit for onward sale to Air Trans Africa (Rhodesia). Canx from C-register 29 Feb 80. Still stored at Sao Tome, in Biafran camouflage with blue top and "Canairelief" titling overpainted, but condition very poor with considerable corrosion.

4833 1049H/01-03-159 17 Feb 58 to REAL Aerovias Brasil (tip-tanks fitted). Reportedly originally allocated PP-AYA, but del as PP-YSA. E-28747 dated 17 Feb 58. Tfd to VARIG when REAL was taken over Aug 61. Made emergency landing at Wilmington, NC in Jul 66 when nos.2 & 3 engines failed while the aircraft was flying over the Atlantic. Repaired. Believed stored at Porto Alegre, Brazil, from Oct 66. Sold to Carolina Aircraft Corp Jan 69 and canx from PP-register 15 Jan 69. Regd N563E. Lsd to Flying W Airways Apr 69, bought by Jul 69 (in payment for L-382s). Sold to Lockheed 9 Sep 69, ret to Carolina Aircraft Corp 23 Sep 69. Lse arranged by W Cobaugh to the Biafran government Oct/Nov 69-Jan 70. Flew into Sao Tome with Alouette helicopter on board 2 Jan 70. Stored at Fort Lauderdale, FL, then sold to Santiago Sablon Sep 71. Lsd to Aircraft Airframe Inc briefly in Oct 71 and also lsd to Vortex Inc briefly in Oct 71. Ret Santiago Sablon until Nov 71. Lsd to Jose A Balboa (Balair Inc) from Nov 72 until Aug 74, but stored at Miami International Airport, FL from 1973 and condition deteriorated. Canx from

PP-YSC 1049H of REAL named "Brasilia I" at Miami International on scheduled passenger service in April 1961. (via George Pennick)

USCAR 1973. Last reported Oct 75, derelict at Miami Intl. Scrapped at Miami late 1975 or early 1976.

4834 1049H/01-03-159 17 Feb 58 to REAL Aerovias Brasil as PP-YSB (tip-tanks fitted). E-28750 dated 17 Feb 58. Tfd to VARIG when REAL was taken over Aug 61. Believed stored at Porto Alegre, Brazil, from Oct 66. Sold to Carolina Aircraft Corp 9 Jan 69 and canx from PP-register 15 Jan 69. Regd N564E. Sold to Flying W Airways 2 Apr 69. Sold to Lockheed Aircraft Corp 9 Sep 69 (payment for L-382s), but ret to Carolina Aircraft Corp 23 Sep 69. Stored at Fort Lauderdale, FL for periods during 1969, but in svce with unknown operator at Oakland, CA Apr 70. Sold to Jose A Balboa t/a Balair Inc 15 Feb 71 (on lse-purchase). Crashed into the sea at 22.05 hrs (local) on 20 Oct 71 south of the Great Inagua Island, Bahamas, killing the crew. The aircraft, reportedly on lse to Gulf Export-Import, was en route Santo Domingo, DR to Miami, FL, with a cargo of processed meat. A US Coast Guard vessel picked the aircraft up on their radar, losing height rapidly, the crew of the vessel saw the aircraft's navigation lights and heard the crash, but no trace of the aircraft or crew was found. Cause: Reportedly struck by lightning, and fuel leaking from wing tanks ignited (the aircraft was known to have fuel leaks & was also fitted with two non-standard engines at the time of the crash). No other reason known for the aircraft's uncontrolled descent.

4835 1049H/01-03-157 11 Feb 58 to Pakistan International Airlines as AP-AJY. E-28758 dated 11 Feb 58. Del via London-Heathrow 25 Feb 58. Inaugurated "Super H" svce Karachi-Dacca 6 Mar 58. Flew last scheduled Super Connie pax svce to Europe, ret London (Heathrow)-Karachi 1 Oct 60. Withdrawn from use at Karachi, Pakistan, after CofA expiry on 18 May 68. Donated to AURI-Indonesian Air Force in 1969 and serialled T-1042. Believed saw brief svce only in Indonesia. Fate unknown, presumably scrapped in the early 1970s.

4836 1049H/01-03-157 1 Mar 58 to Pakistan International Airlines as AP-AJZ. E-28759 dated 26 Feb 58. Del via London-Heathrow 14 Mar 58. Withdrawn from use at Karachi, Pakistan, after CofA expiry on 10 Jul 69. Donated to AURI-Indonesian Air Force in 1969 and serialled T-1041. Believed saw brief svce only in Indonesia. Fate unknown, presumably scrapped in the early 1970s.

4837 1049H/01-03-159 20 Feb 58 to REAL Aerovias Brasil as PP-YSC (tip-tanks fitted). E-28755 dated 20 Feb 58. Named 'Brasilia I' by Nov 60. Tfd to VARIG when REAL taken over Aug 61. Believed stored at Porto Alegre, Brazil, from Oct 66. Sold to Carolina Aircraft Corp Jan 69 and canx from PP-register 8 Jan 69. Regd N565E. Sold to Flying W Airways early 69 and in use in Caribbean and South America, then lsd to Produce International Inc Mar 69 for short period. Ret to Flying W Airways Apr 69. Stored at Fort Lauderdale, FL from Aug 69. Sold to Lockheed Aircraft Corp 9 Sep 69 (in payment for L382s), but ret to Carolina Aircraft Corp 23 Sep 69. Repainted by Apr 70 and carried emblem of unknown company on nose of aircraft. Used little, however, and last reported at Fort Lauderdale in Jul 72, stored, with two engines and parts missing. Scrapped there in late 1972 or early 1973. Canx from USCAR 1972.

4838 1049H/01-03-159 18 Mar 58 to REAL Aerovias Brasil as PP-YSD (tip-tanks fitted). E-28760 dated 14 Mar 58. Tfd to VARIG when REAL taken over Aug 61. Believed stored at Porto Alegre, Brazil, from Oct 66. Sold to Carolina Aircraft Corp 11 Feb 69 and regd N566E. Canx from PP-register 15 Jan 69. Tf to Florida Aircraft Leasing Corp 28 Feb 69, but ret to Carolina Aircraft Corp 18 Mar 69 and sold to Flying W Airways same day. Stored Wilmington, DE summer 69. Sold to Lockheed Aircraft Corp 9 Sep 69, but ret to Carolina Aircraft Corp 30 Sep 69 and stored at Fort Lauderdale, FL until sold to Raitron Inc 3 Jun 70. Sold (lse-purchase) to S Muhammed, Temple 2 of the Holy Nation of Islam Inc 22 Aug 73. Crashed on landing at Gary Municipal Airport, IN at 00.54 hrs (local) 24 Sep 73. Made hard landing, causing undercarriage to collapse, ran off runway and substantially damaged in ensuing fire. No injuries to crew. Was on corporate/executive flight from Los Angeles, CA to Gary, IN via Kansas City, MO. Cause: Improper levelling off on touchdown by co-pilot and inadequate supervision by the captain.

4839 1049H/01-06-166 23 Apr 58 to Trans World Airlines as N5401V, FN 1261 (TT: 18 hrs). In svce 25 Apr 58 (domestic network). To intl network 27 Apr 58, and back to domestic 13 May 58. To intl network again 18 Sep 58. Used on pax, cargo and MATS contract flights up to Aug 59. (TT: 4,442 hrs a/o 31 Aug 59 & a/o 30 Jun 61: 8,218 hrs). Sold to Trans International 2 Sep 61, in svce 3 Sep 61. Sold to Capitol Airways Nov 61 and used as a 108-seater. Later named Capitol International Airways. FN 01V. In all-cargo use and latterly for pilot training 24 Oct 67 at Wilmington, DE. Subsequently withdrawn from use and stored there. Flown for further storage at Sebring, FL in Mar/Apr 70 (TT: 20,650 hrs). Sold to California Airmotive Corp 5 Jul 72. Made last flight Sebring to Miami, FL 10 Jul 72 and stored there. Sold to FHB Maintenance May 73 and gradually parts sold off for spares to keep other Super Constellations in "corrosion corner" flying. Still basically whole in Sep 73. Tfd to Startech from FHB Nov 73, two engines and parts missing by Jun 74. Owned by Startech until at least Aug 74. Broken up approx Nov 74 at Miami. Canx from USCAR 1974.

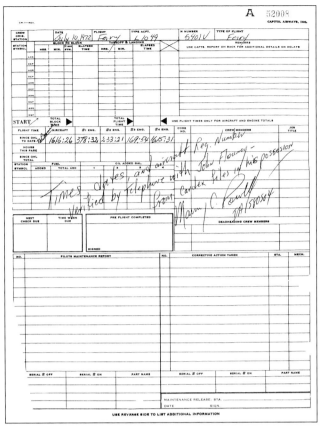

C/n 4839. The last entry in the Capitol Airways flight log for 1049H N5401V shows the aircraft's ferry flight to Sebring in Florida on 10th July 1972. The details contained have been verified by the ultimate purchaser of the aircraft for spares use at Miami International.

4840 1049H/01-06-162 14 Apr 58 to KLM as PH-LKL 'Desiderius Erasmus'. Regd same day, E-28761 dated 15 Apr 58, KLM dely date 17 Apr 58. (Tip-tanks used occasionally). Updated to 1049H/02 late 1958 and to 1049H/06 by Apr 60. Lsd to World Airways 11 Jul 62 to 9 Jul 63 and regd N45516. Canx from PH-register 2 Jul 62. Lsd to Flying Tiger Line, FN 818, 7 Jul 63 (KLM quote 7 Aug 63), sold to Flying Tiger 26 Apr 66 (KLM quote 4 May 66). Still in svce Dec 67, but stored at Kingman, AZ by mid 1968. Sold to Murphree Air International Inc 28 Feb 69, but ntu. Sold to North Slope Supply Co Inc 29 Apr 69 and del to Anchorage, AK early May 69. Stored at Anchorage by 1970 and sold to Unum Inc 2 Feb 71 via Small Business Administration. Remained in storage at Anchorage in ex-Flying Tiger markings, and, probably due to the non-collection of the aircraft, it was seized by the Anchorage Airport Commission and auctioned in an "as-is, where-is" condition in Nov 73. Sold to Aviation Specialties 16 Nov 73, but remained at Anchorage until ferried to Mesa, AZ in Aug 74. Ownership tfd to Aircraft Specialties 26 Aug 74. Sale to Les Specialites de l'Aviation de Quebec Ltee as C-GAZA (allotted 27 Nov 74) fell through. Cvtd to sprayer with fuselage tanks and over-wing spray-booms. Crashed on initial climb-out of Mesa, AZ at 16:40 hrs (local) on 11 May 75. Suffered failure of all four engines and collided with trees and play-house while attempting a forced landing in a rocky dry river bed in the desert near the airport. Destroyed by fire and impact and crew killed. En route to Kansas City, MO. Cause: Engines ran out of ADI (anti-detonation-injection) fluid, resulting in overheating of the engines on take-off and internal damage. Crew believed that the water methanol system had been replenished when in fact it had not. Canx from USCAR 5 Sep 75.

4841 1049H/01-06-162 22 Apr 58 to KLM as PH-LKM 'Hugo de Groot'. Regd same day, E-28762 dated 22 Apr 58, KLM dely date 26 Apr 58. Crashed into the Atlantic Ocean approx 110 nautical miles west of Shannon, Ireland between 03.45 hrs & 03.50 hrs (GMT) on 14 Aug 58. All on board killed. The aircraft was on flight KL 607E Amsterdam-Shannon-Gander-New York. Take-off from Shannon was at 03.05 hrs and the last message received from the aircraft was at 03.40:48 hrs at which time the aircraft was climbing up to its allotted cruise altitude of 16,000 feet and had cleared 12,000 feet. Nothing further was heard from the aircraft. Search & Rescue alert not given until 08.47 hrs (due to confusion between flights KL 607 and KL 607E, "E" denoting 'extra') and wreckage from the Super Constellation was subsequently found at 53 12.5N/11 53W. (TT: 889 hrs). Cause: Unknown with any degree of certainty. The only acceptable hypothesis to the Accident Investigation Board was that of a compound malfunction of the governor of one of the outer propellers which resulted in over-speeding of the propeller to such a degree that an uncontrollable flight condition developed. Canx from PH-register 29 Aug 58. KLM's other two 1049Hs (c/n 4840 & 4843) subsequently used only for all-cargo flights.

4842 1049H/01-06-166 3 May 58 to Trans World Airlines as N5402V, FN 1262 (TT: 6 hrs). In svce (domestic network) 8 May 58. To intl network 18 Sep 58. Used on pax, cargo and MATS contract flights up to Aug 59. (TT: 4,171 hrs a/o 31 Aug 59 & a/o 30 Jun 61: 8,009 hrs). Sold to Trans International 15 Sep 61. Sold to Capitol Airways Nov 61 (TT: a/o 26 Dec 61: 8,070 hrs), and used as a 108-seater. Later named Capitol International Airways, FN 02V. Final use in all-cargo configuration. Stored at Wilmington, DE, probably from 3 Nov 67. Flown for further storage at Sebring, FL in Mar/Apr 70 (TT: 20,761 hrs). Sold to California Airmotive Corp 5 Jul 72, and to Midair Inc, probably in Apr 73. Never deld and remained in storage at Sebring. Sold to Richard Blaine Bergstresser at Sheriff's sale 12 Aug 74, officially tfd 20 Dec 74. Broken up for spares at Sebring. Canx from USCAR 21 Jan.75 as "reduced to produce, engines removed and rest scrapped".

4843 1049H/01-06-162 5 May 58 to KLM as PH-LKN 'Hermannus Boerhaave'. Regd 1 May 58, E-28763 dated 5 May 58, KLM dely date 9 May 58 (tip-tanks used occasionally). Slightly damaged by lightning in flight near Amsterdam 12 Oct 60. Repaired. Slightly damaged when the aircraft tipped on to its tail while being unloaded at London-Heathrow Airport on 14 Jan 61 (evening). Repaired and ret to svce 17 Jan 61. Lsd to World Airways 25 Jul 62 to 31 Jul 63 and regd N45515. Canx 23 Jul 62 from PH-register. Lsd to Flying Tiger Line, FN 819, 8 Aug 63 (KLM quote 7 Aug 63), sold to Flying Tiger 4 May 66. Still in svce Dec 67, but stored at Kingman, AZ by mid-1968. Sold to Murphree Air International Inc 28 Feb 69, but ntu. Sold to North Slope Supply Co Inc 3 Jun 69, but never deld. Still in storage at Kingman in ex-Flying Tiger markings in Nov 69. Sold to R C Wheatley 24 Dec 69, and to D Finkbeiner 26 Jan 70, but ret to North Slope Supply Co Inc 17 Jun 70. Probably sold to Unum Inc on 2 Feb 71 via Small Business Administration. Canx from USCAR 1971. Remained in storage at Kingman with severe structural damage to the leading edge of the port wing, suggesting that the aircraft suffered a fuel explosion in this wing and was the reason for the aircraft eventually being abandoned at Kingman. Reportedly sold to Aircraft Specialties for spares in Aug 73. Hulk of aircraft, less engines, instruments & other useable parts, on display at Kingman from 1974 with bold lettering "Mohave County Airport" on the roof. Titling removed by Sep 75, and derelict, sitting on tail by Jan 76. Last reported there in Nov 76. Presumably scrapped during 1977.

4844 1049H/01-06-166 26 May 58 to Trans World Airlines as N5403V, FN 1263 (TT: 7 hrs). In svce (domestic network) 30 May 58. To intl network 3 Jun 58. Used on pax, cargo and MATS contract flights up to Aug 59. (TT: 4,287 hrs a/o 31 Aug 59 & a/o 30 Jun 61: 7,907 hrs). Sold to Trans International 21 Sep 61. Sold to Capitol Airways Nov 61 and used as 108-seater. Later named Capitol International Airways, FN 03V. Final use in all-cargo configuration. Stored at Wilmington, DE, by mid-1968. Flown for further storage at Sebring, FL in Mar/Apr 70. Sold to California Airmotive Corp 5 Jul 72, and to Midair Inc, probably in Apr 73. Never deld and remained in storage at Sebring. Sold

N469C 1049H of Slick Airways after delivery from Transcontinental SA (Argentina) and still in that airline's colours at Oakland, California in the spring of 1960. (via John T Wible)

to Richard Blaine Bergstresser at Sheriff's sale 12 Aug 74, officially tfd 20 Dec 74. Broken up for spares at Sebring. Canx from USCAR 21 Jan 75 as "reduced to produce, engines removed and rest scrapped".

4845 1049H/01-06-166 29 May 58 to Trans World Airlines as N5404V, FN 1264 (TT: 7 hrs) .In svce (domestic network) same day, to intl network 6 Jun 58. Used on pax, cargo and MATS contract flights up to Aug 59. (TT: 4,282 hrs a/o 31 Aug 59 & a/o 30 Jun 61: 8,102 hrs). Sold to Trans International 10 Sep 61, in svce 11 Sep 61. Sold to Capitol Airways Nov 61 and used as 108-seater. Later named Capitol International Airways, FN 04V. Final use in all-cargo configuration. Stored at Wilmington, DE by mid-1968. Flown for further storage at Sebring, FL in Mar/Apr 70. Sold to California Airmotive Corp 5 Jul 72, and to Midair Inc, probably in Apr 73. Never deld and remained in storage at Sebring. Sold to Richard Blaine Bergstresser at Sheriff's sale 12 Aug 74, officially tfd 20 Dec 74. Broken up for spares at Sebring. Canx from USCAR 21 Jan 75 as "reduced to produce, engines removed and rest scrapped".

4846 1049H/02-06-167 Regd N5405V to Lockheed Aircraft Corp. LADD: 24 Jul 58 to California Eastern Aviation as N6635C. E-28764 dated 21 Jul 58 for lse to Transcontinental SA, regd LV-PKX, reregd LV-FTU after dely. Used by Transcontinental from Aug 58 (tip-tanks fitted). Damaged Buenos Aires 13 Nov 58. Repaired. Ret to California Eastern 15 Dec 59. Lsd to Slick Airways as N468C 8 Mar 60. Ownership tfd mid-1963 to Dynalectron Corp, lse to Slick continued until end 1965. Stored at San Francisco, CA, then lsd to Airlift International 9 Aug 66-Dec 67. Ret to Dynalectron Corp and presumably stored. For sale by Jack Richards Aircraft Co Inc Sep 69. Canx from USCAR 1970, then restored on sale to F & B Livestock Corp 3 Feb 71 as N468C. Fitted with cargo restraining bulkhead by Aeronautical Engineers Inc at Miami, FL in 1972. Remained in svce with F & B Livestock until damaged beyond repair in landing accident at Belize at approx 18.30 hrs (local) on 19 May 76. While en route (empty) from Tegucigalpa, Honduras to Miami, & approx 25 miles off Belize, the aircraft suffered a runaway no.1 propeller, which then came off and damaged no.2 engine cowling and engine, breaking the engine at the top joints with the result that the whole engine was hanging down at an angle. The aircraft returned to Belize, but the port undercarriage would not come down. Four circuits of the airfield were made in an attempt to lower the undercarriage. Nos.3 & 4 engines started overheating, so the aircraft was brought in with only the starboard main and nosewheel undercarriage extended. A successful landing was made, and the aircraft slid off the runway onto some soft sand, settling gently on to the port wing-tip, and ending up approx 20 feet from the runway. No fire and little damage, and no injuries to the crew. Not repaired, and dismantled by local scrap merchant approx two months after the accident. Canx from USCAR 28 Jul 76. Complete fuselage transported to Blue Hole, 50 nm northwest of Belize Intl Airport, & approx 100 mls by road (engines & tail unit presumably scrapped). Fuselage used as store-room by the local Menonite community, with the wings lying alongside, from May 77. Believed still in existence (last reports 1990).

4847 1049H/02-06-167 Regd N5406V to Lockheed Aircraft Corp. LADD: 24 Jul 58 to California Eastern Aviation as N6636C. E-28765 dated 21 Jul 58 for lse to Transcontinental SA, regd LV-PKZ, reregd LV-FTV after dely. Used by Transcontinental from Aug 58 (tip-tanks fitted). Ret to California Eastern 15 Dec 59. Lsd to Slick Airways as N469C 8 Mar 60. Ownership tfd mid-1963 to Dynalectron Corp, lse to Slick continued until early 1966. Stored at San Francisco, CA until lsd to Heiffer Inc early Jul 66. Op charter during Jul 66, also reported as owned subsequently by Aerolessors Inc, and National Aero Leasing Co Inc. Subsequently lsd to LEBCA during summer 1966. Believed owned or op by Aerolessors Inc 1966-1969, but USCAR lists Intertrade Leasing Corp as owner from Apr 67 until USCAR Jan 70. Lsd to Lucien Pickett during Jul 68, t/a Air Mid East, subsequently as Inter-City Airways, in an attempt to fly into Biafra with supplies for the Norwegian and Danish churches. Arrived at Fernando Po from Madrid 25 Jul 68 with large titling "Angel of Mercy" on the cabin roof. Remained at Fernando Po until 12 Aug 68, then ret to USA. Flew on Biafra airlift from Lisbon on lse from (or op by) Aerolessors Inc from at least 23 Sep 68 until 13 Nov 68. Ret to San Juan, PR by Jan 69 & stored at Sebring, FL by Mar 70. Remained in store there, condition deteriorating, until towed to a site near the edge of the airfield in 1977, repainted, and used subsequently by the Civil Air Patrol for maintenance instruction & marked as 'Property of the USAF'. Still in use 1986. Stripped of all paint in early 1981 & renovated in polished metal overall scheme, later repainted with blue & red cheat lines. Sold to the US Army in 1987 for use as a target at the Avon Park Bombing Range, 30 mls north of Sebring, & was to be transported there by helicopter in Oct 87. The scheme fell through & the acft was scrapped at Sebring in Nov 90.

4848 1049H/02-06-160 Laid down for Trans World Airlines & regd N5407V to Lockheed Aircraft Corp. Mod at factory, after TWA option canx, to 1049H/02-06-167 for California Eastern Aviation, but ntu either. Remained at factory and was the last Constellation model to be delivered, when the acft was sold to Slick Airways (regd owner The Slick Corp) in Sep 59. LADD: 30 Sep 59 as N6935C. In svce 1 Oct 59. Sold to Air Carrier Service Corp in Nov 65 and stored at San Francisco, CA until at least Jan 66 in ex-Slick markings. Flown to Oakland,

CA and withdrawn from use for spares by May 66. Dismantled at Oakland 1966/67. Canx from USCAR 1967. Last reported at Oakland derelict in Jun 67. Presumably scrapped 1968/69.

4849 1049H/02-06-160 Laid down for Trans World Airlines & regd N5408V to Lockheed Aircraft Corp. Mod at factory, after TWA option canx, to 1049H/02-06-? for Slick Airways (regd owner The Slick Corp). LADD: 5 Aug 59 as N6936C. (Slick quote 7 Aug 59). In svce 1 Oct 59 until at least Dec 65. Lsd to Airlift International 29 Jun 66. Destroyed in mid-air collision with a USAF McDonnell RF-4C Phantom at 13.13 hrs (GMT) on 22 Jun 67 four miles north of Saigon, Vietnam. The Super Constellation was operating a mail contract flight from Manila, Philippines to Saigon. Crew killed, as the aircraft fell to the ground out of control.

4850 Laid down as 1049H/02-03-168 for Dollar Lines, but ntu, and mod at factory to 1049H/07-06-170 for Trans-Canada Air Lines. Manufactured Jul 58. LADD: 21 Jan 59 to Trans-Canada as CF-TEY, FN 413. E-27683 dated 20 Jan 59. Sold back to LAC 17 Feb 61 (TT: 6,324 hrs) and regd N9752C 24 Mar 61. CF-regn canx 22 Mar 61. Lsd to Trans International 11 Apr 61, sold to Trans International 12 May 61, in svce same day. Sold to Necal Aircraft Leasing 1 Jun 62 and lsd back to Trans International same day. Out of svce by Jan 69 and stored at Oakland, CA. Sold to Central American Airways Flying Service 30 Jan 69. At Burbank, CA in ex-TIA colours with outer wings removed Apr 69-Jun 69 at least. Reregd N74CA with Central American Airways Flying Service 15 Dec 70, but subsequently canx. Believed never entered svce with Central American at this stage. Stored at Houston, TX still in ex-TIA colours in Mar 72. Restored to USCAR by Aug 72 as N74CA with Central American, and entered svce. Stored at varions periods during Central American use, at Detroit-Willow Run, MI in summer 1975, at Fort Lauderdale, FL from Jan 76 until Aug 77, and at Miami, FL during Apr 78. Renamed Central American International. Last flight for Central American in Oct 78, on ferry permit from Willow Run to Bakalar Airport, Columbus, IN for storage. (TT: 20,416 hrs). Stored at Columbus until sold to Gary J Garibaldi via Rhoades Aircraft Sales on 15 May 80, and on to Air Traders International on 6 Jun 80. During high-speed (60 mph) crew familiarization and taxy tests at Columbus on 20 Jun 80, the aircraft taxied into a farm field after the crew were unable to stop the aircraft by the end of the runway. No damage - no.1 propeller had failed to go into reverse thrust due to a broken electrical connection. Repaired. Crashed on take-off from Bakalar Airport, Columbus, IN at 13.59 hrs (EST) on 22 Jun 80, killing three of the crew, including Herman R "Fish" Salmon, former Chief Test Pilot for Lockheed. The aircraft was taking-off on Runway 22 at Bakalar Airport for delivery to Seattle, WA with a cargo of Super Constellation spares. During the take-off run, there was a fire-warning to no.2 engine, and heavy white smoke was seen coming from that engine. While the no.2 engine throttle was being retarded, there was a gradual power decay on the other three engines. The aircraft struck the top of a 35-foot utility pole 3,850 feet beyond the end of the runway, settled in a nose-high attitude into a soybean field and skidded into trees. The wings broke off and the aircraft came to rest approx 4,600 feet beyond the runway end and burst into flames, which destroyed most of the aircraft. Cause: Inadequate and uncoordinated response to the no.2 fire warning and power decay, with contributing factors of less than full power for take-off, and use of less than take-off cowl flaps which precluded adequate engine cooling, plus probability of overloading beyond maximum gross take-off weight with lower grade (100/130) fuel. On crash, aircraft powered by three EA-6 engines and one R3350-42 engine. (TT: 20,416 hrs).

4851 Laid down as 1049H/02-03-168 for Dollar Lines, but ntu, and mod at factory to 1049H/07-06-170 for Trans- Canada Air Lines. LADD: 13 Dec 58 to Trans-Canada as CF-TEZ, FN 414. E-27682 dated 11 Dec 58, TCA quote 12 Dec 58 dely. Struck trees on approach to Malton Airport, Toronto, Ont made emergency wheels-up landing and came to rest 1,370 feet beyond the end of the runway at 21.05 hrs (EST) on 10 Feb 60 in poor visibility. Was on flight TC20 from Winnipeg, Man to Toronto. No injuries. Cause: Crew flew the aircraft below the approved minimum IFR altitude. (TT: 1,560 hrs). Sold back to Lockheed Aircraft Corp 27 Apr 60 (buy-back program), with "repair pending". Stored unrepaired at Toronto until sold to California Airmotive Corp 8 Aug 62. Rebuilt with parts from TCA 1049G c/n **4542** and regd N9740Z. Sold to Tracy Lease & Finance Corp late 1962. Lsd immediately to Slick Airways. Painted up in full Quicktrans colours. Crashed on approach to land at San Francisco, CA, at 12.07 hrs (PST) on 3 Feb 63, killing four of the occupants. The aircraft was on an all-cargo flight from Albuquerque, NM (cargo included 2 Polaris missile guidance capsules) and was approaching the airport in fog with visibility of less than three quarters of a mile. The aircraft, which was flying with an inoperative ILS glide-slope receiver, struck the approach lights 1,170 feet short of the runway threshold, climbed to approx 200 feet, then struck the runway with the port wingtip, veered off the runway and crashed approx 1,900 feet beyond the threshold. Destroyed by impact and subsequent fire. Cause: Continuation of approach after the loss of visual reference below the authorized minimum, and inadequate monitoring by the PAR (Precision Approach Radar) controller.

4852 Laid down as 1049H/02-03-168 for Dollar Lines, but ntu, and mod at factory to unknown configuration. Regd N6924C to Lockheed Aircraft Corp. Lsd to Flying Tiger Line as N6924C, FN 814, 1 Oct 58 (LADD). Ret to LAC 1960 and lsd to Trans International 14 Nov 60 (FAA quote 1 Oct 60), in svce 23 Jan 61. Sold to Trans International 11 May 61. Sold to Necal Aircraft Leasing Corp 1 Jun 62 and lsd back to Trans International same day. Sold to Trans International Feb 63. Sold to Flying Tiger Line 30 Sep 66 and lsd same day to Flying Tiger Air Services, in svce 29 Oct 66, named 'City of Manila' FN 24C. Received damage on 10 Feb 67 when no.2 engine separated from the aircraft while on a ferry flight over Da Nang, South Vietnam. Repaired. Ret to Flying Tiger Line 25 Mar 67. Believed lsd to Flying Tiger Air Services for further brief period until 31 Dec 67 and ret to Flying Tiger Line 1 Jan 68 and stored, presumably at Kingman, AZ. To Pacific Airmotive 7 Dec 68, then sold to Murphree Air International Inc 28 Feb 69 and to North Slope Supply Co Inc 29 Apr 69. Lsd to Interior Airways Apr 69 for brief period. Ret to North Slope Supply Co Inc and stored at Anchorage, AK. Repossessed by Small Business Administration 1 Feb 71 and sold to Unum Inc 2 Feb 71. Flown to Miami, FL by Dec 71. Sold to Skyways International Inc 28 Feb 72 and lsd to (or op by) Brian Shelton t/a Transair Cargo Service Inc from at least 1975. Sold to R B Bergstresser t/a Air Cargo Support Inc Oct 77 & used extensively during the docks strike Oct-Nov 77. Stored at Miami from Nov 77 onwards. Air Cargo Support paid parking dues at Miami until Feb 78. Offer of $15,000 for acft from Maurice Roundy (to be used as a hamburger stall in Maine!) not accepted. Sold to unknown persons and deld at Miami 14 Oct 78. Crashed and caught fire on a three-engined take-off at a dirt strip at Riohacha, near Santa Marta in northern Colombia, probably on 15 Oct 78. The aircraft was being used for an undercover drug-run by the DEA. When the crew heard the Colombian military approaching, they hastily boarded the aircraft. The 1049H started its take-off run on three engines owing to a faulty starter motor on no.4 engine, but in the confusion the undercarriage was retracted prematurely before flying speed had been reached. The aircraft ground-looped to the left, ran off the dirt strip and crashed. Destroyed by fire and impact. The co-pilot (Mel Anderson, of Proimex - qv) was killed when he returned to the cockpit to retrieve the captain's fund, consisting of many thousands of US dollars. The drug flight had been sponsored by the DEA in an attempt to catch some of the drug-dealers in Colombia. Canx from USCAR Oct 81.

4853 Laid down as 1049H/02-03-168 for Dollar Lines, but ntu, and mod at factory to unknown configuration. Regd N6925C to Lockheed Aircraft Corp. Lsd to Flying Tiger Line as N6925C, FN 815, 29 Sep 58 (LADD). Ret to LAC 1960 and lsd to Trans International 14 Nov 60, in svce 21 Dec 60. Sold to

Trans International 11 May 61. Damaged May 62 and sold to Kirk Kerkorian Jun 62. After repairs completed sold to Tracy Lease & Finance Corp Sep 62. Lsd to Slick Airways Sep 62-Aug 63. Sold to Trans International 1 Mar 64. Sold to Flying Tiger Line 30 Sep 66 and to China Airlines 24 Oct 66. Regd B-1809. In svce 2 Dec 66. Used on scheduled svces, then on charter flights only and withdrawn from svce approx 1970. Stored Taipei. Scrapped 28 Aug 72.

4854 onwards. Not used. WV-2/1049A series continued from c/n **4499** with c/n **5500**, see below.

5500 WV-2/1049A-55-137 2 Dec 57 to US Navy as 143226. Navy acceptance date 18 Nov 57. To VW-l Agana 2 Dec 57. To Storage Facility, Litchfield Park, 13 Jun 60. (TT: 2,170 hrs). Tfd to US Army 19 Jun 61. Flown to Ontario, CA for work by LAS. Redesignated EC-121K 24 Aug 62. To BWR Burbank 24 Aug 62. To US Air Force 25 Aug 62. Struck off (BUWEPS Burbank) 26 Nov 62. Bailed to Bendix Corp, New York, NY and cvtd to GRC-121D. Upper and lower radomes removed and converted by LAS for TRAP III program (Terminal Radiation Airborne Program), with three 'turret-like' constructions on upper fuselage where top radome had been. Nick-named 'Triple Nipple'. Del to US Air Force for tests as 56-6956 early in 1964 to ARDC, Wright-Patterson. Redesignated NC-121D. Later to AFSC-ASD, Wright-Patterson. In use with 4950th Test Wg AFSC, Wright-Patterson a/o Dec 68 & until approx Jul 69. (no records exist on this aircraft with the USAF). Flown to MASDC, Davis Monthan, for storage by Nov 69. Dismantled by Mar 71. For sale by DofD (Davis Monthan) 17 Jun 71. (TT: 4,327 hrs). Subsequently scrapped.

5501 WV-2/1049A-55-137 5 Dec 57 to US Navy as 143227. Navy acceptance date 19 Nov 57. To VW-l Agana 5 Dec 57. To Storage Facility, Litchfield Park, 13 Jun 60. Redesignated EC-121K 30 Nov 62. Struck off (Litchfield Park) 21 May 65, (TT: 2,216 hrs). Scrapped approx Oct 65.

5502 WV-2/1049A-55-137 9 Dec 57 to US Navy as 143228. Navy acceptance date 27 Nov 57. To VW-l Agana 9 Dec 57, coded TE-7. To Storage Facility, Litchfield Park 3 Jun 60. Redesignated EC-121K 30 Nov 62. Struck off (Litchfield Park) 21 May 65, (TT: 2,149 hrs). Scrapped approx Oct 65.

5503 WV-2/1049A-55-137 13 Dec 57 to US Navy as 143229. Navy acceptance date 29 Nov 57. To NADC, Johnsville 12 Dec 57. To BAR Facility Burbank 28 Feb 58 & to VW-3 Agana 28 Mar 58, coded PM-2. To Storage Facility, Litchfield Park, 1 Jun 60. Redesignated EC-121K 30 Nov 62. Struck off (Litchfield Park) 21 May 65, (TT: 1,817 hrs). Scrapped approx Oct 65.

5504 WV-2/1049A-55-137 24 Jan 58 to US Navy as 143230. Navy acceptance date 20 Dec 57. To VW-l Agana 24 Jan 58. To Storage Facility, Litchfield Park 3 Jun 60. Redesignated EC-121K 30 Nov 62. Struck off (Litchfield Park) 21 May 65, (TT: 2,104 hrs). Scrapped approx Oct 65.

5505 WV-2/1049A-55-137 13 Mar 58 to US Navy as 145924. First Warning Star to be completed on the production line with no rudder on centre fin. Navy acceptance date 21 Feb 58 (BAR FA Burbank). To VW-3 Agana 13 Mar 58, coded PM-3. To VW-l Agana 19 May 60. To Storage Facility, Litchfield Park, 15 Dec 60. Withdrawn from storage & to BWR FR Burbank 6 Sep 61. Redesignated EC-121K 30 Nov 62. To NAS/NATC, Patuxent, Det Magnet 13 Dec 62. Cvtd by LAS to NC-121K, with removal of dorsal radome, installation of special equipment and observation blisters in rear fuselage. Completed 24 Mar 63, redeld to NATC Patuxent, Det Project ASWEPS, (within Project Magnet), named 'El Coyote' with stylized coyote on forward fuselage. To OASU 1 Jul 65 (Patuxent). VX-8, Patuxent 1 Jul 67, coded JB-924. To VXN-8 1 Jan 69, still coded JB-924/ASWEPS and named 'El Coyote'. To storage Davis Monthan 1 Jun 72. Struck off 31 Jul 72 (TT: 9,057 hrs) and stored at MASDC, Davis Monthan. Sold to Sun Valley Avn 16 Sep 76, subsequently scrapped.

5506 WV-2/1049A-55-137 28 Jan 58 to US Navy as 145925. Navy acceptance date 10 Jan 58 (BAR FA Burbank). To VW-3 Agana 28 Jan 58, coded PM-4. To VW-l Agana 7 Jun 60. To Storage Facility, Litchfield Park, 15 Dec 60. Withdrawn from storage 1961 as replacement for c/n 4302 (qv). To BWR FR Burbank 17 Apr 61 & cvtd for Project Magnet by LAS, Ontario. Radomes removed, demagnetized and fitted with special equipment. To NAS/NATC, Patuxent, Det Magnet, 12 Jul 62. To EC-121K 30 Nov 62. First Antarctic ops Nov 62, named 'Paisano Dos'. To NC-121K 24 Mar 63. Forward fuselage had stylised drawing of "Road Runner". To OASU, Patuxent 1 Jul 65, coded JB. Coded JB-5 by Feb 67. Magnetometer carried in streamlined tip-tank like fairings under the wing centre-section as required (eg 1965/66). To VX-8 1 Jul 67, coded JB-925 & to VXN-8, Patuxent 1 Jan 69, still coded JB-925/ PROJECT MAGNET 'Paisano Dos'. Officially tfd to storage Davis Monthan 18 Dec 72. Struck off (VXN-8 Magnet) 15 May 73 (TT: 11,408 hrs) at Patuxent. Later flown to MASDC, Davis Monthan for storage. Sold to Sun Valley Avn 28 May 76, subsequently scrapped.

5507 WV-2/1049A-55-137 30 Jan 58 to US Navy as 145926. Navy acceptance date 16 Jan 58 (BAR FA Burbank). To VW-l Agana 30 Jan 58. To BWR FR Burbank 14 Feb 61. To Pacific Missile Range, Pt Mugu 8 May 61. Redesignated EC-121K 24 Oct 62. Possibly cvtd to EC-121P. Fitted with two small additional radomes aft of ventral radome by May 63. Tfd NMC Pt Mugu 1 Aug 63, ret PMR Pt Mugu 30 Nov 63. Struck off 20 Nov 75, (TT: 9,466 hrs). Withdrawn from use at Point Mugu, CA and used for spares there until at least Oct 76. Subsequently scrapped on site.

5508 WV-2/1049A-55-137 20 Feb 58 to US Navy as 145927. Navy acceptance date 31 Jan 58 (BAR FA Burbank). To VW-3 Agana 28 Feb 58, coded PM-5. Tfd VW-l Agana 2 Jun 60. To Storage Facility, Litchfield Park, 21 Jun 61. Withdrawn from storage and to VW-11 Argentia 26 Sep 62, coded MJ-927. Redesignated EC-121K 2 Oct 62. Cvtd to EC-121P 5 May 64. Ret to storage at Davis Monthan Aug 65. Withdrawn from storage & to NPRO Dallas (rework) by Feb 67, cvtd to EC-121M. To VQ-1 Atsugi 9 Apr 68, coded PR-26. Written-off 16 Mar 70. Aircraft was landing at Da Nang, South Vietnam with no.3 engine out & prop feathered returning from Tainan, Taiwan. There was a work crew & machinery on the last 500ft of the runway. The aircraft stalled, crashed & cartwheeled into a large USAF maintenance hangar at the southeast corner of the airbase, destroying the hangar and an F-4 Phantom. The Super Constellation broke into three, the cockpit & fuselage forward of the wing slid into a revetment wall & burned. The centre section crashed upside down into a street & burst into flames, while the tail section landed in a softball field. 23 of the 28 crew were killed, one crew in the tail section was unhurt, four in the centre section seriously injured. Struck off (VQ-l) 16 Mar 70, TT: 8,940 hrs.

5509 WV-2/1049A-55-137 25 Feb 58 to US Navy as 145928. Navy acceptance date 10 Feb 58 (BAR FA Burbank). To VW-3 Agana 25 Feb 58, coded PM-6. Tfd VW-l Agana 16 Sep 58. Ret VW-3 Agana 3 Oct 58. To VW-1 27 May 60 (officially, but in fact by Mar 60), coded TE-7 'Road Runner'. Redesignated EC-121K 30 Nov 62. Cvtd to WC-121N by May 67. Withdrawn from use after being damaged beyond repair in a ground accident at Atsugi, Japan 25 Aug 70. During an engine check, the undercarriage was accidentally retracted. Equipment was removed & the airframe scrapped on site. Struck off (VW-l) 3 Dec 70, (TT: 11,260 hrs).

5510 WV-2/1049A-55-137 13 Mar 58 to US Navy as 145929. Navy acceptance date 25 Feb 58 (BAR FA Burbank). To VW-3 Agana 28 Feb 58, coded PM-7. Tfd VW-l Agana 14 Jun 60, coded TE-8. To Storage Facility, Litchfield Park, 21 Jun 61. Redesignated EC-121K 30 Nov 62. Withdrawn from storage 28 Feb 65. Cvtd to WC-121N. To VW-4 Roosevelt Roads 11 Mar 65, later tfd to Jacksonville, coded MH-l by Apr 66, recoded

MH-2 and named 'Faith' by Dec 68 and MH-5 'Faith' by Dec 71. To MASDC, Davis Monthan for storage 5 May 72. Struck off (Davis Monthan) 6 Nov 73, (TT: 8,074 hrs). Still stored Oct 75. Sold to Sun Valley Avn 18 May 76, subsequently scrapped.

5511 WV-2/1049A-55-137 13 Mar 58 to US Navy as 145930. Navy acceptance date 25 Feb 58 (BAR FA Burbank). To VW-l Agana 13 Mar 58. Redesignated EC-121K 9 Nov 62. Coded TE-6 by 1960 'The A-Team', later 'F-Troop'. To MASDC, Davis Monthan, for storage, TOC 18 Feb 71. Struck off (Davis Monthan) 25 May 71, (TT: 12,242 hrs). Sold to Kolar Inc 23 Oct 74, subsequently scrapped.

5512 WV-2/1049A-55-137 3 Mar 58 to US Navy as 145931. Navy acceptance date 25 Feb 58 (BAR FA Burbank). To VW-3 Agana 20 Mar 58, coded PM-8. Tfd VW-l Agana 31 May 60, coded TE-5 'City of Cavite', with drawing of Andy Capp. Redesignated EC-121K 9 Nov 62. Cvtd to WC-121N by Jun 67. Struck off (DCASR Pasadena) 28 Jul 70, (TT: 11,522 hrs). Reported at Ontario, CA in Oct 70 in camouflaged scheme. To MASDC, Davis Monthan, for storage 9 Sep 71 (in VW-l Markings, coded TE-5 still). Sold to Sun Valley Avn 24 May 76, scrapped subsequently.

5513 WV-2/1049A-55-137 27 Mar 58 to US Navy as 145932. Navy acceptance date 25 Feb 58 (BAR FA Burbank). To VW-3 Agana 27 Mar 58, coded PM-9. Tfd VW-l Agana 18 May 60, coded TE-4 'City of Naminue'. Redesignated EC-121K 30 Nov 62. Cvtd to WC-121N by Jul 67. To VQ-l Agana mid-71, coded PR-53. To MASDC, Davis Monthan, for storage 1 Feb 72. Struck off (Davis Monthan) 12 Jul 72, (TT: 12,792 hrs). Sold to Sun Valley Avn 19 May 76, subsequently scrapped.

5514 WV-2/1049A-55-137 16 Apr 58 to US Navy as 145933. Navy acceptance date 25 Feb 58 (BAR FA Burbank). To VW-3 Agana 16 Apr 58, coded PM-1. Tfd VW-l Agana 18 May 60, coded TE-3. Redesignated EC-121K 30 Nov 62. Cvtd to WC-121N by May 67. To MASDC, Davis Monthan, for storage 6 Apr 71. Struck off (Davis Monthan) 12 Jul 72, (TT: 12,785 hrs). Sold to Sun Valley Avn 21 May 76, subsequently scrapped.

5515 WV-2/1049A-55-137 6 May 58 to US Navy as 145934. Navy acceptance date 25 Feb 58 (BAR FA Burbank). To VW-1 Agana 7 May 58. Redesignated EC-121K 30 Nov 62. Coded TE-2 'Draggin Lady'. Cvtd to WC-121N by May 67. On 25 Oct 68 lost starboard tip-tank and three foot of wing when penetrating tropical storm "Judy" nr Kwajalein Atoll. Made safe landing back at Guam. Repaired. To MASDC, Davis Monthan, for storage 22 Mar 71. Struck off (Davis Monthan) 12 Jul 72, (TT: 12,151 hrs). Sold to Sun Valley Avn 18 May 76, subsequently scrapped.

5516 WV-2/1049A-55-137 12 May 58 to US Navy as 145935. Navy acceptance date 26 Feb 58 (BAR FA Burbank). To VW-l Agana 12 May 58. Redesignated EC-121K 30 Nov 62. Coded TE-1 'WW1 Ace', with Snoopy drawing. To WC-121N by Jun 67. To VQ-l Agana mid-71, coded PR-55. To MASDC, Davis Monthan, for storage 16 Nov 71. Struck off (Davis Monthan) 12 Jul 72, (TT: 12,532 hrs). Sold to Sun Valley Avn 25 May 76, subsequently scrapped.

5517 WV-2/1049A-55-137 16 May 58 to US Navy as 145936. Navy acceptance date 1 May 58 (BAR FA Burbank). To VW-2 Patuxent 16 May 58, coded MG-936, VW-2 Det B Sigonella 16 Feb 60, ret VW-2 Patuxent 28 Apr 60. To VW-2 Det B Sigonella 21 Jun 60, ret VW-2 Patuxent 26 Jun 60. To VW-11 Argentia 20 Jun 61, coded MJ-936, named 'Trade Wind'. Redesignated EC-121K 15 Oct 62 & cvtd to EC-121P 21 Feb 64. To Davis Monthan for storage Aug 65, (TT: 6,565 hrs). Withdrawn from storage & to VQ-l Atsugi after 67. Cvtd to EC-121M 13 Feb 67. Named 'Jim's Jeepney' (a/o Oct 70), Coded PR-24 (second use). To VQ-l Agana 1971. Damaged beyond repair by internal ground fire 19 Jul 73 Agana, Guam. Gas turbine APU left running unattended without cover & caught fire, gutting the rear end of the aircraft. Struck off (VQ-l) 22 Sep 73, (TT: 15,571 hrs). Scrapped on site.

5518 WV-2/1049A-55-137 27 May 58 to US Navy as 145937. Navy acceptance date 13 May 58 (BAR FA Burbank). To VW-2 Patuxent 29 May 58, coded MG-937. To VW-2 Det B Sigonella 7 Dec 59, ret VW-2 Patuxent 25 Jan 60. To VW-2 Det B Sigonella 27 Mar 60, ret VW-2 Patuxent 25 Jul 60. To AEW TRAUNIT/AEW TULANT, Patuxent 12 Jun 61 & to VW-11 Argentia 28 Jun 62, coded MJ-937. Redesignated EC-121K 2 Oct 62. To VW-4 Roosevelt Roads 25 Jul 63, ret VW-11 Argentia 10 Jan 64. Cvtd to EC-121P 31 Jan 64. To Davis Monthan 29 Jul 65, (TT: 7,455 hrs). Tfd to NASA by US Navy 3 Nov 65 as NASA 670 for use at Wallops Island, VA. Regn N670NA requested 17 Apr 69, regd 25 Jun 69 officially, NASA notified 14 Aug 69. Ret to MASDC, Davis Monthan, for storage, TOC 6 May 70. N-regn canx 18 Jun 70. Struck off by Navy (Davis Monthan) 21 Dec 70, (TT: quoted as 7,455 hrs, but wrong - see above!). Sold to Kolar Inc 17 Oct 74, subsequently scrapped.

5519 WV-2/1049A-55-137 19 Jun 58 to US Navy as 145938. Navy acceptance date 5 Jun 58 (BAR FA Burbank). To VW-2 Patuxent 20 Jun 58. To VW-2 Det B Chincoteague 11 May 59, Det B Malta 31 Aug 59, ret VW-2 Patuxent 8 Sep 59. To VW-2 Det B Sigonella 16 Jul 60, ret VW-2 Patuxent 1 Sep 60. To AEW TRAUNIT/ AEW TULANT Patuxent 16 Jun 61. To VW-11 Argentia 9 Jun 62, coded MJ-938. Redesignated EC-121K 11 Oct 62. Cvtd to EC-121P 4 Dec 63. To Davis Monthan for storage Aug 65. Withdrawn for storage and to VW-1 Agana by Jun 67 and cvtd to WC-121N, coded TE-8 'I'm so sweet (Skunk). Nobody loves me'. Recoded TE-10 in 1970/71. To VQ-1 Agana, coded PR-52, in 1971. Ret MASDC, Davis Monthan, for storage 13 Dec 71. Struck off (Davis Monthan) 12 Jul 72, (TT: 12,971 hrs). Sold to Sun Valley Avn 21 May 76, subsequently scrapped.

5520 WV-2/1049A-55-137 27 Jul 58 to US Navy as 145939. Navy acceptance date 13 Jun 58 (BAR FA Burbank). To VW-2 Patuxent 28 Jun 58. To VW-2 Det B Sigonella 20 Apr 60, ret VW-2 Patuxent 21 Jul 60. To AEW TRAUNIT/AEW TULANT Patuxent, coded MM-3, 19 Jun 61. To VW-11 Argentia 4 Jun 62, coded MJ-939. Redesignated EC-121K 2 Oct 62. Cvtd to EC-121P 22 Dec 63, named 'Cutty Sark'. To Davis Monthan for storage Aug 65. Withdrawn from storage by Apr 67 and to VW-1 Agana, coded TE-9 'Malfunction Junction', Apr 67. Recoded TE-11 in 1970/71, & also TE-5 at some stage. Reverted to EC-121K 28 Apr 67. To VAQ-33/FEWSG, Norfolk 1971, coded GD-10, named 'Maytag Messerschmitt'. Ret to MASDC, Davis Monthan, for storage 2 Dec 72. Struck off (Davis Monthan) 29 Jul 74, (TT: 13,702 hrs). Sold to Sun Valley Avn 16 Sep 76, subsequently scrapped.

5521 WV-2/1049A-55-137 8 Aug 58 to US Navy as 145940. Navy acceptance date 24 Jul 58 (BAR FA Burbank). To VW-2 Patuxent 9 Aug 58. To VW-2 Det B Chincoteague 1 Dec 58, ret VW-2 Patuxent 15 Dec 58, coded MG-940. To VW-2 Det B Chincoteague 17 Mar 59, ret VW-2 Patuxent 20 May 59. To VW-2 Det B Malta 16 Sep 59, Det B Sigonella 30 Nov 59, ret VW-2 Patuxent 9 Dec 59. To VW-2 Det B Sigonella 15 May 60, ret VW-2 Patuxent 1 Sep 60. To VW-11 Argentia 21 Jun 61, coded MJ-940. Redesignated EC-121K 15 Oct 62. Cvtd to EC-121P 6 Mar 64. To Davis Monthan for storage Aug 65. Withdrawn from storage by Apr 67 and to VQ-l Atsugi. Cvtd to EC-121M 28 Apr 67. Coded PR-25 by 1970. Tfd to VQ-1 Agana 1971. Ret to MASDC, Davis Monthan, for storage 27 Oct 74. Struck off (Davis Monthan) 11 Nov 74, (TT: 18,090 hrs). For sale by DofD (Davis Monthan) 11 Feb 81, TT quoted as 18,147 hrs. Sold to Kolar Inc, scrapped subsequent to Apr 81.

5522 WV-2/1049A-55-165 10 Oct 58 to US Navy as 145941. To BAR M&S Burbank 19 Sep 58. Mod with canoe-shaped upper radome on forward fuselage. To VW-2 Patuxent 11 Oct 58. To VW-2 Det B Chincoteague 1 Dec 58, ret VW-2 Patuxent 28 Feb 59. To AEW TRAUNIT/AEW TULANT Patuxent 23 Jun 61. To VW-11 Argentia 3 Jul 62, coded MJ-941. Redesignated EC-121K 3 Oct 62. Cvtd to EC-121P 11 Jan 64. To Davis Monthan for storage Aug 65. Struck off (AFASDG) 8 Feb 67, (TT: 6,485 hrs). Scrapped by Mar 71.

N1649 1649A prototype flying in loose formation with a Navy WV-2 in late 1956. The 150 ft-span wing is clearly evident in this view. (Lockheed)

THE STARLINERS

1001 Prototype Model 1649 Starliner. First flight 10 Oct 56 as Model 1649A-98-01 regd N1649. Painted with white cabin top extending below windows, polished metal lower surfaces. Still regd N1649 in Jul 60, then reregd N60968 to Lockheed Aircraft Corp. By mid-1963 reregd N1102, still to Lockheed Aircraft Corp and repainted with thin dark blue cheat line and MATS-style dark blue band on fins. Used as company hack until approx 1970. Up for sale Apr 70 and stored at Burbank, CA. Sold to American Jet Industries Inc by Oct 71, and stored at Fox Fld, Lancaster, CA by May 71. Ret to Burbank Nov 72 for refurbishing and painting. Sold in Japan and ferried non-stop from Burbank to Nagoya, Japan, arr 15 Dec 72. Converted into a restaurant at Sanjo, Niigata Prefecture, after flight to Niigata, arr 19 Dec 72. Opened as "Restaurant Shinano" Aug 73, later called "Restaurant Lockheed" (advertised as MacArthur's 'Bataan'). By Sep 79, the aircraft was dismantled at Higashi Shogo, 40 miles from Niigata, awaiting transport to new site near Tokyo, with green cheat line. By early Nov 79, the aircraft was at the Yazu Amusement Park, Narashino, Chiba Prefecture and was owned by the Sanyo Kosan Corp. Site was en route from Narita Airport to Tokyo City. In Nov 79, the aircraft had camouflage-type dark upper surfaces, finishing in a wavy line below the windows and light-coloured lower surfaces, still with the regn N1102 on the fin. By Nov 80, it had a white top, duck-egg blue lower surfaces, and medium blue cheat line. Inside, the original pax seating was on one side, Lockheed test equipment was on the other side, and cockpit intact. It was expected to stay at Narashino for five years and then be moved again to a new site at Nagoya by 1984, but in fact when the Yazu Amusement Park was closed down in 1982, the Starliner was scrapped on site.

1002 1649A-98-15 Regd N7301C and painted in Trans World Airlines colours with FN 301, 'Star of Wyoming'. Used from Jan 57 for type certification tests by LAC and deld to TWA LADD: 4 Sep 57 (TT: 147 hrs 52 mins). In svce 8 Sep 57 (intl network). Later unnamed. (TT: 6,091 hrs a/o 31 May 59). Last svce 31 Aug 61 (TT: 11,000 hrs) and stored at Kansas City, MO from 1 Sep 61. Sold to B MacDonald Keith & Vera M Keith 14 Oct 63, officially to B MacDonald Keith 1 Mar 64, Vera M Keith 2 Mar 64. To Vand Inc 25 Aug 64. Sold to Charles E. Bush t/a Bush Aviation 23 Feb 65 and lsd to World Samplers (travel club) by Aug 65. Also reported owned or lsd by International Flights Centers Inc in 1964 or 1965. In store at Fort Lauderdale, FL in May 66, then lsd to Passaat Inc. Sub-lsd to various airlines during late 1966 (airline strike), and sub-lsd to Aerocondor (Aerovias Condor de Colombia Limitida) 17 Dec 66. Crashed on landing at Bogota Airport, Colombia, at 02.15 hrs (local)/07.55 GMT on 18 Dec 66, while operating a non-scheduled passenger flight from Miami, FL. 17 killed, 39 survivors. The aircraft was flying unpressurized and was attempting to land in thick fog. Approx 80 metres from the end of the runway the aircraft dropped suddenly and struck the bank of the Bogota River with all three undercarriage legs. The nosewheel assembly broke off, aircraft skimmed across the lagoon, breaking off parts of the engines, propellers & fuselage covering, then struck the inner edge of a drainage ditch on the left of the extended centre

Section 12: Constellation Production List

N7306C 1649A of Trans World Airlines, specially named "Spirit of St.Louis", was the first 1649A "Jetstream" to visit London (Heathrow) Airport, with sistership N7307C (c/n 1008) on 2nd June 1957. (Stephen Piercey collection)

line of Runway 12 & approx 10-20 metres before the threshold. The fuselage broke in two, wings and tail also broke off, but acft did not catch fire. Survivors trapped in fuselage for 20 minutes as the emergency doors could not be opened from the inside. Cause: Pilot error. The distance between the aircraft and the ground was misjudged in the variable weather conditions. Contributing factors were that the 1649A was 5,800 lbs above the maximum landing weight, and the manager of Aerocondor was in the cockpit with the pilots and in contact with the control tower, possibly distracting the pilots from flying; the crew was also over-tired due to working long hours after a previous flight had been delayed.

1003 1649A-98-09 11 May 57 to Trans World Airlines as N7302C, FN 302, 'Star of Utah'. (TT: 17 hrs). Used for maintenance training 13 May-1 Jun 57. In svce 2 Jun 57 (intl network). Later unnamed. (TT: 6,947 hrs a/o 31 May 59). Op last TWA piston-engined passenger transatlantic service on flight TW 905 Rome to New York-Idlewild 28 Oct 61. Used on domestic svces until last svce 29 Oct 62 (TT: 13,296 hrs). Stored at Fairfax, KS and wfu 9 Mar 63. Remained in storage until sold to Charles E Bush t/a Bush Aviation 21 Oct 65. Lsd to Flying Ambassadors (travel club) during 1966. Repossessed by First National Bank of Hollywood Corp by 1967 and stored at Fort Lauderdale, FL from Jan 67 at least. Dismantled at Fort Lauderdale May 68 onwards, and broken up there during Oct 68.

1004 1649A-98-15 Used for type certification tests by LAC and deld to Trans World Airlines as N7303C, FN 303, 'Star of Vermont' LADD: 26 May 57 (TT: 84 hrs 42 mins). In svce (domestic network) 1 Jun 57, tf almost immediately to intl network. Later unnamed. (TT: 6,910 hrs a/o 31 May 59). Last svce with TWA 24 Sep 62 (TT: 13,474 hrs) .Withdrawn from use 9 Dec 62 and stored at Kansas City, MO. Used for spares. Hull sold 5 Mar 63 to Patrick G Guirk. Note: This last entry may be an error in TWA records for the owner of the "Flight 42 Cocktail Lounge" - see c/n 1007.

1005 1649A-98-15 Used for type certification tests by LAC and deld to Trans World Airlines as N7304C, FN 304, 'Star of Rhode Island' LADD: 12 Jun 57 (TT: 81 hrs 44 mins). In svce (domestic network) 14 Jun 57, tfd almost immediately to intl network. Made 2 hr 45 min test flight from Los Angeles Intl over the Catalina Island area 10 Jul 57 for Howard Hughes to compare the noise level of the 1649A compared with the 1049G. Flew New York-Lisbon Jetstream inaugural 30-31 Jul 57. Later unnamed with TWA. (TT: 6,791 hrs a/o 31 May 59). Op last scheduled TWA piston-engined passenger flight from New York to London-Heathrow 17 Jan 60. Last svce with TWA 27 Oct 62 (TT: 13,774 hrs). Stored at Kansas City, MO and withdrawn from use 5 Dec 62. Remained in storage until sold to Charles E Bush t/a Bush Aviation 28 Oct 65. Stored at Fort Lauderdale, FL from at least May 66. Repossessed by First National Bank of Hollywood Corp by 1967. Dismantled at Fort Lauderdale from May 68 onwards, and broken up there during Aug-Sep 68.

1006 1649A-98-09 10 May 57 to Trans World Airlines as N7305C, FN 305, 'Star of Idaho'. (TT: 11 hrs) .Used for maintenance training 11-31 May 57. In svce (intl network) 1 Jun 57. Later unnamed. (TT: 7,134 hrs a/o 31 May 59). Withdrawn from svce 9 Sep 60. Sold to Trans Atlantica Argentina SA 12 Sep 60. (TT: 10,894 hrs). E-42357 dated 10 Sep 60 as LV-PXM. Reregd LV-GLH 12 Sep 60. Damaged landing at Rio de Janeiro, Brazil, on 19 Jun 61. No injuries. While landing at Rio, the aircraft hit an earth abutment at the end of the runway. Both main landing gears were sheared off, and the aircraft skidded approx two-thirds of a mile. The fuselage, both inner flaps, the main undercarriage, all engines and propellers sustained severe damage. Cause: Pilot error. Aircraft repairable, but in fact stored unrepaired at Rio until scrapped at unknown date.

1007 1649A-98-09 4 May 57 to Trans World Airlines as N7306C, FN 306, 'Star of Maryland'. (TT: 23 hrs). Used for pilot training 5-30 May 57. In svce (intl network) 1 Jun 57. Renamed

'Spirit of St.Louis' and inaugurated scheduled 1649A svces from New York-Idlewild to London-Heathrow, arr London 2 Jun 57. Still named end Aug 57, but unnamed by 1958. (TT: 6,945 hrs a/o 31 May 59). Last svce with TWA 26 Apr 62. Stored at Mid-Continent Airport, Kansas City, MO. (TT: 13,176 hrs). Used for spares. Hull sold to Normandie Iron & Metals 28 Feb 65. Stripped for spares and hulk sold for conversion into restaurant. Converted into the "Flight 42 Cocktail Lounge" at Kansas City, MO. On site by mid-1965. Painted white with thick black cheat line. Subsequent history unknown, but believed removed within three years.

1008 1649A-98-09 7 May 57 to Trans World Airlines as N7307C, FN 307, 'Star of Montana'. (TT: 22 hrs). Used for domestic and intl maintenance training 8 May-1 Jun 57, including proving flight from New York-Idlewild to London-Heathrow (arr 17 May 57) and to Frankfurt (arr 19 May 57). In svce (intl network) 3 Jun 57. Later unnamed. Inaugurated non-stop polar scheduled services from London-Heathrow to San Francisco, CA on 2 Oct 57- flying time 23 hrs 20 mins, a record at the time for **non-stop** commercial service! (TT: 7,177 hrs a/o 31 May 59). Withdrawn from use by TWA 12 Sep 60 at Kansas City, MO. (TT: 11,227 hrs). Sold to Trans Atlantica Argentina SA 3 Oct 60. E-42358 dated 30 Sep 60 as LV-PXL. Regd LV-GLI 3 Oct 60. Stored at Frankfurt-Rhein Main, Germany after Trans Atlantica ceased ops in Nov 61. Ret to USA Nov 62, stored at Kansas City. Officially reclaimed by Trans World 12 Feb 64 and sold same day (also quoted as 15 Jan 64) as N7307C to the FAA for $38,000. Fitted out and instrumented for safety tests. Destroyed in FAA safety tests at Deer Valley Airport, near Phoenix, AZ on 3 Sep 64 (For further details, see Section 9). Fuselage then prepared by Aviation Safety Engineering Research (AvSER) to a passenger configuration Feb-Mar 65. Emergency evacuation tests carried out day & night 6 Apr 65 & 8 Apr 65. Subsequently scrapped on site.

1009 1649A-98-22 18 May 57 to Trans World Airlines as N7308C, FN 308, 'Star of Oklahoma' (TT: 19 hrs). In svce 2 Jun 57, used on domestic network. Later unnamed. (TT: 7,326 hrs a/o 31 May 59 & a/o 30 Jun 61 11,829 hrs). Sold to Trans Atlantica Argentina SA 30 Aug 61. E-50089 29 Aug 61 as LV-PHW. Reregd LV-HCU 30 Aug 61. Trans Atlantica ceased ops Nov 61. Reclaimed by TWA and stored at Mid-Continent Airport, Kansas City, MO by summer 1962. (TT: 12,630 hrs). Used for spares, restored as N7308C, but believed not carried. Remained in storage, parts missing, until sold to Arizona Aircraft Parts & Sales Co (as scrap) 30 Sep 66. Presumably scrapped late 1966. Canx from USCAR 1966.

1010 1649A-98-22 28 May 57 to Trans World Airlines as N7309C, FN 309, 'Star of Maine' (TT: 18 hrs 37 mins). Used for flight training 29 May-1 Jun 57. In svce 3 Jun 57 (intl network). Later unnamed. (TT: 6,957 hrs a/o 31 May 59). Last svce with TWA 1 Dec 62 (TT: 13,595 hrs). Stored at Mid-Continent Airport, Kansas City, MO until sold to Arizona Aircraft Parts & Sales Co (as scrap) 30 Sep 66. Presumably scrapped late 1966. Canx from USCAR 1966.

1011 1649A-98-11 30 Jun 57 to Air France as F-BHBK 'Lafayette'. E-28736 dated 27 Jun 57, deld Los Angeles -Paris 7-8 Jul 57, CofA issued 22 Jul 57. Damaged when an explosion occurred in no.3 engine, wing and starboard undercarriage damaged by subsequent fire, on 23 Jul 57(!), after the crew had been practising landings and take-offs at Reims Airport, France. Repaired & entered svce 22 Sep 57. Carried joint Air France-Japan A/L titling (a/o Aug 60) for polar flts. Lsd to Air Afrique as 81-seater 1 Nov 61 as F-BHBK, reregd TU-TBB on sale to Air Afrique 17 Apr 62, CofA issued 18 Apr 62. Ret to Air France 15 May 63 (CofA as TU-TBB expired 28 May 63) and restored as F-BHBK, unnamed. Withdrawn from use at Paris (Orly) on 2 Nov 63, prior to CofA expiry on 19 Nov 63. Stored at Orly, canx as wfu 24 May 67, but 20 Apr 67 also quoted, (TT: 13,975 hrs). Stripped for spares at Orly during Aug 67. Fuselage and wing stubs subseqeuntly used for fire-fighting practice at Orly. Most of cabin burnt and fuselage falling apart by May 79, but still extant in hulk form at Orly for fire-training until late 1985/early 1986, when charred fuselage finally scrapped.

1012 1649A-98-22 28 May 57 to Hughes Tool Co as N7310C (TT: 19 hrs 18 mins). Used by Hughes in Trans World colours, based in Nassau, Bahamas for some of the time, but few flts made. Deld to Trans World on 19 Dec 57 (TT: 97 hrs 16 mins). In svce 21 Dec 57 as N7310C, FN 310, name 'Star of Kansas' allocated, but probably never carried. Used on intl network (TT: a/o 31 May 59 4,967 hrs). Last svce with TWA 2 Dec 62 (TT: 11,129 hrs). Withdrawn from use 20 Feb 63. Stored at Kansas City, MO until sold to Delta Aircraft & Equipment Co (also named Delta Aircraft & Engine Parts) 29 Apr 64. Tfd to Charlotte Aircraft Corp autumn 1964. Sold to Alaska Airlines Mar 65 for spares use only. Ferried to Seattle, WA and stored there in ex-TWA markings. Derelict by Oct 65 and scrapped there by Sep 66. Canx from USCAR 1966.

1013 1649A-98-20 31 May 57 to Trans World Airlines as N7311C, FN 311. Name 'Star of the Ebro' allocated, but probably never carried. In svce (intl network) 4 Jun 57. Damaged when wingtip caught the starboard wingtip of parked TWA l049G N7125C at Los Angeles,CA on 16 Dec 58 when taxying out en route to Philadelphia, PA. Minor damage, wing fuel tank punctured but no fire. Flt left LAX with c/n 1016 two hrs & 45 mins late. Acft repaired. (TT: 6,598 hrs a/o 31 May 59). Last pax svce with TWA 17 Aug 60. Cvtd to all-cargo configuration by LAS, the first 1649A all-cargo conversion for TWA. Ret .to Trans World 20 Oct 60, in svce 21 Oct 60. (TT: 11,437 hrs a/o 30 Jun 61). Withdrawn from svce 10 Dec 66 (TT: 18,898 hrs). Stored at Kansas City, MO until sold to California Airmotive Corp 20 Sep 67. Lsd to Trans American Leasing Inc approx Dec 68/Jan 69 (parked at Van Nuys, CA in Jan 69). Damaged in attempted forced landing on a strip at Colchane at an altitude of 13,300 feet near Isluga, province of Iquique, about a mile inside the Chilean border with Bolivia, in the Altiplano region, on 26 Mar 69 after a double engine failure. The aircraft, which was engaged on a whisky & cigarette smuggling trip at the time, overran the strip, hit a banking and reportedly engine fire in no.1 took hold & port wing separated. Cause: After failure of one engine, the Flight Engineer feathered the wrong one by mistake. The aircraft was reported destroyed at the time, but was subsequently found whole, but derelict, and was still on site in 1994. Only parts of centre-section and lower fuselage remaining by 2004.

1014 1649A-98-20 14 Jun 57 to Trans World Airlines as N7312C, FN 312. Name 'Star of the Elbe' allocated, but probably never carried. (TT: 16 hrs 28 mins). In svce (intl network) 17 Jun 57. TWA dely quoted as 12 Jun 57. (TT: 7,062 hrs a/o 31 May 59). Last svce with TWA 26 Dec 62 (TT: 14,279 hrs). Stored at Kansas City, MO until sold to Arizona Aircraft Parts & Sales Co (as scrap) 30 Sep 66. Presumably scrapped late 1966. Canx from USCAR 1966.

1015 1649A-98-20 30 May 57 to Trans World Airlines as N7313C, FN 313. Name 'Star of the Severn' allocated, but probably never carried. (TT: 9 hrs 13 mins). In svce 1 Jun 57 (domestic network), tfd to intl network. Crashed to the ground in the region of Olgiate Olona, Varese, northern Italy, at approx 16.35 hrs (GMT) on 26 Jun 59, while climbing through 11,000 feet after take-off from Milan-Malpensa. All on board killed. The aircraft was flying service TW 891/26 from Athens to Chicago. Take-off from Milan en route to Paris was at 16.20 hrs. At 16.32 hrs the flight reported reaching 10,000 feet. Three minutes later, structural failure, followed by in-flight disintegration occurred. There were scattered thunderstorms in the area at the time. Probable cause: Explosion of fuel vapours in no.7 fuel tank set off, through the outlet pipes, by the igniting of the gasoline vapours issuing from these pipes as a consequence of static electricity discharges which developed on the vent outlets. Probably followed immediately by excess of pressure or further explosion in no.6 fuel tank, causing separation of the starboard wing in flight and subsequent loss of control. (TT: 6,671 hrs).

SECTION 12: CONSTELLATION PRODUCTION LIST

1016 1649A-98-20 22 Jun 57 to Trans World Airlines as N7314C, FN 314. Name 'Star of the Shannon' allocated, but probably never carried. (TT: 20 hrs 50 mins). Used for pilot training 23-30 Jun 57. In svce 1 Jul 57 on domestic network. (TT: 6,709 hrs a/o 31 May 59). Cvtd to 96-pax charter aircraft and re-entered svce 1 Aug 60. (TT: 10,930 hrs a/o 30 Jun 61). Withdrawn from use 29 Mar 65 and stored at Kansas City, MO. Lsd 4 Jun 65 to Moral Rearmament Corp Inc & deld at New York-JFK same day. Op by Starflite Inc for Moral Rearmament, sold to Moral Rearmament Corp Inc 10 Dec 65. In use with the International Air Travel Club as 'Supercalifragilisticexpealidocius' by Jun 66, until at least Sep 66. Sold to Tex Hou Inc 25 Jul 66. Lsd to Air Venturers in Apr 67, then to Holiday Wings (travel club). Ownership tfd to Broadway Enterprises Inc 9 Aug 67. Lse to Holiday Wings continued, carried additional titling "East Texas Flying Clubhouse" by May 68. Sold to Janus Enterprises Inc 15 Aug 68. Lsd to Fly by Night Safaris Inc. While in use with Fly by Night Safaris Inc, the acft was substantially damaged in an aborted take-off at McCarran Fld, Las Vegas, NV at night on 9 Dec 68. While taking-off from Las Vegas, no.3 engine failed at approx 100 mph. The remaining three engines were placed in reverse pitch, but as the aircraft braked, the main undercarriage collapsed, and the aircraft skidded along the runway. A small electrical fire in the baggage compartment was extinguished, after smoke filled the cabin. All 104 pax and crew evacuated within two minutes, with only five pax receiving minor injuries. The take-off had been delayed for 24 hrs due to two flat tyres and an engine running rough. The aircraft was declared to be repairable, but was presumably scrapped at Las Vegas some time during 1969, as no further reports of it were made. Canx from USCAR 1969.

1017 1649A-98-20 24 Jun 57 to Trans World Airlines as N7315C, FN 315. Name 'Star of the Tagus' allocated, but probably never carried. (TT: 15 hrs). In svce (domestic network) 27 Jun 57. (TT: 6,776 hrs a/o 31 May 59). Last pax flight 16 Sep 60. Cvtd to al1-cargo configuration by LAS. Ret to Trans World 1 Dec 60, in svce same day. (TT: 11,029 hrs a/o 30 Jun 61). Made Trans World's last piston-engined aircraft flight (as cargo aircraft) TW591 from Newark, NJ to St Louis & Kansas City, MO 11 May 67. Withdrawn from svce 16 May 67 and stored at Fairfax, KS (TT: 20,280 hrs). Sold to California Airmotive Corp 22 Aug 67 and flown to Fox Field, Lancaster, CA for storage. Stored at Fox Fld until sold to Prudhoe Bay Oil Distributing Co Inc in late 1968 or early 1969. N-regn canx requested by California Airmotive 30 Jun 70, canx from USCAR 12 Jul 70. Stored at Anchorage, AK in ex-TWA colours by Jun 72. Used for spares by West-Air Inc in restoration of c/ns 1018 & 1038 during summer 1974. Ownership tfd to the State of Alaska Department of Public Works 25 Feb 75. Remained in derelict condition at Anchorage. Auctioned at Anchorage in early 1977, but remained unsold. Moved to fire-dump Apr 77 and fins damaged by a truck. Donated by airport authority to Alaska State Transportation Museum (Palmer, AK) in 1978, but scheme fell through and aircraft remained on the fire-dump at Anchorage. Still there in Oct 80. Further useable spares purchased by Aeroborne Enterprises Inc in approx Aug/Sep 80. Hulk of acft, no engines or cargo doors, etc, still on fire-dump in Jan 82, and in pieces by Oct 83. Maine Coast Airways bought what remained of the acft from the Anchorage Fire Svce in 1994 & after removing anything useable as spares, the remains were scrapped at Anchorage in 1995.

1018 1649A-98-20 26 Jun 57 to Trans World Airlines as N7316C, FN 316. Name 'Star of the Tigris' allocated, but probably never carried. (TT: 10 hrs 48 mins). In svce 28 Jun 57, used on intl & domestic networks. (TT: 6,598 hrs a/o 31 May 59). Cvtd to all-cargo configuration by LAS. Deld for conversion after last pax svce 9 Sep 60. Ret to Trans World 21 Nov 60, in svce as all-cargo aircraft 28 Nov 60. (TT: 11,282 hrs a/o 30 Jun 61). Lsd to Alaska Airlines 25 Jan 62, sold to them 31 Dec 62 (1 Jan 64 also quoted, presumably date of final payment). Cvtd to bulk fuel-oil carrier 1968 and sold to Red Dodge Aviation 16 Nov 68. Sold to Prudhoe Oil Distributing Co Inc 2 Dec 68. Believed lsd Interior Airways during 1969. Stored at Anchorage, AK by Apr 72. Sold to Harry E Faulkner dba West-Air Inc 9 Sep 74. Flown to Kenai, AK after restoration for storage during winter 1974-75. Sold to Onyx Aviation Inc 14 Nov 75. Canx from USCAR, then restored to Burns Aviation Inc as N7316C 17 Jan 76. Made last flights for Burns in Jul 76. Flew Fort Lauderdale, FL to Stewart, NY 15 Jul 76, dep Stewart 16 Jul 76, but nosewheel would not retract, so ret to Stewart. Flew Stewart-Gander, Nfld 18 Jul, to Paris (Le Bourget) 21 Jul 76. Ret Le Bourget-Shannon 22 Jul & Shannon-Stewart 28 Jul 76. This was the last flight by a Starliner in Europe. Stored at Stewart, Newburgh, NY. Aircraft up for sale in 1979 for $40,000. Still regd to Burns Aviation Inc, but tied up in legal problems between the Metropolitan Transport Authority (operators of Stewart Airport) and Burns. Transexecutive Aviation Inc reported to be acting as broker for sale of aircraft in 1976. Remained stored at Stewart. Sold to Robert Haer, president of Southwest Aircraft Inc Jul 80. Sale not completed officially as $1,000 per month owed to airport in parking fees, of which only $6,000 were paid. Canx from USCAR Apr 82. Sold to Maurice A Roundy & Jane A Theberge t/a Maine Coast Airways Jun 83. Prepared for dely during Jun-Oct 83. Named 'Star of the Tigris' (& 'Jason's Star' on nosewheel door). Del 9 Nov 83 Stewart, NY to Auburn-Lewiston, ME. Restored to USCAR 31 Jan 84. Stored at Auburn-Lewiston in good condition & engines run up occasionally. Sold to James P A Thompson, regd 19 Apr 06.Ret Maine Coast Airways 27 Dec 06.

1019 1649A-98-20 30 Jun 57 to Trans World Airlines as N7317C, FN 317 (TT: 14 hrs 29 mins). Name 'Star of the Clyde' allocated, but probably never carried. In svce 1 Jul 57 on intl network. (TT: 6,410 hrs a/o 31 May 59). Deld for conversion to all-cargo configuration by LAS 30 Aug 60. Ret to Trans World 9 Nov 60, in svce 10 Nov 60. (TT: 11,141 hrs a/o 30 Jun 61). Withdrawn from svce with TWA 12 May 67 (TT: 20,134 hrs). Stored Mid-Continent Airport, Kansas City, MO. Sold to California Airmotive Corp 11 Aug 67. To Willair International Inc (lse-purchase) in Dec 68. Withdrawn from use at Honolulu, HI by early 1970 and stored. N-regn canx requested by California Airmotive 30 Jun 70, canx from USCAR 12 Jul 70. Broken up at Honolulu, probably during 1973.

1020 1649A-98-11 10 Jul 57 to Air France as F-BHBL 'Rochambeau'. E-28737 dated 5 Jul 57, deld 14 Jul 57 to Paris and CofA issued 22 Jul 57. In svce on Paris-New York Starliner inaugural 17 Aug 57. Damaged taxying Chicago, IL 26 Jul 59. Repaired. Later op as 81-seater. Withdrawn from svce 20 Jan 63 (TT: 12,619 hrs) prior to CofA expiry on 10 May 63 and stored at Paris (Orly). Wfu 20 Apr 67 (TT: 12,619 hrs). F-regn canx 24 May 67. Broken up at Orly Aug 67.

1021 1649A-98-20 19 Jul 57 to Trans World Airlines as N7318C, FN 318. Name 'Star of the Arno' allocated, but probably never carried. (TT: 9 hrs). Used for pilot training 20-29 Jul 57. In svce 30 Jul 57, intl network. (TT: 6,494 hrs a/o 31 May 59). Cvtd to 96-pax charter aircraft and re-entered svce 27 Nov 60. Last svce with TWA 23 Jan 63 (TT: 13,005 hrs). Stored at Fairfax, KS 4 Feb 63 until sold to Charles E Bush t/a Bush Aviation 27 Dec 65. Flown to Fort Lauderdale, FL and stored there by May 66. Repossessed by First National Bank of Hollywood Corp 1968. Broken up at Fort Lauderdale during May 68. Canx from USCAR 1970.

1022 1649A-98-20 24 Jul 57 to Trans World Airlines as N7319C, FN 319. Name 'Star of the Loire' allocated, but probably never carried. (TT: 11 hrs 24 mins). In svce 26 Jul 57. Used on domestic & intl networks, (TT: 6,358 hrs a/o 31 May 59). Deld for conversion to all-cargo configuration by LAS after last pax svce 10 Oct 60. Ret to TWA 22 Dec 60, in svce 29 Dec 60. (TT: 10,965 hrs a/o 30 Jun 61). Sustained damage on 23 Aug 61 at 06.06 hrs (PST) when the propeller struck the ground taxying at Los Angeles Intl Airport after the undercarriage collapsed. Aircraft had arrived from Newark, NJ on a cargo flight. Repaired. Stored at Mid-Continent Airport, Kansas City, MO after withdrawn from use 27 Dec 63 (TT:15,436 hrs) .Sold to Bush Aviation Enterprises and deld to Fort Lauderdale, FL 10 May 66. Still at Fort Lauderdale in Jan 67, but aircraft not paid for and ret to storage at Kansas City by the end of the year. Wfu with Trans World again 5 Apr 68. Sold to Aero-Tech Corp 23 May 68. Scrapped at Kansas City, MO by Aero-Tech mid-1968. Canx from USCAR 1970.

N7322C 1649A Freighter leased to Aerovias Halcon (Argentina) and photographed at Buenos Aires (Ezeiza) in June 1968. Note the airline's emblem on the nose. (Alex Reinhard via Jennifer M Gradidge)

1023 1649A-98-20 26 Jul 57 to Trans World Airlines as N7320C, FN 320. Name 'Star of the Avon' allocated, but probably never carried. (TT: 15 hrs). In svce, domestic & intl networks 27 Jul 57. (TT: 6,734 hrs a/o 31 May 59). Sold to Trans Atlantica Argentina SA 11 Aug 61, (TT: 11,638 hrs). E-50014 dated same day as LV-PHV. Reregd LV-HCD 11 Aug 61. Stored at Paris (Orly) when Trans Atlantica ceased ops in Nov 61. Released by Air France 3 Dec 63. Reregd N7320C by Apr 64 at Orly, and reclaimed by Trans World. Ret to Fairfax, KS 15 Jun 64 (TT: 11,968 hrs) and stored there in ex-Trans Atlantica markings until sold to Charles E Bush t/a Bush Aviation 15 Dec 65. Stored at Fort Lauderdale, FL by May 66, in ex-Argentina colours. Parts missing by May 68 & no engines by Oct 68. Ownership tfd to Aviation Development Corp Jan 69. Remained in storage at Fort Lauderdale and broken up there during May 1970.

1024 1649A-98-20 31 Jul 57 to Trans World Airlines as N7321C, FN 321. Name 'Star of the Euphrates' allocated, but probably never carried. (TT: 17 hrs 54 mins). In svce 2 Aug 57, used on intl & domestic networks. (TT: 6,436 hrs a/o 31 May 59). Cvtd to 96-pax charter aircraft and re-entered svce 16 Dec 60. (TT: 11,038 hrs a/o 30 Jun 61). Withdrawn from use 29 Mar 65 and stored at Kansas City, MO. Sold to Charles E Bush t/a Bush Aviation 12 Oct 65 (FAA quote 8 Oct 65 as transfer date). Lsd to World Samplers Inc (travel club) Nov 65. Sold to Association of Flying Travel Clubs Inc 24 Jan 66, but continued to fly in World Samplers colours until at least Sep 68. Sold to Janus Enterprises Inc 17 Jan 69 & in svce in Mexico Aug 69. To Lodge Service Corp 20 Jul 70. Stored at Houston-Hobby Airport, TX by Mar 72 (and probably much earlier) in World Samplers colours. Sold to Harry Faulkner t/a West-Air Inc 17 Jul 73 and stripped for spares to make c/n 1040 airworthy. Derelict at Houston-Hobby by Jun 74, scrapped shortly afterwards.

1025 1649A-98-20 29 Jul 57 to Trans World Airlines as N7322C, FN 322. Name 'Star of the Po' allocated, but probably never carried. (TT: 11 hrs 13 mins). In svce 30 Jul 57, used on domestic & intl networks. (TT: 6,317 hrs a/o 31 May 59). Deld for conversion to all-cargo configuration by LAS after last pax svce 27 Sep 60. Ret to TWA 13 Dec 60, in svce 16 Dec 60. (TT: 10,785 hrs a/o 30 Jun 61). Withdrawn from svce 16 May 67 (TT: 19,965 hrs) and stored at Fairfax, KS until sold to California Airmotive Corp 29 Aug 67. Stored at Van Nuys, CA Sep 67. Lsd to Aerovias Halcon May-Dec 68. Lsd to Trans American Leasing Inc approx Dec 68. Withdrawn from use at Miami, FL some time during 1970 after one engine failed on take-off on a heavily-loaded cargo flight and the remaining three engines were flown on maximum power around the circuit, causing internal damage. Stored at Miami, FL from autumn 1970. Repossessed by California Airmotive & regn canx requested 30 Jun 70. Canx from USCAR 12 Jul 70. California Airmotive continued to pay parking fees at Miami until 11 Aug 72, when the acft was towed over to the military ramp prior to scrapping. Scrapped approx Feb-Mar 73, probably by Shelton Metals, at Miami Intl.

1026 Laid down as Model 1649A-98-16 for Linee Aeree Italiane as I-LAMA. Completed for LAI, but ntu. Test flown, then remained at the factory (LADD: 2 Jan 58). Sold to Trans World Airlines and deld at Burbank, CA 5 Jun 58 as N8081H (TT: 15 hrs 40 mins). Ferried to Mid-Continent Airport, Kansas City, MO 5 Jun 58 for conversion to TWA standards. Completed 29 Jun 58. Ferried Kansas City Municipal-New York (Idlewild) 30 Jun 58 and entered svce same day (intl network) with FN 329. (TT: 2,823 hrs a/o 31 May 59). Last pax svce with TWA 9 Jan 61, to LAS for conversion to all-cargo configuration same day. Ret to TWA 3 Apr 61, in svce 5 Apr 61. (TT: 7,006 hrs a/o 30 Jun 61). Withdrawn from svce 2 Feb 62 and stored at Mid-Continent Airport, Kansas City, MO. Re-entered svce 3 Jun 62 as non-revenue engine carrier & for all-cargo svces until withdrawn from svce again 30 Dec 66 (TT: 13,745 hrs) and stored at Fairfax, KS until sold to California Airmotive Corp 6 Sep 67. To Willair International Inc on lse-purchase approx Aug 68. Received substantial damage when the aircraft undershot on approach to Stockton Airport, CA at 16.13 hrs (local) on 28 Sep 68. No injuries. On final approach, the starboard main undercarriage struck the seven inch lip of a blast pad 102 feet short of the runway. Starboard undercarriage subsequently collapsed on touchdown and a fire broke out in the engine bay, both starboard propellers bent. Cause: Student pilot misjudged distance and altitude on approach, with inadequate supervision by the captain. Aircraft repairable, but in fact the aircraft was chopped up and melted down for scrap late 1968/early 1969. All remains gone by Aug 69. (USCAR lists California Airmotive as owner until canx 1969).

NB: The four 1649As for LAI were to have been named 'Roman', 'Ambrosian', 'Vesuvian' & 'Sicilian', but the order is unknown. (see also c/ns 1037, 1038, 1039).

1027 1649A-98-11 24 Jul 57 to Air France as F-BHBM 'De Grasse'. E-28738 dated 22 Jul 57, deld Burbank-Paris (Orly) 22-23 Jul 57. CofA issued 8 Aug 57, in svce 22 Aug 57. Damaged when port tyre burst Mexico City 21 Dec 57. Repaired. Damaged on ground at Paris (Orly) 25 Dec 59. Repaired. Disintegrated in mid-air while flying at 20,500 feet at approx 00.30 hrs (GMT) on 10 May 61 over Edjele and crashed at In Amenas, approx 30 miles south of Ghadames, in the Sahara Desert in Libya, killing all on board. The aircraft was en route Brazzaville, Congo to Paris, France on Flight AF406 via Bangui, Central African Republic & Fort Lamy, Chad. It had left Fort Lamy at 21.18 hrs on 9 May 61, en route for Marseilles, France, and the last radio contact was made at 00.10 hrs over Edjele. The aircraft descended at high speed into the desert, with the tail unit and wingtips found nearly 800 yards away from the main wreckage. Cause: Uncertain, possibly shot down in error by French fighters during combat in Algeria. Canx from F-register 14 Jun 61. (TT: 10,014 hrs).

1028 1649A-98-11 8 Aug 57 to Air France as F-BHBN 'La Motte Cadillac'. E-28739 dated 5 Aug 57, del Burbank-Paris (Orly) 10-11 Aug 57. CofA issued 13 Aug 57, in svce 31 Aug 57. Carried joint Air France/Japan Air Lines titling mid-1960 for polar flts. Later used in 81-seater configuration. Withdrawn from svce 30 Oct 63 prior to CofA expiry on 19 Nov 63 and stored at Orly. Wfu 20 Apr 67 (TT: 14,027 hrs). Canx from F-register 24 May 67 & broken up at Paris (Orly) during Aug 67.

1029 1649A-98-20 15 Aug 57 to Trans World Airlines as N7323C, FN 323. Name 'Star of the Aegean Sea' allocated, but probably never carried. (TT: 10 hrs 37 mins). In svce (domestic & intl networks) 16 Aug 57. (TT: 6,574 hrs a/o 31 May 59). Last pax svce with TWA 22 Jan 61, to LAS for conversion to all-cargo configuration same day. Ret to TWA 14 Apr 61, in svce same day. (TT: 10,811 hrs a/o 30 Jun 61). Withdrawn from svce 27 Mar 64 and stored at Mid-Continent Airport, Kansas City, MO. Sold to Charles E Bush t/a Bush Aviation 9 Dec 65 (TT: 15,940 hrs) and flown to Fort Lauderdale, FL. Stored there from at least May 66. Repainted in unusual scheme with all yellow upper surfaces and brown cheat lines by May 68 (no engines installed). Reregd to Bush Aviation Inc 1968. Remained in storage at Fort Lauderdale until Jun 70 (last report) and scrapped there during the latter part of 1970. Canx from USCAR 1970.

1030 1649A-98-20 22 Aug 57 to Trans World Airlines as N7324C, FN 324. Name 'Star of the Danube' allocated, but probably never carried. (TT: 11 hrs 24 mins). In svce on domestic network 24 Aug 57. (TT:6,440 hrs (a/o 31 May 59). Last pax svce with TWA 30 Jan 61, to LAS for conversion to all-cargo configuration same day. Ret to Trans World 28 Apr 61, in svce 5 May 61. Withdrawn from use 20 Jun 64 Mid-Continent Airport, Kansas City, MO. Reported sale to Lineas Aereas Patagonica Argentina SA 19 Oct 64 as LV-ILN unconfirmed. In storage at Mid-Continent Airport, Kansas City, as N7324C with TWA again by Oct 65. Remained in storage there until sold to Aero-Tech Inc 24 May 68 after wfu officially by TWA on 13 May 68 (TT: 15,772 hrs). However, acft del to Miami, FL 18 Apr 68. Sold to American National Bank of Jacksonville 3 May 68 & to Woodrow W Tilton (on lse-purchase) 6 May 68. Lsd to Trans American Leasing Inc May 68. Ownership tfd to Six T Ranch Inc 23 Feb 70. Damaged beyond repair when the aircraft hit trees after take-off at night on a contraband flight from Zandery Airport, Paramaribo, Surinam, in late 1968 or early 1969. Leading edge was damaged, no.2 engine caught fire. Acft returned to Zandery, was declared a write-off and abandoned as landing/parking fees were never paid. Was flying for Trans American Leasing at the time. Stored whole at Zandery, Paramaribo, in ex-TWA colour scheme, condition deteriorated & scrapped approx 1988. Canx from USCAR 1970.

1031 1649A-98-11 22 Aug 57 to Air France as F-BHBO 'Champlain'. E-28740 dated 22 Aug 57, deld Los Angeles-Paris 24-25 Aug 57. CofA issued 28 Aug 57, in svce 7 Sep 57. Lsd to Air Afrique as F-BHBO 15 Oct 61 as 81-seater. Sold to Air Afrique 17 Apr 62 and regd TU-TBA, CofA issued 18 Apr 62. Ret to Air France 19 May 63 and stored. (CofA as TU-TBA expired 7 Jun 63). Regd F-BHBO 'Champlain' again. Withdrawn from svce 27 Nov 63 at Paris (Orly) after CofA expiry on 7 Nov 63. Wfu 20 Apr 67 (TT: 13,608 hrs) & canx from F-register 24 May 67. Broken up at Orly during Aug 67.

1032 1649A-98-11 24 Aug 57 to Air France as F-BHBP 'Jacques Cartier'. E-28742 dated 22 Aug 57, deld 31 Aug 57. CofA issued 9 Sep 57, in svce 30 Sep 57. Carried joint Air France/Japan Air Lines titling Apr 60 for polar flts. Later used in 81-seater configuration. Withdrawn from svce 11 Dec 61 (TT: 11,672 hrs), prior to CofA expiry on 14 Dec 61 and stored at Paris (Orly). Wfu 20 Apr 67 & canx from F-register 24 May 67. Remained in storage until broken up at Orly during Aug 67.

1033 1649A-98-11 29 Aug 57 to Air France as F-BHBQ 'Montcalm'. E-28741 dated 28 Aug 57, deld 1 Sep 57. CofA issued 9 Sep 57, in svce 12 Sep 57. Carried joint Air France/Japan Air Lines titling in Jun 60 for polar flts. Later used as 81-seater. Received minor damage at New York-Idlewild 11 Feb 59. Repaired. Withdrawn from svce 1 Jan 64, the last Air France Starliner in svce, prior to CofA expiry on 2 Jul 64 (TT: 13,741 hrs), and stored at Paris (Orly). Wfu 15 Apr 66 & canx from F-register 20 Apr 67. Broken up at Orly during Jul 67 or Aug 67.

1034 1649A-98-17 25 Sep 57 to Lufthansa as D-ALUB (regn allocated 26 Jun 56). Permit to Fly issued 13 Sep 57, E-28744 dated 24 Sep 57, deld 27 Sep 57 in Germany, CofA issued 2 Dec 57. To LAS for conversion to cargo aircraft Apr 60. Ret to Lufthansa Jul 60 and named 'Isar'. Lsd to World Airways 19 Jul 62, handed over 17 Aug 62, regd N45511 and D-regn canx 22 Aug 62. Lse ended 30 Jan 64. Ret to Lufthansa 17 Feb 64, N-regn canx 20 Feb 64. Restored to register as D-ALUB 31 Mar 64, unnamed. Used mainly on domestic pax svces until withdrawn from use in Nov 65 and canx from D-register 29 Nov 65. Sold to Nordflug GmbH 27 Jan 66 and converted for use as a restaurant the "Nordflug Cafe" at Hartenholm airfield, near Hamburg, West Germany. In Lufthansa colours, with no titling. By 1973 was repainted in the Lufthansa colour scheme originally carried by the 1649A in 1958. Continued in use until destroyed by fire at Hartenholm on 31 Jul 75, remains scrapped.

1035 1649A-98-20 15 Sep 57 to Trans World Airlines as N7325C, FN 325. Name 'Star of the Meuse' allocated, but probably never carried. (TT: 15 hrs 16 mins). In svce (domestic network) 17 Sep 57. (TT: 5,604 hrs a/o 31 May 59). Last svce with Trans World 26 Nov 61 (TT: 10,574 hrs). Stored from 27 Nov 61 at Mid-Continent Airport, Kansas City, MO and used for spares until sold to Arizona Aircraft Parts & Sales Co (as scrap) 30 Sep 66. Probably scrapped late 1966. Canx from USCAR 1966.

1036 1649A-98-11 24 Sep 57 to Air France as F-BHBR 'Marquette'. E-28743 dated 24 Sep 57, deld 27 Sep 57. CofA issued 21 Oct 57, in svce 21 Oct 57. Used on the first 'Over the Pole' training flight 26 Jan-1 Feb 58. Later used in an 81-seater configuration. Withdrawn from svce 11 Nov 63 (TT: 13,690 hrs) and stored at Paris (Orly) prior to CofA expiry on 1 Jul 64. Sold to Trek Airways Pty 19 Apr 66 via Safari Travel (Pty) Ltd, and regd in Luxembourg as LX-LGY in May 66 to Luxair. Painted in Luxair colours, cvtd to 98-seater, and CofA issued 20 May 66. Del Orly-Luxembourg 23 May 66. Operated the last Luxair Starliner flight from London (Gatwick) to Luxembourg on 20 Jan 69, withdrawn from use at Luxembourg-Findel same day. Stored at Luxembourg until sold for Central Intelligence Agency use & regd N4796 on 29 Jul 69. LX-regn canx Aug 69. US-regn canx 1 Aug 69 & removed approx 10 Aug 69. Reregd TF-ERA to Bjorn Sverrisson for one return flight Luxembourg-Tel Aviv, Israel-Luxembourg, dep 17 Aug 69, ret 12 Sep 69. Painted up with Nittler Air Transport International titling 13 Sep 69 at Luxembourg, removed 20 Sep 69. Reregd HP-501, owned by Larry Raab or member of Phoenix group, 28 Oct 69. On lse to Biafran government. Left Luxembourg 28 Oct 69, believed flew to Lisbon or Faro, and op one flight on the Biafran airlift to Sao Tome, dep Sao Tome for Faro, Portugal 11 Jan 70. Returned to storage at Luxembourg by Mar 70 and painted up in Nittler titling again. Flew to Dublin, Ireland 29 Jul 70, possibly to be used for pirate TV scheme with R O'Rahilly. Stored at Douala, Cameroons from at least 1971, still with Nittler (NAT) titling and HP-regn. Scheme to convert the aircraft into a restaurant reportedly fell through due to objections from fire authorities.

F-BHBT the final production 1649A, named "Frontenac" (in small letters behind the radar nose) and delivered to Air France in February 1958 is seen at an unknown location in 1960. (PJM collection)

Towed half a mile from Douala Airport alongside main road to Douala from the airport. Partly derelict but whole in 1980, scrapped by Apr 81.

1037 Laid down as Model 1649A-98-16 for Linee Aeree Italiane as I-LETR (for name, see note after c/n 1026). Completed for LAI, but ntu and remained at the factory (LADD: 2 Jan 58), see note to c/n 1026. Sold to Trans World Airlines and deld at Burbank, CA, 29 Mar 58 as N8082H (TT: 8 hrs 19 mins). Ferried to Mid-Continent Airport, Kansas City, MO 29 Mar 58 for conversion to TWA standards. Completed 1 May 58. In svce same day (domestic network), and to intl network 2 May 58 with FN 327. (TT: 3,446 hrs a/o 31 May 59). Last pax svce with TWA 27 Dec 60, and deld to LAS for conversion to all-cargo configuration. Completed 6 Mar 61, in svce 10 Mar 61. (TT: 7,853 hrs a/o 30 Jun 61). Withdrawn from svce 30 Jun 64. Sold to Charles E Bush t/a Bush Aviation 26 Oct 65. (TT: 12,622 hrs). At Miami, FL, in ex-TWA markings during Mar-May 66. At Fort Lauderdale, FL in Jan 67. Sold to Air Korea 25 Feb 67 and deld from San Francisco, CA approx 8 Mar 67 as HL4003. Air Korea ceased ops Aug 68. Stored, probably at Seoul. Still regd in Aug 70, but no valid CofA. Fate unknown, presumably broken up in Korea in early 1970s.

1038 Laid down as Model 1649A-98-16 for Linee Aeree Italiane as I-LIRA (for name, see note after c/n 1026). Completed for LAI, but ntu and remained at factory (LADD: 2 Jan 58), see note to c/n 1026. Sold to Trans World Airlines and deld at Burbank, CA 16 Apr 58 as N8083H (TT: 2 hrs 37 mins). Ferried to Mid-Continent Airport, Kansas City, MO 16 Apr 58 for conversion to TWA standards. Completed 16 May 58. In svce 18 May 58 (domestic network), and to intl network 20 May 58 with FN 326. (TT: 3,328 hrs a/o 31 May 59). Last pax svce with TWA 20 Dec 60, and deld to LAS for conversion to all-cargo configuration same day. Completed 17 Feb 61, in svce 3 Mar 61. (TT: 8,161 hrs a/o 30 Jun 61). Last cargo svce with Trans World 19 Apr 62. Lsd to Alaska Airlines 29 Apr 62 (FAA quote 17 Apr 62), sold to them 31 Dec 62 (1 Jan 64 also quoted). Withdrawn from use May 67 and used for spares at Seattle, WA. Restored during Nov-Dec 68, and cvtd to bulk fuel-oil carrier. Sold to Red Dodge Aviation Inc 16 Nov 68, and to Prudhoe Bay Oil Distributing Co Inc 2 Dec 68. Believed lsd Interior Airways 1969. Stored at Anchorage, AK by Jun 72. Sold to Harry E Faulkner dba West-Air Inc 9 Sep 74. Flown to Kenai, AK after restoration for storage during the winter 1974-75. Sold to Onyx Aviation Inc 14 Nov 75. Canx from USCAR, then restored to Burns Aviation Inc 17 Jan 76 as N8083H. Planned use for fish charters fell through, and aircraft remained in storage at Kenai. Impounded by 1978 for non-payment of parking charges by City of Kenai. Sold to McNamara & Associates Inc at auction by City of Kenai 24 May 79 for $150 (!), officially sold to Gerald E McNamara 5 Jun 79 and tfd to McNamara & Associates 16 Jul 79. Immediately advertised for sale at US$ 125,000. Tfd back to Gerald E.McNamara 28 Dec 79 (CofRegn 19 Mar 80). Sold to Aeroborne Enterprises Inc 8 May 80, and dep Kenai after six years in storage on 26 Aug 80. Flown to Anchorage, then to Seattle, WA 29 Nov 80, and to Chandler Memorial Fld, AZ by Feb 81 and stored there awaiting a replacement no.3 engine. Sold to Canary Leasing Corp Aug 81 and ferried to Tucson, AZ for rework. In svce by May 82 at Chandler on 6-7 hour "training flights". Rear cargo door strengthened to enable the door to be opened in flight. In use on clandestine ops out of Honduras by Jan 83 (probably flying arms), and in central Colombia by Nov 83. Parked out of use at San Pedro Sula, Honduras by early 1984. Sold to Maine Coast Airways Inc 23 May 86, regd 16 Jun 86 & named 'Star of San Pedro Sula'. Ferried San Pedro Sula via Ft.Lauderdale, FL to Auburn-Lewiston, ME, arriving 1 Jun 86. Stored at Auburn-Lewiston in good condition, engines run up occasionally. Had name 'Brian's Star' on nosewheel door by 1994. Planned restoration to fly 2006. Sold to James P A Thompson, regd 19 Apr 06. Ret Maine Coast Airways 27 Dec 06.

1039 Laid down as Model 1649A-98-16 for Linee Aeree Italiane as I-LODO (for name, see note after c/n 1026). Completed for LAI, but ntu and remained at factory (LADD: 2 Jan 58), see note to c/n 1026. Sold to Trans World Airlines and deld at Burbank, CA 25 Mar 58 (TT: 1 hr) as N8084H. First of four ex-LAI 1649As to be deld to TWA. Ferried to Mid-Continent Airport, Kansas City, MO 25 Mar 58 for conversion to TWA standards. In svce (domestic network) 4 May 58, and to intl network 9 May 58 with FN 328. On 25 Aug 58, a gradual loss of power occurred in no.3 engine, followed by a propeller overspeed. The prop could not be feathered and continued to windmill after the engine froze. The aircraft was diverted to Cut Bank, MT for an emergency landing, and on approach the propeller fell from the engine. This was followed by an engine fire which could not be extinguished in the air. A safe landing was made at Cut Bank and the fire extinguished on the ground. No injuries. Repaired. (TT: 3,659 hrs a/o 31 May 59). Last pax svce with TWA 31 Dec 60, and deld to LAS same day for conversion to all-cargo configuration. Completed 21 Mar 61, in svce 22 Mar 61. (TT: 8,221 hrs a/o 30 Jun 61). Collided with Lake Central Convair 340 (N73138) at Indianapolis, IN at 11.04 hrs on 27 Jan 62 on the ground. Minor damage. Repaired. Withdrawn from use 18 Jan 64 and stored at Mid-Continent Airport, Kansas City, MO. Reportedly sold to Bush Aviation, but believed ntu. Stored at Kansas City Sep 64, being used for spares. Withdrawn from use by TWA 28 Dec 67. Sold to Aero-Tech Corp 13 Jun 68 and broken up by them at Kansas City during Jun-Jul 68. (TT: 12,843 hrs).

1040 1649A-98-17 20 Dec 57 to Lufthansa as D-ALAN (regn allocated 26 Jun 56). Permit to Fly issued 21 Nov 57, E-28749 dated 20 Dec 57, CofA issued 5 Feb 58. Flew Chancellor Adenauer to Japan 12 Mar-2 Apr 60, was first Lufthansa acft to fly over North Pole on ret flt. To LAS for conversion to cargo aircraft May 60. Completed 27 Jul 60 and named 'Neckar'. Flew a London (Heathrow)-Prestwick-Shannon charter for Seaboard 25 Aug 61. Lsd to World Airways 9 Jul 62, regd N45512 and D-regn canx 18 Sep 62. Lse ended 6 Feb 64. Ret to Lufthansa 13 Feb 64, N-regn canx 18 Feb 64 and restored to D-ALAN 24 Apr 64, unnamed. Used mainly on domestic pax svces until sold to Parker & Ransom Aircraft Sales 22

Feb 66 (17 Feb 66 also quoted). D-regn canx 14 Feb 66 and regd NI79AV. Sold to Air Venturers 3 Mar 66, officially 10 Mar 66, and deld to Houston, TX. Lsd to Trans Mediterranean Airways for scheduled Middle East-Europe all-cargo flights Oct 66-Feb 67. Ret to Air Venturers from London (Heathrow) to New York-JFK 18 Feb 67. Ownership tfd to Tex Hou Inc 1 Aug 66. Ret to Air Venturers 1 Oct 67, and to CHS Leasing Corp same day, lsd to Air Venturers. Reregd N974R 28 Oct 68, still with CHS Leasing Corp. Sold to CJS Aircargo Inc 29 Dec 70. Stored at Houston-Hobby Airport, TX by Mar 72, in CJS colours. Sold to Harry E Faulkner dba West-Air Inc 23 Jun 73, and deld from Houston to Bethel, AK approx 15 Jul 73. Ownership tfd to Charles Baldon Aircraft 27 Jun 73, and to Onyx Aviation Inc 18 Oct 73. Stored at Anchorage, AK until 2 Jun 74, when it dep, probably to Houston, TX. Stored at Houston from spring 1975 to spring 1976. Sold to Thomas C.Campbell 15 Jul 75 & named 'Ramatou U' by Sep 76. Lsd to Burns Aviation Inc 28 Apr-7 Jun 76, and arr Miami, FL on del 28 Apr 76 (still in CJS colours and with name 'Ramatou U'). Ownership tfd 20 May 76 to Mel Anderson t/a Proimex Intl Ltd, and stored at Miami same day until 7 Jun 76. Flown to Ft Lauderdale, FL by Jul 76 for storage. Official records show the aircraft was ret to Harry E Faulkner dba West-Air Inc 17 Jul 77, but Hub Aviation at Ft Lauderdale, on whose ramp the aircraft was parked, quote owner as Mel Anderson. Acft for sale at US$ 14,000 (a/o Aug 77) - owner had disappeared while the aircraft was halfway through a major overhaul by Hub Aviation, leaving debts of over US$ 100,000. Acft remained in storage at Ft Lauderdale, engine and parts missing by late 1977, and condition deteriorating. Sold to Aeroborne Enterprises Inc Sep 80 and restoration work on the aircraft started Oct 80 at Ft Lauderdale. Repainted & all 4 engines refitted by Jun 81, but nos.3 & 4 engines removed Dec 81 for c/n 1038. Condition deteriorated until sold to Maine Coast Airways Inc dba Starliner Promotions 13 Mar 86, regd 25 Mar 86. Restoration work began again, named 'Jenny's Star'. First flt for 12 years 18 Aug 88, dep Ft Lauderdale,FL, but made emergency landing at West Palm Beach, FL with no.1 engine feathered & nose-wheel gear problems. Dep West Palm Beach 19 Sep 88, but with runaway no.1 propeller made emergency landing at Sanford, FL, en route to Auburn-Lewiston, ME. Work carried out on acft occasionally in early '90s. Restoration begun in earnest from late 1999. No.1 engine, rudders & instruments replaced with parts from c/n 1018 during 2000, & acft repainted in late 1950s Lufthansa scheme. Special Ferry Permit obtained Oct 01, fast taxy runs carried out 18 Oct 01 & ferried Sanford, FL to Polk City, FL 19 Oct 01. Parked outside Kermit Weeks' "Fantasy of Flight" museum on long term loan. Donated to US Airline Industry Museum Foundation 25 Dec 05, but remains preserved at Polk City.

1041 1649A-98-17 9 Jan 58 to Lufthansa as D-ALER. Permit to Fly issued 21 Nov 57 and E-28752 dated 9 Jan 58. CofA issued 14 Mar 58. Nominally tf to Deutsche Flugdienst 1 Mar 60, but acft retained Lufthansa colours. Used by Lufthansa and subsidiary as required. Lsd to World Airways 5 Oct 62, (TT: 16,351 hrs), regd N45517 and deld 25 Oct 62. D-regn canx 29 Oct 62. Lse ended 12 Feb 64 and sold to Trek Airways (Pty) Ltd same day. E-43834 dated 7 Feb 64. Deld Oakland, CA-Hamburg, West Germany (via Prestwick, UK) 13-14 Feb 64 as ZS-DTM, and deld in Johannesburg, South Africa 17 Feb 64. N-regn canx 5 Mar 64. Op first Trek Starliner flight (Trek 310) on 10 Mar 64 as 98-seater. Used by Trek until 8 Apr 64, and reregd LX-LGZ 4 Apr 64 to Safari Travel Ltd, lsd Luxair. CofA issued 10 Apr 64 and first svce (flight LG410) ex-Luxembourg op 11 Apr 64 to South Africa. First return flight 20-22 Apr 64 from Johannesburg-Luxembourg-London (Gatwick). Ret to Trek Airways (Pty) Ltd 18 May 67 (CofRegn) as ZS-FAB. LX-regn canx 12 May 67 (TT: 20,038 hrs) and CofA issued in South Africa 22 May 67, as 101-seater. Received damage on 27 Apr 68 when taxying out for take-off at Bangkok, Thailand. Port main undercarriage wheel went off hard concrete surface and aircraft sank into the ground through the concrete slabs next to the hard surface. Repaired and ret to South Africa 17 May 68. (TT: 20,263 hrs a/o 15 Aug 68). Used by Trek until expiry of CofA on 15 Sep 69. Stored at Johannesburg, South Africa, and sold to Morris Abkin (for scrap) for SA£2,500 in Dec 69. Canx from ZS-register 11 Dec 69 as "wfu-sold as scrap". Scrapped at Johannesburg during May-Jun 70.

1042 1649A-98-17 17 Jan 58 to Lufthansa as D-ALOL. Regn allocated 26 Jun 56. Permit to Fly issued 27 Dec 57, and E-28753 issued 17 Jan 58. CofA issued 27 Mar 58. Flew Chancellor Adenauer to burial of Foster Dulles in USA May 59. Nominally tfd to Deutsche Flugdienst 1 Mar 60, but aircraft retained Lufthansa colours. Used by Lufthansa and subsidiary as required. Lsd to World Airways 5 Oct 62 and deld 23 Oct 62 as N45520 Frankfurt-Chicago. D-regn canx 10 Oct 62. Lse ended 21 Feb 64 and sold to Trek Airways (Pty) Ltd same day. E-43835 dated 27 Feb 64. Deld Oakland, CA-Hamburg, West Germany 1 Mar 64 as ZS-DVJ (regd 20 Feb 64) in Luxair colours & titles, deld to Johannesburg, South Africa 7 Mar 64. N-regn canx 18 Mar 64. Used as 98-seater, later 101-seater. Cvtd end Apr 65 to 10F/56T configuration for South African Airways. Lsd to South African Airways 7 May-28 Sep 65 and used in Trek scheme with SAA titles on Johannesburg-Perth, Australia route. Ret to Trek and cvtd back to 101-seater. (TT: 14,943 hrs a/o 6 Aug 65). First South African-operated acft to fly the South Atlantic non-stop 15 Feb 66. Tfd to Luxembourg register 18 May 67 as LX-LGX to operate on behalf of Trek Airways. Regd to Safari Travel (Pty) Ltd, lsd Luxair, and canx from ZS-register 18 May 67, CofA issued 23 May 67. (TT: 16,742 hrs a/o 4 Jun 68). Ret to Trek Airways (Pty) Ltd and regd ZS-DVJ 20 Jun 68, canx from LX-register 10 Jun 68. Used by Trek Airways until Apr 69, then stored at Johannesburg, South Africa. (TT: 16,775 hrs a/o 9 Oct 68). Sold to W J Pelser 27 Jul 71, regd 16 Aug 71 and special permit for one flight only from Johannesburg (Jan Smuts) Airport to Wonderboom Airport, Warmbad/Warmbaths issued 17 Aug 71 and renewed 24 Sep 71. Flown out to Warmbad, North Transvaal 9 Oct 71 for planned use as cafe, but plans not implemented. Canx from ZS-register 20 May 72. Resold to Die Afrikaanse Taal-en Kultuurvereniging (ATKV) 1973 and displayed at Klein Kariba, Near Warmbad by Apr 74. Later used as board-room at factory at Klein Kariba, situated north of Warmbad on the route Nl to Beit Bridge. Remained there until donated to South African Airways museum for preservation at end of 1978. Dismantling began at Klein Kariba, Warmbad, 1 May 79 for transport by road back to Johannesburg. Arrived at Johannesburg (Jan Smuts) Airport on 23 May 79 and stored outside, awaiting restoration and reassembly. Still stored outside, restoration began Feb 84, basically complete by Aug 86. Placed on display at Johannesburg 30 Apr 88 (SAA Open Day), officially opened 12 Jan 99. Acft has Trek colours with 'S A Airways' titling. Current.

1043 1649A-98 First of order placed in May 56 for VARIG. Construction canx Mar 57, and VARIG order amended to 1049G 4 Apr 57 (see c/ns 4681, 4684, 4685). Not built.

1044 Originally allocated to Model 1649A-98-17 for Lufthansa, regn D-ALER allotted 26 Jun 56. This regn re-allocated to c/n 1041 (qv). C/n 1044 allocated to Air France as Model 1649A-98-11. LADD: 3 Feb 58 to Air France as F-BHBS. E-28756 dated 31 Jan 58, deld 8 Feb 58. CofA issued 28 Feb 58, in svce 4 Mar 58. Named 'La Salle'. Later mod to 81-seater. Damaged Paris (Orly) 23 Jun 60. Repaired. Withdrawn from svce 31 Aug 63 (TT: 12,678 hrs) prior to CofA expiry on 18 Sep 63 (23 Jan 64?) and stored at Orly Airport. Wfu 20 Apr 67, F-regn canx 24 May 67. Remained in storage at Orly until broken up during Aug 67.

1045 1649A-98-11 12 Feb 58 to Air France as F-BHBT 'Frontenac'. E-28757 dated 12 Feb 58, deld 16 Feb 58. In svce 17 Mar 58. Flew Paris (Orly)-Anchorage, AK-Tokyo inaugural 10 Apr 58. Damaged by vehicle at Paris (Orly) 25 Dec 58. Repaired. Later used as 81-seater. Lsd briefly in Oct 61 to Air Afrique. Damaged when hit vehicle on runway at Orly 8 Mar 62. Repaired. Withdrawn from svce 10 Jan 63 (TT: 11,819 hrs) prior to CofA expiry on 28 Jan 63 and stored at Paris (Orly). Wfu 20 Apr 67, F-regn canx 24 May 67. Remained in storage at Orly until broken up there during Aug 67.

1046 1649A-98 Second of order placed in May 56 for VARIG. Construction canx Mar 57, and VARIG order amended to 1049G 4 Apr 57 (see c/ns 4681, 4684, 4685). Not built.

1047 1649A-98 Originally the last aircraft on the 1649A production line. Construction canx when production cut back from 47 aircraft to 44 aircraft by Mar 57. Not built.

The end of an era: Air France 1649A F-BHBP (c/n 1032) on Burbank's production line alongside the last 1049G for Thai Airways (left), with a National Airlines 1049H & the prototype L188 turbo-prop Electra (background) in the summer of 1957. (Lockheed)

One of Lufthansa's lovely "Super Star" 1649As posed alongside a company 1049G at Hamburg in 1958. (Lufthansa)

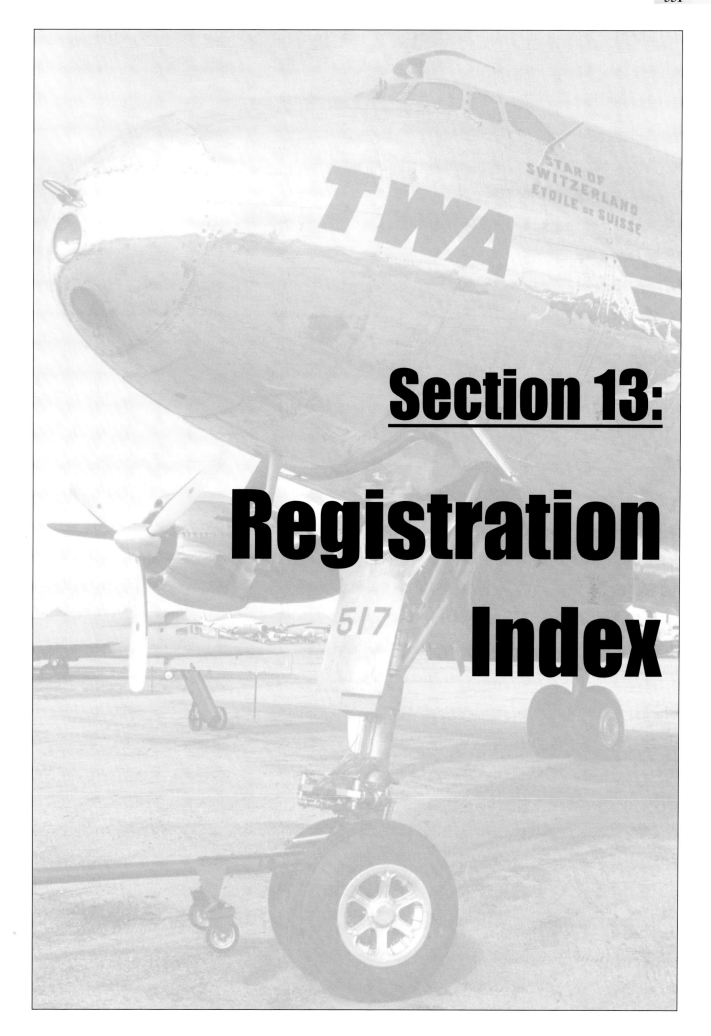

Section 13: Registration Index

Including all known allocations, aircraft subsequently cancelled, registrations and serials not taken up, etc. Numbers in brackets after registrations denote use of same registration more than once.

CIVIL

AP- PAKISTAN
AP-AFQ	4520
AP-AFR	4521
AP-AFS	4522
AP-AJY	4835
AP-AJZ	4836

B- CHINA/TAIWAN
B-1809	4853

C-/CF-/C-G CANADA
CF-AEN	4821
C-FBDB	4809
C-FBFN	4825
CF-BFN	4825
CF-NAJ	4828
CF-NAK	4829
CF-NAL	4831
CF-NAM	4832
CF-PXX	4580
CF-RNR	4544
CF-TEU	4641
CF-TEV	4643
CF-TEW	4682
CF-TEX	4683
CF-TEY	4850
CF-TEZ	4851
CF-TGA	4540
CF-TGB	4541
CF-TGC	4542
CF-TGD	4543
CF-TGE	4544
CF-TGF	4563
CF-TGG	4564
CF-TGH	4565
CF-WWH	4820
C-GAZA	4840
C-GXKO	2601
C-GXKR	2604
C-GXKS	2609

CC- CHILE
CC-CAA	2069

CN- MOROCCO
CN-CCM	2515
CN-CCN	2675
CN-CCO	2676
CN-CCP	2627
CN-CCR	2512

CP- BOLIVIA
CP-797(2)	2548
CP-797(3)	4807
CP-797(4)	4801
CP-998	4805

CS- PORTUGAL
CS-TLA	4616
CS-TLB	4617
CS-TLC	4618
CS-TLD	4808
CS-TLE	4677
CS-TLF	4672
CS-TLH	4557

CU- CUBA
CU-C601	4632
CU-C602	4633
CU-P573	4557
CU-T532	2061
CU-T545	2032
CU-T547	2036
CU-T601	4632
CU-T602	4633
CU-T631	4675

CX- URUGUAY
CX-BBM	2661
CX-BBN	2641
CX-BCS	2640
CX-BEM	4818
CX-BGP	2668
CX-BHC	2565
CX-BHD	2548

CY- CEYLON
CY- ?	2548
CY- ?	2549

D- GERMANY
D-ACED	4637
D-ACID	4640
D-ACOD	4647
D-ACUD	4649
"D-ADAM"	4671
D-ALAB	4637
D-ALAK	4602
D-ALAN	1040
D-ALAP	4637
"D-ALAP"	4671
D-ALEC	4640
D-ALEM	4603
"D-ALEM"	4671
D-ALER(1)	1044
D-ALER(2)	1041
D-ALID	4647
D-ALIN	4604
D-ALOF(1)	4649
D-ALOF(2)	4642
D-ALOL	1042
D-ALOP	4605
D-ALUB	1034

EC- SPAIN
EC-AIN	4550
EC-AIO	4551
EC-AIP	4552
EC-AMP	4673
EC-AMQ	4676
EC-AQL	4553
EC-AQM	4644
EC-AQN	4645
EC-ARN	4678
"EC-ARN"	4825
EC-BEN	4519
EC-WRN	4678

EI- IRELAND
EI-ACR	2548
EI-ACS	2549
EI-ADA	2554
EI-ADD	2555
EI-ADE	2566
EI-ARS	4672

ET- ETHIOPIA
ET-T-35	2608

F- FRANCE
F-BAVN	2676
F-BAZA	2072
F-BAZB	2073
F-BAZC	2074
F-BAZD	2075
F-BAZE	2624
F-BAZF	2625
F-BAZG	2626
F-BAZH	2627
F-BAZI	2513
F-BAZJ	2514
F-BAZK	2515
F-BAZL	2538
F-BAZM	2545
F-BAZN	2546
F-BAZO	2547
F-BAZP	2550
F-BAZQ	2512
F-BAZR	2503
F-BAZS	2628
F-BAZT	2629
F-BAZU	2525
F-BAZV	2526
F-BAZX	2527
F-BAZY	2528
F-BAZZ	2674
F-BBDT	2675
F-BBDU	2676
F-BBDV	2677
F-BECA	1966
F-BGNA	4510
F-BGNB	4511
F-BGNC	4512
F-BGND	4513
F-BGNE	4514
F-BGNF	4515
F-BGNG	4516
F-BGNH	4517
F-BGNI	4518
F-BGNJ	4519
F-BHBA	4620
F-BHBB	4621
F-BHBC	4622
F-BHBD	4623
F-BHBE	4624
F-BHBF	4625
F-BHBG	4626
F-BHBH	4627
F-BHBI	4634
F-BHBJ	4639
F-BHBK	1011
F-BHBL	1020
F-BHBM	1027
F-BHBN	1028
F-BHBO	1031
F-BHBP	1032
F-BHBQ	1033
F-BHBR	1036
F-BHBS	1044
F-BHBT	1045
F-BHMI	4668
F-BHMJ	4669
F-BHMK	4670
F-BHML	4671
F-BRAD	4519
F-BRNH	4513

G- UNITED KINGDOM
G-AHEJ	1975
G-AHEK	1976
G-AHEL	1977

Section 13: Registration Index

Registration	Page
G-AHEM	1978
G-AHEN	1980
G-AKCE	1971
G-ALAK	2548
G-ALAL	2549
G-ALAM	2554
G-ALAN	2555
G-ALAO	2566
G-AMUP	2051
G-AMUR	2065
G-ANNT	2671
G-ANTF	2504
G-ANTG	2505
G-ANUP	2562
G-ANUR	2565
G-ANUV	2551
G-ANUX	2556
G-ANUY	2557
G-ANUZ	2559
G-ANVA	2564
G-ANVB	2589
G-ANVD	2544
G-ARHJ	2051
G-ARHK	2036
G-ARVP	1967
G-ARXE	1965
G-ASYF	2630
G-ASYS	2623
G-ASYT	2631
G-ASYU	2632
G-CONI	2553

HB- SWITZERLAND
Registration	Page
HB-IBI	2068
HB-IBJ	2069
HB-IBY	2070
HB-IEA	1965
HB-IEB	1967
HB-IEC	2061
HB-IED	1980
HB-RSC	4175

HH- HAITI
Registration	Page
HH-ABA	2615

HI- DOMINICAN REPUBLIC
Registration	Page
HI-129	2523
HI-140	2520
HI-207	2522
HI-228	4009
HI-254	4823
HI-260	2070
HI-270	2085
HI-328	2607
HI-329	4536
HI-332	2522
HI-393	2603
HI-515	4192
HI-515CT	4192
HI-532	4155
HI-532CT	4155
HI-542	4825
HI-542CT	4825
HI-548	4202
HI-548CT	4202
HI-583CT	4137

HK- COLOMBIA
Registration	Page
HK-162	2663
HK-163	2664
HK-175	4554
HK-175X	4554
HK-176	4555
HK-176X	4555
HK-177	4556
HK-177X	4556
HK-184	4628
HK-184X	4628
HK-650	2544
HK-651	2557
HK-652	2564
HK-653	2645

HL KOREA
Registration	Page
HL102	2551
HL4002	4819
HL4003	1037
"HL4003"	2061
HL4006	4816

HP- PANAMA
Registration	Page
HP-280	4678
HP-281	4677
HP-467	4678
HP-475	4551
HP-501	1036
HP-526	4815

HS- THAILAND
Registration	Page
HS-TCA(1)	4644
HS-TCA(2)	4672
HS-TCB(1)	4645
HS-TCB(2)	4677
HS-TCC	4678

I- ITALY
Registration	Page
I-LAMA	1026
I-LETR	1037
I-LIRA	1038
I-LODO	1039

LN- NORWAY
Registration	Page
LN- ?	4549
LN- ?	4557

LV- ARGENTINA
Registration	Page
LV-FTU	4846
LV-FTV	4847
LV-GLH	1006
LV-GLI	1008
LV-HCD	1023
LV-HCU	1009
LV-IGS	2540
LV-IIC	2619
LV-ILN	1030
LV-ILW	4166
LV-IXZ	4580
LV-JHF	4801
LV-JIO	4808
LV-JJO	4807
LV-PBH	2619
LV-PCQ	4166
LV-PHV	1023
LV-PHW	1009
LV-PJU	4801
LV-PKW(1)	2069
LV-PKW(2)	4807
LV-PKX	4846
LV-PKZ	4847
LV-PWK	2069
LV-PXL	1008
LV-PXM	1006
LV-PZX	2540

LX- LUXEMBOURG
Registration	Page
LX-IOK	2562
LX-LGX	1042
LX-LGY	1036
LX-LGZ	1041

N/NC- UNITED STATES
Registration	Page
N65	2648
N116	2611
N119	2612
N120	2613
N121	2654
N964	4683
N1060	2523
N1102	1001
N1192	2612
N1206	2613
N1489	2548
N1649	1001
N1880	4820
N1939	2630
N1949	2565
N4624	4617
N4796	1036
N8021	4673
N8022	4676
N8023	4551
N8024	4644
N8025(1)	4645
N8025(2)	4642
N8025(3)	4647
N8025(4)	4640
N8026	4678
N8338	4616
N9463	2602
N9464	2601
N9465	2604
N9466	2607
N9467	2609
N10401	2661
N10403	2622
N27189	4155
N38936	1962
N45511	1034
N45512	1040
N45515	4843
N45516	4840
N45517	1041
N45520	1042
N51006	4350
N51517	4618
N54214	1974
N58921	4562
N60968	1001
N67900	1961
N67930	1967
N67952	1963
N67953	1964
N73544	4175
N74192	1980
N86500	2021
N86501	2022
N86502	2023
N86503	2024
N86504	2025
N86506	2027
N86509	2030
N86511	2035
N86514	2041
N86515	2042
N86516	2043
N86517	2044
N86520	2503
N86521	2642
N86522	2653
N86523	2659
N86524	2660
N86525	2662
N86526	2084
N86527	2525
N86528	2526
N86529	2527
N86530	2528
N86531	2068
N86532	2069
N86533	2071
N86535	2673
N86536	1979
N86682	4679
N88832	2032
N88833	2033
N88836	2036
N88837	2037
N88838	2038
N88846	2046
N88847	2047
N88850	2050
N88855	2055
N88856	2056
N88857	2057
N88859	2059
N88861	2061
N88868	2067
N88879	4192
N90607	2551
N90608	2564
N90621	2559
N90622	2544
N90623	2556
N90624	2589
N90625	2557
N90814	2076
N90815	2077
N90816	2078

N90817	2079	N6003C	2635	N6925C	4853
N90818	2080	N6004C	2636	N6931C	4813
N90823	2085	N6005C	2637	N6932C	4823
N90825	2087	N6006C	2639	N6933C	4826
N90826	2088	N6007C	2643	N6935C	4848
N90827	1965	N6008C	2644	N6936C	4849
N90829	1968	N6009C	2645	N6937C	4830
N90830	1969	N6010C	2646	N7023C	4818
N90831	1970	N6011C	2647	N7101C	4582
N90921	2051	N6012C	2648	N7102C	4583
N90922	2052	N6013C	2649	N7103C	4584
N90923	2053	N6014C	2650	N7104C	4585
N90924	2054	N6015C	2651	N7105C	4586
N90925	2063	N6016C	2654	N7106C	4587
N90926	2064	N6017C	2655	N7107C	4588
N90927	2065	N6018C	2656	N7108C	4589
N91201	2577	N6019C	2657	N7109C	4590
N91202	2578	N6020C	2658	N7110C	4591
N91203	2579	N6021C	2667	N7111C	4592
N91204	2580	N6022C	2668	N7112C	4593
N91205	2581	N6023C	2669	N7113C	4594
N91206	2582	N6024C	2670	N7114C	4595
N91207	2583	N6025C	2671	N7115C	4596
N91208	2584	N6026C	2672	N7116C	4597
N91209	2585	N6201C	4001	N7117C	4598
N91210	2586	N6202C	4002	N7118C	4599
N91211	2587	N6203C	4003	N7119C	4600
N91212	2588	N6204C	4004	N7120C	4601
N93163	4573?	N6205C	4005	N7121C	4648
N93164	4581	N6206C	4006	N7122C	4649
		N6207C	4007	N7123C	4650
N101A	2518	N6208C	4008	N7124C	4651
N102A	2519	N6209C	4009	N7125C	4652
N103A	2520	N6210C	4010	N7126C	4654
N104A	2521	N6211C	4011	N7127C	4656
N105A	2522	N6212C	4012	N7128C	4658
N106A	2523	N6213C	4013	N7131C	4828
N107A	2524	N6214C	4014	N7132C	4829
N108A	2529	N6215C	4523	N7133C	4831
N109A	2530	N6216C	4524	N7134C	4832
N110A	2531	N6217C	4525	N7301C	1002
N112A	2533	N6218C	4526	N7302C	1003
N113A	2534	N6219C	4527	N7303C	1004
N114A	2535	N6220C	4528	N7304C	1005
N115A	2610	N6221C	4529	N7305C	1006
N116A	2611	N6222C	4530	N7306C	1007
N117A	2614	N6223C	4531	N7307C	1008
N118A	2615	N6224C	4532	N7308C	1009
N119A	2616	N6225C	4533	N7309C	1010
N120A	2617	N6226C	4534	N7310C	1012
N121A	2618	N6227C	4535	N7311C	1013
N2717A	2513	N6228C	4536	N7312C	1014
N2735A	1978	N6229C	4537	N7313C	1015
N2736A	1977	N6230C	4538	N7314C	1016
N2737A	1976	N6501C	4163	N7315C	1017
N2738A	2051	N6502C	4164	N7316C	1018
N2739A	2065	N6503C	4165	N7317C	1019
N2740A	1975	N6504C	4166	N7318C	1021
N2741A	1971	N6635C	4846	N7319C	1022
N4192A	4581	N6636C	4847	N7320C	1023
N5595A	2620	N6695C	2671	N7321C	1024
N5596A	2619	N6696C	4619	N7322C	1025
N515AC	4202	N6901C	4015	N7323C	1029
N608AS	2600	N6902C	4016	N7324C	1030
N611AS	2603	N6903C	4017	N7325C	1035
N179AV	1040	N6904C	4018	N7623C	2612
		N6905C	4019	N7624C	2613
N2520B	2081	N6906C	4020	N7772C	4682
N2521B	2082	N6907C	4021	N7776C	4801
		N6908C	4022	N7777C	4803
N468C	4846	N6909C	4023	N7938C	4132
N469C	4847	N6910C	4024	N9712C	4573?
N611C	4602	N6911C	4804	N9714C	4580
N1005C	4557	N6912C	4809	N9715C	4581
N1006C	4802	N6913C	4810	N9716C	4545
N1007C	4805	N6914C	4811	N9717C	4546
N1008C	4806	N6915C	4812	N9718C	4549
N1009C	4807	N6916C	4814	N9719C	4574
N1010C	4808	N6917C	4815	N9720C	4578
N4900C	2663	N6918C	4816	N9721C	4607
N4901C	2671	N6919C	4819	N9722C	4679
N4902C	2566	N6920C	4822	N9723C	4680
N4903C	4619	N6921C	4817	N9751C	4607
N6000C	2070	N6922C	4825	N9752C	4850
N6001C	2633	N6923C	4827	"N91211C"	2587
N6002C	2634	N6924C	4852	N74CA	4850

Section 13: Registration Index

Registration	Number
N105CF	4137
N22CS	2556
N833D	4677
N563E	4833
N564E	4834
N565E	4837
N566E	4838
N9907E	2602
N9812F	2559
N9813F	2589
N9816F	2504
N9830F	2551
N9907F	2602
N4715G	4543
N6231G	4653
N6232G	4655
N6233G	4657
N6234G	4659
N6235G	4660
N6236G	4661
N6237G	4662
N6238G	4663
N6239G	4664
N6240G	4665
N7777G	2553
N548GF	4363
"N53H"	4616
N864H	2068
N1927H	4821
N8081H	1026
N8082H	1037
N8083H	1038
N8084H	1039
N9409H	2074
N9410H	2073
N9412H	2072
N9414H	2075
N4247K	4144
N521KE	2602
N4257L	4335
N442LM	4581
N6687N	2564
N6688N	2557
N6689N	2544
N420NA	4143
N421NA	4159
N422NA	2605
N670NA	5518
N671NA	4475
N749NL	2604
N4115Q	4176
N101R	4818
N102R	4824
N273R	2650
N974R	1040
N8742R	4544
N8743R	4543
N189S	4541
N11SR	4581
N494TW	2601
N4257U	4336
N1552V	2505
N1554V	2555
N1593V	2556
N5172V	4572
N5173V	4575
N5174V	4576
N5175V	4577
N5176V	?
N5177V	?
N5400V	4830
N5401V	4839
N5402V	4842
N5403V	4844
N5404V	4845
N5405V	4846
N5406V	4847
N5407V	4848
N5408V	4849
N5409V	4827
N749VR	2604
N173W	4674
N174W	4636
N1104W	4196
N137X	4650
N173X	2553
N137XR	4650
N5510Y	4186
N2114Z	4137
N9639Z	4565
N9640Z	4641
N9641Z	4643
N9642Z	4683
N9733Z	2573
N9739Z	4541
N9740Z	4851
N9742Z	4563
N9744Z	2561
N9745Z	4576
N9746Z	4161/4674
N9747Z	4572
N9748Z	4577
N9749Z	4162/4636
NASA20	4143
NASA21	4159
NASA420	4143
NASA421	4159
NASA422	2605
NASA670	5518
NASA671	4475

NC (prior to 31 Dec 48)

Registration	Number
NC25600	1961
NC54212	1971
NC54214	1974
NC67901	1969
NC67930	1967
NC67952	1963
NC67953	1964
NC70000	1974
NC86500	2021
NC86501	2022
NC86502	2023
NC86503	2024
NC86504	2025
NC86505	2026
NC86506	2027
NC86507	2028
NC86508	2029
NC86509	2030
NC86510	2034
NC86511	2035
NC86512	2039
NC86513	2040
NC86514	2041
NC86515	2042
NC86516	2043
NC86517	2044
NC86518	2501
NC86519	2502
NC86520	2503
NC86521	2504
NC86522	2505
NC86523	2506
NC86524	2507
NC86525	2508
NC86526	2509
NC86527	2525
NC86528	2526
NC86529	2527
NC86530	2528
NC86531	2545
NC86532	2546
NC86533	2547
NC86534	2548
NC86535	2549
NC86536	1979
NC88831	2031
NC88832	2032
NC88833	2033
NC88836	2036
NC88837	2037
NC88838	2038
NC88845	2045
NC88846	2046
NC88847	2047
NC88848	2048
NC88849	2049
NC88850	2050
NC88855	2055
NC88856	2056
NC88857	2057
NC88858	2058
NC88859	2059
NC88860	2060
NC88861	2061
NC88862	2062
NC88865	2066
NC88868	2067
NC90602	1975
NC90603	1976
NC90604	1977
NC90605	1978
NC90606	1980
NC90616	2066
NC90617	2067
NC90814	2076
NC90815	2077
NC90816	2078
NC90817	2079
NC90818	2080
NC90819	2081
NC90820	2082
NC90821	2083
NC90822	2084
NC90823	2085
NC90824	2086
NC90825	2087
NC90826	2088
NC90827	1965
NC90828	1967
NC90829	1968
NC90830	1969
NC90831	1970
NC90921	2051
NC90922	2052
NC90923	2053
NC90924	2054
NC90925	2063
NC90926	2064
NC90927	2065
NC91201	2577
NC91202	2578
NC91203	2579
NC91204	2580
NC91205	2581
NC91206	2582
NC91207	2583
NC91208	2584
NC91209	2585
NC91210	2586
NC91211	2587
NC91212	2588
NC101A	2518
NC102A	2519
NC103A	2520
NC104A	2521
NC105A	2522
NC106A	2523
NC107A	2524
NC108A	2529
NC109A	2530
NC110A	2531
NC111A	2532
NC112A	2533
NC113A	2534
NC114A	2535

NX *(prior to 31 Dec 48)*
NX6700	1961
NX25600	1961
NX38936	1962
NX54212	1971
NX54214	1974
NX86500	2021
NX86501	2022
NX86502	2023
NX86503	2024
NX86504	2025
NX86505	2026
NX86506	2027
NX86507	2028
NX86508	2029
NX86509	2030
NX86510	2034
NX86511	2035
NX86512	2039
NX88832	2032
NX88836	2036
NX88849	2049
NX88858	2058
NX90827	1965
NX90828	1967
NX90829	1968
NX90921	2051
NX90924	2054
NX101A	2518

OB- PERU
OB-LJM-682	?
OB-R-732	2614
OB-R-733	2518
OB-R-740	2534
OB-R-741	4574
OB-R-742	4546
OB-R-743	2535
OB-R-771	2521
OB-R-785	2519
OB-R-802	2566
OB-R-819	2523
OB-R-833	2610
OB-R-849	2522
OB-R-898	2627
OB-R-899(1)	2549
OB-R-899(2)	2548
OB-R-914	2544
OB-R-915	2557
OB-R-916	2564
OB-R-917	2645
OB-WAA-732	2614
OB-WAB-733	2518
OB-WAC-740	2534

OE- AUSTRIA
OE-IFA	1969
OE-IFE	2551
OE-IFO	2562

PH- NETHERLANDS
PH-AXM	?
PH-AXO	?
PH-AXP	?
PH-AXS	?
PH-AXT	?
PH-AXU	?
PH-AXV	?
PH-AXY	?
PH-LDD	2640
PH-LDE	2641
PH-LDG	2661
PH-LDK	2590
PH-LDN	2621
PH-LDO	2622
PH-LDP	2638
PH-LDR	2540
PH-LDS	2552
PH-LDT	2553
PH-LKA	4553
PH-LKB	4558
PH-LKC	4559
PH-LKD	4560
PH-LKE	4629
PH-LKF	4630
PH-LKG	4631
PH-LKH	4635
PH-LKI	4644
PH-LKK	4645
PH-LKL	4840
PH-LKM	4841
PH-LKN	4843
PH-LKP	4501
PH-LKR	4502
PH-LKS	4503
PH-LKT	4504
PH-LKU	4505
PH-LKV	4506
PH-LKW	4507
PH-LKX	4508
PH-LKY	4509
PH-TAU	2068
PH-TAV	2069
PH-TAW	2070
PH-TAX	2071
PH-TDA	2071
PH-TDB	2544
PH-TDC	2551
PH-TDD	2556
PH-TDE	2557
PH-TDF	2558
PH-TDG	2559
PH-TDH	2564
PH-TDI	2589
PH-TDK	2590
PH-TDN	2621
PH-TDO	2622
PH-TDP	2638
PH-TEN	2083
PH-TEO	2084
PH-TEP	2540
PH-TER	2541
PH-TES	2552
PH-TET	2553
PH-TFD	2640
PH-TFE	2641
PH-TFF	2652
PH-TFG	2661
PH-TFP	4501
PH-TFR	4502
PH-TFS	4503
PH-TFT	4504
PH-TFU	4505
PH-TFV	4506
PH-TFW	4507
PH-TFX	4508
PH-TFY	4509
PH-TFZ	4553
PH-TGK	4558
PH-TGL	4559
PH-TGM	4560

PK- DUTCH EAST INDIES/INDONESIA
PK-ALA	2540
PK- ?	2541
PK- ?	2552
PK- ?	2553

PP- BRAZIL
PP-AYA	4833?
PP-PCB	2048
PP-PCF	2049
PP-PCG	2062
PP-PCR	2060
PP-PDA	2066
PP-PDC	2056
PP-PDD	2033
"PP-PDD"	2071
PP-PDE	2047
PP-PDF	2038
PP-PDG	2037
PP-PDH	2050
PP-PDI	2057
PP-PDJ	2032
PP-PDK	2059
PP-PDP	2052
PP-PDQ	2059
PP-VDA(1)	4582
PP-VDA(2)	4610
PP-VDB(1)	4583
PP-VDB(2)	4611
PP-VDC(1)	4584
PP-VDC(2)	4612
PP-VDD	4681
PP-VDE	4684
PP-VDF	4685
PP- ?	1043
PP- ?	1046
PP-YSA	4833
PP-YSB	4834
PP-YSC	4837
PP-YSD	4838

RX- PANAMA
RX-121	1968
RX-123	1965
RX-124	1967

TF- ICELAND
TF-ERA	1036

TI- COSTA RICA
TI-1044P	2540
TI-1045P	2553

TR- GABON
TR-LNY	4685

TU- IVORY COAST
TU-TBA	1031
TU-TBB	1011

VH- AUSTRALIA
VH-EAA(1)	2562
VH-EAA(2)	4580
VH-EAB(1)	2565
VH-EAB(2)	4581
VH-EAC(1)	2572
VH-EAC(2)	4606
VH-EAD(1)	2573
VH-EAD(2)	4607
VH-EAE(1)	2505
VH-EAE(2)	4578
VH-EAF(1)	2504
VH-EAF(2)	4579
VH-EAG(1)	4539
VH-EAG(2)	4176
VH-EAH	4545
VH-EAI	4546
VH-EAJ	4549
VH-EAK	4573
VH-EAL	4574
VH-EAM(1)	4578
VH-EAM(2)	4801
VH-EAN(1)	4579
VH-EAN(2)	4803
VH-EAO(1)	4580
VH-EAO(2)	4679
VH-EAP(1)	4581
VH-EAP(2)	4680
VH-EAQ	4681
VH-EAR	4682
VH-EAS	4683
VH-EAT	4684
VH-EAU	4685

VP-W RHODESIA
VP-WAW	4685

VT- INDIA
VT-CQP	2506
VT-CQR	2505
VT-CQS	2504
VT-DAR	2619
VT-DAS	2620
VT-DEO	2665
VT-DEP	2666
VT-DGL	4547
VT-DGM	4548
VT-DHL	4613
VT-DHM	4614
VT-DHN	4615
VT-DIL	4646
VT-DIM	4666
VT-DIN	4667
VT-DJW	4686
VT-DJX	4687

Section 13: Registration Index

XA- MEXICO
XA-GOQ	2503
XA-GOS	25xx
XA-LIO	2572
XA-LIP	2573
XA-MAG	2052
XA-MAH	2059
XA-MEU	2620
XA-MEV	2665
XA-MEW	2619
XA-MOA	2534
XA-NAC	4672
XA-NAD	4677
XA-NAF	4678

YV- VENEZUELA
YV-C-AMA	2560
YV-C-AME(1)	2081
YV-C-AME(2	4636
YV-C-AMI(1)	2082
YV-C-AMI(2)	4674
YV-C-AMR	4561
YV-C-AMS	4561
YV-C-AMT	4562
YV-C-AMU	2561
YV-C-ANB	4572
YV-C-ANC	4575
YV-C-AND	4576
YV-C-ANE	4577
YV-C-ANF	4562
YV-C-LBI	4808
YV-C-LBP	4807

ZP- PARAGUAY
ZP-CAS	1964
"ZP-TBV"	4581

ZS- SOUTH AFRICA
ZS-DBR	2623
ZS-DBS	2630
ZS-DBT	2631
ZS-DBU	2632
ZS-DTM	1041
ZS-DVJ	1042
ZS-FAA	4685
ZS-FAB	1041

4R- CEYLON
4R-ACH	4553

4X- ISRAEL
4X-AKA	1965
4X-AKB	1967
4X-AKC	1968
4X-AKD	1980
4X-AKE	2061
4X-AKF	2036
4X-AOK	2036
4X-AOL	2623?
4X-AOM	2631?
4X-121	1968
BK-54	2036 (Class "B")

5B- CYPRUS
5B-CAJ	4683

5N- BIAFRA
5N-07G	4514
5N-83H	4616
5N85H	2662
5N86H	2660

5T- MAURETANIA
5T-TAC(1)	4645
5T-TAC(2)	4166
5T-TAF	4618
5T-TAG	4642
5T-TAH	4647
5T-TAK	4640

5Y- KENYA
5Y-ABF	1977

6V- SENEGAL
6V-AAR	2538

9G- GHANA
9G-28	4683

MILITARY

FRENCH AIR FORCE/CEV
F-SSFF	2625
F-SSFJ	2514
F-SSFM	2545
F-SSFO	2547
F-SSFP	2550
F-SSFT	2629
F-SSFY	2528
F-ZVMV	2503

INDIAN AIR FORCE
BG575	4614
BG576	4666
BG577	4615
BG578	4646
BG579	4687
BG580	4613
BG581	4547
BG582	4548
BG583	4686

INDIAN NAVY
IN315	4614
IN316	4666
IN317	4613
IN318	4547
IN319	4548

INDONESIAN AIR FORCE/AURI
T1041	4836
T1042	4835
T1043	4521

UNITED STATES ARMY AIR FORCE
42-94549	1970
42-94550	1971
42-94551	1972
42-94552	1973
42-94553	1974
42-94554	1975
42-94555	1976
42-94556	1977
42-94557	1978
42-94558	1979
42-94559	1980
42-94560	2021
to	to
42-94609	2070
42-94610(1)	2071
42-94610(2)	3001
42-94611(1)	2072
42-94611(2)	3002
42-94612(1)	2073
42-94612(2)	3003
42-94613(1)	2074
to	to
42-94649(1)	2110
42-94613(2)	3004
to	onwards
42-94649(2)	(order uk)
42-94650	3001
to	to
42-94725	3076
42-94726	3148
42-94727	3149
42-94728	3150
43-10238	3077
to	to
43-10308	3147
43-10309	1961
43-10310	1962
43-10311	1963
43-10312	1964
43-10313	1965
43-10314	1966
43-10315	1967
43-10316	1968
43-10317	1969

UNITED STATES AIR FORCE
"0-30552"	4347
0-43184	4458
0-50539	4354
"03-0552"	4433
4153	4199
43189	4463
43199	4473
43200	4474
48-608	2600
48-609	2601
48-610	2602
48-611	2603
48-612	2604
48-613	2605
48-614	2606
48-615	2607
48-616	2608
48-617	2609
51-3836	4112
51-3837	4113
51-3838	4114
51-3839	4115
51-3840	4116
51-3841	4117
51-3842	4118
51-3843	4119
51-3844	4120
51-3845	4121
52-3411	4329
52-3412	4330
52-3413	4331
52-3414	4332
52-3415	4333
52-3416	4334
52-3417	4335
52-3418	4336
52-3419	4337
52-3420	4338
52-3421	4339
52-3422	4340
52-3423	4341
52-3424	4342
52-3425	4343
53-533	4348
53-534	4349
53-535	4350
53-536	4351
53-537	4352
53-538	4353
53-539	4354
53-540	4355
53-541	4356
53-542	4357
53-543	4358
53-544	4359
53-545	4360
53-546	4361
53-547	4362
53-548	4363
53-549	4364
53-550	4365
53-551	4366
53-552	4367
53-553	4368
53-554	4369
53-555	4370
53-556	4371
53-3398	4372
53-3399	4373
53-3400	4374
53-3401	4375
53-3402	4376
53-3403	4377
53-3404	canx
53-3405	canx
53-7885	4151
53-8157	4161
53-8158	4162
54-151	4170
54-152	4171
54-153	4172
"54-153"	4199
54-154	4173
54-155	4174

Serial	c/n	Serial	c/n	Serial	c/n
54-156	4175	55-138	4411	131392	4312
54-157	4176	55-139	4412	131393	43xx
54-158	4177	55-5262	4413	to	to
54-159	4178	55-5263	4415	131399	43xx
54-160	4179	55-5264	4424	131621	4122
54-161	4180	55-5265	4426	131622	4123
54-162	4181	55-5266	4457	131623	4124
54-163	4182	55-5267	4442	131624	4125
54-164	4183	55-5268	4451	131625	4126
54-165	4184	56-6956	5500	131626	4127
54-166	4185	57-143184	4458	131627	4128
54-167	4186	57-143188	4462	131628	4129
54-168	4187	57-143189	4463	131629	4130
54-169	4188	57-143191	4465	131630	4131
54-170	4189	57-143195	4469	131631	4132
54-171	4190	57-143199	4473	131632	4133
54-172	4191	57-143200	4474	131633	4134
54-173	4192	57-143202	4476	131634	4135
54-174	4193	57-143203	4477	131635	4136
54-175	4194	57-143204	4478	131636	4137
54-176	4195	57-143206	4480	131637	4138
54-177	4196	57-143207	4481	131638	4139
54-178	4197	57-143208	4482	131639	4140
54-179	4198	57-143210	4484	131640	4141
54-180	4199	57-143213	4487	131641	4142
54-181	4200	57-143214	4488	131642	4143
54-182	4201	57-143216	4490	131643	4144
54-183	4202	57-143218	4492	131644	4145
54-2304	4386	57-143222	4496	131645	4146
54-2305	4387	57-143224	4498	131646	4147
54-2306	4388	67-21471	4382	131647	4148
54-2307	4389	67-21472	4385	131648	4149
54-2308	4390	67-21473	4420	131649	4150
54-4048	4101	67-21474	4430	131650	4151
54-4049	4102	67-21475	4436	131651	4152
54-4050	4103	67-21476	4441	131652	4153
54-4051	4105	67-21477	4444	131653	4154
54-4052	4106	67-21478	4452	131654	4155
54-4053	4122	67-21479	4454	131655	4156
54-4054	4123	67-21480	4459	131656	4157
54-4055	4135	67-21481	4462	131657	4158
54-4056	4127	67-21482	4465	131658	4159
54-4057	4138	67-21483	4469	131659	4160
54-4058	4129	67-21484	4476	131660	4161
54-4059	4130	67-21485	4477	131661	4162
54-4060	4133	67-21486	4478	135746	4313
54-4061	4109	67-21487	4480	135747	4314
54-4062	4137	67-21488	4481	135748	4315
54-4063	4139	67-21489	4482	135749	4316
54-4064	4141	67-21490	4484	135750	4317
54-4065	4143	67-21491	4487	135751	4318
54-4066	4146	67-21492	4488	135752	4319
54-4067	4147	67-21493	4489	135753	4320
54-4068	4148	67-21494	4490	135754	4321
54-4069	4149	67-21495	4491	135755	4322
54-4070	4150	67-21496	4492	135756	4323
54-4071	4152	67-21497	4493	135757	4324
54-4072(1)	4153	67-21498	4496	135758	4325
54-4072(2)	4134	67-21499	4497	135759	4326
54-4073	4154	67-21500	4498	135760	4327
54-4074	4157			135761	4328
54-4075	4158	**UNITED STATES NAVY**		137887	4344
54-4076	4159	124437	2612	137888	4345
54-4077	4167	124438	2613	137889	4346
54-4078	4168	126512	4301	137890	4347
54-4079	4169	126513	4302	137891	4378
55-118	4391	128323	4303	137892	4379
55-119	4392	128324	4304	137893	4380
55-120	4393	128325	4305	137894	4381
55-121	4394	128326	4306	137895	4382
55-122	4395	128434	4101	137896	4383
55-123	4396	128435	4102	137897	4384
55-124	4397	128436	4103	137898	4385
55-125	4398	128437	4104	140311	4167
55-126	4399	128438	4105	140312	4168
55-127	4400	128439	4106	140313	4169
55-128	4401	128440	4107	141289	4413
55-129	4402	128441	4108	141290	4414
55-130	4403	128442	4109	141291	4415
55-131	4404	128443	4110	141292	4416
55-132	4405	128444	4111	141293	4417
55-133	4406	131387	4307	141294	4418
55-134	4407	131388	4308	141295	4419
55-135	4408	131389	4309	141296	4420
55-136	4409	131390	4310	141297	4421
55-137	4410	131391	4311	141298	4422

Section 13: Registration Index

c/n	serial		c/n	serial		c/n	serial
141299	4423		143184	4458		143219	4493
141300	4424		143185	4459		143220	4494
141301	4425		143186	4460		143221	4495
141302	4426		143187	4461		143222	4496
141303	4427		143188	4462		143223	4497
141304	4428		143189	4463		143224	4498
141305	4429		143190	4464		143225	4499
141306	4430		143191	4465		143226	5500
141307	4431		143192	4466		143227	5501
141308	4432		143193	4467		143228	5502
141309	4433		143194	4468		143229	5503
141310	4434		143195	4469		143230	5504
141311	4435		143196	4470		145924	5505
141312	4436		143197	4471		145925	5506
141313	4437		143198	4472		145926	5507
141314	4438		143199	4473		145927	5508
141315	4439		143200	4474		145928	5509
141316	4440		143201	4475		145929	5510
141317	4441		143202	4476		145930	5511
141318	4442		143203	4477		145931	5512
141319	4443		143204	4478		145932	5513
141320	4444		143205	4479		145933	5514
141321	4445		143206	4480		145934	5515
141322	4446		143207	4481		145935	5516
141323	4447		143208	4482		145936	5517
141324	4448		143209	4483		145937	5518
141325	4449		143210	4484		145938	5519
141326	4450		143211	4485		145939	5520
141327	4451		143212	4486		145940	5521
141328	4452		143213	4487		145941	5522
141329	4453		143214	4488		145942	55xx
141330	4454		143215	4489		to	to
141331	4455		143216	4490		145956	55xx
141332	4456		143217	4491			
141333	4457		143218	4492			

NOTES

1) *The following registrations and serials have been reported in various sources for Constellation aircraft, but are believed to be incorrect:-*

CF-IHB	– misreading of CF-NAJ
CX-BEN	– misreading of CX-BEM, or possibly a second CAUSA 1049H that was not taken up
N53H	– probable misreading of 5N83H
N480C	– probable misreading of N469C
N9970E	– misreporting of N9907E
N9970F	– misreporting of N9907F
ZP-TVB	– misprint for ZP-TBV
4X-ACK	– misreading of 4X-AOK

2) *Unknown construction numbers:-*

N5176V & N5177V registrations allocated to a fifth & sixth aircraft for Northwest Orient Airlines, but order cancelled.

OB-LJM-682 allocated in 1962 to an unknown Constellation, in all probability for CICASA (see Prospective Operators).

PH-AXM to PH-AXY series. These were the registrations allocated to KLM's original order for L49s in 1941 which were not taken up owing to the US entry into the war.

XA-GOS was allocated to a 749 for Guest Aerovias Mexico, but the order was cancelled. The c/n was probably in the 250x batch.

3) *Problems*

In addition to several problems concerning identities/fates of individual aircraft mentioned in the main sections, the following aircraft have not so far been identified:-

A US-registered Constellation arrived at 'Happy Valley' (Puerto Cabezas), Nicaragua, with members of the CIA (Central Intelligence Agency) to discuss the invasion of Cuba with B-26s. Insignia was overpainted.

In about 1960, a Constellation was used as the "star" of the feature film called 'Rebel Flight to Cuba'.

Some TWA 049s received individual names in 1946 that have not yet been tied in with individual aircraft:-"California Sunbeam" was used on 24 April 46 for an aircraft that was testing a new ventilation & heating system. It must have been allocated to one of the Domestic batch of 049s with Fleet numbers 501 to 509, as the tests involved a flight from California to Houston, Texas.

"Cherokee Sky Chief" was used in early 1946 (a picture of the aircraft appears in TWA's history "Legacy of Leadership" on page 156), but the individual aircraft still remains unidentified.

A Pan American 049 was named "Clipper Southern Cross" for the South Africa inaugural service in Feb-Mar 48.

A number of United States Navy modex numbers (and individual aircraft names) are still unknown. Any additional details on these would be welcomed by the author. The largest gaps are in the Pacific-based barrier and AEW squadrons.

AIR-BRITAIN MEMBERSHIP

If you are not currently a member of Air-Britain, the publishers of this book, you may be interested in what we have on offer to provide for your interest in aviation.

About Air-Britain
Formed nearly 60 years ago, we are the world's most progressive aviation society, and exist to bring together aviation enthusiasts with every type of interest. Our members include aircraft historians, aviation writers, spotters and pilots - and those who just have a fascination with aircraft and aviation. Air-Britain is a non-profit organisation, which is independently audited, and any financial surpluses are used to provide services to the world-wide membership which currently stands at around 4,000, some 700 of whom live overseas.

Membership of Air-Britain
Membership is open to all. A basic membership fee is charged and every member receives a copy of the quarterly house magazine, Air-Britain Aviation World, is entitled to use all the Air-Britain specialist services and to buy **Air-Britain publications at discounted prices** (one-third off the cover price of this book for example!). A membership subscription includes the choice to add any or all of our other three magazines, News and/or Archive and/or Aeromilitaria. Air-Britain also publishes 10-20 books per annum (around 70 titles in stock at any one time). Membership runs January - December each year, but new members have a choice of options periods to get their initial subscription started - see below.

Air-Britain Aviation World is the quarterly 48-page house magazine containing not only news of Air-Britain activities, but also a wealth of features, often illustrated in colour, on many different aviation subjects, contemporary and historical, contributed by our members.

Air-Britain News is the world aviation news monthly, containing data on aircraft registrations worldwide and news of Airlines and Airliners, Business Jets, Local Airfield News, Civil and Military Air Show Reports, Preservation reports and International Military Aviation News. An average 160 pages of lavishly-illustrated information for the dedicated enthusiast.

Air-Britain Archive is the quarterly 48-page specialist journal of civil aviation history. Packed with the results of historical research by Air-Britain specialists into aircraft types, overseas registers and previously unpublished facts about the rich heritage of civil aviation. Averaging around 100 photographs per issue, some in colour.

Air-Britain Aeromilitaria is the quarterly 48-page unique source for meticulously researched details of military aviation history edited by the acclaimed authors of Air-Britain's military monographs featuring British, Commonwealth, European and U.S. Military aviation articles. Illustrated in colour and black & white.

Other Benefits
Additional to the above, members have exclusive access to the Air-Britain e-mail Information Exchange Service (ab-ix) where they can exchange information and solve each other's queries, and to an on-line UK airfield residents database. Other benefits include numerous Branches, use of the Specialists Information Service; Air-Britain trips; and access to black & white and colour photograph libraries. During the summer we also host our own popular FLY-IN. Each autumn, we host an Aircraft Recognition Contest.

Membership Subscription Rates - from £18 per annum.
Membership subscription rates start from as little as £18 per annum (2007), and this amount provides a copy of 'Air-Britain Aviation World' quarterly as well as all the other benefits covered above. Subscriptions to include any or all of our other three magazines vary between £25 and £62 per annum (slightly higher to overseas).

*** Join now for two years 2007-2008 at the same time and save £5.00 off the total ***

Join on-line at www.air-britain.co.uk. Or, write to 'Air-Britain' at 1 Rose Cottages, 179 Penn Road, Hazlemere, High Wycombe, Bucks HP15 7NE, UK, alternatively telephone/fax on 01394 450767 (+44 1394 450767) or e-mail Barry.Collman@air-britain.co.uk and ask for a membership pack containing the full details of subscription rates, samples of our magazines and a book list.

Recent titles from Air-Britain include (Non-members prices quoted):

HIGHWAYS TO THE EMPIRE - Long-Distance Flying Between the Wars, Colin Cruddas. The international activities of Sir Alan Cobham and other pioneers of Empire and transatlantic routes and record-breaking, profusely illustrated. A4 hardback 256pp. (£37.50)   ISBN: 0 85130 334 X

THE TRIPLE ALLIANCE - The Predecessors of the first British Airways, Neville Doyle. The story of Hillman's Airways, Spartan Air Lines and United Airways Ltd who amalgamated in 1935 to form British Airways Ltd. Fully illustrated A4 hardback 128pp. (£22.50)   ISBN: 0 85130 286 6

THE de HAVILLAND DRAGON/RAPIDE FAMILY, John F Hamlin. Complete histories of all DH.84, DH.86, DH.89 and DH.90 biplane transports with an introduction to the development of each type. Background histories of the UK operators who used them. Over 450 photos plus colour plates and side-views. A4 hardback 256 pp. (£29.95)   ISBN: 0 85130 344 7

THE STORY OF THE de HAVILLAND DRAGON TYPES, Colin N Dodds. The comprehensive design and development history of the Dragon, Express, Rapide and Dragonfly types with stories of their operators, crews, dramatic events and routine activities worldwide. Almost 400 illustrations, many in colour. A4 hardback 272pp. (£37.50)   ISBN: 0 85130 363 3

DC-1, DC-2, DC-3: THE FIRST SEVENTY YEARS, Jennifer Gradidge. The fully-updated complete history of the development, use and individual histories of all Douglas DC-1, DC-2 and DC-3 aircraft including Li-2 production and turboprop conversions. Fully indexed and well-illustrated in colour and black & white. Two volumes totalling approx 740pp A4 hardback. (£63.75)   ISBN: 0 85130 332 3

AIRCRAFT MUSEUMS AND COLLECTIONS OF MAINLAND EUROPE, Bob Ogden. New title covering all of Europe (except UK & Eire) and Western Russia, with location and admission details, background information and detailed listing of all aircraft involved. Maps and a type index are included as are illustrations in colour and black & white. A5 hardback 608pp. (£28.00)   ISBN: 0 85130 375 7

Air-Britain publishes a range of books for the aviation enthusiast and historian:

A series of civil titles published annually covers the UK and European civil Registers, worldwide Airline Fleets, Business Jets and there is also a series of low-priced "Quick Reference" books on these topics. Non-annual books include the history of manufacturers, of airliner types and of complete civil registers. The comprehensive list of military titles includes detailed RAF and RN type histories, squadron histories and RAF serial registers together with other products of painstaking historical research. Full details of these, many other Air-Britain titles, and membership details and benefits may be obtained from the address given on page 2 of this book or by using our secure on-lineSales site on **www.air-britain.co.uk**

Remember that members receive substantial discounts on the prices of all Air-Britain publications.